PHILOSOPHY OF RELIGION

A Reader and Guide

General Editor

William Lane Craig

Section Editors

**Kevin Meeker, J. P. Moreland,
Michael Murray, Timothy O'Connor**

RUTGERS UNIVERSITY PRESS

New Brunswick, New Jersey

First published in the United States 2002
by Rutgers University Press, New Brunswick, New Jersey

First published in Great Britain 2002
by Edinburgh University Press Ltd
22 George Square, Edinburgh

Library of Congress Cataloging-in-Publication Data and British Library
Cataloguing-in-Publication Data are available upon request

ISBN 0-8135-3120-9 (cloth)
ISBN 0-8135-3121-7 (pbk.)

Printed in Great Britain

CONTENTS

GENERAL INTRODUCTION

William Lane Craig

The last half-century has witnessed a veritable revolution in Anglo-American philosophy. On 8 April 1966, *Time* magazine carried a lead story for which the cover was completely black except for three words emblazoned in bright, red letters against the dark background: 'IS GOD DEAD?' The story described the so-called Death of God movement then current in American theology. According to the movement's protagonists, traditional theism was no longer tenable and had to be once and for all abandoned. Ironically, however, at the same time that theologians were writing God's obituary, a new generation of young philosophers was rediscovering His vitality.

Back in the 1940s and 1950s it had been widely believed among philosophers that talk about God, being in principle non-verifiable, was meaningless – actual nonsense. In response, philosophers interested in religious questions offered trenchant critiques of this verificationist viewpoint along with searching analyses of religious language, thereby sparking a renaissance of interest in Philosophy of Religion. The turning point probably came in 1967 with the publication of Alvin Plantinga's *God and Other Minds*, which applied the tools of analytic philosophy to questions in the Philosophy of Religion with an unprecedented rigour and creativity. Just a few years after its famous Death of God issue, *Time* ran a similar red-on-black cover story, only this time the question read, 'IS GOD COMING BACK TO LIFE?' So it must have seemed to those theological morticians of the 1960s!

During the 1970s interest in Philosophy of Religion continued to grow, and in 1980 *Time* ran another major story entitled 'Modernizing the Case for God', in which it described the movement among contemporary philosophers to refurbish the traditional arguments for God's existence. *Time* marvelled,

> In a quiet revolution in thought and argument that hardly anybody
> could have foreseen only two decades ago, God is making a comeback.
> Most intriguingly, this is happening not among theologians or ordinary
> believers, but in the crisp intellectual circles of academic philosophers,
> where the consensus had long banished the Almighty from fruitful
> discourse.[1]

According to the article, the noted American philosopher Roderick Chisholm
believes that the reason that atheism was so influential in the previous
generation is that the brightest philosophers were atheists; but today, he
observes, many of the brightest philosophers are theists, using a tough-minded
intellectualism in defence of that belief.

Today Philosophy of Religion flourishes in young journals such as the
*International Journal for Philosophy of Religion, Religious Studies, Sophia,
Faith and Philosophy, Philosophia Christi, American Catholic Philosophical
Quarterly* and other journals devoted to the discipline, not to mention the
standard non-specialist journals, as well as in professional societies such as the
Society of Christian Philosophers, the Evangelical Philosophical Society, the
American Catholic Philosophical Society and other smaller groups. Publishing
in Philosophy of Religion is booming, as is evident from the plethora of
available textbooks (also testimony to the tremendous interest among students for courses on the subject) such as Rowe and Wainwright's *Philosophy
of Religion* (1989), Stewart's *Philosophy of Religion* (1996), Basinger *et al.*'s
Philosophy of Religion (1996), Pojman's *Philosophy of Religion* (1998),
Murray and Stump's *Philosophy of Religion* (1998), and Clark's *Readings
in the Philosophy of Religion* (2000).[2]

Although Philosophy of Religion has been recognised as a delineated sub-
discipline of philosophy as far back as Hegel, who had lectured on the subject,
analytic Philosophy of Religion, the dominant form of the field today, is thus a
young movement which came to prominence in the debates over religious
language. As it appears on the contemporary scene, there are actually two
rather different disciplines going under the name of Philosophy of Religion.
What I have described thus far is a sub-discipline of philosophy pursued by
professional philosophers, who would typically participate in a professional
society like the American Philosophical Association. But Philosophy of
Religion is also a sub-discipline of Religious Studies, where it is typically
carried out by professors of Religion or Theology who are active profession-
ally in societies like the American Academy of Religion. These two approaches
to Philosophy of Religion have a very different texture. Loosely speaking, we
may say that the former is concerned with philosophising about problems
raised by religious truth claims, whereas the latter tends to philosophise about
the phenomenon of religion itself. The latter therefore resembles more closely
than the former the discipline of comparative religion; and when its advocates
do reflect on a problem of philosophical significance they often lack the

conceptual tools furnished by training in analytic philosophy. The contemporary resurgence of interest in Philosophy of Religion is due almost entirely to the revolution that has taken place among professional analytic philosophers, whose work the practitioners of Religious Studies are finding increasingly difficult to ignore.

My overall aim in assembling this Reader and Guide is to acquaint the student with the very best of cutting-edge work in analytic philosophy on key topics in the Philosophy of Religion. I have therefore elected to assign specialists to choose the selections and to write the Introductions to the different topical sections of the book. The anthology is comprised of six sections, each of which opens with a substantial introductory essay surveying the contemporary discussion of the relevant topic.

1. Religious epistemology
2. Natural theology
3. Coherence of theism
4. Problem of evil
5. The soul and life everlasting
6. Christian theology

These are, in my opinion, the most important topics in the Philosophy of Religion, though I am acutely aware that owing to limitations of space other important topics (for example, the problem of miracles, religious experience, non-Christian religions) have been omitted. Even within each section, difficult decisions were necessary with respect to the omission of material. I encouraged the section editors to make quality their primary criterion in selecting essays. Ideally one should like to include articles pro and contra on each issue, but that would have necessitated the omission of the some of the best work on each question.

Given the crowded field of textbooks in Philosophy of Religion, one might ask what distinguishes our volume from its many competitors. Four distinctive features of this text come to mind:

1. Our volume focuses largely on contemporary Philosophy of Religion. Many of the other textbooks include historical sources as background reading for the contemporary debate. Our volume gains more space for current discussions by foregoing these.
2. The volume's serving as both a Reader and a Guide is unique. No other anthology of readings that I know of includes substantive essays written by specialists on various areas introducing each of the respective topics.
3. The selected readings represent the best of cutting-edge work in each area. Few, if any, of our competitors feature selections dealing with such important and intriguing issues as the Anthropic Principle,

middle knowledge, evidential arguments from evil, property/substance dualism, substitutionary atonement, and so on.

4. The anthology presents a sympathetic view of the topics it treats. Too many of the current textbooks leave the impression that arguments for the existence of God, for example, are all unsound or inconclusive or that theists have not been able to answer the Problem of Evil, thereby doing the student a disservice. Our desire is to highlight some of the best of recent work which is sympathetic to religious belief.

NOTES

1. 'Modernizing the Case for God', *Time*, 7 April 1980, pp. 65–6.
2. William Rowe and William Wainwright, *Philosophy of Religion* (Belmont, CA: Wadsworth Publishing Co., 1989); Melville Y. Stewart, *Philosophy of Religion: An Anthology of Contemporary Views* (Belmont, CA: Wadsworth Publishing Co., 1996); Michael Peterson, William Hasker, Bruce Reichenbach and David Basinger (eds), *Philosophy of Religion: Selected Readings* (Oxford: Oxford University Press, 2001); Louis P. Pojman, *Philosophy of Religion: An Anthology* (Belmont, CA: Wadsworth Publishing Co., 1998); Michael J. Murray and Eleonore Stump, *Philosophy of Religion: The Big Questions* (Malden, MA: Blackwell Publishing Co., 1999); and Kelly James Clark, *Readings in Philosophy of Religion* (Peterborough, Ontario: Broadview Press, 2000).

PART I
RELIGIOUS EPISTEMOLOGY

RELIGIOUS EPISTEMOLOGY: INTRODUCTION

Kevin Meeker

Religious epistemology, which (roughly stated) is the philosophical study of religious belief or knowledge, sounds like a daunting and impractical topic. But in many ways it deals with some very practical issues. Some questions that religious epistemologists often ask include the following: is it intellectually respectable to believe that God exists?; are religious beliefs in general rational?; can we know that God exists?; and, which religious beliefs ought one to adopt? Let us linger on the fourth question for a moment. Everyone provides his or her own answer to this question. Atheists, for instance, decide that religious beliefs ought to be rejected. Even agnostics have concluded that it is better to suspend judgement on religious matters rather than either to accept or to deny the existence of God. To be sure, religious 'believers' and 'non-believers' alike often 'absorb' or 'adopt' their beliefs from those around them. Yet most are aware that many others hold opposing religious views. Despite an awareness of this disagreement, most maintain their beliefs. So, even if most people never recall consciously considering the fourth question, the beliefs that they continue to hold and the practices that they continue to follow represent at the very least a tacit answer to this question. Everyone then possesses some nascent religious epistemology (that is, has answered questions in the discipline) that guides a significant aspect of his or her life. Clearly religious epistemology is a very practical topic.

Let us then consider questions like those just mentioned. Is it rational to believe that God exists? Does one need to be able to provide arguments to be intellectually respectable in believing that God exists? Answering these questions requires some rudimentary understanding of 'rationality'. Unsurprisingly, philosophers often distinguish various types of rationality, such as epistemic rationality and prudential rationality. For example, suppose that Alice refrains from reading *The National Enquirer* because she wants to try her best to follow credible evidence and acquire and maintain true beliefs. Philosophers would say that she is acting in an epistemically rational manner. To change the example, suppose that Albert exercises regularly, eats healthy food, and gets enough sleep. Albert is acting in a prudentially rational manner insofar as he is trying his utmost to do what is in his own best interest. We can thus evaluate religious beliefs from these distinct perspectives.

One of the most provocative arguments in the history of philosophy sprang from the pen of Blaise Pascal in the seventeenth century. In essence, Pascal argued that one has pragmatic or prudential reasons to believe in God. In trying to decide whether or not God exists, Pascal claims:

> Reason cannot decide this question. Infinite chaos separates us. At the far end of this infinite distance a coin is being spun which will come down heads or tails. How will you wager? Reason cannot make you choose either, reason cannot prove either wrong . . . you must wager. There is no choice, you are already committed. Which will you choose then? . . . Since a choice must be made, let us see which offers you the least interest. You have two things to lose: the true and the good; and two things to stake: your reason and your will, your knowledge and your happiness; and your nature has two things to avoid: error and wretchedness. Since you must necessarily choose, your reason is no more affronted by choosing one rather than the other. This one point is cleared up. But your happiness? Let us weigh up the gain and the loss involved in calling heads that God exists. Let us assess the two cases: if you win, you win everything, if you lose, you lose nothing. Do not hesitate then; wager that he does exist. 'That is wonderful. Yes, I must wager, but perhaps I am wagering too much.' Let us see: since there is an equal chance of gain and loss, if you stood to win only two lives for one you could still wager, but supposing you stood to win three?
>
> You would have to play (since you must necessarily play), and it would be unwise of you, once you are obliged to play, not to risk your life in order to win three lives at a game in which there is an equal chance of losing and winning. But there is an eternity of life and happiness. That being so, even though there were an infinite number of chances, of which one only were in your favour, you would still be right to wager one in order to win two; and you would be acting wrongly, being obliged to play, by refusing to stake one life against three in a game, where out of an infinite number of chances there is one in your favour, if there were an infinity of an infinitely happy life to be won. But there is here an infinity of an infinitely happy life to be won, one chance of winning against a finite number of chances of losing, and what you are staking is finite. That leaves no choice; wherever there is infinity, and where there are not

infinite chances of losing against that of winning, there is no room for hesitation, you must give everything. And thus, since you are obliged to play, you must be renouncing reason if you hoard your life rather than to risk it for an infinite gain, just as likely to occur as a loss amounting to nothing.[1]

This passage comes from notes that Pascal had jotted down in anticipation of writing a book defending the rationality of Christianity. Because of Pascal's early death, his project never came to fruition; so he never polished up or elaborated the ideas in the preceding passage.

In our first selection, Ian Hacking discusses 'The Logic of Pascal's Wager' and argues that Pascal, a brilliant mathematician and probability theorist, employs sophisticated principles of decision theory to argue that one ought to believe in God. More specifically, Hacking discerns three distinct versions of the argument in the above passage. The first version of the argument states roughly that if one believes in God and God exists, then one attains infinite happiness (salvation). But if God does not exist, then believing in God is not any more detrimental than if one is an atheist and God does not exist. Alternatively, if one does not believe in God and God does exist, then one loses infinite happiness. From this perspective, one has 'everything to gain and nothing to lose' by believing in God; so clearly the prudentially rational course of action is to believe in God. Of course, some may protest that being a theist in a godless world does exact a heavy price of forgoing many pleasures in this life. The second version of the argument claims that even if the odds of God's existing are 50/50, because the payoff of betting on God is infinite and the cost is at best finite, it is still prudentially rational to be a theist. Finally, the third version shows that even if it is unlikely that God exists, as long as there is *some* chance, no matter how slight, that God exists, it is still prudentially rational to believe in God. In presenting the details of these versions of the Wager, Hacking contends that they are logically valid arguments. That is, Hacking maintains that if the premises of Pascal's arguments are true, then the conclusions are true. Nevertheless, he contends that each argument has one contestable premise. One of Hacking's main complaints is that Pascal assumes that our choices are simply between atheism/agnosticism and Christianity. While Hacking points out that there are other alternatives from which to choose, he also notes that Pascal discusses other such alternatives in different parts of the *Pensées* and clearly aims his Wager arguments at those who would consider atheism/agnosticism or Christianity as the only realistic choices.

Fair enough; but a nagging question still remains: is Pascal's Wager at all helpful for the vast majority of people living today – those who seem to have more than two realistic alternatives? This question or charge, usually called the 'many gods objection', is probably the most common and vexing criticism of Pascal's Wager. The heart of the objection is this: there are many different gods or religions that offer infinite happiness (salvation). So which one should we choose? George Schlesinger deals with this question (as well as others) in the second selection entitled 'A Central Theistic Argument'. He contends that believing in the existence of an omnipotent, omniscient and perfectly good Creator – in the words of Anselm 'a being than which none greater can be conceived' – is rational in part because this theistic hypothesis is more probable and simpler than all other hypotheses (for example, that Zeus exists). Interestingly enough, Schlesinger also argues that because other theistic arguments, such as the teleological and cosmological arguments, also face the many gods objection, appeals to simplicity and the like will be critical in defending those arguments as well. It would be interesting to keep this point in mind while reading about such arguments in Part 2 of this book on natural theology.

Another problem with Pascal's Wager is that it runs against the grain of a deeply entrenched (especially since the Enlightenment) philosophical assumption: evidentialism. Evidentialists claim that prudential considerations should have no (or very little) bearing on what we believe. In the memorable words of W. K. Clifford, 'it is wrong, always, everywhere, and for any one, to believe anything upon insufficient evidence'.[2] A consequence of this position is that religious believers are not entitled to their theistic belief unless they can provide good arguments for the claim that God exists. Pointing out, à la Pascal, that it is prudentially beneficial to accept belief in God will cut no ice with the evidentialists. As I have mentioned, Part 2 on natural theology will present arguments that attempt to meet this challenge.

Recently, though, some philosophers have challenged the evidentialist thesis in a unique way. Alvin Plantinga, for example, controversially argues that the belief that God exists is (or can be) a 'properly basic' belief. In other words, Plantinga contends that believers can be perfectly rational in believing in God even if they cannot support such a belief with arguments or any other evidential considerations. To put this point yet another way, Plantinga is concerned with the question of whether or not theistic believers are within their intellectual rights in believing in God even if they do not have evidence. Even more recently, Plantinga has downplayed questions of intellectual rights and duties to push the discussion a notch further by examining the concept of knowledge and asking whether we can know that God exists in the absence of evidentiary support. So what is knowledge? Knowledge at a minimum includes true belief. I cannot know that Sacramento is the capital of California if I do not believe that it is. Likewise, if I were to believe that San Diego is the capital of California, then I would not know that because I would have a false belief. But more is needed. If I simply guess on a multiple choice exam that Albany is the capital of New York (as opposed to Binghamton, Buffalo, New York City, Rochester and Syracuse), then even if I believe it, I do not know it to be the case; it is just a lucky guess. So we need something besides a lucky guess to convert a true belief into knowledge. What precisely do we need?

Plantinga calls that property that distinguishes knowledge from mere true belief 'warrant'. And he argues that we should understand warrant in terms of proper functioning. Just as your liver should help to detoxify your blood (when it is functioning properly) so too your mind should form beliefs in certain circumstances (when it is functioning properly). So for Plantinga a belief is warranted (roughly speaking) just in case it is produced by properly functioning cognitive faculties that are designed to arrive at the truth in the given environment and do so reliably.[3]

The details of Plantinga's theory need not concern us here; what is important is that we can read this theory as an attempt to develop a positive theory in support of his claim that belief in God is properly basic. One difference, though, is that now Plantinga argues that theistic belief is (or can be) properly basic with respect to warrant (as opposed to rationality) and thus more strongly opens up the possibility that believers can know that God exists even without arguments to back up this belief.

Our third selection entitled 'Is Belief in God Rationally Acceptable?' provides a taste of Plantinga's initial arguments defending the proper basicality thesis. In the first part of this selection ('Is Belief in God Properly Basic?'), he claims that evidentialism stems from a theory he labels 'classical foundationalism'. Foundationalists in general hold that our beliefs should conform to a certain structure: all our beliefs should be basic or based on other beliefs that eventually terminate in basic beliefs. For example, Dr Jane Smith's belief that Jack has a cold is partially based on her belief that Jack is sneezing and has a runny nose. It is also partially based on the belief that Jared, Jack's brother, recently was diagnosed with a cold. It is easy to see how these latter two beliefs provide evidence for the former, as evidentialists would like. In contrast, my belief that 1+1=2 is not based on any belief; it is basic. More specifically, one need not provide an argument for the truth of 1+1=2 because this belief is self-evident (that is, one cannot help but assent to the proposition when one understands it). A key distinguishing feature of classical foundationalism is, according to Plantinga, its requirement that basic beliefs should be self-evident, incorrigible (that is, a belief – for instance, 'I exist' or 'there is a pain in my finger' – that cannot be doubted) or 'evident to the senses' (for example, there is a book on my desk). Because theistic belief is not self-evident, incorrigible, or evident to the senses, it must have evidential support to be rationally acceptable. Although Plantinga rejects classical foundationalism, he does not reject foundationalism *tout court*. That is, while Plantinga agrees with the general foundationalist claim that our beliefs should be basic or based on beliefs that eventually terminate in basic beliefs, he renounces the classical foundationalist criterion for properly basic beliefs. More specifically, as we have seen, he argues that the belief 'God exists' is (or can be) a properly basic belief and thus does not need to be supported by arguments or any other evidential considerations.

How does Plantinga defend such controversial claims? One reason the criterion proposed by classical foundationalists is not acceptable according to Plantinga is that it does not meet its own standards. That is, the belief that properly basic beliefs must be either self-evident, incorrigible, or evident to the senses is itself neither self-evident, nor incorrigible, nor evident to the senses. So it is not properly basic. Moreover, Plantinga contends that classical foundationalists have not provided any argument for their claims; and without such an argument it seems that such beliefs are not based on beliefs that are themselves self-evident, incorrigible, or evident to the senses. Hence, it appears that classical foundationalism is irrational. Beyond these self-inflicted wounds, Plantinga insists that classical foundationalism is too restrictive. For beliefs such as 'I visited Amsterdam last year' or 'I had a cheese sandwich for lunch' are not based on any beliefs; neither are they self-evident, nor incorrigible, nor evident to the senses. Nevertheless, they are clearly rationally acceptable, contrary to what classical foundationalism would suggest.

To develop a better theory of proper basicality, Plantinga contends that we must investigate instances of properly basic beliefs and nonbasic beliefs and hypothesize what characteristics distinguish them from each other. Such an investigation would reveal that beliefs are properly basic if they are grounded in the right experience or circumstance. Thus my belief that 'I had a cheese sandwich for lunch' is properly basic because it arises from my memory in the appropriate circumstances. Although Plantinga admits that it is difficult to explain what exactly counts as good grounds or right circumstances, he maintains that belief in God can be properly basic when grounded in the appropriate experiences. So someone beholding the pristine emerald waters off Destin, Florida, may form the belief that 'this is God's handiwork' and be perfectly rational in doing so, despite lacking any supporting arguments, because the belief wells up in the appropriate circumstances.

Interestingly enough, because epistemologists were already realising the deficiencies of classical foundationalism, Plantinga's arguments could not be so easily ruled out. In other words, as epistemologists developed alternative theories of knowledge in the light of the waning influence of classical foundationalism, Plantinga's controversial position that allowed belief in God to be properly basic garnered much attention and provoked heated debate. Although his articulation of this theory in this tumultuous epistemo-logical milieu was quite innovative, he credited many of the original insights found in his position to thinkers in the Reformed Calvinist tradition. As a result, the name 'Reformed Epistemology' was most commonly associated with Plantinga's views and those closely allied to it. Interestingly enough, then, just as the disintegration of classical foundationalism in the broader episte-mological context softened up the ground for Plantinga and other Reformed Epistemologists in Philosophy of Religion, so too Plantinga's more recent theory of warrant, which sprang up in a Philosophy of Religion context, has grown to become a contender in the general epistemological arena. This fruitful cross-fertilisation is one reason that many philosophers consider religious epistemology to be the most exciting areas of Philosophy of Religion today.

One important response to Reformed Epistemology and Plantinga in particular is to be found in Philip L. Quinn's 'On Finding the Foundations of Theism'.[4] In this essay, Quinn questions several of Plantinga's general epistemological theses. For example, he argues that Plantinga's attacks on classical foundationalism are less than decisive. Moreover, he questions if Plantinga's own method of theorising about proper basicality will in the end show that the belief that God exists is properly basic. More specifically, Quinn contends that, while Plantinga may be right that in some circumstances belief in God is properly basic, it is not for most intellectually sophisticated believers today. Why is that? The problem is that properly basic beliefs can be sabotaged or, as philosophers like to say, defeated. Take an example. Suppose that upon walking down the aisle in the supermarket, you see a bottle of clear liquid marked 'Natural Spring Water' and accordingly form the belief 'that is water in that bottle'. Imagine further that you read a story in a reliable local newspaper that many supermarkets in the area have recently received shipments of bottles that were mistakenly filled with a clear liquid that was not water. Upon remembering the information of the article, you no longer believe that the liquid in the bottle is water. Your belief, although originally properly basic, is thus undermined or defeated by other information; one cannot rationally accept it anymore in such circumstances. Quinn argues that theistic belief is also defeated by such things as the presence of evil in the world and atheistic explanations of religious belief. Of course, once a belief is defeated, it does not follow that one could never rationally hold it again. Suppose I also hear that the story about the fake water was a hoax – a story slipped in by a prankster unbeknownst to the usually vigilant editors of the paper. Then the defeater (that is, the information in the story) is itself defeated. Quinn suggests analogously that natural theology (arguments for the existence of God) and attacks on the problem of evil may be needed to establish the rationality of belief in God, so that theistic belief is not properly basic but requires evidential support.

In the second part of our third selection ('Intellectual Sophistication and Basic Belief in God') Plantinga takes up Quinn's challenge and argues that the presence of evil in the world and other types of consideration do not provide very strong defeaters for properly basic theistic belief. In addition, Plantinga argues that, even if one did have defeaters for theistic belief, a theist would not need to provide evidence for the existence of God: refuting the argument against theistic belief would be sufficient to retain rational or warranted theistic belief. While Quinn thinks that such refutations would provide warrant for theistic beliefs, rendering them nonbasic, Plantinga believes that they simply nullify the defeaters and preserve the status of theistic beliefs as properly basic. Finally, Plantinga argues that some properly basic beliefs (including the belief that God exists) could be such that they are to be preferred even in the face of defeaters.

Our last selection, then, contains Quinn's reply to Plantinga ('Defeating Theistic Beliefs'). As one might expect, Quinn takes the challenge to theistic belief from the problem of evil and other considerations to be stronger than Plantinga does. Thus he believes that natural theology and other theistic arguments could be much more important to the rationality or warrant or theistic belief than Plantinga allows.

Before closing our discussion, we should consider Plantinga's latest thoughts on such matters, which are contained in his recent book *Warranted Christian Belief*.[5] This book is devoted to a full-scale defence of the claim that theistic beliefs, and even specifically Christian beliefs (such as 'Jesus atoned for our sin') are (or can be) properly basic with respect to warrant. His arguments touch on many issues in this book, most of which would take us too far afield for our purposes. But he provides a fascinating new argument that has potentially momentous implications for the question of whether belief in God is properly basic with respect to warrant. If Christian belief is false, and there is no God, then Plantinga admits that belief in God is probably not warrant-basic. After all, if there is no God, then how can we possess a faculty that produces belief in God reliably? It is difficult to see how anyone without such a reliable faculty could be warranted in believing in God without evidence or arguments.[6] Alternatively, if Christian belief is true, and we were created by an omnipotent, loving God, then it is reasonable to think that theistic belief is warrant-basic. In Plantinga's own words:

> [God] would of course intend that we be able to be aware of his presence and to know something about him. And if that is so, the natural thing to think is that he created us in such a way that we would come to hold such true beliefs as that there is such a person as God, that he is our creator, that we owe him obedience and worship, that he is worthy of worship, that he loves us, and so on. And if *that* is so, then the natural thing to think is that the cognitive processes that *do* produce belief in God are aimed by their designer at producing that belief. But then the belief in question will be produced by cognitive faculties functioning properly according to a design plan successfully aimed at truth: it will therefore have warrant.[7]

So how exactly does this argument affect his debate with Quinn and the importance of natural theology?

Let us approach this question by considering a thought experiment. In a world of genetic engineering and the human genome project, some people believe that it will be possible one day to have 'designer babies'. No matter how practical such designing really is, it seems that we can at least imagine what we would do if we could 'design' our children. Suppose, then, that we had staggering control over designing our offspring. We would want them to know that we loved them; we would like them to be able to sense this; and we would want them to be able to recognise this love very easily. We would not want them to need to reason like this: 'Mom and Dad have done X for me; most of the time when people do X for others, they love them; therefore, Mom and Dad love me.' In other words, we would want them to be able to know, in a properly basic way, without needing to rely on arguments, that we love them. Of course, this does not mean that we would like them to be unfamiliar with any evidence supporting the claim that their parents love them. If their peers, say, tried to unsettle them by charging that their parents did not love them, we would desire that they have access to (or be in possession of) evidence of our love so that they could dispute such charges. But presumably we would also desire that their immediate acquaintance with our love would be strong enough that they would not doubt it even if they were pummelled with such charges.

This thought experiment suggests that Plantinga is correct in saying that if Christian theism is true, then theistic belief is probably warrant-basic. For God, as a loving parent, would presumably design us to be able to grasp such beliefs in a basic way. Moreover, God would presumably not want challenges (such as the presence of evil in the world) to shake us enough so that we lose faith. Note, however, that it seems that this thought experiment also shows that God would desire that we be in possession of (or have access to) evidence for our beliefs (or at least evidence to undermine challenges to our beliefs). If this is right, then it seems that natural theology is important, even if it is not necessary for believers to know that God exists.

An interesting upshot of Plantinga's position is that questions of religious epistemology cannot be answered in isolation from other issues in Philosophy of Religion. For the answer to the question 'Can one be warranted in holding theistic belief without arguments?' will depend on whether one thinks that God exists. So natural theology, the problem of evil and similar issues are interesting and significant not only in themselves but also in helping to shape one's opinion in religious epistemology.[8]

NOTES

1. Blaise Pascal, *Pensées*, translated with an Introduction by A. J. Krailsheimer (New York: Penguin Books, 1966), pp. 150–1 (number 418).
2. William K. Clifford, 'The Ethics of Belief', *Lectures and Essays* (New York: Macmillan, 1901), p. 183.
3. Plantinga's general epistemological thoughts appear in *Warrant: The Current Debate* (New York: Oxford University Press, 1993), and *Warrant and Proper Function* (New York: Oxford University Press, 1993). The first book was an overview and criticism of the contemporary epistemological landscape that paves the way for his positive account in the second book.
4. *Faith and Philosophy* 2, 4 October 1985, pp. 469–86.
5. Alvin Plantinga, *Warranted Christian Belief* (New York: Oxford University Press, 2000).
6. For the details of Plantinga's argument, see *Warranted Christian Belief*, pp. 186–8.

7. *Warranted Christian Belief*, pp. 188–9. Plantinga does not explicitly say in this quoted passage that if God exists, then belief in God is probably warrant-basic. But 'Is Belief in God Warrant-Basic?' (p. 186) is the title of the section in which this passage appears and, appropriately enough, the title of the subsection is 'If True, Probably So'.

8. I would like to thank Michael Bergmann, William Lane Craig and Michael Murray for helpful comments on earlier versions of this introduction. Any deficiencies that remain are, of course, my responsibility.

I.I

'THE LOGIC OF PASCAL'S WAGER'

Ian Hacking

Pascal's wager is the name of some game-theoretic considerations that concern belief in God.[1] I show that Pascal briefly presents three distinct arguments, each with different premises. In each case, the conclusion does follow from the premisses. In each case, there is at least one unacceptable premiss. I am concerned here only with the logic of the wager, that is, with the question of whether the conclusion does follow from the premisses.

My aims are twofold. First, Pascal's wager has been extensively studied, especially in recent times when the existential and nondeductive character-istics of the argument have seemed more important to moralists and theo-logians than traditional, more deductive ways to God. Despite such studies, the logic of Pascal's three arguments has never been set out. Moralists tend not to study decision theory. Pascal invented it. This chapter may help the moralists who read his thoughts to understand his invention.[2]

Second, I have the historical aim, divorced from morality, of stating a bit of the history of probability. Pascal's arguments show that it was possible to have a deep understanding of what we now call decision theory, even in the seventeenth century. Possible, but not easy: Pascal's distinctions escaped most of his readers. Yet despite misunderstanding, Pascal's was a decisive turning point in probability theory. Pascal is celebrated for the probability corre-spondence with Fermat, but that is not his most profound contribution to probability.[3] Pascal's thought showed that the mathematics of games of chance had quite general applications. He made it possible for *the doctrine*

Ian Hacking, 'The Logic of Pascal's Wager', *American Philosophical Quarterly*, 9, 2 (1972), pp. 186–92.

of chances (a theory involving "objective" frequencies, whose primitive concept is expectation or average winnings) to become *the art of conjecture* (a "subjective" theory about degrees of confidence).[4]

DECISION THEORY

Decision theory is the theory of deciding what to do when it is uncertain what will happen. *Given* an exhaustive list of possible hypotheses about the way the world is, the observations or experimental data relevant to these hypotheses, together with an inventory of possible decisions, and the various utilities of making these decisions in various possible states of the world, *determine* the best decision.

A special case of this problem occurs when no experiments are made. In the thought that concerns us, Pascal deliberately "ties his hands" and refuses to look at any observations or experimental data bearing on the existence of a Christian God. He is writing for those who will not countenance miracles, or the doctors of the church, or the witness of the faithful. So we may restrict our attention to the logic of decision when there is no experimental data.

Among the valid argument forms investigated by decision theory, I show three apprehended by Pascal. I call them "valid" in the sense now favored by logicians. A valid argument form is one in which the conclusion follows from the premisses. Colloquially, of course, a valid argument is one that is pertinent and persuasive. Nowhere in this article do I imply that Pascal's arguments are persuasive. But this is not because they are invalid (in the logician's sense) but because the premisses of the arguments are, at best, debatable. The three argument forms that concern us follow.

Dominance

The simplest special case occurs when one course of action is better no matter what the world is like. Schematically, suppose that we have some exhaustive set of possible states of affairs: we label the states $S_1, S_2 \ldots$ Suppose that in some state S_i the utility U_i1 of performing act A_1 is greater than the utility of U_i2 of performing act A_2. In no other state of affairs is the utility of performing A_1 less than A_2. Then, under no circumstances could A_2 have happier consequences than A_1, and under some circumstances A_1 could be better than A_2, A_1 is said to dominate A_2. If one act dominates all others, the solution to our decision problem is *"perform the dominant act."*

Expectation

The argument from dominance does not consider how likely are various states of affairs. Even if dominating A_1 is better only in a very unlikely state of affairs, then, because A_1 can never fare worse than any other act, it is worthwhile performing A_1. But suppose no action dominates, although we do think we know which states of affairs are more likely than others. Suppose we can assess the probability of each state of affairs. Then (no matter what one means by "probability") one argues as follows. We have assigned a probability p_1 to each possible state of affairs S_i in some exhaustive set. Let U_{ij} stand for the utility of doing A_j if S_i actually obtains. The *expected value*, or *expectation*, of A_j is the average[5] value of doing A_j: namely, $\Sigma_i p_i U_{ij}$. An argument from *expectation* concludes with the advice "*Perform an act with highest expectation.*"

Dominating Expectation

It may happen that we do not know, or cannot agree on, the probabilities of the various states of affairs. We can at best agree on a set of probability assignments to the states S_i. For example, suppose we agree that the coin is biased toward heads but disagree how great is the bias; at least we agree that the probability of "next toss gives heads" exceeds one in two. If in some admissible probability assignment, the expectation of A_1 exceeds that of any other act, whereas in no admissible assignment is the expectation of A_1 less than that of any other act, then A_1 has dominating expectation. The argument from dominating expectation concludes: "*Perform an act of dominating expectation.*"[6]

The three argument schemes are mutually consistent. If one act does dominate the rest, then it will be recommended by all three arguments. If there is no dominating act but an act of highest expectation, then that act will also be the act of dominating expectation. The argument from dominance is the rarest, most special case. The argument from dominating expectation is more widely applicable.

Pascal's procedure in the thought "*Infini-rien*" is to offer an argument from dominance. Then, if its premises be rejected, to offer an argument from expectation. Then, if the second lot of premises be rejected, to offer an argument from dominating expectation.

PASCAL'S THOUGHT

Immense scholarship has been lavished on *infini-rien*: it consists of two pieces of paper covered on both sides by handwriting going in all directions, full of erasures, corrections, insertions, and afterthoughts.[7] There is endless speculation about when and how Pascal wrote these two pages; every blot of ink or raindrops on them has been given minute analysis. We do not presume to trespass on this critical work, and take for granted Lafuma's text.

"Infini-rien" has also attracted a great deal of philosophical scholarship from moralists and theologians alike. Although they have been aware of the rough lines of Pascal's argument, their own analyses have been defective because they have not noticed that Pascal has three distinct arguments. First, he offers an argument from dominance. But dominance occurs only if a certain premiss is admitted. If it is rejected, a new tack must be pursued. We get an argument from expectation. Yet this requires an implausible assignment of probabilities. So the argument is changed again to an argument from dominating expectation. Not all the links forged by Pascal are transparent, but it is remarkable how these two scratched sheets that constitute "Infini-rien" conform to this analysis. The details follow.

The argument is directed, as the *Port Royal* editors say from the start, at the sort of person who "not being convinced of the proofs of religion, and still less by the arguments of atheists, remains suspended between a state of faith and one of unbelief."[8] This assertion is extremely important. A decision program requires an exhaustive partition of possibilities. It is taken as a premiss of the argument that either there is no God or else there is a God whose characteristics are correctly reported by the Church. Mohammedanism, for example, is not admitted as a possibility. It is a corollary that Pascal's argument is good for any decision problem with the same formal structure. "An Imam could reason just as well this way," as Diderot remarked.[9]

Pascal's partition may be out of place today. But this is one thought from a book of thoughts; the other thoughts contain other reasons bearing on this partition. There are also other arguments directed at other special groups; for example, the arguments directed at Orthodox Jews whose partition, of course, is not at all like that of the Parisian about town. "God is, or he is not." This is the way Pascal abbreviates the partition of the Parisian. "Which way should we incline? Reason cannot answer." That is, there is no valid proof or disproof of God's existence. Instead, we adopt the following model:

> A game is on at the other end of an infinite distance, and heads or tails is going to turn up. Which way will you bet?

The model is then reinforced. When reason cannot answer, a sensible person can say that he or she will not play the game. But in our case, by the mere fact of living, we are engaged in play. We either believe in God, or we do not.

A decision problem requires a partition of possible actions. As Pascal sees it, you either act with complete indifference to God or you act in such a way that you will, in due course, believe in his existence and his edicts. There is no cant to Pascal. He accepts as a piece of human nature that belief is catching: if you go along with pious people, give up bad habits, follow a life of "holy water and sacraments" intended to "stupefy one" into belief, you will become a believer. Pascal is speaking to one unsure whether to follow this path or whether to be indifferent to the morality of the church. The two possible acts are *not* "Believe in God" and "Do not believe." One cannot decide to believe in God. One can decide to act so that one will very probably come to believe in God. Pascal calls that the wager that God is. To wager that God is not is to stop bothering about such things.

THE ARGUMENT FROM DOMINANCE

The decision problem is constituted by two possible states of the world and two possible courses of action. If God is not, then both courses of action are pretty much on a par. You will live your life and have no bad effects either way from supernatural intervention. But if God exists, then wagering that there is no God brings damnation. Wagering that God exists can bring salvation. Salvation is better than damnation. Hence the wager "God is" dominates the wager "he is not." The decision problem is solved.

The argument is valid. The premises are dubious, if not patently false. Few nonbelievers now can suppose that Pascal's partition exhausts the possibilities. If we allow just one further alternative, namely the thesis of some fundamentalist sects, that Jehovah damns all who toy with "holy water and sacraments," then the Catholic strategy no longer dominates. That is, there is one possible state of affairs in which the Catholic strategy does not have the best payoff.

It is a question for the historian whether Pascal's argument from dominance could ever have been effective. Perhaps some Parisians three centuries ago did believe, say, on the evidence of alleged revelation, that if there is any supernatural truth, it is that truth professed by the Church. Such people may have found the argument persuasive.

From the very first, a fallacious correction has sometimes been urged. M. J. Orcibal has found the following contemporary note by Daniel Huet: "this reasoning suits all religions; that which proves too much proves nothing. It proves only the necessity of having some religion, but not the Christian religion."[10] This is a mistake; unless one has independent grounds for excluding the proposition of an eccentric religion, that all and only religious people are damnable. This point has been nicely made recently by James Cargile.[11]

One premiss needed for Pascal's argument is that faith is catching. His interlocutor does protest that perhaps a treatment of holy water and sacraments is not going to work. The theme is not well developed.[12] Also, many of us will share William James's suspicion that a person who becomes a believer for the reasons urged by Pascal is not going to get the payoffs hoped for.[13] Although all these questions are crucial to the merit of the argument as a piece of apologetics, they are irrelevant to its logical validity. The conclusion does follow from the premisses.

THE ARGUMENT FROM EXPECTATION

Pascal is more worried by another premiss, as yet hardly stated. We assumed that if God is not, then either course of action has roughly equal utility. But this is untrue. The libertine is giving up something if the choice is to adopt a pious form of life. The libertine likes sin. If God is not, the worldly life is preferable to the cloistered one. The wager "God is" does not dominate, for there is one circumstance (God is not) in which accepting this wager, that is, adopting the pious life, has lower utility than the other wager. When dominance is challenged, we require an argument from probabilities.

The transition is swift, perhaps too swift. Having heard the argument from dominance, the interlocutor says, "Very well. But suppose I am asked to stake too much?" This remark is obscure unless seen in the light of the present analysis. The interlocutor is protesting that to follow the pious life something must be given up. Perhaps the stakes are too much, that is, perhaps there is a significant difference between the utility of the two actions under the hypothesis that there is no God. So Pascal has to introduce the policy of maximizing expectation. If the chances of heads and tails are equal and there are equal payoffs for either outcome, it is a matter of indifference whether we bet on heads. But if heads pays twice as much as tails, then clearly we bet on heads. In the agnostic's existential situation, the optimal payoff if there is no God is a worldly life. The optimal payoff if there is a God is salvation, of incomparably greater value. Hence, if there is an equal chance of God's existence or nonexistence, the expectation of choosing the pious life exceeds that of choosing the worldly one. The argument from expectation concludes, act so that you will come to believe in God.

THE ARGUMENT FROM DOMINATING EXPECTATION

The argument from expectation can hardly be maintained. Although it is valid, it requires a monstrous premiss of equal chance. We have no good reason for picking one half as the chance of God's existence. This argument can work only for people who are, in the strongest sense, exactly as unsure whether God exists as they are unsure whether he does not exist. Against all other agnostics, another argument is called for.

The argument from expectation with an equal probability distribution requires only that salvation, if God is, is more valuable than sinful pleasures, when there is no God. But salvation is infinitely preferable to the joys of the worldly life. No matter how great may be the daily pleasures of the libertine, they are finite. Salvation, according to Pascal, is infinitely blessed.

Moreover, although we have no idea of the chance that God exists, it is not zero. Otherwise there would be no problem. There is a finite positive chance that God exists. No matter what this finite chance is—no matter how small—the expectation of the pious strategy with infinite reward exceeds that of the worldly one. Hence, the pious strategy must be followed. This is an argument from dominating expectation.

SUMMARY

All three arguments are valid. None are convincing. All rely on dubious premisses. The arguments are worthless as apologetics today, for no present agnostic who understood the arguments would ever be moved to accept all the premisses.

The most dubious premiss is the partition, with its concomitant assignment of utilities. God is (and belief in him brings salvation) or God is not (and nonbelievers who have heard the Word are damned). It is no criticism of Pascal that he assumes this partition: he is directing his argument at his fellows who accept it. He knew this, and so did his editors. All three arguments assume this partition and the assigned utilities.

Many questions of morality and theology may be adduced against the wager. What is striking is that Pascal raised the logically relevant questions. There is a logically special feature of the argument from dominance, which is challenged if the utility of a libertine life exceeds that of a pious one, in the event that there is no God. To allow for this difficulty, we move to the second argument form, employing probabilities. An equal distribution of probabilities has some appeal, but that special logical feature is in turn abandoned as we move to the third argument form.

NOTES

1. Blaise Pascal, *Pensées sur la religion et sur quelque autres sujets*, the first edition, *édition de Port Royal*, was in 1670. The standard text is that of Louis Lafuma (Paris, 1951); or *Oeuvres Complètes*, ed. Lafuma (Paris, 1963). Pascal's wager is the fragment headed "Infini-rien," which is number 418 of Lafuma. Many older editions and translations use Leon Brunschvieg's numeration, where "Infini-rien" is 233.

2. Pascal did not invent the notion that belief in God is better than disbelief because belief brings salvation if there is a God and costs little if there is no God. He invented the concepts of decision theory that create valid argument forms out of this earlier idea. For precursors of Pascal (who did not understand Pascal's logic) see Georges Brunet, *Le Pari de Pascal* (Paris, 1956), p. 62.

3. The 1654 letters to Fermat are in the *Oeuvres Complètes*, op. cit., pp. 43–49. There are several fabulous anecdotes about the origin of this correspondence in general circulation: for a good anecdote, consult Oystein Ore, "Pascal and the Invention of Probability Theory," *American Mathematical Monthly* 67 (1960), pp. 409–19. For a complete historical background, see Jean Mesnard, *Pascal et les Roannez* (Bruges, 1965).

4. The art of conjecture and what used to be called the subjective theory of probability begins with Jacques Bernoulli, *Art conjectandi* (Basel, 1713). Carnap has argued that interpretations of probability as objective long-run frequencies commence only in the nineteenth century (*Logical Foundations of Probability* [Chicago, 1950], p. 42). In fact, the frequency-style interpretation is the oldest, although Pascal began to change all that. Proofs of this opinion will be published elsewhere. The doctrine of chances is an old name for the study of physical properties of games of chance, although the most celebrated work of that title, by Abraham de Moivre, was published five years after the appearance of Bernoulli's masterpiece.

5. Someone unacquainted with probability jargon may wonder why the expectation is called an "average." This innocent question probes quite deep. The answer depends on what one means by probability. If probability is long-run frequency, then the expectation is quite literally the average profit. For example, if act A_j is "bet on heads" and a coin falls heads two-thirds of the tosses, and if the payoff for a correct bet is $5, while the fine for an incorrect one is $4, the average profit on A_j is

$$\tfrac{2}{3}(\$5) + \tfrac{1}{3}(-\$4) = \$2$$

If probabilities are personal degrees of confidence, the expectation is not, strictly speaking, an average. The validity of this argument form, under this interpretation, may be derived from a joint analysis of personal probability and utility, as in F. P. Ramsey, "Truth and Probability," in *The Foundations of Mathematics* (London, 1931), pp. 156–98. If probabilities are long-run frequencies and one is repeatedly wagering, then maximizing expectation is justified as bringing the best average profits. If one wagers only once, however, the validity of this pattern of argument may be questioned.

6. If probabilities are my personal degrees of confidence, then I may assign unique probabilities to each state S_i and get along with expectation. Even so I may need dominating expectation in arguing with others. Like Pascal, I may say, "Our probability assessments differ, but at least we agree the probabilities lie in this range, and there is still an inference from dominating expectation."

7. For a photograph, see, for example, Henri Gouhier, *Blaise Pascal, commentaires* (Paris, 1966), or G. Brunet, op. cit., n. 2.

8. For example, in the 6th (unnumbered) page of the preface to the edition of Amsterdam, 1677.

9. Denis Diderot, *Pensées philosophiques*, LIX, *Oeuvres*, ed. J. Assézat (Paris, 1875–877), Vol. I, p. 167.

10. M.J. Orcibal, "Le fragment infini-rien et ses sources," p. 183, n. 89 in *Blaise Pascal, l'homme et l'oeuvre*, Cahiers de Royaumont (Paris, 1956).

11. James Cargile, "Pascal's Wager," *Philosophy* 41 (1966): 250–57.

12. One may pedantically urge a partition into three states of affairs: God is not; God is, and one will come to believe by being pious; and God is, but one will not come to believe by being pious. The pious strategy still dominates, under the initial assignment of utilities favored by Pascal.

13. William James, "The Will to Believe," *The Will to Believe and other Essays in Popular Philosophy* (London, 1897).

1.2

'A CENTRAL THEISTIC ARGUMENT'

George Schlesinger

INTRODUCTION

Pascal's wager is as a rule more easily appreciated than any other argument in support of religious belief. After all, the locution (which represents the essential structure of the wager), "I have nothing to lose and everything to gain by doing such and such," is a common one and readily understood by everybody.

At the same time the wager has been the target of a number of objections. I propose here to deal with three of these; two are widely known, whereas the third is of very recent origin. Finally, I also point out that the gravest objection to the wager requires a reply that is based on an argument indispensable in the context of nearly all other theistic proofs. Hence, that argument may well be regarded as the most central theistic argument.

The first objection has no great logical force but carries considerable psychological weight. It is unique insofar that it contends not so much that the wager violates the rules of sound thinking and is therefore invalid but rather that it is repugnant, and, in a religious context, it is especially unseemly. The second objection contends that even if the argument were logically impeccable it would lead nowhere. The last one, surprisingly enough, claims that it is overly effective, so much so that it should not at all matter what an individual does or fails to do, because he or she is by virtue of the wager in a maximally advantageous position anyway with regard to eternal salvation.

George Schlesinger, 'A Central Theistic Argument', in Jeff Jordan (ed.), *Gambling on God: Essays on Pascal's Wager* (Lanham, MD: Rowman & Littlefield, 1994), pp. 83–99.

THE WAGER AND GREED

It is common knowledge that many well-intentioned individuals reject the wager for reasons that do not require much philosophical sophistication. They find it mercenary. They believe it appeals to the scheming, calculating self and are thus repelled by it. Without delving deep into theological issues, it has seemed to many that applying betting rules, relevant to moneymaking ventures, to a supposedly infinitely more exalted subject to lure skeptics by appealing to their grasping instincts offends religious proprieties.

People have found absurd the very notion that there may be any comparison between the seeker of a transcendent goal in life and a patron of a gambling house. We need not assume that greed as such is held generally in our highly acquisitive society in intense contempt. In the present context, however, it appears to offend the very spirit of what one is supposed to pursue. The essence of religion is generally perceived as the conviction that all profane, self-seeking ambitions are incompatible with the quest for piety. The religious seeker is not one to be mired in self-indulgent pursuits but passionately devotes oneself to much nobler and more ultimate concerns.

Now of course Pascal was quite explicit in saying that the skeptic's wagering on God is no more than a first step, and those who take no further steps will have achieved nothing. However, his advice to the wagerer is to start behaving as one would if one actually believed, because Pascal believed that such conduct is likely to lead to a truly dedicated life in the service of God. By starting to observe the rituals of religion, associating with pious persons, and studying the sacred literature, individuals are likely to transform their sentiments and feelings and eventually acquire genuine belief.

Yet Pascal's reply has failed to satisfy many of his critics. If grasping is incompatible with the spirit of religion, then it is not to be used as a vehicle with which to reach any destination. Noble ends are debased when pursued by ignoble means.

Pascal's supporters at this stage are usually inclined to offer distinctions between means that do not and means that do justify their end. I believe a more important point should be made: we are free to assume that no objective is ever hallowed enough that it should be impermissible to reach it by anything but impeccable means.

First, a relatively simple point about the offensiveness of greed. Suppose there is a person of an extraordinarily high income who gives away almost all his money to charity, retaining only what is necessary for bare existence. Furthermore, this individual does not seek the gratitude of the beneficiaries of these donations nor the admiration of the community. In fact, this person always makes every possible effort to ensure that no one should be aware of these humanitarian activities. Despite all this, it is conceivable that he could be charged with selfishness and greed: he is surely aware of his almost unparalleled, heroic, moral accomplishments. Evidently therefore he is a highly greedy individual;

what he apparently craves is not material possessions nor the prestige accorded for outstanding philanthropy but the ability to relish the knowledge that he has outdone practically everyone in his contempt for stinginess, in his indifference for fame and praise, and the ability to enjoy the deep satisfaction of having been able to reach the pinnacle of otherdirectedness and the heights of noble magnanimity free of the slightest taint of petty self-regard.

Clearly, if we were to take this line, then we would be forced to conclude that every act which fulfills some wish is greedy and selfish and no freely willed act would ever be free of sin. Thus, the sensible thing to say is that the pursuit of a quest is deplorable when it brings harm either to others or to oneself in the sense that it debases the questing individual (which Pascal calls "poisonous pleasures") who could instead strive for more refined, higher order, life-enhancing pleasures.

Now the pleasure that Pascal holds up before his "calculating clients" is of the most exalted kind, one that is simply inaccessible to an individual who has not spent life passionately serving the Master of the Universe and thereby developing and perfecting one's soul, without which one lacks the capacity to partake in the transmundane bliss available to the select few. Only the suitably groomed soul, when released from its earthly fetters, will bask in the radiance of the Divine presence and delight in the adoring communion with a loving God. If craving for such an end is a manifestation of greed, then it is the manifestation of a noble greed that is to be acclaimed. Therefore, only if one were to assume that the ultimate reward of the righteous is the satisfaction of some cruder yearnings could one charge a follower of Pascal with trying to enkindle our unseemly mercenary motives.

PRACTICE AND BELIEF

However, a more important point needs to be made as well. The essence of true religion is not the intellectual assent to a set of propositions nor is it the verbal profession of certain beliefs. It is a full commitment and devotion, having one's heart and soul virtually consumed by a deep reverence and love of God. Maimonides wrote:

> What is the proper love of God? It is the love of the Lord with a great and very strong love so that one's soul shall be tied to the love of the Lord, and one should be continually enraptured by it, like a lovesick individual . . .[1]

The immediate question one is bound to ask is, how does one achieve such a state of mind? Belief might be obtained through compelling arguments, or credible evidence, but surely exaltation or love is not an epistemic universal and cannot be planted into one's heart by the methodological rules of knowledge acquisition.

A very brief answer has been hinted at by the sagacious Hillel, who, as the famous story goes, was approached by someone demanding to be taught the whole Law while standing on one foot. Hillel agreed and informed the man that the single sentence, "Whatever is hateful to you do not do it to your fellow-human," contains the essence of all there is to be learned.[2] Hillel's fascinating precis of the Law raises many problems. One of them is in Leviticus 19:18: it says, "You shall love your fellow-human as yourself." Why did he believe it necessary to change the wording of the Scriptures? This particular question may have a simple answer, namely, Hillel realized that one cannot be commanded to have certain sentiments; I could be ordered to act or to refrain from acting in a certain way but not to love someone I happen to dislike. Thus, to reach the stage that the Scripture prescribes where one actually loves other human beings, we have to begin with the kind of behavior that is always associated with such a sentiment, that is, our practical conduct toward our fellow humans should be like that toward our own self: never actually do anything injurious to their interests. Desirable behavior is assumed to generate eventually desirable feelings.

Hillel's insight should be applied in the context of one's relation to God as well. The twelfth-century poet-philosopher Judah Halevi was quite explicit on this point, "Man can reach God only by doing His commands" (*Cuzari*, 2,46). Good thoughts, on their own, are too fleeting and insubstantial, and physical acts are concrete; when one has trained oneself to act in accordance with the dictates of religion and actual behavior closely resembles the behavior of those who possess truly deep religious sentiments, then one has provided oneself with the proper grounds on which fervent love for the Divine may grow. The theory behind this view may be compared with what today is called "behavior modification." This kind of therapy is based on the belief that it is possible to induce feelings of aversion to what is harmful and a natural desire for what is beneficial through adopting certain patterns of behavior. On the more extreme version of this view (as held by Halevi), it is not merely possible but essential to begin one's journey toward authentic theism by looking on the practices mandated by religion as the proper first step toward genuine piety. On this view, the wagerer who starts out satisfying the demands of faith before having acquired actual belief is not merely doing what is calculating and mercenary nor even that which is merely commendable but is engaged in what is absolutely indispensable for reaching the noble objective that is sought.

ARE THERE INFINITELY MANY EQUALLY VIABLE HYPOTHESES?

The second, oft-repeated objection is a relatively powerful, clearly articulated objection, known as the "many-gods objection." Pascal has been charged with making the unwarranted assumption that the problem facing the agnostic is confined to the question of which of two options to choose. In reality, however, in addition to the God of the theist, there are any number of other possible ones as well. How is the wagerer to assess the relative benefits associated with betting on Osiris, Baal, Dagon, Zeus, or Blodenwedd? Pascal provides no argument to guide us to the right deity, worshiping whom one is most likely to secure oneself eternal salvation.

Before attempting to advance any reply, I should point out that though the objection is, as already mentioned, a serious one, we find in the literature several versions, depicting a far more threatening portrayal of the difficulty than it is in reality. Richard Gale, for example, sees the following devastating consequences of the many-gods objection:

> from the fact that it is logically possible that God exists it does not follow that the product of the probability of his existence and an infinite number is infinite. In a fair lottery with a denumerable infinity of tickets, for each ticket it is true that it is logically possible that it will win, but the probability of its doing so is infinitesimal and the product of an infinitesimal and an infinite number is itself infinitesimal. Thus the expected gain of buying a ticket is not infinite but infinitesimal. There is at least a denumerable infinity of logically possible deities . . . and thus betting on any one of them the expected gain is zero according to this argument.[3]

The opponents of the wager have had the tendency to magnify the gravity of the problem by overcalculating the number of alternatives available for the religious seeker and hence depicting Pascal's counsel as quite hopelessly arbitrary. For example, J.L. Mackie, who lists a number of possible deities that seem to have escaped Pascal's notice, also mentions,

> that there might be a god who looked with more favor on honest doubters or atheists who, in Hume's words, proportioned their belief to the evidence, than on mercenary manipulators of their own understanding. Indeed, this would follow from the ascription to God of moral goodness in any sense we can understand.[4]

Also fairly often heard is the argument that among the infinitely many possible deities, we must not overlook one who grants eternal reward to those who firmly deny the existence of a theistic God and punishes all those who believe in him.

Richard Gale goes even further, suggesting that

> there is the logically possible deity who rewards with infinite felicity all and only those who believe in him and step on only one sidewalk crack in the course of their life, as well as the two-crack deity, the three-crack deity, and so on ad infinitum.[5]

There are several lines one may adopt to meet this kind of objection. One may be based on the realization that Pascal is addressing individuals who, though they may be hardened in their disbelief, do have a notion of what genuine religion is about. In other words, though they deny its truth, they acknowledge its meaningfulness and understand that it is based on a highly optimistic view of human potential and of the sublime possible level of existence it postulates. It is a necessary presupposition of the wager that one understands that the notion of "genuine religion" is conceptually associated with a number of other exalted notions, and those people whom Pascal addresses are to be assumed to have a basic grasp of the sublime concerns of its devout practitioners. Divine worship in an authentic sense (as distinct from a pagan sense, where one is trying to propitiate the supernatural powers on whose whims one's fate depends) is in no way to be likened to a commercial transaction. Whatever the probability of the existence of an afterlife worth seeking with all one's might is, it is certainly not to be viewed as a place to which one may be admitted after one has paid the amount demanded by its Divine Proprietor. "The service of God is not intended for God's perfection; it is intended for our own perfection," says Maimonides. On this view, an individual who has devoted his or her life to Divine service has nurtured and refined his or her soul, rendering it capable of receiving and finding felicity in the celestial radiance available for those prepared to absorb it. In brief, the wagerer is supposed to appreciate that in the context of theism, highly involved systems of theologies have been developed over the centuries, theologies that have an internal coherence and consist of many propositions with an appeal to the intellect as well as to the nobler, human sentiments.

Nothing of this sort exists in the context of, say, the sidewalk deity. It is difficult to conceive a reason why one should come to love such a being or why one should desire to be in its proximity. Of course, one might claim that without any rhyme or reason it capriciously rewards those who obey its arbitrary demands. Still, a Pascalian would insist that because a good portion of theistic belief is in harmony with natural, noble aspirations and is embedded in highly developed theology, it has to be ascribed a considerably higher probability than those with little appeal to the human mind and heart.

Thus, we are permitted to assert the following: if we were to agree that different deities have different probabilities, then even if there are infinitely many candidates for the office of the Master of the Universe it does not follow that each has zero probability. One may, if one wants to, ascribe a finite value to the probability of the existence of each one of them and yet obtain a sum total of all these (which is the value of the probability of the infinite disjunction of "Zeus exists OR Baal exists OR etc."), an amount that does not exceed one. This should be the case if the various finite probabilities are members of a convergent series, for instance, the sum of the series $\frac{1}{2} + \frac{1}{4} + \frac{1}{8} + \ldots$ never actually reaches one. This should be sufficient to lay to rest Gale's fear that if "there is at least a denumerable infinity of logically possible deities . . . [then] betting on any one of them the expected gain is zero."

THE CRITERION FOR BETTING WHEN THE EXPECTED UTILITIES ARE INFINITE

I submit a crucial point, one that is contrary to what numerous philosophers hold, namely, that when each possible outcome carries an infinite expected value, it is rational to bet on the outcome most probable to occur. Are there solid grounds for my hypothesis? Let me first point out that grounds are provided for this view by common sense (which in itself would not be sufficient to establish my point). Anyone wishing to verify this experimentally may consider the following two cases, A and B:

A = Of the billions of people alive at the present moment, one and only one is going to enjoy eternal salvation, whereas the rest vanish into nothingness after completing their lives upon this earth. A truly randomizing device is going to determine the identity of the single lucky individual.

B = Of the billions of people alive at the present moment, one and only one is going to vanish into nothingness after completing one's existence upon this planet; the rest are going to enjoy eternal salvation. A truly randomizing device is going to determine the identity of the one unlucky individual.

Now, without offering preliminary explanations, ask any number of individuals (and you may include among them some mathematicians) which case they would prefer to obtain? If my experience is reliable to any degree, rarely if ever does anybody argue: although if B is true then I am a billion times more likely to be among the blessed, this is quite irrelevant; the expected utilities are equal and therefore it makes no difference which is true.

Now let us look at a truly compelling argument. In cases where the mathematical expectations are infinite, the criterion for choosing the outcome to bet on is its probability. In all betting situations the sum I am charged to participate I am charged with certainty, whereas the prize I may receive is uncertain. Fairness demands that I be compensated through being charged less than the value of the prize and proportionately so, that is, the lower the probability of winning, the less I should be charged. Thus, it is obvious that the same set of rules cannot apply in case the prize is infinite, as in other cases. Justice cannot demand that the cost for being permitted to bet should equal the expected utilities, because then the fair cost should be infinite. But that is absurd: why should I definitely pay an infinite amount for a less than certain chance of winning back the same amount? It is evident therefore that the situation demands that a different principle must be guiding a wagerer faced with the problem of which of the various outcomes—each associated with infinite utilities—to choose. Because neither expected utilities nor the magnitude of the prize can serve as one's criterion, by elimination it should be reasonable to be guided by the value of the probability: wager on the outcome that is most likely to materialize.

DEITIES WITH DIFFERENT DEGREES OF PLAUSIBILITY

Let us consider a number of possible solutions to the many-gods problem. First, it is reasonable that a scrupulously just deity who ensures that each person's celestial reward is in direct proportion to the amount of energy and time invested throughout one's earthly life to the refinement of one's soul so as to increase its susceptibility to that reward, is considerably more probable than a fancy-bred capricious power whose awards are not in any obvious way related to earning, meriting, or the enhanced quality of the receptivity or atonement of the worshipper. Thus, we regard it at least fairly plausible that a deity may exist who does not hand out compensation or reimbursement for the trouble his adherents have gone through in serving him but who is so exalted that it seems reasonable to assume that the highest form of felicity is to center one's life around him. The most important task is to do everything in one's power to adjust and attune one's soul so that it has the capacity of fully resonating with the celestial radiance in which it will be submerged. A mere century or two ago theists did not recoil from using such locutions and were unembarrassed by what today may strike some as inflated grandiloquence. Thus we find the eighteenth-century poet and theologian M. H. Luzatto making (in his widely studied *Mesilat Yesharim*) the brief statement, because he regarded the matter too obvious to require elaboration, "Man came into the world only to achieve nearness to God." Surely such a view is bound to permeate every act and every thought of its adherent; it is part of an inclusive outlook on life and belongs to an extensive system of interconnected propositions.

Furthermore, in the context of the sublime God of the theist, many found it not unreasonable to view life's many trials and tribulations as instruments of soul-making or in any case as means to an end that may surpass our understanding. On the other hand, when referring to deities devoid of the various glorious Divine attributes, it seems more natural to speak like Gloucester: "As flies to wanton boys, are we to the gods/They kill us for their sport."

Thus, the hypothesis is that "a God of faithfulness and without iniquity [one who is] just and right . . ." (Deuteronomy 31:4), who therefore can be a source of emulation and inspiration and whose attributes altogether resonate with our nobler sentiments, makes a great deal of sense and it is therefore reasonable to ascribe a higher probability to his existence than to an unprincipled, arbitrarily acting, wanton god. And if this is conceded, then it should also seem sensible to hold that the greater those sublime properties, the greater the likelihood the one exemplifying them exists. Hence, the being greater than which is inconceivable, who possesses them to a maximum degree, is to be regarded more probable than any other deity.

SIMPLICITY

The Cambridge statistician H. Jeffreys has shown in the 1920s that whenever we have a finite set of experimental results there are indefinitely many hypotheses that satisfy each result. The only way to select the hypothesis to be adopted is by following the principle of simplicity: of all the equally well-confirmed hypotheses, select the one that is simpler than all the others. It is crucial to realize that Jeffreys does not refer to the simplicity of structure of the systems involved or the simplicity of use and so on; he refers solely to descriptive simplicity and says that among the various expressions that represent the law, we are to adopt the one consisting of the minimal number of terms. It is also worth noting that Jeffreys' is not a prescriptive but a descriptive principle: scientists have followed it for hundreds of years without explicitly being aware of it, simply because it has never been articulated before that of the indefinitely many alternative hypotheses present in all cases.

Many people willingly concede that the rules of rational reasoning are invariant with subject matter. Consequently, after Pascal has convinced us that we should wager on some supernatural power, we are confronted with the problem of which of the many possible such powers to adopt. In the absence of any facts to assist us, it stands to reason that we should have to use Jeffreys' principle. It is fairly easy to see that the theistic hypothesis is the simplest in the sense specified by Jeffreys.

It is the simplest because it is the only hypothesis that may be expressed with the use of a single predicate: to describe the God of the theist all that is needed is that he is an absolutely perfect being. By contrast, a statement positing the existence of any deity less than absolutely perfect will be relatively complex. For example, though there is a large body of ancient Greek literature concerning Zeus, there are still many aspects of Zeus' character that remain unknown to us. We know for instance that he was sometimes asleep, but we have no idea how many hours of sleep he needed and what effect sleeplessness had on him. We also know that he ate and drank, but not how much or whether he occasionally overgorged himself or how long he could go without any food at all, and so on.

THE PRINCIPLE OF SUFFICIENT REASON

Finally, I should advance an argument based on the principle of sufficient reason why the wagerer should go for the being greater than which is not conceivable. Before doing so, I believe it is necessary to defend the principle because many contemporary philosophers deny its validity. J. L. Mackie was speaking for a large number of adherents of empiricism when he said, "There is no sufficient reason to regard the principle of sufficient reason to be valid."[6] Levelheaded empiricists are not supposed to subscribe to a priori principles. For this reason, the majority of contemporary writers strongly object to ascribing equal probabilities on the basis of the principle of indifference, which is no more than a variation on the principle of sufficient reason (PSR).

It seems to me that these objections are based on a serious misconception. They are mostly based on the refusal to acknowledge that "experience is mute" and that it is necessary to assume some unconfirmed principles before we are able to surmise what it tells us. As a matter of fact, no empirically confirmed statement can be found anywhere that did not rely on the PSR. The following illustrate the wide range of its application.

1. It is universally held that there is, for instance, overwhelming inductive evidence that the melting point of gold is 1064 degrees Celsius. It is common knowledge, however, that it is illegitimate to argue inductively from biased sample classes. Thus, the question arises why do physicists feel entitled to maintain that 1064 degrees Celsius is likely to remain the melting point of gold when all their evidence is based on a biased sample class: all the samples of gold hitherto melted occurred in a universe in which the density of matter (which keeps decreasing) was higher, the scaling factor (which is constantly increasing) was lower, and the velocity of the universe's expansion (which according to some cosmologists keeps decreasing all the time) was higher than at this crucial moment.

   The answer is not that we have no grounds on which to assume that these changes are relevant to the melting point of any metal. In the past, serious biases turned out to be factors we never suspected before of having relevance: all swans were thought to be white, and the fact that the sample class on which this conclusion was based included only non-Australian swans had not occurred to anyone to be of concern. The presumed law that matter cannot be destroyed was based on the failure of every conceivable attempt to do so; you may break, grind, melt, boil and evaporate, or burn to ashes any lump of matter without succeeding to alter the amount in which it continues to exist. The fact that no relevant observations have been made under exceedingly large pressures and temperatures, the kind of which prevail at the center of the sun where matter does diminish through part of it transforming into energy, did not seem to constitute a source of worry. Indeed, at the pre-twentieth century knowledge of what processes take place on the subatomic level, there was no reason why one should suspect that pressure and temperature had relevance to the issue of the conservation of matter. Similarly, our knowledge of physics may be still too deficient for us to be able to see why the scaling factor of the universe should influence the melting point of anything.

The correct answer has to be that we are aware of the possibility of having arrived at our conclusion through the use of a biased sample class, and consequently there are two lines of action available to us. One is to make no predictions at all. This, of course, would imply the complete paralysis of the scientific enterprise, which we should want to resist if at all possible. The alternative is to make use of the principle of sufficient reason. In the particular context of the melting point of gold, we then proceed in the following manner; in the past the melting point of gold has always been observed to be 1064 degrees Celsius. In the future it may be different. However, there is no good reason to believe that the melting point will be higher than it will be lower or vice versa. Thus, as long as not proven otherwise, we make the unique prediction that it will be neither higher nor lower but will continue to remain the same as in the past.

2. It was mentioned before that whenever we have a finite set of experimental results there are indefinitely many hypotheses that satisfy each result and that the accepted practice is to select the hypothesis to be adopted by following the principle of simplicity: of all the equally well-confirmed hypotheses, select the one that is simpler than all the others. What justification is there for this rule? One is the PSR. Should we suggest that some alternative hypothesis be adopted it will immediately be asked: what reason is there to make this particular choice? Why not select a simpler or a more complicated hypothesis? However, the simplest hypothesis has an edge over all others. It is unique. It is the only one in connection with which it is not possible to ask why not choose a simpler hypothesis. We thus justify our selection on the basis of the chosen hypothesis having a significant feature no other hypothesis has. The most complex hypothesis would also have such a feature except that it does not exist (just as the largest integer does not exist).

3. A strong illustration of how compelling the PSR is is the fact that even mathematicians have found it useful as a principle of plausible reasoning. L. C. Larson in his highly influential book poses the problem: of all the rectangles which can be inscribed in a given circle, which has greatest area? Larson suggests,

> The principle of insufficient reason leads to suspect the rectangle of maximum area that can be inscribed in a circle is a square.

He then goes on to give a rigorous proof of his conjecture without regarding it as necessary to elaborate how precisely the principle led him to it. It is reasonable to assume that what Larson had in mind was that if it were suggested that the sought-after rectangle was one with length x and width $x+n$ then of course the rectangle with length $x+n$ and width x must also have the maximum area. And if there are indeed two rectangles with maximum area, then, of course, there are infinitely many couples that might possibly be the ones we are after. There is, however, one rectangle that is unique in the sense that it has no counterpart: the rectangle with equal length and width. It "stands to reason" that this is the privileged figure we are after.

4. Some 2400 years ago Democritus argued,

> that there are infinite worlds, hypothesizing that the void is infinite; for why would this part of the void be filled by a world, but that part not? So, if there is a world in one part of the void, then also in all the void. So, since the void is infinite, the worlds will be infinite too.

Democritus' hypothesis would warrant detailed study; here I can point out only first of all that his "worlds," unlike what we mean when referring to various possible worlds, are not necessarily causally separated from one another and also that he thought of the actual world as having tiny size as compared with what we believe it to be. Yet his hypothesis may be said to have survived to this very day in the form of the far-reaching cosmological principle. It asserts that the universe is the same (i.e., the distribution of galaxies, stars, and planets) everywhere in space (apart from irregularities of a local nature), or that the universe is homogeneous.

The reasoning behind Democritus' hypothesis is once more based on the PSR. Suppose it were suggested that there exist some finite number n worlds. We would be at loss to offer a reason why it was not a number less or greater than n. However, if n is infinite then a unique reason can be given why it is not larger than n.

This last example is of special significance as it shows that the PSR, which is customarily associated with the name of Leibniz, who indeed applied it to numerous issues, was known and made use of two thousand years before him. It provides therefore further evidence of the universal appeal of the PSR and its central role in all our conceptual schemes.

Suppose someone subscribed to a religion that was based on the belief that the deity governing the universe was very benevolent but not absolutely so, possessing merely 95 percent of full benevolence. (It is not important for our purposes to describe how we compute the numerical degree of benevolence.) We might then ask an adherent of this religion: why not ascribe to your deity 96 percent or 94 percent benevolence? No reasonable answer seems available. On the other hand, the theist, when faced with a similar inquiry, might appeal to the PSR. If one settles for any number, like 95 percent, no sufficient reason seems to be available: why not have more or why not have less. However, a reason may be offered for 100 percent benevolence: it is of a unique magnitude, as it is impossible to have more. Suppose someone were to ask: but by the same principle you might as well ascribe 0 percent benevolence and explain your doing so by saying that having less than it is impossible? To this, as mentioned before, the theist reply would be that such a being is not a fit deity to worship, and thus one is to ascribe considerably lower probability to its existence.

Why Wager at All?

We are now in the position to reply to an ingenious objection raised by Antony Duff. Duff points out that the wager works regardless how small the probability, as long as its value is not zero, and that one is going to be the recipient of infinite salvation. If so, he argues, it is quite superfluous that I should follow Pascal's advice and begin acting religiously and make every effort to acquire faith, because,

> suppose I take no steps to make it more likely that I will come to believe in God. There must be some probability, however small, that I will nonetheless come to believe in Him . . . and that probability is enough to generate an infinite expected value for my actions.[7]

Now we have at least two answers to Duff's objection. The briefer answer is to recall the idea advanced previously that it is untenable to maintain that because of the infinitude of the reward it makes no difference how probable is its acquisition. We are instead to assume that it is important to try and increase the probability of obtaining the prospective prize.

The second answer would be based on the principle that a rational wagerer will always want to bet on the outcome associated with the highest expected utilities. But is it possible to gain anything more than infinite salvation? The answer is, in an appropriate sense, yes! An infinitely long string, for example, may be increased in width, or in mass per unit length, and so on. Similarly, eternal life, which of course is infinitely long and cannot be increased in length, may vary in the degree of its depth, intensity, exquisiteness, and so on, during every moment for the eternal duration of that felicitous state. Once we are prepared to entertain the possibility of an afterlife, we are likely to find it reasonable to go along with the traditional view that the magnificence of posthumous reward varies directly with the quality and the portion of the time at one's disposal as well as the magnitude of the exertion invested in acts of piety.

It should also be recalled that as soon as an individual embarks on the road that offers the best chance to lead to the acquisition of genuine religious faith, one is already set on the path of the righteous and is already engaged in the service of God. Clearly, therefore, one who acts upon Pascal's call at once, rather than waiting for the not entirely improbable inspiration to light unassisted upon him at some later time, places oneself in a far more favorable position with respect to the amount of time spent on the purification of one's soul. Thus, even if we conceded that in the context of eternal salvation the value of probability plays no role, the individual following Duff's advice would engage in a conduct associated with a prize of lower quality and thus with lower expected utilities.

A Common Feature to Almost All Theistic Argument

One of the most commonly cited theistic proofs is the Argument from Design. It is based on the wonders of nature we see around us that are unlikely to be, or perhaps unthinkable that they should be, the results of blind forces. Now even if we regard the argument absolutely compelling, it establishes at most—as was pointed out by Hume—that there exists a creator who is many hundreds times more powerful and intelligent than ourselves. But such a creator's power and intelligence may still fall infinitely short of Omnipotence and Omniscience. About benevolence the argument says even less, and the same goes for Omnipresence or Immutability.

Another famous argument is the Cosmological Argument. It shares all the weaknesses just mentioned in connection with the Argument from Design. Indeed, it should be obvious that all other arguments in support of theism (with the exception of the Ontological Argument, of which only a few would claim to have achieved full clarity) face the many-gods objection.

Thus, an individual making use of any of numerous known arguments for the existence of God can get no further than to conclude that there exists some supernatural power and intelligence behind the material universe. That individual is thus facing the need to choose among the various candidates who may fulfill this function.

It seems reasonable to conjecture that whatever is deemed the best justification for the theist's choice in one context is also likely to be so in other contexts as well. Therefore, the most acceptable reply to the many-gods objection may well be regarded as an argument of wide application and thus of central importance in the context of theistic arguments in general.

One of the striking features of Pascal's wager is surely the fact that the most often cited stumbling block it runs into has been the many-gods objection, whereas in the context of theistic arguments, I venture to suggest that this may be read as an indication of the unique strength of the wager. The reason why the many-gods objection has been raised less frequently in the context of theistic arguments was because skeptics felt able to clip the wings of a putative argument at the very initial stages, before it could get off the ground and thus prevent even the conclusion that some supernatural being is to be assumed.

Thus, the Argument from Design is nipped in the bud by insisting that the universe does not exhibit any signs of design; the Cosmological Argument has been cut short because of its alleged, unwarranted, basic assumption that there can be no uncaused contingent particulars. On the other hand, it seems that no serious defect could be discovered in Pascal's wager before it reached the relatively advanced stage of establishing the reasonableness of assuming the existence of some transmundane force.

NOTES

1. *Mishneh Torah*, Hilkhot Teshuvah, x.
2. *Shabbat*, 31b.
3. *On the Nature and Existence of God* (Cambridge, 1991), p. 350.
4. *The Miracle of Theism* (Oxford, 1982), p. 203.
5. Gale, op. cit., p. 350.
6. "Three steps toward Absolutism," *Space, Time and Causality*, ed. R. Swinburne (Dordrecht, 1981), p. 6.
7. "Pascal's Wager and Infinite Utilities," *Analysis* 46 (1986): 107.

1.3

'IS BELIEF IN GOD RATIONALLY ACCEPTABLE?'

Alvin Plantinga

I. Is Belief in God Properly Basic?

Many philosophers have urged the *evidentialist* objection to theistic belief; they have argued that belief in God is irrational or unreasonable or not rationally acceptable or intellectually irresponsible or noetically substandard, because, as they say, there is insufficient evidence for it[1]. Many other philosophers and theologians—in particular, those in the great tradition of natural theology—have claimed that belief in God is intellectually acceptable, but only because the fact is there is sufficient evidence for it. These two groups unite in holding that theistic belief is rationally acceptable only if there is sufficient evidence for it. More exactly, they hold that a person is rational or reasonable in accepting theistic belief only if she has sufficient evidence for it—only if, that is, she knows or rationally believes some *other* propositions which support the one in question, and believes the latter on the basis of the former. In [4] I argued that the evidentialist objection is rooted in *classical foundationalism*, an enormously popular picture or total way of looking at faith, knowledge, justified belief, rationality and allied topics. This picture has been widely accepted ever since the days of Plato and Aristotle; its near relatives, perhaps, remain the dominant ways of thinking about these topics. We may think of the classical foundationalist as beginning with the observation that some of one's beliefs may be *based upon* others; it may be that there are a pair of propositions A and B such that I believe A *on the basis of B*.

Alvin Plantinga, 'Is Belief in God Rationally Acceptable?', from: 'Is Belief in God Properly Basic?', *Nous*, 15 (1981), pp. 41–51; and 'Intellectual Sophistication and Basic Belief in God', from 'The Foundations of Theism: A Reply', *Faith and Philosophy*, 3, 3 (July 1986), pp. 298–313.

Although this relation isn't easy to characterize in a revealing and non-trivial fashion, it is nonetheless familiar. I believe that the word "umbrageous" is spelled u-m-b-r-a-g-e-o-u-s: this belief is based on another belief of mine: the belief that that's how the dictionary says it's spelled. I believe that $72 \times 71 = 5112$. This belief is based upon several other beliefs I hold: that $1 \times 72 = 72$; $7 \times 2 = 14$; $7 \times 7 = 49$; $49 + 1 = 50$; and others. Some of my beliefs, however, I accept but don't accept on the basis of any other beliefs. Call these beliefs *basic*. I believe that $2 + 1 = 3$, for example, and don't believe it on the basis of other propositions. I also believe that I am seated at my desk, and that there is a mild pain in my right knee. These too are basic to me; I don't believe them on the basis of any other propositions. According to the classical foundationalist, some propositions are *properly* or *rightly* basic for a person and some are not. Those that are not are rationally accepted only on the basis of *evidence*, where the evidence must trace back, ultimately, to what is properly basic. The existence of God, furthermore, is not among the propositions that are properly basic; hence a person is rational in accepting theistic belief only if he has evidence for it.

Now many Reformed thinkers and theologians[2] have rejected *natural theology* (thought of as the attempt to provide proofs or arguments for the existence of God). They have held not merely that the proffered arguments are unsuccessful, but that the whole enterprise is in some way radically misguided. In [8], I argue that the Reformed rejection of natural theology is best construed as an inchoate and unfocused rejection of classical foundationalism. What these Reformed thinkers really mean to hold, I think, is that belief in God need not be based on argument or evidence from other propositions at all. They mean to hold that the believer is entirely within his intellectual rights in believing as he does even if he doesn't know of any good theistic argument (deductive or inductive), even if he doesn't believe that there is any such argument, and even if in fact no such argument exists. They hold that it is perfectly rational to accept belief in God without accepting it on the basis of any other beliefs or propositions at all. In a word, they hold that *belief in God is properly basic*. In this paper I shall try to develop and defend this position.

But first we must achieve a deeper understanding of the evidentialist objection. It is important to see that this contention is a *normative* contention. The evidentialist objector holds that one who accepts theistic belief is in some way irrational or noetically substandard. Here "rational" and "irrational" are to be taken as normative or evaluative terms; according to the objector, the theist fails to measure up to a standard he ought to conform to. There is a right way and a wrong way with respect to belief as with respect to actions; we have duties, responsibilities, obligations with respect to the former just as with respect to the latter. So Professor Blanshard:

> everywhere and always belief has an ethical aspect. There is such a thing
> as a general ethics of the intellect. The main principle of that ethic I hold

to be the same inside and outside religion. This principle is simple and sweeping: Equate your assent to the evidence. [1], p. 401

This "ethics of the intellect" can be construed variously; many fascinating issues—issues we must here forebear to enter—arise when we try to state more exactly the various options the evidentialist may mean to adopt. Initially it looks as if he holds that there is a duty or obligation of some sort not to accept without evidence such propositions as that God exists—a duty flouted by the theist who has no evidence. If he has no evidence, then it is his duty to cease believing. But there is an oft remarked difficulty: one's beliefs, for the most part, are not directly under one's control. Most of those who believe in God could not divest themselves of that belief just by trying to do so, just as they could not in that way rid themselves of the belief that the world has existed for a very long time. So perhaps the relevant obligation is not that of divesting myself of theistic belief if I have no evidence (that is beyond my power), but to try to cultivate the sorts of intellectual habits that will tend (we hope) to issue in my accepting as basic only propositions that are properly basic.

Perhaps this obligation is to be thought of *teleologically*: it is a moral obligation arising out of a connection between certain intrinsic goods and evils and the way in which our beliefs are formed and held. (This seems to be W. K. Clifford's way of construing the matter.) Perhaps it is to be thought of *aretetically*: there are valuable noetic or intellectual states (whether intrinsically or extrinsically valuable); there are also corresponding intellectual virtues, habits of acting so as to promote and enhance those valuable states. Among one's obligations, then, is the duty to try to foster and cultivate these virtues in oneself or others. Or perhaps it is to be thought of *deontologically*: this obligation attaches to us just by virtue of our having the sort of noetic equipment human beings do in fact display; it does not arise out of a connection with valuable states of affairs. Such an obligation, furthermore, could be a special sort of moral obligation; on the other hand, perhaps it is a *sui generis* non-moral obligation.

Still further, perhaps the evidentialist need not speak of duty or obligation here at all. Consider someone who believes that Venus is smaller than Mercury, not because he has evidence of any sort, but because he finds it amusing to hold a belief no one else does—or consider someone who holds this belief on the basis of some outrageously bad argument. Perhaps there isn't any obligation he has failed to meet. Nevertheless his intellectual condition is deficient in some way; or perhaps alternatively there is a commonly achieved excellence he fails to display. And the evidentialist objection to theistic belief, then, might be understood, as the claim, not that the theist without evidence has failed to meet an obligation, but that he suffers from a certain sort of intellectual deficiency (so that the proper attitude toward him would be sympathy rather than censure).

These are some of the ways, then, in which the evidentialist objection could be developed; and of course there are still other possibilities. For ease of exposition, let us take the claim deontologically; what I shall say will apply *mutatis mutandis* if we take it one of the other ways. The evidentialist objection, therefore, presupposes some view as to what sorts of propositions are correctly, or rightly, or justifiably taken as basic; it presupposes a view as to what is *properly* basic. And the minimally relevant claim for the evidentialist objector is that belief in God is *not* properly basic. Typically this objection has been rooted in some form of *classical foundationalism*, according to which a proposition *p* is properly basic for a person *S* if and only if *p* is either self-evident or incorrigible for *S* (modern foundationalism) or either self-evident or "evident to the senses" for *S* (ancient and medieval foundationalism). In [4] I argued that both forms of foundationalism are self-referentially incoherent and must therefore be rejected.

Insofar as the evidentialist objection is rooted in classical foundationalism, it is poorly rooted indeed: and so far as I know, no one has developed and articulated any other reason for supposing that belief in God is not properly basic. Of course it doesn't follow that it *is* properly basic; perhaps the class of properly basic propositions is broader than classical foundationalists think, but still not broad enough to admit belief in God. But why think so? What might be the objections to the Reformed view that belief in God is properly basic?

I've heard it argued that if I have no evidence for the existence of God, then, if I accept that proposition, my belief will be groundless, or gratuitous, or arbitrary. I think this is an error; let me explain.

Suppose we consider perceptual beliefs, memory beliefs, and beliefs which ascribe mental states to other persons: such beliefs as

(1). I see a tree,

(2). I had breakfast this morning,

and

(3). That person is angry.

Although beliefs of this sort are typically and properly taken as basic, it would be a mistake to describe them as *groundless*. Upon having experience of a certain sort, I believe that I am perceiving a tree. In the typical case I do not hold this belief on the basis of other beliefs; it is nonetheless not groundless. My having that characteristic sort of experience—to use Professor Chisholm's language, my being appeared treely to—plays a crucial role in the formation and justification of that belief. We might say this experience, together, perhaps, with other circumstances, is what *justifies* me in holding it; this is the *ground* of my justification, and, by extension, the ground of the belief itself.

If I see someone displaying typical pain behavior, I take it that he or she is in pain. Again, I don't take the displayed behavior as *evidence* for that belief; I don't infer that belief from others I hold; I don't accept it on the basis of other beliefs. Still, my perceiving the pain behavior plays a unique role in the formation and justification of that belief; as in the previous case, it forms the ground of my justification for the belief in question. The same holds for memory beliefs. I seem to remember having breakfast this morning; that is, I have an inclination to believe the proposition that I had breakfast, along with a certain past-tinged experience that is familiar to all but hard to describe. Perhaps we should say that I am appeared to pastly; but perhaps this insufficiently distinguishes the experience in question from that accompanying beliefs about the past not grounded in my own memory. The phenomonology of memory is a rich and unexplored realm; here I have no time to explore it. In this case as in the others, however, there is a justifying circumstance present, a condition that forms the ground of my justification for accepting the memory belief in question.

In each of these cases, a belief is taken as basic, and in each case properly taken as basic. In each case there is some circumstance or condition that confers justification; there is a circumstance that serves as the *ground* of justification. So in each case there will be some true proposition of the sort

(4). In condition C, S is justified in taking p as basic.

Of course C will vary with p. For a perceptual judgment such as

(5). I see a rose-colored wall before me,

C will include my being appeared to in a certain fashion. No doubt C will include more. If I'm appeared to in the familiar fashion but know that I'm wearing rose-colored glasses, or that I am suffering from a disease that causes me to be thus appeared to, no matter what the color of the nearby objects, then I'm not justified in taking (5) as basic. Similarly for memory. Suppose I know that my memory is unreliable; it often plays me tricks. In particular, when I seem to remember having breakfast, then, more often than not, I *haven't* had breakfast. Under these conditions I am not justified in taking it as basic that I had breakfast, even though I seem to remember that I did.

So being appropriately appeared to, in the perceptual case, is not sufficient for justification; some further condition—a condition hard to state in detail—is clearly necessary. The central point, here, however, is that a belief is properly basic only in certain conditions; these conditions are, we might say, the ground of its justification and, by extension, the ground of the belief itself. In this sense, basic beliefs are not, or are not necessarily, *groundless* beliefs.

Now similar things may be said about belief in God. When the Reformers claim that this belief is properly basic, they do not mean to say, of course, that there are no justifying circumstances for it, or that it is in that sense groundless or gratuitous. Quite the contrary. Calvin holds that God "reveals and daily discloses himself to the whole workmanship of the universe," and the divine art "reveals itself in the innumerable and yet distinct and well-ordered variety of the heavenly host." God has so created us that we have a tendency or disposition to see his hand in the world about us. More precisely, there is in us a disposition to believe propositions of the sort *this flower was created by God* or *this vast and intricate universe was created by God* when we contemplate the flower or behold the starry heavens or think about the vast reaches of the universe.

Calvin recognizes, at least implicitly, that other sorts of conditions may trigger this disposition. Upon reading the Bible, one may be impressed with a deep sense that God is speaking to him. Upon having done what I know is cheap, or wrong, or wicked I may feel guilty in God's sight and form the belief *God disapproves of what I've done*. Upon confession and repentence, I may feel forgiven, forming the belief *God forgives me for what I've done*. A person in grave danger may turn to God, asking for his protection and help; and of course he or she then forms the belief that God is indeed able to hear and help if he sees fit. When life is sweet and satisfying, a spontaneous sense of gratitude may well up within the soul; someone in this condition may thank and praise the Lord for his goodness, and will of course form the accompanying belief that indeed the Lord is to be thanked and praised.

There are therefore many conditions and circumstances that call forth belief in God: guilt, gratitude, danger, a sense of God's presense, a sense that he speaks, perception of various parts of the universe. A complete job would explore the phenomenology of all these conditions and of more besides. This is a large and important topic; but here I can only point to the existence of these conditions.

Of course none of the beliefs I mentioned a moment ago is the simple belief that God exists. What we have instead are such beliefs as

> (6). God is speaking to me,
> (7). God has created all this,
> (8). God disapproves of what I have done,
> (9). God forgives me,

and

> (10). God is to be thanked and praised.

These propositions are properly basic in the right circumstances. But it is quite consistent with this to suppose that the proposition *there is such a person as God* is neither properly basic nor taken as basic by those who believe in God. Perhaps what they take as basic are such propositions as (6)–(10), believing in the existence of God on the basis of propositions such as those. From this point of view, it isn't exactly right to say that it is belief in God that is properly basic; more exactly, what are properly basic are such propositions as (6)–(10), each of which self-evidently entails that God exists. It isn't the relatively high level and general proposition *God exists* that is properly basic, but instead propositions detailing some of his attributes or actions.

Suppose we return to the analogy between belief in God and belief in the existence of perceptual objects, other persons, and the past. Here too it is relatively specific and concrete propositions rather than their more general and abstract colleagues that are properly basic. Perhaps such items are

(11). There are trees,

(12). There are other persons,

and

(13). The world has existed for more than 5 minutes,

are not in fact properly basic; it is instead such propositions as

(14). I see a tree,

(15). That person is pleased,

and

(16). I had breakfast more than an hour ago,

that deserve that accolade. Of course propositions of the latter sort immediately and self-evidently entail propositions of the former sort; and perhaps there is thus no harm in speaking of the former as properly basic, even though so to speak is to speak a bit loosely.

The same must be said about belief in God. We may say, speaking loosely, that belief in God is properly basic; strictly speaking, however, it is probably not that proposition but such propositions as (6)–(10) that enjoy that status. But the main point, here, is that belief in God or (6)–(10), are properly basic; to say so, however, is not to deny that there are justifying conditions for these beliefs, or conditions that confer justification on one who accepts them as basic. They are therefore not groundless or gratuitous.

A second objection I've often heard: if belief in God is properly basic, why can't *just any* belief be properly basic? Couldn't we say the same for any bizarre abberation we can think of? What about voodoo or astrology? What about the belief that the Great Pumpkin returns every Halloween? Could I properly take *that* as basic? And if I can't, why can I properly take belief in God as basic? Suppose I believe that if I flap my arms with sufficient vigor I can take off and fly about the room; could I defend myself against the charge of irrationality by claiming this belief is basic? If we say that belief in God is properly basic, won't we be committed to holding that just anything, or nearly anything, can properly be taken as basic, thus throwing wide the gates to irrationalism and superstitution?

Certainly not. What might lead one to think the Reformed epistemologist is in this kind of trouble? The fact that he rejects the criteria for proper basicality purveyed by classical foundationalism? But why should *that* be thought to commit him to such tolerance of irrationality? Consider an analogy. In the palmy days of positivism, the positivists went about confidently wielding their verifiability criterion and declaring meaningless much that was obviously meaningful. Now suppose someone rejected a formulation of that criterion— the one to be found in the second edition of A. J. Ayer's *Language, Truth and Logic*, for example. Would that mean she was committed to holding that

(17). Twas brillig; and the slithy toves did gyre and gymble in the wabe

contrary to appearances, makes good sense? Of course not. But then the same goes for the Reformed epistemologist; the fact that he rejects the Classical Foundationalist's criterion of proper basicality does not mean that he is committed to supposing just anything is properly basic.

But what then is the problem? Is it that the Reformed epistemologist not only rejects those criteria for proper basicality, but also seems in no hurry to produce what he takes to be a better substitute? If he has no such criterion, how can he fairly reject belief in the Great Pumpkin as properly basic?

This objection betrays an important misconception. How do we rightly arrive at or develop criteria for meaningfulness, or justified belief, or proper basicality? Where do they come from? Must one have such a criterion before one can sensibly make any judgments—positive or negative—about proper basicality? Surely not. Suppose I don't know of a satisfactory substitute for the criteria proposed by classical foundationalism; I am nevertheless entirely within my rights in holding that certain propositions are not properly basic in certain conditions. Some propositions seem self-evident when in fact they are not; that is the lesson of some of the Russell paradoxes. Nevertheless it would be irrational to take as basic the denial of a proposition that seems self-evident to you. Similarly, suppose it seems to you that you see a tree; you would then be irrational in taking as basic the proposition that you don't see a tree, or that there aren't any trees. In the same way, even if I don't know of some illuminating criterion of meaning, I can quite properly declare (17) meaningless.

And this raises an important question—one Roderick Chisholm has taught us to ask. What is the status of criteria for knowledge, or proper basicality, or justified belief? Typically, these are universal statements. The modern foundationalist's criterion for proper basicality, for example, is doubly universal:

(18). For any proposition A and person S, A is properly basic for S if and only if A is incorrigible for S or self-evident to S.

But how could one know a thing like that? What are its credentials? Clearly enough, (18) isn't self-evident or just obviously true. But if it isn't, how does one arrive at it? What sorts of arguments would be appropriate? Of course a foundationalist might find (18) so appealing, he simply takes it to be true, neither offering argument for it, nor accepting it on the basis of other things he believes. If he does so, however, his noetic structure will be self-referentially incoherent. (18) itself is neither self-evident nor incorrigible; hence in accepting (18) as basic, the modern foundationalist violates the condition of proper basicality he himself lays down in accepting it. On the other hand, perhaps the foundationalist will try to produce some argument for it from premises that are self-evident or incorrigible: it is exceedingly hard to see, however, what such an argument might be like. And until he has produced such arguments, what shall the rest of us do—we who do not find (18) at all obvious or compelling? How could he use (18) to show us that belief in God, for example, is not properly basic? Why should we believe (18), or pay it any attention?

The fact is, I think, that neither (18) nor any other revealing necessary and sufficient condition for proper basicality follows from clearly self-evident premises by clearly acceptable arguments. And hence the proper way to arrive at such a criterion is, broadly speaking, *inductive*. We must assemble examples of beliefs and conditions such that the former are obviously properly basic in the latter, and examples of beliefs and conditions such that the former are obviously *not* properly basic in the latter. We must then frame hypotheses as to the necessary and sufficient conditions of proper basicality and test these hypotheses by reference to those examples. Under the right conditions, for example, it is clearly rational to believe that you see a human person before you: a being who has thoughts and feelings, who knows and believes things, who makes decisions and acts. It is clear, furthermore, that you are under no obligation to reason to this belief from others you hold; under those conditions that belief is properly basic for you. But then (18) must be mistaken; the belief in question, under those circumstances, is properly basic, though neither self-evident nor incorrigible for you. Similarly, you may seem to remember that you had breakfast this morning, and perhaps you know of no reason to suppose your memory is playing you tricks. If so, you are entirely justified in taking that belief as basic. Of course it isn't properly basic on the criteria offered by classical foundationalists; but that fact counts not against you but against those criteria.

Accordingly, criteria for proper basicality must be reached from below rather than above; they should not be presented as *ex Cathedra*, but argued to and tested by a relevant set of examples. But there is no reason to assume, in advance, that everyone will agree on the examples. The Christian will of course suppose that belief in God is entirely proper and rational; if he doesn't accept this belief on the basis of other propositions, he will conclude that it is basic for him and quite properly so. Followers of Bertrand Russell and Madelyn Murray O'Hare may disagree, but how is that relevant? Must my criteria, or those of the Christian community, conform to their examples? Surely not. The Christian community is responsible to *its* set of examples, not to theirs.

Accordingly, the Reformed epistemologist can properly hold that belief in the Great Pumpkin is not properly basic, even though he holds that belief in God is properly basic and even if he has no full-fledged criterion of proper basicality. Of course he is committed to supposing that there is a relevant *difference* between belief in God and belief in the Great Pumpkin, if he holds that the former but not the latter is properly basic. But this should prove no great embarrassment; there are plenty of candidates. These candidates are to be found in the neighborhood of the conditions I mentioned in the last section that justify and ground belief in God. Thus, for example, the Reformed epistemologist may concur with Calvin in holding that God has implanted in us a natural tendency to see his hand in the world around us; the same cannot be said for the Great Pumpkin, there being no Great Pumpkin and no natural tendency to accept beliefs about the Great Pumpkin.

By way of conclusion for this section then: being self-evident, or incorrigible, or evident to the senses is not a necessary condition of proper basicality. Furthermore, one who holds that belief in God *is* properly basic is not thereby committed to the idea that belief in God is groundless or gratuitous or without justifying circumstances. And even if he lacks a general criterion of proper basicality, he is not obliged to suppose that just any or nearly any belief— belief in the Great Pumpkin, for example —is properly basic. Like everyone should, he begins with examples; and he may take belief in the Great Pumpkin as a paradigm of irrational basic belief.

[. . .]

II. INTELLECTUAL SOPHISTICATION AND BASIC BELIEF IN GOD

In [7] (hereafter R&BG) I suggested that such propositions as

(5). God is speaking to me,

(6). God disapproves of what I have done,

and

(7). God forgives me for what I have done (numbering in this section is from Quinn's paper)

are properly basic for at least some believers in God; there are widely realized sets of conditions, I suggested, in which such propositions are indeed properly basic. And when I said that these beliefs are properly basic, I had in mind what Quinn ([9], pp. 20–21) calls the *narrow* conception of the basing relation: I was taking it that a person S accepts a belief A on the basis of a belief B only if (roughly) S believes both A and B and could correctly claim (on reflection) that B is part of his *evidence* for A. S's belief that there is an error in some argument *against* p will not typically be a belief on the basis of which he accepts p and will not be part of his evidence for p (See R&BG, pp. 84–85).

This is important for the following reason. In arguing that belief in God is properly basic, I meant to rebut the claim made by the evidentialist objector: the claim that the theist who has no evidence for theism is in some way irrational. What the evidentialist objector objects to, however, is not just believing in God without having a response to such objections to theism as the argument from evil. He concedes that the theist may perfectly well have an answer to that objection and to others; but as long as she has no evidence *for* the existence of God, he says, she can't rationally believe. As the evidentialist objector thinks of evidence, then, you don't have evidence for a belief just by virtue of refuting objections against it; you must also have something like an argument *for* the belief, or some positive reason to think that the belief is true. I think this conception of evidence is an appropriate conception; but in any event it is the relevant conception, since it is this conception of evidence that the evidentialist objector has in mind in claiming that the theist without evidence is irrational.

As I see it, then, propositions like (5)–(7) are properly basic for many persons, including even such intellectually sophisticated adults as you and I. Quinn disagrees: "I conclude that many, perhaps most, intellectually sophisticated adult theists in our culture are seldom if ever, in conditions which are right for propositions like those expressed by (5)–(7) to be properly basic for them" (p. 481). Why so? I think Quinn is inclined to agree, first, that there *are* conditions in which such beliefs are properly basic for a person; such conditions might be those of a child brought up by believing parents, or perhaps of an adult in a culture in which sceptics had not produced the sorts of alleged reasons for rejecting theistic belief that are at present fashionable. The problem for intellectually sophisticated adults in our culture, he says, is that many potential *defeaters* of theistic belief are available; and we have substantial reason to think them true. One kind of defeater for a belief (the kind Quinn is concerned with here) is a proposition incompatible with the belief; Quinn cites

(12). God does not exist

as a potential defeater of theism. And the problem for the intellectually sophisticated adult theist in our culture, says Quinn, is that many substantial reasons for believing (12) have been produced.

There are defeaters for theistic belief, then; and in the presence of defeaters, an otherwise properly basic belief may no longer be properly basic. More exactly, according to Quinn

> it seems plausible to suppose that conditions are right for propositions like those expressed by (5)–(7) to be . . . properly basic for me only if (i) either I have no sufficiently substantial reason to think that any of their potential defeaters is true, or I do have some such reason, but for each such reason I have, I have an even better reason for thinking the potential defeater in question is false, and (ii) in either case my situation involves no epistemic negligence on my part (p. 483; call this principle 'Q*').

Quinn goes on to say that he is not in this fortunate condition with respect to theistic belief; he knows of substantial reason, he says, to think that (12) is true, and it is not the case that for each such reason he has, he has an even better reason for thinking (12) false. So (by Q*) belief in God is not properly basic for him; and he suspects the same goes for most of the rest of us.

Now here I find myself in solid disagreement. We must first ask what these "very substantial reasons for thinking that what (12) expresses is true" (p. 481) *are*. What would be some examples of such substantial reasons for atheism? Quinn's answer: "After all, nontrivial atheological reasons, ranging from various problems of evil to naturalist theories according to which theistic belief is illusory or merely projective, are a pervasive, if not obstrusive, component of the rational portion of our intellectual heritage" (p. 481). So these substantial reasons for thinking theism false would be the atheological argument from evil together with theories according to which theistic belief is illusory or merely projective; here perhaps Quinn has in mind Marxist and Freudian theories of religious belief.

I should remark immediately that the Marxist and Freudian theories he alludes to don't seem to be even reasonably cogent if taken as reasons for believing (12), or as evidence for the nonexistence of God, or as reasons for rejecting belief in God. Freud's jejune speculations as to the psychological origin of religion and Marx's careless claims about its social role can't sensibly be taken as providing argument or reason for (12), i.e., for the nonexistence of God; so taken they present textbook cases (which in fact are pretty rare) of the genetic fallacy. If such speculations and claims have a respectable role to play, it is instead perhaps that of providing a naturalistic explanation for the wide currency of religious belief, or perhaps that of attempting to discredit religious belief by tracing it to a disreputable source. But of course that doesn't constitute anything like evidence for (12) or a reason to think theism false. One might as well cite as evidence for the existence of God St. Paul's claim (Romans 1) that failure to believe in God is a result of sin and rebellion against God. None of the naturalistic theories according to which theism is illusory or merely projective seem to me to have any strength at all as arguments or evidence for the nonexistence of God—although they may be of interest in other ways.

This leaves us with the atheological argument from evil as the sole substantial reason for thinking (12) true. And initially this argument seems much stronger as a reason for rejecting theistic belief. But is it really? Until recently, most atheologians who urged an atheological argument from evil held that

(10). God exists and is omniscient, omnipotent and wholly good

is logically incompatible with the proposition

(11). there are 10^{13} turps of evil

(where (11) is just a way of referring to all the evil our world in fact displays). At present, I think atheologians have given up the claim that (10) and (11) are incompatible, and quite properly so.[3] What they now say is that (10) is *unlikely* or *improbable* with respect to (11); and Quinn (himself, of course, no atheologian) says, "What I know, partly from experience and partly from testimony, about the amount and variety of non-moral evil in the universe confirms highly for me the proposition expressed by (12)" (p. 481). But is this really true? Does what Quinn and the rest of us know about the amount and variety of non-moral evil in the world confirm highly the nonexistence of God? This is not the place to enter a discussion of that difficult and knotty problem (difficult and knotty at least in part because of the difficult and confusing character of the notion of confirmation); for what it is worth, however, I can't see that it does so at all. So far as I can see, no atheologian has given a successful or cogent way of working out or developing a probabilistic atheological argument from evil; and I believe there are good reasons for thinking that it can't be done.[4] I am therefore very much inclined to doubt that (11) "highly disconfirms" (10) for Quinn. At the least what we need here is some explanation to show just how (or even approximately how) this disconfirmation is supposed to go.

So first, these alleged substantial reasons for rejecting theism warrant a good deal of scepticism. But secondly, even if we concede that there are such reasons, Quinn's conclusion won't follow; this is because (Q*), as it stands, is pretty clearly false. The suggestion is that if I have a substantial reason for thinking some defeater of a proposition (for example, its denial) is true, then I can't properly take the proposition as basic unless I have an even stronger reason for thinking the defeater in question false. But surely this is to require too much. Suppose an atheologian gives me an initially convincing argument for thinking that (10) is in fact extremely unlikely or improbable on (11). Upon grasping this argument, perhaps I have a substantial reason for accepting a defeater of theistic belief, namely that (10) is extremely improbable on (11). But in order to defeat this potential defeater, I need not know or have very good reason to think that it is *false* that (10) is improbable on (11); it would suffice to show that the atheologian's argument (for the claim that [10] is improbable on [11]) is unsuccessful. To defeat this potential defeater, all I need to do is refute this argument; I am not obliged to go further and produce an argument for the denial of its conclusion. Quinn takes

(12). God does not exist

to be a potential defeater for the propositions (5)–(7); but to defeat the potential defeater offered by an argument for (12) I need not necessarily have some argument *for* the existence of God. There are undercutting defeaters as well as rebutting defeaters.[5]

There is another and more subtle point here. Quinn seems to be thinking along the following lines: suppose I take some proposition as basic, but have substantial evidence from other things I believe for some defeater of this proposition—a proposition incompatible with it, let's say. Then (according to Q*) I am irrational if I continue to accept the proposition in question, unless I also have good evidence for the falsehood of that defeater. So if I accept a proposition **p**, but believe or know other things that constitute strong evidence for some defeater **q** of **p**, then, says Q*, if I am not to be irrational in continuing to accept **p** as basic, I must have a reason for thinking **q** false—a reason that is stronger than the reasons I have for thinking **q** true.

Now my question is this: could **p** *itself* be my reason for thinking **q** false? Or must that reason be some proposition distinct from **p**? Consider an example. I am applying to the National Endowment for the Humanities for a fellowship; I write a letter to a colleague, trying to bribe him to write the Endowment a glowing letter on my behalf; he indignantly refuses and sends the letter to my chairman. The letter disappears from the chairman's office under mysterious circumstances. I have a motive for stealing it; I have the opportunity to do so; and I have been known to do such things in the past. Furthermore an extremely reliable member of the department claims to have seen me furtively entering the chairman's office at about the time when the letter must have been stolen. The evidence against me is very strong; my colleagues reproach me for such underhanded behavior and treat me with evident distaste. The facts of the matter, however, are that I didn't steal the letter and in fact spent the entire afternoon in question on a solitary walk in the woods; furthermore I clearly remember spending that afternoon walking in the woods. Hence I believe in the basic way

> (13). I was alone in the woods all that afternoon, and I did not steal the letter.

But I do have strong evidence for the denial of (13). For I have the same evidence as everyone else that I was in the chairman's office and took the letter; and this evidence is sufficient to convince my colleagues (who are eminently fairminded and initially well disposed towards me) of my guilt. They are convinced on the basis of what they know that I took the letter; and I know everything they know.

So I take (13) as basic; but I have a substantial reason to believe a defeater of (13). According to Q*, if I am to be rational in this situation, I must have even better reason to believe that this potential defeater is false. Do I? Well, the only reason I have for thinking this potential defeater false is just (13) itself; I don't have any *independent* reason to think the defeater false. (The warrant I have for (13) is a *nonpropositional* warrant; it is not conferred upon (13) by virtue of my believing that proposition, on the basis of some other proposition, for I don't believe (13) on the basis of any other proposition.)

In this situation it is obvious, I take it, that I am perfectly rational in continuing to believe (13) in the basic way. The reason is that in this situation the positive epistemic status or warrant that (13) has for me (by virtue of my memory) is greater than that conferred upon its potential defeater by the evidence I share with my colleagues. We might say that (13) *itself* defeats the potential defeater; no further reason for the denial of this defeater is needed for me to be rational. Suppose we say that in this sort of situation a proposition like (13) is an *intrinsic* defeater of its potential defeater. When a basic belief **p** has more by way of warrant than a potential defeater **q** of **p**, then **p** is an intrinsic defeater of **q**—an intrinsic defeater-defeater, we might say. (A belief **r** is an *extrinsic* defeater-defeater if it defeats a defeater **q** of a belief **p** distinct from **r**.)

So my question here is this: how is Quinn thinking of these reasons for thinking the defeating proposition false? I am *inclined* to believe that he intends Q* to be read in such a way that these reasons have to be *extrinsic* defeater-defeaters; but if so, then his principle, I think, is clearly false. On the other hand, perhaps it is to be understood as saying something like

> Q** If you believe **p** in the basic way and you have reason to believe a defeater **q** of **p**, then if you are to be rational in continuing to believe **p** in this way, **p** must have more warrant for you then **q** does.

I am not certain this principle is correct, but I am also not inclined to dispute it. The central point to see, however, is that if a belief **p** is properly basic in certain circumstances, then it has warrant or positive epistemic status in those circumstances in which it is properly basic—warrant it does not get by virtue of being believed on the evidential basis of other propositions. (By hypothesis it is not believed on the evidential basis of other propositions.) To be successful, a potential defeater for **p** must have as much or more warrant as **p** does. And **p** can withstand the challenge offered by a given defeater even if there is no independent evidence that serves either to rebut or undercut the defeater in question; perhaps the nonpropositional warrant that **p** enjoys is itself sufficient (as in the above case of the missing letter) to withstand the challenge.

But how does all this apply in the case in question, the case of belief in God and the alleged defeaters Quinn mentions? As follows. If there are circumstances in which belief in God is properly basic, then in those circumstances such belief has a certain degree of warrant or positive epistemic status. Now suppose a potential defeater arises: someone claims that the existence of 10^{13} turps of evil makes theism improbable, or he claims that theistic belief arises out of nothing more reputable than a kind of widespread human neurosis. Two questions then arise. First how does the degree of nonpropositional warrant enjoyed by your belief in God compare with the warrant possessed by the alleged potential defeater? It could be that your belief, even though accepted as basic, has more warrant than the proposed defeater and thus constitutes an intrinsic defeater-defeater. When God spoke to Moses out of the burning bush, the belief that God was speaking to him, I daresay, had more by way of warrant for him than would have been provided for its denial by an early Freudian who strolled by and proposed the thesis that belief in God is merely a matter of neurotic wish fulfillment. And secondly, are there any extrinsic defeaters for these defeaters? Someone argues that the existence of 10^{13} turps of evil is inconsistent with the existence of God; I may then have an extrinsic defeater for this potential defeater. This defeater-defeater need not take the form of a proof that these propositions are indeed consistent; if I see that the argument is unsound, then I also have a defeater for it. But I needn't do even that much to have a defeater. Perhaps I am no expert in these matters but learn from reliable sources that someone else has shown the argument unsound; or perhaps I learn that the experts think it is unsound, or that the experts are evenly divided as to its soundness. Then too I have or may have a defeater for the potential defeater in question, and can continue to accept theistic belief in the basic way without irrationality.

By way of conclusion for this section then: Quinn claims that intellectually sophisticated adult theists in our culture are seldom in epistemic circumstances in which belief in God is properly basic; for they have substantial reason to think that some potential defeater of theism is true, and do not have, for each such defeater, even stronger reason to think it is false. But first, it isn't necessary that they have reason *independent* of their belief in God for the falsehood of the alleged defeaters. Perhaps the nonpropositional warrant enjoyed by your belief in God is itself sufficient to turn back the challenge offered by the alleged defeaters, so that your theistic belief is an intrinsic defeater-defeater. And second, extrinsic defeaters of the alleged defeaters need not be evidence for the falsehood of those defeaters; they may instead undercut the alleged defeaters; they may be, for example, refutations of atheological arguments. (And here Christian philosophers can clearly be of service to the rest of the Christian community.) My opinion (for what it is worth) is that for many theists, the nonpropositional warrant belief in God has for them is indeed greater than that of alleged potential defeaters of theistic belief—for example, Freudian or Marxist theories of religion. Furthermore, there are powerful extrinsic defeaters for the sorts of potential defeaters of theism Quinn suggests. The atheological argument from evil, for example, is formidable; but there are equally formidable defeaters for this potential defeater. I am therefore inclined to believe that belief in God is properly basic for most theists—even intellectually sophisticated adult theists.

REFERENCES

[1] Blanshard, Brand, *Reason and Belief* (London: Allen & Unwin, 1974).
[2] Clifford, W. K., "The Ethics of Belief," *Lectures and Essays* (London: Macmillan, 1879).
[3] Flew, A. G. N., *The Presumption of Atheism* (London: Pemberton Publishing Co., 1976).
[4] Plantinga, A., "Is Belief in God Rational?" in *Rationality and Religious Belief*, ed. C. Delaney (Notre Dame: University of Notre Dame Press, 1979).
[5] Plantinga, A., *The Nature of Necessity* (Oxford: The Clarendon Press, 1974).
[6] Plantinga, A., "The Probabilistic Argument from Evil," *Philosophical Studies*, 1980, pp. 1–53.

[7] Plantinga, A., "Reason and Belief in God," in *Faith and Rationality*, ed. A. Plantinga and N. Wolterstorff (Notre Dame: University of Notre Dame Press, 1983).

[8] Plantinga, A., "The Reformed Objection to Natural Theology," *Proceedings of the American Catholic Philosophical Association*, 1980.

[9] Quinn, Philip L., "On Finding the Foundations of Theism," *Faith and Philosophy*, 1985, pp. 469–486.

[10] Russell, Bertrand, "Why I Am Not a Christian," *Why I Am Not a Christian* (New York: Simon & Schuster, 1957).

[11] Scriven, Michael, *Primary Philosophy* (New York: McGraw-Hill, 1966).

NOTES

1. See, for example, [1], pp. 400ff., [2], pp. 345ff., [3], p. 22, [10], pp. 3ff., and [11], pp. 87ff. In [4] I consider and reject the evidentialist objection to theistic belief.

2. A Reformed thinker or theologian is one whose intellectual sympathies lie with the Protestant tradition going back to John Calvin (not someone who was formerly a theologian and has since seen the light).

3. See for example Chapter IX of [5].

4. See [6].

5. I owe these terms to John Pollock. The distinction between undercutting and rebutting defeaters is of central importance to apologetics. If the propriety of basic belief in God is threatened by defeaters, there are two ways to respond. First, there is *negative* apologetics: the attempt to refute the arguments brought *against* theism (the atheological argument from evil, the claim that the conception of God is incoherent, and so on). Second, there is *positive* apologetics: the attempt to develop arguments *for* the existence of God. These are both important disciplines; but it is only the first, clearly enough, that is required to defeat those defeaters.

I.4

'DEFEATING THEISTIC BELIEFS'

Philip L. Quinn

The intellectually sophisticated adult theist in our culture is an ideal type I constructed in my earlier paper for the purpose of making vivid certain questions about the defeasibility of theistic beliefs such as

(14). God is speaking to me,
(15). God disapproves of what I have done,

and

(16). God forgives me for what I have done.[1]

Such a person is supposed to know a good deal about standard objections to belief in God. These objections include various versions of the problem of evil as well as the tradition of explaining theistic belief projectively that stems from Feuerbach and comes down to us through Freud and Durkheim. Can such theistic beliefs as (14)–(16) be properly basic for the intellectually sophisticated adult theist in our culture? If so, under what conditions?

The answer I proposed to the latter question was framed in terms of the following principle:

(23). Conditions are right for propositions like (14)–(16) to be properly basic for me "only if (i) either I have no sufficiently substantial reason to think that any of their potential defeaters is true, or I do have some such reason, but for each such reason I have, I have an

Philip L. Quinn, 'Defeating Theistic Beliefs', from 'The Foundations of Theism Again: A Rejoinder to Plantinga', in Linda Zagzebski (ed.), *Rational Faith* (Notre Dame, IN: University of Notre Dame Press, 1993), pp. 35–47.

> even better reason for thinking the potential defeater in question is false, and (ii) in either case any situation involves no epistemic negligence on my part." (p. 483)

Plantinga's reply contains an attack on this principle; he thinks it is pretty clearly false and can be shown to be so. Suppose, he says, an atheologian gives me an initially convincing argument for thinking that

(24). God exists and is omniscient, omnipotent, and wholly good

is extremely improbable on

(25). There are 10^{13} turps of evil.[2]

Plantinga's analysis of the situation proceeds as follows:

> Upon grasping this argument, perhaps I have a substantial reason for accepting a defeater of theistic belief, namely that (24) is extremely improbable on (25). But in order to defeat this potential defeater, I need not know or have very good reason to think that it is *false* that (24) is improbable on (25); it would suffice to show that the atheologian's argument (for the claim that [24] is improbable on [25]) is unsuccessful. To defeat this potential defeater, all I need to do is refute this argument; I am not obliged to go further and produce an argument for the denial of its conclusion. (FT, p. 309)

There are, he reminds us in terminology borrowed from John Pollock, undercutting defeater-defeaters as well as rebutting defeater-defeaters.

But does this show that (23) is false? I think not. Suppose that the only potential defeater of theistic belief I need to worry about is

(26). (24) is extremely improbable on (25),

and assume also that the only reason I have for accepting (26) is the argument the atheologian gives me. On these assumptions, if I do show that the atheologian's argument is unsuccessful by refuting it, then I have no sufficiently substantial reason to think that any potential defeater of theistic belief is true, for surely an argument I know to be unsuccessful because I myself have refuted it gives me no reason to accept its conclusion. So it is not a consequence of (23) that, once I encounter the atheologian's argument, theistic belief ceases to be properly basic for me unless I have a good reason for thinking that (26) is false. Even if I have no argument for the denial of (26), I can satisfy both (ii) and the first disjunct of (i) in the consequent of (23) by showing that the atheologian's argument fails. Hence even if I lack a good reason for the falsity of (26), (23) does not preclude theistic belief from being properly basic for me both before I am given the atheologian's argument and after I have refuted it. It seems to me that Plantinga has failed to notice the fact that, although the atheologian's argument is a substantial reason for accepting a defeater of theistic belief if it is undefeated, it is not a substantial reason for accepting such a defeater if it has been undercut by a successful refutation. Therefore I am not persuaded that he has shown (23) to be false by means of this line of argument.

Nor am I persuaded by the possibility of there being intrinsic defeater-defeaters, though I must admit that this possibility had not occurred to me before Plantinga pointed it out. An intrinsic defeater-defeater is a basic belief that has more by way of warrant than some of its potential defeaters. Suppose that one of my basic theistic beliefs has so much warrant that it remains properly basic for me even after I have acquired a substantial reason for thinking one of its potential defeaters is true because that reason, though substantial, confers less warrant on the defeater in question than my basic theistic belief has in its own right. On this assumption, the antecedent of (23) is satisfied. But if I am not epistemically negligent, the consequent of (23) holds as well because the second disjunct of condition (i) is satisfied. Though I do have a substantial reason for thinking that a potential defeater of my basic theistic belief is true, for the only such reason I have, I have an even better reason, namely, my basic theistic belief itself, for thinking the potential defeater in question is false. The existence of intrinsic defeater-defeaters would falsify (23) if it were read in such a way that my reason for thinking the defeater in question is false has to be an extrinsic defeater-defeater. But since, as I have acknow-ledged, I did not have the distinction between extrinsic and intrinsic defeater-defeaters in mind when I formulated (23), it was certainly not my intention that it be so understood. Nor need it be read in that way.

But are there such things as intrinsic defeater-defeaters? The example Plantinga gives convinces me that there are. A letter that could embarrass me disappears from my department chair's office under mysterious circum-stances. I had motive, means, and opportunity to steal it, and a reliable member of the department testifies to having seen me furtively entering the office around the time the letter must have disappeared. I have been known to steal things in the past. This circumstantial evidence persuades my colleagues, who are fair-minded people, that I am guilty, and I have all the evidence they do. Yet the fact of the matter is that I spent the whole afternoon in question on a solitary walk in the woods, and I clearly remember having done so. It is one of my basic beliefs that

> (27). I was alone in the woods all that afternoon, and I did not steal the letter.

The evidence I share with my colleagues gives me a substantial reason to believe a defeater of (27), but the warrant (27) has for me in virtue of my memory is greater than that conferred on this defeater by that evidence. Hence (27) is an intrinsic defeater-defeater.

It is worth noting that the power of this example to persuade depends critically on what we may assume about the case. One such assumption is quite explicit; it is said that my memory of the walk in the woods is clear. If it were not clear, the warrant (27) has for me in virtue of my memory might well be less than that conferred on its defeater by the circumstantial evidence I share with my colleagues. But there are also some tacit assumptions. Thus, for example, I suppose (27) would not have much, if any, warrant for me if I suffered from certain sorts of memory disorder or even had a sufficiently substantial reason to consider myself thus afflicted and no reason to think otherwise.

And, of course, from the fact that some basic memorial beliefs are intrinsic defeater-defeaters, it does not follow without further ado that basic theistic beliefs are ever intrinsic defeater-defeaters. Nonetheless I am willing to grant that some basic theistic beliefs are or, at least, could be intrinsic defeater-defeaters. Another example Plantinga gives illustrates the point. He remarks, with what I take to be some asperity: "When God spoke to Moses out of the burning bush, the belief that God was speaking to him, I daresay, had more by way of warrant for him than would have been provided for its denial by an early Freudian who strolled by and proposed the thesis that belief in God is merely a matter of neurotic wish fulfillment" (FT, p. 312). But having the experience of being spoken to out of a burning bush is one thing; having a deep sense that God is speaking to one upon reading the Bible is quite another. Even if the former experience is part of a condition in which (14) has more warrant for Moses than would have been provided for its denial by the casual proposal of an early Freudian, it does not follow that the latter experience is part of a condition in which (14) has more warrant for a contemporary theist than is provided for its denial by the results of current psychoanalytic inquiry. So from the assumption that (14) is an intrinsic defeater-defeater for Moses it does not follow that it is also an intrinsic defeater-defeater for the intellectually sophisticated adult theist in our culture. It may be; but, then again, it may not. For all that has been said so far, when contemporary theists form the belief that God is speaking to them upon reading the Bible, that basic theistic belief has less warrant for them than at least some of its potential defeaters and so is not a defeater of all its defeaters. And perhaps basic theistic beliefs such as (14)–(16) do not have enough warrant in the circumstances described by Plantinga, in which the believer reads the Bible, feels guilty or feels forgiven, to defeat any potential defeaters of theism but those the believer has only relatively insubstantial reasons to think true.

If basic theistic beliefs such as (14)–(16) do not in such circumstances have enough warrant to serve as intrinsic defeater-defeaters of all the potential defeaters of theism, natural theology might come to the theist's rescue. Suppose there is a sound deductive argument for the existence of God. If the theist comes to see that it is valid and to know its premiss and bases belief in God on those premiss, belief in God will come to have a great deal of warrant for the theist. The increment in warrant might well be sufficiently large that belief in God comes to have more warrant for the theist than all its potential defeaters. So this is another way in which natural theology might improve the theist's epistemic situation. Its fate, then, may turn out to be no small matter even if it is conceded to the Reformed Epistemologist that belief in God can be properly basic in certain special conditions.

Whether or not basic theistic beliefs such as (14)–(16) are intrinsic defeater-defeaters depends both on how much warrant they have and on how much warrant potential defeaters of theistic belief have. How much warrant do basic theistic beliefs have? It is not easy to say. For what it is worth, my view is that they do not have a great deal of warrant except in extraordinary conditions such as those we may imagine to be present in Plantinga's Moses example. As I see it, such basic theistic beliefs as (14)–(16) have only modest amounts of warrant in conditions in which the theist reads the Bible, feels guilt, or feels forgiven. Plantinga says: "It could be that your belief, even though accepted as basic, has more warrant than the proposed defeater and thus constitutes an intrinsic defeater-defeater" (FT, p. 312). It could indeed; this might even be the case for all proposed defeaters, not just for one. I accept this weak modal claim because I think the Moses example establishes it. But I have never been spoken to out of a burning bush. Nor, I daresay, have many other contemporary theists been thus addressed. Of course, even if I am right in thinking that basic theistic beliefs such as (14)–(16) have only modest amounts of warrant in ordinary conditions, they would still be intrinsic defeater-defeaters if the potential defeaters of theistic belief had even less warrant.

How much warrant do potential defeaters of theistic belief have? Much needs to be said on this topic, and I have space here to say only a little bit of it. I think both the evidential problem of evil and projective explanations of theistic belief provide substantial reasons for thinking the following defeater of theistic belief is true:

(28). God does not exist.

In his reply Plantinga argues that these reasons for rejecting theism warrant a good deal of skepticism. I do not find his arguments convincing for reasons I shall briefly explain.

My claim about evil is this: "What I know, partly from experience and partly from testimony, about the amount and variety of non-moral evil in the universe confirms highly for me the proposition expressed by (28)" (p. 481). It is worth bearing in mind that this claim is consistent with (28) being highly disconfirmed by my total evidence. Plantinga's counterclaim is this: "So far as I can see, no atheologian has given a successful or cogent way of working out or developing a probabilistic atheological argument from evil; and I believe there are good reasons for thinking that it can't be done" (FT, p. 309).[3] But even if it is the case that it cannot be shown that (28) is highly probable given the amount and variety of non-moral evil in the universe, it does not follow that it cannot be shown that (28) is highly confirmed by that evil unless it is also assumed that confirmation is to be understood probabilistically. I do not accept this additional assumption. It seems to me that the failure of philosophers of science in the Carnapian tradition to work out a satisfactory probabilistic confirmation theory gives me reason enough not to accept it. I do not for a minute doubt that in science, observation statements sometimes confirm theoretical hypotheses. I take intuitively clear cases of scientific confirmation and disconfirmation as data against which philosophical accounts of confirmation are to be tested. Such data have an epistemic presumption in their favor, as I see it, and so should be rejected only for good reasons. And I am inclined to think that the claim that (28) is highly confirmed by the non-moral evil in the universe is another such datum for confirmation theory.

The treatment of projection theories in Plantinga's reply is very harsh. He dismisses them with this remark: "Freud's jejune speculations as to the psychological origin of religion and Marx's careless claims about its social role can't sensibly be taken as providing argument or reason for (28), i.e., for the nonexistence of God; so taken they present textbook cases (which in fact are pretty rare) of the genetic fallacy" (FT, p. 308). There are, I admit, some textbook cases of the genetic fallacy in Freud's writings; I enjoy seeing students discover this in class discussions of *The Future of an Illusion*. But to construe Freud's contribution to our understanding of religion as nothing but jejune speculation and bad argument strikes me as uncharitable in the extreme. There is, I suggest, a great deal more to his legacy than that, and things get even more complicated when we take into account sociological projection theories such as Durkheim's.

I believe it is useful to think of projection theories of religious belief as constituting a research program in the human sciences.[4] This research program has not and is not likely to come up with a theory having the explanatory power of Newtonian mechanics, but that is probably too much to hope for in any research in the human sciences. The unifying idea of the research program is that there is in us a mechanism of belief formation and maintenance that involves projecting attributes of individual humans or their societies outwards and postulating entities in which the projected attributes are instantiated. The existence of the postulated entities is supposed to play no role in explaining the formation or persistence of belief in the postulates. The various theories that make up this research program attempt to specify in some detail the workings of the projection mechanism; typically they consist of hypotheses about its inputs and outputs. If such hypotheses can explain religious beliefs in a wide variety of circumstances, leaving unexplained no more anomalies than other good theories, then appeal to some principle of economy such as Ockham's razor can be made to justify the conclusion that the entities whose existence is postulated as a result of the operation of the projection mechanism do not exist because they are explanatorily idle. To the extent that such hypotheses have explained religious beliefs, that conclusion has warrant. I believe that projection hypotheses have so far achieved a real, but limited, success in explaining religious beliefs of some sorts, and I think this success does give the intellectually sophisticated adult theist in our culture a substantial reason for thinking that (28) is true.

This is another point at which natural theology might perform useful services. Suppose the natural theologian presented us with an abductive argument for the existence of God according to which divine activity is the best explanation of a wide variety of phenomena, including, but not restricted to, theistic beliefs. The successes of the projection theorist's research program would undercut this argument to some extent, but they would leave untouched the claim that divine activity is the best explanation of phenomena other than theistic beliefs. Though the strength of the abductive argument would be diminished, it might retain enough force to confer a good deal of warrant on belief in the existence of God. If that were so, theists could accept the successes of projection theories with equanimity, for they could view the projection mechanisms discovered by the human sciences as secondary causes divinely ordained to serve as generators of theistic belief.

Of course the research program of the projection theorists is open to being criticized in the same ways that other scientific research programs are criticized by scientists and philosophers of science. Thus, for example, it might be argued that although the program was progressive back around the beginning of the twentieth century, when Freud and Durkheim were making contributions to it, it has more recently been degenerating and ought now to be abandoned. Or it might be argued that projection hypotheses explain only religious beliefs that are "primitive" or "pathological" and that the best explanation of the religious beliefs of mature theists involves the truth of theism and the existence of God. I myself am inclined to believe that an argument for the conclusion that the truth of theism is part of the best explanation of theistic belief might well be, when all is said and done, the best way for theists to reply to projection theorists. But I think it is a mistake to ignore the explanatory successes of projection theories and the warrant they confer on a potential defeater of theistic belief such as (28). Dismissing the work of projection theorists as a combination of jejune speculation and bad argument would not do justice to their real accomplishments.

So I am convinced that defeaters of theistic belief have a good deal of warrant. It seems to me they have enough to insure that, for the intellectually sophisticated adult theist in our culture, basic theistic beliefs such as (14)–(16) are not intrinsic defeater-defeaters unless such a theist is in extraordinary circumstances of the sort that are assumed in Plantinga's Moses example. If such a theist is not thus circumstanced, then theistic beliefs such as (14)–(16) will be properly basic only if the theist has extrinsic defeater-defeaters for defeaters of theism like (28).

For simplicity's sake, I have up to this point been conducting the discussion in terms of the idealized figure of the intellectually sophisticated adult theist in our culture. How should my conclusions be applied to actual adult theists? In considering this question I wish to proceed more cautiously than I did in my previous paper. An answer to this question is bound to be speculative unless it is based on empirical knowledge of the doxastic situations of adult theists.

Imagine a large research project whose first phase aims at finding out how many adult theists there are in the United States who both have propositions such as those expressed by (14)–(16) among their basic beliefs and know a good deal about non-moral evil and projective theories of religious belief. A follow-up phase of the project is designed to learn more about such people in order to subdivide them into three groups. In the first group will be people in conditions in which their basic theistic beliefs are intrinsic defeater-defeaters of the defeaters of theism that derive warrant from what they know of non-moral evil and projective theories. In the second group will be people who have extrinsic defeater-defeaters of such defeaters of theism. Anyone who satisfies both these conditions will be arbitrarily placed in the first group. Those who satisfy neither conditions will be placed in the third group; they are people whose basic theistic beliefs are not properly basic and who are to some extent irrational. In determining the membership of the second group, a generous communitarian account of what it is to have the requisite defeater-defeaters is to be adopted. That one know exactly how to solve the evidential problem of evil or to respond on behalf of theism to projection theorists is not necessary. It would suffice to have it on the authority of a reliable informant that the experts had reached consensus on these matters, the trouble of course being that, as things actually stand at present, it is well known that there is no such expert consensus and so testimony to that effect could hardly come from a reliable informant.

Now it strikes me as rather silly to try to predict, in advance of doing the imagined research, the actual numbers of people who would wind up in each of the three groups. But, given his views, I would expect Plantinga to predict that a very large percentage of the total will be in the first or second groups, leaving the third group sparsely populated. So it is understandable that he should think little of importance hangs on the fate of natural theology, since few people need it in order to escape from irrationality in theistic belief. Given my views, however, I am willing to predict that a large percentage of the total will be in the third group, rendering it thickly populated. Therefore I believe a great deal hangs on the fate of natural theology, for it seems to me that many people need it, or, at least, need assurances that the experts of the relevant community have it, if their theistic beliefs are to avoid irrationality. My hunch is that this is the issue on which Plantinga and I disagree most deeply, and the prospects of progress toward agreement do not seem to me good.

But I wish to conclude by paying tribute to Plantinga's achievement. I think he has succeeded in identifying a view of theistic belief that, though it may be inchoately present in the Calvinian theological tradition, has never before been seriously discussed by analytic philosophers of religion. And I think he has by this time said enough about the view to show that it has real promise of developing coherently into a religious epistemology worthy of respect. What he has not shown, in my opinion, is that it is superior to alternatives that display similar promise of coherent development.[5]

NOTES

1. Philip L. Quinn, "In Search of the Foundations of Theism," *Faith and Philosophy* 2 (1985); Plantinga's response appears in Alvin Plantinga, "The Foundations of Theism: A Reply" (hereafter FT), *Faith and Philosophy* 3 (1986). I include page references to this paper of mine and to FT parenthetically in the text.
2. A turp is $1/10^{13}$ times all the evil there is in the actual world.
3. In a footnote Plantinga refers the reader who is interested in finding out what those reasons are to Alvin Plantinga, "The Probabilistic Argument from Evil," *Philosophical Studies* 35 (1979).
4. In this paragraph and the next I make use of ideas derived from Imre Lakatos, "Falsification and the Methodology of Scientific Research Programmes," in *Criticism and the Growth of Knowledge*, ed. Imre Lakatos and Alan Musgrave (Cambridge: Cambridge University Press, 1970). Those who doubt that there are such things as human *sciences* could, I believe, translate my talk about research programs into talk about traditions of inquiry of the sort contained in Alasdair MacIntyre's recent writings. See Alasdair MacIntyre, *Whose Justice? Which Rationality?* (Notre Dame: University of Notre Dame Press, 1988); and Alasdair MacIntyre, *Three Rival Versions of Moral Enquiry* (Notre Dame: University of Notre Dame Press, 1990).
5. I am grateful to Alvin Plantinga for spending most of an afternoon discussing a draft of this paper with me. It takes a rare kind of generosity to help one's critics improve their arguments.

SUGGESTED READING

Alston, William P. (1991), *Perceiving God*, Ithaca, NY: Cornell University Press.

Gale, Richard (1991), *On the Existence and Nature of God*, Cambridge: Cambridge University Press.

Geivett, Douglas and Brendan Sweetman (eds) (1992), *Contemporary Perspectives in Religious Epistemology*, Oxford: Oxford University Press.

Hasker, William (1998), 'The Foundations of Theism: Scoring the Quinn–Plantinga Debate', *Faith and Philosophy* 15, 1, pp. 52–67.

Jordan, Jeff (ed.) (1994), *Gambling on God*, Lanham, MD: Rowman and Littlefield.

McCarthy, Gerald D. (ed.) (1986), *The Ethics of Belief Debate*, Atlanta, GA: Scholars Press.

Mackie, J. L. (1982), *The Miracle of Theism*, Oxford: Clarendon Press.

Phillips, D. Z. (1988), *Faith after Foundationalism*, London and New York: Routledge.

Plantinga, Alvin (2000), *Warranted Christian Belief*, Oxford: Oxford University Press.

Plantinga, Alvin and Nicholas Wolterstorff (eds) (1983), *Faith and Rationality*, Notre Dame, IN: University of Notre Dame Press.

Rescher, Nicholas (1985), *Pascal's Wager*, Notre Dame, IN: University of Notre Dame Press.

Swinburne, Richard (1981), *Faith and Reason*, Oxford: Clarendon Press.

Wykstra, Stephen (1989), 'Toward a Sensible Evidentialism: On the Notion "Needing Evidence" ', in William Rowe and William Wainwright (eds), *Philosophy of Religion*, New York: Harcourt Brace Jovanovich, pp. 426–37.

Zagzebski, Linda (ed.) (1983), *Rational Faith*, Notre Dame, IN: University of Notre Dame Press.

PART II
NATURAL THEOLOGY

NATURAL THEOLOGY:
INTRODUCTION

William Lane Craig

Natural theology is that branch of theology which seeks to provide rational warrant for the proposition that God exists on the basis of argument and evidence independent of authoritative divine revelation. Although it was for a very long time taken for granted that Hume and Kant had demolished all prospects of a successful natural theology, the authors of our selections develop their arguments in full cognisance of the Humean-Kantian *Angriff*, maintaining that their theistic arguments are not susceptible to the customary objections.

Cosmological Argument

The cosmological argument is a family of arguments which seek to demonstrate the existence of a Sufficient Reason or First Cause of the existence of the cosmos. The arguments can be grouped into three basic types: the *kalam* cosmological argument for a First Cause of the beginning of the universe, the Thomist cosmological argument for a sustaining Ground of Being of the world, and the Leibnizian cosmological argument for a Sufficient Reason why something exists rather than nothing.

The *kalam* cosmological argument derives its name from the Arabic word designating medieval Islamic scholasticism, the intellectual movement largely responsible for developing the argument. It aims to show that the universe had a beginning at some moment in the finite past and, since something cannot come out of nothing, must therefore have a transcendent cause, which brought the universe into being. Classical proponents of the argument sought to demonstrate that the universe began to exist on the basis of philosophical arguments against the existence of an infinite, temporal regress of past events. Contemporary interest in the argument arises largely out of the startling empirical evidence of astrophysical cosmology for a beginning of space and time.

By contrast the Thomist cosmological argument seeks a cause which is first, not in the temporal sense, but in the sense of rank. On Aquinas's Aristotelian-inspired metaphysic, every existing finite thing is composed of essence and existence and is therefore radically contingent. A thing's essence is a set of properties which serve to define what that thing is. Now if an essence is to be instantiated or exemplified, there must be continually conjoined with that essence an act of being. Essence is thus in potentiality to being. No substance can actualise itself; for in order to bestow being upon itself it would have to be already actual. Any finite substance is therefore sustained in existence by a First Cause of being. This Cause cannot be composed of essence and existence and, hence, requires no sustaining cause. This being's essence just *is* existence. In a sense, this being has no essence; rather it is the pure act of being, unconstrained by any essence. It is, as Thomas says, *ipsum esse subsistens*, the act of being itself subsisting. Thomas identifies this being with the God whose name was revealed to Moses as 'I am' (Exod. 3:15).

Leibniz sought to develop a version of the cosmological argument from contingency without the Aristotelian metaphysical underpinnings of the Thomist argument. 'The first question which should rightly be asked,' he wrote, 'is this: why is there something rather than nothing?'[1] Leibniz meant this question to be truly universal, not merely to apply to finite things. On the basis of his Principle of Sufficient Reason, that 'no fact can be real or existent, no statement true, unless there be a sufficient reason why it is so and not otherwise',[2] Leibniz held that this question must have an answer. It will not do to say that the universe (or even God) just exists as a brute fact.[3] There must be an explanation why it exists. He went on to argue that the Sufficient Reason cannot be found in any individual thing in the universe, nor in the collection of such things which comprise the universe, nor in earlier states of the universe, even if these regress infinitely. Therefore, there must exist an ultra-mundane being which is metaphysically necessary in its existence, that is to say, its non-existence is impossible. It is the Sufficient Reason for its own existence as well as for the existence of every contingent thing.

In the first selection is this section Stephen Davis presents a disarmingly simple formulation of the Leibnizian argument. One of the principal objections to Leibniz's argument is that his Principle of Sufficient Reason seems evidently false. There cannot be an explanation of why there are any contingent states of affairs at all; for if such an explanation is contingent, then it, too, must have a further explanation; whereas if it is necessary, then the states of affairs explained by it must also be necessary. Davis avoids this objection by taking his premiss (2) to mean that any *thing* which exists must have an explanation of its existence, either in the necessity of its own nature or in some external ground. This premiss is compatible with the obtaining of states of affairs which are brute facts. What Davis's principle excludes is that there could exist things – substances exemplifying properties – which just exist inexplicably. This principle seems quite plausible, at least more so than its contradictory, which is all that is required for a successful argument. On this analysis, there are two kinds of being: necessary beings, which have no external ground of their existence, and contingent beings, whose existence is accounted for by causal factors outside themselves. Davis's move in premiss (1) is adroit, for this premiss is, in effect, the contrapositive of the typical atheist response to Leibniz that on the atheistic world-view the universe simply exists as a brute contingent. The atheist implicitly recognises that if the universe has an explanation, then God exists as its explanatory ground. Since the universe is obviously a thing (especially evident in its very early stages when its density was so extreme that distinct things, not even subatomic particles, could exist within it), it follows that God exists.

It is open to the atheist to retort that while the universe has an explanation of its existence, that explanation lies not in an external ground but in the necessity of its own nature; in other words, (1) is false. The universe is a metaphysically necessary being. This was the suggestion of David Hume, who demanded, 'Why may not the material universe be the necessarily existent being?' . . .?' Indeed, 'How can anything, that exists from eternity, have a cause, since that relation implies a priority in time and a beginning of existence?'[4]

This is an extremely bold suggestion on the part of the atheist. We have, I think we can safely say, a strong intuition of the universe's contingency. A possible world in which no concrete objects exist certainly seems conceivable. We generally trust our modal intuitions on other matters; if we are to do otherwise with respect to the universe's contingency, then the atheist needs to provide some reason for such scepticism other than his desire to avoid theism.

Still, it would be desirable to have some stronger argument for the universe's contingency than our modal intuitions alone. Enter the *kalam* cosmological argument. For an essential property of a metaphysically necessary *ens realissimum* (ultimate being) is that it be eternal, without beginning or end. But it is precisely the aim of the *kalam* cosmological argument to show that the universe is not eternal but had a beginning. The universe must therefore be contingent in its existence. Not only so; the *kalam* argument shows the universe to be contingent in a very special way: it came into existence out of nothing. The atheist who would answer Leibniz by holding that the existence of the universe is a brute fact, an exception to the Principle of Sufficient Reason, is thus thrust into the very awkward position of maintaining not merely that the universe exists eternally without explanation, but rather that for no reason at all it magically popped into being out of nothing, a position which might make theism look like a welcome alternative.

TELEOLOGICAL ARGUMENT

Widely thought to have been demolished by Hume and Darwin, the teleological argument for God's existence has come roaring back into prominence in recent years. The scientific community has been stunned by its discovery of how complex and sensitive a nexus of conditions must be given in order for the universe to permit the origin and evolution of intelligent life.

The discovery of this cosmic fine-tuning has led many scientists to conclude that such a delicate balance cannot be dismissed as coincidence but cries out for explanation. In a sense more easy to discern than to articulate this fine-tuning of the universe seems to manifest the presence of a designing intelligence. The inference to design is best thought of, not as an instance of reasoning by analogy (as it is often portrayed), but as a case of inference to the best explanation.[5] John Leslie speaks of the need for what he calls a 'tidy explanation'. A tidy explanation is one that not only explains a certain situation but also reveals in doing so that there is something to be explained. Leslie provides a whole retinue of charming illustrations of tidy explanations at work.[6] Suppose, for example, that Bob is given a new car for his birthday. There are millions of licence plate numbers, and it is therefore highly unlikely that Bob would get, say, CHT 4271. Yet that plate on his birthday car would occasion no special interest. But suppose Bob, who was born on 8 August 1949 finds BOB 8849 on the licence plate of his birthday car. He would be obtuse if he shrugged this off with the comment, 'Well, it had to have *some* licence plate, and any number is equally improbable . . .'

A full-fledged theory of design inference has recently been offered by William Dembski. He furnishes a ten-step Generic Chance Elimination Argument,[7] which delineates the common pattern of reasoning that he believes underlies chance-elimination arguments. Dembski's analysis can be used to formalize what Leslie grasped in an intuitive way. What makes an explanation a tidy one is not simply the fact that the *explanandum* is some improbable event, but the fact that the event also conforms to some independently given pattern, resulting in what Dembski calls 'specified complexity'. It is this specified complexity that tips us off to the need for an explanation in terms of more than mere chance.

Is the teleological argument a sound and persuasive argument? The key to detecting design is to eliminate the two competing alternatives of physical necessity and chance. The crucial question with respect to the first alternative is whether there is some unknown Theory of Everything which would explain the way the universe is. According to this alternative, the universe has to be the way it is, and there was really no chance or little chance of the universe's not being life-permitting. Now on the face of it, this alternative seems extraordinarily implausible. It requires us to believe that a life-prohibiting universe is virtually physically impossible. But surely it does seem possible. If the primordial matter and anti-matter had been differently proportioned, if the universe had expanded just a little more slowly, if the entropy of the universe were marginally greater, any of these adjustments and more would have prevented a life-permitting universe, yet all seem perfectly possible physically. The person who maintains that the universe must be life-permitting is taking a radical line which requires strong proof. But as yet there is none; this alternative is simply put forward as a bare possibility.

Moreover, there is good reason to reject this alternative. Even if the laws of nature were necessary, one would still have to supply initial conditions. As P. C. W. Davies states,

> Even if the laws of physics were unique, it doesn't follow that the physical universe itself is unique . . . the laws of physics must be augmented by cosmic initial conditions. . . . There is nothing in present ideas about 'laws of initial conditions' remotely to suggest that their consistency with the laws of physics would imply uniqueness. Far from it . . . It seems, then, that the physical universe does not have to be the way it is: it could have been otherwise.[8]

Sometimes it is said that we really do not know how much certain constants and quantities could have varied from their actual values. But this admitted uncertainty becomes less important when the number of variables to be fine-tuned is high. For example, the chances of all 50 known variables being finely-tuned, even if each variable has a 50 per cent chance of being its actual value, is less than 3 out of 10^{17}.

What, then, of the alternative of chance? It is sometimes alleged that it is meaningless to speak of the probability of our finely-tuned universe's existing because there is, after all, only one universe. But John Barrow provides the following illustration which clarifies the sense in which our life-permitting universe is improbable.[9] Take a sheet of paper and place upon it a red dot. That dot represents our universe. Now alter slightly one or more of the finely-tuned constants and physical quantities which have been the focus of our attention. As a result we have a description of another universe, which we may represent as a new dot in the proximity of the first. If that new set of constants and quantities describes a life-permitting universe, make it a red dot; if it describes a universe which is life-prohibiting, make it a blue dot. Now repeat the procedure arbitrarily many times until the sheet is filled with dots. What one winds up with is a sea of blue with only a few pinpoints of red. That is the sense in which it is overwhelmingly improbable that the universe should be life-permitting. There are simply vastly more life-prohibiting universes in our local area of possible universes than there are life-permitting universes.

Issues pertinent to the so-called Anthropic Principle arise here. As formulated by Barrow and Tipler, the Anthropic Principle states that any observed properties of the universe which may initially appear astonishingly improbable can only be seen in their true perspective after we have accounted for the fact that certain properties could not be observed by us, were they to obtain, because we can only observe those compatible with our own existence. Most Anthropic theorisers recognise that the Anthropic Principle can only legitimately be employed when it is conjoined to a Many Worlds Hypothesis, according to which a World Ensemble of concrete universes exists, actualising a wide range of possibilities.[10] The Many Worlds Hypothesis is essentially an effort on the part of partisans of the chance hypothesis to multiply their probabilistic resources in order to reduce the improbability of the occurrence of fine-tuning. The very fact that they must resort to such a remarkable hypothesis is a backhanded compliment to the design hypothesis in that they recognize that the fine-tuning does cry out for explanation. But is the Many Worlds Hypothesis as plausible as the design hypothesis? This is the hottest issue in contemporary debate over the fine-tuning and is tackled by Robin Collins in the reading for this section.

AXIOLOGICAL ARGUMENT

Can we be good without God? At first the answer to this question may seem so obvious that even to pose it arouses indignation. For while theists undoubtedly find in God a source of moral strength and resolve which enables them to live lives that are better than those they would otherwise live, nevertheless it would be arrogant and ignorant to claim that those who do not share a belief in God do not often live good moral lives. But wait! It would, indeed, be arrogant and ignorant to claim that people cannot be good without *belief* in God. But that was not the question. The question was: can we be good without God? When we ask that question, we are posing in a provocative way the meta-ethical question of the objectivity of moral values. Are the values we hold dear and guide our lives by mere social conventions akin to driving on the left versus right side of the road or mere expressions of personal preference akin to having a taste for certain foods? Or are they valid independently of our apprehension of them, and, if so, what is their foundation? Moreover, if morality is just a human convention, then why should we act morally, especially when it conflicts with self-interest? Or are we in some way held accountable for our moral decisions and actions?

Many philosophers have argued that if God exists, then the objectivity of moral values, moral duties and moral accountability is secured, but that if God does not exist, then morality is just a human convention, that is to say, morality is wholly subjective and non-binding. We might act in precisely the same ways that we do in fact act, but in the absence of God, such actions would no longer count as good (or evil), since if God does not exist, objective moral values do not exist. Thus, we cannot truly be good without God. Alternatively, if we do believe that moral values and duties are objective, that provides moral grounds for believing in God.

Consider the hypothesis that God exists. According to classical theism, objective moral values are rooted in God.[11] God's own holy and perfectly good nature supplies the absolute standard against which all actions and decisions are measured. Moreover, God's moral nature is expressed in relation to us in the form of divine commands which constitute our moral duties or obligations. Finally, on classical theism God holds all persons morally accountable for their actions. Thus, the moral choices we make in this life are infused with an eternal significance.

Contrast the atheistic hypothesis. If God does not exist, then what is the foundation for moral values? More particularly, what is the basis for the value of human beings? If God does not exist, then it is difficult to see any reason to think that human beings are special or that their morality is objectively valid. Moreover, why think that we have any moral obligations to do anything? Who or what imposes any moral duties upon us? Philosopher of science Michael Ruse writes,

> The position of the modern evolutionist . . . is that humans have an awareness of morality . . . because such an awareness is of biological worth. Morality is a biological adaptation no less than are hands and feet and teeth . . . Considered as a rationally justifiable set of claims about an objective something, ethics is illusory. I appreciate that when somebody says 'Love thy neighbor as thyself,' they think they are referring above and beyond themselves . . . Nevertheless . . . such reference is truly without foundation. Morality is just an aid to survival and reproduction . . . and any deeper meaning is illusory . . .[12]

As a result of socio-biological pressures, there has evolved among *homo sapiens* a sort of 'herd morality' which functions well in the perpetuation of our species in the struggle for survival. But there does not seem to be anything about *homo sapiens* that makes this morality objectively binding. Human beings are just accidental by-products of nature which have evolved relatively recently on an infinitesimal speck of dust lost somewhere in a hostile and mindless universe and which are doomed to perish individually and collectively in a relatively short time. Some action, say, rape, may not be biologically or socially advantageous and so in the course of human evolution has become taboo; but on the atheistic view it is difficult to see why there is really anything really wrong about raping someone.

Moreover, if atheism is true, there is no moral accountability for one's actions. Even if there were objective moral values and duties under naturalism, they are irrelevant because there is no moral accountability. As the Russian writer Fyodor Dostoyevsky rightly said: 'If there is no immortality, then all things are permitted.'[13] Given the finality of death, it really does not matter how we live. Acts of self-sacrifice become particularly inept on a naturalistic world-view. Considered from the socio-biological point of view, such altruistic behaviour is merely the result of evolutionary conditioning which helps to perpetuate the species. Good sense dictates that we should resist, if we can, the socio-biological pressures to such self-destructive activity and choose instead to act in our best self-interest. Life is too short to jeopardise it by acting out of anything but pure self-interest. Sacrifice for another person is just stupid.

We thus come to radically different perspectives on morality depending upon whether or not God exists. These different implications might in turn serve as moral justification for belief in the existence of God.

For example, if we do think that objective moral values exist, then we shall be led logically to the conclusion that God exists. If moral values are gradually discovered, not invented, then our gradual and fallible apprehension of the moral realm no more undermines the objective reality of that realm than our gradual, fallible perception of the physical world undermines the objectivity of that realm. Most of us think that we do apprehend objective values. As Ruse himself confesses, 'The man who says that it is morally acceptable to rape little children is just as mistaken as the man who says, 2+2=5.'[14] Or consider the nature of moral obligation. The international community recognizes the existence of universal human rights, and many persons are even willing to speak of animal rights as well. But the best way to make sense of such rights is in terms of agreement or disagreement of certain acts with the will or commands of a holy, loving God.

Finally, take the problem of moral accountability. Here we find a powerful practical argument for believing in God. To believe that God does not exist and that there is thus no moral accountability would be quite literally de-moralising, for then we should have to believe that our moral choices are ultimately insignificant, since both our fate and that of the universe will be the same regardless of what we do. By 'de-moralization' one means a deterioration of moral motivation. It is hard to do the right thing when that means sacrificing one's own self-interest and to resist temptation to do wrong when desire is strong, and the belief that ultimately it does not matter what one chooses or does is apt to sap one's moral strength and so undermine one's moral life. By contrast there is nothing so likely to strengthen the moral life as the beliefs that one will be held accountable for one's actions and that one's choices do make a difference in bringing about the good. Theism is thus a morally advantageous belief, and this, in the absence of any theoretical argument establishing atheism to be the case, provides practical grounds to believe in God and motivation to accept the conclusions of the theoretical arguments in support of theism.

NOÖLOGICAL ARGUMENT

Plato indicted the atheistic physicalists of his day because they were 'ignorant of the nature and power of the soul' (*Laws* 10.891c, 892). Some contemporary philosophers of mind, such as Adams and Swinburne, have similarly argued that theism best explains the nature and power of mind.[15] What I have called the noölogical argument is thus intimately connected with one's views on the nature of the soul or mind (*noûs*) discussed in Part 5. The argument is that property or substance dualism with respect to the mind/body problem is best accounted for on a theistic as opposed to atheistic world-view.

The argument from mental properties/substances to God can take a variety of forms. Some have argued that the standard neo-Darwinian theory of biological evolution cannot explain the emergence of mind in the evolutionary process.[16] Others construct a creationist argument based on the radically different nature of mind from matter and the necessity of a causal account of mind.[17]

The argument defended by J. P. Moreland in the selected reading for this section, however, avoids such controversial creationist theses. Leaving the origin of mind an open question, Moreland presents a non-etiological argument for theism based on the unnaturalness of mind in an atheistic or naturalistic ontology. He argues that on a theistic metaphysic, one already has an instance of unembodied mind in the being of God; therefore it is hardly surprising that finite, embodied minds should also exist in the world. But on a naturalistic world-view, minds, being immaterial substances distinct from their respective bodies, are so strange and out of place that their existence is not at all to be expected on such a world-view.

Thus, when Moreland speaks of an explanation for the correlations between mental event types and specific physical event types, he is not asking for a causal account of why, for example, a certain conscious volition of mine is correlated with my arm's rising. Rather he is asking for an explanation of why there exist these two realms of the world operating in causal harmony with one another. His comparison of his argument with the axiological argument is instructive: there the question is why there exist two realms, the physical and the moral, which are intimately related; here the question is why there exist the interacting realms of the physical and the mental. His claim is that a personal explanation in terms of an agent, his intentions and his power is called for and that theism provides just such an agent. Therefore, given property or substance dualism we should infer theism as the best explanation of the nature of the world.

ONTOLOGICAL ARGUMENT

Anselm of Canterbury, having argued in his *Monologion* for the existence of God by means of axiological and cosmological arguments, remained dissatisfied with the complexity of his demonstration and yearned to find a single argument which would, on its own, prove that God exists. It was then that he hit upon the conception of God as 'the greatest conceivable being' (*aliquid quo nihil maius cogitari possit*), which provided the key to his new argument. Anselm argued that once a person truly understands the notion of a greatest conceivable being, then he will see that such being must exist, since if it did not, it would not be the *greatest* conceivable being. God's existence, then, is truly inconceivable for him who rightly understands 'God' (*Proslogion* 2–3).

Anselm's argument, which has come to be known as the ontological argument, went on to assume a variety of forms.[18] But the common thread in such arguments is that they try to deduce the existence of God from the very concept of God, together with certain other necessary truths. It is claimed that once we understand what God is – the greatest conceivable being or the most perfect being or the most real being – then we shall see that such a being must in fact exist.

In Plantinga's version of the argument, reprinted here, he appropriates Leibniz's insight that the argument assumes that the concept of God is possible, that is to say, that it is possibly instantiated or, employing the semantics of possible worlds, that there is a possible world in which God exists. Plantinga conceives of God as a being which is 'maximally excellent' in every possible world, where maximal excellence entails such excellent-making properties as omniscience, omnipotence and moral perfection. Such a being would have what Plantinga calls 'maximal greatness'. Now maximal greatness is possibly instantiated, that is to say, there is a possible world in which a maximally great being exists. But then this being must exist in a maximally excellent way in every possible world, including the actual world. Therefore, God exists.

Although Plantinga thinks that the ontological argument is sound and non-question-begging, still he did not regard it as 'a successful piece of natural theology' because the key premiss, 'Possibly, maximal greatness is exemplified', can be rationally denied. Plantinga later confessed that he had set the bar for 'success' in natural theology unreasonably high. For he believes that 'the ontological argument provides as good grounds for the existence of God as does any serious philosophical argument for any important philosophical conclusion'.[19]

The principal issue to be settled is what warrant exists for thinking the key premiss to be true. It is crucial in this regard to keep in mind the difference between metaphysical and merely epistemic possibility. One is tempted to say, 'It's possible that God exists, and it's possible that He doesn't!' But this is true only with respect to epistemic possibility; if God is conceived as a maximally great being, then His existence is either necessary or impossible, regardless of our epistemic uncertainty. Thus, the epistemic entertainability of the key premiss (or its denial) does not guarantee its metaphysical possibility.

It might be said that the idea of a maximally great being is intuitively a coherent notion and, hence, possibly instantiated. In this respect, the idea of God differs from putatively parallel notions like the idea of a maximally great island or of a necessarily existent lion. The properties that go to make up maximal excellence have intrinsic maxima, whereas the excellent-making properties of islands (if there even are such properties!) do not. Any animal which could exist in a universe comprised of a singularity of infinite density just is not a lion; whereas a maximally excellent being could transcend such physical limitations. Still, the argument from intuition is inconclusive because it seems intuitively coherent in the same way to conceive of a quasi-maximally great being, say, one which is in every other respect maximally excellent save that it does not know truths about future contingents. Why is the key premiss of the ontological argument more plausibly true than a parallel premiss concerning quasi-maximal greatness?

Plantinga provides a clue when he says that if we 'carefully ponder' the key premiss and the alleged objections to it, if we 'consider its connections with other propositions we accept or reject' and we still find it compelling, then we are within our rational rights in accepting it. Such a procedure is a far cry from the sort of a priori theorising decried by the modal sceptic. Even if we cannot determine a priori whether maximal greatness is possibly exemplified, we may come to believe on the basis of a posteriori considerations that it is possible that a maximally great being exists. For example, other theistic arguments like the Leibnizian cosmological argument and the axiological argument may lead us to think that it is plausible that a maximally great being exists. The one argument leads to a metaphysically necessary being which is the ground of existence for any conceivable finite reality and the other to a locus of moral value which must be as metaphysically necessary as the values it grounds. In the second selection reprinted here, Quentin Smith provides a conceptualist argument for an infinite, metaphysically necessary Mind to ground all truths and other *abstracta*. On the basis of considerations like these,[20] one might well consider oneself to be warranted in believing that it is possible that a maximally great being exists.

The question which arises at this point is whether the ontological argument has not then become question-begging. For it might seem that the reason one thinks that it is possible that a maximally great being exists is that one has good reasons to think that a maximally great being does exist. But this is to think of the project of natural theology in too linear a fashion. The theistic arguments need not be taken to be like links in a chain, in which one link follows another so that the chain is only as strong as its weakest link. Rather they are like links in a coat of chain mail, in which all the links reinforce one another so that the strength of the whole exceeds that of any single link. The ontological argument might play its part in a cumulative case for theism, in which a multitude of factors simultaneously conspires to lead one to the global conclusion that God exists. In that sense Anselm was wrong in thinking that he had discovered a single argument which, standing independently of all the rest, served to demonstrate God's existence in all His greatness. Nevertheless, his argument does encapsulate the thrust of all the arguments together to show that God, the Supreme Being, exists.

NOTES

1. G.W. Leibniz, 'The Principles of Nature and of Grace, Based on Reason', in G. W. Leibniz, *Leibniz Selections*, ed. P. Wiener (New York: Charles Scribner's Sons, 1951), p. 527.
2. G. W. Leibniz, 'The Monadology', in Leibniz, *Leibniz Selections*, p. 539.
3. Swinburne has recently broached an inductive version of the Leibnizian cosmological argument which allows that the explanatory Ultimate is a brute fact (Richard Swinburne, *The Existence of God*, rev. edn [Oxford: Clarendon Press, 1991], ch. 7). The really interesting feature of Swinburne's argument is thus not its inductive form, but its conclusion to a metaphysically contingent God. Swinburne's claim is that in answer to the question, 'Why is there something rather than nothing?' we must come to the brute existence of some contingent being. This being will not serve to explain its own existence (and, hence, Leibniz's question goes unanswered), but it will explain the existence of everything else. Swinburne argues that God is the best explanation of why everything other than the brute Ultimate exists because as a unique and infinite being God is simpler than the variegated and finite universe.
4. David Hume, *Dialogues concerning Natural Religion*, ed. with an Introduction by Norman Kemp Smith, Library of Liberal Arts (Indianapolis: Bobbs-Merrill, 1947), pt. IX, p. 190.
5. See Peter Lipton, *Inference to the Best Explanation* (London: Routledge, 1991).
6. John Leslie, *Universes* (London: Routledge, 1989), p. 225 of Index of Concepts under 'stories'.
7. William A. Dembski, *The Design Inference: Eliminating Chance through Small Probabilities*, Cambridge Studies in Probability, Induction, and Decision Theory (Cambridge: Cambridge University Press, 1998), pp. 184–5; cf. pp. 167–74.
8. Paul Davies, *The Mind of God* (New York: Simon & Schuster, 1992), p. 169.
9. John Barrow, *The World within the World* (Oxford: Clarendon Press, 1988).
10. For a demonstration of the fallaciousness of employing the principle in the absence of a World Ensemble see William Lane Craig, 'Barrow and Tipler on the Anthropic Principle vs. Divine Design', *British Journal for the Philosophy of Science*, 38 (1988), pp. 389–95.
11. To say that there are objective moral values is to say that something is right or wrong independently of whether anybody believes it to be so. It is to say, for example, that Nazi anti-Semitism was morally wrong, even though the Nazis who carried out the Holocaust thought that it was good; and it would still be wrong even if the Nazis had won World War II and succeeded in exterminating or brainwashing everybody who disagreed with them.
12. Michael Ruse, 'Evolutionary Theory and Christian Ethics', in Michael Ruse, *The Darwinian Paradigm* (London: Routledge, 1989), pp. 262, 268–9.
13. Fyodor Dostoyevsky, *The Brothers Karamazov*, trans. C. Garnett (New York: Signet Classics, 1957), bk II, ch. 6; bk V, ch. 4; bk XI, ch. 8.
14. Michael Ruse, *Darwinism Defended* (London: Addison-Wesley, 1982), p. 275.
15. Robert Adams, 'Flavors, Colors, and God', in Robert Adams, *The Virtue of Faith* (Oxford: Oxford University Press, 1987); Richard Swinburne, *The Evolution of the Soul* (Oxford: Clarendon Press, 1986), pp. 183–96.
16. J. J. Haldane, 'Atheism and Theism', in J.J.C. Smart and J.J. Haldane, *Atheism and Theism*, Great Debates in Philosophy (Oxford: Blackwell, 1996), pp. 106–12 and references in the Index under 'mind, and matter'.
17. Stuart C. Hackett, *The Reconstruction of the Christian Revelation Claim* (Grand Rapids, MI: Baker, 1984), pp. 107–11.
18. In his very thorough survey, Oppy identifies six basic types of ontological argument (Graham Oppy, *Ontological Arguments and Belief in God* [Cambridge: Cambridge University Press, 1995]). However, Oppy classifies an argument as ontological if it

proceeds from considerations that are entirely internal to the theistic world-view (p. 1), a criterion far too vague for useful classification.

19. Alvin Plantinga, 'Reason and Belief in God', typescript dated in October 1981, pp. 18–19. This paragraph was inadvertently omitted in the published version of the essay, with the result that Mavrodes's reference to it in the same book has no referent. Fortunately, a nearly identical paragraph appears in Alvin Plantinga, 'Self-Profile', in James E. Tomberlin and Peter van Inwagen (eds), *Alvin Plantinga*, Profiles 5 (Dordrecht: D. Reidel, 1985), p. 71. Cf. Alvin Plantinga, *Warranted Christian Belief* (Oxford: Clarendon Press, 2000), p. 69.

20. Considerations of simplicity might also come into play here. For example, it is simpler to posit one metaphysically necessary, infinite, omniscient, morally perfect being than to think that three separate necessary beings exist instantiating these respective excellent-making properties. Similarly, with respect to quasi-maximally great beings, Swinburne's contention seems plausible that it is simpler (or perhaps less ad hoc) to posit either zero or infinity as the measure of a degreed property than to posit some inexplicably finite measure. Thus, it would be more plausible to think that maximal greatness is possibly instantiated than quasi-maximal greatness. If the latter is possibly instantiated, why not the former? But if the former is possibly instantiated, there is reason to think that the latter is not, since a maximally great being could refrain from creating a quasi-maximally great being, i.e., there is a possible world in which no quasi-maximally great being exists. But then the existence of such a being is impossible.

COSMOLOGICAL ARGUMENT

2.1

'THE COSMOLOGICAL ARGUMENT AND THE EPISTEMIC STATUS OF BELIEF IN GOD'

Stephen T. Davis

I

The Cosmological Argument for the existence of God (CA) is a venerable and frequently debated theistic proof. It has been discussed by philosophers at least since the third century B.C., when a version of it appeared in Plato.[1] Since then it has been both attacked and defended throughout the history of philosophy. There have been important discussions of it in the ancient, medieval, modern, and contemporary periods.[2] There is no one "Cosmological Argument;" what we refer to by that name is of course a whole cluster of related arguments that revolve around certain common and recognizable themes. Virtually every author who discusses the CA has a favorite version.

In the present paper I wish to focus on what I will call the "generic cosmological argument" (GCA). I can find no philosopher to whom to attribute this precise version, although it clearly has affinities with eighteenth century versions of the CA, especially those of Leibniz and Clarke.[3] Moreover, the GCA contains several themes that we associate with Aquinas' versions of the CA, especially the "Third Way."[4] Here, then, is what I am calling the GCA:

(1). If the universe can be explained, then God exists.
(2). Everything can be explained.

Stephen T. Davis, 'The Cosmological Argument and the Epistemic Status of Belief in God', *Philosophia Christi*, series 2, 1, 1 (1999), pp. 5–15.

(3). The universe is a thing.
(4). Therefore, the universe can be explained.
(5). Therefore, God exists.

Let me now set out to clarify the GCA. First, three terms need definition. By the term, "the universe" (or "the world"), I simply mean the sum total of everything that has ever existed or will exist (minus God, if God exists). By the term "God," I mean some sort of divine reality or divine realities. I do not think the CGA, even if it is an entirely successful theistic proof, necessarily proves the existence of the God of theism—unique, all-powerful, all-knowing, loving, etc. But if the GCA is successful, it certainly does prove the existence of *some* sort of divine reality or necessary being[5] (which of course could possibly be the God of theism). So whenever I use the word "God" in this paper I mean it as shorthand for the more complex set of possibilities just noted. By the term "thing" I simply mean a being or entity ("substance," as earlier philosophers would have called it)—something that has an identity distinct from other things and is a property-bearer.

Second, let me briefly discuss the premises of the GCA. Premise (1) simply claims that if there is any explanation of the existence of the universe, then God must exist and provide that explanation. This premise seems perfectly sensible because if God exists then the explanation for the existence of the universe is just this: "God created it." And this seems about the only sort of explanation that *could* be given. If no God or Godlike creator of the universe exists, it seems that the universe will have no explanation whatsoever for its existence. Its existence will be what we might call a brute fact. It is just there, and that is all that can be said.

Premise (2) is a version of a principle that philosophers call the "principle of sufficient reason" (PSR). There are many versions of the PSR; I will interpret it to mean simply this: *Everything that exists has a reason for its existence.*[6] That is, if something x exists, there must be a reason or explanation why x exists. Defenders of the PSR usually admit that the PSR cannot be proven, since it constitutes one of the basic axioms of rational thought against which all other claims or statements are measured. That is, we standardly try to argue for the truth of a proposition by means of other propositions that are more evident or certain than it; but in the case of the PSR (so this argument goes), there are no propositions more certain or evident than it that can be used in this way.

But the PSR—so its defenders claim—is rationally indispensable in that it is presupposed in all rational thought. Richard Taylor says that you cannot argue for the PSR without assuming it; he calls the PSR "a presupposition of reason itself."[7] We encounter thousands of existing things every day, and our assumption always is that there is some reason or explanation why they exist. Suppose one day you were to encounter something unusual—a strange animal, or an automobile completely unknown to you. You would dismiss as absurd any such statement as "There is no reason why it exists; it's just there—that's all." That is, your commitment to the truth of the PSR would make you reject out of hand any suggestion that the existence of the thing is entirely random or inexplicable, a brute fact. Moreover, it needs to be pointed out that there are *no* existing things about which we know that they have no explanation for their existence.

Premise (3) represents what we might call the "lumping together" strategy that we see in many versions of the CA. The typical move is to lump together all the existing things, or all the contingent things that have ever existed or will exist, and call it "reality" or "the world" or "the universe." Then causal questions are asked about this huge aggregate—questions like, "Who made it?" or "Where did it come from?" or "Why is it here?" or "What is its cause?" Premise (3) simply says that the huge aggregate that we call "the universe" is itself a thing about which such causal questions can coherently be asked.

Suppose a critic of the GCA wanted to deny premise (3). If so, the response to the critic would be to point out that the universe has the two essential characteristics of "things." First, it has an identity apart from other things; the universe is not the same thing as the earth or as my computer, for example. Second, the universe is a property-bearer. That is, it has certain unique properties like a certain pressure, density, temperature, space-time curvature, etc. In its very early history everything was so smashed together that there wasn't even atomic structure, so that the only thing there was the universe itself. Accordingly, premise (3) seems highly plausible.

Premise (4) is entailed by (2) and (3). That is, if it is true, as premise (3) says, that the universe is a thing; and if it is true, as premise (2) says, that everything can be explained; then it strictly follows, as premise (4) says, that the universe can be explained. It is impossible for (2) and (3) to be true and (4) false. The conclusion of the GCA follows from (1) and (4). If it is true, as (1) says, that *if* the universe can be explained, then God exists; and if it is true, as (4) says, that the universe *can* in fact be explained; then it strictly follows, as (5) says, that God exists. Because of the argument form known as *modus ponens*, it is impossible for (1) and (4) to be true and (5) false.

II

Now the GCA looks at first glance to have promise as a theistic proof. But some have argued that it commits the fallacy of begging the question, and accordingly fails.[8] (There are, of course, other objections that are standardly raised against the CA,[9] but with one exception—an objection we will consider in Section IV—we will focus in the present paper just on the "question-begging" objection.)

In order to clarify this objection to the GCA (it also constitutes an objection to most versions of the CA), let me refer to the transcript of a famous debate in 1948 on BBC radio. The debaters were Bertrand Russell, the famous atheist philosopher, and Frederick Copleston SJ, the eminent historian of philosophy;

the debate topic was the existence of God. In a discussion of the CA, Copleston remarked, "Well, my point is that what we call the world is intrinsically unintelligible, apart from the existence of God."[10] Copleston thus in effect endorsed premise (1) of the GCA. But Russell consistently took the position that the world has no explanation, and that it is illegitimate to ask for an explanation of the world. Russell thus in effect insisted on denying premise (2) of the GCA, which is the PSR. "I should say that the universe is there, and that's all," Russell said; "the notion of the world having an explanation is a mistake."

The debate over the CA then ground to an inconclusive halt, with Russell unwilling to grant the PSR and Copleston unable to convince him of its truth. As Copleston wrote at the end of his own discussion of Aquinas' Five Ways, "If one does not wish to embark on the path which leads to the affirmation of transcendent being . . . one has to deny the reality of the problem, assert that things 'just are' and that the existential problem in question is a pseudo-problem. And if one refuses even to sit down at the chess-board and make a move, one cannot, of course, be checkmated."[11]

What the Russell–Copleston debate shows, according to some critics, is that at least some versions of the CA, including the GCA, fail as theistic proofs because they commit the fallacy of begging the question. Now there are many ways in which an argument can beg the question. At issue here is the question-begging that is engaged in when one's argument contains a premise or premises that will only be acceptable to those who already accept the conclusion. As an illustration, notice this theistic proof:

(6). Either God exists or 7+5=13;
(7). 7+5 does not=13;
(8). Therefore, God exists.[12]

This argument is certainly formally valid; it is impossible for (6) and (7) to be true and (8) false. And to theists (those who believe in the existence of God), it is also sound; that is, they hold both its premises (i.e., [6] and [7]) to be true. Now nearly everybody will grant the truth of (7), and theists are happy also to grant the truth of (6). But the problem here is that no sensible person who denies or doubts the conclusion of the argument (i.e., no sensible atheist or agnostic) will grant the truth of (6). There is no reason to grant (6) apart from a prior commitment to the existence of God. Thus the (6)–(8) theistic proof is an unsuccessful theistic proof because it begs the question.

Returning to the GCA, the criticism we are discussing argues that it begs the question at the point of premise

2. Everything can be explained,

that is, at the point where the PSR is introduced. Let me explain the objection in this way: it is clear to all concerned that the GCA is formally valid; so the deepest question we can ask about it is whether its premises are true. Well, premises (1) and (3) appear to be beyond reproach, and can be accepted by any sensible person. But what about (2)? Well, there is a certain set of rational persons who will be much inclined to consider premise (2) true as well, that is, inclined to accept the truth of the PSR. These people may accordingly consider the GCA to be both valid and sound (again, we are ignoring other possible objections to the GCA). That is, these folk might well consider the GCA a successful proof of the existence of God.

The people whom I have in mind are of course theists, that is, people who already believe in the existence of God. Those folk quite naturally accept the suggestion that everything can be explained. This is because they hold that the universe and everything in it (the whole of reality minus God) can be explained in some such terms as, "God created it." But here is the crucial point: there is also a certain set of rational persons who will be much inclined to reject premise (2). These folk are atheists. No atheist like Bertrand Russell will have the slightest inclination to grant the truth of premise (2). Such persons will hold that the PSR is false because there is at least one existing thing—the universe itself—that has always existed and cannot be explained. Its existence is simply a brute fact.

If the defender of the GCA can find a way of arguing convincingly for the truth of the PSR that does not appeal to or presuppose the existence of God, then the GCA might well constitute (depending of course on whether other objections to it can also be answered) a successful theistic proof. In the absence of such an argument, the GCA, according to the objection that we are considering, fails because it requires a premise that should not be granted by those at whom the GCA is aimed, viz, atheists and agnostics. Thus, since even defenders of the PSR admit that it cannot be proved, the GCA fails as a theistic proof. One of its crucial premises will only be acceptable to those who already accept its conclusion.

The point is not that only theists accept the PSR. Some atheists affirm it. The point is, as Bertrand Russell saw, that atheists *should not* affirm the PSR. In order to be consistent, they must insist that there is no explanation of why there is any reality at all. Accordingly—so the objection we are considering concludes—the GCA begs the question.

III

But perhaps the objection that the GCA fails as a theistic proof because it begs the question is too hasty. It seems correct to say that rational theists quite naturally accept the PSR and that rational atheists and agnostics do not, or should not, do so. But does it follow that the GCA, or indeed any version of the CA that relies on the PSR, accordingly begs the question? Perhaps the answer to that question will depend on the aim, goal, or purpose of the GCA. Suppose the goal of the GCA is *to convince all atheists and agnostics to believe in the existence of God* or *to constitute an argument that rationally **should** convince all atheists and agnostics to believe in the existence of God*. Then, of course, the objection to the GCA that we are considering would appear to stand. The GCA would be a failure as a theistic proof. It would achieve neither purpose because rational atheists and agnostics will reject its second premise.

But suppose the goal of the GCA is instead *to strengthen the belief of theists in the existence of God* or *to show theists that they can **know** that God exists*. If something like this is the purpose or goal of the GCA, then the objection to the GCA that we are considering appears to fail. It will not matter that atheists and agnostics rationally should reject the GCA's second premise. Since the theists at whom the argument is aimed all accept its second premise, the GCA might well (again depending on what is to be said about other objections that might be raised against it) constitute a successful proof of the existence of God.

But it seems that most theistic proofs in the history of philosophy, including the many versions of the CA that we find there, are offered with at least some sort of apologetic purpose in mind, that is, with some such goal in the mind of the theistic prover as that of showing—showing to any rational person—that belief in God can be a rational belief. Theistic proofs have rarely been offered, so far as I can see, for intramural use only, for believers only. I will take it, then, that the actual aim or goal of the GCA is to *demonstrate the existence of God* and thus to *demonstrate the rationality of belief in the existence of God*. That is, what a successful theistic proof aims to do is substantiate the theist's belief in God, give a convincing reason for it, show that it is credible, show that it is *true*. But to whom is it to be demonstrated? Let me suggest that theistic proofs aim to demonstrate the rationality of theistic belief to all rational persons (whoever exactly they are), theists *or* atheists.

One way to do this, of course, is to convince folk that the premises of the theistic proof under consideration are more plausible than their denials. The premise with which we are concerned is of course premise (2) of the GCA:

(2). Everything can be explained.

Which then is more rational or plausible, premise (2) or its denial, which we can call:

(2'). It is false that everything can be explained?

And that question, in the context of the current discussion, amounts to this: Is it possible to argue convincingly for the truth of the PSR in such a way as not to appeal to or presuppose the existence of God?[13]

It is surely possible to argue for the truth of the PSR without invoking or presupposing God. The question is whether it is possible to do so *convincingly*. The argument standardly used by defenders of the PSR is the one briefly suggested above, viz, that the PSR is an indispensable requirement of reason. That is, it is an intuition shared by all rational folk (except perhaps atheists and agnostics when they are objecting to the CA) about the way reality operates. It is a kind of natural belief or basic assumption that all rational people quite normally make. In this way—so defenders of the PSR say—it is not unlike the belief that

9. My epistemic faculties do not systematically mislead me.

Of course our faculties for gaining true beliefs about and even knowledge of the world (faculties like memory, perception, reasoning, etc.) *sometimes* mislead us; but any attempt to argue that they do not *systematically* mislead us would involve assuming the reliability of our epistemic faculties. So no rational person can deny (9).

The point can be made in a slightly different way: just as it is necessary for our survival as living organisms on the earth that we accept (9), so it is necessary for our survival that we accept the PSR. Imagine the life of someone who seriously doubted the PSR. Such a person would—so it seems—live in constant fear that no matter what precautions she took dangerous things might always pop into existence in her vicinity uncaused—things like hungry lions or speeding trains or deep chasms or armed terrorists. Thus—so the argument concludes—human nature compels us to accept the PSR.

Is this a convincing argument? Perhaps it is to everyone but the Bertrand Russells of this world. Such folk will surely grant that tigers, lions, chasms, and terrorists do not pop into existence uncaused; but they will still insist on the rationality of holding the *whole* of reality, that is, the universe itself, to be uncaused. Moreover—so they will ask—who says that the demands of human reason are all satisfied? Is reality bound to agree with our presuppositions, even presuppositions that otherwise seem rational? In short, even if it is true that reason demands that we hold that the PSR is true, that does not show that the PSR is true.

IV

As noted earlier, there are several objections that are often raised against the CA beside the begging-the-question criticism with which we have been principally concerned. Although I am ignoring most of them in the present paper, there is one that seems relevant to our discussion, and should be considered. The objection is this: If GCA is a successful argument, the "god" or necessary being that it proves to exist is not the God of theism or even any lesser god-like sentient being, but rather the universe, or physical matter itself. And an argument that proves the existence or indeed the necessary existence of the universe itself hardly does much to bolster the epistemic status of belief in God.

But it does not seem sensible to consider the universe, or physical reality, to be a necessary being. I cannot quite prove this by arguing that "Everything in the universe is a contingent thing; ergo the universe is a contingent thing," for that argument might well commit the fallacy of composition. Sometimes such arguments are clearly fallacious ("Every member of the human race has a mother; ergo the human race has a mother"); although at other times they are perfectly acceptable ("All the tiles in this mosaic are blue; ergo the whole mosaic is blue"). Whether or not the inference goes through in the case of the world's contingency, it is still a meaningful fact about the universe that none of its members is necessary.

And that fact strongly suggests that there is *no* telling reason to consider the universe a necessary being. If we knew that the universe were everlasting, that *might* suggest it is a necessary thing. But those who would so argue would still have to overcome the obstacle of Richard Taylor's trenchant argument to the effect that something can be both everlasting and contingent. Suppose, he says, contrary to fact, that the sun and the moon are both everlasting. Then moonlight would also be everlasting—but still contingent, because it would (everlastingly) depend for its existence on sunlight.[14] Moreover, we do not know that the universe—physical reality—is everlasting. Indeed, all indications are that it began at the Big Bang some 16.5 billion years ago (or whenever it occurred). And we have no basis whatsoever—no physics—for suggesting that or even whether anything existed before the Big Bang.

And a truly telling point against the objection to the GCA that we are considering is this: even if the universe were everlasting, it would still make sense to ask: Why should it exist at all? That is, why is there a reality at all? Why is there anything and not nothing? There is no absurdity at all in the idea of there being nothing at all, no universe. (No one would be there to notice that state of affairs, of course, but that does nothing to rule out the possibility.) It follows that there is nothing about the universe that implies or even suggests that it is a necessary being. Accordingly, the objection to the GCA that we are considering fails.

Where then have we arrived? What does our discussion imply about the epistemic status of belief in God? If the purpose of the GCA is *to demonstrate to any rational person that belief in the existence of God is rational*, then our conclusion ought to be that the GCA (assuming it emerges unscathed by other criticisms) *can* constitute a successful theistic proof. This is because defenders of the GCA, as we have seen, are perfectly capable of making a rational case for its truth that does not invoke or presuppose God. It seems that even atheists will be able to understand (though they might not agree with or be convinced by) the argument that the PSR is a demand of rational thought. A strong case can be made—a case that any sensible person can understand— that belief in the PSR is rational.

But theists can also understand (though they might not agree with or be convinced by) the argument that while the PSR applies well to existing items like animals, automobiles, and houses (things that have finite lifespans, things that come into and later pass out of existence), it does not apply to the megathing of the universe itself. Bertrand Russell might be right that it is a mistake to expect that reality itself has an explanation.

But which then is more plausible,

(2). Everything can be explained,

or

(2′). It is false that everything can be explained?

Since, as we have seen, commitment to (2′) does not entail commitment to the absurd notion that things like animals, automobiles, and houses can come into existence uncaused (one can consistently hold that the universe itself is the only exception to the PSR), it does not seem possible to show which is more plausible.[15] We appear to be left with the possibility that the theist's belief in the existence of God might well be rational (given the theist's rational acceptance of [2]) and that the atheist's disbelief in the existence of God might well also be rational (given the atheist's rational acceptance of [2′]).

But it is important to note that even this relatively irenical conclusion—that both atheists and theists can be rational—has an important consequence. If the conclusion of this paper is correct (and again if the GCA can withstand other objections that might be raised against it), then belief in God (or some Godlike being or beings who is or are responsible for the existence of the universe) is rational.

This is not a trivial conclusion. Why? Because no objection to theism is more common than the objection that in believing in God theists are being soft-headed, gullible, and credulous; they are violating the ethics of belief; they are setting a poor epistemic example. Thus Kai Nielsen (I could have quoted almost a host of others): "For someone living in the twentieth century with a good philosophical and a good scientific education, who thinks carefully about the matter . . . for such a person it is irrational to believe in God".[16] In the light of the GCA, this objection to theism collapses.[17]

Notes

1. See Edith Hamilton and Huntington Cairns (eds.), *The Collected Dialogues of Plato* (New York: Pantheon, 1961), 1455–1479 (*Laws* 894A–899C).
2. There are several good surveys of the literature. See, for example, William L. Craig, *The Cosmological Argument from Plato to Leibniz* (New York: Barnes and Noble, 1980). See also the essays collected in Donald R. Burrill (ed.), *The Cosmological Arguments* (Garden City, New York: Anchor Books, 1967).
3. See Gottfried Leibniz, "On the Ultimate Origin of Things," in Philip P. Wiener (ed.), *Leibniz: Selections* (New York: Charles Scribner's Sons, 1951), 345–355, and the selections from Samuel Clarke's *A Demonstration of the Being and Attributes of God* in D. Raphael (ed.), *British Moralists 1650–1800* (Oxford: Oxford University Press, 1969).

4. See Thomas Aquinas, *Summa Theologica* (New York: Benzinger Brothers, 1947), 1, 2, 3 (13–14).

5. Let us say that a necessary being (NB) is a being that (1) is everlasting; there is no moment when it does not exist; and (2) depends for its existence on no other being. In some strong sense of the word "cannot," a NB cannot not exist. A contingent being (CB), on the other hand, is a being that can either exist or not exist; if it exists it (1) has a finite lifespan (it does not exist, and then exists, and then ceases existing); and (2) depends for its existence, as long as it exists, on another being or other beings. Some contingent things exist (horses) and some do not (unicorns). Thus CBs, unlike NBs, can fail to exist.

6. A slightly weaker version of the PSR says this: Everything that comes into existence has a reason for its existence. I opt for the stronger version so that the PSR will apply to the universe even if it turns out that the universe is everlasting (there is no moment of time when it does not exist) and thus did not come into existence. This is because even if the universe is eternal, the question, "Why should it exist instead of not exist?" is still a legitimate question. One problem with the stronger version of the PSR is that it requires that even necessary beings (if there are any) have a reason for their existence. But then we will say that the reason for the existence of a given necessary being B is simply that B is a necessary being.

7. Richard Taylor, *Metaphysics*, 4th edition (Englewood Cliffs, New Jersey: Prentice-Hall, 1992), 101.

8. As indeed I argued in Stephen T. Davis, *God, Reason, and Theistic Proofs* (Edinburgh: Edinburgh University Press, 1997), 144–146. The present paper represents a correction of the argument presented there. John Hick has also argued that the CA begs the question. See his (ed.) *The Existence of God* (New York: Macmillan, 1964), 6–7

9. For discussion of them, see *God, Reason, and Theistic Proofs*, 70–76.

10. See Hick, *The Existence of God*, 174–177.

11. Reprinted in Hick, *The Existence of God*, 93.

12. This argument is discussed by Alvin Plantinga in *The Nature of Necessity* (Oxford: Clarendon Press, 1974), 217–218.

13. It should be noted that attempts have been made to argue against the PSR, but they are not convincing. (1) Some have argued that since quantum physics, at least on some interpretations, allows for undetermined and inexplicable events, it can also allow for things to come into existence uncaused. But even if indeterministic interpretations of certain quantum events are correct, the conservation laws in physics still rule out things coming into existence uncaused. (2) Others argue that the uncaused and totally random coming-into-existence of something is not logically contradictory, and indeed is perfectly conceivable. Both points are true, but prove nothing. There are lots of reasons why a given proposition might be intellectually unacceptable besides its being logically contradictory. And in some sense of the word "conceive" I surely can conceive of, say, a poodle popping into existence in my office for no cause or reason. But that does nothing to show that belief that such an event can actually occur is plausible.

14. Taylor, *Metaphysics*, 101.

15. There is a problem with the atheist's theory which I will note but not explore. It was originally pointed out by A. N. Prior: it cannot be the case that only certain things and not others come into existence uncaused because, before they exist, there is just nothing that would determine that only things of that kind can come into existence uncaused. Why then is it that animals, automobiles, and houses cannot come into existence uncaused, but the universe can? See A. N. Prior, "Limited Indeterminism," *Papers on Time and Tense* (Oxford: Clarendon Press, 1968), 65.

16. J. P. Moreland and Kai Nielsen (eds.), *Does God Exist? The Great Debate* (Nashville, Tennessee: Thomas Nelson, 1990), 48.

17. I would like to thank William Lane Craig for his helpful comments on an earlier draft of this paper.

2.2

THE *KALAM* COSMOLOGICAL ARGUMENT

William Lane Craig

In my opinion the version of the cosmological argument which is most likely to be a sound and persuasive proof for the existence of God is the *kalam* cosmological argument based on the impossibility of an infinite temporal regress of events. The argument may be formulated in three simple steps:

1. Whatever begins to exist has a cause.
2. The universe began to exist.
3. Therefore, the universe has a cause.

The point of the argument is to demonstrate the existence of a first cause which transcends and creates the entire realm of finite reality. Having reached that conclusion, one may then inquire into the nature of this first cause and assess its significance for theism.

WHATEVER BEGINS TO EXIST HAS A CAUSE

The first premiss is rooted in the metaphysical principle that 'something cannot come out of nothing' and is so intuitively obvious that I think scarcely anyone could sincerely believe it to be false. I therefore think it somewhat unwise to argue in favour of it, for any proof of the principle is likely to be less obvious than the principle itself, and, as Aristotle remarked, one ought not to try to prove the obvious via the less obvious. The proposition that 'Out of nothing, nothing comes' seems to me to be a sort of metaphysical first principle whose truth impresses itself upon us. In any case, the first premiss, even if taken as a mere inductive generalisation, seems as secure as any truth rooted in experience.

It is therefore not a little surprising to find atheists attempting to defeat the argument by attacking the first premiss. For example, the late J. L. Mackie turned his main guns on this first premiss, writing, 'there is *a priori* no good reason why a sheer origination of things, not determined by anything, should be unacceptable, whereas the existence of a god [*sic*] with the power to create something out of nothing is acceptable'.[1] Indeed, he believed that *creatio ex nihilo* raises problems: (1) if God began to exist at a point in time, then this is as great a puzzle as the beginning of the universe; (2) if God existed for infinite time, then the same arguments would apply to His existence as would apply to the infinite duration of the universe; and (3) if it be said that God is timeless, then this, says Mackie, is a complete mystery.

Now notice that Mackie never denies, much less refutes, the principle that whatever begins to exist has a cause. Rather, he simply demands what good reason there is a priori to accept it. He writes, 'As Hume pointed out, we can certainly conceive an uncaused beginning-to-be of an object; if what we can thus conceive is nevertheless in some way impossible, this still requires to be shown.'[2] But, as many philosophers have noted, imaginability is in no way a reliable guide to metaphysical possibility. Just because I can imagine in my mind's eye an object, say a horse, coming into existence from nothing, that in no way suggests that a horse really could come into existence that way. The fact that there is no formal contradiction in 'a horse's popping into being out of nothing' does not defeat the claim of the defender of the *kalam* argument that such a thing is metaphysically impossible. Does anyone in his right mind believe that, say, a raging tiger could suddenly come into existence uncaused, out of nothing, in this room right now? The same applies to the universe: if there were absolutely nothing prior to the existence of the universe – no God, no space, no time – how could the universe possibly have come to exist?

In fact, Mackie's appeal to Hume at this point is counter-productive. For Hume himself clearly believed the causal principle. In 1754 he wrote to John Stewart,

> But allow me to tell you that I never asserted so absurd a Proposition as *that anything might arise without a cause*: I only maintain'd, that our Certainty of the Falsehood of that Proposition proceeded neither from Intuition nor Demonstration, but from another source.[3]

Even Mackie, in response to the claim of atheist scientist Peter Atkins that the universe came into being out of nothing by sheer chance, demurred: 'I myself find it hard to accept the notion of self-creation *from nothing*, even *given* unrestricted chance. And how *can* this be given, if there really is nothing?'[4] Moreover, Mackie concedes, 'Still this [causal] principle has some plausibility, in that it is constantly confirmed in our experience (and also used, reasonably, in interpreting our experience).'[5] So, leaving a priori intuitions aside, why not at least accept the truth of the causal principle as plausible and reasonable – at the very least more so than its denial?

The answer is that in this particular case the theism implied by affirming the principle is, in Mackie's thinking, even more unintelligible than the denial of the principle. It makes more sense to believe that the universe came into being uncaused out of nothing than to believe that God created the universe out of nothing.

But is this really the case? Consider the three alternatives Mackie raises concerning *creatio ex nihilo*. Certainly, the proponent of the *kalam* argument would not hold (1) that God began to exist or (2) that God has existed for an infinite number of, say, hours, or any other unit of time. But what is wrong with (3), that God is, without creation, timeless? I would argue that God exists timelessly without creation and temporally since creation. This may be 'mysterious' in the sense of 'wonderful' or 'awe-inspiring', but it is not, so far as I can see, unintelligible; and Mackie gives us no reason to think that it is. Moreover, there is also an alternative which Mackie failed to consider: (4) prior to creation God existed in an undifferentiated time in which hours, days and so forth simply do not exist. Because this time is undifferentiated, it is not incompatible with the *kalam* argument based on the impossibility of an infinite temporal regress of events. It seems to me, therefore, that Mackie is entirely unjustified in rejecting the first step of the argument as not being intuitively obvious, plausible and reasonable.

The Universe Began to Exist

If we agree that whatever begins to exist has a cause, what evidence is there to support the crucial second premiss, that 'the universe began to exist'? This premiss may be supported by both deductive and inductive arguments from metaphysics and physics.

1. Argument from the Impossibility of an Actually Infinite Number of Things

This argument can also be formulated in three steps:

1. An actually infinite number of things cannot exist.
2. A beginningless series of events in time entails an actually infinite number of things.
3. Therefore, a beginningless series of events in time cannot exist.

Since the universe is not distinct from the temporal series of past events, the demonstration that the series of temporal events had a beginning implies that the universe began to exist. Let us examine more closely each of the argument's two premises.

1. *An actually infinite number of things cannot exist.* In order to understand this first premiss, we need to differentiate clearly between

an actual infinite and a potential infinite. A potential infinite is a collection that is increasing toward infinity as a limit but never gets there. Such a collection is really indefinite, not infinite. For example, any finite distance can be subdivided into potentially infinitely many parts. One can keep on dividing parts in half forever, but one will never arrive at an actual 'infinitieth' division or come up with an actually infinite number of parts. By contrast, an actual infinite is not growing toward infinity; it is infinite, it is 'complete'. A collection is actually infinite just in case a proper part of the collection can be put into a one-to-one correspondence with the whole collection, so that the proper part has the same number of members as the whole (Principle of Correspondence). This notion of infinity is employed in set theory to designate sets that have an infinite number of members, such as {1, 2, 3, . . .}. The argument, then, is not that a potentially infinite number of things cannot exist, but that an actually infinite number of things cannot exist. For if an actually infinite number of things could exist, this would spawn all sorts of absurdities.

Perhaps the best way to bring this home is by means of an illustration. Let me use one of my favourites, Hilbert's Hotel, a product of the mind of the great German mathematician David Hilbert.[6] Let us imagine a hotel with a finite number of rooms. Suppose, furthermore, that all the rooms are full. When a new guest arrives asking for a room, the proprietor apologises, 'Sorry, all the rooms are full', and the new guest is turned away. But now let us imagine a hotel with an infinite number of rooms and suppose once more that 'all the rooms are full'. There is not a single vacant room throughout the entire infinite hotel. Now suppose a new guest shows up, asking for a room. 'But of course!' says the proprietor, and he immediately shifts the person in room #1 into room #2, the person in room #2 into room #3, the person in room #3 into room #4, and so on, out to infinity. As a result of these room changes, room #1 now becomes vacant and the new guest gratefully checks in. But remember, before he arrived, all the rooms were full! Equally curious, according to the mathematicians, there are now no more persons in the hotel than there were before: the number is just infinite. But how can this be? The proprietor just added the new guest's name to the register and gave him his keys – how can there not be one more person in the hotel than before?

But the situation becomes even stranger. For suppose an infinity of new guests show up at the desk, each asking for a room. 'Of course, of course!' says the proprietor, and he proceeds to shift the person in room #1 into room #2, the person in room #2 into room #4, the person in room #3 into room #6, and so on out to infinity, always putting each former occupant into the room number twice his own. Because any natural number multiplied by two always equals an even number, all the guests wind up in even-numbered rooms. As a result, all the odd-numbered rooms become vacant, and the infinity of new guests is easily accommodated. And yet, before they came, all the rooms were full! And again, strangely enough, the number of guests in the hotel is the same after the infinity of new guests check in as before, even though there were as many new guests as old guests. In fact, the proprietor could repeat this process *infinitely many times*, and yet there would never be one single person more in the hotel than before.

But Hilbert's Hotel is even stranger than the German mathematician made it out to be. For suppose some of the guests start to check out. Suppose the guest in room #1 departs. Is there not now one less person in the hotel? Not according to the mathematicians – but just ask Housekeeping! Suppose the guests in rooms ##1, 3, 5 check out. In this case an infinite number of people have left the hotel, but according to the mathematicians, there are no fewer people in the hotel – but don't talk to those people in Housekeeping! In fact, we could have every other guest check out of the hotel and repeat this process infinitely many times, and yet there would never be any fewer people in the hotel.

Now suppose the proprietor does not like having a half-empty hotel (it looks bad for business). No matter! By shifting occupants as before, but in reverse order, he transforms his half-vacant hotel into one that is jammed to the gills. One might think that by these manoeuvres the proprietor could always keep this strange hotel fully occupied. But one would be wrong. For suppose that the persons in rooms ##4, 5, 6 . . . checked out. At a single stroke the hotel would be virtually emptied, the guest register reduced to but three names, and the infinite converted to finitude. And yet it would remain true that the *same* number of guests checked out this time as when the guests in rooms ##1, 3, 5 . . . checked out! Can anyone believe that such a hotel could exist in reality?

Hilbert's Hotel is absurd. Since nothing hangs on the illustration's involving a hotel, the above sorts of absurdities show in general that it is impossible for an actually infinite number of things to exist.[7] There is simply no way to avoid these absurdities once we admit the possibility of the existence of an actual infinite. Students sometimes react to such absurdities as Hilbert's Hotel by saying that we really do not understand the nature of infinity and, hence, these absurdities result. But this attitude is simply mistaken. Infinite set theory is a highly-developed and well-understood branch of mathematics, so that these absurdities can be seen to result precisely because we do understand the notion of a collection with an actually infinite number of members.

These considerations also show how superficial Mackie's response to this premiss is.[8] He thinks that the absurdities are resolved by noting that for infinite groups the axiom that 'the whole is greater than its part' does not hold, as it does for finite groups. But far from being the solution, this is precisely the problem. Because in infinite set theory this axiom is denied, one gets all sorts of absurdities, like Hilbert's Hotel, when one tries to translate that theory into reality. Mackie's response does nothing to prove that the envisioned situations are not absurd, but only reiterates, in effect, that if an actual infinite were to exist and the Principle of Correspondence were valid with respect to it, then the relevant situations would result, which is not in dispute. Moreover, the contradictions that result when guests check out of the hotel are not even prima facie resolved by Mackie's analysis. (In trans-finite arithmetic, inverse operations of subtraction and division are prohibited because they lead to contradictions; but in reality, one cannot stop people from checking out of the hotel if they want to!) Hence, it is plausible that an actually infinite number of things cannot exist.[9]

2. *A beginningless series of events in time entails an actually infinite number of things.* This second premiss seems pretty obvious. If the universe never began to exist, then prior to the present event there have existed an actually infinite number of previous events. Thus, a beginningless series of events in time entails an actually infinite number of things, namely, events.

3. *Therefore a beginningless series of events in time cannot exist.* If the above two premisses are true, then the conclusion follows logically. The series of past events must be finite and have a beginning. Since, as I said, the universe is not distinct from the series of events, the universe therefore began to exist.

2. Argument from the Impossibility of Forming an Actually Infinite Collection of Things by Successive Addition

This argument is distinct from the foregoing argument, for it does not deny that an actually infinite number of things can exist. It denies that a collection containing an actually infinite number of things can be formed by adding one member after another. This argument, too, can be formulated in three steps:

1. The series of events in time is a collection formed by successive addition.
2. A collection formed by successive addition cannot be actually infinite.
3. Therefore, the series of events in time cannot be actually infinite.

Let us take a closer look at each of the three premisses.

1. *The series of events in time is a collection formed by successive addition.* This seems rather obvious. The past did not spring into being whole and entire but was formed sequentially, one event occurring after another. Notice, too, that the direction of this formation is 'forward' in the sense that the collection of events grows with time. Although we sometimes speak of an 'infinite temporal regress' of events, in reality an infinite past would be an 'infinite temporal progress' of events with no beginning and its end in the present.

2. *A collection formed by successive addition cannot be actually infinite.* This is the crucial step. Sometimes this is called the impossibility of counting to infinity or the impossibility of traversing the infinite. This impossibility has nothing to do with the amount of time available: no matter how much time one has at one's disposal, an actual infinite cannot be so formed. For no matter how many numbers one counts or how many steps one takes, one can always add or take one more before arriving at infinity.

   Now someone might say that while an infinite collection cannot be formed by beginning at a point and adding members, nevertheless an infinite collection could be formed by never beginning but ending at a point, that is to say, ending at a point after having added one member after another from eternity. But this method seems even more unbelievable than the first method. If one cannot count *to* infinity, how can one count down *from* infinity? If one cannot traverse the infinite by moving in one direction, how can one traverse it by moving in the opposite direction?

   Indeed, the idea of a beginningless temporal series of events ending in the present seems absurd. To give just one illustration: consider Tristram Shandy, who, in the novel by Sterne, writes his autobiography so slowly that it takes him a whole year to record the events of a single day. According to Bertrand Russell, if Tristram Shandy were immortal, then the entire book could be completed, since by the Principle of Correspondence to each day there would correspond one year, and both are infinite.[10] Russell's assertion is wholly untenable, however, since the future is in reality a potential infinite only. Though he write for ever, Tristram Shandy would only get farther and farther behind, so that instead of finishing his autobiography he would progressively approach a state in which he would be infinitely far behind. But he would never reach such a state because the years and, hence, the days of his life would always be finite in number, though indefinitely increasing.

   But let us turn the story about: suppose Tristram Shandy has been writing from eternity past at the rate of one day per year. Should not Tristram Shandy now be infinitely far behind? For if he has lived for an infinite number of years, Tristram Shandy has recorded an equally infinite number of past days. Given the thoroughness of his autobiography, these days are all consecutive days. At any point in the past or present, therefore, Tristram Shandy has recorded a beginningless, infinite series of consecutive days. But now the question inevitably arises: Which days are these? Where in the temporal series of events are the days recorded by Tristram Shandy at any given point? The answer can only be that *they are days infinitely distant from the present*. For there is no day on which Tristram Shandy is writing which is finitely distant from the last recorded day. This may be seen through an incisive analysis of the Tristram Shandy paradox given by Robin Small.[11] He points out that if Tristram Shandy has been writing for one year's time, then the most recent day he could have recorded is one year ago. But if he has been writing two years, then that same day could not have been recorded by him. For since his intention is to record consecutive days of his life, the most recent day he could have recorded is the day immediately after a day at least two years ago. This is because it takes a year to record a day, so that to record two days he must have two years. Similarly, if he has been writing three years, then the most recent day recorded could be no more recent than three years and two days ago. In other words, the longer he has written the further behind he has fallen. In fact, the recession into the past of the most recent recordable day can be plotted according to the formula (present date $-n$ years of writing)$+n-1$ days. But what happens if Tristram Shandy has, *ex hypothesi*, been writing for an infinite number of years? The most recent day of his autobiography recedes to infinity, that is to say, to a day infinitely distant from the present. Nowhere in the past at a finite distance from the present can we find a recorded day, for by now Tristram Shandy is infinitely far behind. The beginningless, infinite series of days which he has recorded are days which lie at an infinite temporal distance from the present. But there is no way to traverse the temporal interval from an infinitely distant event to the present, or, more technically, for an event which was once present to recede to an infinite temporal distance. Since the task of writing one's autobiography at the rate of one year per day seems obviously coherent, what follows from the Tristram Shandy story is that an infinite series of past events is absurd.

But now a deeper absurdity bursts into view. For even if every recorded past event lies at only a finite distance from the present, still, if the series of past events is actually infinite, we may ask, why did Tristram Shandy not finish his autobiography yesterday or the day before, since by then an infinite series of events had already elapsed? No matter how far along the series of past events one regresses, Tristram Shandy would have already completed his autobiography. Therefore, at no point in the infinite series of past events could he be finishing the book. We could never look over Tristram Shandy's shoulder to see if he were now writing the last page. For at any point an actually infinite sequence of events would have transpired and the book would have already been completed. Thus, at no time in eternity will we find Tristram Shandy writing, which is absurd, since we supposed him to be writing from eternity. And at no point will he finish the book, which is equally absurd, because for the book to be completed he must at some point have finished.

These illustrations reveal the absurdities involved in trying to form an actually infinite collection of things by successive addition. Hence, set theory has been purged of all temporal concepts; as Russell says, 'classes which are infinite are given all at once by the defining properties of their members, so that there is no question of "completion" or of "successive synthesis".'[12] The only way an actual infinite could come to exist in the real world would be by being created all at once, simply in a moment. It would be a hopeless undertaking to try to form it by adding one member after another.

Mackie's objections to this premiss are off the target.[13] He thinks that the argument illicitly assumes an infinitely distant starting point in the past and then pronounces it impossible to travel from that point to today. If we take the notion of infinity 'seriously', he says, we must say that in the infinite past there would be no starting point whatever, not even an infinitely distant one. Yet from any given point in the past, there is only a finite distance to the present.

Now I know of no proponent of the *kalam* argument who assumed that there was an infinitely distant starting point in the past. On the contrary, the beginningless character of the series of past events only serves to underscore the difficulty of its formation by successive addition. The fact that there is no beginning at all, not even an infinitely distant one, makes the problem worse, not better. It is thus not the proponent of the *kalam* argument who fails to take infinity seriously. To say the infinite past could have been formed by adding one member after another is like saying someone has just succeeded in writing down all the negative numbers, ending at -1. And, we may ask, how is Mackie's point that from any given moment in the past there is only a finite distance to the present even relevant to the issue? The defender of the *kalam* argument could agree to this without batting an eye. For the issue is how the whole series can be formed, not a finite portion of it. Does Mackie think that because every finite segment of the series can be formed by successive addition, the whole infinite series can be so formed? That is as logically fallacious as saying that because every part of an elephant is light in weight, the whole elephant is light in weight. Mackie's point is therefore irrelevant. It seems that this premiss of the argument remains undefeated by his objections.

3. *Therefore, the series of events in time cannot be actually infinite*. Given the truth of the premisses, the conclusion logically follows. If the universe did not begin to exist a finite time ago, then the present moment would never arrive. But obviously it has arrived. Therefore, we know that the universe is finite in the past and began to exist.

(3) Argument Based on the Isotropic Expansion of the Universe

In 1917, Albert Einstein made a cosmological application of his newly discovered gravitational theory, the General Theory of Relativity (GTR). In so doing he assumed that the universe is homogeneous and isotropic and that it exists in a steady state, with a constant mean mass density and a constant curvature of space. To his chagrin, however, he found that GTR would not permit such a model of the universe unless he introduced into his gravitational field equations a certain 'fudge factor' Λ in order to counterbalance the gravitational effect of matter and so ensure a static universe. Unfortunately, Einstein's static universe was balanced on a razor's edge, and the least perturbation would cause the universe either to implode or to expand. By taking this feature of Einstein's model seriously, the Russian mathematician Alexander Friedman and the Belgian astronomer Georges Lemaître were able to formulate independently in the 1920s solutions to the field equations which predicted an expanding universe.

The monumental significance of the Friedman–Lemaître model lay in its historization of the universe. As one commentator has remarked, up to this time the idea of the expansion of the universe 'was absolutely beyond comprehension. Throughout all of human history the universe was regarded as fixed and immutable and the idea that it might actually be changing was inconceivable.'[14] But if the Friedman–Lemaître model were correct, the universe could no longer be adequately treated as a static entity existing, in effect, timelessly. Rather the universe has a history, and time will not be a matter of indifference for our investigation of the cosmos.

In 1929 the astronomer Edwin Hubble showed that the red shift in the optical spectra of light from distant galaxies was a common feature of all measured galaxies and was proportional to their distance from us. This red shift was taken to be a Doppler effect indicative of the recessional motion of the light source in the line of sight. Incredibly, what Hubble had discovered was the isotropic expansion of the universe predicted by Friedman and Lemaître on the basis of Einstein's GTR. It was a veritable turning point in the history of science. 'Of all the great predictions that science has ever made over the centuries,' exclaims John Wheeler, 'was there ever one greater than this, to predict, and predict correctly, and predict against all expectation a phenomenon so fantastic as the expansion of the universe?'[15]

According to the Friedman–Lemaître model, as time proceeds, the distances separating galactic masses become greater. It is important to understand that as a GTR-based theory, the model does not describe the expansion of the material content of the universe into a pre-existing, empty space, but rather the expansion of space itself. The ideal particles of the cosmological fluid constituted by the matter and energy of the universe are conceived to be at rest with respect to space but to recede progressively from one another as space itself expands or stretches, just as buttons glued to the surface of a balloon would recede from one another as the balloon inflates. As the universe expands, it becomes less and less dense. This has the astonishing implication that as one reverses the expansion and extrapolates back in time, the universe becomes progressively denser until one arrives at a state of infinite density at some point in the finite past.[16] This state represents a singularity at which space–time curvature, along with temperature, pressure, and density, becomes infinite. It therefore constitutes an edge or boundary to space–time itself. P.C.W. Davies comments,

> If we extrapolate this prediction to its extreme, we reach a point when all distances in the universe have shrunk to zero. An initial cosmological singularity therefore forms a past temporal extremity to the universe. We cannot continue physical reasoning, or even the concept of spacetime, through such an extremity. For this reason most cosmologists think of the initial singularity as the beginning of the universe. On this view the Big Bang represents the creation event; the creation not only of all the matter and energy in the universe, but also of spacetime itself.[17]

The term 'Big Bang', originally a derisive expression coined by Fred Hoyle to characterise the beginning of the universe predicted by the Friedman–Lemaître model, is thus potentially misleading, since the expansion cannot be visualised from the outside (there being no 'outside', just as there is no 'before' with respect to the Big Bang).

The standard Big Bang model, as the Friedman–Lemaître model came to be called, thus describes a universe which is not eternal in the past, but which came into being a finite time ago. Moreover – and this deserves underscoring – the origin it posits is an absolute origin out of nothing. For not only all matter and energy, but space and time themselves come into being at the initial cosmological singularity. As Barrow and Tipler emphasise, 'At this singularity, space and time came into existence; literally nothing existed before the singularity, so, if the Universe originated at such a singularity, we would truly have a creation *ex nihilo*.'[18] On such a model the universe originates *ex nihilo* in the sense that at the initial singularity it is true that 'There is no earlier space–time point' or it is false that 'Something existed prior to the singularity'.

Now such a conclusion is profoundly disturbing for anyone who ponders it. For, in the words of one astrophysical team, 'The problem of the origin [of the universe] involves a certain metaphysical aspect which may be either appealing or revolting.'[19] Revolted by the stark metaphysical alternatives presented to us by an absolute beginning of the universe, certain theorists have been understandably eager to subvert the Standard Model and restore an eternal universe. The history of twentieth-century cosmology has been the history of the repeated falsification of such non-standard theories and the corroboration of the Big Bang theory. It has been the overwhelming verdict of the scientific community that none of these alternatives theories is superior to the Big Bang theory. Again and again models aimed at averting the prediction of the Standard Model of an absolute beginning of the universe have been shown either to be untenable or to fail to avert the beginning after all. For example, some theories, like the Oscillating Universe (which expands and re-contracts forever) or the Chaotic Inflationary Universe (which continually spawns new universes), do have a potentially infinite future but turn out to have only a finite past.[20] Vacuum Fluctuation Universe theories (which postulate an eternal vacuum out of which our universe is born) cannot explain why, if the vacuum was eternal, we do not observe an infinitely old universe.[21] The Quantum Gravity Universe theory propounded by James Hartle and Stephen Hawking, if interpreted realistically, still involves an absolute origin of the universe even if the universe does not begin in a so-called singularity, as it does in the Standard Big Bang theory.[22] Hawking sums up the situation: 'Almost everyone now believes that the universe, and time itself, had a beginning at the Big Bang.'[23]

4. Argument Based on Thermodynamic Properties of the Universe

If this were not enough, there is a second inductive argument for the beginning of the universe based on the evidence of thermodynamics. According to the Second Law of Thermodynamics, processes taking place in a closed system always tend toward a state of equilibrium. For example, if we had a bottle containing a sealed vacuum, and we introduced into it some molecules of gas, the gas would spread itself out evenly throughout the bottle. It would be virtually impossible for the molecules to retreat, for example, into one corner of the bottle and remain. This is why, when we walk into a room, the air in the room never separates suddenly into oxygen at one end and nitrogen at the other. It is also why, when we step into the bath, we may be confident that it will be an even temperature instead of frozen solid at one end and boiling at the other. It is clear that life would not be possible in a world in which the Second Law of Thermodynamics did not operate.

Now our interest in the law is what happens when it is applied to the universe as a whole. The universe is, on a naturalistic view, a gigantic closed system, since it is everything there is and there is nothing outside it. What this seems to imply then is that, given enough time, the universe and all its processes will run down, and the entire universe will come to equilibrium. This is known as the heat death of the universe. Once the universe reaches this state, no further change is possible. The universe is dead.

There are two possible types of heat death for the universe. If the universe will eventually re-contract, it will die a 'hot' death. Beatrice Tinsley describes such a state:

> If the average density of matter in the universe is great enough, the mutual gravitational attraction between bodies will eventually slow the expansion to a halt. The universe will then contract and collapse into a hot fireball. There is no known physical mechanism that could reverse a catastrophic big crunch. Apparently, if the universe becomes dense enough, it is in for a hot death.[24]

If the universe is fated to re-contraction, then as it contracts the stars gain energy, causing them to burn more rapidly so that they finally explode or evaporate. As everything in the universe grows closer together, the black holes begin to gobble up everything around them, and eventually begin themselves to coalesce. In time, 'All the black holes finally coalesce into one large black hole that is coextensive with the universe',[25] from which the universe will never re-emerge.

But suppose, as is more likely, that the universe will expand forever. Tinsley describes the fate of this universe:

> If the universe has a low density, its death will be cold. It will expand forever at a slower and slower rate. Galaxies will turn all of their gas into stars, and the stars will burn out. Our own sun will become a cold, dead remnant, floating among the corpses of other stars in an increasingly isolated Milky Way.[26]

At 10^{30} years the universe will consist of 90 per cent dead stars, 9 per cent supermassive black holes formed by the collapse of galaxies, and 1 per cent atomic matter, mainly hydrogen. Elementary particle physics suggests that thereafter protons will decay into electrons and positrons, so that space will be filled with a rarefied gas so thin that the distance between an electron and a positron will be about the size of the present galaxy. At 10^{100} years, some scientists believe that the black holes themselves will dissipate by a strange effect predicted by quantum mechanics. The mass and energy associated with a black hole so warp space that they are said to create a 'tunnel' or 'wormhole' through which the mass and energy are ejected in another region of space. As the mass of a black hole decreases, its energy loss accelerates, so that it is eventually dissipated into radiation and elementary particles. Eventually all black holes will completely evaporate and all the matter in the ever expanding universe will be reduced to a thin gas of elementary particles and radiation. Equilibrium will prevail throughout, and the entire universe will be in its final state, from which no change will occur.

Now the question that needs to be asked is this: if given enough time the universe will reach heat death, then why is it not in a state of heat death now, if it has existed forever, from eternity? If the universe did not begin to exist, then it should now be in a state of equilibrium. Like a ticking clock, it should by now have run down. Since it has not yet run down, this implies, in the words of one baffled scientist, 'In some way the universe must have been *wound up*.'[27]

Some theorists have tried to escape this conclusion by adopting an oscillating model of the universe which never reaches a final state of equilibrium. But wholly apart from the physical and observational difficulties confronting such a model, the thermodynamic properties of this model imply the very beginning of the universe that its proponents sought to avoid. For entropy increases from cycle to cycle in such a model, which has the effect of generating larger and longer oscillations with each successive cycle. As one scientific team explains,

> The effect of entropy production will be to enlarge the cosmic scale, from cycle to cycle . . . Thus, looking back in time, each cycle generated less entropy, had a smaller cycle time, and had a smaller cycle expansion factor then [*sic*] the cycle that followed it.[28]

Thus, as one traces the oscillations back in time, they become progressively smaller until one reaches a first and smallest oscillation. Zeldovich and Novikov therefore conclude, 'The multicycle model has an infinite future, but only a finite past.'[29] In fact, astronomer Joseph Silk estimates on the basis of current entropy levels that the universe cannot have gone through more than 100 previous oscillations.[30]

Even if this difficulty were avoided,[31] a universe oscillating from eternity past would require an infinitely precise tuning of initial conditions in order to perdure through an infinite number of successive bounces. A universe rebounding from a single, infinitely long contraction is, if entropy increases during the contracting phase, thermodynamically untenable and incompatible with the initial low entropy condition of our expanding phase. Postulating an entropy decrease during the contracting phase in order to escape this problem would require us to postulate inexplicably special low entropy conditions at the time of the bounce in the life of an infinitely evolving universe. Such a low entropy condition at the beginning of the expansion is more plausibly accounted for by the presence of a singularity or some sort of quantum creation event.

Indeed, thermodynamics may provide good reasons for affirming the reality of the singular origin of space–time postulated by the Standard Model. Penrose states, 'I have gradually come around to the view that it is actually misguided to ask that the space–time singularities of classical relativity should disappear when standard techniques of quantum (field) theory are applied to them.'[32] For if the initial cosmological singularity is removed, then 'we should have lost what seems to me to be the best chance we have of explaining the mystery of the second law of thermodynamics'.[33] What Penrose has in mind is the remarkable fact that as one goes back in time the entropy of the universe steadily decreases. Just how unusual this is can be demonstrated by means of the Bekenstein–Hawking formula for the entropy of a stationary black hole. The total observed entropy of the universe is 10^{88}. Since there are around 10^{80} baryons in the universe, the observed entropy per baryon must be regarded as extremely small. By contrast in a collapsing universe the entropy would be 10^{123} near the end. Comparison of these two numbers reveals how absurdly small 10^{88} is compared to what it might have been. Thus, the structure of the Big Bang must have been severely constrained in order that thermodynamics as we know it should have arisen. So how is this special initial condition to be explained? According to Penrose, we need the initial cosmological singularity, conjoined with the Weyl Curvature Hypothesis, according to which initial singularities (as opposed to final singularities) must have vanishing Weyl curvature.[34] In standard models, the Big Bang does possess vanishing Weyl curvature. The geometrical constraints on the initial geometry have the effect of producing a state of very low entropy. So the entropy in the gravitational field starts at zero at the Big Bang and gradually increases through gravitational clumping. The Weyl Curvature Hypothesis thus has the time asymmetric character necessary to explain the second law. By contrast, the Hartle–Hawking model 'is very far from being an explanation of the fact that past singularities have small Weyl curvature whereas future singularities have large Weyl curvature'.[35] On Hawking's time symmetrical theory, we should have white holes spewing out material, in contradiction to the Weyl Curvature Hypothesis, the Second Law of Thermodynamics and probably also observation.[36] If we remove the initial cosmological singularity, we render the Weyl Curvature Hypothesis irrelevant and 'we should be back where we were in our attempts to understand the origin of the second law'.[37]

Could the special initial geometry have arisen sheerly by chance in the absence of a cosmic singularity? Penrose's answer is decisive:

> Had there not been any constraining principles (such as the Weyl curvature hypothesis) the Bekenstein–Hawking formula would tell us that the probability of such a 'special' geometry arising by chance is at least as small as about one part in $10^{1000B(3/2)}$ where B is the present baryon number of the universe [$\sim 10^{80}$].[38]

Thus Penrose calculates that, aiming at a phase space whose regions represent the likelihood of various possible configurations of the universe, 'the accuracy of the Creator's aim' would have to have been one part in $10^{10(123)}$ in order for our universe to exist.[39] He comments, 'I cannot even recall seeing anything else in physics whose accuracy is known to approach, even remotely, a figure like one part in $10^{10(123)}$.[40] Thus, the initial cosmological singularity may be a virtual thermodynamical necessity.

So whether one adopts a re-contracting model, an ever-expanding model, or an oscillating model, thermodynamics implies that the universe had a beginning. According to P. C. W. Davies, the universe must have been created a finite time ago and is in the process of winding down. Prior to the creation, says Davies, the universe simply did not exist. Therefore, he concludes, even though we may not like it, we must say that the universe's energy was somehow simply 'put in' at the creation as an initial condition.[41]

So we have two inductive arguments that the universe began to exist. First, the expansion of the universe implies that the universe had a beginning. Second, thermodynamics shows the universe began to exist. Therefore, on the basis of both philosophical argument and scientific evidence, I think we are justified in accepting our second premiss, that the universe began to exist.

THE UNIVERSE HAS A CAUSE

From the first premiss – that 'whatever begins to exist has a cause' – and the second premiss – that 'the universe began to exist' – it follows logically that 'the universe has a cause'. This conclusion ought to stagger us, to fill us with awe, for it means that the universe was brought into existence by something which is greater than and beyond it.

But what is the nature of this first cause of the universe? A conceptual analysis of what properties must be possessed by such an ultra-mundane cause enables us to recover a striking number of the traditional divine attributes. An analysis of what it is to be cause of the universe reveals that

4. If the universe has a cause, then an uncaused, personal Creator of the universe exists, who *sans* the universe is beginningless, changeless, immaterial, timeless, spaceless, and enormously powerful.

From (3) and (4), it follows that

5. Therefore, an uncaused, personal Creator of the universe exists, who *sans* the universe is beginningless, changeless, immaterial, timeless, spaceless, and enormously powerful.

As the cause of space and time, this entity must transcend space and time and therefore exist atemporally and non-spatially, at least *sans* the universe. This transcendent cause must therefore be changeless and immaterial, since time-lessness entails changelessness, and changelessness implies immateriality. Such a cause must be beginningless and uncaused, at least in the sense of lacking any antecedent causal conditions. Ockham's Razor will shave away further causes, since we should not multiply causes beyond necessity. This entity must be unimaginably powerful, since it created the universe out of nothing.

Finally, and most strikingly, such a transcendent cause is plausibly to be regarded as personal. As Swinburne points out, there are two types of causal explanation: scientific explanations in terms of laws and initial conditions and personal explanations in terms of agents and their volitions.[42] A first state of the universe cannot have a scientific explanation, since there is nothing before it, and therefore it can be accounted for only in terms of a personal explanation. Moreover, the personhood of the cause of the universe is implied by its timelessness and immateriality, since the only entities we know of which can possess such properties are either minds or abstract objects, and abstract objects do not stand in causal relations. Therefore the transcendent cause of the origin of the universe must be of the order of mind. This same conclusion is also implied by the origin of a temporal effect from a timeless cause. For if the cause of the universe were an impersonal set of necessary and sufficient conditions, it could not exist without its effect. The only way for the cause to be timeless and changeless but for its effect to originate *de novo* a finite time ago is for the cause to be a personal agent who freely chooses to bring about an effect without antecedent determining conditions. This type of causation is called 'agent causation', and because the agent is free he can initiate new effects by freely bringing about conditions which were not previously present. A finite time ago a Creator endowed with free will could have acted to bring the world into being at that moment. In this way, God could exist changelessly and eternally but choose to create the world in time. By 'choose' one need not mean that the Creator changes His mind about the decision to create, but that He freely and eternally intends to create a world with a beginning. By exercising His causal power, He brings it about that a world with a beginning comes to exist. So the cause is eternal, but the effect is not. In this way, then, it is possible for the temporal universe to have come to exist from an eternal cause, through the free will of a personal Creator. Thus, we are brought, not merely to a transcendent cause of the universe, but to its personal Creator.

These purely philosophical arguments for the personhood of the cause of the origin of the universe receive powerful scientific confirmation from the observed fine-tuning of the universe, which bespeaks intelligent design. Without wanting to go into a discussion of the teleological argument, let me simply say that the incredibly complex and delicately balanced nexus of initial conditions necessary for intelligent life seems to be most plausibly explained if that nexus is the product of intelligent design, that is to say, if the cause of the beginning of the universe is a personal Creator. The scientific evidence thus serves to underscore the conclusion to which philosophical argument has led us. So we have both good philosophical and scientific reasons for regarding the cause of the universe as an uncaused, beginningless, timeless, spaceless, immaterial, changeless, powerful, personal Creator.

Now certain thinkers have objected to the intelligibility of this conclusion. For example, Adolf Grünbaum has marshalled a whole troop of objections against inferring a Creator of the universe.[43] As these are very typical, a brief review of his objections should be quite helpful. Grünbaum's objections fall into three groups. Group I seeks to cast doubt upon the concept of 'cause' in the argument for a cause of the universe.

1. When we say that everything has a cause, we use the word 'cause' to mean something that transforms previously existing materials from one state to another. But when we infer that the universe has a cause, we must mean by 'cause' something that creates its effect out of nothing. Since these two meanings of 'cause' are not the same, the argument is guilty of equivocation and is thus invalid.
2. It does not follow from the necessity of there being a cause that the cause of the universe is a conscious agent.
3. It is logically fallacious to infer that there is a single conscious agent who created the universe.

But these objections do not seem to present any insuperable difficulties:

1. The univocal concept of 'cause' employed throughout the argument is the concept of something which brings about or produces its effects. Whether this production involves transformation of already existing materials or creation out of nothing is an incidental question. Thus, the charge of equivocation is groundless.
2. The personhood of the cause does not follow from the cosmological argument proper, but from an analysis of the notion of a first cause of the beginning of the universe, confirmed by Anthropic considerations.
3. The inference to a single cause of the origin of the universe seems justified in the light of the principle, commonly accepted in science, that one should not multiply causes beyond necessity. One is justified in inferring only causes such as are necessary to explain the effect in question; positing any more would be gratuitous. Since the universe is a single effect originating in the Big Bang event, we have no grounds for inferring a plurality of causes.

The objections of Group II relate the notion of causality to the temporal series of events:

(1) Causality is logically compatible with an infinite, beginningless series of events.
(2) If everything has a cause of its existence, then the cause of the universe must also have a cause of its existence.

Both of these objections, however, seem to be based on misunderstandings.

1. It is not the concept of causality which is incompatible with an infinite series of past events. Rather the incompatibility, as we have seen, is between the notion of an actually infinite number of things and the series of past events. That causality has nothing to do with it may be seen by reflecting on the fact that the philosophical arguments for the beginning of the universe would work even if the events were all spontaneous, causally non-connected events.
2. The argument does not presuppose that everything has a cause. Rather the operative causal principle is that 'whatever begins to exist has a cause'. Something that exists eternally and, hence, without a beginning would not need to have a cause. This is not special pleading for God, since the atheist has always maintained the same thing about the universe: it is beginningless and uncaused. The difference between these two hypotheses is that the atheistic view has been shown to be untenable.

Group III objections are aimed at the alleged claim that creation from nothing surpasses all understanding:

1. If creation out of nothing is incomprehensible, then it is irrational to believe in such a doctrine.
2. An incomprehensible doctrine cannot explain anything.

But these objections are also unsuccessful:

1. Creation from nothing is not incomprehensible in Grünbaum's sense. By 'incomprehensible' Grünbaum appears to mean 'unintelligible' or 'meaningless'. But the statement that a finite time ago a transcendent cause brought the universe into being out of nothing is clearly a meaningful statement, not mere gibberish, as is evident from the very fact that we are debating it. We may not understand how the cause brought the universe into being out of nothing, but then it is even more incomprehensible, in this sense, how the universe could have popped into being out of nothing without any cause, material or productive. One cannot avert the necessity of cause by positing an absurdity.
2. The doctrine, being an intelligible statement, obviously does constitute a purported explanation of the origin of the universe. It may be a personal rather than a scientific explanation, but it is no less an explanation for that.

Grünbaum has one final objection against inferring a cause of the origin of the universe: the cause of the Big Bang can be neither after the Big Bang (since backward causation is impossible) nor before the Big Bang (since time begins at or after the Big Bang). Therefore, the universe's beginning to exist cannot have a cause.[44] But this argument pretty clearly confronts us with a false dilemma. For why could God's creating the universe not be simultaneous (or coincident) with the Big Bang? On the view I've defended, God may be conceived to be timeless or relatively timeless without creation and in time at and subsequent to the first moment of creation. None of Grünbaum's objections, therefore, seems to undermine the credibility of the *kalam* cosmological argument for a personal Creator of the universe.

Thus, we have been brought to the remarkable conclusion that an uncaused, personal Creator of the universe exists, who *sans* the universe is beginningless, changeless, immaterial, timeless, spaceless and enormously powerful. And this, as Thomas Aquinas laconically remarked, is what everyone means by 'God'.

NOTES

1. J. L. Mackie, *The Miracle of Theism* (Oxford: Clarendon Press, 1982), p. 94.
2. Mackie, *Theism*, p. 89.
3. David Hume, *The Letters of David Hume*, 2 vols, ed. J. Y. T. Greig (Oxford: Clarendon Press, 1932), 1: 187.
4. J. L. Mackie, critical notice of *The Creation*, by Peter Atkins, *Times Literary Supplement* (5 February 1982), p. 126.
5. Mackie, *Theism*, p. 89.
6. The story of Hilbert's Hotel is related in George Gamow, *One, Two, Three, Infinity* (London: Macmillan, 1946), p. 17.
7. What is the logical structure of the argument here? The proponent of the argument has two options open to him. On the one hand, he could argue that if an actual infinite were to exist, then the Principle of Correspondence would be valid with respect to it and that if an actual infinite were to exist and the Principle of Correspondence were to be valid with respect to it, then the various counter-intuitive situations would result. Therefore, if an actual infinite were to exist, the various counter-intuitive situations would result. (A $\Box\!\!\rightarrow$ B; A & B $\Box\!\!\rightarrow$ C; $\therefore$ A $\Box\!\!\rightarrow$ C). But because these are absurd and so really impossible, it follows that the existence of an actual infinite is impossible ($\neg\Diamond$C; $\therefore$ $\neg\Diamond$A).

   On the other hand, the proponent of the argument might call into question the premiss that if an actual infinite were to exist, then the Principle of Correspondence would be valid with respect to it. There is no reason to think that the principle is universally valid. It is merely a convention adopted in infinite set theory. Now, necessarily, if an actual infinite were to exist, then either the Principle of Correspondence or Euclid's maxim that 'The whole is greater than its part' would apply to it. ($\Box$[A $\Box\!\!\rightarrow$ B $\vee$ C]). But since the application of either of these two principles to an actual infinite results in counter-intuitive absurdities, it is plausible that if the existence of an actual infinite were possible, then if an actual infinite were to exist, neither of these two principles would be valid with respect to it. ($\Diamond$A $\rightarrow\neg$[A$\Box\!\!\rightarrow$ B $\vee$ C]). It therefore follows that the existence of an actual infinite is impossible, since the counterfactual that 'If an actual infinite were to exist, then neither principle would be valid with respect to it' is necessarily false ($\therefore$ $\neg\Diamond$A).
8. Mackie, *Theism*, p. 93.
9. Students frequently ask if God, therefore, cannot be infinite. The question is based on a misunderstanding. When we speak of the infinity of God, we are not using the word in a mathematical sense to refer to an aggregate of an infinite number of finite parts. God's infinity is, as it were, qualitative, not quantitative. It means that God is metaphysically necessary, morally perfect, omnipotent, omniscient, eternal, etc.
10. Bertrand Russell, *The Principles of Mathematics*, 2nd edn (London: Allen & Unwin, 1937), pp. 358–9.

11. Robin Small, 'Tristram Shandy's Last Page', *British Journal for the Philosophy of Science*, 37 (1986), pp. 214–15.
12. Bertrand Russell, *Our Knowledge of the External World*, 2nd edn (New York: W. W. Norton, 1929), p. 170.
13. Mackie, *Theism*, p. 93.
14. Gregory L. Naber, *Spacetime and Singularities: An Introduction* (Cambridge: Cambridge University Press, 1988), pp. 126–7.
15. John A. Wheeler, 'Beyond the Hole', in *Some Strangeness in the Proportion*, ed. Harry Woolf (Reading, MA: Addison-Wesley, 1980), p. 354.
16. This is not to say that the density measurement takes on the value of a trans-finite cardinal number. Rather, the density is the mass divided by volume, and, since division by zero is impossible, the density of the universe at the initial cosmological singularity is said to be 'infinite' in this sense.
17. P. C. W. Davies, 'Spacetime Singularities in Cosmology', in J. T. Fraser (ed.), *The Study of Time III* (New York: Springer Verlag, 1978), pp. 78–79.
18. John Barrow and Frank Tipler, *The Anthropic Cosmological Principle* (Oxford: Clarendon Press, 1986), p. 442.
19. Hubert Reeves, Jean Audouze, William A. Fowler and David N. Schramm, 'On the Origin of Light Elements', *Astrophysical Journal*, 179 (1973), p. 912.
20. See I. D. Novikov and Ya. B. Zeldovich, 'Physical Processes near Cosmological Singularities', *Annual Review of Astronomy and Astrophysics*, 11 (1973), pp. 401–2; A. Borde and A. Vilenkin, 'Eternal Inflation and the Initial Singularity', *Physical Review Letters*, 72 (1994), pp. 3305, 3307.
21. Christopher Isham, 'Creation of the Universe as a Quantum Process' in R. J. Russell, W. R. Stoeger and G. V. Coyne (eds), *Physics, Philosophy and Theology: A Common quest for Understanding* (Vatican City: Vatican Observatory, 1988), pp. 385–7.
22. See John D. Barrow, *Theories of Everything* (Oxford: Clarendon Press, 1991), pp. 67–8.
23. Stephen Hawking and Roger Penrose, *The Nature of Space and Time*, The Isaac Newton Institute Series of Lectures (Princeton, NJ: Princeton University Press, 1996), p. 20.
24. Beatrice Tinsley, 'From Big Bang to Eternity?' *Natural History Magazine* (October 1975), p. 103.
25. Duane Dicus et al., 'The Future of the Universe', *Scientific American* (March 1983), p. 99.
26. Tinsley, 'Big Bang', p. 105.
27. Richard Schlegel, 'Time and Thermodynamics', in J.T. Fraser (ed.), *The Voices of Time* (London: Penguin, 1968), p. 511.
28. Duane Dicus et al., 'Effects of Proton Decay on the Cosmological Future', *Astrophysical Journal*, 252 (1982), pp. 1, 8.
29. Novikov and Zeldovich, 'Physical Processes near Cosmological Singularities', pp. 401–2.
30. Joseph Silk, *The Big Bang*, 2nd edn (San Francisco: W. H. Freeman, 1989), pp. 311–12.
31. See D. Hochberg, C. Molina-Paris and M. Visser, 'Tolman Wormholes Violate the Strong Energy Condition', *Physical Review D*, 59 (1999) forthcoming.
32. Roger Penrose, 'Some Remarks on Gravity and Quantum Mechanics', in M. J. Duff and C. J. Isham (eds), *Quantum Structure of Space and Time* (Cambridge: Cambridge University Press, 1982), p. 4.
33. Penrose, 'Remarks on Gravity', p. 5.
34. Weyl curvature is the curvature of space–time which is not due to the presence of matter and is described by the Weyl tensor. Space–time curvature due to matter is described by the Ricci tensor. Together they make up the Riemann tensor giving the metric for space–time.

35. Hawking and Penrose, *Nature of Space and Time*, p. 129.
36. Hawking and Penrose, *Nature of Space and Time*, p. 130.
37. Penrose, 'Remarks on Gravity', p. 5.
38. Penrose, 'Remarks on Gravity', p. 5.
39. Roger Penrose, 'Time-Asymmetry and Quantum Gravity', in C. J. Isham, R. Penrose and D. W. Sciama (eds), *Quantum Gravity 2*, (Oxford: Clarendon Press, 1981), p. 249; cf. Hawking and Penrose, *Nature of Space and Time*, pp. 34–5.
40. Penrose, 'Time-Asymmetry', p. 249.
41. P. C. W. Davies, *The Physics of Time Asymmetry* (London: Surrey University Press, 1974), p. 104.
42. Richard Swinburne, *The Existence of God*, rev. edn (Oxford: Clarendon Press, 1991), pp. 32–48.
43. Adolf Grünbaum, 'The Pseudo-Problem of Creation in Physical Cosmology', in John Leslie (ed.), *Physical Cosmology and Philosophy*, Philosophical Topics (New York: Macmillan, 1990), pp. 92–112.
44. Adolf Grünbaum, 'Pseudo-Creation of the Big Bang', *Nature*, 344 (1990), p. 85.
45. Thomas Aquinas, *Summa Theologiae* 1a. 2.3.

TELEOLOGICAL ARGUMENT
2.3

'THE PREREQUISITES OF LIFE IN OUR UNIVERSE'

John Leslie

[. . .]

Newton's blending of Science with theism is something glorious. [. . .] I shall appeal chiefly to recent evidence, often discussed in connection with the Anthropic Principle. (a) Many suggest that basic characteristics of the observable cosmos—the strengths of its main forces, the masses of its particles, its early expansion speed, the photon to baryon ratio—and so forth are remarkably "fine tuned" for producing life. (b) Instead of introducing God to explain the fine tuning, they typically propose that there exist countless "universes" (that is largely or entirely separate systems, perhaps of immense size and that force strengths, particle masses, expansion speeds and so on vary from universe to universe. Sooner or later, somewhere, conditions permit life to evolve. The Anthropic Principle reminds us that, obviously, *only such a somewhere could be observed by living beings*. (c) But an alternative interpretation could be offered. This is that there exists just a single universe. Its force strengths and particle masses are the same everywhere [. . .] [and] were selected with a view to making life possible. They were selected by a Mind or by a more abstract Creative Principle[1] which can reasonably be called "God."

John Leslie, 'The Prerequisites of Life in our Universe', in G. V. Coyne (ed.), *Newton and the New Direction in Science* (Vatican City: Speculo Vaticana, 1988), pp. 97–119.

II

[. . .]

Run a model cosmos backwards. Unless its parts are very carefully positioned, chaos ensues. [. . .] It is commonly argued that a chaotic Big Bang, probably beginning in a singularity (a region beyond which the past histories of light rays cannot extend) which is "ragged" rather than point-like, could be expected because chaos would result from running a randomly selected universe backwards; and further, that the chaos of such a Bang could evolve towards cosmic smoothness only at the price of producing vastly much disorder on a smaller scale—vastly much heat or vastly many black holes.

(Black holes are very disorderly, "very high entropy" systems.) Here, special importance attaches to the fact that instantaneous action at a distance is impossible. [. . .] Lack of instantaneous communication would mean that regions coming out of a Big Bang could not know of one another until light had had time to pass between them. Hence their movements could be expected to be thoroughly uncoordinated. When they made contact, friction might bring about some large-scale uniformity, but in so doing it would produce life-excluding temperatures or black holes. This is the Smoothness Problem. P. C. W. Davies wrote that frictional smoothing away of even a tiny amount of early roughness "would increase the primeval heat billions of times," disastrously. And "if the primeval material was churned about at random it would have been overwhelmingly more probable for it to have produced black holes than stars": "the odds against a starry cosmos" become "one followed by a thousand billion billion zeros, at least."[2] R. Penrose similarly calculated[3] that in the absence of new physical principles which ensured a smooth beginning "the accuracy of the Creator's aim" when he placed a pin to select our orderly world from the space of physically possible ones would need to have been "at least of the order of one part in $10^{10^{123}}$".

[. . .]

Any solution to the Problem must allow for life-encouraging local departures from smoothness: the galaxies. Volumes of gas must condense into stars. Yet if the entire universe behaved similarly, collapsing upon itself, then this could yield swift disaster.

[. . .]

[O]ur cosmos was from very early instants expanding at a speed placing it very close to the line dividing continued explosion from gravitational implosion. Tiny early deviations from this line would grow immensely, as was stressed by R. H. Dicke in 1970. He calculated[4] that a 0.1 per cent early speed increase would have yielded a present-day expansion thousands of times faster than what we find. An equivalent decrease would have led to recollapse when the cosmos was a millionth its present size.

Such calculations have since been refined. In 1978 Dicke said[5] that a decrease of one part in a million when the Big Bang was a second old would have produced recollapse before temperatures fell below 10,000 degrees; with an equally small increase "the kinetic energy of expansion would have so dominated gravity that minor density irregularities could not have collected into bound systems in which stars might form." And S. W. Hawking estimated that even a decrease by one part in a million million when the temperature was 10^{10} degrees "would have resulted in the Universe starting to recollapse when the temperature was still 10,000 degrees."[6] The fine tuning must be more accurate, the more one pushes back the time at which it is carried out.

Another way of expressing the need for fine tuning is to consider early cosmic densities, which are closely related to expansion speeds. If we can trace things back to the Planck time 10^{-43} seconds after the Bang started, then the density must seemingly have been within about one part in 10^{60} of the "critical density" at which space is precisely flat, this placing it precisely on the line between collapse and continued expansion.[7] [. . .] The Expansion Speed Problem can thus be restated as a Flatness Problem. Why is space not more curved?

Many now claim that Smoothness and Flatness Problems can both be solved by an Inflationary Scenario. A. H. Guth and others developed such a scenario to explain the absence of magnetic monopoles. At very high temperatures the four main forces of Nature—gravity, electromagnetism, and the strong and weak nuclear forces—are thought to have been only aspects of a single force; there may also have been just one kind of particle. As temperature dropped the forces split apart in symmetry-breaking phase transitions: compare how water, on freezing, loses its complete rotational symmetry, its property of looking the same in all directions, and takes on the more limited symmetry of ice crystals. Now, the phase transitions could proceed in different ways. It would be highly probable that in areas that were causally separated, light rays not having had time to link them, they would in fact proceed differently: a million monkeys are unlikely to type always the same sequence of letters! The outcome would be vastly many domains with different symmetries, and topological knots where these came into contact. Such knots would be magnetic monopoles. These would be so heavy and so numerous that the universe would recollapse very rapidly.[8] But this disaster could have been averted if any monopole-creating phase transition were associated with an exponentially fast inflation of space. And such inflation (like the growth of a warren in which each rabbit gives birth to ten others) might occur at early instants. It could push monopoles and domain walls far beyond the reach of any telescope.

Massive inflation could give us extremely flat space: a greatly inflated balloon has a very flat surface. And the Smoothness Problem might find much the same answer as the Expansion Speed or Flatness Problem. In the absence of inflation the visible universe would have grown from perhaps 10^{83} initially separated regions, tremendous turbulence resulting when these made contact. Inflation, though, could mean that our horizon was deep within a single such region, one whose parts formed a coordinated whole because they had interacted at pre-inflationary moments. (Inflation would have hurled them asunder far faster than the speed of light. General relativity permits such velocities when expansion of space produces them.)

However, the two Problems seem only to have been solved by introducing others. Model-builders have difficulties in getting inflation started, in persuading it to end without excess turbulence ("the Graceful Exit Problem"), and in having it produce irregularities neither too small nor too large to allow galaxies to grow. Even when you cunningly select your Grand Unified Theory to achieve the desired results—which can look suspiciously like the "fine tuning" which the inflationary hypothesis is so often praised for rendering unnecessary—you may still be forced to postulate a gigantic space containing rare regions, perhaps ones already very unusually smooth, in which inflation of the right type occurs.[9] Further, in the most popular models the inflation is powered by repulsion of the sort Einstein introduced when he gave a nonzero value to the cosmological constant. Though appearing naturally in General Relativity's equations, this constant has long been treated as being zero and thus disregarded. Einstein remarked that his use of it had been his greatest blunder: instead of employing it to keep everything static he should, he said, have predicted the cosmic expansion. Yet Einstein's puzzle of how the cosmos could be kept static has been replaced by that of how it could avoid immediate collapse, for today's physics fills space with fields of so great an energy density (in particular in the form of quantum vacuum fluctuations in which particles attain a fleeting existence) that gravity could be expected to roll everything up into a sphere measuring 10^{-33} cm.

To deal with this new puzzle two components of the cosmological constant, "bare lambda" and "quantum lambda," are viewed as cancelling each other with an accuracy of better than one part in 10^{50}. How this beautiful result is achieved is totally unclear. While we could invent mechanisms to perform the trick, it can seem best to treat such precise cancellation as a question of Chance—that is, of what would be quite likely to happen somewhere inside any sufficiently gigantic Reality—or else of Divine Selection. For it could seem that the cancellation cannot be dictated by any fundamental law, since the quantum activity of the vacuum involves many fields each contributing in a temperature-dependent way, the masses of a host of scalar particles seeming crucial to the outcome.[10] Nor could one explain it as a product of an inflation which occurred appropriately, for this would put the cart before the horse. Inflation could occur appropriately only if the cancellation were already enormously accurate,[11] though it would be still more accurate afterwards. (Today[12] the cosmological constant is zero to one part in 10^{120}.)

A change in the presently measured strengths either of gravitation or of the weak nuclear force by as little as one part in 10^{100} could end this cancellation, on which our lives depend.[13] And it seems that inflation would result in galaxy-producing density fluctuations only if a Grand Unified Force had a coupling constant (a measure of how strongly this Force affected particles) of only 10^{-7}, which could be thought "unnaturally small."[14]

[. . .]

III

[. . .]

Moreover suns and planets can seem to depend on impressively much "fine tuning." Thus, the Big Bang needed to deliver atoms usable in stellar fusion reactions, not ones which had already undergone fusion. Two things were crucial: the high expansion speed when atoms first formed—they were rushed apart before they could fuse—and *the extreme weakness of the nuclear weak force*. The weak force controls proton-proton fusion, a reaction 10^{18} times slower than one based on the other nuclear force, the strong force. But for this, "essentially all the matter in the universe would have been burned to helium before the first galaxies started to condense"[15] so there would be neither water nor long-lived stable stars, which are hydrogen-burning. (Helium-burners remain stable for times too short for the evolution of life as we know it.) Again, the weak force's weakness makes our sun "burn its hydrogen gently for billions of years instead of blowing up like a bomb."[16]

Had the weak force been appreciably stronger then the Big Bang's nuclear burning would have proceeded past helium and all the way to iron. Fusion-powered stars would then be impossible.

Notice, though, that the weak force could not have been much *weaker* without again giving us an all-helium universe. (There are thus *two* threats to hydrogen, one setting an upper and the other a lower limit to the values of the weak force compatible with life as we know it.) For at early moments neutrons were about as common as protons, things being so hot that the greater masses of the neutrons, which made them harder to generate, had little importance. The weak force, however, could make neutrons decay into protons. And it was just sufficiently strong to ensure that when the first atoms formed there were enough excess protons to yield roughly 70 percent hydrogen. Without a proton excess there would have been helium only.[17]

Again, weakening the weak force would ruin the proton-proton and carbon-nitrogen-oxygen cycles which make stars into sources of the heat, the light and the heavy elements which life appears to need.[18]

How do these heavy elements get to be outside stars, to form planets and living things? The weak force helps explain this. When stars explode as supernovae they lose their heavy-element-rich outer layers. (Elements heavier than iron, which play an important role in Earth's organisms, can be synthesized only during the explosions.) Now, these layers are blasted off by neutrinos which interact with them via the weak force alone. Its extreme weakness, which allows neutrinos to pass through our planet more easily than bullets through air, permits also their escape from a supernova's collapsing core. Still, the force is just strong enough to hurl into space the outer-layer atoms needed for constructing astronomers!

[. . .]

The *nuclear strong force*, too, must be neither over-strong nor over-weak for stars to operate life-encouragingly. "As small an increase as 2%" in its strength "would block the formation of protons out of quarks," preventing the existence even of hydrogen atoms,[19] let alone others. If this argument fails then the same small increase could still spell disaster by binding protons into diprotons: all hydrogen would now become helium early in the Bang[20] and stars would burn by the strong interaction[21] which, as noted above, proceeds 10^{18} times faster than the weak interaction which controls our sun. A yet tinier increase, perhaps of 1 percent, would so change nuclear resonance levels that almost all carbon would be burned to oxygen.[22] A somewhat greater increase, of about 10 percent, would again ruin stellar carbon synthesis, this time changing resonance levels so that there would be little burning beyond carbon's predecessor, helium.[23] One a trifle greater than this would lead to "nuclei of almost unlimited size,"[24] even small bodies becoming "mini neutron stars."[25] All which is true despite the very short range of the strong force. Were it long-range then the universe would be "wound down into a single blob."[26]

Slight *decreases* could be equally ruinous. The deuteron, a combination of a neutron and a proton which is essential to stellar nucleosynthesis, is only just bound: weakening the strong force by "about 5%" would unbind it[27] leading to a universe of hydrogen only. And even a weakening of 1 percent could destroy[28] "a particular resonance in the carbon nucleus which allows carbon to form from ^{4}He plus ^{8}Be despite the instability of ^{8}Be" (which is, however, stable enough to have a lifetime "anomalously long" in a way itself suggesting fine tuning).[29] "A 50% decrease would adversely affect the stability of all the elements essential to living organisms":[30] any carbon, for example, which somehow managed to form would fast disintegrate.

I. L. Rozental estimates that the strong force had to be within 0.8 and 1.2 of its actual strength for there to be deuterons and all elements of atomic weight greater than four.[31]

Electromagnetism also needs to fall inside narrow limits if the stars are to encourage anything like life as we know it. For one thing, it is the strong force's strength by comparison with electromagnetism (it is some hundreds of times stronger) which is the real topic of the above remarks about carbon synthesis and about the deuteron's being luckily just bound while the diproton is equally luckily just unbound. Again, electromagnetic repulsion between protons prevents most of their collisions from resulting in proton-proton fusion, this explaining how stars can burn so slowly: each second our sun generates thousands of times less energy per gram than the human body. The strength of electromagnetism by comparison with gravity is crucial here.

[. . .]

Davies holds[32] that Carter has shown that changes either in electromagnetism or in gravity "by only one part in 10^{40} would spell catastrophe for stars like the sun." In the background is Dicke's remark of 1957 that a star's radiation rate varies as the inverse seventh power of the dielectric constant so that if electromagnetism were appreciably stronger "all stars would be cold. This would preclude the existence of man."[33]

[. . .]

Similar points could next be made about *the gravitational force*.

Some of them could be viewed as rephrasings of the statements of Carter and others about electromagnetism's needing to be appropriately strong by comparison with gravity, or of the remark that the weak force must be weak if any hydrogen is to come out of the Bang. Others would be reworkings of the point that the cosmic expansion speed must be "just right" if galaxies are to form: thus, gravity may need an appropriate strength if inflation is to occur, or maybe inflation is a false hypothesis and the speed had to be fine-tuned from the very start by immensely accurate choice of the gravitational constant. Again, gravity must be extremely weak for the universe to avoid fast collapse. Other points are at least in part new. (a) One reason stars live so long is that they are so huge (for besides providing more to burn, size slows down the burning because radiation's random walk to the stellar surface takes millions of years) and yet are compressed so little by gravity. Though the figure varies with whether we consider electron-electron or proton-proton interactions, we can say roughly that gravity is an astonishing 10^{39} times weaker than electromagnetism. Were it appreciably *stronger* than it is, stars would form from smaller amounts of gas; and/or would blaze more fiercely (Teller calculated in 1948 that the radiation increases as the seventh power of the gravitational constant);[34] and or would collapse more easily to form white dwarfs, neutron stars or black holes. Were it a million times stronger (which would leave it 10^{33} times weaker than electromagnetism, while we lack any well-developed theory saying that it had to be at all weaker) then stars would be a billion times less massive and burn a million times faster.[35] With even tenfold strengthening, a star with as much matter as our sun would burn only a million years.[36] (b) Were gravity ten times *less strong*, it would be doubtful whether stars and planets could form.[37] And any appreciable weakening could mean that "all stars would be chemically homogeneous due to convective mixing and one would not get the onion-skin shell structure which characterizes presupernova models":[38] hence, perhaps, no supernovae scattering heavy elements. (c) As things are, clouds the right size to form stable stars are just able to cool fast enough to avoid fragmentation.[39] Tinkering with gravity could destroy this happy phenomenon. (d) If the protogalaxies formed by fragmentation of larger clouds then, J. Silk has argued,[40] this required gravity's strength to be interestingly close to its actual value. (e) Violent events at the galactic core presumably exclude life from many galaxies. In Cygnus A "the level of hard, ionizing radiation is hundreds of times more intense than on the surface of the earth."[41] Strengthening gravity could make every galaxy this nasty.

One last factor crucial to the stars is the *neutron-proton mass difference*. As S. W. Hawking says,[42] if this "were not about twice the mass of the electron, one would not obtain the couple of hundred or so stable nucleides that make up the elements and are the basis of chemistry and biology." Here are the reasons.[43] The neutron is the heavier of the two particles, by about one part in a thousand. Less energy thus being tied up in a neutron, decays of neutrons into protons would have yielded a universe of protons only, with hydrogen the only possible element, had neutrons not become bound to protons in atoms. Here the presence of electrons and the Pauli Principle discourage their decay; but even that would not prevent it were the mass difference slightly greater. And were it *smaller* (one-third of what it is), neutrons *outside* atoms would *not* decay; all protons would thus change irreversibly into neutrons during the Bang, whose violence produced frequent proton-to-neutron conversions. There could then be no atoms: the universe would be neutron stars and black holes. *The mass of the electron* enters the picture like this. If the neutron mass failed to exceed the proton mass by a little more than the electron mass then atoms would collapse, their electrons combining with their protons to yield neutrons. (Proton mass: 938.28 MeV. Electron: 0.51. Total: 938.79. And the neutron weighs in at 939.57.)

[. . .]

Neutrons and protons differ in their quark content so their very fortunate mass difference can be explained as a reflection of the "up" quark's being slightly lighter than the "down." But such explanation may succeed only in pushing puzzlement back a step. (A believer in God need not think that each fortunate phenomenon is directly due to divine choice, lacking all further explanation. [. . .] The seeming failure of the simplest Grand Unified Theory, "minimal SU [5]," as evidenced by failure to see sufficiently many proton decays,[44] should, however, discourage the idea that some Principle of Simplicity is the only factor selecting Nature's laws. Hugely many alternative GUTs now compete for the physicist's attention. God had an immensely rich field from which to choose.)

IV

[. . .]

Even the proton is now believed liable to decay—which can be viewed as beneficial since the factors involved are probably responsible for *how matter came out of the Bang in any quantity instead of annihilating with antimatter to produce a universe of light.*

Roughly, the actual excess was of one proton for every hundred million proton-antiproton pairs. Too many more protons, and the universe would quickly collapse, assuming that its expansion rate reflected the number of photons per proton; or it would become a collection of neutron stars and black holes; or at the very least, there would be helium everywhere instead of hydrogen. Too many *fewer*, and there would be over-rapid expansion coupled with radiation pressures guaranteeing that protagalaxies and stars could not condense: any massive bound systems managing to form despite the expansion would trap radiation which stopped the fragmenting into the smaller bodies on whose existence life depends.[45]

Proton decay, moreover, must please be slow. Proton lives of 10^{16} years, about 10^6 times the present age of the universe, would mean (says M. Goldhaber) that even the decays occurring *in you* would kill you with their radiation.[46]

All this implies that the masses of the superheavy bosons must fall inside interestingly narrow limits: for instance, they must be at least one hundred million times heavier than the proton if protons are to be stable enough.[47] Again, making the electromagnetic constant larger than 1/85 would result in too many proton decays for there to be long-lived, stable stars (while 1/180 is a lower limit suggested by GUTs).[48] And if high levels of radiation must be lethal then 1/85 would itself be too large as the stability of living organisms would then be more sensitive than that of stars.

[. . .]

The Pauli Principle's "spreading out" of the atom by keeping electrons in a hierarchy of orbits is decidedly fortunate. Could electrons take just any orbit then, (i) thermal buffetings would at once knock them into new orbits, so destroying the fixed properties which underlie the genetic code and the happy fact that atoms of different kinds behave very differently, and (ii) atoms would quickly collapse, their electrons spiralling inwards while radiating violently. Now, the "wave-particle" natures of atomic particles could give us some insight into the Principle. For consider sound waves: air in an organ pipe likes to vibrate at a particular frequency or at simple multiples thereof. Observe, however, that *bosons* also have wave-particle natures yet are not restricted by the Pauli Principle. If electrons behaved like bosons then all could occupy the lowest possible orbit and there could be no chemistry.

[. . .]

F. D. Kahn similarly pointed out that water molecules, benzine rings, DNA, and so forth, have structures that "persist owing to the great difference between the mass of an electron and the mass of an atomic nucleus."[49] At stake is "the existence of chemistry (and also chemists)" since chemistry needs atoms "full of open space with well-defined central nuclei."[50] Electromagnetism's comparative weakness is involved too, as is the fact that electrons cannot feel the hundreds-of-times-more-powerful strong nuclear force. (Kahn added that such reflections threw severe doubt on the possibility of *non-chemical life* based on the strong force rather than on electrons and electromagnetism.

[. . .]

Theists should not be too opposed to the idea of fundamental principles which dictate this or that fortunate phenomenon; for though such principles may be comparatively simple, they will still be impressively intricate and very far from being logically inevitable. Even the simplest modern GUT due to H. Georgi and S. Glashow, now thought to be too crude, involves twenty-four force fields.[51] Hugely many more complex theories now compete for the physicist's attention. And claims to have derived this or that quantity "from basic principles" typically gloss over the fact that some other quantity, often the mass of a force-conveying "messenger particle" like the pion, had first to be put in by hand.

[. . .]

Finally, long-lasting particles exist only because of *space's topological and metrical properties*. For instance, it seems to be three-dimensional, which was not a logical inevitability. Currently popular Kaluza-Klein theories suggest that it in fact has at least ten dimensions, seven now being invisible because each became very tightly rolled up, compacted. The real difficulty is of understanding how the others could remain uncompacted in view of the enormous energy density of a "vacuum" crammed with quantum fluctuations: see the discussion of the Flatness Problem.

[. . .]

This paper has stressed that *quantitative* considerations contribute strongly to a modern Design Argument. Tiny changes in fundamental constants would have made life's evolution very unlikely. Look again at that figure of one part in 10^{100}, representing how accurately gravity may have to be adjusted to the weak force for the cosmos not to suffer swift collapse or explosion. Recall the claim that changing by one part in 10^{40} the balance between gravity and electromagnetism could have made stars burn too fast or too slowly for life's purposes. Think of the many other claims I reported.

True, few such claims involve figures as huge as 10^{100}; but they often compensate for this by being very firmly established. And my survey has been far from comprehensive. For instance I did not mention how fast the cosmos would have collapsed if electron neutrinos, often thought to have a small mass, had weighed even a hundredth of what the electron does.[52] (The Bang produced some billion of them for every proton.) I was silent, too, about P. W. Atkins's calculation[53] that a 1 per cent increase in electromagnetism's strength could have doubled the years needed for intelligent life to evolve, while doubling it could have meant that 10^{62} years would be needed. Atkins comments that were atoms more tightly knit then only "prods like nuclear explosions" could have much probability of inducing changes in living structures made from them.

Observe that argument on these lines need not appeal to any need for an ozone layer to defend us against ultraviolet rays; or for ice to float so as to form a protective cover over ponds; or for there to be calcium, chlorine, magnesium, potassium, phosphorus, sodium and sulfur (mineral elements essential to the actual organisms on our planet). It need not even be assumed (though Wale[54] and others give powerful grounds for it) that without carbon as a basis for complex chains and water's special properties there would be no life in our universe. The big point is instead the one insisted on by Rozental: that small changes in fundamental constants—force strengths, masses, Planck's constant, and so forth—would have meant the total absence of "nuclei, atoms, stars and galaxies": "not merely slight quantitative changes in the physical picture but rather the destruction of its foundations."[55] Presumably this would mean the absence not just of observers made of carbon and water, but of absolutely all observers. There would be no fire, crystals, wind-shaken bubbles; and even if there were still things "reproducing" much as fire does, that would be a long way from anything worth calling life.

[. . .]

We need not claim that *of all logically possible universes* only a small fraction would contain life. We need look only at universes in "the local area" of possibilities, ones much like ours in their basic laws but differing in their force strengths, particle masses, expansion speeds, and so on. A parable may help. A wasp on a wall is surrounded by a fairly wide area free of all insects. Just one bullet is fired. It hits the wasp. Was it fired by an expert, probably? In tackling this we need not care whether *distant* areas of the wall bear many insects. There is only one insect *locally*!

In cosmology our wasp becomes a small "window" inside which various constants had to fall, for life to evolve. The local area becomes an area (or volume) of possibilities, measurable with the help of axes giving possible values for those constants. And "hitting a window" can be impressive even when the area might have one or two other small windows. (A pioneering paper by I. L. Rozental, I. Novikov and A. Polnarey illustrates this. With axes showing various strengths of gravity and electromagnetism, they find one tiny window of possible life-encouragingness in addition to the one inside which the actual strengths lie.[56] But more research could well reveal that the second window is illusory. For when we list ten reasons for thinking that a strength or mass or other constant must fall inside narrow limits if life is to evolve, we are not just guarding against error by giving ten arguments for one conclusion. Rather, we are offering ten grounds for saying that tinkering with this constant, or with a balance between it and others, will result in disaster *somewhere*.)

[. . .]

However, this can suggest that any "fine-tuning" might be accounted for without bringing in God's creative choice. Perhaps life-encouraging force strengths and particle masses are just what would be bound to occur some-where in any sufficiently gigantic Reality. Such a Reality could be split into immensely many huge domains, perhaps almost all of them ones in which symmetries had broken in ways not compatible with life.

VI

[. . .]

[We could adopt] the today quite popular idea of a "World Ensemble", a large-U Universe with very many regions ("small-u universes," worlds) that are largely or wholly separate, and vary widely. (1) Wheeler has proposed perpetual oscillations: Big Bang, Big Squeeze, Big Bang, and so on. At each Squeeze information about properties is lost. Successive Bangs thus have differing amounts of matter, force strengths, particle masses, and so on, so each might count as a new World. (2) Many Worlds Quantum Theory, originated by H. Everett III, has Reality forever branching into Worlds almost fully separate. Every set of possibilities that quantum mechanics recognizes becomes real in some branch. (3) Following E. P. Tryon, many describe Worlds appearing as quantum fluctuations, *ex nihilo* or in an already existing Superspace. (4) Linde has toyed with an eternally expanding de Sitter space, forever boiling with bubble Worlds in which the energy density of the vacuum is lower. (5) G. F. R. Ellis and G. B. Brundrit remind us that if the universe is "open" then it is standardly thought to contain infinitely much material. Outside the region we can see (a "bubble" of an epistemic sort), who can say what might not be happening? (6) Guth's inflationary cosmos, now getting to be the Standard Cosmos, is gigantic and with domains individuated by the various ways in which symmetries broke. Guth and P. J. Steinhardt suggest that our domain stretches 10^{35} light years; the cosmos may be 10^{25} times larger. (7) Et cetera (for example, the many-celled cosmos of F. Hoyle and J. V. Narlikar).

All or most of these approaches[57] (the Hoyle-Narlikar one is the possible exception) allow for early symmetry-breaking in which force strengths and masses are settled largely by chance, different strengths and masses thus appearing in different Worlds.

[. . .]

Thus some fairly well-developed Ensemble stories offer to explain why there are living beings who observe a situation "fine-tuned" to life's needs. Even if most "lunches" in an Ensemble are poisonous, sooner or later there will exist a life-encouraging World. Only such a World could be seen by living beings (Anthropic Principle). God need not enter into this.

VII

How might a modern Newton react? Perhaps as follows.

A) World Ensembles are very speculative. The main evidence for them is the apparent fine-tuning, but God could account for *that*.

B) God might act through laws which produced an Ensemble, relying on Chance to generate life-encouraging Worlds. True, we should now be tempted to attribute life-encouraging properties to Chance alone, dismissing the God hypothesis as an unnecessary extra; yet the evidence for that hypothesis would not have been eroded entirely. For one thing, any World Ensemble explanation of fine-tuning is in difficulties unless we assume inflation (for why don't we see domain walls, and so forth). Now, as discussed earlier, inflation of any appropriate kind may itself need much fine-tuning (particularly if quantum fluctuations are to be inflated to produce density variations from which galaxies can grow.[58] And even if inflation of that kind were dictated by the Unified Theory which applies to our cosmos, there would be the question, more pressing now that "minimal SU(5)" has failed,[59] of why *just that* Theory applies.

C) To answer this last question we might postulate an Ensemble in which every possible Unified Theory is exemplified somewhere. But would it not be simpler to introduce God to select the Theory appropriately, and to answer also why there is any world at all?

D) Let us list factors which appear very fortunate and also unable to vary from World to World as readily as a force strength or a particle mass.

    i) Our world *is complex*: even at high temperatures, any formula describing it must have many terms, this being what makes possible a complex hierarchy of forces and particles when the Big Bang cools and symmetries break. Yet *it is simple enough to be understood*. This is necessary if consciousness is to evolve; for where would be the evolutionary advantage of being conscious of the world, without at all understanding it?

126

[. . .]

ii) *Special Relativity*. Life can develop in different inertial systems no matter how fast they move towards or away from one another. (Not inevitable. Depends on space's having signature +++ − and on how light's speed enters into this. Life might well have been impossible in various systems because forces propagating in certain directions found it hard or impossible to catch up with the particles ahead of them.)

iii) *Quantization* and *Least Action*. Energy is not dissipated uselessly but concentrated in bursts or propagated in straight lines; also (see above) electrons do not spiral into atomic nuclei; and so forth.

iv) *Renormalizability*. Life exists only because quantum fluctuations, added to fluctuations-of-fluctuations, and so on, do not yield infinite results; nor do infinities arrive by, for example, "virtual" point-particles materializing indefinitely close to one another. Only recently has anyone had much idea of how such infinities might be avoided. (Many of them may cancel one another. And instead of being infinitely divisible, space may become "foam" at about 10^{-33} cm; or point-particles may be replaced by "super-strings.")

v) The still perplexing fact that there is *an "Arrow of Time"*, a direction of entropy increase. (The suggestion looked at above, that the cosmos starts off with low gravitational entropy, could give only a partial explanation; for why is such entropy ever low, and why is there a dimension along which it can grow higher? As Penrose says, we are here "groping at matters that are barely understood at all from the point of view of physics" and may have to accept time-asymmetric basic laws).[60]

vi) Rozental holds that if particles had no spin there would be neither electromagnetism nor gravity; and that had all hadrons lacked isotopic spin, complex stable nuclei would not exist.[61] Yet spins for particles are odd enough to have been laughed at when first proposed.

vii) *Baryon Conservation* and other bizarre conservation principles, linked to strange and beautiful symmetry principles.

VIII

I have glimpsed only the vague outlines of this huge field; and in this paper many relevant philosophical topics (probability theory; indirect observation; why anything ever needs explanation; and so forth) have received no mention. Still, two results can be stated.

First: In a field so complex, no very firm conclusions will be justified even a million years from now. The early instants of the Big Bang, the presence of vastly many mini-universes, are far beyond direct experience. The same applies, I would say, to the reality of God.

Second: There are nonetheless good grounds for thinking of the visible universe as remarkably fine-tuned for producing life. Now, despite the extent to which it goes beyond direct experience, the World Ensemble interpretation of this is straightforward enough to be powerful. And the same could be true of the theistic interpretation.

Notes

1. A Neoplatonist Creative Principle is defended in many of my writings: particularly in *Value and Existence* (Oxford: 1979) and in articles in *American Philosophical Quarterly* 7 (1970); *Mind* 87 (1978); *International Journal for Philosophy of Religion* 11 (1980); and *Religious Studies* (to appear).
2. *Other Worlds* (London: 1980), pp. 160–1 and 168–9.
3. *Quantum Gravity* 2 (Oxford: 1981), eds. C. J. Isham, R. Penrose, D. W. Sciama, pp. 248–9.
4. *Gravitation and the Universe* (Philadelphia: 1970), p. 62.
5. Page 514 of R. H. Dicke and P. J. E. Peebles in *General Relativity* (Cambridge: 1979), eds. S. W. Hawking and W. Israel.
6. Page 285 of *Confrontation of Cosmological Theories with Observational Data* (Dordrecht: 1974), ed. M. S. Longair.
7. B. J. Carr, *Irish Astronomical Journal* 15 (1982), p. 244; cf. p. 20 of P. C. W. Davies's superb "The Anthropic Principle," in *Particle and Nuclear Physics* 10 (1983), pp. 1–38, or p. 411 of J. D. Barrow's and F. J. Tipler's impressively wide-ranging *The Anthropic Cosmological Principle* (Oxford: 1986).
8. Page 433 of Barrow and Tipler, cf. A. H. Guth, *Physical Review* D 23 (1981), p. 352.
9. See, e.g., *The Very Early Universe* (Cambridge: 1982), eds. G. W. Gibbons, S. W. Hawking, T. C. Siklos, pp. 271, 393ff.; or A. D. Mazenko, G. M. Unruh, R. M. Wald, *Physical Review* D 31 (1985), pp. 273–82.
10. Pages 28–30 of Davies, "The Anthropic Principle."
11. See p. 413 of Barrow and Tipler; or pp. 6, 26, 475–6, of *The Very Early Universe*.
12. S. W. Hawking, *Phil. Trans. Roy. Soc. London* A 310 (1983), p. 304.
13. Davies, "The Anthropic Principle," p. 28.
14. Barrow and Tipler, p. 434.
15. F. Dyson, *Scientific American* 225 (1971), p. 56.
16. Ibid.
17. Davies, *Other Worlds*, pp. 176–7.
18. J. Demaret and C. Barbier, *Revue des Questions Scientifiques* 152 (1981), p. 500.
19. J. D. Barrow and J. Silk, *Scientific American* 242 No. 4 (1980), pp. 127–8.
20. Davies, "The Anthropic Principle," p. 8, and I. L. Rozental, *Elementary Particles and the Structure of the Universe* (Moscow: 1984, in Russian), p. 85.
21. Dyson, p. 56.
22. F. Hoyle, *Astrophys. J. Suppl.* 1 (1954), p. 121; E. E. Salpeter, *Physical Review* 107 (1957), p. 516.
23. I. L. Rozental, *Structure of the Universe and Fundamental Constants* (Moscow: 1981), p. 8.
24. B. J. Carr and M. J. Rees, *Nature* 278 (1979), p. 611.
25. B. Carter in *Atomic Masses and Fundamental Constants*: 5 (New York: 1976), eds. J. H. Sanders and A. H. Wapstra, p. 652.
26. P. W. Atkins, *The Creation* (Oxford: 1981), p. 13.

27. Davies, "The Anthropic Principle," p. 7.
28. M. J. Rees, *Quart. J. of the Royal Astron. Soc.* 22 (1981), p. 122, with the figure of about 1 percent coming from a conversation of that year; cf. the above-cited works of Hoyle and Salpeter.
29. Barrow and Tipler, pp. 252–3.
30. Ibid., p. 327.
31. *On Numerical Values of Fundamental Constants* (Moscow: 1980), p. 9; on the question of atomic weights above four he cites E. E. Salpeter, *Astrophys J.* 140 (1964), p. 796.
32. P. C. W. Davies, *Superforce* (New York: 1984), p. 242.
33. *Reviews of Modern Physics* 29 (1957), pp. 375–6.
34. *Physical Review* 73, p. 801.
35. M. J. Rees, *Phil. Trans. Roy. Soc. London* A 310 (1983), p. 312.
36. R. Breuer, *Das Anthropische Prinzip* (Munich: 1983), p. 228.
37. Ibid.
38. Carr and Rees, p. 611.
39. Barrow and Tipler, p. 339.
40. *Nature* 265 (1977), p. 710.
41. I. S. Shklovskii and C. Sagan, *Intelligent Life in the Universe* (New York: 1966), p. 124.
42. *Physics Bulletin*, Cambridge, 32, p. 15.
43. Barrow and Tipler, pp. 371, 399–400; Davies, "The Anthropic Principle," pp. 9–10, and *The Forces of Nature* (Cambridge: 1979), pp. 100–102, 172; Rozental, *Elementary Particles*, pp. 78–84.
44. Davies, *Superforce*, pp. 137–8.
45. Carr and Rees, p. 610; Demaret and Barbier, pp. 478–80, 500; D. V. Nanopoulos, *Physics Letters* 91B, pp. 67–71; Davies, "The Anthropic Principle," pp. 24–5; Barrow and Tipler, p. 418.
46. H. Pagels, *Perfect Symmetry*. (New York: 1985), pp. 275–9.
47. Weinberg, p. 157.
48. Barrow and Tipler, pp. 358–9.
49. *The Emerging Universe* (Charlottesville: 1972), eds. W. C. Saslaw and K. C. Jacobs, p. 79.
50. Barrow and Tipler, p. 297.
51. Davies, *Superforce*, p. 131.
52. Davies, "The Anthropic Principle," p. 15.
53. *The Creation*, pp. 10–12.
54. *Cosmochemical Evolution and the Origins of Life* (Dordrecht: 1974), eds. J. Oro, S. L. Miller, C. Ponnamperuma, R. S. Young, pp. 7, 24.
55. *Soviet Physics: Uspekhi* 23 (1980), p. 296.
56. *Izvest. Akad. Nauk Estonskoi SSR Fiz. Matemat.* 31 (1982) pp. 284–9.
57. Wheeler in *Gravitation* (San Francisco: 1973), ch. 44, and *Quantum Gravity* (Oxford: 1975), eds. C. J. Isham, R. Penrose and D. W. Sciama, pp. 538–605 and esp. 556–7; Everett and others in *The Many-Worlds Interpretation of Quantum Mechanics* (Princeton: 1973), eds. B. S. DeWitt and R. N. Graham; Tryon, *Nature* 246 (1973), pp. 396–7, and *New Scientist* 101 (1984), pp. 14–16; Linde in *The Very Early Universe*, p. 239; Ellis and Brundrit, *Quart. J. of the Royal Astron. Soc.* 20 (1979), pp. 37–41; Guth and Steinhardt, *Scientific American* 250 (1984), pp. 116–128; Hoyle, *Ten Faces of the Universe* (San Francisco: 1977), ch. 6.
58. See, e.g., Linde on p. 216 of *The Very Early Universe*.
59. Davies, *Superforce*, pp. 137–8.
60. Pages 581–638, and esp. 594, of *General Relativity*.
61. *Uspekhi* paper, p. 302.

2.4

'DESIGN AND THE MANY-WORLDS HYPOTHESIS'

Robin Collins

INTRODUCTION

In the last thirty years, the argument from the fine-tuning of the cosmos has steadily gained in popularity, often being considered the strongest single argument for the existence of God. The 'fine-tuning' of the cosmos refers to the claim that the fundamental parameters or constants of physics and the initial conditions of the universe are set just right for life to occur.[1] To give two of many examples, if the strong force coupling constant, which determines the strength of the strong force that binds protons and neutrons together in the nucleus, were slightly less, the electrical repulsion between protons would cause all atoms except hydrogen to break apart, thus eliminating the possibility of complex life forms such as ourselves; in contrast, if this constant were slightly greater, all the hydrogen would have been burned to helium, thus causing stars to burn too quickly for life to evolve (Barrow and Tipler 1986: p. 322). Similarly, it is estimated that unless the cosmological constant were near zero to one part in 10^{120} of its 'natural' value derived from current theories in particle physics, the universe would either expand too rapidly, or collapse too quickly, for life to develop (Guth 1997: p. 284).[2]

In light of these scientific findings, many theists have argued that the fine-tuning of the cosmos strongly supports the hypothesis that the universe was intelligently designed for life, arguing that it is highly implausible to attribute this sort of fine-tuning to chance or to claim that it needs no explanation. In response to this theistic or intelligent design explanation of the fine-tuning, however, many atheists have offered an alternative explanation, what I will

Robin Collins, 'Design and the Many-Worlds Hypothesis' (© June 2000).

call the 'many-universes hypothesis', but which in the literature goes under a variety of names, such as many-worlds hypothesis, the many-domains hypothesis, the world-ensemble hypothesis, the multiuniverse hypothesis, etc. According to this hypothesis, there are a very large – perhaps infinite – number of universes, with the fundamental parameters of physics varying from universe to universe.[3] Of course, in the vast majority of these universes the parameters of physics would not have life-permitting values. Nonetheless, in a small proportion of universes they would, and consequently it is no longer improbable that universes such as ours exist that are fine-tuned for life to occur.

There are two major versions of the many-universe hypothesis, what could be called the metaphysical version and what could be called the physical version. In the metaphysical version the universes are thought to exist on their own without being generated by any physical process, whereas in the physical versions some particular real physical process is postulated that generates the many universes. Princeton University philosopher David Lewis and University of Pennsylvania astrophysicist Max Tegmark, for example, both propose a version of the metaphysical many-universe hypothesis. According to Lewis (1986), every possible world actually exists parallel to our own. Thus, for instance, there exists a reality parallel to our own in which I am president of the United States and a reality in which objects can travel faster than the speed of light. Dream up a possible scenario, and it exists in some parallel reality, according to Lewis. Alternatively, according to Tegmark's hypothesis, 'everything that exists mathematically exists physically' (1998, p. 1), by which he means that every self-consistent mathematical structure is in one-to-one correspondence with some physical reality (1998, pp. 1–3). Tegmark calls this hypothesis the 'ultimate ensemble hypothesis', and claims it explains why there exists a universe such as ours in which the laws of nature and the parameters of physics are life-permitting.

Besides these sorts of metaphysical many-universe hypotheses, a variety of physical many-universe hypotheses has also been offered. For example, one of the first many-universe models that was proposed was the so-called oscillating Big Bang model, which essentially is a version of the Big Bang theory. According to the Big Bang theory, the universe came into existence in an 'explosion' (that is, a 'bang') somewhere between 10 and 15 billion years ago. According to the oscillating Big Bang theory, our universe will eventually collapse back in on itself (what is called the 'Big Crunch') and then from that 'Big Crunch' will arise another 'Big Bang', forming a new universe, which will in turn itself collapse, and so on. According to those who use this model to attempt to explain the fine-tuning, during every cycle the parameters of physics and the initial conditions of the universe are reset at random. Since this process of collapse, explosion, collapse and explosion is assumed to have been going on for all eternity, eventually a fine-tuned universe will occur, indeed infinitely many of them.

More recently, a variety of other physical many-universe scenarios has been proposed, such as the so-called vacuum fluctuation models, first proposed by Edward Tyron (1973). According to the vacuum fluctuation models, our universe, along with these other universes, were generated by quantum fluctuations in a pre-existing superspace. Imaginatively, one can think of this pre-existing superspace as a infinitely extending ocean full of soap, and each universe generated out of this superspace as a soap bubble which spontaneously forms on the ocean.

Even more recently, Pennsylvania State University gravitational physicist Lee Smolin (1997) has offered a many-universes scenario based on a highly speculative scenario regarding black holes. According to Smolin's speculation, by tearing and rearranging the fabric of space-time, black holes can give rise to new universes with different parameters, and even lower-level laws, of physics. Thus, once a single universe exists, it will spawn new universes via black holes, and these new universes will spawn further universes, and so on.

Since the early 1980s, what could be called the inflationary many-universe hypothesis has steadily gained popularity, being based on so-called inflationary cosmology, which is the cosmological theory first proposed by Alan Guth in 1980 to explain the Big Bang and various features of the universe, such as the large-scale uniformity of matter in space. Despite the variety of many-universe scenarios that has been proposed, both metaphysical and physical, the inflationary scenario is the only one that goes beyond mere speculation. The reason is twofold. First, unlike the other scenarios, inflationary cosmology has significant scientific evidence in its favour, being widely regarded as the most viable theory of the origin of the universe available today. Second, a many-universe scenario naturally arises out of what are widely considered the most plausible models of inflationary cosmology, the so-called chaotic inflationary models. So, although speculative, an inflationary many-universe hypothesis deserves to be taken particularly seriously.[4]

Because it is widely considered to be by far the most physically plausible scenario, I shall focus on the inflationary many-universe scenario here. In the rest of this paper, I shall first explain why an inflationary many-universes scenario might be able to offer a viable explanation of the fine-tuning, but then go on to explain why there still remains a powerful case for design from physics and cosmology. Further, much of the evidence for design that I shall present cannot be naturally explained by any many-universe scenario, and thus circumvents any objection to design based on the many-universe hypothesis, whether the inflationary version or some other version.

INFLATIONARY MANY-UNIVERSE SCENARIO

According to inflationary cosmology, our universe started from an exceedingly small region of space that underwent enormous expansion due to an hypothesised inflaton field which both caused the expansion and imparted a constant, very large energy density to space as it expanded. The expansion caused the temperature of space to decrease, in analogy to what happens when a gas expands. This in turn caused one or more 'droplet' universes to form, much as water droplets are formed when water vapour is cooled upon expanding, as when moist air goes over a mountain range producing rain. As each droplet universe is formed, the energy of the inflaton field is converted into a burst of 'normal' mass-energy thereby giving rise to a standard Big-Bang expansion of the kind we see in our universe.

In chaotic inflation models – widely considered the most plausible – space expands so rapidly that it becomes a never ending source of droplet universes, much as a rapidly expanding, continually replenished supply of water vapour would serve as an unending source of water droplets. Thus, an enormous number of universes naturally arises from this scenario.

In order to get the initial conditions and parameters of physics to vary from universe to universe, however, there must be a further physical mechanism to cause the variation. Whether a mechanism exists that allows for enough variation to explain the fine-tuning depends on the fundamental physical theory governing elementary particles and forces. The particular versions of the so-called grand unified theories currently being widely explored by physicists, for instance, only allow for a very limited number of variations of the parameters of physics, about a dozen or so in the case of the simplest model (Linde 1990a, p. 33). Merely to account for the fine-tuning of the cosmological constant, however, would require trillions upon trillions upon trillions upon trillions of variations, since it is estimated that it is fine-tuned to one part in 10^{120}.

To see this, note that, at least in the case of the cosmological constant, to say that a parameter is fine-tuned to 1 part in 10^{120} means that the life-permitting range of the parameter is 1 in 10^{120} of what physicists take as the natural range of values given by the background physical theory. Thus, to account for this fine-tuning by means of a many-universes hypothesis would require around 10^{120} variations in the parameters of physics. If, for example, there were only ten different values for the cosmological constant among the universes, we would still find it very surprising for the cosmological constant to fall into the life-permitting range in any of the universes. The same could be said for many of the other cases of fine-tuning.

Here is where superstring theory could come to the rescue. Superstring theory is widely considered the only currently feasible candidate for a truly fundamental physical theory (Greene 1999: p. 214), and is certainly the only currently viable physical theory that seems to allow for enough variation among universes of the parameters of physics to explain the fine-tuning. According to superstring theory, the ultimate constituents of matter are strings of energy that undergo quantum vibrations in a 10 (or 11) dimensional space–time, 6 or 7 dimensions of which are 'compactified' to extremely small sizes and are hence unobservable. The shape of the compactified dimensions, however, determines the modes of vibration of the strings, and hence the types and masses of fundamental particles, along with many characteristics of the forces between them. Thus, universes in which compactified dimensions have different shapes will have different parameters of physics and differing lower-level laws governing the forces.

Now, if the universe started in an extremely high energy state, the various compactified dimensions would undergo rapid variations in shape. As the temperature of a region of expanding space cools, a droplet universe is likely to form. Such a universe will fall into a local minimum of energy, called a vacuum state, of the space of possible compactified shapes, thus determining the shape of the compactified dimensions for that universe. Consequently, the number of variations in the shape of the compactified dimensions among universes, and hence the variation in the parameters and lower-level laws of physics governing the forces is determined by the number of vacua of string theory – that is, the number of local minima of energy. The number of vacua is unknown, but most string theorists hope that it is small so that string theory would virtually determine the parameters and laws of physics; nonetheless, as far as we know, the number could be enormous enough to explain the fine-tuning.

Thus, it is in the realm of real physical plausibility that a viable inflationary many-universes scenario could be constructed that would account for the fine-tuning of the parameters of physics and the initial conditions of the cosmos. Nonetheless, it should be noted that despite the current popularity of both inflationary cosmology and superstring theory, both are highly speculative. For instance, as Michio Kaku states in his recent textbook on superstring theory, 'Not a shred of experimental evidence has been found to confirm . . . superstrings' (1999: p. 17). The major attraction of string theory is its mathematical elegance and the fact that many physicists think that it is the only game in town that offers significant hope of providing a truly unified physical theory of gravitation with quantum mechanics (Greene 1999: p. 214).[5]

It should be stressed, however, that even if superstring theory or inflationary cosmology turn out to be false, they have opened the door to taking the many-universes explanation of the fine-tuning as a serious physical possibility since some other physical mechanisms could give rise to multiple universes with a sufficiently large number of variations in the parameters of physics. The only way we could close this door is if we discovered that the ultimate laws of physics did not allow either many-universes or enough variation in the parameters and laws of physics among universes.

Now that I have established the positive case for taking the many-universes hypothesis seriously as a possible explanation for the fine-tuning of the parameters of physics, I shall turn to the case for design.

THE CASE FOR DESIGN

The Many-Universe Generator Needs Design

In this subsection, I shall present the case for design based on the assumption that the physical many-universe (i.e., 'universe generator') scenario is by far the most plausible. (In the next subsection, I shall present the case for design that applies as well to those who find the metaphysical many-universe scenario plausible.) I begin by noting that even if a 'many-universes generator' exists it seems to need to be 'well designed' in order to produce life-sustaining universes. And this is true whether such a generator is based in inflationary cosmology or something else. After all, even a mundane item like a bread machine, which only produces loaves of bread instead of universes, must be well designed to produce decent loaves of bread.

As a test case, consider whether this line of reasoning works for the inflationary type many-universe scenario. In order for many universes to be generated in this scenario, there must be one or more mechanisms that: (1) cause the expansion of a small region of space into a very large region; (2) in the process allow for the generation of the very large amount of mass-energy needed for a universe containing matter instead of merely empty space; and (3) allow for the conversion of the mass-energy of inflated space to the sort of mass-energy we find in our universe.

Glossing over the details, in inflationary models, the first two conditions are met via two factors. The first factor is the postulated inflaton field that gives the vacuum (i.e., empty space) a positive energy density. The second factor is the peculiar nature of Einstein's equation of general relativity, which dictates that space expands at an enormous rate in the presence of a large near-homogenous positive energy density. Finally, because the inflaton field gives a constant positive energy density to empty space, as space expands the total amount of energy within the space in question must enormously increase. This in turn generates the needed energy for the formation of matter in the universe. As one text in cosmology explains, 'the vacuum acts as a reservoir of unlimited energy, which can supply as much as is required to inflate a given region to any required size at constant energy density' (Peacock 1999: p. 26).

So, we effectively have a sort of 'conspiracy' between at least two different factors: the inflaton field that gives empty space a positive energy density and Einstein's equation. These two harmoniously work together to inflate small regions of space enormously while at the same time imparting to them the positive energy density necessary for a universe with significant mass-energy. Without either factor, there would neither be regions of space that inflate nor would those regions have the mass-energy necessary for a universe to exist. If, for example, the universe obeyed Newton's theory of gravity instead of Einstein's, the vacuum energy of the inflaton field would at best simply create a gravitational attraction causing space to contract, not to expand.[6] Finally,

Einstein's equivalence of mass and energy, $E=mc^2$, along with the assumption that there is a coupling between the inflaton field and the matter fields, allows the energy of the inflaton field to be converted to 'normal' mass-energy.

In addition to the above conspiracy of factors, the initial state of space that generates the many-universes must start with a high value for the energy density of the inflaton field. For example, if the inflaton field started out at a near zero value, as is its current value in our universe, no inflation could occur.

Moreover, as we saw above, there must be some mechanism that allows for enough variation in the parameters of physics to account for the fine-tuning. This would require that the fundamental structures of physical laws have the right form, as might be the case in string theory but is not the case, for example, in the typical grand unified theories that are being studied today, as mentioned above. As Joseph Polchinski notes in his textbook on string theory (1998, vol. 2: pp. 372–3), there is no reason to expect a generic field to have an enormous number of stable local minima of energy, which would be required if there is to be a large number of variations in the parameters of physics among universes.

In addition to all this, some of the background laws of physics must be right for the universes generated to be life-permitting. For example, without the principle of quantisation all electrons would be sucked into the atomic nuclei and hence atoms would be impossible; without the Pauli-exclusion principle, electrons would occupy the lowest atomic orbit and hence complex and varied atoms would be impossible; without a universally attractive force between all masses, such as gravity, matter would not be able to form sufficiently large material bodies (such as planets) for life to develop or for long-lived stable energy sources such as stars to exist.

Although some of the laws of physics can vary from universe to universe in string theory, these background laws and principles are entailed by the very structure of string theory and therefore cannot be explained as a many-universes selection effect. Further, since the variation among universes would consist of variation of the masses and types of particles, and the form of the forces between them, complex structures would almost certainly be atom-like and stable energy sources would almost certainly require aggregates of matter. Thus, the above background laws seem necessary for there to be life in any of the many universes generated in this scenario, not merely a universe with our specific types of particles and forces.

In sum, even if an inflationary/superstring many-universe generator exists, it along with the background laws and principles could be said to be an 'irreducibly complex' system, to borrow a phrase from biochemist Michael Behe (1996), with just the right combination of laws and fields for the production of life-permitting universes: if one of the components were missing or different, such as Einstein's equation or the Pauli-exclusion principle, it is unlikely that any life-permitting universes could be produced. In the absence of alternative explanations, the existence of such a system suggests design.

It should also be noted that the inflationary scenario does not explain where the mass-energy of the universe, and the laws of physics, came from. The answer that they always existed is most likely ruled out within inflationary scenarios (See Guth 1997: p. 249; and Guth 2000: p. 16). This suggests a need for an ontologically transcendent being that is responsible for the existence of the universe, though I shall not pursue this form of the cosmological argument here.

Finally, it should be stressed that theists need not be opposed to the inflationary many-universe hypothesis. Indeed, there are several reasons one could give in support of a theistic version of it. First, as described above, the fact that so many factors in contemporary cosmology and particle physics conspire together to make the inflationary many-universe scenario viable gives theists significant reasons for taking it as a serious possibility. Second, science has progressively shown that the visible universe is vastly larger than we once thought, with a current estimate of some 300 billion galaxies with 300 billion stars per galaxy. Thus, it makes sense that this trend will continue and physical reality will be found to be much larger than a single universe. Finally, since theists have traditionally believed that God is infinite and infinitely creative, it only makes sense that creation would reflect these attributes of God, and hence that physical reality would be much larger than one universe, perhaps even infinitely larger.

Apparent Design of Physical Law

Next, I shall turn to the various features of the laws of nature that both suggest design and cannot be explained by any many-universes hypothesis, whether physical or metaphysical. I shall only be able to give the briefest sketch of them here, however. These features of the laws are: (1) their simplicity; (2) their beauty, harmony and elegance; (3) their intelligibility; and (4) what I shall call their 'discoverability'.

I shall begin with the simplicity of the laws. Although no adequate definition of what is meant by calling the laws of nature simple has ever been given, both scientists and philosophers almost unanimously agree that they manifest a surprising degree of simplicity. Indeed, when constructing a new law of nature in some domain, scientists routinely look for the simplest law that adequately accounts for the extant data and which meets the other constraints imposed by various background assumptions.

Besides simplicity, there is also the beauty of the laws of nature. As Nobel prize-winning theoretical physicist Steven Weinberg stresses in his book *Dreams of a Final Theory* (1992), beauty is widely recognised by physicists as being an important characteristic of the laws of nature, one which has served as a highly successful guide to discovering the fundamental laws of nature in the twentieth century. Indeed, Weinberg devotes all of Chapter 6 of his book to discussing and emphasising the role that considerations of beauty have played in physics. Weinberg, who is a convinced atheist, even admits that 'sometimes nature seems more beautiful than strictly necessary' (1992: p. 250).

This use of beauty and elegance as a fundamental guiding principle was to a large extent inaugurated by Einstein in his development of general relativity, though it was certainly implicitly used by earlier physicists. For example, following Einstein's lead, Paul Dirac, one of the most important figures in the development of quantum mechanics is the twentieth century, made mathematical beauty the foremost criterion in developing a physical theory. According to theoretical physicist and historian of physics Oliver Darrigol,

> the notion of mathematical beauty was an integral part of [Dirac's] strategy. [According to Dirac,] one first had to select the most beautiful mathematics—not necessarily connected to the existing basis of theoretical physics—and then interpret them in physical terms. (1992: p. 304)

Today, this use of beauty and elegance as a guide is particularly evident in the popularity of string theory, which as mentioned above is almost entirely motivated by considerations of elegance, having no experimental support in its favour (Greene 1999: p. 214).

As embodied in the mathematical structure of physical theory, some of these elements of beauty are: (1) simplicity with variety; (2) proportion and harmony; (3) symmetry; (4) inevitability; (5) ingenuity; and (6) having an 'interesting twist' or a 'strangeness of proportion'.[7]

The above elements are largely constitutive of the so-called classical concept or type of beauty, but I will only significantly discuss that of simplicity with variety here. Simplicity with variety was the defining feature of beauty or elegance stressed by William Hogarth in his 1753 classic *The Analysis of Beauty*, where he famously used a line drawn around a cone to illustrate this notion. According to Hogarth, simplicity apart from variety, such as a straight line, is boring, neither elegant nor beautiful.

Now, the laws of nature seem to manifest just this sort of simplicity with variety: we inhabit a world that could be characterised as a world of fundamental simplicity that gives rise to the enormous complexity needed for intelligent life. In physics, this simplicity with variety is particularly evident in the way in which whole classes of diverse physical phenomena and laws of nature are encompassed by common contingent principles of great simplicity and elegance. For instance, consider the so-called gauge principle of fundamental particle physics which undergirds our current understanding of at least three, and arguably all four, of the four forces of nature. The mathematical form of three of the four forces of nature, the strong force, the weak force, and electromagnetism, all obey the gauge principle, and the gauge principle served as a crucial guide in constructing the modern theory of these forces. Further, a principle very much like the gauge principle is what guided Einstein in the construction of his theory of general relativity, which is currently our best theory of the gravitational force. Yet, as Ian Atchison and Anthony Hey point out in their text *Gauge Theories in Particle Physics*, there is no compelling logical reason why this principle must hold (1989: pp. 59–60). Rather, they claim, this principle has been almost universally adopted as a fundamental principle by elementary particle physicists because it is 'so simple, beautiful and powerful (and apparently successful)' (1989: p. 60). Further, as Alan Guth points out, the original 'construction of these [gauge] theories was motivated mainly by their mathematical elegance' (1997: p. 124). Thus, the gauge principle provides a good example of a contingent principle of great simplicity and elegance that encompasses a wide range of phenomena, namely the interactions between all the particles in the universe.[8]

Other examples of principles that encompass large classes of diverse phenomena are the law of energy conservation, the least action principle, the second law of thermodynamics, various quantum principles, such as the superposition principle and the Pauli-exclusion principle and the like. Further, though we will not argue in detail for it here, it does not seem that one can plausibly think of these principles as in themselves having any causal power to dictate the lower-level phenomena or laws. Rather, the 'causation' or dependence is in the other direction: it is because the laws and phenomena are what they are that these principles universally hold, not the other way around. An analogy from architecture might be helpful to illustrate this point: insofar as the placement of windows in a building follows higher-level principles, it is not because the principles somehow in themselves have a special power to make the windows have the right positions. Rather, it is because of the position of the windows that the higher-level principles hold. Further, insofar as the higher-level principles could be said to have a causal efficacy to determine the placement of the windows, it is only via the causal powers of an intelligent agent, such as the people who constructed the building.

One reason for claiming that these principles have no intrinsic causal powers is that except for being an intention or thought in some mind, human or transcendent, it is difficult to see how these higher-level principles could be anything over and above merely the patterns into which the laws and phenomena of nature fall. For example, they do not appear to be reducible to the causal powers of actual entities, as some philosophers claim about the laws of nature.[9] Instead, insofar as entities possess causal powers, the principles describe the arrangement of the causal powers of a diverse class of such entities – for example, the fundamental particles – and therefore cannot be the powers of any given entity.

Thus, just as the positions of windows in a building are often arranged just right so that certain higher-level architectural principles are met, the laws of nature and various phenomena give the appearance of being arranged just right, or even 'fine-tuned', so that a few simple, higher-level physical principles are universally valid. Although this idea of the laws being arranged just right or 'fine-tuned' is difficult rigorously to spell-out, several specific examples will help illustrate the idea. One example is the so-called peaceful coexistence of the principles of special relativity with those of quantum mechanics, which many authors have pointed out is quite 'miraculous', since it depends on certain special features of quantum dynamics – namely, the absolute linearity of the central equation of quantum mechanics, the Schrödinger equation, and the particular form of the rule governing the so-called 'collapse of the state vector'.[10]

Another example occurs with the gauge principle mentioned above, in which many of the laws and phenomena of physics, such as the mathematical form of the forces between elementary particles, are arranged in just the right way for the gauge principle to apply. A particularly interesting case of this occurs with regard to the weak force. The gauge principle applies in a relatively straightforward way to the electromagnetic and strong force, but initially it appeared that it could not be used to determine the mathematical form of the weak force, which is one of the four forces of nature and is responsible for many cases of the transmutation and decay of nuclei and elementary particles. The problem was that a straightforward application of the gauge principle requires that the particle carrying the weak force be massless, which in turn implies that the weak force would be long range. Not only was this contrary to the experimental data, but if the weak force were long range, life would probably be impossible.[11] It took ten years for physicists to see their way around this problem. Using the previous work of Sheldon Glashow, Steven Weinberg and Abdus Salam developed a solution: introduce a new field, called a Higgs field, with a special mathematical form, often referred to as a 'Mexican hat' potential because when represented on a graph its form resembles that of a Mexican hat. The introduction of this field allowed Weinberg and Salam not only to apply the gauge principle to the weak force, but it allowed them to produce a theory that unites the electromagnetic and weak force, the so-called Glashow–Weinberg–Salam electroweak theory. This theory has since been significantly confirmed by experiment.

Without the Higgs field, therefore, one would either not have an extremely short-range force like the weak force, which as mentioned above would probably mean a lifeless universe, or the gauge principle would be violated. Once again, the point of this example is that nature appears to be arranged in just the right way – such as by including a Higgs field of the right form – to guarantee that certain simple higher-level principles are satisfied, while at the same time guaranteeing a life-permitting universe.

Theoretical physicist Paul Davies offers even further examples of this sort of seemingly ingenious construction of nature that allow the higher-level principles of physics to remain valid, even in very bizarre circumstances. For example, he discusses how black holes initially appear to violate the second law of thermodynamics, but that upon further careful and subtle analysis, 'it turns out not to be so, but only when quantum physics is taken into account' (1984: p. 231). Thus, Davies concludes,

> The three branches of physics [general relativity, quantum mechanics and thermodynamics] mutually support each other, even for a system as bizarre as a black hole . . . The black hole provides a good example, then, of how physics hangs together coherently, sometimes for the most subtle of reasons. (1984: p. 231)

Finally, as further testimony to the above point, consider what Steven Weinberg and other physicists have called the 'inevitability' of the laws of nature (e.g., see Weinberg 1992: pp. 135–53, 235–7). The inevitability that Weinberg refers to is not the inevitability of logical necessity (1992: p. 235), but rather that the mathematical structure of the laws of nature are encompassed by a few general principles, as with the gauge principle discussed above. The reason Weinberg refers to this as the 'inevitability' of the laws of nature is that the requirement that these principles be met often severely restricts the possible mathematical forms the laws of nature can take, thus rendering them in some sense 'inevitable'. This inevitability of the laws is particularly evident in Einstein's general theory of relativity. As Weinberg notes, 'once you know the general physical principles adopted by Einstein, you understand that there is no other significantly different theory of gravitation to which Einstein could have been led' (1992: p. 135). As Einstein himself said, 'To modify it [general relativity] without destroying the whole structure seems to be impossible' (quoted in Weinberg 1992: p. 135).

One way of thinking about this inevitability is as a sort of fine-tuning. If one imagines a space of all possible laws, the set of laws and physical phenomena we have are just those that meet the higher-level principles. Of course, in analogy to the case of the fine-tuning of the parameters of physics, there are bound to be other sets of laws that meet some other relatively simple set of higher-level principles. But this does not take away from the fine-tuning of the laws, or the case for design, anymore than the fact that there are many possible elegant architectural plans for constructing a house takes away from the design of a particular house. What is important is that the vast majority of variations of these laws end up causing a violation of one of these higher-level principles, as Einstein noted about general relativity. Further, for those who are aware of the relevant physics, it is easy to see that in the vast majority of such cases, such variations do not result in new, equally simple higher-level principles being satisfied. It follows, therefore, that these variations almost universally lead to a less elegant and simple set of higher-level physical principles being met. Thus, in terms of the simplicity and elegance of the higher-level principles that are satisfied, the laws of nature we have appear to be a tiny island surrounded by a vast sea of possible law structures that produce a far less elegant and simple physics.

Now, this simplicity and elegance cannot be explained by the many-universes hypotheses, since there is no reason to think that intelligent life could only arise in a universe with simple, elegant underlying physical principles. Certainly a somewhat orderly macroscopic world is necessary for intelligent life, but there is no reason to think this requires a simple and elegant underlying set of physical principles. This is especially clear when one considers how radically different the framework and laws of general relativity and quantum mechanics are from the world of ordinary experience: although the regularities of the everyday world are probably derived from the underlying laws of quantum mechanics and general relativity, they do not reflect the structure of those laws. Indeed, it is this difference in structure that has largely given rise to the interpretive problems of quantum mechanics and general relativity. Thus, there is little reason to expect the sort of macroscopic order necessary for intelligent life to be present in the underlying, microscopic world.

In sum, therefore, the apparent delicate arrangement and fine-tuning of the laws of nature in order to meet a few simple, contingent, higher-level principles seem strongly to suggest design. As theoretical physicist Paul Davies notes with regard to these and related features of the laws of nature,

> A common reaction among physicists to remarkable discoveries of the sort discussed above is a mixture of delight at the subtlety and elegance of nature, and of stupefaction: 'I would never have thought of doing it that way.' If nature is so 'clever' it can exploit mechanisms that amaze us with their ingenuity, is that not persuasive evidence for the existence of intelligent design behind the physical universe? If the world's finest minds can unravel only with difficulty the deeper workings of nature, how could it be supposed that those workings are merely a mindless accident, a product of blind chance? . . . Once again, the crossword puzzle analogy is appropriate here. Uncovering the laws of physics resembles completing a crossword in a number of ways. . . . In the case of the crossword, it would never occur to us to suppose that the words just happened to fall into a consistent interlocking pattern by accident . . . (1984: pp. 235–6)

Another feature of the fundamental structure of the physical world that seems to suggest design is its intelligibility. As Albert Einstein once remarked, 'the most unintelligible thing about the universe is that it is intelligible at all'. One aspect of this intelligibility is the fact that those human intuitions, categories and concepts we consider significant apply surprisingly well and serve as surprisingly good guides to the underlying order of things. We have already seen this in the applicability of the categories of simplicity and beauty to the underlying order, which are special cases of this more general notion of the intelligibility of nature. This more general notion also includes human intuitions about the way nature should be, along with additional categories such as naturalness, all of which are central to both theory confirmation and development. As Albert Einstein remarked, 'There is no logical path leading to these laws [of nature], but only intuition, supported by sympathetic under-standing of experience' (quoted in Miller 1996: p. 369).

The final way in which the laws of nature and the structure of physical reality suggest design is in what I will call their discoverability: that is, the laws of nature seem to be carefully arranged so that they are discoverable by beings with our level of intelligence. I believe that this feature of the laws suggests not only design, but also that it fits into a larger pattern indicative of a particular providential purpose for human beings, such as that of developing a sophis-ticated science and technology, but I cannot argue for that here.

Of course, the fact that the fundamental structure of the world displays a simplicity, elegance and intelligibility greatly contribute to its discoverability, as I have indicated above. Although I cannot present them here, more specific examples of this 'fine-tuning' for discoverability are presented by philosopher Mark Steiner in his book, *The Applicability of Mathematics as a Philosophical Problem*, in which he concludes that the world is much more 'user-friendly' than seems explicable under naturalism (1998: p. 176). Although I do not think that Steiner has yet made an entirely compelling case, his work does show, I believe, that there is potentially a significant case to be made for the discoverability of the laws of nature, a case that needs to be spelled-out by further research.

Alternative Non-design Explanations

Above I have claimed that the simplicity, beauty, intelligibility and discover-ability of the laws of nature all point to design. But there are alternative explanations. For brevity's sake, I shall focus primarily on these alternatives for the case of beauty.

The first alternative explanation is to claim that this so-called beauty is purely subjective, simply the result of our reading into nature anthropo-morphic patterns in the same way as humans have read various meaningful patterns – such as the Bear or the Big Dipper – into the random pattern of stars in the night sky. The major problem with this explanation is that it does not account for the surprising success of the criterion of beauty in the physical sciences. We would not expect patterns that are merely subjective to serve as a basis for theories that make highly accurate predictions, such as quantum electrodynamics's successful prediction, to nine significant digits, of the quantum correction to the g-factor of the electron. The second problem is that there are significant objective aspects of beauty, at least in the classical sense of beauty, that one can clearly demonstrate in the realm of physics, such as that of symmetry.

The second attempt at offering an alternative explanation is to invoke evolution, claiming that, long before the rise of science, natural selection programmed into us the category of beauty because it was of survival value. Although evolution might be able to explain why we have a category of beauty, it cannot explain why it applies so well to the underlying order of the world, since such applicability was obviously irrelevant to our survival during the long course of human evolution. At most, evolution can only explain why beauty applies to the everyday world of those things necessary for our survival, what philosopher Patricia Churchland has called the four Fs: feeding, fleeing, fighting and reproducing. But, as often noted, it is in the underlying world that considerations of beauty as a guide have met with the most impressive success, at least in terms of producing theories that are extraordinarily predictively fruitful. This is just the opposite of what this evolutionary explanation would lead one to expect. Further, this evolutionary explanation leaves unexplained why the underlying world exhibits those objective features – such as simplicity with variety, symmetry, harmony and proportion so characteristic of beauty. Theism, in contrast, naturally explains these characteristics, and thus provides a better explanation of them.

A second kind of evolutionary explanation is that presented by Steven Weinberg: through a process of trial and error since the scientific revolution, we have learned that nature is a certain way, and then we have come to consider the way nature is beautiful (1992: p. 158). That is, Weinberg suggests that, after the scientific revolution, scientists unconsciously modified their criteria of beauty to fit nature. The problem with this explanation is that we can point to objective features of the underlying world – its symmetry, its simplicity in variety, its inevitability – that clearly fit the general criteria of the so-called classical conception of beauty, a category of great human significance that originated long before the scientific revolution. Further, the mere fact that scientists use the term 'beautiful' instead of some other category to describe the underlying order indicates that they sense a deep congruence between the order of nature and those features normally associated with beauty in other, non-scientific contexts. It is this congruence that Weinberg's evolutionary explanation fails to explain.

The third alternative explanation invokes some metaphysical principle of beauty and simplicity – such as that the basic structure of the world is more likely to be simple and beautiful than complex and ugly – to account for the simplicity and beauty of the laws. Not only does such a principle seem implausible, but also it would need to be supplemented with a parallel principle to account for the intelligibility and discoverability of the laws of nature, along with a many-universes hypothesis to account for the fine-tuning for life of the parameters of physics. The only way I can see of making the existence of such principles plausible is by appealing to some unified overarching hypothesis that implies these lower-level principles, such as the theistic hypothesis.

The final alternative is merely to claim that the simplicity and beauty of the laws of nature are simply a brute fact that requires no explanation. One could always adopt this position, but then given that theism naturally explains these features of the laws of nature, the atheist must admit that theism offers a better explanation of them than atheism, and thus that they support theism over atheism. Why? Because a natural, non-ad hoc explanation of a phenomenon x is always better than no explanation at all. And theism does seem to offer such a natural explanation: for example, given the classical theistic conception of God as the greatest possible being, and hence a being with a perfect aesthetic sensibility, it is not surprising that such a God would create a world of great subtlety and beauty at the fundamental level.

These non-design responses get even more implausible when we consider other aspects of the laws of nature that suggest design, such as their discoverability and intelligibility. An even further implausibility arises when we reflect on the emergence within our universe of consciousness and highly abstract and theoretical thought as occurs in philosophy, mathematics and advanced physics, something seemingly inexplicable by an unguided evolutionary process since it does not appear either to have been of significant survival value, or to be a natural by-product of anything of significant survival value, during the long course of human biological evolution.[12] This is especially true given the strong case that many believe can be made for the irreducibility of consciousness to physical processes or states.

CONCLUSION

Finally, it is worth reflecting on the sort of inference that I have invoked in my argument. It involves what philosophers call a cumulative case argument in which many factors, such as the fine-tuning, the simplicity, the beauty, the intelligibility and discoverability of the laws of nature, all point in the same direction, and seem difficult to explain on any other hypothesis. In this sense, the above case is very similar to the sort of arguments offered for scientific theories, such as the theory of evolution by descent with modification. As evolutionary biologist and geneticist Edward Dodson summarises the case for evolution,

> All [pieces of evidence] concur in *suggesting* evolution with varying degrees of cogency, but most can be explained on other bases, albeit with some damage to the law of parsimony. The strongest evidence for evolution is the concurrence of so many independent probabilities. That such different disciplines as biochemistry and comparative anatomy, genetics and biogeography should all point toward the same conclusion is very difficult to attribute to coincidence. (p. 68)

The case for design as I have presented it is of the same form and, I believe, will be found to be of comparable strength upon further research and elaboration.

NOTES

1. The fundamental parameters or constants of physics are the fundamental numbers (such as the gravitational constant G in Newton's law of gravity, $F=Gm_1m_2/r^2$) that help determine the basic structure of the universe. For a careful development of the fine-tuning argument, see my 'The Fine-tuning Design Argument', in Michael Murray (ed.), *Reason for the Hope Within*, Eerdmans Press, 1999. For some substantial treatments of the evidence of fine-tuning, see Leslie (1989), Davies (1982, 1984), Barrow and Tipler (1986), and Rozental (1988).

2. The cosmological constant is a fundamental physical parameter that can be thought of as corresponding to the energy density of empty space.

3. I define a 'universe' as any region of space–time that is disconnected from other regions in such a way that the parameters of physics in that region could differ significantly from the other regions.

4. For a critique of inflationary cosmology, see John Earman and Jesus Mosterin 1999. For an accessible introduction to inflationary cosmology, see Alan Guth 1997. For recent experimental confirmation of inflationary cosmology, see 'Cosmology from Maxima_1, Boomerang and COBE/DMR CMB Observations', July 2000, at the astrophysics website, http://arXiv.org/abs/astro_ph/0007333.

5. The sort of inflationary/superstring many-universe explanations of the fine-tuning discussed above have been suggested by a number of authors, such as Linde (1990a: p. 306; 1990b: p. 6) and Greene (1999: pp. 355–63). To date, however, no one has adequately verified or *developed* the physics of superstring theory or inflationary cosmology, let alone the combination of the two, so this scenario remains highly speculative.

6. In addition, the near-homogenous energy density requirement imposed by the particular form of Einstein's equation guarantees an almost smooth early universe which probably is essential for the development of life. (As Davies argues, even a small amount of turbulence in the early universe would most likely generate too much heat for life to develop (1980: pp. 156–61)). Further, however, the existence of quantum perturbations guarantees that the universe is not completely smooth, and hence allows for the formation of galaxies which are almost certainly dependent on slightly inhomogeneous distributions of mass-energy in the early universe (see Rozental 1988: pp. 48–53). Thus, the particular form of Einstein's equation, along with the principles of quantum mechanics, work together to allow the right amount of inhomogeneities to develop. If, for instance, Einstein's equation required an inhomogeneous energy density for inflation to occur, it is unlikely that inflation could produce any life-permitting universes.

7. For example, see S. Chandrasekhar (1987: chapter 4) for a discussion of this last criterion. Also see A. Zee (1986), for a very accessible account of the role that considerations of beauty have played in modern physics.

8. The gauge principle is highly technical and difficult to understand without much advanced training in physics, and thus beyond the scope of this paper to explain further.

9. For example, see Rom Harré and Edward Madden (1975).

10. See, for instance, N. Gisin 1989: especially pp. 364, 366.

11. The reason the existence of life is dependent on the weak force is that the weak force is crucially involved in the transmutation of elements, such as the formation of deuterium from protons in the sun. Thus it plays a key role in the sun's being a life-sustaining source of energy. For more information of the role the weak force plays in the existence of life, see Davies (1982), Rozental (1988), and Leslie (1989).

12. The argument that unguided naturalistic evolution cannot explain human consciousness or our capacity for theoretical reasoning has been advocated by both atheists and theists. See, for instance, Paul Davies (1993), Thomas Nagel (1997: pp. 130–43), and Alvin Plantinga (1993: ch. 12).

REFERENCES

Aitchison, Ian and Anthony Hey (1989), *Gauge Theories in Particle Physics: A Practical Introduction*, 2nd edn, Bristol, England: Adam Hilger Publishing Company.

Barrow, John and Frank Tipler (1986), *The Anthropic Cosmological Principle*, New York: Oxford University Press.

Behe, Michael (1996), *Darwin's Black Box: The Biochemical Challenge to Evolution*, New York: The Free Press.

Chandrasekhar, S. (1987), *Truth and Beauty: Aesthetics and Motivations in Science*, Chicago, IL: University of Chicago Press.

Darrigol, Oliver (1992), *From c-Numbers to q-Numbers: The Classical Analogy in the History of Quantum Theory*, Los Angeles, CA: University of California Press.

Davies, Paul (1980), *Other Worlds: a Portrait of Nature in Rebellion, Space, Superspace, and the Quantum Universe*, New York: Simon and Schuster.

—(1982), *The Accidental Universe*, Cambridge: Cambridge University Press.

—(1984), *Superforce: The Search for a Grand Unified Theory of Nature*, New York: Simon and Schuster.

Davies, P. C. W. (1993), 'The Intelligibility of Nature', in Robert John Russell, Nancey Murphy and C. J. Isham (eds), *Quantum Cosmology and the Laws of Nature: Scientific Perspectives on Divine Action*, 2nd edn, Berkeley, CA: The Center for Theology and the Natural Sciences Publications, pp. 149–64.

Dodson, Edward (1984), *The Phenomena of Man Revisited: A Biological Viewpoint on Teilhard de Chardin*, New York: Columbia University Press.

Earman, John and Jesus Mosterin (1999), 'A Critical Look at Inflationary Cosmology', *Philosophy of Science*, 66 (March), pp. 1–49.

Gisin, N. (1989), 'Stochastic Quantum Dynamics and Relativity', *Helvetica Physica Acta*, vol. 62, pp. 363–71.

Greene, Brian (1999), *The Elegant Universe: Superstrings, Hidden Dimensions, and the Quest for the Ultimate Theory*, New York: W. W. Norton and Company.

Guth, Alan (1997), *The Inflationary Universe: The Quest for a New Theory of Cosmic Origins*, New York: Helix Books.

—(2000), 'Inflation and Eternal Inflation', at the government astrophysics website, http://arXiv:astro-ph/0002156, February 2000.

Harré, Rom and Edward Madden (1975), *Causal Powers: A Theory of Natural Necessity*, Oxford: Basil Blackwell.

Hogarth, William (1753), *The Analysis of Beauty*.

Kaku, Michio (1999), *Introduction to Superstrings and M-Theory*, 2nd edn, New York: Springer-Verlag.

Leslie, John (1989), *Universes*, New York: Routledge.

Lewis, David (1986), *On the Plurality of Worlds*, New York: Basil Blackwell.

Linde, Andrei (1990a), *Particle Physics and Inflationary Cosmology*, translated by Marc Damashek, Longhorne, PA: Harwood Academic Publishers.

—(1990b), *Inflation and Quantum Cosmology*, New York: Academic Press.

Miller, Arthur (1996), *Insights of Genius: Imagery and Creativity in Science and Art*, New York: Copernicus.

Nagel, Thomas (1997), *The Last Word*, New York: Oxford University Press.

Peacock, John (1999), *Cosmological Physics*, Cambridge: Cambridge University Press.

Plantinga, Alvin (1993), *Warrant and Proper Function*, Oxford: Oxford University Press.

Polchinski, Joseph (1998), *String Theory*, vols 1 and 2, Cambridge Monographs in Mathematical Physics, Cambridge: Cambridge University Press.

Rozental, I. L. (1988), *Big Bang, Big Bounce: How Particles and Fields Drive Cosmic Evolution*, New York: Springer-Verlag.

Smolin, Lee (1997), *The Life of the Cosmos*, New York: Oxford University Press.

Steiner, Mark (1998), *The Applicability of Mathematics as a Philosophical Problem*, Cambridge, MA: Harvard University Press.

Tegmark, Max (1998), 'Is "the Theory of Everything" Merely the Ultimate Ensemble Theory?', *Annals of Physics*, 270, pp. 1–51.

Tyron, Edward (1973), 'Is the Universe a Vacuum Fluctuation?' *Nature*, vol. 246, pp. 396–7.

Weinberg, Steven (1992), *Dreams of a Final Theory*, New York: Vintage Books.

Zee, A. (1986), *Fearful Symmetry: The Search for Beauty in Modern Physics*, Princeton, NJ: Princeton University Press.

AXIOLOGICAL ARGUMENT

2.5

'THE VALUE DIMENSION OF THE COSMOS: A MORAL ARGUMENT'

Stuart C. Hackett

[. . .]

Selfhood, even on the human level, is not, of course, an isolated matter. It involves membership in what I will call the community of selves or persons, and this in turn engulfs all the relations in which persons appropriately stand in association with each other. In order to see what those relations themselves encompass, I propose to make what to some will seem an astounding assumption which I will expend little energy to defend as reasonable, since I firmly believe that it is an assumption which, for most of us, has but to be clearly understood in order to be accepted as virtually beyond serious question. That assumption is that persons, merely as such and just on account of their personhood, possess intrinsic value or worth. What that means is that persons are not to be construed as merely means or instruments of further ends, but rather as ends in themselves. Material objects, human experiences, and even particularized human activities (solving a problem, playing a game of tennis, eating lunch, or listening to a musical performance) may all appropriately be regarded as possessing primarily, if not exclusively, extrinsic worth—that is, they are all means or instruments to further ends. But this, I shall assume, is not the case with persons. Because of their incidental social relations to us, they may inevitably find a place among the means to the achievement of our own personal goals; but if that exhausts their significance

Stuart C. Hackett, 'The Value Dimension of the Cosmos: A Moral Argument', *Reconstruction of the Christian Revelation Claim* (Grand Rapids, MI: Baker Book House Company, 1984), pp. 111–17, 152–6.

for us, then our regard for them lacks the propriety which it can only possess if we construe them as ends in themselves, along with our own personhood as similarly possessing the same sort of intrinsic worth.

While I have referred to this thesis of intrinsic personal worth as an assumption, it is certainly not a groundless assumption, in my opinion. Persons, as we know them on the human level, characteristically pursue goals which are, at least to some extent and in cases where something of recognized importance is at stake, the objects of their implicit or even explicit choice. Furthermore, they make value judgments about the worth of these goals—indeed, it is difficult to see how responsible choice can proceed at all here unless some alternative goals are judged as more deserving of our acceptance than others, since not to judge in this way would be to judge irresponsibly by allowing our goals to be determined by accidental causes (such as emotional whims, public sentiment, or political pressure) which contribute nothing to their worth in a rationally grounded sense. Now if a person introspectively analyzes the grounds which in his most lucid moments he would regard as appropriate for making such choices and such judgments of worth with respect to his own goals, he will, I think, clearly see that those goals are alone deserving of rational choice which implement or seem likely to implement his own personal well-being as a self and/or the analogous personal well-being of other selves whose circumstances are likely to be affected by his choices. In other words, in aiming at significant goals, a person implicitly accepts his own intrinsic worth and that of other persons as the rational basis of the worth of his choice, so that those goals themselves are judged appropriate, in the final analysis, because they are extrinsic means for actualizing the intrinsic worth of persons. Action toward any end, then, if it is rational, presupposes one's own worth as an intrinsic end. Otherwise, the whole process of making choices becomes trivial and absurd in the most objectionable existential sense.

The same conclusion (namely, that persons possess intrinsic worth in a unique sense) can be illustratively discerned if we consider two further points: First, that any other proposed candidates for the status of intrinsic worth in this sense turn out to be patently ridiculous on analysis—the pursuit for example, of power, wealth, knowledge, pleasure, or even health—all these ends are so obviously instrumental means to the well-being of persons as selves that any supposition that they are themselves intrinsically valuable becomes virtually ludicrous, except to a person who is self-deceived or confused. It may be good to pursue any or all of these goals, but not unconditionally; yet the recognition and acceptance of the intrinsic worth of persons is, on the contrary, the unconditional goal which makes all these conditional goals plausible within limits. And it then follows from this insight that personal well-being does not consist in every individual's getting what he wants as a matter of idiosyncratic preference or hedonistic pleasure—for preferences and pleasures are themselves to be evaluated by their role in fulfilling, or deteriorating, the meaning of personhood.

Now if persons are in this way possessed of intrinsic worth, it is further reasonable to believe that the community of persons is a moral or ethical community in which the members have duties and obligations toward themselves and each other as intrinsic ends, so that, at least in regard to persons, the universe is pervaded by an objective moral order which ideally defines the network and principles of these duties, obligations, and responsibilities. I call this moral order objective because the morally binding character of these principles is not a function of individually and culturally variable states of feeling, preference, opinion, or response. The authority of such principles is not constituted by our opting for them in any sense; it is instead an authority that we recognize and discover as binding on us precisely because conformity to these principles implements and expresses the intrinsic worth of persons whether any individual person accepts this authority or not—so that, far from it being the case that we legislate these principles by opting for them, it is rather the case that our legislative options are themselves to be evaluated by these principles considered as objective. How could I sincerely respect the moral authority of a principle whose binding force lay solely in my idiosyncratic preference? Of course, the doctrine of moral objectivism I am contending for here has been subject to a long tradition of negative criticism; and in due season I shall have to grapple with the main core of this criticism. Suffice it to say for now that, if there were no intrinsic moral worth in the objective sense, then there would be no reasonable standard for evaluating preferences themselves. And, in fact, without any objective intrinsic worth, there could, by definition, be no extrinsic or instrumental ends, since there would be no terminating goals of which such intermediate ends would be the means. Or shall we judge as reasonable the supposition that each end is an extrinsic means to other ends which are extrinsic to still others and so on without logical limit? That would reduce the pursuit of any of these ends to absurdity. Just as a contingent entity depends ontologically on an ultimately necessary ground, so an extrinsic goal depends morally on an intrinsically valuable end. If everything is, valuationally considered, for the sake of something else and nothing is for its own sake, then, in the last analysis, nothing can reasonably be judged to be for the sake of something else either.

We are now in a position to analyze the implications of the concept of intrinsic personal worth and of the objective moral order of being which that concept involves. It is not difficult to see that if moral authority, as I have urged, is objective to any particular finite self, then the ultimate basis of that authority cannot reasonably be identified with that particular self or even with the whole community of finite moral selves, for that moral authority would retain its binding force even if any particular finite self had never existed. Granted that finite moral selves possess, as I have argued, intrinsic moral worth, this must in some sense be a derived, though genuinely intrinsic, moral worth. What that disclosure suggests is that there is an ultimate and unconditionally intrinsic moral worth that is independent of finite moral selves but yet participated in, or instantiated, by these finite selves. Clearly, this ultimate intrinsic worth could not attach to anything in the impersonal order of nature or to that order as a whole, since such impersonal entities, singly or collectively considered, have no more than an extrinsic or instrumental significance, not an intrinsic one in the sense we are here considering. It then follows that if there is an ultimate and absolute intrinsic good or worth, it must transcend both the impersonal natural order and also the realm of finite personal selves. But this Ultimate Good cannot, in that case, be less than personal in nature, so that the most plausible explanation of intrinsic moral worth is the supposition that it is ultimately an aspect of transcendent personal selfhood or the Absolute Mind which we have already confronted at the conclusion of earlier arguments. If that is the case, I could not possess derived intrinsic worth as a finite person unless God as Absolute Person possessed ultimate and unconditional intrinsic worth.

It will, however, be helpful to develop a frontal and summary answer to the following direct question. Granted that the Absolute Good, in the moral sense, must transcend the realm of contingent, finite entities and persons, why must that transcendent good itself be personal in the explicitly theistic sense? The argument just concluded provides a considerable part of the answer to this question, since it attempts to take intrinsic personal worth as the basic content of the good in the moral sense, and then attempts as well to argue that the derived intrinsic worth of finite persons must be grounded in the absolute and ultimate intrinsic worth of God as transcendent personal reality. There is also the further analogical argument that since every case of recognized moral obligation within actual human moral experience may plausibly be interpreted as involving the responsibility on the part of a person or persons to some person or persons as object of that responsibility—and since the transcendent good is the ultimate ground and object of all moral responsibility, even to finite persons—then it is reasonable to conclude that the transcendent good itself is, by this analogy with human moral experience, itself personal.

Again, if the transcendent objectivity of the good is accepted but its identity with Ultimate Personal Mind (God) is not acknowledged, then the good would have to be interpreted as some sort of abstract essence (Plato) or principle (Kant). But the transcendent status of essences in general is fully intelligible only if these essences are regarded as constitutive principles of Ultimate Personal Mind.[1] Hence, since the good is, by hypothesis in this case, at least a transcendent essence, its status also is fully intelligible only if the good is therefore such a constitutive principle of Ultimate Personal Mind or God, in the theistic sense.

It is important to be reminded, furthermore, that the ultimate intrinsic good must be wholly self-contained in its worth; and that would mean that the entire basis of its worth would be inherent in itself—for if it depended on anything else for its worth, its value would be extrinsic or instrumental in relation to that other entity and not really intrinsic at all in the posited sense. Now it clearly follows from this analysis that the transcendent good must be ontologically identical with self-existent being. But God is, by theistic definition, the only self-existent being. Indeed, a plurality of self-existent beings is rationally objectionable, since, if there were more than one such being, each would stand limited in its being by the others, and none would be truly self-existent and independent at all. Of course, my earlier arguments have concluded precisely the existence of God as a self-existent Being whose nature is that of personal intelligent mind and will. So, if the transcendent good is self-contained in its worth and therefore identical with God as self-existent Being, then the good must also be identical with God as Ultimate Personal Mind.

Perhaps the most notorious answer to the original question—why the ultimate good must be personal—is found in Immanuel Kant's principal argument for the reasonableness of belief in a personal God, although it should be made clear that Kant did not himself believe that the conclusion of this argument represented any genuine extension of speculative, theoretical knowledge in contrast to reasonable belief on moral grounds; and I myself, in expounding this argument, will not be bound by the details involved in Kant's way of posing it. If, as has been argued, the universe is an objective moral order, then within such an order moral obligation would imply, in part, both a responsibility, on the part of any moral agent, to make amends for immorality, and also an order of reality in which existence is both adapted to moral ends and at the same time involves effects proportionate to the state of one's moral conduct and character. More pointedly, reality would not be an objective moral order if there were not finally an ideal proportion between moral virtue and personal well-being, as well as between moral vice and personal ill-being. Moral agents, other circumstances being equal, should enjoy precisely that state of overall well-being which matches the developing or deteriorating state of their moral character. Nor is this to be taken hedonistically, as if well-being were to be wholly defined in terms of the accumulated experience of pleasures and pains. It is rather to be understood in terms of the circumstances and means essential to provide an individual with the possibility of both being and becoming a better person through the implementation of respect for the moral law and acceptance of whatever truth about reality the authority of that law, correctly understood, would imply. However, the possibility of achieving such a state of moral well-being involves such an arrangement of the circumstances of persons as to constitute in effect a purposively adapted order of the entire universe. But such an adaptive order is fully intelligible only as the complex effect of such a directive control over the universe as would require the operation of personal intelligent will—so that God, thus construed, is the only conceivable ground for the ideal proportion between moral virtue and well-being which an objective moral order of reality would require.

If, now, we put together in a single framework all of these considerations, in answer to the question why the transcendent good must be personal, they appear both singly and unitedly to provide a fully plausible basis for believing reasonably that God as Ultimate Personal Mind is the transcendent locus and even the reality of that essential or absolute goodness which alone makes moral objectivity fully conceivable. But I do not wish to leave this argument without responding to a very common rejoinder to the effect that if, as I have argued, morality is contingent in this way on the reality of God theistically construed, then it would follow that, if God did not exist, there would be no such thing as objective morality. And it might even follow as well that, if a person did not believe in the reality of God so understood, he would not for that reason be bound by moral law, since he would by hypothesis be deprived of any subjective basis for its authority. The last of these two suggestions is, I think, clearly mistaken, since a person is objectively bound by the truth and its implications for his existence, whether or not he accedes to that truth—so that believing even in the moral law (much less in God) is in no sense a necessary condition of its authority over the individual. Hence, the moral institution of life can clearly survive, even if without a fully adequate foundation in thought, whatever the idiosyncratic metaphysical beliefs of various individuals may turn out to be. And what of the suggestion that there would be no such thing as objective morality if God did not exist? That, I submit, is essentially correct—for if our previous arguments for the existence of God are essentially correct in their structure and conclusion, then it clearly follows that nothing at all would either exist or be conceivable; and, hence, objective morality, like all the rest of being and possibility, would, as it were, be swept away. It is, however, reasonably clear that this is not the case, else there would be nothing to discuss and certainly no one to discuss it. In fact, I think this last question (whether objective morality would cease if there were no God) boggles the mind of the average reflective individual only because (1) he does not fully understand the implications of the question, and (2) he confuses it with the earlier question as to whether *belief* in God is a necessary subjective condition of objective moral authority.

[. . .]

But, of course, as I long ago conceded (and now, at least, without reluctance), the persuasive thrust of even the most plausible speculative arguments of this sort is person-relative. An objectively rational basis does not always, or perhaps even characteristically, provide a subjectively effective motive for commitment, since such motives are as variable in their result as the complex of altered factors which constitute the unparalleled uniqueness of individual persons.

NOTE

1. Hackett presents a conceptualist argument for God's existence earlier in the book; cf. Smith's essay in this section 1 (Ed.).

NOÖLOGICAL ARGUMENT

2.6

'SEARLE'S BIOLOGICAL NATURALISM AND THE ARGUMENT FROM CONSCIOUSNESS'

J. P. Moreland

In the last few decades, there has been an avalanche of activity in the epistemology of science. I shall apply a set of insights from studies in the conditions of scientific theory acceptance to an assessment of John Searle's biological naturalism. More specifically, an important factor in scientific theory acceptance is whether or not a specific paradigm has a rival. If not, then certain epistemic activities, for example, labeling some phenomenon as basic for which only a description and not an explanation is needed, may be quite adequate not to impede the theory in question. But the adequacy of those same activities can change dramatically if a sufficient rival position is present. Now Searle's philosophy of mind is a certain sort of naturalist theory and its claim to superiority is one that countenances only rival naturalist theories. What I hope to show is that irrespective of how his biological naturalism compares to rival naturalist theories of mind, the crucial arguments supporting his position are defective in light of what is sometimes called the theistic argument from consciousness (AC). To make my case, I shall (1) underscore briefly two important issues in theory acceptance that clarify the impact of a rival paradigm on theory adjudication; (2) formulate a general statement of AC; and (3) critique the salient features of Searle's biological naturalism in light of AC.

Before I proceed, it is important to state the central features of contemporary scientific naturalism.[1] Roughly, scientific naturalism is the view that

J. P. Moreland, 'Searle's Biological Naturalism and the Argument from Consciousness', *Faith and Philosophy*, 15, 1 (January 1998), pp. 68–91.

the spatio-temporal universe of entities studied by the physical sciences is all there is. Scientific naturalism includes (1) different aspects of a naturalist epistemic attitude (e.g., a rejection of so-called first philosophy along with an acceptance of either weak or strong scientism); (2) an etiological account of how all entities whatsoever have come to be, constituted by an event causal story (especially the atomic theory of matter and evolutionary biology) described in natural scientific terms; and (3) a general ontology in which the only entities allowed are those that bear a relevant similarity to those thought to characterize a completed form of physics.

The ordering of these three ingredients is important. Frequently, the naturalist epistemic attitude serves as justification for the naturalist etiology which, in turn, helps to justify the naturalist's ontological commitment. Moreover, naturalism seems to require a coherence among what is postulated in these three different areas of the naturalistic turn. For example, there should be a coherence among third person scientific ways of knowing, a physical, evolutionary account of how our sensory and cognitive processes came to be, and an ontological analysis of those processes themselves. Any entities that are taken to exist should bear a relevant similarity to entities that characterize our best physical theories, their coming-to-be should be intelligible in light of the naturalist causal story, and they should be knowable by scientific means.

Though Searle would disagree, most naturalists embrace strict physicalism because it seems to be implied by the constraints placed on philosophy of mind by the coherence of these three aspects of naturalism. William Lyons's statement is representative of most naturalists on this point: "[Physicalism] seem[s] to be in tune with the scientific materialism of the twentieth century because it [is] a harmonic of the general theme that all there is in the universe is matter and energy and motion and that humans are a product of the evolution of species just as much as buffaloes and beavers are. Evolution is a seamless garment with no holes wherein souls might be inserted from above."[2] Interestingly, Lyons's reference to souls being "inserted from above" appears to be a veiled reference to the explanatory power of theism given the existence of the mental. Let us begin in earnest, then, and probe these issues more fully.

Two Issues in Scientific Theory Acceptance

There are two issues involved in adjudicating between rival scientific theories relevant to the debate about consciousness. The first is whether to take some phenomenon as **basic** or as something to be explained in terms of more basic phenomena. For example, attempts to explain uniform inertial motion are disallowed in Newtonian mechanics because such motion is basic on this view, but an Aristotelian had to explain how or why a particular body exhibited uniform inertial motion. Thus, what may be basic to one theory is derived in another.

Issue two is the **naturalness** of a postulated entity in light of the overall theory of which it is a part. A postulated entity should be at home with other entities in the theory. Some entity (particular thing, process, property, or relation) e is natural for a theory T just in case it bears a relevant similarity to other entities that populate T in e's category of formal ontology.[3] More work needs to be done on making precise what I mean by "e's category of formal ontology." But I think that I can make this tolerably clear, at least for my purposes, by noting that if e is in a category such as substance, force, property, event, relation, or cause, e should bear a relevant similarity to other entities of T in that category. This is a formal definition and the material content given to it will depend on the theory in question. Moreover, given rivals R and S, the postulation of e in R is ad hoc and question-begging against advocates of S if e bears a relevant similarity to the appropriate entities in S, and in this sense is "at home" in S, but fails to bear this relevant similarity to the appropriate entities in R.

Naturalness is relevant to assessing rivals by providing a criterion for identifying question-begging arguments or ad hoc adjustments by advocates of a rival theory. Naturalness can also be related to basicality by providing a means of deciding the relative merits of accepting theory R which depicts phenomenon e as basic, versus embracing S which takes e to be explainable in more basic terms. If e is natural in S but not in R, it will be difficult for advocates of R to justify the bald assertion that e is basic in R and that all proponents of R need to do is describe e and correlate it with other phenomena in R as opposed to explaining e. Such a claim by advocates of R will be even more problematic if S provides an explanation for e.

THE ARGUMENT FROM CONSCIOUSNESS

Theists such as Robert Adams[4] and Richard Swinburne[5] have advanced an argument from consciousness for the existence of God which can be presented as follows:

(1) Mental events are genuine non-physical mental entities that exist.
(2) Specific mental event types are regularly correlated with specific physical event types.
(3) There is an explanation for these correlations.
(4) Personal explanation is different from natural scientific explanation.
(5) The explanation for these correlations is either a personal or natural scientific explanation.
(6) The explanation is not a natural scientific one.
(7) Therefore, the explanation is a personal one.
(8) If the explanation is personal, then it is theistic.
(9) Therefore, the explanation is theistic.

In my view, premises (3) and (6) are the most crucial ones for the success of AC since they are the premises most likely to come under naturalist attack. Let us set them aside for the moment. We are assuming the truth of premise (1) and with a slight modification, Searle's version of biological naturalism entails it. There have been a number of variants on (1) that have been cited as problems which science cannot explain but which can be given a theistic personal explanation: (a) the existence of mental properties themselves;[6] (b) the fact that mental properties have come to be exemplified in the spatio-temporal world; (c) the nature of the relation, for example, causal or supervenient, between mental and physical entities;[7] (d) the fact that certain particular mental events are correlated with certain particular physical events; (e) the fact that the correlations mentioned in d are regular; (f) the existence of libertarian freedom and the type of agency necessary for it;[8] (g) the aptness of our noetic equipment to serve as truth gatherers in our noetic environment;[9] and (h) the evolutionary advantage of having mental states as opposed to the evolution of organisms with direct stimulus-response mechanisms that have no mental intermediaries.[10]

What about premise (2)? Physicalist treatments of the mental, multiple realization, and the existence/irreducibility of laws in the special sciences are irrelevant here because we are granting the existence of genuine mental events constituted by mental properties. Thus, physicalist attempts to avoid the reduction of psychological to physical laws by denying such laws in the first place do not count against (2).[11] For example, both the functionalist account of the mental offered by Fodor and the anomalous monism of Davidson deny the existence of general exceptionless psychological or psycho-physical laws. But both positions depict the mental as being realized by the physical and, moreover, are most naturally associated with token physicalism when it comes to an ontological analysis of individual mental events.[12] But if mental and physical events are what the argument from consciousness takes them to be, then it seems reasonable for individual events of both kinds to be instances of general types of events that could in principle be correlated.

Premise (2) would be accepted by an advocate of supervenient physicalism since there are two desiderata for this position: non-reductive physicalism plus the dependency of supervenient entities on the physical. If one accepts premise (1) but denies (2), then the mental becomes too autonomous for naturalism. An example of such a view is weak dualism according to which the mind is a Humean bundle of mental states that neither belong to nor depend on a specific body but which at best are more or less generally associated with specific physical states. It would seem, then, that given (1), (2) is uncontroversial for a naturalist like Searle.

The main justification for premise (4) is the difference between libertarian and event causal theories of agency. J. L. Mackie rejected (4), claiming that personal explanation is simply a sub-class of event causal explanation. Moreover, divine action, as it figures into Swinburne's account of personal explanation, involves the direct fulfillment of an intention on the part of God. But, argued Mackie, since human action is a type of efficient event causality between the relevant prior mental state, for example, an intending, and a fulfillment which runs through and depends on a number of intermediate events which are part of a complex physical mechanism, there is a disanalogy between human intentional acts in which intentions are fulfilled indirectly and those of a god in which, supposedly, intentions are directly fulfilled. On Mackie's view, this disanalogy makes alleged divine action and the relevant sort of personal explanation mysterious and antecedently improbable. Thus, (4) is false and, even if it is true, it makes theistic personal explanation less, not more, probable.

Is Mackie's argument successful against (4)? I don't think so. For one thing, *pace* Mackie, it is not at all clear that libertarian agency and the associated form of personal explanation are not to be preferred as accounts of human action to event causal accounts. Obviously, we cannot delve into this issue here, but if libertarian agency is correct, then Mackie is wrong in his claim that (4) is false.

Secondly, a defence of (4) may only require a **concept** of libertarian agency and personal explanation, even if we grant a causal theory of action for human acts. If we have such a clear conception, then even if human acts do not fall under it, under the right circumstances, it could be argued that a form of explanation clearly available to us is now to be employed. What those circumstances are and whether they obtain are more centrally related to premises (3) and (6) of AC and not (4). But since Mackie criticized (4) on the grounds that if true it would make theistic explanation antecedently improbable, I want briefly to say something about what could justify the claim that a personal explanation of the libertarian sort should actually be used.

There have been a number of attempts to state necessary and sufficient conditions for personal action in event causal terms with John Bishop's account being the most sophisticated to date. But Bishop admits that our concept of agency is different from and irreducible to event causality and is, in fact, libertarian.[13] For Bishop, the pervasiveness and power of the libertarian conception of agency places the burden of proof on the defender of a causal theory of action. Bishop claims that his own causal theory works only for worlds relevantly similar to ours in being naturalistic worlds. He does not offer an analysis of action true across all possible worlds because he admits that our concept of action is libertarian and there are worlds in which it obtains. His justification of this minimal task is a prior assumption of naturalism, but such an assumption is clearly question-begging against AC. So if we have a clear, powerful, and prima facie justified libertarian conception of agency, Mackie's point about the mysteriousness and antecedent improbability of anything answering to this concept is seriously overstated. Since my purpose is to bring AC to bear on criticizing Searle's biological naturalism, it is important to note that Searle agrees with Bishop that our commonsense concept of freedom is libertarian, even though he also says that "our conception of physical reality simply does not allow for radical [libertarian] freedom."[14]

Now, if we grant the non-physicality of mental states, then a causal theory of action for human acts will boil down to the claim that person P does some act e (raising one's hand to vote) if and only if some event b (the hand going up) which instantiates the type of state intrinsic to e-ing is caused by the appropriate mental state in the appropriate way. Note carefully that, regardless of the details of such an account, it will amount to nothing more than a causal correlation between certain physical states and the relevant mental events. According to premises (2) and (3) of AC, these correlations need and have an explanation. A causal theory of action will not do for the origin, regularity, and precise nature of these correlations, since these are what constitute a causal theory of action in the first place. If a causal theory of action presupposes mental states, then it will be impotent to explain the existence, regularity, and precise nature of those mental states themselves unless, of course, a divine causal theory of action is used. If this is so, and if we possess a clear concept of libertarian agency and personal explanation as Searle admits, then there is no good reason why a theist cannot use this type of explanation in this case.

However, when it comes to defending AC, I think one could deny a libertarian view of agency and personal explanation altogether and still defend (4). After all, some Christian theists, for example certain Calvinists, employ a causal theory for divine action. One could argue that there is some difference between normal physical event causality in physics and a causal theory of personal action. At the very least, the latter utilizes appropriately related mental states as parts of causal chains. Since (4) simply notes that there is a distinguishable difference between personal and natural scientific explanation, the alternative we are now considering may be all that AC needs to rebut Mackie. Bishop claims that for a naturalist any causal theory of action must be combined with a strict physicalist theory of mental states.[15] I agree. I also reject a causal theory of action. But setting this aside, since we are assuming the reality of mental states, Bishop's physicalist rendition of the causal theory of action simply does not apply here and a suitable statement of the nature and role of mental states in a causal theory could be all that is needed to distinguish personal from natural scientific explanation according to (4).

There are two sides to (5): Is personal explanation different from natural scientific explanation and are there other explanations for the facts mentioned in (1) and (2) besides these two? We have already dealt with the first question in conjunction with (4). Regarding question two, I think it is safe to say that, given the current intellectual climate, a personal theistic or a naturalistic explanation would exhaust at least the live, if not the logical, options. It is true that Thomas Nagel suggested that pan-psychism may be necessary to explain the mental.[16] But it is widely recognized that pan-psychism has serious problems in its own right, for example, explaining what an incipient or proto-mental entity is or how the type of unity that appears to characterize the self could emerge from a mere system of parts standing together in various causal and spatio-temporal relations.[17] Moreover, pan-psychism is arguably less reasonable than theism on other grounds, though I cannot pursue this point here. Further, it is not clear that pan-psychism is an **explanation** of the phenomena in question. As Geoffrey Madell notes, "the sense that the mental and the physical are just inexplicably and gratuitously slapped together is hardly allayed by adopting . . . a pan-psychist . . . view of the mind, for [it does not] have an explanation to offer as to why or how mental properties cohere with physical."[18] Interestingly, Nagel's own argument suggestive of pan-psychism turns on a failure to consider a theistic explanation of the mental, coupled with an admission of the inadequacy of a natural scientific explanation:

> One unsettling consequence of such a theory [of mental/physical duality] is that it appears to lead to a form of panpsychism—since the mental properties of the complex organism must result from some properties of its basic components, suitably combined; and these cannot be merely physical properties or else in combination they will yield nothing but other physical properties. If any two hundred pound chunk of the universe contains the material needed to construct a person, and if we deny both psychophysical reductionism and a radical form of emergence, then everything, reduced to its elements, must have proto-mental properties.[19]

Actually, Nagel's statement is a near precis of AC. He accepts (1) and (2) in his denial of reductionism, he accepts (3) in his rejection of radical emergence which, I take it, would amount to the claim that the emergence of the mental from the physical is a brute case of something coming from nothing without explanation, and his whole argument rests on the acceptance of (6) as an implicit premise. Elsewhere, Nagel expresses a view about freedom and personal explanation very similar to Searle's, namely, that libertarian freedom is what we take ourselves to have, yet we cannot have it, given naturalism and the external, scientific point of view.[20] Apparently, Nagel would accept some version of (4). That leaves (5) and, so far as I know, Nagel does not argue for the relative merits of theism versus pan-psychism. At the very least, we may be able to say this: If the other premises of AC are accepted, then scientific naturalism is false and there is an intramural debate left between theists and pan-psychists.

(7) follows from previous steps in the argument and asserts the adequacy of a personal explanation for the facts expressed in (1) and (2). One may reject (7) (or [5]) on the grounds that personal explanation, theistic or otherwise, doesn't give us any real understanding of an explanandum, especially one like (1) and (2). Sometimes this objection assumes that an explanation must cite a mechanism before it can count as adequate. My response to this problem

centers on the difference between libertarian and event causality and their associated forms of explanation.

Advocates of libertarian agency employ a form of personal explanation that stands in contrast to a covering law model. To understand this form of explanation, we need to look first at the difference between a basic and non-basic action. Often more than one thing is accomplished in a single exercise of agency. Some actions are done by doing others, for example, I perform the act of going to the store to get bread by getting into my car and by driving to the store. Basic actions are fundamental to the performance of all others but are not done by doing something else. In general, S's F-ing is basic if there is no other non-equivalent action description 'S's Y-ing' such that it is true that S F-ed by Y-ing. My endeavoring to move my arm to get my keys is a basic action. A non-basic action contains basic actions as parts which serve as means for realizing the ultimate intention of that non-basic action. To fulfill a non-basic intention, I must form an action plan: a certain ordered set of basic actions that I take to be an effective means of accomplishing my non-basic intention. The action plan that constitutes going to the store to get bread includes the acts of getting my keys and walking to my car.[21]

In my view, an action is something contained wholly within the boundaries of the agent. Thus, strictly speaking, the results of an action are not proper parts of that action. A basic result of an action is an intended effect brought about immediately by the action. If I successfully endeavor to move my finger, the basic result is the moving of the finger. Non-basic results are more remote intended effects caused by basic results or chains of basic results plus more remote intended effects. The firing of the gun or the killing of Lincoln are respective illustrations of these types of non-basic results.

With this in mind, a personal explanation (divine or otherwise) of some basic result R brought about intentionally by person P where this bringing about of R is a basic action A will cite the *intention* I of P that R occur and the basic *power* B that P exercised to bring about R. P, I, and B provide a personal explanation of R: agent P brought about R by exercising power B in order to realize intention I as an irreducibly teleological goal. To illustrate, suppose we are trying to explain why Wesson simply moved his finger (R). We could explain this by saying that Wesson (P) performed an act of endeavoring to move his finger (A) in that he exercised his ability to move (or will to move) his finger (B) intending to move the finger (I). If Wesson's moving his finger was an expression of an intent to move a finger to fire a gun to kill Smith, then we can explain the non-basic results (the firing of the gun and the killing of Smith) by saying that Wesson (P) performed an act of killing Smith (I_3) by endeavoring to move his finger (A) intentionally (I_1) by exercising his power to do so (B), intending thereby to fire the gun (I_2) in order to kill Smith. An explanation of the results of a non-basic action (like going to the store to get bread) will include a description of the action plan.[22]

By way of application, the adequacy of a personal explanation does not consist in offering a mechanism, but rather, in correctly citing the relevant person, his intentions, the basic power exercised, and in some cases, offering a description of the relevant action plan. Thus, if we have some model of God and His intentions for creating a world suitable for human persons (from revelation or otherwise), we can make reference to God, His intentions for creating a world with persons with mental states regularly correlated with their environment, and the adequacy of His power to bring about the basic results captured in (1) and (2).

Premise (8) seems fairly uncontroversial. To be sure, Humean style arguments about the type, size, and number of deities involved could be raised at this point, but again, these issues would be intramural theistic problems of small comfort to someone like Searle committed to naturalism.[23] And if we take live options only, then it seems fair to limit our alternatives in (5) to theistic or naturalistic. If that is acceptable, at least for the purposes of arguing against Searle and other naturalists like him, then (8) should not be objectionable.

SEARLE'S BIOLOGICAL NATURALISM

I hope I have said enough to show that the crucial premises of AC in dispute are (3) and (6). Rather than consider these directly, it will be more profitable to look at them in light of Searle's biological naturalism. Searle has some pretty harsh things to say about the last fifty years or so of work in the philosophy of mind.[24] Specifically, he says that the field has contained numerous assertions that are obviously false and absurd and has cycled neurotically through various positions precisely because of the dominance of strict physicalism as the only live option for a naturalist. Searle's statement of the reason for this neurotic behavior is revealing:

> How is it that so many philosophers and cognitive scientists can say so many things that, to me at least, seem obviously false? . . . I believe one of the unstated assumptions behind the current batch of views is that they represent the only scientifically acceptable alternatives to the anti scientism that went with traditional dualism, the belief in the immortality of the soul, spiritualism, and so on. Acceptance of the current views is motivated not so much by an independent conviction of their truth as by a terror of what are apparently the only alternatives. That is, the choice we are tacitly presented with is between a 'scientific' approach, as represented by one or another of the current versions of 'materialism,' and an 'unscientific' approach, as represented by Cartesianism or some other traditional religious conception of the mind.[25]

In other words, philosophy of mind has been dominated by scientific naturalism for fifty years and scientific naturalists have advanced different versions of strict physicalism, however implausible they may be in light of what is obviously known by us about consciousness, because strict physicalism was seen as a crucial implication of taking the naturalistic turn. For these naturalists, if one abandons strict physicalism one has rejected a scientific naturalist approach to the mind/body problem and opened himself up to the intrusion of religious concepts and arguments about the mental.

Searle offers his analysis of the mind as a naturalistic account because, he says, no one in the modern world can deny "the obvious facts of physics—for example, that the world is made up entirely of physical particles in fields of force . . ."[26] An acceptance of naturalism is constituted by an acknowledgment of the atomic theory of matter and evolutionary biology both of which allow for micro to micro or micro to macro causal explanations, but not macro to micro ones.[27] According to Searle, dualism in any form is widely rejected because it is correctly considered to be inconsistent with the scientific world-view.[28] He also claims that because people educated in the contemporary scientific world-view know how the world works, the existence of God is no longer a serious candidate for truth.[29] But a commitment to naturalism and a concomitant rejection of dualism have blinded people to the point that they feel compelled to reject what is obvious to experience, namely, the obvious nature of consciousness and intentionality.

Searle's own solution to the mind/body problem is biological naturalism: consciousness, intentionality, and mental states in general, are emergent biological states and processes that supervene upon a suitably structured, functioning brain. Brain processes cause mental processes which are not reducible to the former. Consciousness is just an ordinary, that is, physical feature of the brain and, as such, is merely an ordinary feature of the natural world.[30] Despite the frequent assertions by a number of philosophers that Searle is a property dualist, he denies the charge and seems puzzled by it.[31] However, in my view, Searle is indeed a property dualist and an epiphenomenalist one at that, though he also denies the latter charge as well.[32] To show this, let us consider the charge of property dualism first. Searle's characterizations of neurophysiological and mental states are exactly those of the property dualist who insists that mental and physical properties are to be characterized in a certain way and that they are two, different types of properties. In light of Searle's descriptions of the mental and physical, it is obvious why most philosophers charge him with property dualism and the burden of proof is on him to show why he is not.

Searle's response to this problem is twofold.[33] First, he seems to think that a property dualist must accept the entire Cartesian metaphysics. Second, he says that dualists accept a false dichotomistic vocabulary in which something is either physical or mental but cannot be both. So biological naturalism is to be distinguished from property dualism in that the former does not include the entire Cartesian apparatus and it rejects this dichotomistic vocabulary. Now if this is how Searle distinguishes biological naturalism from property dualism, then his response is inadequate. For one thing, it is absurd to claim that one must accept the entire Cartesian metaphysics to be a property dualist. Thomas Aquinas was a certain sort of property (and substance) dualist, but obviously he did not accept the Cartesian apparatus.[34] Swinburne defends Cartesian property and substance dualism without accepting Descartes' entire metaphysical scheme.[35] Moreover, Searle's own view has a dichotomistic vocabulary in which he distinguishes normal physical (e.g., neurophysiological) properties from emergent biological "physical" (i.e., mental) properties. So he has simply replaced one dualism with another one.

But perhaps there is a different and deeper distinction between (at least) Cartesian property dualism and biological naturalism for Searle. For the property dualist mental and physical properties are so different that it is inconceivable that one could emerge from the other by natural processes. However, for the biological naturalist, biological physical properties are normal physical properties in this sense: they are like solidity, liquidity, or the properties of digestion or other higher-level properties that can emerge by means of natural processes. I don't wish to comment further on this claim here except to say that Searle's employment of it to distinguish biological naturalism from property dualism amounts to nothing more than a mere assertion combined with a few undeveloped examples (e.g., liquidity) that are supposed to be good analogies to emergent mental states. But this assertion is simply question-begging in light of AC and, as I will show later, it amounts to an abandonment of naturalism. At the very least, one should stop and ask why, if Searle's solution to the mind/body problem is at once obvious and not at all problematic for naturalists, a field of philosophy dominated by naturalists for fifty years has missed this obvious solution?

Searle's response to this question involves a specification of why it is that emergent mental states have no deep implications. We will look at this issue shortly, but for now I want to show that Searle's biological naturalism implies an epiphenomenalist view of emergent mental states in spite of his denial that this is so. Searle's position is epiphenomenalist for at least three reasons. First, Searle takes scientific naturalism to imply that there is no macro to micro causation and, on this point, most naturalists would agree. Jaegwon Kim says "a physicalist must, it seems, accept some form of the principle that the physical domain is causally closed—that if a physical phenomenon is causally explainable, it must have an explanation within the physical domain."[36] He goes on to say that "Causal powers and reality go hand in hand. To render mental events causally impotent is as good as banishing them from our ontology."[37] For these reasons, Kim claims that a naturalist should be a strict and not a supervenient physicalist because the latter implies a problematic epiphenomenal view of the mental. David Papineau has endorsed the same point.[38]

Second, Searle distinguishes two types of emergent features. Emergent$_1$ features are caused by micro-level entities and do not exercise independent causality. Emergent$_2$ features are caused by micro-level entities and **are** capable of exercising independent causality once they exist. Searle rejects the existence of emergent$_2$ features because, among other things, they would violate the transitivity of causality. Since he holds that conscious states are emergent$_1$, it is hard to see how those states could have causal efficacy.

Third, Searle holds to the causal reduction of the mental. In causal reduction, the existence and "powers" of the emergent but causally reduced entity are explained by the causal powers of the reducing, base entities. It is hard to see how he could hold this and avoid epiphenomenalism. I conclude then, that despite protests to the contrary, Searle's biological naturalism is a certain type of epiphenomenalist property dualism.

Why are there no deep metaphysical implications that follow from Searle's biological naturalism? Why is it that biological naturalism does not represent a rejection of scientific naturalism which, in turn, opens the door for religious concepts about and arguments from the mental? Searle's answer to this question is developed in three steps. First, he cites several examples of emergence (e.g., liquidity) that he takes to be unproblematic for a naturalist and argues by analogy that the emergent properties of consciousness are likewise unproblematic.

Step two is a formulation of two reasons why, appearances to the contrary notwithstanding, consciousness isn't a problem for naturalists. First, Searle says that naturalists are troubled by the existence of irreducible mental entities because they are misled into thinking that the following is a coherent question that needs an answer: "How do unconscious bits of matter produce consciousness?"[39] Many "find it difficult, if not impossible to accept the idea that the real world, the world described by physics and chemistry and biology, contains an ineliminably subjective element. How could such a thing be? How can we possibly get a coherent world picture if the world contains these mysterious conscious entities?"[40]

For Searle, the question of how matter produces consciousness is simply a question about how the brain works to produce mental states even though individual neurons in the brain are not conscious. This question is easily answered in terms of specific though largely unknown neurobiological features of the brain. However, Searle thinks that many are misled into thinking this question is about something deeper and more puzzling. Setting consciousness aside, in all other cases of entities arranged in a part/whole hierarchy of systems, we can picture or image how emergent features arise because these systems and all their features are objective phenomena. Our problem is that we try to image how consciousness could arise from a system of unconscious bits of matter in the same way, but this is not possible because consciousness itself is not imageable and we can't get at it through a visual metaphor. Once we give up trying to imagine consciousness, any deep puzzlement about the emergence of consciousness, given naturalism, evaporates and the only question left is one about how the brain produces mental states.

There is another reason Searle offers as to why the emergence of consciousness has no deep metaphysical significance.[41] In standard cases of reduction, for example, heat and color, an ontological reduction (color is nothing but a wavelength) is based on a causal reduction (color is caused by a wavelength). In these cases we can distinguish the appearance of heat and color from the reality, place the former in consciousness, leave the latter in the objective world, and go on to define the phenomenon itself in terms of its causes. We can do this because our interests are in the reality and not the appearance. The ontological reduction of heat to its causes leaves the appearance of heat the same. However, when it comes to mental states like pain, even though an ontological reduction cannot be found, there is a similar causal pattern, for example, pain is caused by such and such brain states. So why do we regard heat as ontologically reducible but not pain? In the case of heat, we are interested in the physical causes and not the subjective appearances, but with pain it is the subjective appearance itself that interests us. If we wanted to, we could reduce pain to such and such physical processes and go on to talk about pain appearances analogous to the heat case. However, in the case of consciousness, the reality is the appearance. Since the point of reductions is to distinguish and separate reality from appearance in order to focus on underlying causes by definitionally identifying the reality with those causes, the point of a reduction for consciousness is missing since it is the appearance itself that is the reality of interest. Therefore, the irreducibility of consciousness has no deep metaphysical consequences and is simply a result of the pattern of reduction that expresses our pragmatic interests.

In step three, Searle claims that an adequate scientific explanation of mental emergence is a set of very detailed, even lawlike correlations between specific mental and physical states.[42] Searle rejects an argument by Thomas Nagel which denies that mere correlations amount to a scientific explanation. In terms of AC, Nagel would accept premise (6) and deny that Searle's correlations count as scientific explanations. Searle rejects (6) and believes such correlations count as adequate scientific explanations. Nagel claims that in other cases of emergence like liquidity, a scientific explanation doesn't just tell us what happens, it explains why liquidity must emerge when a collection of water molecules gather under certain circumstances. In this case, scientific explanation offers physical causal necessity: given certain states of affairs, it is causally necessary that liquidity emerge and it is inconceivable that it not supervene. But, argues Nagel, no such necessity and no answer to a why question is given by a mere correlation between mental states and physical states in the brain.

Searle's response to Nagel is threefold.[43] First, he says that some explanations in science do not exhibit the type of causal necessity Nagel requires, for example, the inverse square law is an account of gravity that does not show why bodies have to have gravitational attraction. This response is question-begging against Nagel because the inverse square law is merely a description of what happens and not an explanation of why it happens. Interestingly, Newton himself took the inverse square law to be a mere description of how gravity works but explained the nature of gravity itself (due to his views about action at a distance, the nature of spirit, and the mechanical nature of corpuscularian causation by contact) in terms of the activity of the Spirit of God. The point is not that Newton was right, but that he distinguished a description of gravity from an explanation of what it is and his explanation cannot be rebutted by citing the inverse square law. Rather, one needs a better explanatory model of gravity. So Searle's own example actually works against him.

Moreover, even if we grant that covering law explanations are, in fact, explanations in some sense, they are clearly different from explanations that offer a model of why things must take place given the model and its mechanisms. Since the argument from consciousness assumes the correlations and offers an answer to the why question, Searle's solution here is not really a rival explanation, but merely a claim that such correlations are basic, brute facts that just need to be listed. In light of what we have already seen, there are at least two further difficulties with Searle's claim.

First, given AC and the nature of theory adjudication among rivals, it is question-begging and ad hoc for Searle to assert that these correlations are basic since the correlations themselves, along with the entities and properties they relate are natural and bear a relevant similarity to other entities, proper- ties, and relations in theism (e.g., God as spirit who can create and causally interact with matter), but are unnatural given the naturalist epistemology, grand story, and ontology. In this regard, Terence Horgan says that "in any metaphysical framework that deserves labels like 'materialism', 'naturalism', or 'physicalism', supervenience facts must be explainable rather than being *sui generis*."[44] And D. M. Armstrong goes so far as to admit that "I suppose that if the principles involved [in analyzing the single all-embracing spatio-tem- poral system which is reality] were completely different from the current principles of physics, in particular if they involved appeal to mental entities, such as purposes, we might then count the analysis as a falsification of Naturalism."[45]

Horgan and Armstrong say this precisely because mental entities, the supervenience relation, or a causal correlation between mental and physical entities simply are not natural given a consistent naturalist paradigm. Their reality constitutes a falsification of naturalism for Horgan and Armstrong and, given AC, they provide evidence for theism. It is question-begging and ad hoc simply to adjust naturalism as does Searle, given the presence of AC as a rival explanation.

Second, Swinburne's version of AC points out that a correlation can be either an accidental generalization or a genuine law (which exhibits at least physical necessity) and we distinguish the two in that laws are (but accidental correlations are not) non-circular correlations that fit naturally into theories that (1) are simple, (2) have broad explanatory power, and (3) fit with background knowledge from other, closely related scientific theories about the world. By "fit" Swinburne means the degree of naturalness of the correlation and entities correlated in light of both the broader theory of which the correlation is a part and background knowledge. Now Searle admits that mental phenomena are absolutely unique compared to all other entities in that they "have a special feature not possessed by other natural phenomena, namely, subjectivity."[46] Unfortunately, it is precisely this radical uniqueness that makes mental phenomena unnatural for a naturalist world-view and which prevents Searle from distinguishing an accidental correlation from a genuine law of nature regarding mental and physical correlations.

So much, then, for Searle's first response to Nagel. His second response is that the apparent necessity of some scientific causal explanations may just be a function of our finding some explanation so convincing that we cannot conceive of certain phenomena behaving differently. Medievals may have thought modern explanations of the emergence of liquidity mysterious and causally contingent. Similarly, our belief that specific mind/brain correlations are causally contingent may simply be due to our ignorance of the brain.

It is hard to see what is supposed to follow from Searle's point here. Just because one can be mistaken in using conceivability as a test for causal necessity, it doesn't follow that conceivability is never a good test for it. Only a case-by-case study can, in principle, decide the appropriateness of its employment. Now when it comes to things like liquidity or solidity, Nagel is right. Precisely because of what we know about matter, we cannot conceive of certain states of affairs obtaining and these properties being absent. That Medievals would not be so convinced is beside the point since they were ignorant of the relevant atomic theory. If they possessed the correct theory, their intuitions would be as are ours. But when it comes to the mental and physical, they are such different entities, and the mental is so unnatural given the rest of the naturalist ontology, that there is no clearly conceivable necessity about their connection. And this judgment is based, not on what we don't know about the two types of states, but on what we do know. Moreover, a more detailed correlation in the future will not change the situation one bit. There is no non-circular or non-ad-hoc way to formulate such a correlation and we will merely be left with a more detailed dictionary of correlations that will leave intact the same type of problem of causal necessity true of less detailed correlations. Our current lack of belief in such a causal necessity is not due to ignorance of more and more details of the very thing that lacks the necessity in the first place. Rather, it is based on a clear understanding of the nature of the mental and physical, an understanding that Searle himself accepts.

This is why it will not do for naturalists to claim that they are not committed to anything ultimately or utterly brute (like the divine will), just to there being something unexplained at any given time but which can be explained through deeper investigation. No scientific advance in our knowledge of the details of mental/physical correlations will render either the existence of mental entities or their regular correlation with physical ones anything other than utterly brute for the naturalist.

But Searle had another line of defence against Nagel: Even if we grant Nagel's point about the lack of causal necessity in the mental/physical case, nothing follows from this. Why? Because in the water and liquidity case, we can picture the relation between the two in such a way that causal necessity is easily a part of that picture. But since consciousness is not pictureable, we are not able to imagine the same sort of causal necessity. Yet that does not mean it is not there.

Here Searle simply applies his earlier point that, given naturalism, our puzzlement about the emergence of consciousness from unconscious bits of matter is due to our attempt to picture consciousness. Now it seems to me that this point is just false and egregiously so. I, for one, have no temptation to try to picture consciousness. And other naturalists have put their finger on the real difficulty about the emergence of consciousness. D. M. Armstrong states that

> It is not a particularly difficult notion that, when the nervous system reaches a certain level of complexity, it should develop new properties. Nor would there be anything particularly difficult in the notion that when the nervous system reaches a certain level of complexity it should affect something that was already in existence in a new way. But it is a quite different matter to hold that the nervous system should have the power to create something else [mental entities], of a quite different nature from itself, and create it out of no materials.[47]

Along similar lines, Paul Churchland says,

> The important point about the standard evolutionary story is that the human species and all of its features are the wholly physical outcome of a purely physical process . . . If this is the correct account of our origins, then there seems neither need, nor room, to fit any non-physical substances or properties into our theoretical account of ourselves. We are creatures of matter. And we should learn to live with that fact.[48]

Churchland puts his finger on two reasons the naturalist should opt for strict physicalism—there is neither need nor room for anything else. Regarding need, I take it he means that everything we need in order to explain the origin and workings of human beings can be supplied by physicalist causal explanations. Regarding room, entities do not come into existence ex nihilo nor do radically different kinds of entities emerge from purely physical components placed in some sort of complex arrangement. This is what Nagel was getting at when he rejected radical emergence. What comes from the physical by means of physical processes will also be physical.

Searle is simply wrong about the problem being the imageability of consciousness. The problem here for naturalism is ontological, not epistemological as most naturalists have seen. What is curious about Searle's reduction of an ontological problem to an epistemological one is that his entire work on biological naturalism is replete with criticisms of other naturalists for doing this very thing in other areas of the philosophy of mind. Could it be that Searle's own misidentification of the ontological problem here is "neurotic" in just the sense that he applies to his naturalist colleagues: if one takes the emergence of consciousness as an ontological problem, then biological naturalism will, in fact, give cause for introducing religious concepts and explanations for the mental as expressed in AC?

I conclude, therefore, that Nagel is right and Searle is wrong: premise (6) of AC is correct and Searle's correlations are not examples of scientific explanation which count against (6). But what about premise (3)? Why isn't it reasonable to take mental entities and their regular correlations with physical entities to be utterly brute natural facts for which there is no explanation? The answer is provided by the arguments just mentioned about why Searle's correlations are not really scientific explanations. Mental entities are not natural or at home in the naturalist epistemology, etiology, and ontology. Given theism and AC as a rival explanatory paradigm, and given the fact that mental entities and correlations are natural for theism, it is question-begging and ad hoc simply to announce that these entities and correlations are natural entities.

Searle could reply that biological naturalism is not question-begging because we already have reason to believe that naturalism is superior to theism prior to our study of the nature of the mental. The only support Searle gives for this claim, apart from a few sociological musings about what it means to be a modern person, is that it is an obvious fact of physics that the world consists **entirely** of physical particles moving in fields of force. It should be clear, however, that this claim is itself question-begging and clearly false. When there is a statement in a physics text about the world in its entirety, it is important to note that this is not a statement of physics. It is a philosophical assertion that does not express any obvious fact of physics. Moreover, it is a question-begging assertion by naturalists prior to a consideration of the evidence and arguments for theism, including AC. If Searle denies this, then he should inform advocates of AC of exactly what obvious fact of physics they deny in their employment of the argument.

Most naturalists have seen this and have opted for strict physicalism in order to avoid abandoning naturalism and legitimizing the introduction of religious concepts and explanations into the picture. It may be "neurotic" to deny consciousness, as Searle points out. But it is far from "neurotic" to be driven to do so in terms of a prior commitment to naturalism, and AC makes clear why this is the case.

But perhaps there is a naturalist rejoinder at this point in the form of a *tu quoque* against theists and AC. J. L. Mackie advanced just such an argument.[49] According to Mackie, theists like John Locke admitted that God could superadd consciousness to systems of matter fitly disposed and, therefore, as a result of Divine intervention, matter may give rise to consciousness after all. Thus, Locke leaves open the possibility that a mere material being might be conscious given theism. Mackie then asks this question: "But if some material structures could be conscious, how can we know **a priori** that material structures cannot **of themselves give rise to** consciousness?"[50] He concludes that this Lockean admission opens the door for the naturalist to assert the emergence of consciousness from fitly disposed matter as a brute fact.

In my view, Mackie's argument carries no force against AC because a main part of AC consists in the recognition that mental/physical correlations exist, they are not explicable within the constraints of scientific naturalism, and they require a personal theistic explanation if they are to be explained at all. In this sense, the idea that, in one way or another, God could "superadd" thinking or other mental states to matter is required for AC to go through.[51] However, as I have tried to show, it does not follow from this "Lockean admission" that it is a brute, naturalistic fact that material structures of themselves can give rise to consciousness or that adequate naturalistic explanations can be given for this. Indeed, Locke himself constructed detailed arguments to show that mental states like thinkings are not within the natural powers of matter nor could they arise from material structures without an original Mind to create and attach those mental states to matter.[52] Locke's view that God could superadd thinking to a material substance just as easily as to a spiritual substance was a conclusion he drew from the omnipotence of God along with the claim that "thinking matter" is not a contradiction and, thus, possible for God to bring about. I am not defending Locke's way of arguing that God could superadd thinking to matter. In fact, I do not think it is correct as he formulated it but, clearly, Locke would not have believed that Mackie's naturalistic conclusion can justifiably be drawn from his own (Locke's) admission of the possibility of Divine omnipotence adding a faculty of thought to a material structure.

Mackie cannot simply assert that material structures have the power to give rise to consciousness and also claim to be operating with a naturalistic depiction of matter. According to David Papineau, matter with emergent mental potentiality is not the sort of matter countenanced by naturalists. This is why, when Papineau attempts to characterize the physical in terms of a future ideal physics, he places clear boundaries on the types of changes allowed by naturalism for developments in physical theory. According to Papineau, the naturalist will admit that future physics may change some features of what we believe about matter, but in light of a naturalist commitment and the past few hundred years of development in physics, future physics will not need to be supplemented by psychological or mental categories.[53]

Given theism, we cannot say a priori just what capacities or states God will correlate with specific physical states. But given naturalism, and the commitment to the role of physics in naturalism, along with a view of the physical that is required by physics, we can say that mental potentiality is just not part of matter. Thus, it is question-begging and ad hoc against AC for Mackie to adjust naturalism to allow that material structures of themselves can give rise to consciousness.

There is one final issue in Searle's defence of biological naturalism that needs to be addressed, viz, his claim that the emergence of consciousness fits a broad pattern of emergence, for example, cases of liquidity, solidity, digestion, and, therefore, since the latter present no problem for naturalism, neither does the former. I offer three responses. First, if we take liquidity or solidity to be the degree of rigidity, flexibility, or viscosity of a collection of particles, then these properties are not good analogies to consciousness because they turn out to be nothing more than group behavior of particles placed in a relatively compressed, stable, ordered structure for solids or a more viscous, less compact arrangement for liquids. So there is no problem about emergence here since we can easily understand how liquidity and solidity are related to groups of material particles as they are depicted in physical theory.

Second, when we are dealing with genuinely emergent properties that are categorially different from what physical theory takes to characterize subvenient entities, I think that it could be argued that the naturalist has the same difficulty here as with the emergence of consciousness. Recall Searle's point about the pragmatics of reduction: we reduce heat to its causes because we happen to be interested in the objective causes and not the subjective appearances, but in cases of, for example, pain, we are interested in the painful appearance itself, so we do not reduce pain to its causes. In my view, the decision to reduce heat to its causes is not primarily a scientific matter nor is it a matter of our pragmatic interest. I think it has been a function of two things. First, if we take heat, color, liquidity, or solidity to be identical to the qualia we experience in certain circumstances (e.g., heat is identical to warmth, red is a color not a wavelength, liquidity is wetness), then an ontological puzzle arises analogous to the one about the emergence of mental states: How could warmth emerge in a physical structure as a result of increased atomic agitation? Second, there was a way of avoiding this question in light of a widely held Lockean view of secondary qualities and sense perception. We can locate these secondary qualities in consciousness and identify them as appearances of the real objective phenomena, viz, the objective causes for our experiences of secondary qualities. John Yolton has shown that during late seventeenth and early eighteenth century debates about materialism, immaterialist philosophers (e.g., Ralph Cudworth) regularly argued against the idea that mental entities could emerge from properly structured matter.[54] A standard rebuttal to this claim was that light and heat were very different from matter but could be generated in material bodies given the right conditions. So mind could likewise emerge. Cudworth and others responded by asserting that light, heat, and other secondary qualities were not in material bodies, but were sensations in minds and, thus, the problem does not arise as to how they could arise in a material structure devoid of such qualities prior to the right conditions obtaining. It is clear from this debate at the very beginning of the emergence of modern materialism that one philosophical motive for locating secondary qualities in consciousness was to avoid a straightforward metaphysical problem: *ex nihilo nihil fit*.

If I am right about this, then the ontological puzzle is really the driving force behind what Searle calls normal naturalist cases of emergence. The problem is that these cases are not natural any more than the emergence of consciousness and that is why they were located in consciousness. For example, both secondary qualities like redness or warmth and painfulness are dissimilar to the properties that constitute an ideal physics. Jaegwon Kim has argued that in Nagel-type reductions, the relevant bridge laws should be taken as biconditionals and not as conditionals, because we need materially equivalent correlations between entities (or terms) in the reduced and base theories in order to assert identities between the entities in question.[55] Moreover, says Kim, the identity of reduced and base entities is preferable to mere correlations because the latter raise potentially embarrassing questions as to why such precise correlations arise in the first place. Kim's point is not confined to mental and physical correlations. All a naturalist can do with them (if we keep these so-called secondary qualities or other categorially distinct emergent qualities in the external world) is to offer a detailed correlation to describe regular relations between physical structures and emergent entities. No amount of knowledge whatever of subvenient entities would take us one inch toward predicting or picturing why these particular entities regularly emerge in such and such circumstances and not others. In discussions of emergence over a century ago, it was precisely their unpredictability from knowledge of subvenient entities that was identified as the hallmark of an emergent property. In more modern terms, it is the inability to either image or understand why warmth emerges regularly here and not somewhere else, or why it emerges at all given our knowledge of molecular agitation. Note carefully that Searle himself seems to accept pictureability as a necessary condition for the acceptance of a claim that one entity emerges from another in the "normal" cases, but pictureability is no more available for heat (warmth) emerging from matter than it is for mental states.[56] Nagel's conceivability test applies here just as it does for mental states.

However, even if I am wrong about this, there is a third response that can be given to Searle. There are two features of mental states that make their emergence disanalogous to, say, the properties of digestion. First, mental states are so peculiar and different from all other entities in the world, that it is far more difficult to see how they could emerge from physical states than it is for the so-called normal cases. Second, mental states are quite natural in a theistic world-view and have a higher prior probability given theism over against naturalism even if we agree that, say, the emergence of the properties of digestion is equally natural and probable on both world hypotheses.

In my view, these two features of mental states make them more analogous to value properties than to characteristics of digestion. Mackie argued that the supervenience of moral properties would constitute a refutation of naturalism and evidence for theism: "Moral properties constitute so odd a cluster of properties and relations that they are most unlikely to have arisen in the ordinary course of events without an all-powerful god to create them."[57] Presumably, Mackie's reasons for this claim involve some of the points I have just made above: moral properties have the two features that make them natural for theism but unnatural for naturalism. No matter how far future physics advances our understanding of matter, it will not make the emergence of moral properties the least bit more likely, more pictureable, or more natural.[58] And the same claim could easily be made for mental properties even if features of digestion are granted equally natural for theism and naturalism.

Searle himself admits that of all the entities in the world, mental states are absolutely unique and radically different from all the others. And as we saw earlier, Armstrong is willing to accept that more ordinary physical or biological properties could emerge when the nervous system reaches a certain level of complexity. But he could not accept the natural emergence of mental states from matter because mental states are of "a quite different nature" from states accepted by naturalists. The jump from physical states to mental states was too far for Armstrong's naturalism to allow, so he adopted strict physicalism as the only acceptable naturalist solution. I admit that the problem with my third response to Searle is that it requires one to weigh the difference between acceptable and unacceptable cases of emergence. But to the degree that mental entities are taken as radically unique and very different from all other types of physical or even biological entities, then to that degree the analogy between the emergence of mental states and other cases of emergence is weakened. And to that degree, the emergence of the mental would be radical as Nagel calls it or unnatural as Adams and Swinburne claim. After all, naturalists have not spent the last fifty years trying to eliminate or reduce solidity or the properties of digestion as they have mental states. This is because the latter are rightly seen as a threat to naturalism even if the former are not.

In any case, I have tried to show that AC is an important rival to Searle's biological naturalism and its presence changes the epistemic status of the latter. As B. F. Skinner noted just before his death, "Evolutionary theorists have suggested that 'conscious intelligence' is an evolved trait, but they have never shown how a nonphysical variation could arise to be selected by physical contingencies of survival."[59] If that is so, then it may well be that the reality of mental entities provides evidence for theism and counts against naturalism.[60]

NOTES

1. Cf. Alex Rosenberg, "A Field Guide to Recent Species of Naturalism," *British Journal for the Philosophy of Science* 47 (1996): 1–29.
2. William Lyons, "Introduction," in *Modern Philosophy of Mind*, ed. by William Lyons (London: Everyman, 1995), p. lv. In context, Lyons remark is specifically about the identity thesis, but he clearly intends it to cover physicalism in general.
3. Actually, there is a slightly different and more detailed characterization of "natural for a theory T" that could be used: e is natural for a theory T just in case either e is a central, core entity of T or e does not bear a relevant dissimilarity to the central, core entities of T in e's category of formal ontology. And entity e is more central or core to T than entity f, just in case e is more deeply ingressed in T than f. I shall continue to use the simpler description since there is no relevant difference between them for our purposes. One further point: I have characterized naturalness in terms of some entity e, but, with appropriate adjustments, naturalness could also be cashed out in terms of the vocabulary, methodology, or type of explanation that constitutes a theory.
4. See Robert Adams, "Flavors, Colors, and God," reprinted in *Contemporary Perspectives on Religious Epistemology*, ed. by R. Douglas Geivett, Brendan Sweetman (N.Y.: Oxford University Press, 1992), pp. 225–40.
5. See Richard Swinburne, *The Existence of God* (Oxford: Clarendon, 1979), chapter 9; *The Evolution of the Soul* (Oxford: Clarendon Press, 1986), pp. 183–96; *Is There a God?* (Oxford: Oxford University Press, 1996), pp. 69–94; "The Origin of Consciousness," in *Cosmic Beginnings and Human Ends*, ed. by Clifford N. Matthews and Roy Abraham Varghese (Chicago and La Salle, Illinois: Open Court, 1995), pp. 355–78.
6. Cf. D. M. Armstrong, "Naturalism: Materialism and First Philosophy," *Philosophia* 8 (1978): 262.
7. Cf. Terence Horgan, "Nonreductive Materialism and the Explanatory Autonomy of Psychology," in *Naturalism*, ed. by Steven J. Wagner and Richard Warner (Notre Dame: University of Notre Dame Press, 1993), pp. 313–14.
8. John Bishop, *Natural Agency* (Cambridge: Cambridge University Press, 1989), 36–44, 74–6. Selmer Bringsjord rejects Swinburne's version of AC because it focuses on the regular correlations of specific types of mental and physical events. But Bringsjord thinks that a version of AC that starts with agent causation is likely to be successful. See "Swinburne's Argument from Consciousness," *Philosophy of Religion* 19 (1986): 140–1.
9. See Alvin Plantinga, *Warrant and Proper Function* (N.Y.: Oxford University Press, 1993), pp. 194–237.
10. Swinburne, *Evolution of the Soul*, pp. 191–5.
11. Howard Robinson has argued persuasively that attempts by Peacocke and Davidson to embrace physicalism but avoid reductionism actually fail because of a confusion about the nature of reduction. See Howard Robinson, *Matter and Sense* (Cambridge: Cambridge University Press, 1982), pp. 22–34. Such accounts do avoid analytic reduction, claims Robinson, but they entail a topic neutral reduction of persons to complexly organized physical entities combined with a token physical analysis of mental events. For an argument that shows that the holism of the mental does not entail a denial of strict psycho-physical laws, see John Foster, "A Defence of Dualism," in *The Case for Dualism*, ed. by John R. Smythies and John Beloff (Charlottesville: University of Virginia Press, 1989), pp. 15–17.

12. For a careful naturalist defence of this claim, see David Papineau, *Philosophical Naturalism* (Cambridge: Cambridge University Press, 1993), pp. 9–51, especially pp. 36–43.
13. Bishop, *Natural Agency*, pp. 58, 72, 69, 95–6, 103–4, 110–11, 114, 126–7, 140–1, 144. Bishop also admits that a causal analysis of agency requires a physicalist view of the mental if the account is to satisfy the constraints that are part of a naturalist theory of agency. See pp. 8, 43, 103.
14. John Searle, *Minds, Brains, and Science* (Cambridge, Mass.: Harvard University Press, 1984), p. 98.
15. Bishop, *Natural Agency*, pp. 8, 43, 103.
16. Thomas Nagel, *The View from Nowhere* (N. Y.: Oxford, University Press, 1986), pp. 49–53.
17. For a critique of pan-psychism in the process of defending AC, see Stephen R. L. Clark, *From Athens to Jerusalem* (Oxford: Clarendon Press, 1984), pp. 121–57.
18. Geoffrey Madell, *Mind and Materialism* (Edinburgh: Edinburgh University Press, 1988), p. 3.
19. Nagel, ibid., p. 49.
20. Ibid., pp. 110–37.
21. There is some debate about whether each of these basic actions requires its own intending. Richard Swinburne argues that in performing actions which take a long time (writing a chapter), we do not exercise a separate volition for each intentional action (e.g., willing to write the first sentence) that is part of the long-term act. Rather, we just intend to bring about the long-term effect by bringing about a generally conceived series of events and the body unconsciously selects a particular routine to accomplish that effect. See Swinburne, *Evolution of the Soul*, pp. 94–5. I leave the matter open except to note that to the degree that a non-basic action contains sub-acts of a discontinuous nature (picking up keys, getting into a car versus a series of steps in taking an hour-long walk), then it is more likely that sub-intentions are required to characterize adequately those sub-acts.
22. Thus, we see that there are at least three kinds of intentional actions: basic actions with a basic intent (simply intentionally moving my finger), basic actions with non-basic intents (ultimate intents that have other intents as means, e.g. intentionally squeezing my finger to fire a gun to kill Smith), and non-basic actions (those that contain sub-acts—sub endeavorings and intending—as parts, e.g., going to the store to buy bread).
23. Cf. Michael Martin, *Atheism: A Philosophical Justification* (Philadelphia: Temple University Press, 1990), p. 220.
24. John Searle, *The Rediscovery of the Mind* (Cambridge, Mass.: MIT Press, 1992), chapters 1 and 2. Cf. Tyler Burge, "Philosophy of Language and Mind: 1950–1990," *The Philosophical Review* 101 (January 1992): 3–51, especially 29–51.
25. Searle, *Rediscovery of the Mind*, pp. 3–4. Cf. p. 31.
26. Ibid., p. 28.
27. Ibid., pp. 85–91.
28. Ibid., pp. 3, 13–16.
29. Ibid., pp. 90–1.
30. Ibid., pp. xii, 13–19, 25–8, 85–93.
31. Ibid., pp. 13, 16.
32. Ibid., pp. 13, 126.
33. Ibid., pp. 2–4, 13–16.
34. Cf. J. P. Moreland, "Humanness, Personhood, and the Right to Die," *Faith and Philosophy* 12 (January 1995): 95–112; J. P. Moreland and Stan Wallace, "Aquinas vs. Descartes and Locke on the Human Person and End-of-Life Ethics," *International Philosophical Quarterly* 35 (September 1995): 319–30.
35. Cf. Swinburne, *Evolution of the Soul*, especially chapter 8.
36. Jaegwon Kim, "Mental Causation and Two Conceptions of Mental Properties,"

unpublished paper delivered at the American Philosophical Association Eastern Division Meeting, Atlanta, Georgia, December 27–30, 1993, p. 21.

37. Ibid., p. 23.

38. Papineau, *Philosophical Naturalism*, pp. 9–32.

39. Searle, *Rediscovery of the Mind*, p. 55. Cf. pp. 32, 56–7, where Searle considers and rejects as incoherent a closely related question formulated in terms of intelligence and intelligent behavior and not consciousness. If intelligence and intelligent behavior are interpreted from a third-person perspective in behavioristic terms (e.g., as regular and predictable behavior), then it is false that bits of matter are not intelligent. If first-person subjective criteria are formulated for intelligence, then the question reduces to the one asked in terms of consciousness. So this is the correct question to ask on Searle's view.

40. Ibid., p. 95.

41. Ibid., pp. 118–24.

42. Ibid., pp. 89, 100–4.

43. Ibid., pp. 101–4.

44. Horgan, "Nonreductive materialism," pp. 313–14.

45. Armstrong, "Naturalism": 262.

46. Searle, *Rediscovery of the Mind*, p. 93.

47. D. M. Armstrong, *A Materialist Theory of Mind* (London: Routledge & Kegan Paul, 1968), p. 30.

48. Paul Churchland, *Matter and Consciousness* (Cambridge, Mass.: MIT Press, 1984), p. 21. Cf. Arthur Peacocke and Grant Gillett, eds., *Persons and Personality* (Oxford: Basil Blackwell, 1987), p. 55.

49. J. L. Mackie, *The Miracle of Theism* (Oxford: Clarendon Press, 1982), pp. 120–1. See also, Clifford Williams, "Christian Materialism and the Parity Thesis," *International Journal for Philosophy of Religion* 39 (February 1996): 1–14.

50. Mackie, *Miracle of Theism*, p. 121.

51. Locke's point about God superadding thinking to matter can be understood as an argument against substance dualism. So understood, Locke is not claiming that thinkings themselves are material or that God is not required to explain their correlation with material states. Rather, he is asserting that there is a parity between material and spiritual substances as fitting candidates to contain the faculty of thought. For an exposition of this understanding of Locke, see Williams, "Christian Materialism and the Parity Thesis." I do not agree with this rendition of the parity thesis—it seems to require a topic-neutral account of consciousness and thinking and it fails to take into account the fact that the immateriality of the self is known both by first-person acquaintance and by reasoning to the precise type of immateriality that constitutes the essence of a substantial soul from the immaterial effects that express its capacities—but, fortunately, this rendition is not relevant to AC per se since property/event dualism is all AC needs to make its case.

52. John Locke, *An Essay Concerning Human Understanding*, 4, 10, 10–17 (pp. 313–19 of the 1959 Dover edition).

53. Papineau, *Philosophical Naturalism*, pp. 29–32.

54. John W. Yolton, *Thinking Matter: Materialism in Eighteenth-Century Britain* (Minneapolis: University of Minnesota Press, 1983), pp. 4–13, especially 6–7.

55. Jaegwon Kim, *Philosophy of Mind* (Boulder, Colorado: Westview Press, 1996), pp. 214–15. See G. K. Chesterton's claim that the regular correlation between diverse entities in the world is magic that requires a Magician to explain it. See *Orthodoxy* (John Lane Company, 1908; repr., San Francisco: Ignatius Press, 1950), chapter five.

56. Searle, *Rediscovery of the Mind*, pp. 102–3.

57. Mackie, *Miracle of Theism* (Oxford: Clarendon Press, 1982), p. 115. Cf. J. P. Moreland and Kai Nielsen, *Does God Exist?* (Buffalo, N.Y.: Prometheus, 1993), chapters 8–10. Mackie found it easy to deny the objectivity of moral properties and

opted for a form of moral subjectivism. But he could not bring himself to deny the mental nature of qualia. So he adopted a solution for qualia similar to Searle's. I shall not look at Mackie's case because Searle's is more forceful and better developed. Moreover, part of Mackie's case rests on his critique of AC and I have already discussed some of his major points of critique.

58. It could be argued that the supervenience of moral properties does not imply theism and, thus, they are of no help to AC. I offer two responses to this claim. First, the supervenience of such properties (as depicted by Mackie) would at least entail some form of ethical non-naturalism, e.g., Platonism, and this would count against naturalism. Given that non-theistic and theistic versions of non-naturalism are the remaining live options, each would receive some degree of confirmation from the falsity of a rival paradigm (naturalism), and the debate would be moved to what I take to be an intramural discussion between the other paradigms. Elsewhere I have argued that theistic non-naturalism gets the better of this dialog. See Moreland and Nielsen, *Does God Exist?*, p. 123. Second, in the reference just cited, I use the existence of moral properties as part of an inference to the best explanation, so even if their existence does not *imply* theism, they may still lend support to it, especially vis-à-vis naturalism.

59. B. F. Skinner, "Can Psychology Be a Science of Mind?" *American Psychologist* 45 (November 1990): 1207. Jaegwon Kim has claimed that substance dualism is to be rejected as deeply puzzling and mysterious but that property dualism is more acceptable because it does not face this difficulty. See his *Philosophy of Mind*, pp. 211–12. If the thesis of this article is correct, Kim is wrong about this.

60. I would like to thank William Lane Craig, Greg Ganssle, William Wainwright, and an anonymous referee for their helpful comments on an earlier draft of this paper.

ONTOLOGICAL ARGUMENT
2.7

'THE ONTOLOGICAL ARGUMENT'

Alvin Plantinga

Although the Ontological Argument for the existence of God looks, at first sight, like a verbal sleight of hand or a piece of word magic, it has fascinated philosophers ever since St. Anselm had the good fortune to formulate it. Nearly every major philosopher from that time to this has had his say about it. Such comment, furthermore, has been by no means exclusively adverse; the argument has a long and illustrious line of defenders extending to the present and at the moment including, among others, Professors Charles Hartshorne and Norman Malcolm. What accounts for this fascination? First, many of the most knotty and difficult problems in philosophy meet in this argument: is existence a property? Are existential propositions ever necessarily true? Are existential propositions about what they seem to be about? How are we to understand negative existentials? Are there, in any respectable sense of 'are', some objects that do not exist? If so, do they have any properties? Can they be compared with things that do exist? These issues and a score of others arise in connection with St. Anselm's argument.

Second: we noted that the argument has about it an air of egregious unsoundness or perhaps even trumpery and deceit; yet it is profoundly difficult to say exactly where it goes wrong. The fact, I think, is that no philosopher has ever given a really convincing, conclusive, and *general* refutation—one relevant to all or most of the myriad forms the argument

Alvin Plantinga, 'The Ontological Argument', from 'God and Necessity', *The Nature of Necessity* (Oxford: Clarendon Press, 1974), pp. 196–221.

takes.[1] Too often philosophers are content to remark that Kant refuted St. Anselm by showing that "existence is not a predicate" and that "one cannot build bridges from the conceptual realm to the real world". But Kant never specified a sense of "is a predicate" such that, in that sense, it is clear both that existence is *not* a predicate and that St. Anselm's argument requires it to be one.[2] Nor are the mere claims that no existential propositions are necessary (or the above comment about bridge building) impressive as refutations of St. Anselm—after all, he claims to have an *argument* for the necessity of at least one existential proposition. I shall take a fresh look at this argument—from the perspective of possible worlds. These ideas permit a much clearer understanding of the argument; and they may enable us to see (as I shall claim) that at least one version of the argument is sound.

[. . .]

Of course there are many versions of the argument. (And I wish to remark parenthetically that the existence of many importantly different versions makes most of the 'refutations' one finds in textbooks look pretty silly.) Professors Charles Hartshorne[3] and Norman Malcolm,[4] for example, find two quite distinct versions of the argument in St. Anselm's writings. In the first of these St. Anselm holds that *existence* is a perfection; he holds some version of the view that a being is greater in a world in which it exists than it is in a world in which it does not. But in the second version, say Malcolm and Hartshorne, it is *necessary* existence that is said to be a perfection. What does *that* mean? Take a world like α and consider two things, A and B that exist in it, where A exists not only in α but in every other world as well while B exists in some but not all worlds. According to the doctrine under consideration, A is so far forth greater in α than B is. Of course B may have some other properties—properties that make for greatness—that A lacks. It may be that on balance it is B that is greater in α. For example, the number 7 exists necessarily and Socrates does not; but it would be peculiar indeed to conclude that the number seven is therefore greater, in α, than Socrates is. The point is only that necessary existence is a great-making quality—it is one of the qualities that must be considered in comparing a pair of beings with respect to greatness. But then it is plausible to suppose that the maximum degree of greatness includes necessary existence—that is to say, a possible being has the maximum degree of greatness in a given world only if it exists in that world and furthermore exists in every other world as well. The argument may accordingly be stated as follows:

(32). There is a world W in which there exists a being with maximal greatness,

and

(33). A being has maximal greatness in a world only if it exists in every world.

W, therefore, includes the existence of a being with maximal greatness who exists in every world. So there is an essence E, exemplified in W, that entails the property *exists in every world*. So it is impossible in W that E not be exemplified. But what is impossible does not vary from world to world. Hence E is exemplified, and necessarily exemplified, in *this* world. So there is a greatest possible being, and it exists necessarily.

What this argument shows is that if it is even *possible* that God, so conceived, exists, then it is true that he does, and, indeed, necessarily true that he does. As it is stated, however, there is one fairly impressive flaw: even if an essence entailing *is maximally great in* W is exemplified, it does not so far follow that this essence entails *is maximally great in* α. For all we have shown so far, this being might be at a maximum in some world W, but be pretty insignificant in α, our world. So the argument does not show that there is a being that enjoys maximal greatness in fact; it shows at most that there is a being that in some world or other has maximal greatness.

Is there a way to remove this flaw? Perhaps. Why, after all, should we think that necessary existence is a perfection or great-making quality? Because the greatness of a being in a world W depends not merely upon the qualities it has in W; what it is like in other worlds is also relevant. In the course of an attempt to *disprove* God's existence J. N. Findlay puts this point as follows:

> Not only is it contrary to the demands and claims inherent in religious attitudes that their object should *exist* "accidentally"; it is also contrary to these demands that it should *possess its various excellences* in some merely adventitious manner. It would be quite unsatisfactory from the religious stand point, if an object merely *happened* to be wise, good, powerful, and so forth, even to a superlative degree . . . And so we are led on irresistibly, by the demands inherent in religious reverence, to hold that an adequate object of our worship must possess its various excellence in some necessary manner.[5]

I think there is sense in what Findlay says. His point is that the greatness of a being in a world W does not depend merely upon its qualities and attributes in W; what it is like in other worlds is also to the point. Those who worship God do not think of him as a being that happens to be of surpassing excellence in *this* world but who in some other worlds is powerless or uninformed or of dubious moral character. We might make a distinction here between *greatness* and *excellence*; we might say that the *excellence* of a being in a given world W depends only upon its (non world-indexed) properties in W, while its greatness in W depends not merely upon its excellence in W, but also upon its excellence in other worlds. The limiting degree of greatness, therefore, would be enjoyed in a given world W only by a being who had maximal excellence in W and in every other possible world as well. And now perhaps we do not need the supposition that necessary existence is a perfection; for a being has no properties at all and *a fortiori* no excellent-making properties in a world in which it does not exist. So existence and necessary existence are not themselves perfections, but necessary conditions of perfection.

We may state this argument more fully as follows.

(34). The property *has maximal greatness* entails[6] the property *has maximal excellence in every possible world.*

(35). *Maximal excellence* entails *omniscience, omnipotence,* and *moral perfection.*

(36). *Maximal greatness* is possibly exemplified.

But for any property *P*, if *P* is possibly exemplified, then there is a world *W* and an essence *E* such that *E* is exemplified in *W*, and *E* entails *has P in W*. So

(37). There is a world *W** and an essence *E** such that *E** is exemplified in *W** and *E** entails *has maximal greatness in W**.

If *W** had been actual, therefore, *E** would have been exemplified by an object that had maximal greatness and hence (by (34)) had maximal excellence in every possible world. So if *W** had been actual, *E** would have been exemplified by a being that for any world *W* had the property *has maximal excellence in W*. But every world-indexed property of an object is entailed by its essence. Hence if *W** had been actual, *E** would have entailed, for every world *W*, the property *has maximal excellence in W*; hence it would have entailed the property *has maximal excellence in every possible world*. That is, if *W** had been actual, the proposition

(38). For any object *x*, if *x* exemplifies *E**, then *x* exemplifies the property *has maximal excellence in every possible world*

would have been necessarily true. But what is necessarily true does not vary from world to world. Hence (38) is necessary in every world and is therefore necessary. So

(39). *E** entails the property *has maximal excellence in every possible world.*

Now a being has a property in a world *W* only if it exists in that world. So *E** entails the property *exist in every possible world*. *E** is exemplified in *W**; hence if *W** had been actual, *E** would have been exemplified by something that existed and exemplified it in every possible world. Hence

(40). If *W** had been actual, it would have been impossible that *E** fail to be exemplified.

But again, what is impossible does not vary from world to world; hence it is *in fact* impossible that E^* fail to be exemplified; so E^* is exemplified; so

(41). There exists a being that has maximal excellence in every world.

That is, there actually exists a being that is omniscient, omnipotent, and morally perfect; and that exists and has these properties in every possible world. This being is God.

A similar but simpler version of the argument could go as follows. Let us say that *unsurpassable greatness* is equivalent to *maximal excellence in every possible world*. Then

(42). There is a possible world in which unsurpassable greatness is exemplified.

(43). The proposition *a thing has unsurpassable greatness if and only if it has maximal excellence in every possible world* is necessarily true.

(44). The proposition *whatever has maximal excellence is omnipotent, omniscient, and morally perfect* is necessarily true.

Now here we should notice the following interesting fact about properties. Some, like *is a human person*, are instantiated in some but not all worlds. On the other hand, however, there are such properties as *is a person in every world*. By the principle that what is necessary or impossible does not vary from world to world, this property cannot be instantiated in some worlds but not in others. Either it is instantiated in *every* world or it is not instantiated at all. Using the term "universal property", we might say that

D$_2$ P is a universal property if and only if P is instantiated in *every* world or in *no* world.

But clearly the property *possesses unsurpassable greatness* is universal in this sense, for this property is equivalent to the property of having maximal excellence in every world; since the latter is universal, so is the former.

From (42) and (43), therefore, it follows that

(45). *Possesses unsurpassable greatness* is instantiated in every world.

But if so, it is instantiated in this world; hence there actually exists a being who is omnipotent, omniscient, and morally perfect and who exists and has these properties in every world.

What shall we say of these arguments? Clearly they are valid; and hence they show that if it is even possible that God, so thought of, exists, then it is true and necessarily true that he does. The only question of interest, it seems to me, is whether its main premiss—that indeed unsurpassable greatness is possibly exemplified, that there is an essence entailing unsurpassable greatness—is *true*. I think this premiss is indeed true. Accordingly, I think this version of the Ontological Argument is sound.

Now some philosophers do not take kindly to the Ontological Argument; the claim that it or some version of it is sound is often met with puzzled outrage or even baffled rage. One objection I have heard is that the formulation of the last section (call it Argument A) may be valid, but is clearly *circular* or *question-begging*. Sometimes this *caveat* has no more substance than the recognition that the argument is indeed valid and that its premiss could not be true unless its conclusion were—which, of course, does not come to much as an objection. But suppose we briefly look into the complaint. What is it for an argument to be circular? In the paradigm case, one argues for a proposition A_1 on the basis of A_2, for A_2 on the basis of A_3, . . . for A_{n-1} on the basis of A_n, and for A_n on the basis of A_1. Whatever the merits of such a procedure, Argument A is clearly not an example of it; to conform to this pattern one who offered Argument A would be obliged to produce in turn an argument for its main premiss—an argument that involved as premiss the conclusion of A or some other proposition such that A's conclusion was proximately or ultimately offered as evidence for it.

So the argument is not obviously circular. Is it question-begging? Although surely some arguments *are* question-begging, it is by no means easy to say what this fault consists in or how it is related to circularity. But perhaps we can get at the objector's dissatisfaction by means of an example. Consider Argument B:

(46). Either 7+5=13 or God exists.
(47). $7+5 \neq 13$.

Therefore

(48). God exists.

This argument is valid. Since I accept its conclusion and therefore its first premiss, I believe it to be sound as well. Still, I could scarcely claim much for it as a piece of Natural Theology. Probably it will never rank with Aquinas's Third Way, or even his much less impressive Fourth Way. And the reason is that indeed this argument is in some way question-begging, or at least dialectically deficient. For presumably a person would not come to believe (46) unless he already believed (48). Not that the alternative is *impossible*—it *could* happen, I suppose, that someone inexplicably find himself with the belief that (46) (and (47)) is true, and then go on to conclude that the same holds for (48). But that certainly would not be the general case. Most people who believe (46) do so only because they already believe (48) and infer the former from the latter. But how do these considerations apply to Argument A?

It is by no means obvious that anyone who accepts its main premiss does so only because he infers it from the conclusion. If anyone *did* do that, then for him the argument is dialectically deficient in the way B is; but surely Argument A need not be thus dialectically deficient for one who accepts it.

A second objection: there are plenty of properties that are *non-compossible* with maximal greatness; that is, their possibility is incompatible with that of the latter. Consider, for example, the property of *near-maximality*, enjoyed by a being if and only if it does not exist in every possible world but has a degree of greatness not exceeded by that of any being in any world. This property is possibly exemplified only if there is a world *W* in which there exists a being who does not exist in every world and whose greatness could not be exceeded. And clearly near-maximality is possibly exemplified only if maximal greatness is *not* possibly exemplified. Or more simply, consider the property of no-maximality, the property of being such that there is no maximally great being. If this property is possible, then maximal greatness is not. But, so claims the objector, these properties are every bit as plausibly possible as maximal greatness. So if Argument A is sound, so is Argument C:

(49). Near-maximality is possibly exemplified
(50). If near-maximality is possible, then maximal greatness is not

Therefore

(51). Maximal greatness is impossible.

Since A and C cannot both be sound, he continues, we must conclude that neither is.

But of course here there is confusion. Agreed: A and C cannot both be sound; but why conclude that *neither* is? Consider Argument D:

(52). No-maximality is possibly exemplified
(53). If no-maximality is possibly exemplified, then maximal greatness is impossible.

Therefore

(54). Maximal greatness is impossible.

Logic tells us that A and D cannot both be sound; but it also tells us they cannot both be *un*sound; one is sound and the other is not.

I have also heard the following rider to the last objection. There are vast numbers of properties not compossible with maximal greatness. There are near-maximality and no-maximality, as we have seen, but any numbers of others as well. For example, there is the intersection of no-maximality with such a property as *being Socrates*; this is a property exemplified by something only in the event that that thing is Socrates and there is no maximally great being. Clearly there are as many properties of this sort as you please; for each it seems fairly plausible, initially, at least, to claim that it is possibly exemplified; but each is non-compossible with maximal greatness. So in all probability the latter is impossible; granted, it does not initially *look* impossible, but its claims are outweighed by the claims of the indefinitely many non-compossible properties that look as possible as it.

This argument has little to recommend it. Indeed there are any number of fairly plausible properties that are not compossible with maximal greatness; but there are just as many (and just as plausible) whose possibility *entails* that of the latter: *being a maximally great creator of Socrates*, *being a maximally great creator of Plato*, *etc.* For any number *n* there is the property of being maximally great and creating just *n* persons; and the possibility of each of these properties will be precisely as plausible, as that of maximal greatness itself.

It must be conceded, however, that Argument A is not a successful piece of natural theology. For the latter typically draws its premises from the stock of propositions accepted by nearly every sane man, or perhaps nearly every rational man. So, for example, each of St. Thomas's Five Ways begins by appealing to a premiss few would be willing to contest: such propositions as that some things are in motion; or that things change; or that there are contingent beings. And (36), the central premiss of Argument A, is not of this sort; a sane and rational man who thought it through and understood it might none the less reject it, remaining agnostic or even accepting instead the possibility of no-maximality.

Well then, why accept this premiss? Is there not something improper, unreasonable, irrational about so doing? I cannot see why. Philosophers sometimes suggest that certain scientific theories—quantum mechanics, perhaps—require us to give up certain laws of logic—the Principle of Distribution,[7] for example. If we can accept the denial of the Distributive Law in the interests of simplifying physical theory, we should be able to accept (36) in order to do the same for Theology. More seriously, suppose we consider analogous situations. Previously, I have examined the question whether

(55). There are or could be possible but unactual objects

is true. This proposition resembles (36) in that if it is *possible*, it is true and indeed necessarily true. The same goes for its denial. Furthermore, there are plenty of initially plausible propositions that are not compossible with (55); and plenty more that are not compossible with its denial. There seems to be no argument against this proposition that need compel a determined advocate; and there are none for it. Shall we conclude that it is improper or irrational or philosophically irresponsible to accept (55) or its negation? Surely not. Or consider Leibniz's Law:

(56). For any objects x and y and property P, if $x=y$, then x has P if and only if y has P.

Some philosophers reject (56); various counterexamples have been alleged; various restrictions have been proposed. None of these "counterexamples" are genuine in my view; but there seems to be no compelling argument for (56) that does not at some point invoke that very principle. Must we conclude that it is improper to accept it, or to employ it as a premiss? No indeed. The same goes for any number of philosophical claims and ideas. Indeed, philosophy contains little else. Were we to believe only what is uncontested or for which there are incontestable arguments from uncontested premises, we should find ourselves with a pretty slim and pretty dull philosophy. Perhaps we should have *Modus Ponens*; certainly not much more. The policy of accepting only the incontestable promises security but little else.

So if we carefully ponder Leibniz's Law and the alleged objections, if we consider its connections with other propositions we accept or reject and still find it compelling, we are within our rights in accepting it—and this whether or not we can convince others. But then the same goes for (36). Hence our verdict on these reformulated versions of St. Anselm's argument must be as follows. They cannot, perhaps, be said to *prove* or *establish* their conclusion. But since it is rational to accept their central premiss, they do show that it is rational to *accept* that conclusion. And perhaps that is all that can be expected of any such argument.

Notes

1. See *God and Other Minds* (Ithaca: Cornell University Press), 1990, Chapter 2.
2. *God and Other Minds*.
3. *Man's Vision of God* (Harper & Row, Inc.), 1941.
4. "Anselm's Ontological Arguments", *Philosophical Review*, 69 (1960).
5. "Can God's Existence be Disproved?", *Mind*, 57 (1948), pp. 108–18.
6. Where, we recall, a property P entails a property Q if there is no world in which there exists an object x that has P but lacks Q.
7. See Hilary Putnam's "Is Logic Empirical?", in *Boston Studies in Philosophy of Science*, Vol. 5 (Dordrecht: D. Riedel, 1969), pp. 216–41.

2.8

'THE CONCEPTUALIST ARGUMENT FOR GOD'S EXISTENCE'

Quentin Smith

I

The conceptualist argument for God's existence (or at least the versions I shall develop in this paper) involves three main premises, conceptualism, actualism, and a premise about the necessary uniqueness of a certain divine attribute.

Conceptualism with respect to propositions is the theory that it is necessarily the case that propositions are effects of mental causes. It is necessarily true that for any x, if x is a proposition, then x is an effect of some propositional attitude. It may be said that the conceiving of a proposition (which may be taken as an element common to all propositional attitudes) is what sustains the proposition in existence, such that the proposition exists by virtue of this conceiving. Conceptualism should not be defined as the thesis that it is necessarily the case that propositions are accusatives of propositional attitudes, since this precludes a philosopher from being both a platonist and an Anselmian theist. An Anselmian theist holds that God exists in every possible world and thus that in every possible world every proposition is an accusative of God's propositional attitudes; this could be held consistently with platonism, the thesis that propositions exist necessarily and by virtue of their natures, and not by virtue of being conceived by some mind. Conceptualism entails that it is necessary that every proposition is an accusative of some propositional attitude, but this entailment is not the thesis of conceptualism, which is that it is necessary that every proposition is an effect of some propositional attitude.

Quentin Smith, 'The Conceptualist Argument for God's Existence', *Faith and Philosophy*, 11, 1 (January 1994), pp. 38–49.

It has been objected to this distinction that if conceptualism entails the accusative thesis, then an Anselmian theist is still precluded from being a platonist. But this objection is unwarranted, since the Anselmian theist can hold the entailment (the accusative thesis) without holding the proposition that entails it (the conceptualist thesis). The Anselmian theist would be precluded from being a platonist if the accusative thesis entailed the conceptualist thesis, but there is no such entailment.

One reason I call my conceptualist arguments "versions" of the conceptualist argument is that they include the thesis of *actualism*, and I do not wish to preclude the possibility that conceptualist arguments without this premise may be constructed. *Actualism* is the theory that defines possibilities in terms of a subclass of actualities, namely, propositions.[1] "It is possible that there is a red unicorn" is analyzed as meaning "There exists the possibly true proposition *that some unicorn is red*." The versions of the conceptualist argument I shall construct involve the claim that the conjunction of conceptualism, actualism and a third premise about the uniqueness of a certain divine attribute entails Anselmian theism, the thesis that God exists in every possible world.

II

One version of the conceptualist argument begins as follows. If actualism is true, then there exist propositions in every possible world; this follows from the fact that possibilities are possibly true propositions. If actualism and conceptualism are both true, it follows that there is some mind in every possible world. If there is some possible world W in which there is no mind, then either (1) the propositions in W are not effects of some mind(s), which contradicts conceptualism, or (2) the possibilities in W are not propositions, which contradicts actualism, or (3) there are no possibilities in W, which contradicts the assumption that W is possible. But "there exists some mind in every possible world" does not entail that God exists in every possible world. Indeed, it does not even entail that God actually exists, since different minds exist in different worlds and no divine mind may actually exist. Perhaps the only minds that actually exist are human and animal minds.

A missing link in the argument is a statement to the effect that there exists at least one proposition that can be an accusative (and thus an effect) only of a divine mind. A possible candidate for this statement is that there exists a certain proposition that can be an accusative only of an omniscient mind. The actual world is an infinitely complex conjunction (not a set!)[2] of all true propositions; it is an accusative only of an omniscient mind.[3] It follows that an omniscient mind actually exists.

It may be objected to this line of reasoning that there could actually exist an infinite number of non-omniscient minds, such that for each different part (conjunct) of the actual world, there is a different non-omniscient mind that knows that part. This would allow us to say that there exists the actual world, that there is no part of this world that is not an accusative of some mind, but that no divinity exists.

The response to this objection is that it commits the fallacy of composition. "Each part of the actual world is an accusative" no more entails "the actual world is an accusative" than "each conjunct of p is an accusative" entails "p is an accusative." If *that red is a color* is an accusative" of John's mind and *that green is a color* is an accusative of Jane's mind, that does not entail *that red is a color and green is a color* is an accusative of some mind. For the latter to be an accusative, there must be some mind that grasps the conjunction of the two propositions that John and Jane separately grasp. Thus, if the actual world and not just each of its parts is an accusative, there must be some mind that grasps the conjunction of all true propositions and this mind will be omniscient. Furthermore, there must be some mind that grasps the actual world, for a conjunction of all true propositions is itself a proposition and every proposition is an accusative of some mind.

A similar argument shows that God exists in every possible world. Each possible world W is a maximal conjunction of propositions, such that every proposition or its negation is a conjunct of W. Each merely possible world W′ is such that it might have been actual; if W′ had been actual, then W′ would have contained only true conjuncts. This entails (given conceptualism) that if W′ were to be actual, W′ would be an accusative of an omniscient mind. This is logically equivalent to the assertion that if W′ were to be actual, an omniscient mind would be actual. Given a third premise that is entailed by the necessary coextensivity of the divine attributes, the premise that there possibly exists no x such that x is omniscient and different than God, it follows that God exists in every possible world.

But this version of the conceptualist argument for Anselmian theism is not complete as it stands, since it is open to the objection that an omniscient mind is not required by the conceptualist and actualist premises but merely a mind that conceives possible worlds. Conceptualism states that a proposition is an effect of some mind and a proposition need not be known or even believed to be an effect of a mind; it need merely be conceived. Accordingly, in order for the maximal proposition that is the actual world to be an effect of some mind, it need not be known by a mind but merely conceived, and the same holds for each other world. Thus the conceptualist and actualist premises entail merely that there is a mind that conceives possible worlds, not that there is an omniscient mind. Accordingly, a supplemental premise is needed about the relation between the divine attribute of omniscience and the attribute of conceiving everything that God knows. The premise is that

(1). Necessarily, only God is omniscient and if a being x knows every true proposition, then there is no being y different from x that conceives every proposition that x knows.

Obviously, if God knows every true proposition, he conceives every true proposition and (1) adds to this obvious claim the assertion that only God conceives every proposition that God knows. Thus, we need the supplementary premise (1) in order for the conceptualist argument for Anselmian theism to go through.

(1) is not needed to rule out the possibility that there be a nondivine mind that knows every true proposition and yet believes some false ones, since this possibility is precluded for other reasons. For each true proposition p, if x knows p, then p is justified for x, which implies that x does not believe not-p. It follows from this that if x knows all truths, then x has no false beliefs.

I am assuming for the sake of simplicity that there are no indexical propositions (although there are indexical sentences), such as the propositions *that I am Quentin Smith* and *that I am here rather than there*, since God would not believe all of these propositions. If there are indexical propositions, then "God knows all true propositions" should be taken to mean "God knows all true nonindexical propositions."

A different argument for Anselmian theism may be constructed using the conceptualist and actualist premiss and a different third premise, viz., that it is impossible that there exists an x such that x is a necessarily existent mind and different from God. I take it to be a sound modal intuition that there is some possible world in which there are no contingently existent minds. In this world, however, there will be propositions (given actualism) and some mind(s) (given conceptualism). Since the mind(s) cannot be contingently existent, the mind(s) must be necessarily existent. Given the premise that it is impossible that there exists an x such that x is a necessarily existent mind and different from God, it follows that there is only one necessarily existent mind in this world and that this mind is God.

Another version of the conceptualist argument can be constructed that does not rely on the modal intuition that there is a possible world devoid of contingent minds. Instead, one may rely on the premise that there is some possible world in which contingent minds exist at some but not all times. Since some propositions exist at all times, there will be times at which propositions exist but are not accusatives of contingent minds. Since the propositions must be accusatives of some mind(s), it follows that at these times they are accusatives of some necessary mind(s). Given the premise that it is impossible that there exists an x such that x is a necessarily existent mind and different from God, it follows that there is only one necessary mind of which these propositions are accusatives and that this mind is God.

This last argument requires the additional premise that in the possible world mentioned, propositions exist at times. This premise is obviously false on some definitions of "time," for example, the Einsteinian definition that entails that something is in time if and only if it is connectable to a physical event by a light or slower signal. But there are other more liberal definitions of "time" that entail that propositions exist in time. It may be argued[4] that a sufficient condition of existing in time is that something acquire or lose any *n*-adic property, such as the property of being an accusative of John's mind. Given this partial definition of "time," it follows that the propositions exist in time in the world in question and that this version of the conceptualist argument goes through.

[. . .]

III

Many philosophers would hold that the key premise needing support to make the conceptualist argument compelling is the premise that conceptualism is true. I would like here to examine the claim that humans are not in an epistemic situation where they can conclusively establish or refute this premise and that in this respect this premise is similar to some of the key premises of some of the traditional types of theistic argument, such as the cosmological and ontological arguments. But this is not the same point that Plantinga makes about conceptualism, that there are no good arguments for it but that there is a strong intuition that it is true. My point rather is that it is false that every rational person would find conceptualism intuitively plausible, but true that (a) there are no rationally compelling arguments for or against conceptualism and that (b) a rational person may find conceptualism intuitively plausible but an equally rational person may find platonism or nominalism intuitively plausible. I shall suggest that the relevant premises in the conceptualist and some other theistic arguments are synthetic a priori propositions that are neither self-evident nor capable of being demonstrated to all rational persons.

A person is rational if and only if her beliefs are compatible with (i) the observational facts of common sense, (ii) the currently warranted scientific theories, (iii) the principles of inductive and deductive logic, and (iv) set theory and mathematics. Since there probably exists no person all of whose beliefs meet these conditions, the notion of a rational person should be tacitly understood as relativized to the proposition or argument under discussion: a person is rational with respect to a proposition p or argument A if and only if her set of beliefs about p or A are compatible with (i) the observational facts of common sense, (ii) the currently warranted scientific theories, (iii) the principles of inductive and deductive logic, and (iv) set theory and mathematics. For example, a person is rational with respect to the argument *All humans are mortal: Socrates is human; therefore, Socrates is mortal*, if the person's set of beliefs about this argument is the unit set [belief that it is sound].

My definition of a rational person is not meant to analyze the ordinary meaning of "rational person," since my definition is much too restrictive, but it is useful for the purposes of explaining the epistemic status of the premises in the theistic arguments I shall discuss. Ordinarily, we would call a person "rational" even if the person violated some of the conditions; for example, Frege was a "rational person" in the ordinary sense even though his views on sets entailed a contradiction in first order logic.

The definition of a rational person is controversial or ambiguous at least inasmuch as it is controversial which logic (tense logic, modal logic, para-consistent logic, etc.), scientific theory (string theory, supergravity, etc.), set theory, etc. is to be chosen, but these controversies will not affect the following discussion.

One point of contention between conceptualists and platonists concerns the truth value of

(5). Necessarily, every proposition is an effect of some mind.

The truth value of (5) cannot be settled by observation or induction, if only for the reason of (5)'s modal operator. If not an a posteriori statement, it is either analytically or synthetically a priori. Now it is dubious at best to regard (5) as analytically true. The concept of a proposition includes such concepts as *having relations or properties among its parts, having parts that are ordered to each other in a certain way*, and *being a bearer of a truth value* (assuming the principle of bivalence). Perhaps the concept of a proposition also includes the concept *being understandable* or *possibly, being an object of a propositional attitude*, but even if these latter concepts are included they do not entail conceptualism since a platonist would freely admit that each proposition can be grasped by some possible mind. But it is implausible to think that the concept of a proposition includes the concept of *being the effect of some mind*.

Perhaps the concept of a *judgement* includes the concept of *being the result of an act of judgement*, but even if "judgement" (in one of its uses) expresses this mentalist concept, it is not an analytic truth that every proposition is a judgement.

This suggests the view that (5) is a synthetic a priori truth or falsehood. (5) is synthetic if only for the reason that neither of the two concepts expressed by "is an effect of some mind" and "is not an effect of any mind" is a part of the concept expressed by "proposition." (5) is a priori in that its true value is not knowable by virtue of empirical observations but by virtue of reflection on the proposition itself (or by reflection upon other a priori propositions that entail or are entailed by it.

Now it is clear that (5) if true is not *self-evident*, where a synthetic a priori proposition p is self-evident if and only if any person who is rational with respect to p would believe p simply by virtue of understanding p. An example of a synthetic a priori proposition that is self-evident is *that no body can be simultaneously red all over and green all over*. (5) is not self-evident since there exist persons, viz. some platonists and nominalists, who are rational with respect to (5) and yet both understand and reject (5). I would suggest that (5) also does not have a rationally compelling proof. A proof of a synthetic a priori proposition is rationally compelling if and only if any person who is rational with respect to the proof and who understood the proof would believe the premiss true and the conclusion validly derived. An example of a rationally compelling proof is *that no body can be one color all over and simultaneously be a different color all over; red is a different color than green; therefore, no body can be simultaneously red all over and green all over.* I believe it would be acknowledged that there exists in the literature no rationally compelling proof of the truth or falsity of (5), and I cannot think of how any such proof could possibly be constructed.

If (5) is neither self-evident nor provable in a rationally compelling way, it may be *rationally acceptable.* A synthetic a priori proposition p is rationally acceptable (and no more) for a person x if and only if, (1) neither p nor not-p are self-evident or compellingly provable and (2) p appears true to x even after x has considered possible objections to p and considered p's relations to other relevant propositions that x believes or disbelieves, and (3) x is rational with respect to p.

If (5) is rationally acceptable (and no more), then the conceptalist argument for God's existence is not a rationally compelling proof. Rather, it is a *rationally acceptable* argument. An argument A for a thesis T is rationally acceptable (and no more) to x if and only if (1) A is not a rationally compelling proof of T and there is no rationally compelling proof of not-T, (2) A appears sound to x even after x has considered possible objections to A and considered A's relations to other relevant arguments he accepts or rejects, and (3) x is rational with respect to A.

I think the conceptualist argument for God's existence may be compared in this respect with the other traditional arguments for God's existence, especially with the cosmological and ontological arguments. A key premise of some forms of the cosmological argument is the principle of sufficient reason, which has at least two versions. One strong version is

(6). Necessarily, everything that exists has a reason why it exists;

and one weak version is

(7). Necessarily, everything that begins to exist has a reason why it exists.

These are not analytic principles and their modal operator prevents them from being merely inductive generalizations. Thus, it is plausible to regard (6) and (7) as synthetic a priori truths if true at all. But it is notorious, however, that some philosophers who are rational with respect to (6) and (7) believe (6) or (7) and other philosophers who are similarly rational disbelieve (6) and (7). If this is the case, and the other conditions of a rational acceptable argument are met, then the cosmological argument is not a rationally compelling but merely a rationally acceptable argument for God's existence.

The same holds for the ontological argument. In Plantinga's version, for example, the premise

(8). Unsurpassable greatness is possibly exemplified

is taken by Plantinga to be a proposition a rational person could accept or reject.[5] Plantinga does not characterize this proposition as synthetic and a priori, but it is obviously not an empirical generalization and the sentence that expresses it is not reducible to a tautology by substitution of synonyms for synonyms. It seems natural, then, to regard it as a synthetic a priori truth if true. Given Plantinga's own admission that a rational person could accept or reject (8), the ontological argument in Plantinga's version is not a rationally compelling argument for God's existence.

If none of the other theistic arguments (e.g., the teleological argument or the argument from mystical experience) is rationally compelling, then the best the theist can hope for is to establish the rational acceptability of theism. The explicit formulation of the conceptalist argument for theism in this paper thus may be interpreted as contributing to establishing the rational acceptability of theism.

[. . .]

However, this way of understanding the argument of this paper must be made with qualifications, for I have not discussed the issue of whether there is a rationally compelling argument for atheism. If there is such an argument, then no argument for theism is rationally acceptable. But the issue of atheological arguments falls outside the scope of this paper.

NOTES

1. Other versions of actualism define possibilities in terms of other sub-classes of actualities, such as states of affairs (Plantinga), properties (Stalnaker) and sentences (Hintikka). See Alvin Plantinga, *The Nature of Necessity* (New York: Oxford University Press, 1974), Robert Stalnaker, "Possible Worlds," in *The Possible and the Actual*, ed. M. Loux (Ithaca: Cornell University Press, 1979), pp. 225–234, and Jaakko Hintikka, "The Modes of Modality," in ibid, pp. 65–79.
2. The power-set axiom precludes the possibility that there is a set of all truths. See Selmer Bringsjord, "Are There Set Theoretic Possible Worlds?," *Analysis* 45.1 (1985), Christopher Menzel, "On Set Theoretic Possible Worlds," *Analysis* 46.2 (1986), and Patrick Grim, "On Sets and Worlds: A Reply to Menzel," *Analysis* 46.4 (1986).
3. The actual world should not be confused with *the universe*, the aggregate of all (created) concrete objects, inclusive of all organisms, matter, energy, and space-time positions. Propositions are abstract objects and thus are not parts of the universe. Nor should the actual world be confused with *the aggregate of all that exists*, what I have elsewhere termed "the world-whole" (*The Felt Meanings of the World*: West Lafayette, Purdue University Press, 1986). The aggregate of all that exists contains all concrete and abstract objects. The accusative of an omniscient mind is the actual world, not the universe or the aggregate of all that exists. However, an omniscient mind knows about the universe and the aggregate of all that exists by virtue of

knowing the true maximal proposition that is the actual world, since this proposition contains true propositions about everything in the universe and in the aggregate of all that exists.

4. This is argued in Quentin Smith, "A New Typology of Temporal and Atemporal Permanence," *Noûs* 23 (1989), pp. 307–30, and "Time and Propositions," *Philosophia* 20 (1990), pp. 279–94.
5. Plantinga, *The Nature of Necessity* (Oxford: Clarendon Press, 1974), pp. 219–20.

Sections I and II of the present essay are largely based on "Actualism, Conceptualism and Theism," co-authored by Quentin Smith and William F. Vallicella and read at the Chicago APA meeting in April, 1991. The response given by Robert Oakes was especially helpful in stimulating the rewriting of this essay and the development of section III. I should also like to thank William Lane Craig, Paul Draper, Brian Leftow, Keith Chrzan and particularly William F. Vallicella for helpful comments that contributed to this version.

SUGGESTED READING

GENERAL

Davis, Stephen T. (1997), *God, Reason, and Theistic Proofs*, Reason and Religion, Grand Rapids, MI: Wm. B. Eerdmans.

Hick, John (ed.) (1964), *The Existence of God*, Problems of Philosophy Series, New York: Macmillan.

Mackie, J. L. (1982), *The Miracle of Theism*, Oxford: Clarendon Press.

COSMOLOGICAL ARGUMENT

Burrill, Donald R. (1967), *The Cosmological Argument*, Garden City, NY: Anchor Books.

Craig, William Lane (1980), *The Cosmological Argument from Plato to Leibniz*, Library of Philosophy and Religion, London: Macmillan.

Craig, William Lane and Quentin Smith (1993), *Theism, Atheism, and Big Bang Cosmology*, Oxford: Clarendon Press.

TELEOLOGICAL ARGUMENT

Barrow, John D. and Frank J. Tipler (1986), *The Anthropic Cosmological Principle*, Oxford: Clarendon Press.

Denton, Michael (1998), *Nature's Destiny: How the Laws of Biology Reveal Purpose in the Universe*, New York: Free Press.

Hume, David (1947), *Dialogues Concerning Natural Religion*, edited with an

Introduction by Norman Kemp Smith, The Library of Liberal Arts, New York: Bobbs-Merrill.

Leslie, John (1989), *Universes*, London: Routledge.

AXIOLOGICAL ARGUMENT

Adams, Robert M. (1987), *The Virtue of Faith*, Oxford: Oxford University Press.

Hick, John (1971), *Arguments for the Existence of God*, New York: Seabury Press.

Sorley, William R. (1930), *Moral Values and the Idea of God*, New York: Macmillan.

Taylor, A. E. (1930), *The Faith of a Moralist*, London: Macmillan.

NOÖLOGICAL ARGUMENT

Adams, Robert (1987), 'Flavors, Colors, and God', in Robert Adams, in *The Virtue of Faith*, Oxford: Oxford, University Press.

Swinburne, Richard (1986), *The Evolution of the Soul*, Oxford: Clarendon Press.

ONTOLOGICAL ARGUMENT

Hick, John H. and Arthur C. McGill (1967), *The Many-faced Argument*, New York: Macmillan.

Oppy, Graham (1995), *Ontological Arguments and Belief in God*, Cambridge: Cambridge University Press.

PART III
THE COHERENCE OF THEISM

THE COHERENCE OF THEISM: INTRODUCTION

William Lane Craig

One of the respects in which contemporary Philosophy of Religion has developed most dramatically is its treatment of the attributes of God, or what has come to be called the coherence of theism. During the previous generation the concept of God was often regarded as fertile ground for anti-theistic arguments. The difficulty with theism, it was said, was not merely that there are no good arguments for the existence of God, but, more fundamentally, that the notion of God is incoherent.

This anti-theistic strategy backfired, however, as it evoked a prodigious literature devoted to the philosophical analysis of the concept of God, thereby refining and strengthening theistic belief. Since the concept of God is under-determined by the biblical data, philosophers working within the Judaeo-Christian tradition enjoy considerable latitude in formulating a philosophically coherent and biblically faithful doctrine of God. Theists thus found that anti-theistic critiques of certain conceptions of God could actually be quite helpful in framing a more adequate conception. Thus, far from undermining theism, the anti-theistic critiques have served mainly to reveal how rich and variegated and challenging is the concept of God.

NECESSITY

Ever since Aristotle, God has been conceived in Western philosophical theology as a necessarily existent being (*ens necessarium*). For Aristotle God's necessary existence probably meant simply His immunity to generation and corruption. This conception connects with the contemporary notion of God's 'factual' necessity: given that God exists, it is impossible that He ever came into or will go out of existence. He is uncaused, eternal, incorruptible and indestructible. During the Middle Ages, however, Islamic philosophers such as al-Farabi began to enunciate an even more powerful conception of God's necessity: God's non-existence is logically impossible. This conception of necessary existence lay at the heart of Anselm's ontological argument: if God's non-existence is logically impossible, it follows that He must exist. God is a logically necessary being.

Powerful theological and philosophical reasons can be given for taking God's existence to be logically necessary. Philosophically, the conception of God as the greatest conceivable being implies His necessary existence in this sense, since logically contingent existence is not as great as necessary existence. Certain forms of the contingency argument for God's existence terminate in a logically necessary being, for only such a being can supply an adequate answer to the question, 'Why is there something rather than nothing?' The conceptualist argument also entails the existence of a logically necessary being in order to ground the realm of abstract objects. The moral argument leads naturally to such a being, since moral values and principles are not plausibly logically contingent. Theologically speaking, a God who just happens to exist (even eternally and without cause) seems less satisfactory religiously than one whose non-existence is impossible.

Since the critiques of Hume and Kant, however, philosophers have until recently widely rejected the notion of God as a logically necessary being. It was often said that to speak of a logically necessary being is flatly a category mistake; propositions are logically necessary or contingent with respect to their truth value, but beings are no more necessary or contingent than they are true or false. If one replied that the theist means to hold that the proposition *God exists* is necessarily true, then the response was that existential propositions are uniformly contingent. Besides, the proposition *God does not exist* is not a contradiction, so that *God exists* cannot be logically necessary. Moreover, many philosophers insisted that necessary/contingent truth is merely a result of linguistic convention, so that it becomes merely conventional to assert that God necessarily exists.

Philosophical reflection over the last quarter century has largely overturned these critiques. The development of possible worlds semantics has provided a useful means of expressing the theist's claim. To say that God is a logically necessary being is to say that God exists in every possible world ('God' in this case being a proper name and, hence, rigidly designating its referent), that is, the proposition *God exists* is true in every possible world. There is no good reason to think that such an existential proposition cannot be true in every possible world, for many philosophers make precisely similar claims about the necessary existence of various abstract objects like numbers, properties, propositions and so forth. Though abstract, such objects are thought by many philosophers to exist, in Plantinga's words, just as serenely as your most solidly concrete object.[1] Thus, it would be special pleading to privilege these objects with necessary existence while denying the possibility of God's existing necessarily.

Furthermore, the modality operative in possible worlds semantics is not strict logical necessity/possibility, but broad logical necessity/possibility. Strictly speaking there is no logical impossibility in the proposition *The Prime Minister is a prime number*; but we should not want to say, therefore, that there is a possible world in which this proposition is true. Broad logical possibility is usually construed in terms of actualisability and is therefore often understood as metaphysical possibility. There are no clear criteria which can be applied mechanically to determine whether a proposition is metaphysically necessary/impossible. One chiefly has to rely on intuition or conceivability. Propositions which are not strictly logically contradictory may nonetheless be metaphysically impossible, for example, *This table could have been made of ice* or *Socrates could have been a hippopotamus*. Similarly, propositions which are neither tautologous nor analytic may nonetheless be metaphysically necessary, for example, *Gold has the atomic number 79*, *Whatever begins to exist has a cause*, or *Everything that has a shape has a size*. Intuitions may differ over whether some proposition is metaphysically necessary/impossible. Thus, with respect to the proposition *God exists*, the fact that the negation of this proposition is not a contradiction in no way shows that the proposition is not metaphysically necessary. Similarly, the proposition that *Nothing exists* is not a logical contradiction, but that does not show that the proposition is broadly logically possible. If one has some reason to think that a metaphysically necessary being exists, then it would be question-begging to reject this conclusion solely on the grounds that it seems possible that nothing should exist.

Finally, as for the conventionalist theory of necessity, such a construal of modal notions is not only unjustified but enormously implausible. As Plantinga points out,[2] the linguistic conventionalist confuses sentences with propositions. We can imagine situations under which the sentence 'Either there are some carnivorous cows or there aren't any' would not have expressed the proposition it in fact does and so might have been neither necessary nor true; but that goes no distance toward proving that the proposition it does express is neither necessary nor true. Moreover, it seems quite incredible to think that the necessity of this proposition is in any wise affected by our determination to use words in a certain way. Could it really be the case that there are carnivorous cows and there are not any?

The conception of God as a necessary being in a broadly logical sense thus seems a coherent notion.[3] Still, not all philosophers of religion are convinced. In our first selection in this section Robert Prevost weighs Richard Swinburne's misgivings about the logical necessity of God's being.

ETERNITY

God's eternity has been the constant affirmation of monotheistic faith, and it follows as well from divine necessity. For if God exists necessarily, it is impossible that He not exist; therefore He can never go out of or come into being. God just exists, without beginning or end, which is a minimalist definition of what it means to say that God is eternal.

But there is considerable disagreement concerning the nature of divine eternity. Plato, Plotinus, Augustine, Boethius, Anselm and Aquinas argued that God transcends time and therefore has His whole life at once (*tota simul*). Alternatively, Aristotle may well have taken God's eternity to be everlasting temporal duration, and Duns Scotus sharply criticised the atemporalist view of Aquinas. Isaac Newton, the father of modern physics, in his General Scholium to his great *Principia Mathematica*, founded his doctrine of absolute time upon God's infinite temporal duration, and in our day process thinkers like Whitehead and Hartshorne have vigorously asserted the temporalist view.

Why think that God exists timelessly? Perhaps the most persuasive argument in favour of divine timelessness is based on the incompleteness of temporal life.[4] Shakespeare's melancholy lines,

> 'Tomorrow and tomorrow and tomorrow
> Creeps in this petty pace from day to day
> To the last syllable of recorded time'[5]

are a poignant reminder of the evanescence of temporal life. Our yesterdays are gone, and our tomorrows we do not yet have. The fleeting present is our only claim on existence. There is thus a transiency and incompleteness to temporal life that seems incompatible with the life of a most perfect being.

On the other hand, there do seem to be good reasons, too, for affirming divine temporality. If God is really related to the world, then it is extraordinarily difficult to see how God could remain untouched by the world's temporality. Stump and Kretzmann tried to craft an Eternal-Temporal simultaneity relation to answer this difficulty[6] but their formulation turned out to be explanatorily vacuous, or, once reformulated, viciously circular.[7] Leftow broached a theory according to which temporal entities exist in eternity as well as in time and so can be causally related to God,[8] but his theory was vitiated by serious category mistakes.[9]

Furthermore, divine omniscience would seem to require that God exist temporally in order to know the truth of propositions expressed by tensed sentences. Hermetically sealed in timeless eternity, God could not know such facts as whether Christ has died or has yet to be born. All He could know would be tenseless truths like *Christ dies in* AD 33. But such ignorance is inconsistent with the standard account of omniscience and is surely incompatible with God's maximal cognitive excellence. To date no satisfactory account of how a timeless God could know tensed truths has been forthcoming.[10]

Whether God is timeless or temporal is, in the end, apt to depend upon the nature of time itself. One of the central questions in the philosophy of time is whether time is dynamic or static.[11] On the dynamic theory of time there is an objective difference between past, present and future, and temporal becoming is real. On the static theory the difference between past, present and future is either purely subjective or else analysable in terms of the tenseless relations *earlier than*, *simultaneous with*, and *later than*, and all events in time are equally real. In the selection included here Alan Padgett argues that divine timelessness is plausible if a static theory of time is correct, but that if time is dynamic then God must be temporal in virtue of His real, causal relation to the world. If Padgett is correct that divine timelessness stands or falls with the static theory of time, then philosophers of religion must explore more extensively the issues central to the debate between the static and dynamic theories of time.

OMNISCIENCE

On the standard account of omniscience, for any person S, S is omniscient if and only if S knows every true proposition and believes no false proposition. If God does exist in time, then the standard account entails that if there are true propositions expressed by future-tense sentences, then God has literal fore-knowledge of the future. So if it is true that 'Jones will mow his lawn next Saturday', then God, being omniscient, must know and have always known the proposition expressed by this sentence. But this raises two difficult questions: (1) If God has always believed this and God cannot be mistaken, then is not Jones fated to mow his lawn come Saturday?; and (2) If Jones's action is truly free, then how can God foreknow it?

The first question raises the issue of fatalism, the view that everything that happens happens of necessity. Ancient Greek fatalism was purely logical: if it is true that some event will happen, then it will necessarily happen. For the Church Fathers fatalism took on a theological colouring: if God foreknows that some event will happen, then it will necessarily happen. Almost every major Christian philosophical theologian after Origen had something to say about this question, the vast majority defending the compatibility of fore-knowledge and freedom, but some, like Martin Luther and Jonathan Edwards, denying it.

Aristotle had sought to avoid fatalism by denying the validity of the Principle of Bivalence for future contingent propositions; that is, propositions about future contingents are neither true nor false. Since no truths remain unknown by God, such a position would be compatible with divine omniscience; but such a solution was not open to the Church Fathers in the light of the biblical doctrine that God has foreknowledge (Greek: *prognosis* (Acts 2:23; I Pet. 1:1–2, 19–20)) and the many biblical examples of detailed prophecies of future events (e.g., Mk 14:18, 30). Some contemporary philosophers, notably the Polish logician Jan Łukasiewicz, have followed Aristotle's lead, but few have found this course attractive in view of the logical dislocations and implausibilities attending this position.[12]

Theists who deny divine foreknowledge have therefore felt obliged to redefine omniscience in such a way that God's ignorance of true future contingent propositions does not count against His being omniscient. For example, it is typically proposed that S is omniscient if and only if S knows only and all true propositions which are such that it is logically possible for S to know them. But it is not clear what more beyond truth is required for a proposition to be logically possible to know, in which case the revision is pointless. Revisionists will say that true future contingent propositions are logically impossible to know, for if one knows them, then they are not contingently true. But the revisionist's reasoning is fallacious. For any future contingent proposition p, even if one grants that it is impossible that both God knows p and p is contingently true, it does not follow from the fact that p is contingently true that it is impossible that God knows p. It only follows that He does not in fact know p. Thus, even on the revisionist definition of omniscience, God must know future contingent propositions, since it is logically possible for Him to know them.

What, then, of fatalism? If the fatalist's reasoning is to be valid, then there must be a peculiar modality of temporal necessity which characterises propositions like *God believed p*. But this notion is notoriously obscure, and on the fullest explications of it propositions about God's beliefs concerning the future turn out *not* to be temporally necessary.[13] This is the conclusion of Alvin Plantinga in our first selection. Plantinga defends the Ockhamist position that while free agents do not have the power to undo the past, they do have the power to act in such a way that if they were to act in that way the past would have been different. The conclusions to which this leads, though startling, are not unique to divine foreknowledge but are also implied by retro-causation, time travel, precognition and the Special Theory of Relativity.[14]

If divine foreknowledge and future contingency are compatible, how could God know future contingents? One of the most interesting developments in contemporary Philosophy of Religion has been the rediscovery of Luis Molina's doctrine of middle knowledge (*scientia media*). According to Molina, logically prior to the divine decree to create a world, God possesses not only knowledge of everything that could happen (natural knowledge) but also everything that would happen in any appropriately specified set of circumstances (middle knowledge). He then decrees to create certain free creatures in certain circumstances and, thus, on the basis of His middle knowledge and His knowledge of His own decree, God has foreknowledge of everything that will happen (free knowledge).

Of course, basing divine foreknowledge in divine middle knowledge raises inevitably the question of the basis of God's middle knowledge, and here the Molinist's best course may be simply to state that subjunctive conditional propositions about how some creature would freely act in a set of circumstances which is fully specified (usually called counterfactuals of creaturely freedom) are bivalent and some are true and therefore simply innately known by God. After all, if such propositions are bivalent, then God's knowledge of the present is alone sufficient for His knowing which truth values now inhere in such propositions.

Detractors of middle knowledge typically claim that if such counterfactuals are bivalent, they are uniformly false, since there is (especially prior to the divine decree) no ground of their truth. Proponents of this so-called 'grounding objection' have, however, never clearly articulated or defended the theory of truth which it tacitly presupposes. It appears to assume some version of what is called 'Truthmaker Theory', according to which true propositions are made to be true by certain entities in the world.[15] Truthmaker Theory is a controversial position, however, and even its proponents typically reject 'truthmaker maximalism', the doctrine that all types of true propositions have truthmakers. No grounding objector has yet to answer Plantinga's retort: 'It seems to me that some counterfactuals of freedom are at least possibly true than that the truth of propositions must, in general, be grounded in this way.'[16] Moreover, acceptable truthmakers for counterfactuals of creaturely freedom are available. In our second selection in this section, Alfred Freddoso, the gifted translator of Molina's *Concordia*, argues that counterfactuals of creaturely freedom are grounded by the fact that a relevant indicative proposition would have grounds of its truth. Thus, the truthmaker of some counterfactual of creaturely freedom $F^t(p)$ *on* H is the fact or state of affairs that p *would have a truthmaker under the relevant condition*.

Does God, then, have middle knowledge? If there are true counterfactuals of creaturely freedom – an assumption which we constantly make in everyday life, which is biblically warranted (e.g., 1 Cor. 2:8), and which is plausible in the light of the Law of Conditional Excluded Middle for such counterfactuals – then these must be known by an omniscient God logically prior to His creative decree, lest God, in decreeing which counterfactuals are true, is made the author of evil.

The mention of evil serves to highlight one of the greatest strengths of the doctrine of middle knowledge: it enables us to give an account of providence which preserves human freedom without sacrificing divine sovereignty. Initially, it might be thought that a God endowed with middle knowledge could prevent all evils whilst realising His goals for human history. But this is not necessarily the case. A provident God endowed with middle knowledge can permit the existence of evils which are to all appearances gratuitous but which in the overarching providential plan of God for human history have morally sufficient reasons that we finite, limited observers cannot even dimly discern owing to the incomprehensible complexity involved in the conspiration of factors contributing to the production of the agents and the circumstances willed by God for the ultimate achievement of His purposes.

OMNIPOTENCE

Although one of the biblical names of God is *El-Shaddai* (God Almighty), the concept of omnipotence has remained poorly understood owing to its recalcitrance to analysis. Few thinkers, aside from Descartes, have been willing to affirm that the doctrine means that God can do just anything – for example, make a round triangle. Such a view has been construed as affirming universal possibilism, the doctrine that there are no necessary truths. For on this view an omnipotent deity could have brought it about that even logical contradictions be true and tautologies be false, as inconceivable as this may seem to us. But such a doctrine seems incoherent. For is the proposition *There are no necessary truths* itself necessarily true or not? If so, then the position is self-refuting. If not, then that proposition is possibly false, that is, God could have brought it about that there are necessary truths. Using possible worlds semantics, we may say that there is, therefore, a possible world in which God brings it about that there are propositions which are true in every possible world. But if there are such propositions, then there is no world in which it is the case that there are no propositions true in every possible world, that is, it is not possible that there are no necessary truths, which contradicts universal possibilism.

Moreover, Descartes' position is incredible. It asks us to believe, for example, that God could have brought it about that He created all of us without His existing, that is, there is a possible world in which God does not exist and He created all of us. This is simply nonsense.

One must therefore delineate more carefully what is meant by omnipotence. Customarily, broadly logical limits are not taken to be infringements upon omnipotence, since something that is broadly logically impossible is not really a thing at all. Thus, it is no diminution of God's omnipotence to deny that He can make a stone too heavy for Him to lift, for 'a stone too heavy for God to lift' is as logically impossible a description as 'a round triangle' and thus describes nothing at all.[17]

Shall we say, then, that an agent S is omnipotent if and only if S can do anything which is logically possible? No, for certain actions are logically possible (sinning, failing) but not logically possible for God. If God cannot do an action because it is logically impossible for Him to do it, that ought not count against His omnipotence. Shall we say, then, that S is omnipotent if and only if S can do anything which is such that S's doing it is logically possible? No, such a definition is too lax, allowing beings who are clearly limited (say, essentially incapable of creating the universe) to count as omnipotent. Suppose, then, that we give up trying to find a general definition of omnipotence and say that God is omnipotent if and only if He can do anything which is such that God's doing it is logically possible. Such a recourse is unacceptable because apart from a general account of what it is to be omnipotent, it tends to trivialise God's omnipotence, since any essential incapacity in God would be automatically and by sheer definition excluded from counting against His omnipotence. Moreover, as we shall see in the discussion of the Problem of Evil, there may be logically possible worlds which are not feasible for God because the wrong counterfactuals of creaturely freedom are true. Thus, although 'God actualises a world of free creatures without evil' describes a logically possible state of affairs, such a state of affairs may not be feasible for God because the creatures would freely go wrong if God tried to actualise such a world. God's inability to actualise such a logically possible state of affairs should not, however, count against His omnipotence because that inability is due to creaturely free choices, and it is logically impossible to make someone freely do something.

In his 1973 survey article 'Omnipotence', Peter Geach, a fine analyst, more or less threw up his hands when it came to defining omnipotence and advised that we should simply speak ambiguously in the biblical terminology of God's being almighty.[18] There the discussion stalled until the remarkable piece 'Maximal Power' by Flint and Freddoso appeared in 1983. Their article exemplifies contemporary Philosophy of Religion at its very best. Flint and Freddoso took what was widely viewed as an insoluble problem, brought to it Flint's expertise in counterfactual discourse and Freddoso's in temporal modality, and through a rigorous and painstaking analysis formulated an adequate explication of omnipotence (a.k.a. 'maximal power').

Flint and Freddoso's analysis is closely connected with the Ockhamist solution to theological fatalism and Molina's doctrine of middle knowledge. In their final formulation (D) condition (i) is intended to preserve God's omnipotence in the face of His inability to decree the truth of counterfactuals of creaturely freedom. For the so-called 'world-type-for-God' just is the set of true counterfactuals of creaturely freedom known to Him via His middle knowledge logically prior to His creative decree. Because it is logically impossible to make someone do a certain act freely, God cannot be expected to be able to actualise states of affairs which are described by counterfactuals not in His world-type. Condition (ii) is meant to safeguard omnipotence against God's inability to bring about different past events than those that occurred. It needs to be kept in mind that Ockham's solution to theological fatalism does not require that one have the power to actualise past states of affairs; it requires only that one have the power to actualise some present or future state of affairs, and if one were to do so, then God would have foreknown that and so would have actualised some state of affairs earlier on. In this same connection it needs to be kept firmly in mind that when they speak of two worlds' sharing the same 'history', Flint and Freddoso are not talking about the historian's history, but about a series of highly abstract submoments which does not include such states of affairs as Christ's prediction of Judas's betrayal or God's promising that Israel shall be saved. An omnipotent agent need not have the power to actualise past events, and so their definition is framed in terms of worlds having the same series of submoments up to time t. On their analysis, then, an agent is omnipotent, roughly speaking, just in case he can do anything which it is logically possible for anyone sharing the same world-type and history to do at that point.

GOODNESS

Believers in the monotheistic tradition have always held that God is perfectly good, and Christians have thought of God as the font of all varieties of goodness, whether moral, metaphysical, aesthetic and so forth. Here our interest is in God's moral goodness. Some versions of the axiological argument for God's existence imply that goodness is somehow rooted in God Himself. But ever since Plato the claim that moral values and duties are founded in God has been criticised as problematic. In a famous dilemma in his dialogue *Euthyphro*, Plato asks, in effect, whether something is good because it is approved by God or whether something is approved by God because it is good. Either horn of this dilemma has been said to lead to untenable consequences. If we say that some action is good or right for the mere reason that God wills it, then morality is fundamentally arbitrary. God could have willed that cruelty be good and love evil, and we should have been obliged to hate others and seek to do them harm. Not only is this unconscionable, but it appears to make the claim that God is good vacuous. To claim that God is good seems to mean no more than that God does whatever He wants!

Alternatively, if God wills that we perform some action because it is the right or a good thing to do, then moral values are not based in God after all but exist independently of Him. Such an alternative is taken to be incompatible with classical theism because it compromises the sovereignty and aseity of God. God is Himself duty-bound to obey certain moral principles not of His own creation, but, as it were, imposed on Him. Evidence that moral value is independent of God is sometimes said to be found in the fact that we can apprehend moral values and duties quite independently of belief in God.

In sorting through the tangle of issues raised by this objection, we shall find it helpful to distinguish clearly various areas of Moral Theory:[19]

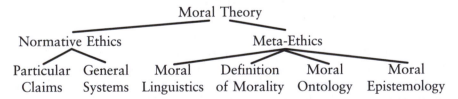

The claim that moral values and duties are rooted in God is a Meta-Ethical claim about Moral Ontology, not about Moral Linguistics or Epistemology. It is fundamentally a claim about the metaphysical status of moral properties, not a claim about the meaning of moral sentences or about the justification or knowledge of moral principles.

These distinctions serve to sweep away in a single stroke all those objections to theistic Meta-Ethics based on linguistic or epistemological considerations. For example, the theist should not be understood to be offering a definition of 'good' or 'right' in theistic terms (e.g., 'willed by God').[20] Therefore objections to the effect that we can understand the meaning of statements like 'Torture of political prisoners is wrong' without reference to God are quite beside the point. Similarly, when it is said that the statement 'God is good' becomes trivial on theistic Meta-Ethics, this objection misconstrues the theistic position as a meaning-claim. A statement like 'God is good' may be taken as a synthetic statement expressing a proposition which is metaphysically necessary both *de dicto* (the proposition is true in all possible worlds) and *de re* (goodness is an essential property of God). Or again, the theist will agree quite readily that we do not need to know or even believe that God exists in order to recognise our moral duties or discern objective moral values.

Although theistic meta-ethics assumes a rich variety of forms, there has been in recent years a resurgence of interest in Divine Command Morality, which understands our moral duties as our obligations to God in light of His moral commands, for example, 'You shall love the Lord your God with all your heart', 'You shall love your neighbour as yourself', and so on. Our moral duties are determined by the commands of a just and loving God. For any state of affairs p, letting 'Rp' represent 'p is required', 'Pp' 'p is permitted', 'Fp' 'p is forbidden', and 'Cp' 'p is commanded by God', and letting 'GJL' represent 'God is just and loving', we can adapt a schema of Philip Quinn's[21] to explicate the notions of moral requirement, permission and forbiddenness as follows:

$$(\forall p)\ (Rp \equiv GJL \ \& \ Cp)$$
$$(\forall p)\ (Pp \equiv GJL \ \& \ \sim C \sim p)$$
$$(\forall p)\ (Fp \equiv GJL \ \& \ C \sim p)$$

Since our moral duties are grounded in the divine commands, they are not independent of God nor, plausibly, is God bound by moral duties, since He does not issue commands to Himself.

If God does not fulfil moral duties, then what content can be given to the claim that He is good? Here Kant's distinction between following a rule and acting in accordance with a rule has proved helpful. God may act naturally in ways which for us would be rule-following and so constitutive of goodness in the sense of fulfilling our moral duties, so that God can be said similarly to be good in an analogical way. Nonetheless, the fact that God is not duty-bound should alert us to the fact that He may well have prerogatives (e.g., taking human life at His discretion) which are forbidden to us.

The above also supplies the key to the arbitrariness objection. For our duties are determined by the commands, not merely of a supreme potentate, but of a just and loving God. God is essentially compassionate, fair, kind, impartial and so forth, and His commandments are reflections of His own character. Thus, they are not arbitrary, and we need not trouble ourselves about counterfactuals with impossible antecedents like 'If God were to command child abuse . . .' God may be said to be good in the sense that He possesses all these moral virtues – and He does so essentially and to the maximal degree! Thus, God's axiological perfection should not be understood in terms of duty-fulfillment, but in terms of virtue. This conception helps us to understand the sense in which God is to be praised: not in the sense of commendation for fully executing His duties or even for His acts of supererogation, but rather in the sense of adoration for His axiological perfection.

The question might be pressed as to why God's nature should be taken to be definitive of goodness. But unless we are nihilists, we shall have to recognise some ultimate standard, and God seems to be the least arbitrary stopping point. Moreover, God's nature is singularly appropriate to serve as such a standard. For by definition, God is a being worthy of worship. And only a being which is the locus and source of all value is worthy of worship.

In the selection chosen for this section, William Alston presents his answer to the Euthyphro dilemma along the lines of a Moral Ontology provided by a Divine Command Definition of Morality. He argues that God plays the role normally assigned by moral realists to the Platonic Ideas and that, therefore, God's commands, issuing from the divine nature, are not arbitrary, but metaphysically necessary.

NOTES

1. Alvin Plantinga, *The Nature of Necessity*, Clarendon Library of Logic and Philosophy (Oxford: Clarendon Press, 1974), p. 132.
2. See remarks of Alvin Plantinga, 'Self-Profile', in James E. Tomberlin and Peter Van Inwagen (eds), *Alvin Plantinga*, Profiles 5 (Dordrecht: D. Reidel, 1985), pp. 71–3.
3. To accept the concept of God as a logically necessary being is not automatically to endorse the ontological argument. One could simply affirm that the concept of God is such that any individual instantiating that concept exists in every possible world if he exists in any world. The question is whether such an individual possibly exists.
4. God's atemporality could be successfully deduced from His simplicity and immutability, for if God is absolutely simple, He stands in no real relations whatsoever, including temporal relations of *earlier/later than*, and if God is absolutely immutable, then He cannot change in any way, which, if He is in time, He must do, at least extrinsically, as things co-present with Him change. But these extra-biblical doctrines are extremely problematic and now widely rejected so that founding one's view of divine eternity on them would be a case of proving the obscure by the more obscure. For a thorough discussion, see Christopher Hughes, *On a Complex Theory of a Simple God*, Cornell Studies in Philosophy of Religion (Ithaca, NY: Cornell University Press, 1990).
5. *Macbeth* V, v, 21.
6. Eleonore Stump and Norman Kretzmann, 'Eternity', *Journal of Philosophy*, 78 (1981), pp. 429–58; Stump and Kretzmann, 'Eternity, Awareness, and Action', *Faith and Philosophy*, 9 (1992), pp. 463–82.

7. See Paul Helm, *Eternal God* (Oxford: Clarendon Press, 1988), pp. 31–3; Brian Leftow, *Time and Eternity*, Cornell Studies in Philosophy of Religion (Ithaca, NY: Cornell University Press, 1991), pp. 167–75.
8. Brian Leftow, 'Eternity and Simultaneity', *Faith and Philosophy*, 8 (1991), pp. 148–79.
9. See my 'The Special Theory of Relativity and Theories of Divine Eternity', *Faith and Philosophy*, 11 (1994), pp. 19–37.
10. See my 'Omniscience, Tensed Facts, and Divine Eternity', *Faith and Philosophy*, 17 (2000), pp. 225–41.
11. For a good introduction, see Richard M. Gale, 'The Static versus the Dynamic Temporal: Introduction', in R. M. Gale (ed.), *The Philosophy of Time: A Collection of Essays* (New Jersey: Humanities Press, 1968), pp. 65–85; on the current debate, see L. Nathan Oaklander and Quentin Smith (eds), *The New Theory of Time* (New Haven: Yale University Press, 1994).
12. For discussion, see my *Divine Foreknowledge and Human Freedom: The Coherence of Theism: Omniscience*, Brill's Studies in Intellectual History 19 (Leiden: E. J. Brill, 1991), ch. 4.
13. See Alfred J. Freddoso, 'Accidental Necessity and Logical Determinism', *Journal of Philosophy* 80 (1983), pp. 257–78; cf. Craig, *Divine Foreknowledge*, ch. 9. Plantinga's analysis is non-standard in that it breaks apart the hard fact/soft fact distinction from temporal necessity/contingency, so that propositions about hard facts can be temporally contingent. Temporally necessary propositions are usually taken just to be those stating 'hard' facts.
14. For a survey of these parallel discussions, see Craig, *Divine Foreknowledge*, chs 6, 10, Appendix I.
15. For an account, see Kevin Mulligan, Peter Simons and Barry Smith, 'Truth-Makers', *Philosophy and Phenomenological Research*, 44 (1984), pp. 287–321.
16. Alvin Plantinga, 'Reply to Robert Adams', in Tomberlin and Van Inwagen (eds), *Alvin Plantinga*, p. 378.
17. If one insists that this description is a broadly logically possible state of affairs, then omnipotence must not be an essential property of God. In that case the paradox would be resolved by affirming that God could make a stone too heavy for Him to lift, but that if He were to do so then He would no longer be omnipotent. Most theologians would, however, take omnipotence to be essential to God.
18. P. T. Geach, 'Omnipotence', *Philosophy*, 48 (1973), pp. 7–20.
19. See Walter Sinnott-Armstrong, 'Moral Skepticism and Justification', in Walter Sinnott-Armstrong and Mark Timmons (eds), *Moral Knowledge?* (New York: Oxford University Press, 1996), pp. 4–5.
20. The theist does offer a Definition of Morality in the sense that moral values and duties are to be explicated in terms of God's nature and will rather than of self-interest, social contract, common happiness, or what have you. But his aim is not to analyse the meaning of moral terms; rather he aims to provide an ontological grounding for objective moral values and duties.
21. Philip L. Quinn, *Divine Commands and Moral Requirements* (Oxford: Clarendon, 1978), pp. 34–5.

NECESSITY
3.1

'DIVINE NECESSITY'

Robert Prevost

I

Traditional language about God's necessity suggests that God has been taken to be a logically necessary being. Leibniz, for example, states:

> if there is a reality in essences or in possibilities or indeed in the eternal truths, this reality is based upon something existent and actual, and, consequently, in the existence of the necessary Being in whom essence includes existence or in whom possibility is sufficient to produce actuality . . . Therefore God alone (or the Necessary Being) has this prerogative that if he be possible he must necessarily exist, and, as nothing is able to prevent the possibility of that which involves no bounds, no negation, and consequently, no contradiction, this alone is sufficient to establish *a priori* his existence.[1]

It is clear that Leibniz meant something akin to logical necessity. He believes, for example, that the ontological argument is valid, but that it simply needs to be augmented by demonstrating that God is indeed a logically possible being. If God is possible, Leibniz argues, he exists.[2] Further, he uses God's absolute, or metaphysical, necessity in the cosmological argument to satisfy the principle of sufficient reason. Swinburne, commenting on Leibniz's cosmological argument, says:

Robert Prevost, 'Divine Necessity', from 'Necessity and Explanation', *Possibility and Theistic Explanation* (Oxford: Clarendon Press, 1990), pp. 130–50.

> Leibniz has . . . deployed the principle of sufficient reason as a meta-physically necessary truth. The principle boils down to the claim that everything not metaphysically necessary has an explanation in some-thing metaphysically necessary. A being has metaphysical necessity according to Leibniz, if from its 'essence existence springs'; i.e. if it could not but exist.[3]

The principle of sufficient reason is satisfied by the existence of God because God's existence 'springs' from his essence in a logically necessary way: it is of the essence of God that he exists.

For Thomistic arguments, the existence of composite beings raises the question of God's existence. The metaphysical requirement for the existence of composite beings entails the existence of a being that is not composite, one whose essence is identical with its existence. This being, as Thomas reminds us, is commonly called God.

The Thomistic metaphysical analysis requires that actual existence precede potential existence. Any actual existence in this world, or any possible world, because it is composite, requires for its constant 'actualization' a being that is not composite, namely, God. No possible world that does not include God could be actual. Therefore, since nothing can come about without God's also keeping it in existence, nothing, in Thomas's view, is truly possible if God does not exist. This metaphysical fact about existence is consonant with interpreting Thomas's concept of God in terms of logical necessity. For Thomas (and Leibniz) the set of possible worlds which contain God is coextensive with the set of all possible worlds. Therefore, it would be wrong to drive a sharp wedge between logical necessity and the necessity attaching to a being of pure act.

This conclusion is confirmed by the way the necessity of God's existence functions in traditional arguments, both philosophical and theological. If by definition God is a necessary being, in the sense of logical necessity, cosmo-logical questions simply do not arise with respect to God. His existence is self-explanatory in a way that the existence of no other being is. The existence of a necessary being answers the question 'Why something rather than nothing?'

God's logically necessary existence also distinguishes him from any other kind of being. Leibniz, for example, argues that the world could not have this kind of absolute or metaphysical necessity: 'For the present world is necessary physically or hypothetically, but not absolutely or metaphysically . . . and so there must exist something different from the plurality of beings, that is the world, which, as we have allowed and have shown, is not of metaphysical necessity.'[4] Anselm, describing God as 'that than which no greater could be conceived', derives from that description God's logically necessary existence. The point is that, for both Anselm and Leibniz, what uniquely identifies God is or entails his logical necessity.

The theological role of necessity relates to this sense of God's ultimacy. The theological doctrine of creation points to God as the source of all existence:

nothing could exist except through his agency. A weaker sense of necessity might be consistent with this religious intuition, but it seems more adequate, as a description of God, to attribute to him absolute ultimacy, that is, not only ultimacy in this world, but ultimacy in every possible world.

Swinburne, in contrast to the tradition, explicitly denies that God is logically necessary. He explains God's necessary existence in this way: to say that God is a necessary being is 'to say that the existence of God is a brute fact which is inexplicable—not in the sense that we do not know its explanation, but in the sense that it does not have one—it is a terminus of complete explanation.[5] God is a necessary being because he is the ultimate brute fact: God simply has no explanation.[6] This concept of necessity, he believes, captures the sense of ultimacy and independence appropriate to God. God is not dependent on anything 'the description of which is not entailed by' his existence.[7]

One consequence of this definition is that necessity is predicated of whatever is the 'brute fact' of the universe. Swinburne states: 'If there is no God or any similar being, "the universe exists" would be a necessary proposition. For in that case the universe would not depend for its existence on anything else. The existence of the universe would be an ultimate brute fact.'[8]

A further consequence of this definition of necessity is that God's necessity is not relevant to the explanatory power of theism. In traditional arguments for God's existence, the logical necessity of God provided the means to halt the regress of sufficient reasons. But, by Swinburne's definition, the concept of necessity can have no relevance to the question of God's existence. In fact the description of anything as the necessary being of the universe is simply a recognition that it is the brute fact of existence.

[. . .]

II

The description of God as a logically necessary being is a contentious description. For example, in his debate with Copleston, Russell, following in the tradition of Hume and Kant, stipulates that logical necessity is solely the property of propositions and, therefore, concludes that God cannot be a logically necessary being.[9]

The notion that God is a logically necessary being cannot be separated from the idea that God, in the strongest possible sense, is conceived of as a perfect being, that is, the ultimate source of existence, the supremely valuable being in the universe, and the 'adequate object of religious worship' (hereafter I shall refer to this as God's ultimacy).[10] Swinburne, characterizing this ultimacy, speaks of God as the 'personal ground of being'. Anselm, also trying to capture this sense of God's absoluteness, describes God as 'that than which no greater can be conceived'. The motivation for claiming that God is a logically necessary being stems from the conviction that God is necessarily the ultimate being in the universe. the reason anyone countenances the possibility of the claim that God is logically necessary is in this connection. If such a being is possible, and if God is not identical with that being, then God would not have the ultimacy appropriate to his nature.

Anselm's articulation of the ontological argument presupposes the perfection of God. Anselm has been criticized for making existence a property of perfection, and, if the criticisms voiced by Hume and Kant are correct, then his way of stating what it means to be 'that than which no greater can be conceived' is surely mistaken. However, others have suggested that Anselm's categories are not the only categories that can express God's logical necessity.

It is a virtue of Plantinga's treatment of the ontological argument that he expresses God's ultimacy in terms of logical necessity without slipping into the same problems as Anselm.

[. . .]

Plantinga provides a cogent alternative interpretation of the ontological argument based not on the concepts of existence and perfection, but on the notion of possible worlds. God's absolute ultimacy, and his logical necessity, are defined in terms of existing in all logically possible worlds. By approaching the concept of God this way he intends to take what is cogent in the traditional arguments and to leave behind the problems associated with the particular conceptuality of Anselm's original statement. Thus, rather than construing existence as a perfection of the most perfect being, Plantinga uses the concepts of maximal excellence and maximal greatness. A maximally excellent being is one who has omniscience, omnipotence, and moral perfection. A maximally great being is one who possesses the property of being maximally excellent in all logically possible worlds. God is maximally excellent, but, because he is the absolutely ultimate being, he will also be maximally great, that is, if a maximally great being is possible.[11]

[. . .]

This discussion clarifies to some extent what it means to claim that God is a logically necessary being. God is a logically necessary being if God is, in Plantinga's terms, either maximally great, or, in terms mentioned earlier in this section, the ultimate being of the universe.

Swinburne discusses two objections to the possibility of God's being logically necessary. He first considers and rejects Russell's objection that logical necessity is solely a property of propositions and not things. He responds to this objection by providing particular counter-examples such as numbers. For example, the existence of a prime number between 9 and 13 illustrates the fact that some things do exist by logical necessity. There is a prime number between 9 and 13, namely 11, and it exists by logical necessity. That is, there are no possible worlds where the number 11 does not exist.

Though, admittedly the importance of this sort of example is limited—since God is not exactly like a number—it does demonstrate that our language contains propositions which state the existence of logically necessary things. And, any attempt, Swinburne concludes, to make the principle—only propositions are logically necessary—include these sorts of counter-examples and also exclude beings such as God has so far proved elusive. Thus, this objection, to Swinburne's mind, gives no reason for rejecting the idea and possibility of God's existing by logical necessity.

He argues, however, that a second, more substantive, objection is conclusive. If God is a logically necessary being, then any proposition entailed by the proposition stating his existence will itself be logically necessary. In the case of God's logically necessary existence, however, this leads to extremely counter-intuitive results. For example, the proposition 'God exists' entails the proposition 'There is a non-embodied person' (since God is a spirit). Therefore, if the proposition 'God exists' is logically necessary, so is the proposition 'There is a non-embodied person'. And if the latter proposition is logically necessary, its negation is logically impossible.[12] It follows then that the proposition 'All persons are embodied' is logically impossible. Yet, according to Swinburne, the proposition 'All persons are embodied' seems to be coherent, that is, seems to be possible. 'Of course,' he comments, 'there just might be contradictions buried in the statements which we have been considering, but in the absence of argument to the contrary we ought to assume what clearly appears to be the case that there are no such buried contradictions, and so that ["God exists"] is not logically necessary. Atheism is a coherent supposition.'[13] Thus, he concludes, God is not a logically necessary being.

His general premise in this argument is indubitably correct: propositions entailed by a logically necessary proposition must also be logically necessary. And it seems correct to say that, if God exists necessarily, there are no possible worlds where only embodied persons exist. But Swinburne draws from that implication the conclusion that God cannot be logically necessary. This conclusion is much stronger than his argument can actually support.

Swinburne's test for coherence contains two contrasting elements. With the first, which I shall call the deductive test, he tries to demonstrate the incoherence of the proposition 'God is a logically necessary being'. This, as we saw above, involves deducing a further proposition which is then tested for its coherence. If the entailment proves to be incoherent, then the original proposition is also incoherent. With the second element he tests the coherence of the entailment. Here he uses the 'obvious-contradiction' test. Unless there is an obvious contradiction in a proposition, then we are entitled to take the proposition to be coherent. With the second test, he concludes that the proposition 'All persons are embodied' is coherent. And using the first test, since the coherence of 'All persons are embodied' entails the incoherence of 'God is logically necessary', he concludes that the latter proposition must be incoherent.

Each of these methods has some intuitive plausibility. But a question remains whether their use in this context can prove the incoherence of the proposition that God is a logically necessary being. The problem is that Swinburne's argument invites a *tu quoque* response. If he used the deductive method to prove the incoherence of the proposition 'All persons are embodied' and tested the coherence of the implication by seeking an obvious contradiction, then he could just as cogently prove that it is logically impossible that all persons are embodied. The proposition 'All persons are embodied' entails the proposition 'No persons are non-embodied'. Thus, if the proposition 'All persons are embodied' is coherent, then its logical entailment 'No persons are non-embodied' will also be coherent. However, the entailment 'No persons are non-embodied' is inconsistent with propositions such as 'The maximally great being loves everyone'.

By definition the concept 'maximally great being' entails that there is at least one non-embodied person in every logically possible world. Hence, either the proposition 'The maximally great being loves everyone' is coherent and the proposition 'No persons are non-embodied' is not; or the proposition 'No persons are non-embodied' is coherent, and the proposition 'The maximally great being loves everyone' is not. But the concepts in the proposition 'The maximally great being loves everyone' are not obviously contradictory, that is, there is no obvious contradiction in the assertion that a maximally great being loves everyone. Hence, recalling Swinburne's argument above, though there may be a buried contradiction, until that is proved, it is reasonable to assume that the proposition 'The maximally great being loves everyone' is coherent and the proposition 'All persons are embodied' is not.

What seems unreasonable about his method is that it is far too lenient. Since it is more difficult to prove that a contradiction exists, it allows virtually any entailment to be coherent and to count against the possibility that God is logically necessary. Furthermore, if Swinburne used the 'obvious-contradiction' test on the proposition that God is a maximally great being, that proposition would turn out coherent also. If he weakened his demand with respect to the proposition 'God is a logically necessary being' or strengthened his demand with respect to the proposition 'All persons are embodied', he would be forced to admit that neither proposition, given these particular tests, can be shown to be incoherent. Thus, the most he can say is that either 'God is a logically necessary being' is possible or 'All persons are embodied' is possible, but that both cannot be.

Even if the concepts of 'person' or 'embodiment' in propositions such as 'All persons are embodied' are internally consistent with each other, it would not show that those propositions are coherent. A proposition can be logically impossible for reasons other than the internal incoherence of the concepts used to state it. Keith Ward, in examining a similar proposition, makes this point in this way:

> At first . . . it seems strange to say that 'No being exists which knows more than I do' is self-contradictory. Taken on its own, of course, it does not contradict itself. It is necessarily false, not because the phrase contains a self-contradiction, but because it contradicts another assertion which is necessarily true, namely, 'There is an omniscient being', and that the latter phrase is entailed by one that is necessarily true; it is not enough simply to look hard at the statement itself . . . To say that 'God exists' is logically necessary is not to trivialize the concept of God by making his existence a matter of verbal definition. 'God exists' is not made true by an arbitrary set of axioms. It is made true by the existence of God, and what makes it non-contingent is that there is no possible world in which God does not exist.[14]

Ward's point is this. The impossibility which attaches to propositions like 'No being exists which knows more than I do' or 'All persons are embodied' cannot appropriately be evaluated by examining the concepts of person and embodiment, and, for that reason, Swinburne's argument fails to show that the concept of God as a logically necessary being is impossible.

Swinburne believes that the logical possibility of 'All persons are embodied' depends on the lack of an internal contradiction in the concepts. But the impossibility involved is not a consequence of a contradiction between the concept of person and embodiment. The contradiction involves predicating the property 'being embodied' of all the persons which exist in a particular logically possible world. Our linguistic conventions permit us to predicate of persons, as an accidental property, both embodiment and non-embodiment. But we cannot determine the possible extension of these concepts in a possible world by examining just the concepts themselves. In any possible world the term 'person' will pick out all those objects which are persons. If God's existence is logically necessary, then there is no world where the concept 'all persons' does not pick out God. Therefore, on this view, since every possible world includes at least one non-embodied person, the contradiction which makes propositions such as 'All persons are embodied' logically impossible occurs at the point of predicating the property of 'being embodied' of every person which exists in that particular possible world. That is to say, the proposition 'All persons are embodied' is logically necessarily false not because the concepts of 'person' and 'embodiment' are internally inconsistent but because, given the existence of a maximally great being, the concept 'all persons' picks out a non-embodied person in every possible world. Swinburne's mistake is to assume that, because a statement contains concepts which are internally consistent, it describes a truly possible state of affairs.

Swinburne's argument against the possibility of God being logically necessary fails, therefore, on two counts. In the first place, he inconsistently applies the various tests for coherence and incoherence, which leads to a question about what his argument actually proves. Both propositions 'God is a logically necessary being' and 'All persons are embodied' have no obvious contradictions, and each of them entails the impossibility of propositions which have no obvious contradictions. The correct conclusion to draw is that his test shows that not both of the propositions can be possible, though we cannot show which is the impossible one. In the second place, there is a question about what the apparent coherence of the proposition 'All persons are embodied' demonstrates. Even if the internal consistency of the concepts which make up the proposition 'All persons are embodied' is granted, it is not evident that it would show the impossibility of the proposition 'God is a logically necessary being'.

There is another test for logical possibility which may prove more helpful in determining the coherence of God's logically necessary existence. If one can, from factual premises, show that a proposition is probably true, then this constitutes a coherence proof for it, since a proposition must be coherent to be true.[15] It may be the case that this method is more appropriate for deciding the coherence of the concept of a maximally great being than the other method.

Two questions, however, can be raised concerning this method of determining the coherence of 'God is maximally great'. First, though Swinburne, in fact, concedes that the only way to prove satisfactorily the coherence of the concept of God is to prove that God exists, it is not obvious which concept of God a proof of his existence would show to be coherent: that God is a maximally excellent being or that God is a maximally great being. And secondly, Swinburne gives a third argument against speaking of God as a logically necessary being: a logically necessary being, he argues, cannot explain a logically contingent universe. If his argument is correct, it is questionable whether any argument could be taken as a proof of the coherence of the proposition 'God is a logically necessary being'. In the next section, therefore, I shall address the issue of how a logically necessary God can serve as an explanation.

III

Swinburne affirms the logical contingency of God's existence because of problems concerning the explanatory relation between logically necessary and logically contingent propositions. He states:

> Nor can anything logically necessary provide any explanation of anything logically contingent. For a full explanation is . . . such that the *explanandum* (i.e. the phenomenon requiring explanation) is deducible from it. But you cannot deduce anything logically contingent from anything logically necessary. And a partial explanation is in terms of something which in the context makes the occurrence of the *explanandum* probable, without which things would probably have gone some other (logically possible) way. Yet a world in which some logically

necessary truth did not hold is an incoherent supposition, not one in which things would probably have gone some other way. These are among many reasons why it must be held that God is a logically contingent being, although maybe one necessary in some other ways.[16]

[. . .]

There is a contingent universe which needs explaining, and, by Swinburne's judgement, God's existence best explains it. However, if God is logically necessary, his existence cannot explain something contingent like the universe. If God were logically necessary, then that which is deduced from the fact that he exists, namely, the universe, itself would be logically necessary. But, in his view, the possibility of explanation rests on the possibility that one thing would occur rather than another. If the universe exists by logical necessity, it could not be other than it is and, for that reason, would not be more liable for explanation than, say, a prime number; but if the universe could truly have been different—or even not at all—then either it does not exist by logical necessity or a logically necessary truth does not hold. Since it is incoherent to suppose that there is a possible world where a logical truth does not hold, the universe must not exist by logical necessity.

Two aspects of the argument can be separated from one another. First, Swinburne argues that a logically contingent proposition cannot be deduced from a logically necessary one; and secondly, he argues that a logically necessary being cannot cause a logically contingent universe. As I see it, the first conclusion is true, but the second is not. The issue concerns the nature of the logically necessary being and whether it is his logical necessity which is involved in the causal explanation of the universe.

It is important to put Swinburne's discussion into context. He has developed his understanding of causal explanation carefully and has identified a number of other kinds of explanation. Complete explanation, for example, is a special case of full explanation. He says: 'A complete explanation of the occurrence of E is a full explanation of its occurrence in which all the factors cited are such that there is no explanation (either full or partial) of their existence or operation in terms of factors operative at the time of their existence or operation.'[17] Yet a further sort of explanation he calls ultimate explanation: 'I define an ultimate explanation of E as a complete explanation of E, in which the factors C and R cited are such that their existence and operation have no explanation either full or partial in terms of other factors.'[18] The difference between these two is that a complete explanation may have a further explanation, though not by factors operative at the time; while an ultimate explanation has no further explanation at all.

Swinburne defines absolute explanation as a special case of ultimate explanation. Absolute explanation not only has no further explanation, but 'the existence and operation of each of the factors cited is either self-explanatory or logically necessary'.[19] However, he believes that no such explanations exist because nothing can explain itself nor, as we noted earlier, can anything logically contingent follow from something logically necessary. Both of these reasons for denying the possibility of absolute explanation find their force in the fact that he is speaking of causal explanation. Obviously something cannot cause itself; so it cannot be self-explanatory in that way. And, if explanation is defined in terms of deductive entailment, any entailment following from a logically necessary proposition must itself be logically necessary. But, since the universe is logically contingent, an explanation of the universe must also be logically contingent. Therefore, if something does exist with logical necessity, it cannot be the explanation of the universe (nor anything else logically contingent).

Swinburne is correct on this point: nothing contingent is entailed by anything logically necessary. It also follows that, in the context of a causal explanation where, as Swinburne argues, a full explanation deductively entails that which is to be explained, there can be no absolute explanation, if that which is to be explained is logically contingent. But it does not follow from this that God cannot be a logically necessary being. Even if we grant Swinburne's concept of explanation, this conclusion would not follow. He would need to show that, if God is a logically necessary being, God's choices and actions are logically necessary as well. This Swinburne has not done.

If we speak of God as a personal being, his choices, decisions, and actions must be contingent. This is entirely consistent with the claim that God is a logically necessary being. Though the logically contingent cannot be deduced from the logically necessary, the logically contingent can be deduced from the conjunction of a logically necessary truth, namely, God exists, and a logically contingent truth, namely, God had the intention to create the universe. It is not from the sheer existence of God that the universe is deduced: rather it is the contingent action of the personal God which explains the existence of the universe. The crucial issue then is whether something can exist by logical necessity and at the same time be a person.

If God is a maximally great being, he necessarily exists. This will be problematic only if maximal greatness is incompatible with being personal. But, since the concept of maximal greatness is defined in terms of the personal qualities, such as omniscience and omnipotence, there is at least no obvious incompatibility present. The properties which are essential to being a person, such as having beliefs, appear compatible with the property of 'existing in all possible worlds'.

[. . .]

A similar issue arises in Swinburne's account over the relationship between God's necessity and his personhood. It appears that he believes one cannot hold these two attributes together. And given his concern for explanation, he abandons logical necessity.

One does not need, however, to pose such stark alternatives. Once one separates the logical necessity of God's existence from the contingency of his actions, there is no need to deny that God is logically necessary. Only if one holds something similar to the Thomistic concept of God as pure act is one driven to the extreme conclusion that logical necessity and personality are incompatible. Once the two properties are properly separated, there is no need to believe that they are incompatible; God has both. Keith Ward puts it as follows:

> As for the necessary not entailing the contingent, that is, of course, quite correct. It is, indeed, a particular form of the crucial difficulty about the relation of creation to necessity with which I am centrally concerned. It clearly requires making God, the self-explanatory being, contingent in some respects . . . I think Swinburne's mistake, and that of most other theists who have discussed the issue, is to insist that God is either necessary in all respects, or contingent in all respects—just the ultimate contingent fact. Whereas . . . we can have both necessity and contingency in God. And we need both.[20]

The case against the logical necessity of God's existence, therefore, is insufficient to show that the concept is incompatible with causal explanation.

It is evident, however, that the logical necessity of God's existence cannot enter into the *explanans* of causal explanation. For that reason, it may be objected that, even if the concept of a logically necessary being is coherent, it is simply redundant. There is no need to postulate such a God because logical necessity can play no role in the explanatory power of a hypothesis. Hence, we return to a question posed at the end of the last section. There I maintained that Swinburne's argument against taking God to be a logically necessary being was inconclusive and that it may be possible to demonstrate the coherence of the concept of a maximally great being by giving an argument for the existence of one. But in this section I have agreed with Swinburne that, if the concept is coherent, the fact that God is a logically necessary being cannot be significant for causal explanation. In the next and final section I shall show that the conflict can be resolved.

IV

Traditionally God's logical necessity has played a central role in arguments for God's existence. Kant is correct when he identifies this concept of God as one core element in the teleological and cosmological arguments. As we saw earlier, Leibniz completes the cosmological argument with a metaphysically necessary being, and Thomas with a being of pure Act.[21] The more contemporary arguments such as Swinburne's move away from the centrality of God's logical necessity toward the explanatory power of theism as a hypothesis where the necessity of God, even in its weaker form, has no role to play.

It seems to me that both positions are in error: the former because it makes God's logical necessity do too much and the latter because it makes it do too little. In contrast to the traditional arguments, one must admit that the principle of sufficient reason and the principle of existential causality are at best highly controversial and therefore inadequate as general proofs for the existence of God.[22] Against contemporary usage it must be admitted that necessity, namely, logical necessity, has a significant part in the explanatory power of theism.

To see this we might look again at the role of the logically necessary being in traditional arguments. At least two functions come to mind. The first is to halt the regress of causes. Of a necessary being no further questions can be asked. The second function is to provide a sense of ultimacy to the explanation. It eliminates any vagueness or ambiguity in the answer to the question 'Why is there something rather than nothing at all?' If God is personal, then we can speak of Him as the cause of the universe. And if God is also logically necessary, then we can speak of Him as the absolute explanation of the universe. This is a further explanatory function of the theistic hypothesis. There is no mystery about the ultimate foundation of existence, for causal questions and ultimacy questions come together in the one logically necessary person: God.

If God is, as Swinburne argues, the logically contingent ultimate brute fact of existence, there are some questions which even an appeal to God's existence cannot answer. Swinburne notes that science cannot explain why 'there are any states of affairs at all; it can explain only why, given that there are such states, this state is followed by that state'.[23] And he implies with this assertion that the existence of God can. The existence of 'any states of affairs at all' is too big for science and is therefore a starting point for the argument for theism. The way he states this, however, conceals a crucial ambiguity. If God is logically contingent, his existence is but one instance of the states of affairs which make up this world. Moreover, if his existence is a brute fact, his existence is a state of affairs which cannot be explained. Hence, in this sense, even the appeal to God cannot answer why there are any states of affairs at all. Swinburne admits that '*a priori* the existence of anything at all logically contingent, even God, may seem vastly improbable, or at least, not very probable. (Hence, "the mystery of existence".)'[24] God's existence, therefore, explains not why there are any states of affairs at all but only why, given that there is an initial state of affairs, there is this particular set of state of affairs.

It is important to put this into the context of an integrative theistic explanation. The capacity of a world hypothesis such as theism to explain both causally and purposively is an aspect of the integrative power of the hypothesis. The logical necessity of God's existence represents a third integrative concept. Theism makes sense of the universe in part by eliminating the ultimate mystery of the universe. Many, sensing that there must be some ultimate purpose and ultimate ground for existence, ask, 'Why is there anything at all?'[25] Theism has always served to provide an answer to this sort of question, a question that Swinburne's strictly causal formulation of the theistic hypothesis cannot answer.

What is at issue here is the nature of the cumulative case for theism as an explanatory hypothesis. Normally, God's logically necessary existence is not seen as part of the argument for theism. The mistake is either to make the entire case for theism rest upon this claim, as in the ontological argument, or to allow it no part in the theistic hypothesis, as in Swinburne's inductive approach. If we can understand God's logical necessity as a significant component of an integrative explanation, we have the possibility of a more powerful cumulative-case argument than is heretofore available.

I have argued that God's logical necessary existence is neither incoherent nor explanatorily irrelevant. Its value is within a properly understood cumulative case for God's existence. In this context we can see how the ontological argument is supported by the other evidential considerations and it contributes to the explanatory power of theism. It is a mistake to consider the different arguments in isolation and to fail to recognize how they answer different questions and how they mutually support one another. Mackie makes a step toward understanding the reciprocal support these arguments give each other. Given Plantinga's restatement of the ontological argument he questions whether it is reasonable to accept the premiss that God is a possible being. In his answer he appeals to the 'simplest' conclusion as the most justified. He argues:

> Surely the more extravagant is that which asserts that maximal greatness is realized in some possible world. For this carries with it the requirement that a maximally excellent being—and, indeed, a maximally great one—should exist in every possible world, whereas the rival premise that no maximality is realized in some possible world, still allows maximal excellence to be realized in some possible worlds though not in others. The latter, then, is less restrictive, less extravagant, and so on very general grounds the more acceptable.[26]

Mackie is correct as far as he goes. The more 'extravagant' hypothesis is less simple and, for that reason, less acceptable. He bases his conclusion, however, on too narrow a base. Once the overriding concern becomes one of evidence, it is simply false to imply that simplicity would be the sole factor in deciding the reasonableness of accepting God's possibility. A justification for the possibility of God will incorporate all the evidence and exploit all the resources of explanatory power the theistic hypothesis may have. This will include not only the simplicity of the hypothesis, but also the capacity of theism to answer questions about the cause of the universe and the meaning of existence.

These considerations are important with respect to the nature of God as a logically necessary being. Given that theism is a causal explanation of the universe, it is essential that God has the ability to make contingent choices and is free to do or to refrain from acting. In these respects God's choices are contingent. But, if God is not also a logically necessary being, theism loses some of its integrative power, for it does not answer the most ultimate questions about the nature of existence.

[. . .]

Notes

1. G. F. W. Leibniz, *Discourse on Metaphysics*, trans. G. R. Montgomery (La Salle, Ill., 1927).
2. *New Essays Concerning Human Understanding*, appendix 10, in John Hick (ed.), *The Existence of God* (London, 1964), pp. 37–9.
3. *The Existence of God*, p. 127.
4. 'On the Ultimate Origination of Things' in *The Philosophical Writings of Leibniz*, trans. Mary Morris (London, 1934), p. 33.
5. *The Existence of God*, pp. 92–3.
6. That is, God has no causal explanation.
7. Richard Swinburne, *The Coherence of Theism* (Oxford, 1977), pp. 250–1.
8. Ibid.
9. Russell and Copleston, 'The Debate', in Hick (ed.), *The Existence of God*, pp. 168–72.
10. This is my attempt to articulate the point made in the previous section with reference to Leibniz and Anselm. Cf. J. N. D. Findlay's discussion of the 'religiously adequate object of worship' in 'Can God's Existence be Disproved?', *Mind*, 52 (1948), pp. 108–18.
11. Alvin Plantinga, *The Nature of Necessity* (Oxford, 1974), pp. 214–15.
12. *The Coherence of Theism*, p. 265.
13. Ibid.
14. Keith Ward, *Rational Theology and the Creativity of God* (Oxford, 1982), pp. 43–4.
15. Swinburne, *The Coherence of Theism*, pp. 45–9.
16. Hick (ed.), *The Existence of God*, p. 76.
17. *The Existence of God*, pp. 74–5.
18. Ibid., p. 75.
19. Ibid., p. 76.
20. *Rational Theology*, p. 8.
21. See sect. 1.
22. See William Rowe, *The Cosmological Argument* (Princeton, NJ, 1975), pp.73ff.
23. *The Existence of God*, pp. 71–2.
24. Ibid., p. 130.
25. Cf. Ronald Hepburn, 'From World to God', in Basil Mitchell (ed.), *The Philosophy of Religion* (Oxford, 1971).
26. John L. Mackie, *The Miracle of Theism* (Oxford, 1983), p. 61.

ETERNITY
3.2

'GOD AND TIMELESSNESS'

Alan Padgett

[. . .]

One central tenet of theism which does impact upon the doctrine of eternity is the sustaining of creation by God. To say that he sustains the created universe is to say that no episode of the universe would exist if it were not for the power of God supporting that episode in being. By an episode of the universe we mean the mereological sum of all episodes of real objects at a given period of time in the history of the universe. This excludes the deistic notion that God sets up the universe and its laws and does not need to support each episode in existence by a direct act. I will also assume the truth of this doctrine, as almost every theist does. I consider this doctrine, in fact, far more central to theism than any particular notion of eternity, and therefore the doctrine of eternity we adopt should conform to the idea that God sustains the world.

THE POSSIBILITY OF TIMELESS CAUSATION

Nelson Pike has recently argued that the idea of God directly sustaining each episode in the history of the universe is inconsistent with the traditional doctrine of eternity. He holds that an absolutely timeless God could not create anything in time (*God and Timelessness*, 97–120). For "the production-verb

Alan Padgett, 'God and Timelessness', from 'A Coherent Model of Absolute Timelessness', *God, Eternity and the Nature of Time* (New York: St. Martin's Press, 1990), pp. 56–76, 150.

carries clear implications regarding the temporal position of the product relative to the creative-activity" (p. 105). Pike's point may be true of humans, and human language, but must it always hold for a God? Merely because an effect is in time, does it necessarily follow that the agent who causes it is in time? Pike nowhere demonstrates that, *of logical necessity*, every datable effect implies an agent with location or extension in time. Granted, the effect itself will have a date, but does every datable effect logically imply an agent who exists at some time? Let's state this question as a positive principle:

(1). The occurrence of any temporal effect brought about by an agent implies that the agent in question is temporal.

Our question, then, is whether (1) is true of logical necessity.

The only type of agency human beings regularly have acquaintance with is agency in time. While some imagination is needed to allow a timeless agent to have a datable effect, there seems nothing logically contradictory in the idea itself. Although Pike claims there is something essentially temporal in production-verbs (p. 107), could this not be true of *any* description of action in a natural language? Most languages have tenses or similar indications of temporality for action-verbs. Of course such languages will thus give a time-aspect to all verbs. Perhaps the temporal aspects of our language must be set aside for the purposes of metaphysical accuracy. Further, all humans are in time and act in time. In fact all agents on earth are in time. So naturally we assume that agency logically implies temporality. But human language must not be allowed to limit the reality of God.

One could give an argument for (1) as follows. Science has taught us that every temporal effect has a prior, temporal cause. The effects of God's acts are temporal, thus God must be temporal, if he really affects the physical world. But the premise of this argument simply begs the question against divine timeless agency. Whether or not every temporal effect has a temporal cause is the very issue at stake. Furthermore, this premise applies to things and events in this space–time universe. All such things and events already have a temporal location: but God need not have one.

Another argument for (1) could run as follows. In order to bring anything about, an agent must change. Anything that changes is in time in some way. Ergo, any agent must be in time. But is it true that an agent must, of logical necessity, change in order to bring anything about? If a huge unchanging mass replaced the sun in the center of our solar system, other things being basically equal, the planets would still orbit this huge mass because of its gravity. Thus the huge mass would be a necessary cause of the orbiting of its planets, but it would not have to change in order to do so. The problem with this response is, the huge mass *is not an agent*. Surely the agent must, in order to cause some intended new effect, act differently at different times. Acting differently is a real change, and whatever undergoes real change is in time. Therefore, (1) is true of logical necessity. I can find nothing wrong with this objection, granting the assumption that *God acts differently*. Yet perhaps God only seems to act differently. Perhaps God's timeless, eternal, unchanging act is always the same "in eternity." Such a view is at least worthy of exploration.

In the case of God, he could sustain the universe of matter-energy without himself being in time. Yet at each moment of time we would be tempted to say from our perspective, "now God is sustaining the universe." In other words, it would seem to us that "now" God affects the universe, when in fact this act might be timeless in the absolute sense. Only from a *prima facie* human point of view – that is, only from a point of view within the structures of time – does the date of the effect seem to give the cause a date. Humans are naturally inclined to infer temporal causes from temporal effects. From a non-human point of view outside of the structures of time, the cause of the universe need not have a date. This basically Augustinian point (*Confessions*, 11.31) is well expressed in our age by Robert Neville (*God the Creator*, 104):

> [The power of God's creative] activity can be said eternally to have a temporal structure or form. Hence, although its productive activity is not temporal, from a point within time the power's activity may be viewed as coming before and after, and in serial order. This follows from the fact that what is productive of the determinations of being cannot be temporal so long as time is a determination of being.

If time is created by God, how can God be limited to temporal existence? Since God creates time, his creative activity (the defender of the traditional argument will urge) gives reality its temporal structure, but without he himself necessarily being temporal.

[. . .]

God can timelessly and changelessly exert exactly the same power, in exactly the same way, to affect the entire universe, with its internal temporal structure. By one, single, timeless act God could sustain the universe, even though from a human perspective this act would seem temporal. In Neville's words, this act will give time its structure, and thus will seem datable, based on the date of its effect, from a human point of view: but in fact it is an absolutely timeless act.

This conception of how God could be absolutely timeless and yet sustain the universe depends upon the idea of a timeless causal process. Such an idea is difficult to imagine. Stephen Davis writes that "we have on hand no acceptable concept of atemporal causation, i.e. of what it is for a timeless cause to produce a temporal effect." (*Logic and the Nature of God*, 13). Despite this problem, unless one is going to argue that time is not contingent, then a timeless world is possible. And on such a world, God might have created something. On such a timeless world, nothing would change, since change implies time. But even so, the existence of, say, a timeless angel would depend upon God. For God could have (timelessly) chosen not to create that one angel. God's choice to create the angel would be logically prior to the existence of the angel; but since time would not exist, the existence of the angel would not be temporally antecedent to the existence of God. Both the angel and God would alike be timelessly eternal, but God would still be the cause of the angel's existence. Despite the remarks of Davis, there is nothing logically contradictory about such an idea. In fact, Davis himself admits as much (p. 21).

[. . .]

Here the objector may point out that the actual world is not timeless, but an ever changing reality. One can accept this point as true, without abandoning the position we are advocating here. The power of this point is best made in a revised version of (1):

> (1'). The occurrence of an effect (which is itself a change) implies a change in some cause of the effect.

Surely (1') is true: if the light goes out on my desk, this change or effect is the result of some change in the causes of the light. For example, the electric current may have ceased, or the bulb may have broken. Because the effect happened, and so some change occurred, we rightly infer some change in the causes of the effect. This principle is sound. Some causes may be unchanging, but at least one cause must change, if an effect takes place. The application of (1') to our problem is also clear. If God is the only ultimate cause of changing things (that is, if God sustains by a direct act the changing episodes of the universe) then God, too, must undergo some change. He undergoes a change, in that he does different things at different times, and acting differently entails a real change for the agent in question. If I am running, or thinking, or writing and then I stop, I have really changed: the same holds if I begin such activities.

I suggest that in any universe where God exists, things do not just happen without any reason. So in any universe where God exists, (1') will be true. Thus God, too, must really change since he directly causes different effects, and so acts differently.

But this objection can be turned. Let us allow, at least at this point in the argument, that the stasis theory of time is true. Further, let us allow that God's sustaining activity relates to the fundamental ontological status of things and events. Now on the stasis theory of time, no particular episode or event is timeless, because they will all have dates. But the totality of the world, considered from a four-dimensional perspective, is both timeless and changeless. If we include in "the totality of the world" all events, things, and happenings *and their dates* (i.e. the before-after relations they have with each other, and any system(s) of reference for dating events in such an order) then the world will be timeless. The world as a whole does not occur at any time, because all dates are internally defined. What is true of the parts is not true of the whole, for all possible changes and times are contained within the whole. All changes and times will occur within the world; outside or beyond the four-dimensional universe, there will not be any change or time. As Helm writes:

> A timeless being may not act within the universe, yet it makes sense to say that such a being produces (tenseless) the universe. The production of the universe is thus not the production of some event or complex of events in time; it is the production of the whole material universe, time included (*Eternal God*, p. 69).

God could thus sustain the four-dimensional space–time universe, just like he sustained the angel in the above example. For the fundamental ontological status of things is eternally the same. Changes in the sense of things having incompatible properties at different dates will still occur. But things and events will not change in their fundamental ontological status. Things and events will exist at the time they exist, no matter when "now" is according to humans. It is this fundamental ontological change that is at issue when we consider the act of God sustaining the world. And it is this sort of fundamental ontological change of status that the stasis theory denies. Such a conception of how a timeless God can sustain the world including dates depends upon the stasis theory of time, which some theologians advocating the traditional doctrine of eternity have rejected. We will have to see whether they may have been inconsistent on this point.

Given this idea of God sustaining the world, *pace* Pike, God could act eternally without changing and without being temporal. The question is, can a timeless God sustain the world without changing, if the process theory of time is true? We put the question this way because of the close relationship between change and time. If God had to change in order to sustain each different episode in the history of our world, then even if he need not be "in our time," he will not be timeless in the absolute sense.

[. . .]

DIALOGUE WITH SELECT DEFENDERS OF DIVINE TIMELESSNESS

We now turn our attention to certain representative theologians who have argued for absolute timeless divine eternity. We will see that the views held by these theologians lead to the stasis theory of time. Thomas Aquinas will represent ancient theologians. Among modern thinkers Eleonore Stump and Norman Kretzmann have been selected for dialogue.

Of all those thinkers in Christian tradition who have defended the doctrine of divine timeless eternity, Thomas Aquinas is one of the great minds. His genius did not lie in originality so much as in the penetrating nature of his thought, the thoroughness of his investigation, and his pursuit of clear and coherent theology. Thomas culled from previous centuries the best arguments for the timelessness of God. Among his theological predecessors, Augustine argued that God was timeless because of God's immutability. Boethius emphasized the issue of divine foreknowledge and human freedom as an important point in favor of the timelessness of God. Anselm argued that God was timeless and spaceless on the basis of divine simplicity. Thomas Aquinas used and refined all of these arguments. What is more, the arguments of several modern philosophers on this issue are a re-presentation of the Thomistic view.[1] So it is that we turn first to the writings of Aquinas in considering the relationship between God and time.

Recall the fundamental Thomistic notion of divine timelessness. God is simple, and thus immutable and eternal. Since God does not change or move, God is not in time. Further, all of time is present to God "at once" in eternity. Here we may recall the image of a circle evoked by Aquinas (SCG, I.66). The center of the circle is outside the circumference, but all of the circumference is present to the center. God's eternity is like the center of the circle: he is outside of time, yet all of time is present to him.

This view of God creates a problem if one holds to the process theory of time, a problem which Duns Scotus clearly saw. Assuming this theory of time, things and events do change their fundamental ontological status with the passage of time. Since God maintains the fundamental ontological status of things, God must change over time. On the process view, the future and its events and episodes are not real. Thus future effects of God's direct sustaining act would not be real. Would not God have to change in order to bring about such new effects of his direct actions? Aquinas considered this objection (SCG, II.32), and his response was, "newness of the effect does not demonstrate newness of action in God, since His action is His essence" (SCG, II.35). In seeking to understand this response, we will need to distinguish between "will" as used by Aquinas and what modern philosophers call "intention."

By "intention" here we simply mean any conscious purposing to do or to be doing. When used of the divine Agent, this term will include what philosophers have called "trying," "intention," and "motive." Of course when God tries to do something, it always gets done! Distinctions drawn by philosophers between these terms are important for human agency, but less important when speaking of God. But we should draw a distinction between God's "intention," or trying, which coexists with the act intended, and God's "design." By "design" we mean an agent's plans or purposes. God's design can be unchanging from all eternity; he can decide to act at time X, and need never change his mind (see Creel, *Divine Impassibility*). However, to accomplish anything, an agent must add to her actual ability to bring about the intended effect, the particular instance of intention. If I always have the power to raise my arm, and I design to do so at time X, I must also add the intention to raise my arm at time X, in order to raise my arm at time X. We shall call this ability to bring about an intended effect one's "power-to-act." In order to act any agent must use or put forth power-to-act, or cease to do so for those effects one wishes to stop.[2]

Since God acts in sustaining the universe, he must exert his sustaining power-to-act in accordance with changing circumstances in our time. But does this mean he would have to change from an eternal perspective? It does not follow that God would have to be in our time to so act, as previously argued. But some kind of change in accordance with the changing circumstances of human time seems to be called for on the basis of principle (1'). If a timeless God does not change in any way, how can he sustain the changing universe? Would he not have to change to do so (not, indeed, in his design, but in his intention and power-to-act)? Thus it seems *prima facie* that a timeless God could not have a temporal effect, or he would have to change over time (that is, he would have to do different things at different times). But why could God not act *timelessly* in such a way as to bring about a temporal effect? This, in essence, is the response of Aquinas.

The divine simplicity assures that the divine will is the divine existence: "as his intellect is his own existence, so is his will" (ST Ia, q. 19, a. 1). As Pure Act, God's activity and his existence are unified in the Being of God. For this reason, God timelessly and changelessly does the same thing, and anything that God wills gets done! God does not "will" (which for Aquinas includes design, intention and power-to-act) that when future time F is present, then God will cause A. Rather, he timelessly wills A-at-F (see also Sturch, "The Problem of Divine Eternity"). He timelessly wills that each effect take place, in its temporal relationships within the process of time. This is seen more clearly from Aquinas' view of divine foreknowledge.

For Aquinas, strictly speaking God does not have foreknowledge. God sees everything in his eternal, timeless "present" (understanding "present" here to be analogous to the temporal present). He uses the image of an observer in a high tower, who can see all the men passing along a road, while the travelers themselves can only see the men next to each other (*Aristotle: On Interpretation*, I. 14, sec. 19). God is like the observer in the tower, watching the passage of time. "God is wholly outside the order of time, stationed as it were at the summit of eternity, which is wholly simultaneous, and to Him the whole course of time is subject to one simple intuition." (*op. cit.*, sec. 20). In the same way, God acts throughout time in one, single, simple and eternal act which has multiple temporal effects.

But a problem clearly arises with this view, from a process perspective. God's sustaining power-to-act need not be "in time" if God is timeless. And it does not automatically follow that because God's power-to-act brings about a temporal effect, his power-to-act must itself be temporal. Certainly God's power-to-act seems to occur at a certain date *from our point of view*. But it does not follow from this consideration alone that God's power-to-act is temporal itself, rather than being the timeless foundation of all temporal structure. Would it not be possible, then, for God to will timelessly a certain effect take place, at a certain time? If by "will" one means design, no problem arises. But the problem is this: if God's "will" includes intention and power-to-act, as it does for Aquinas, then God cannot timelessly "will" that a certain effect take place at some non-present time if the process view of time is correct.

To see why, say that God will sustain an episode of the universe, *E*, at a future time, *F*. Since *F* is future, all episodes of things and events at time *F* do not exist. It's not merely that they do not exist now – they do not exist in any sense. It is true that they *will exist*; but this is just a species of non-existence *tout court*. Can God "will" something that does not exist? If God is eternally, immutably "willing" *E*-at-*F*, can *E* not exist (tenselessly, perhaps) at *F*? Surely *E*-at-*F* must exist in some way, if God changelessly forever "wills" *E*-at-*F*! But since God's will is actively sustaining any episode whenever it exists, this model of divine timeless agency leads to the stasis theory of time, according to which all states of affairs are equally real, whether past, present or future. According to the process view of time, God cannot changelessly "will" *E*-at-*F*, because *E*-at-*F* does not changelessly exist. Yet anything that God "wills" to exist does exist. Since God "wills" *E*-at-*F* to exist, and God's will does not change, *E* is existing in some sense at *F* (ST, Ia, q.19, a.4 and 6). Since God is eternally and immutably "willing" *E*-at-*F*, then *E*-at-*F* must be existing in some way also eternally and immutably. Thus *E* exists (tenselessly?) at *F* no matter what time humans call "now."

According to Aquinas, all things ultimately find their cause in God: God is present by his activity in all things, and throughout time (ST, Ia, q.8 and 10). All items at every time in the history of the universe are eternally willed by God. Thus all items at every time in the history of the universe exist (tenselessly). These ideas, taken together, lead to the stasis theory of time (see also Craig, "Was Thomas Aquinas a B-Theorist of Time?"). If God is pure act, and if God puts forth unchanging, simple, eternal power-to-act that *E* exist at *F*, then *E*-exists-at-*F* immutably and eternally. It is not merely that God intends to sustain *E*, when *F* is the present time. This would make God's pure act depend upon changing circumstances. Rather, God eternally puts forth power-to-act as well as intention (i.e., "Will") in the single, eternal act by which he sustains all things. And since God sustains all things and events at every time, all things that exist at some time, exist (tenselessly). Thus the stasis theory of time is correct. This, at least, seems to be the implication of Aquinas' answer to how God can sustain a changing universe without himself changing: "newness of the effect does not demonstrate newness of action in God, since His action is His essence" (SCG, II. 35, cf. I.79).

We have seen that Aquinas' view of God's simplicity, immutability and eternity lead to the stasis theory of time. Whether or not Aquinas himself actually held to this theory of time is another question, of course (see Quinn,

"The Doctrine of Time in St. Thomas"). But perhaps more modern defenders of divine timelessness can and will avoid this implication.

Like other defenders of the traditional doctrine of eternity, Stump and Kretzmann deny the *prima facie* incoherence of divine timelessness with temporal action on the part of God. They define timeless eternity as an unending and illimited life of timeless duration, which is "lived" completely, all at once ("Eternity", 430–433). Given such a view, they develop the idea of an "eternal–temporal simultaneity" based upon the relativity of all simultaneity.

[. . .]

Stump and Kretzmann's definition of timeless eternity is an important clarification of the traditional doctrine of eternity. This definition is generally helpful and enlightening given certain refinements. However, Stump and Kretzmann not only define eternity, they describe its properties. At the center of their description of divine eternity is the concept of "ET-simultaneity," and to this concept we now turn.

Simultaneity between God's eternity and all of human time is central to Stump and Kretzmann's account of a timeless God. In order to describe how a timeless God could act in, and know of, the temporal world Stump and Kretzmann develop the idea of an "ET" (eternal–temporal) simultaneity ("Eternity," 434–440).[3] They define ET-simultaneous as (p. 439):

For every x and for every y, x and y are ET-simultaneous if:

(i) either x is eternal [timeless] and y is temporal, or vice versa; and
(ii) for some observer A, in the unique eternal reference frame, x and y are both present – i.e., either x is eternally present and y is observed as temporally present, or vice versa; and
(iii) for some observer, B, in one of the infinitely many temporal reference frames, x and y are both present – i.e., either x is observed as eternally present and y is temporally present, or vice versa.

One problem with this definition is equivocation. The "present" of a timeless eternity cannot be the same as the temporal present. Stump and Kretzmann state that an eternal being "has present existence in some sense of the word 'present'" (p. 434). But "present" is a temporal term, and eternity is non-temporal according to their definition. Yet one can see an analogy between the eternal "present" and the temporal present.

Let us allow that an eternal being has a "present-like" existence. While one could grant that a timeless being exists in a present-like, atemporally successive mode of being, Stump and Kretzmann glide all too easily over the distinction between a temporal present and a timeless present-like instant. They state that x is temporal and y is atemporal (or vice verse) *and* that x and y

are both "present." But one is temporally present, and the other is atemporal, and not really a part of our temporal system. The fundamental problem then, of how a timeless present-like being could share a moment of time with some temporally present event, is inherent within this very definition.

[. . .]

The conception of how a timeless God sustains a temporal universe depends upon one's understanding of time. As noted before, if the stasis view of time is correct, then God need not change over time in order to sustain the world. The events and things which exist at particular times are all equally real. They do not pass out of being, but exist (tenselessly). Since they exist tenselessly, God's eternal sustaining act can also exist, without God having to change in accordance with process. Of course it would seem to us that God was changing, but this would only be because we experienced the subjective distinction between past, present and future. In reality, and for God, this distinction would be an illusion. This theory of time allows divine timelessness and divine agency to be reconciled.[4]

Stump and Kretzmann are not willing to travel this philosophical path. They insist on the genuine reality of process, and reject the stasis theory of time ("Eternity," 441–444). Instead they appeal to the idea of ET-simultaneity. But their definition of ET-simultaneity does not address the fundamental problem of the simultaneity of a timeless present-likeness and a temporal present. In order to deal with this problem, Stump and Kretzmann turn to the Special Theory of Relativity.

In defending their idea of ET-simultaneity, Stump and Kretzmann appeal to the Special Theory of Relativity. This brings us to the central error made by Stump and Kretzmann: their misunderstanding of this very theory. In order to give some plausibility to their claim that a timeless present-like instant could be simultaneous with the temporal present, Stump and Kretzmann point out the *relativity of simultaneity* in the Special Theory of Relativity (STR). Their defence of ET-simultaneity depends on the relativity of simultaneity in the STR (p.437f.) Stump and Kretzmann claim that this discussion of relativity is merely a heuristic device (p. 440). But even so, surely this idea is necessary to the demonstration of the coherence of ET-simultaneity, given the dependence of their explanation of its coherence upon relativity. Given its *prima facie* incoherence, the plausibility of ET-simultaneity greatly depends upon their interpretation of relativity.

Stump and Kretzmann state that due to the STR "there is no absolute state of being temporally simultaneous with, any more than there is an absolute state of being to the left of" (p. 438). This is a popular, but false, opinion. There are a number of absolutes in relativity theory, when by "absolute" we mean "the same for all physically possible observers." One such absolute is the round-trip speed of light, which is the same in all frames. Another absolute is found in what A.A. Robb called "conical order" (*A Theory of Space and Time*, 15f.).

Conical order is the temporal order of absolute past, absolute simultaneity and absolute future, according to the STR. This particular absolute is quite important for our dialogue with Stump and Kretzmann. Two events are absolutely simultaneous, in our sense, if they occur at the same time in the same place. If one observer finds that two things occur at the same time and place, all observers will find that they are simultaneous. Two events are absolutely past if one is in the past "light-cone" of the other. An event is in your "light-cone" if it is physically possible for a photon to travel from you to the event. Since causation can at best spread at the speed of light, anything in the causal past or future of my here-now is in my light-cone. Further, two events are absolutely future if one is in the future light-cone of the other.

[. . .]

So there *are* absolute temporal relations in the STR. It is simply not the case that "being simultaneous" is as relative as "being to the left of." In fact, *no event in my causal future or past can be simultaneous with my here-now*. We shall see that the very witness that Stump and Kretzmann bring into court contradicts their case.

What follows, then, from this misunderstanding of the STR by Stump and Kretzmann? Two things: first, Stump and Kretzmann commit the fallacy of false analogy. They use the analogy of the relative simultaneity between two events outside of their light-cones to support some notion of God's timeless cause being simultaneous with its effect. But if two events are outside of each other's light-cones, then *they cannot be causally connected*. On the STR, only events inside of the light-cone can be causally connected. Since Stump and Kretzmann want some sort of causal connection between God and the world to hold, they should not have appealed to the relativity of simultaneity between events that – by the very nature of things – cannot be causally connected. Second, the attempt by Stump and Kretzmann to explain away the *prima facie* contradiction in ET-simultaneity fails. Because simultaneity is not as "relative" as they need it to be to make sense of ET-simultaneity, the full force of the contradiction stands. The very idea that a timeless present-like instant could share a moment of time with the temporal present is just as incoherent as it was when the argument began.

Given this critique of Stump and Kretzmann, we are now in a better position to consider whether God could act once, changelessly, "from eternity," and have all of the effects of this divine cause occur at different times. Just for the sake of argument, assume that the process theory of time is true. Say that God acts such that, at some time $T4$, some episode B of an object was sustained. Further, at the present time, $T5$, God acts so as to sustain a different object's episode, C, which is in the same place as B. Now $T4$ and $T5$ are some distance apart in time, and not Zero Time Related. Can the same divine, eternal, immutable act sustain both B and C? Since $T5$ is not, B no longer exists, and so is not being sustained, either in our time or in eternity, by any act of God. Since God's sustaining of C is direct, he cannot (logically cannot) sustain C by an act whose effect is dated at $T4$, and by some causal chain indirectly sustains C-at-$T5$. Furthermore, the present effect of God's eternal act at $T5$ is Zero Time Related with the eternal intention of God; but this same eternal intention and act cannot also be Zero Time Related to B, since B and C are not themselves Zero Time Related. By a single, timeless act God can sustain C and any episode Zero Time Related to C. But since the divine sustaining is a direct act which must be Zero Time Related to its effect, the same divine act cannot sustain both C and B. At the present time ($T5$) B is not real, and so a different act (different, that is, than the act which sustained B) is now called for if God is to sustain C. The particular intention plus power-to-act, such that B-at-$T4$ is sustained, can only sustain episodes Zero Time Related to $T4$. Possibly, this includes episodes of object at $T4$ and the immediate next episode. I don't in fact think that this is the case; rather, it makes more sense to me to say that God puts forth a different act to sustain each different episode of every object. But the point to be made is the same, since the entire past and future of all objects must be sustained by God, not just the immediate next episode. No other disjunct episode of an object can be sustained by that particular act, since no other disjunct episode of that object is Zero Time Related to it. These considerations show that the possibility of God acting once, timelessly and changelessly, yet still sustaining all of the episodes of all objects, is ruled out if the process theory of time is true.[5] Thus God's direct action upon the present time cannot sustain an episode at another past or future time, disjunct from the present. Thus God must change over time, and the traditional doctrine of eternity must be false.

But couldn't God *timelessly* will that a certain effect take place at a certain time ("Eternity," 449)? Again, if by "will" one means only design, this view is possible. But if God's "will" includes design, intention and power-to-act, and if the stasis theory of time is false, then God cannot timelessly "will" that a certain effect take place at some future time, since the effects of his "will" do not yet exist. So Stump and Kretzmann have missed the fact, due in part to their misunderstanding of the STR, that, given their assumptions about time, God cannot both be timeless and sustain a changing temporal world.

What follows from our dialogue with Stump and Kretzmann? The central point made above is that their notion of eternity is incongruent with the truth universally affirmed by Christian theologians that God sustains the universe, unless the stasis theory of time is true. If Stump and Kretzmann wish to hold on to their concept of eternity, and yet reject the stasis theory of time, then they must reject the doctrine that God sustains everything in its being (*esse*). But surely the latter doctrine is far more central to theology than absolute timelessness. For Stump and Kretzmann, then, there remains a choice between the stasis theory of time or the doctrine that God sustains the world, if they are going to be consistent and hold to absolute divine timelessness.

Just because the stasis theory of time follows from the arguments of

Aquinas, or Stump and Kretzmann, does not automatically mean it follows from all traditional theories of eternity. I have closely examined the thought of Aquinas, Stump and Kretzmann on the doctrine of divine timelessness. In each case, when the ability of God to sustain a changing, temporal world is insisted upon, these representatives have led us to the stasis theory of time. Yet it is also possible to reach this conclusion directly from the assumptions that defenders of absolute timelessness make.

AN ARGUMENT FROM ABSOLUTE DIVINE TIMELESSNESS TO THE STASIS THEORY OF TIME

Given certain assumptions, it is possible to argue from the traditional doctrine of eternity to the stasis theory of time without having to consider a particular exponent of divine timelessness. In order to do so it will be important to summarize what we have learned about absolutely timeless eternity from the representative defenders already examined.

In dialogue with them we have learned, first, that any discussion of absolutely timeless eternity must admit that talk of such a timeless being is talk of a durationless existence with no temporal location nor extension. Thus any succession or extension in the life of God is logical, not temporal. Second, divine timelessness understood in this way entails the absolute immutability of God. "Absolute immutability" means not only the Biblical doctrine that God is unchanging in his abilities and character, but also the Augustinian doctrine that God does not change in any way whatsoever, apart from merely relative changes (*City of God*, 22.2: "They find God changed because *they* have undergone a change"). With these common assumptions in mind, we now assume the process view of time, to discover what results will follow.

Take a particular example of a direct sustaining divine act: God sustains an episode of the universe, E, at a certain time, $T2$. At one time in the past, call it $T1$, no episode which is part of E existed in any way. At a subsequent time, $T2$, God directly puts forth sustaining power-to-act so as to hold in being all the episodes of things and events in E. Finally, at a later time $T3$ no episode of E exists in any way. Assume that God immutably and eternally designed so to act at time $T2$, and only at $T2$. If it is not $T2$, then God is not sustaining E: he is not putting forth this specific power-to-act. Nor can God do so. For if he did so (immutably and eternally) then E would have to exist (or E-at-$T2$ would tenselessly exist, perhaps; see next paragraph). Even God, therefore, must wait until time $T2$ to act in the specified manner. At time $T2$, and at no other time, can he so act. God's sustaining power must change between $T1$ and $T2$, or either (a) E-at-$T2$ would already exist, and hence the stasis theory of time would be true; or (b) E would not come into existence at $T2$. The argument based on this example can be applied equally well to any sustaining act of God. If God sustains the episodes of a changing, temporal universe, then God changes over time with respect to his power-to-act, and cannot be timeless in the traditional sense. This argument assumes that the process theory is true.

On the other hand, if the stasis theory of time is correct, God does not have to change to act in the specified way at $T2$. He can timelessly act so as to sustain E (or any other episode) and it will be sustained at $T2$ and only at $T2$, since E tenselessly exists-at-$T2$ in order to be effected by the power of God. This could equally well be put the other way around: E exists (tenselessly) at $T2$, because God is eternally putting forth power-to-act so as to sustain E-at-$T2$. Thus a model of God's timeless, changeless activity, which sustains the universe at every moment of time, leads to the stasis theory of time. Assuming that God sustains the universe, the traditional doctrine of eternity is true if and only if the stasis theory of time is true.

What responses might be made to this argument? One might question whether design, intention and power-to-act can be separated in God. The one "will" of God includes them all, one might argue; whatever God wills is done. But if we do not make this distinction, then it will follow that God must change his "will" in order to act in the way specified in the above example.

Another objection might be that if the above argument is correct, God must wait until a certain time is present in order to sustain events at that time. But (a) all times are equally present to an absolutely timeless God, and (b) such a notion does not suit the dignity and power of God.

All times may indeed be present to God, if God is absolutely timeless and the stasis theory of time is correct. However, on the process view there is one and only one present for any agent. For "present" simply selects those possible objects which really exist. And even God cannot act upon a non-existent object. Therefore, on process assumptions, even God cannot sustain a non-present, non-existing episode.

But another aspect of this conclusion, that God must wait for circumstances in order to act, seems odd or inappropriate. God, after all, is the source of all being, the source of the existence of all that exists. God does not have to wait until a particular time in order to act, it might be objected. He can act anywhere, at any time, since he already acts everywhere at all times. He can cause whatever he wants to exist, whenever he wants, in order to sustain it.

But returning to the above example, if God in eternity creates E in time (assuming, say, that $T2$ is future) then E will not exist at $T2$ and only at $T2$. And God cannot act in eternity in such a way as to bring about E-at-$T2$, since $T2$ is not yet (we assume, remember, that the process theory of time is true). It is logically impossible for some time to both be present and future. So it is logically impossible for God to act in eternity in such a way as to bring about E-at-$T2$, as long as $T2$ is not the present time. Only if $T2$ is the present time, then, will E exist at $T2$ and only at $T2$. Since God sustains E at $T2$, even he must wait until $T2$ if in his eternal design he wishes to sustain E at $T2$ and at no other time. So the fact remains that God would have to change to act in this way, if the process theory is correct.

This section has led us in one direction. Any model of absolute divine timelessness that wishes to retain the important notion of God sustaining the world should also affirm the stasis theory of time.

[. . .]

NOTES

1. For example, Mascall, *He Who Is*; Davies, *Thinking about God*.
2. This assumes that the agent's power-to-act is a necessary cause of the effect's continuance, as it will be in cases where God is the agent.
3. The idea of ET-simultaneity has been criticized by others but not thoroughly enough, nor along the lines I follow with respect to the Special Theory of Relativity. See Davis, *Logic*, 16–24: Lewis. "Eternity Again"; Fitzgerald, "Stump and Kretzmann on Time and Eternity", and Nelson, "Time(s), Eternity and Duration."
4. This point was made by Walker, "Time, Eternity and God" as early as 1919; and in more recent times, by Kellett. "Time and Eternity," Hebblethwaite, "Some Remarks," 434–436, Craig, "Was Thomas Aquinas a B-Theorist of Time?", Mellor, "History Without the Flow of Time," and Lewis, "God and Time." Note that Hebblethwaite and Lewis reject the stasis theory.
5. The analogy between time and space is sometimes used to argue that a spaceless God can act on objects at every point of space; so also an absolutely timeless God can act on every point of time from outside of it, even given the process view of time (e.g. Hasker, "Concerning the Intelligibility of 'God is Timeless'"). But this simply misunderstands the analogy between time and space. God can act on the here-now; God can act on the now at different places; and God can act on the here at different times. None of this implies that God can "timelessly" act on the here at all dates "at once." This is true of both space and time. As Here-Now exists, so There-Now exists over there; but it is absurd to say that There-Now exists *here*. Likewise, as Here-Now exists, Here-Then existed back then; but it is absurd to think that Here-Then exists *now*! Careful analysis of the analogy between space and time undermines the conclusions that Hasker wishes to draw.

REFERENCES

Craig, William Lane (1985), "Was Thomas Aquinas a B-Theorist of Time?" *New Scholasticism* 59, pp. 475–83.

Creel, Richard (1985), *Divine Impassibility* (Cambridge: Cambridge University Press).

Davies, Brian (1985), *Thinking about God* (London: Geoffrey Chapman).

Davis, Stephen T. (1983), *Logic and the Nature of God* (London: Macmillan).

Fitzgerald, Paul (1985), "Stump and Kretzmann on Time and Eternity," *Journal of Philosophy* 82, pp. 260–9.

Hasker, William (1983), "Concerning the Intelligibility of 'God is Timeless'," *New Scholasticism* 58, pp. 170–95.

Hebblethwaite, Brian (1979), "Some Reflections on Predestination, Providence and Divine Foreknowledge," *Religious Studies* 15, pp. 433–48.

Helm, Paul (1988), *Eternal God: A Study of God without Time* (Oxford: Oxford University Press).

Kellet, B. H. (1971), "Time and Eternity," *Church Quarterly* 3, pp. 317–25.

Lewis, J. Delmas (1984), "Eternity Again: A Reply to Stump and Kretzmann," *International Journal for Philosophy of Religion* 15, pp. 73–9.

Lewis, J. Delmas (1985), "God and Time," Ph.D. thesis, University of Wisconsin-Madison.

Mascall, E. L. (1966), *He Who Is* (London: Darton, Longman & Todd).

Mellor, D. H. (1986), "History without the Flow of Time," *Neue Zeitschrift für systematische Theologie und Religionsphilosophe* 28, pp. 68–76.

Nelson, Herbert J. (1987), "Time(s), Eternity and Duration," *International Journal for Philosophy of Religion* 22, pp. 3–19.

Neville, Robert Cummings (1968), *God the Creator: On the Transcendence and Presence of God* (Chicago: University of Chicago Press). Reprinted with corrections and a new Preface (Albany: State University of New York Press).

Pike, Nelson (1970), *God and Timelessness* (London: Routledge & Kegan Paul).

Quinn, John M. (1960), "The Doctrine of Time in St. Thomas," Ph.D. Thesis, Catholic University of America.

Robb, A. A. (1913), *A Theory of Time and Space* (Cambridge: Heffer and Sons).

Stump, Eleonore and Norman Kretzmann (1981), "Eternity," *Journal of Philosophy* 77, pp. 429–58.

Sturch, R. L. (1974), "The Problem of Divine Eternity," *Religious Studies* 10, pp. 487–93.

Walker, Leslie (1919), "Time, Eternity and God," *Hibbert Journal* 18, pp. 36–48.

OMNISCIENCE
3.3

'ON OCKHAM'S WAY OUT'

Alvin Plantinga

Two essential teachings of western theistic religions – Christianity, Judaism, and Islam – are that God is omniscient and that human beings are morally responsible for at least some of their actions. The first apparently implies that God has knowledge of the future and thus has foreknowledge of human actions; the second, that some human actions are *free*. But divine foreknowledge and human freedom, as every twelve-year-old Sunday School student knows, can seem to be incompatible; and at least since the fifth century A.D. philosophers and theologians have pondered the question whether these two doctrines really do conflict. There are, I think, substantially two lines of argument for the *incompatibility thesis* – the claim that these doctrines are indeed in conflict; one of these arguments is pretty clearly fallacious, but the other is much more impressive.

I. Foreknowledge and the Necessity of the Past

[. . .]

The argument essentially appeals to two intuitions. First, although the past is not necessary in the broadly logical sense (it is possible, in that sense, that Abraham should never have existed), it *is* necessary in *some* sense: it is fixed, unalterable, outside anyone's control. And second, whatever is "necessarily

Alvin Plantinga, 'On Ockham's Way Out', *Faith and Philosophy*, 3 (1986), pp. 235–69.

connected" with what is necessary in some sense, is itself necessary in that sense; if a proposition A, necessary in the way in which the past is necessary, entails a proposition B, then B is necessary in that same way. If [the] argument is a good one, what it shows is that if at some time in the past God knew that I will do A, then it is necessary that I will do A – necessary in just the way in which the past is necessary. But then it is not within my power to refrain from doing A, so that I will not do A freely. So suppose God knew, eighty years ago, that I will mow my lawn this afternoon. This foreknowledge is a "thing that is past."[1] Such things, however, are now necessary; " 'tis now impossible, that it should be otherwise than true, that that thing has existed." So it is now necessary that God had that knowledge eighty years ago; but it is also *logically* necessary that if God knew that I will mow my lawn today, then I will mow my lawn today. It is therefore now necessary that I will mow; it is thus not within my power to refrain from mowing; hence though I will indeed mow, I will not mow freely.

[The] argument is for what we might call "theological determinism"; the premise is that God has foreknowledge of the "acts and wills of moral agents" and the conclusion is that these acts are necessary in just the way the past is. Clearly enough the argument can be transformed into an argument for *logical* determinism, which would run as follows. It was true, eighty years ago, that I will mow my lawn this afternoon. Since what is past is now necessary, it is now necessary that it was true eighty years ago that I will mow my lawn today. But it is logically necessary that if it was true eighty years ago that I will mow my lawn today, then I will mow my lawn today. It is therefore necessary that I will mow my lawn – necessary in just the sense in which the past is necessary. But then it is not within my power not to mow; hence I will not mow freely.

Here is where a Boethian bystander might object as follows. [The] argument involves divine *fore*knowledge – God's having known at some time in the past, for example, that Paul will mow his lawn in 2005. Many theists, however, hold that God is *eternal*[2] and that his eternity involves at least the following two properties. First, his being eternal means, as Boethius suggested, that everything is *present* for him; for him there is no past or future. But then God does not know any such propositions as *Paul will mow in 2005*; what he knows, since everything is present for him, is just that Paul mows in 2005. And secondly, God's being eternal means that God is atemporal, "outside of time" – outside of time in such a way that it is an error to say of him that he knows some proposition or other *at a time*. We thus cannot properly say that God *now* knows that Paul mows in 2005, or that at some time in the past God knew this; the truth, instead, is that he knows this proposition *eternally*. But then [the] argument presupposes the falsehood of a widely accepted thesis about the nature of God and time.

I am inclined to believe that this thesis – the thesis that God is both atemporal and such that everything is present for him – is incoherent. If it *is* coherent, however, [the] argument can be restated in such a way as not to presuppose its falsehood. For suppose in fact Paul will mow his lawn in 2005. Then the proposition *God (eternally) knows that Paul mows in 2005* is now true. That proposition, furthermore, was true eighty years ago; the proposition *God knows (eternally) that Paul mows in 2005* not only *is* true *now*, but *was* true *then*. Since what is past is necessary, it is now necessary that this proposition was true eighty years ago. But it is logically necessary that if this proposition was true eighty years ago, then Paul mows in 2005. Hence his mowing then is necessary in just the way the past is. But, then it neither now is nor in future will be within Paul's power to refrain from mowing.

Of course this argument depends upon the claim that a proposition can be true *at a time* – eighty years ago, for example. Some philosophers argue that it does not so much as make sense to suggest that a proposition *A* is or was or will be true at a time; a proposition is true or false *simpliciter* and no more true at a time than, for example, true in a mail box or a refrigerator.[3] (Even if there is no beer in the refrigerator, the proposition *there is no beer* is not true in the refrigerator.) We need not share their scruples in order to accommodate them; the argument can be suitably modified. Concede for the moment that it makes no sense to say of a *proposition* that it was true at a time; it nonetheless makes good sense, obviously, to say of a sentence that it expressed a certain proposition at a time. But it also makes good sense to say of a sentence that it expressed a truth at a time. Now eighty years ago the sentence

(5). God knows (eternally) that Paul mows in 2005

expressed the proposition that God knows eternally that Paul mows in 2005 (and for simplicity let us suppose that this proposition was the only proposition it expressed then). But if in fact Paul will mow in 2005, then (5) also expressed a truth eighty years ago. So eighty years ago (5) expressed the proposition that Paul will mow in 2005 and expressed a truth; since what is past is now necessary, it is now necessary that eighty years ago (5) expressed that proposition and expressed a truth. But it is necessary in the broadly logical sense that if (5) then expressed that proposition (and only that proposition) and expressed a truth, then Paul will mow in 2005. It is therefore necessary that Paul will mow then; hence his mowing then is necessary in just the way the past is.

Accordingly, the claim that God is outside of time is essentially irrelevant. In what follows I shall therefore assume, for the sake of expository simplicity, that God does indeed have foreknowledge and that it is quite proper to speak of him both as holding a belief at a time and as having held beliefs in the past. What I shall say, however, can be restated so as to accommodate those who reject this assumption.

[. . .]

II. OCKHAM'S WAY OUT

[. . .]

[We] are all inclined to believe that the past, as opposed to the future, is fixed, stable, unalterable, closed. It is outside our control and outside the control even of an omnipotent being.

Strictly speaking, however, it is not alterability that is here relevant; for the future is no more alterable than the past. What after all, would it be to alter the past? To bring it about, obviously, that a temporally indexed proposition which is true and about the past before I act, is false thereafter. On January 1, 1982, I was not visiting New Guinea. For me to change the past with respect to that fact would be for me to perform an action A such that prior to my performing the action, it is true that on January 1, 1982, I was not in New Guinea, but after I perform the action, false that I was not in New Guinea then. But of course I can't do anything like that, and neither can God, despite his omnipotence.

But neither can we alter the future. We can imagine someone saying, "Paul will in fact walk out the door at 9:21 A.M.; hence *Paul will walk out at 9:21 A.M.* is true; but Paul has the power to refrain from walking out then; so Paul has the power to alter the future." But the conclusion displays confusion; Paul's not walking out then, were it to occur, would effect no alteration at all in the future. To alter the future, Paul must do something like this: he must perform some action A at a time t before 9:21 such that prior to t it is true that Paul will walk out at 9:21, but after t (after he performs A) false that he will. Neither Paul nor anyone – not even God – can do something like that. So the future is no more alterable than the past.

The interesting asymmetry between past and future, therefore, does not consist in the fact that the past is unalterable in a way in which the future is not; nonetheless this asymmetry remains. Now, before 9:21, it is within Paul's power to make it false that he walks out at 9:21; after he walks out at 9:21 he will no longer have that power. In the same way, in 1995 B.C. God could have brought it about that Abraham did not exist in 1995 B.C.; now that is no longer within his power.

Recognizing this asymmetry, Ockham, like several other medieval philosophers, held that the past is indeed in some sense necessary: it is *necessary per accidens*:

> I claim that every necessary proposition is *per se* in either the first mode or the second mode. This is obvious, since I am talking about all propositions that are necessary *simpliciter*. I add this because of propositions that are necessary *per accidens*, as is the case with many past tense propositions. They are necessary *per accidens*, because it was contingent that they be necessary, and because they were not always necessary.[4]

Here Ockham directs our attention to propositions about the past: past tense propositions together with temporally indexed propositions, such as

(8). *Columbus sails the ocean blue* is true in 1492

whose index is prior to the present time. Such propositions, he says, are accidentally necessary if true; they are *accidentally* necessary because they *become* necessary. Past tense propositions become necessary when they become true; temporally indexed propositions such as (8), on the other hand, do not become true – (8) was always true – but they become necessary, being necessary after but not before the date of their index. And once a proposition acquires this status, says Ockham, not even God has the power to make it false.

In *Predestination, God's Foreknowledge, and Future Contingents*, Ockham goes on to make an interesting distinction:

> Some propositions are about the present as regards both their wording and their subject matter (*secundum vocem et secundum rem*) Where such propositions are concerned, it is universally true that every true proposition about the present has (corresponding to it) a necessary one about the past: – e.g., 'Socrates is seated,' 'Socrates is walking,' 'Socrates is just,' and the like.
>
> Other propositions are about the present as regards their wording only and are equivalently about the future, since their truth depends on the truth of propositions about the future. Where such (propositions) are concerned, the rule that every true proposition about the present has corresponding to it a necessary proposition about the past is not true.[5]

Ockham means to draw the following contrast. Some propositions about the present "are about the present as regards both their wording and their subject matter"; for example,

(9). Paul is seated.

Such propositions, we may say, are *strictly* about the present; and if such a proposition is now true, then a corresponding proposition about the past

(10). Paul was seated

will be accidentally necessary from now on. Other propositions about the present, however, "are about the present as regards their wording only and are equivalently about the future"; for example,

(11). Paul correctly believes that the sun will rise on January 1, 2010.

Such a proposition is "equivalently about the future," and it is not the case that if it is true, then the corresponding proposition about the past

(12). Paul correctly believed that the sun will rise on January 1, 2010

in this case – will be accidentally necessary from now on. (Of course we hope that [12] will be accidentally necessary after January 1, 2010.)

What Ockham says about the present, he would say about the past. Just as some propositions about the present are "about the present as regards their wording only and are equivalently about the future," so some propositions about the past are about the past as regards their wording only and are equivalently about the future; (12) for example, or

(13). Eighty years ago, the proposition *Paul will mow his lawn in 2005* was true

or (to appease those who object to the idea that a proposition can be true at a time)

(14). Eighty years ago, the sentence "Paul will mow his lawn in 2005" expressed the proposition *Paul will mow his lawn in 2005* and expressed a truth.

These propositions are about the past, but they are also equivalently about the future. Furthermore, they are not necessary *per accidens* – not yet, at any rate. We might say that a true proposition like (12)–(14) is a *soft* fact about the past, whereas one like

(15). Paul mowed in 1981

– one *strictly* about the past – is a *hard* fact about the past.[6]

Now of course the notion of aboutness, as Nelson Goodman has reminded us,[7] is at best a frail reed; *a fortiori*, then, the same goes for the notion of being *strictly* about. But we do have *something* of a grasp of this notion, hesitant and infirm though perhaps it is. It may be difficult or even impossible to give a useful criterion for the distinction between hard and soft facts about the past, but we do have *some* grasp of it, and can apply it in many cases.

The idea of a hard fact about the past contains two important elements: *genuineness* and *strictness*. In the first place, a hard fact about the past is a genuine fact about the past. This cannot be said, perhaps, for (13). It is at least arguable that if (13) is a fact about the past at all, it is an *ersatz* fact about the past; it tells us nothing about the past except in a Pickwickian, Cambridgian sort of way. What it really tells us is something about the future: that Paul will mow in 2005. (12) and (14), on the other hand, do genuinely tell us something about the past: (12) tells us that Paul believed something and (14) that a certain sentence expressed a certain proposition.

But (12) and (14) aren't *strictly* about the past; they also tell us something about what will happen in 2005. It may be difficult to give criteria, or (informative) necessary and sufficient conditions for either genuineness or strictness; nevertheless we do have at least a partial grasp of these notions.

Accordingly, let us provisionally join Ockham in holding that there is a viable distinction between hard and soft facts about the past. The importance of this distinction, for Ockham, is that it provides him with a way of disarming the arguments for logical and theological determinism from the necessity of the past. Each of those arguments, when made explicit, has as a premise

(16). If *p* is about the past, then *p* is necessary

or something similar. Ockham's response is to deny (16); *hard* facts about the past are indeed accidentally necessary, but the same cannot be said for soft facts. Such propositions as (13) and (14) are not hard facts about the past; each entails that Paul will mow his lawn in 2005, and is therefore, as Ockham says, "equivalently about the future." Not all facts about the past, then, are hard facts about the past; and only the hard facts are plausibly thought to be accidentally necessary. (16), therefore, the general claim that all facts about the past are accidentally necessary, is seen to be false – or at any rate there seems to be no reason at all to believe it. And this dissolves any argument for theological determinism which accepts (16) in its full generality.

I believe Ockham is correct here; furthermore, there is no easy way to refurbish [the determinist's] argument. Given Ockham's distinction between hard and soft facts, what [the] argument needs is the premise that such propositions as

(17). God knew eighty years ago that Paul will mow in 2005

are hard facts about the past. Clearly, however, (17) is not a hard fact about the past; for (like [13] and [14]), it entails

(18). Paul will mow his lawn in 2005;

and no proposition that entails (18) is a hard fact about the past.

Let me be entirely clear here; I say that none of (13), (14), and (17) is a hard fact about the past, because each entails (18). In so saying, however, I am not endorsing a *criterion* for hard facthood; in particular I am not adopting an "entailment" criterion, according to which a fact about the past is a hard fact about the past if and only if it entails no proposition about the future. No doubt *every* proposition about the past, hard fact or not, entails *some* proposition about the future; *Socrates was wise*, for example, entails *It will be true from now on that Socrates was wise*; and *Paul played tennis yesterday* entails *Paul will not play tennis for the first time tomorrow*. What I *am* saying is this: No proposition that entails (18) is a hard fact about the past, because no such proposition is *strictly* about the past. We may not be able to give a criterion for being strictly about the past; but we do have at least a rough and intuitive grasp of this notion. Given our intuitive grasp of this notion, I think we can see two things. First, no conjunctive proposition that contains (18) as a conjunct is (now, in 1986) strictly about the past. Thus *Paul will mow his lawn in 2005 and Socrates was wise*, while indeed a proposition about the past, is not *strictly* about the past. And second, hard facthood is closed under logical equivalence: any proposition equivalent (in the broadly logical sense) to a proposition strictly about the past is itself strictly about the past.[8] But any proposition that entails (18) is equivalent, in the broadly logical sense, to a conjunctive proposition one conjunct of which is (18); hence each such proposition is equivalent to a proposition that is not a hard fact about the past and is therefore itself not a hard fact about the past. Thus the argument fails.

Similar comments apply to Pike's argument for the incompatibility of essential divine omniscience with human freedom.[9] Pike puts his argument in terms, not of God's fore*knowledge*, but, so to speak, of God's fore*belief*; and the essential premise of the argument is

(iv*)   For any persons S and S*, if at some time in the past S* held a certain belief, then it is not within the power of S to perform an action such that if he were to perform it, then S* would not have held that belief then.

His essential insights, I think, are two: first, it seems natural to think of propositions of the sort *eighty years ago, S believed p* as hard facts about the past (and thus as plausible candidates for accidental necessity); and secondly, if God is essentially omniscient, then such a proposition as *God believed eighty years ago that p* entails *p*. (To these insights he adds the idea, not in my view an insight, that it is not within anyone's power to perform an action which is such that if he were to perform it, then what is *in fact* a hard fact about the past wouldn't have been a fact at all.)

Unfortunately, the second of these insights is incompatible with the first. If God is essentially omniscient, then

(19).   Eighty years ago, God believed the proposition that Paul will mow his lawn in 2005

entails that Paul will mow in 2005. By the above argument, then, (19) is not strictly about the past and is therefore not a hard fact about the past. But then we no longer have any reason to accept (iv*). Perhaps it is plausible to accept (iv*) for S^* stipulated not to be essentially omniscient, or stipulated to be such that propositions of the sort S^* *believed that* p are hard facts about the past.[10] But given the possibility of essential divine omniscience, (iv*) in its full generality has nothing whatever to recommend it; for if God is essentially omniscient, then such propositions as (19) are not hard facts about the past.

We can see the same point from a slightly different perspective. Pike is assuming, for purposes of argument, that God is essentially omniscient. Suppose we add, as classical theism also affirms, that God is a necessary being. What follows is that God both exists and is omniscient in every possible world; hence in every possible world God believes every true proposition and believes no false propositions. But then *truth* and *being believed by God* are equivalent in the broadly logical sense; it is then necessary that for any proposition p, p is true if and only if God believes p. It follows that

> (20). Eighty years ago, God believed that Paul will mow in 2005

is equivalent in the broadly logical sense to

> (21). Eighty years ago, it was true that Paul will mow in 2005.

Here again we can accommodate our colleagues ("atemporalists," as we may call them) who do not believe that propositions can be true at times; for (20), given the plausible (but widely disputed) assumption that necessarily, for any time t there is a time t^* eighty years prior to t, is also equivalent to

> (22). Paul will mow in 2005.

Even without the "plausible assumption," (20) is equivalent to

> (23). There is (i.e., is, was, or will be) such a time as eighty years ago, and Paul will mow in 2005.

Clearly enough none of (21), (22), and (23) is a hard fact about the past; but (20) is equivalent in the broadly logical sense to at least one of them; hence (20) is not a hard fact about the past. Furthermore, (20) is inconsistent with Paul's being free to mow in 2005 only if (23) is; and no one, presumably, except for the most obdurate logical fatalist, will hold that (23) is incompatible with Paul's being free to mow in 2005.[11] So if, as traditional theism affirms, God is both a necessary being and essentially omniscient, then theological determinism is logically equivalent to logical determinism; divine foreknowledge is incompatible with human freedom only if the latter is inconsistent with the existence of true propositions detailing future free actions.

Ironically enough, from Ockham's perspective it is the suggestion that God is omniscient but not *essentially* omniscient that is plausibly thought to create a problem. Return, once more, to

(20). Eighty years ago, God believed that Paul will mow in 2005.

If God is not essentially omniscient, then (20) does not entail that Paul will mow in 2005; at any rate we no longer have any reason to suppose that it does. But then we are deprived of our only reason for denying that (20) is strictly about the past. From an Ockhamist perspective, it follows that (20) is accidentally necessary. But an Ockhamist would also certainly hold that even if God is not *essentially* omniscient, nevertheless his omniscience is counter-factually independent of Paul's actions; that is to say, there isn't anything Paul can do such that if he were to do it then God would not have been or would no longer be omniscient. If Paul were to refrain from mowing his lawn in 2005, therefore, God would not have believed, eighty years ago, that Paul will mow then. But Ockham also thinks it is or will be within Paul's power to refrain from mowing then. From Ockham's point of view, then, the facts are these: if God is not essentially omniscient, then there is an accidentally necessary proposition P – (20) as it happens – and an action Paul can perform, such that if he were to perform it, then P would have been false. Ockham is not very explicit about accidental necessity; nevertheless he would have held, I think, that it is not within anyone's power to perform an action which is such that if he were to perform it, then a proposition which is in fact accidentally necessary would have been false. From Ockham's point of view, therefore, divine foreknowledge threatens human freedom only if God is not essentially omniscient.

[. . .]

If God is essentially omniscient, then the facts about what God *believed* are not, in general, hard facts about the past; but then there is no reason to suppose that none of us can act in such a way that God would not have believed what in fact he does believe.

NOTES

1. Jonathan Edwards, *Freedom of the Will*, 1745, section 12.
2. See E. Stump and N. Kretzmann, "Eternity," *Journal of Philosophy* (1981): 429–58.
3. See, for example, Peter van Inwagen, *An Essay on Free Will* (Oxford: Oxford University Press, 1983), pp. 35ff.; and Nelson Pike, *God and Timelessness* (New York: Schocken Books, 1970), pp. 67ff. Pike's objection is not to temporally indexed propositions as such, but to alleged propositions of the sort *It is true at T_1 that S does A at T_2*.
4. William of Ockham, *Ordinatio*, I, Prologue, q.6.
5. William of Ockham, *Predestination, God's Foreknowledge, and Future Contingents*, tr. with Introduction, Notes, and Appendices by Marilyn Adams and Norman Kretzmann (Ithaca: Cornell University Press, 1969), pp. 46–47.
6. See Nelson Pike, "Of God and Freedom: A Rejoinder," *Philosophical Review*, 1966, p. 370, and Marilyn Adams, "Is the Existence of God a 'Hard' Fact?" *Philosophical Review*, 1966, pp. 493–94.
7. Nelson Goodman, "About," *Mind* (1962).

8. I think it is clear that hard facthood *is* closed under broadly logical equivalence; this argument, however, does not require the full generality of that premise. All it requires is that no proposition strictly about the past is equivalent in the broadly logical sense to a conjunction one conjunct of which, like (18), is a contingent proposition paradigmatically about the future.

9. Nelson Pike, "Divine Omniscience and Voluntary Action," *Philosophical Review*, 1965, p. 33.

10. Even so restricted, (iv*) is by no means obviously true: couldn't I know my wife or child so well that, while I correctly believe that she will do A, it is within her power to do B instead; and if she were to do B, then I would have believed that she will do B? It isn't easy to see why not.

11. More exactly, anyone who thinks *both* that such propositions as (23) are either true or false *and* that (23) is incompatible with Paul's being free to mow in 2005, will be a logical fatalist.

3.4

'ON DIVINE MIDDLE KNOWLEDGE'

Alfred J. Freddoso

DIVINE KNOWLEDGE: NATURAL, MIDDLE, AND FREE

[M]iddle knowledge derives its name from the fact that it stands 'midway' between natural knowledge and free knowledge. Like natural knowledge but unlike free knowledge, middle knowledge is prevolitional, with the result that God has no more control over the states of affairs He knows through His middle knowledge than He does over the states of affairs He knows through His natural knowledge. Like free knowledge but unlike natural knowledge, middle knowledge is such that the states of affairs known through it might have failed to obtain, with the result that what God knows through His middle knowledge may vary from one possible world to another just as what He knows through His free knowledge may vary from one possible world to another. So God has middle knowledge only if He knows some metaphysically contingent states of affairs over which He has no control.

There is another way in which middle knowledge lies between natural and free knowledge. Natural knowledge has among its objects all the *possible* future contingents, whereas free knowledge has among its objects all *actual* or *absolute* future contingents. By contrast, middle knowledge has as its objects *conditional* or *subjunctive* future contingents that stand 'between' the actual and the merely possible. By His natural knowledge God knows that it is metaphysically possible but not metaphysically necessary that Adam will sin if placed in the garden; by His free knowledge He knows that Adam will in fact

Alfred J. Freddoso, 'On Divine Middle Knowledge', in 'Introduction', from Luis de Molina, *On Divine Foreknowledge*, translated with an introduction and notes by Alfred J. Freddoso (Ithaca, NY: Cornell University Press, 1988), pp. 47, 68–75.

be placed in the garden and will in fact sin. What He knows by His middle knowledge, on the other hand, is something stronger than the former but weaker than the latter, namely, that Adam will sin *on the condition* that he be placed in the garden. So God has middle knowledge only if He knows all the conditional future contingents.

God has middle knowledge if and only if He has comprehensive *prevolitional* knowledge of *conditional future contingents*.

[. . .]

The Ground for Conditional Future Contingents

Bañezians object that conditional future contingents cannot obtain before God's act of will or hence be objects of God's prevolitional knowledge. Thus Garrigou-Lagrange:

> Before the divine decree, there is no object for the *scientia media*, because the conditionally free act of the future is not determined either in itself or in another . . . The *scientia media* does not precede the divine decree, because there is no cause in which this conditioned future is determined; for it is not determined in the divine cause or in human liberty or in the circumstances; and if it is said that God knows infallibly this conditioned future by exploring the circumstances, then this theory would end in determinism of the circumstances. Thus the *scientia media*, which is devised to save human liberty, would destroy it.[1]

Bañezians go on to infer that since God does indeed know conditional future contingents, He must be able, in a way that does not threaten human freedom, to decree that they obtain.

Robert Adams disagrees with this inference, but is in full sympathy with the charge that Molinism does not provide adequate grounding for conditional future contingents. Since his presentation of the argument is the most sophisticated I know of, I will quote it at length. After citing the biblical passage concerning David and Saul, Adams writes:

> This passage was a favorite proof text for the Jesuit theologians. They took it to prove that God knew the following two propositions to be true:
> (1) If David stayed in Keilah, Saul would besiege the city.
> (2) If David stayed in Keilah and Saul besieged the city, the men of Keilah would surrender David to Saul . . .
> I do not understand what it would be for [these] propositions to be true, given that the actions in question would have been free, and that David did not stay in Keilah. I will explain my incomprehension.

First we must note that middle knowledge is not simple *fore* knowledge . . . For there never was nor will be an actual besieging of Keilah by Saul, nor an actual betrayal of David to Saul by the men of Keilah, to which those propositions might correspond.

Some other grounds that might be suggested for the truth of (1) and (2) are ruled out by the assumption that the actions of Saul and the men of Keilah are and would be free in the relevant sense. The suggestion that Saul's besieging Keilah follows by *logical* necessity from David's staying there is implausible in any case. It would be more plausible to suggest that Saul's besieging Keilah follows by *causal* necessity from David's staying there . . . But both of these suggestions are inconsistent with the assumption that Saul's action would have been free.

Since necessitation is incompatible with the relevant sort of free will, we might seek non-necessitating grounds for the truth of (1) and (2) in the actual intentions, desires and character of Saul and the Keilahites . . .

But the basis thus offered for the truth of (1) and (2) is inadequate precisely because it is not necessitating. A free agent may act out of character, or change his intentions, or fail to act on them. Therefore the propositions which may be true by virtue of correspondence with the intentions, desires and character of Saul and the men of Keilah are not (1) and (2) but

(5) If David stayed in Keilah, Saul would *probably* besiege the city.

(6) If David stayed in Keilah and Saul besieged the city, the men of Keilah would *probably* surrender David to Saul.

(5) and (6) . . . will not satisfy the partisans of middle knowledge. It is part of their theory that God knows infallibly what definitely would happen, and not just what would probably happen or what free creatures would be likely to do.[2]

I will join Adams here in speaking of propositions rather than states of affairs. The leading principle of his objection is that a proposition p is true only if there are what we might call *adequate metaphysical grounds* for the truth of p. He then argues inductively that there are not and indeed cannot be adequate metaphysical grounds for the truth of the alleged objects of middle knowledge—at least not if a strong libertarian account of freedom and causal indeterminism is correct. It follows that there are not and cannot be true conditional future contingents. In keeping with contemporary parlance, we might thus aptly say that Adams espouses *antirealism* with respect to conditional future contingents.

As Alvin Plantinga has pointed out, the notion of adequate metaphysical grounds appealed to here is far from pellucid.[3] Still, the objection to Molinism posed by Adams and (albeit less precisely) by Garrigou-Lagrange seems to have considerable intuitive appeal. So I will assume that the fundamental notion underlying the objection has at least some validity and attempt to flesh it out sympathetically.

We must, it is clear, draw a basic distinction between the grounds for the truth of metaphysically necessary propositions and the grounds for the truth of metaphysically contingent propositions. The former will presumably involve just the constant and necessary relations of natures or properties to each other. (Of course, it need not be that all of these relations are self-evident to us or even so much as conceivable by us.) But, the claim goes, such grounds are inadequate to underwrite the truth of metaphysically contingent propositions. These require *causal* grounding in order to be true. That is, they must be *caused to be true* by some agent or agents, since it is not of their nature to be true.

The idea of metaphysical grounding is commonly invoked in similar fashion by those who espouse antirealism with respect to *absolute* future contingents, that is, by those who deny that there are or can be contingent truths about the absolute, as contrasted with the conditional, future. They typically claim that there are at present no adequate metaphysical grounds for, say, Peter's freely denying Christ at some future time *T*, and that the proposition *Peter will freely sin at T* thus cannot now be true—even if it turns out that when *T* is present Peter freely denies Christ. And they support their antirealism regarding *absolute* future contingents with arguments exactly like the one Adams produces for the case of *conditional* future contingents. Specifically, they note that the causal history of the world up to the present does not logically entail Peter's sinning at *T*; nor does the world now have a deterministic natural tendency toward this state of affairs. Perhaps, because of Peter's character and the present likelihood of a test of his virtue occurring at *T*, it is now true that the world is tending, albeit nondeterministically, toward his sinning at *T*. That is, perhaps the proposition *Peter will probably sin at T* is now true, where the probability in question is metaphysical rather than epistemic. But, of course, this proposition might now be true even if the proposition *Peter is sinning* turns out to be false when *T* is present. So there are not and cannot be adequate metaphysical grounds at present for the truth of the absolute future contingent *Peter will sin at T*.

Sophisticated Molinists will not only welcome but insist on this parallel between antirealism regarding conditional future contingents and antirealism regarding absolute future contingents. Indeed, they will go so far as to claim that the former entails the latter. For on the Molinist view the absolute future is conceptually posterior to, and emerges by divine decree from, the many conditional futures that define the creation situation God finds Himself in.

[. . .]

The most promising Molinist strategy for dealing with the "grounding" objection is, I believe, to build upon the arguments against antirealism regarding the absolute future. I cannot do this exhaustively here but will instead concentrate on just one such argument, an argument having to do with prediction viewed both retrospectively and prospectively.

Suppose that John has ruefully predicted beforehand that Peter will deny Christ at time T. Then, after Peter's denial at T, John can reasonably maintain that his prediction was true and thus that he spoke the truth before T when he asserted the proposition *Peter will deny Jesus*. So it is reasonable to hold that this proposition was true before T.

The same point can be made more starkly in the case of random events. Suppose I predict that on the next toss the coin in your hand will come up heads. And suppose for the sake of argument that the coin's coming up one way or the other is wholly indeterminate, so that prior to the toss the world is not tending, even nondeterministically, either toward the coin's coming up heads or toward its coming up tails. In that case

    (P) The coin will probably come up heads,

and

    (Q) The coin will probably come up tails

are both false, where the probability in question is objective or metaphysical. Suppose, finally, that when you toss the coin, it in fact comes up heads. In that case it is perfectly reasonable for me to claim that my prediction was true, that is, that I spoke the truth in asserting beforehand the proposition *The coin will come up heads*. So it is reasonable for me to maintain that this proposition was true before you tossed the coin, even though neither (P) nor (Q) were true at that time.

So much for the retrospective argument. The prospective argument appeals to common intuitions about what we are asserting when we make predictions about the future. If I know that you have promised to meet me for dinner at 6:00 P.M. and know further that you are a very reliable person, then I am highly justified in asserting that you will in fact meet me at 6:00 P.M. To be sure, my *evidence* for this assertion consists in my beliefs about your character and in other beliefs about the world's present tendencies. But *what* I assert is the nonmodal proposition

    (R) You will meet me at 6:00 P.M.

and not the 'probabilistic' proposition

    (S) You will probably meet me at 6:00 P.M.,

where the probability is, once again, objective or metaphysical. This is so even if, when challenged, I hedge my prediction by saying something like "She will *probably* meet me at 6:00 P.M." For normally the probability so expressed is *epistemic* rather than *metaphysical*. That is, the hedging is indicative of my wavering confidence in the truth of (R) rather than of my firm belief in (S). Or so, at least, many of us would be prone to claim.

But if there are true absolute future contingents, what are the metaphysical grounds for their truth? Notice, exactly the same question can be raised about past-tense propositions that are true in the present. What are the grounds for the present truth of, say, the proposition *Socrates drank hemlock*? Let *p* stand for present-tense propositions and *P* for the past-tense propositional operator. The proper response, I think, is that there are *now* adequate metaphysical grounds for the truth of a past-tense proposition *Pp* just in case there *were* at some past time adequate metaphysical grounds for the truth of its present-tense counterpart *p*. Likewise, a realist about the absolute future will claim that there are *now* adequate metaphysical grounds for the truth of a future-tense proposition *Fp* just in case there *will* be at some future time adequate metaphysical grounds for the truth of its present-tense counterpart *p*. So in order for propositions about the past or the future to be true now, it is not required that any agent *now* be causing them to be true. Rather, it is sufficient that some agent has caused or will cause the corresponding present-tense propositions to be true.

But if this is so, then it seems reasonable to claim that there are now adequate metaphysical grounds for the truth of a conditional future contingent $F^t(p)$ on *H* just in case there *would* be adequate metaphysical grounds at *t* for the truth of the present-tense proposition *p* on the condition that *H* should obtain at *t*. At any rate, the argument leading up to this claim is exactly the same as before. Take the case of Peter and John. John might just as easily make his prediction by asserting the conditional proposition *If Peter were tempted anytime soon to deny Jesus, he would succumb*. And after Peter's denial John may reasonably maintain that what he had asserted was true. Indeed, even if Peter had luckily been spared any such temptation, John could still reasonably maintain that what he had asserted was true—and he might even be able to convince Peter of this.

Again, in the coin tossing example, I could just as easily have said, "If you tossed the coin, it would come up heads." As before, both

(T) If you tossed the coin, it would probably come up heads,

and

(U) If you tossed the coin, it would probably come up tails

would be false. But after the toss is completed and the coin comes up heads, it seems perfectly reasonable for me to claim that I spoke the truth when I asserted beforehand the proposition *If you tossed the coin, it would come up heads*, even though both (T) and (U) were then false. What's more, unless conditional future contingents are unlike all other conditional propositions, they can be true even if their antecedents are false. So given that the proposition in question was true when I made the prediction, I may reasonably claim that it would still have been true even if the coin had never been tossed. Of course, in that case we would never have found out whether or not the proposition was true, but that is another matter.

The prospective argument likewise goes as before. Knowing you well, I might say with confidence, "If you promised to meet me at 6:00 P.M., you would do so." To be sure, my *evidence* for this assertion consists in my beliefs about your character and about tendencies the world would have if you were to make the promise in question. Still, *what* I assert is the proposition

> (V) If you promised to meet me at 6:00 P.M., you would meet me at 6:00 P.M.,

and not the probabilistic proposition

> (W) If you promised to meet me at 6:00 P.M., you would probably meet me at 6:00 P.M.,

where the probability in question is metaphysical. Once again, of course, a third party might challenge my prediction and even induce me to qualify it by saying, "Well, she would *probably* meet me." But the probability thus invoked would at least normally be epistemic, reflecting my wavering confidence in (V) rather than my unflinching confidence in the weaker (W).

The position I am urging has some far-reaching consequences for the semantics of subjunctive conditionals. I am suggesting, in effect, that when such conditional propositions are not probabilistic, the connection between antecedent and consequent is not reducible to any logical or, more important, causal connection. This suggestion cuts against the spirit, if not the letter, of the standard possible-worlds semantics for subjunctive conditionals. For it is usually assumed that the similarities among possible worlds invoked in such semantics are conceptually prior to the acquisition of truth-values by the subjunctive conditionals themselves. The intuitive idea seems to be that the truth-value of a subjunctive conditional p depends asymmetrically on the categorical (including causal) facts about the world at which p is being evaluated, so that until the full range of such categorical facts is in place, the truth-value of p is still indeterminate. On this view, then, the determination of the true conditional future contingents is posterior to the determination of which possible world is actual. This is the source of one of Kenny's complaints about middle knowledge:

> Prior to God's decision to actualize a particular world those counter-factuals [about the behavior of free humans] cannot yet be known: for their truth-value depends . . . on which world is actual . . . The problem is that what makes the counterfactuals true is not yet there at any stage at which it is undecided which world is the actual world. The very truth-conditions which the possible-world semantics were introduced to supply are absent under the hypothesis that it is undetermined which world the actual world is.[4]

I will not tarry over the moot question of whether the standard possible-worlds semantics for subjunctive conditionals in fact implies or presupposes that the acquisition of truth-values by such conditionals is conceptually posterior to and dependent on the determination of which world is actual. It is clear, however, that on the Molinist view the dependence runs in just the opposite direction when the conditionals in question are conditional future contingents. For Molinists hold that conditional future contingents delimit prevolitionally the range of worlds God is able to actualize. If the standard possible-worlds semantics for subjunctive conditionals presupposes otherwise, then Molinists will have to modify it or propose an alternative capable of sustaining realism with respect to conditional future contingents. There are, in any case, independent grounds for having doubts about the standard semantics, for example, its inability to accommodate the intuitively plausible belief that subjunctive conditionals with impossible antecedents may differ from one another in truth-value.[5]

My aim here has merely been the negative one of showing that the grounding objection is not conclusive. I believe I have succeeded in this. But, as Michael Dummett has suggested, the doctrine of middle knowledge is the most vivid and perhaps the most extreme example of philosophical realism in the history of thought.[6] And I freely admit that the positive task of elaborating a metaphysical and semantic foundation for this doctrine is enormous and has hardly yet begun.

NOTES

1. Reginald Garrigou-Lagrange, *God: His Existence and Nature* (St. Louis: Herder, 1936), p. 465.
2. Adams, R. M., 'Middle Knowledge and the Problem of Evil', *American Philosophical Quarterly* 14 (1977): 109–117, esp. pp. 110–11.
3. See "Replies to My Colleagues," in James E. Tomberlin and Peter van Inwagen, eds., *Alvin Plantinga* (Dordrecht, Boston: D. Reidel, 1985), pp. 374–375. Plantinga suggests that counterfactuals of freedom relating to *God's* free action are routinely accepted as true by Christians.
4. Anthony John Patrick Kenny, *The God of the Philosophers* (Oxford: Clarendon Press; New York: Oxford University Press, 1979), p. 70. For more on the possible-worlds semantics for subjunctive conditionals, see David K. Lewis, *Counterfactuals* (Cambridge: Harvard University Press, 1973); and Robert Stalnaker, "A Theory of Conditionals," in N. Rescher, ed., *Studies in Logical Theory* (Oxford: Blackwell, 1968), pp. 98–112, reprinted in W. L. Harper, R. Stalnaker and G. Pearce, eds., *Ifs: Conditionals, Belief, Decision, Chance and Time* (Dordrecht: Reidel, 1981), pp. 41–55.
5. For a brief discussion of this point, see my "Human Nature, Potency and the Incarnation," *Faith and Philosophy* 3 (1986): 27–53, esp. pp. 43–45.
6. See Dummett's *Truth and Other Enigmas* (Cambridge, Mass., 1978), p. 362.

OMNIPOTENCE
3.5

'MAXIMAL POWER'

Thomas P. Flint and Alfred J. Freddoso

Christians profess that God is almighty. He has created the world and conserves it in being. Whatever can or does occur is within his control. His great power guarantees the fulfillment of his providential designs.

[. . .]

We will begin by proposing five conditions of philosophical adequacy for an account of maximal power, indicating in the footnotes which of these conditions are not satisfied by one or another of the numerous recent attempts to explicate omnipotence. Then we will present an analysis which meets all five conditions.

I

1. Our first condition of adequacy is that an analysis of maximal power should be stated in terms of an agent's power to actualize or bring about states of affairs. (Since we are assuming that there is an exact isomorphism between states of affairs and propositions, we can also speak equivalently of an agent's power to make propositions true.) Though this condition is now widely accepted, some writers have employed the alternative strategy of casting their accounts of

Thomas P. Flint and Alfred J. Freddoso, 'Maximal Power', in Alfred J. Freddoso (ed.), *The Existence and Nature of God* (Notre Dame, IN: University of Notre Dame Press, 1983), pp. 81–113.

omnipotence in terms of an agent's ability to perform tasks, where a task is expressed linguistically by the nominalization of a verb phrase rather than, like a state of affairs, by the nominalization of a complete declarative sentence. The problems with this alternative strategy are well known. Suppose we claim that an agent S is omnipotent just in case S can perform any logically possible task, that is, any task which is possibly such that someone performs it. This proposal rules out Smith as omnipotent simply on the ground that Smith cannot perform the logically possible task of saying something which is (at the same time) being said only by Jones. Yet it is clear intuitively that this fact about Smith in no way points to a lack of power on his part. Moreover, when we attempt to amend our analysis by claiming that S is omnipotent just in case S has the power to perform any task that it is logically possible *for S* to perform, we find that we are forced to count as omnipotent the notorious weakling Mr. McEar, who is capable of scratching his left ear but essentially incapable of performing any other task.[1]

Such difficulties are obviated by our first condition. For the state of affairs of Smith's saying something which is being said only by Jones is logically impossible and thus unproblematically not within anyone's power to actualize, whereas the state of affairs of Jones's (or: someone's) saying something which is being said only by Jones may well be one which agents other than Jones can actualize and which we should expect an omnipotent being to have the power to actualize.

Nevertheless, even though our first condition is commonplace today, few writers on omnipotence have explicitly entertained the following question: Is it possible for one agent to actualize (and hence to have the power to actualize) a state of affairs consisting in or at least involving in some way the free actions of other agents? If we assume a compatibilist account of freedom, the answer to this question is uncontroversially affirmative. For it is obviously possible for a suitably powerful and aptly situated agent to bring it about that another agent has desires or needs and also opportunities that are together causally sufficient for his behaving freely (in this compatibilist sense) in a specified way. So on this view of freedom, bringing about the free actions of others is not relevantly different from actualizing states of affairs that in no way involve the free actions of others. In both sorts of cases the agent in question simply does something which, in conjunction with other operative causal factors, is sufficient for the obtaining of the state of affairs in question.

However, we believe along with many others that there are good reasons for rejecting this account of freedom in favor of the position that every free action must involve the occurrence of an event for which there is no antecedent sufficient causal condition – an event, that is, which has only an agent and no other event as its cause. Given this libertarian conception of freedom, there is a clear and familiar sense of 'actualize' in which it is logically impossible for one agent to actualize another agent's free actions. Following Alvin Plantinga, we call this sense of actualization *strong actualization*.[2] Roughly, an agent S strongly actualizes a state of affairs p just when S causally determines p's obtaining, that is, just when S does something which in conjunction with other operative causal factors constitutes a sufficient causal condition for p's obtaining. Since an agent's freely performing (or, perhaps better, freely endeavoring to perform) a given action cannot have a sufficient causal condition, it follows straightforwardly that no such state of affairs can be strongly actualized by anyone other than the agent in question.

But even granted the libertarian conception of freedom, there is a weaker sense of actualization – discussed in rather different contexts by both Plantinga and Roderick Chisholm[3] – in which one agent can actualize (and hence can have the power to actualize) the free actions of another. In such cases the agent in question, by his actions or omissions, strongly brings it about that another agent S is in a situation C, where it is true that if S were in C, then S would freely act in a specified way. For instance, a mother might actualize her child's freely choosing to have Rice Krispies for breakfast by limiting his choices to Rice Krispies and the hated Raisin Bran. Or she might bring it about that the child freely donates his allowance to a relief agency by telling him poignantly of the plight of those who do not have enough to eat. In short, it is a familiar truth that one agent may contribute causally to the free actions of another in any number of ways which stop short of being incompatible with the other's acting freely. In such cases it seems perfectly legitimate to say that the one has actualized the other's acting freely in the way in question. Again adopting Plantinga's terminology, we will call this sense of actualization *weak actualization*. Further, it is not only the free actions of another which a given agent may weakly actualize. In addition, an agent S may weakly actualize a state of affairs p *through the mediation of* the free actions of another agent S^*. This occurs when S weakly actualizes S^*'s freely acting in such a way as to bring about p. Thus, in the second of the above examples, the mother weakly actualizes not only her son's freely donating his allowance to a relief agency but also – among others – the state of affairs of someone's hunger being alleviated.

We want to insist that in an analysis of omnipotence the term "actualize" (or "bring about") should be construed broadly to include both strong and weak actualization. For it is intuitively evident that a person's power is normally judged in large measure by his ability to influence the free actions of others in one or another of the ways intimated above, for example, by restricting their options, or by providing them with information or opportunities, or by commanding them, or by persuading or dissuading them, etc. So an omnipotent being should be expected to have the maximal amount of this sort of power. This underscores nicely the impressive nature of maximal power, extending as it does even to the free actions of others. On the other hand, even though the use of this liberal sense of actualization helps us to capture the pervasiveness of an omnipotent agent's power, it also points to an almost universally ignored limitation on that power. We will discuss this limitation below.[4]

2. Our second condition is that an omnipotent being should be expected to have the power to actualize a state of affairs p only if it is logically possible that someone actualize p, that is, only if there is a possible world W such that in W someone actualizes p. We take this claim to be self-evident.

One generally acknowledged consequence of this condition of adequacy is that the scope of an omnipotent agent's power is limited to logically contingent states of affairs, where a logically contingent state of affairs is one that possibly obtains and also possibly fails to obtain. However, it should be obvious that an analysis of maximal power will not by itself determine just which states of affairs are logically contingent and which are not. Indeed, one could trivialize the consequence in question by espousing the extreme view, sometimes attributed to Descartes, that every state of affairs is logically contingent. Or one might weaken it considerably by embracing the slightly more modest position – and perhaps this is what Descartes actually had in mind – that many allegedly paradigmatic necessary truths, for example, logical laws or simple mathematical truths, are in fact logically contingent. We do not endorse such views, but nothing we say about maximal power itself will rule them out. Their truth or falsity must be decided independently.

Also, we will explicitly assume below that all states of affairs (and propositions) are tensed. If this assumption is correct, then it is reasonable to think that at least some logically contingent past-tense states of affairs are not possibly such that someone actualizes them.[5] For instance, one might hold that even though it is logically possible for someone to bring it about that Jones will someday be in Chicago, it is logically impossible that anyone ever bring it about that Jones has already been in Chicago. Again, however, an account of maximal power will not by itself decide whether such a claim is true.[6]

3. Many contemporary philosophers not only have accepted our first two conditions of adequacy but also have taken them to be sufficient

by themselves. This is evident from the widespread acceptance, until fairly recently, of analyses equivalent to the following:

(A) *S* is omnipotent if and only if for any state of affairs *p*, if there is a world *W* such that in *W* someone actualizes *p*, then *S* has the power to actualize *p*.

However, philosophers at least as far back as Aristotle have realized that if the past is in some sense necessary, then there are further, purely temporal, restrictions on the power of any agent. The medievals, in fact, had a moderately well articulated theory of temporal (*per accidens*) modality, from which it follows that at any given time there are states of affairs which meet the condition specified in (A) and yet are such that they cannot be within the power of any agent to actualize. Interestingly, even those like Aquinas, who held that God is not "in time," recognized this sort of restriction on God's power.

So, for instance, suppose that Jones played basketball two days ago. Then, the claim goes, not only is it *true* now that Jones once played basketball, but it is also *necessary* now that Jones once played basketball. That is, in any possible world just like ours prior to the present moment *t*, it is true at *t* and at every moment after *t* that Jones once played basketball. And from this it follows that no one can *now* have the power to actualize the following state of affairs:

(1) Its being the case that it will be true at some time that Jones has never played basketball.

For it is a minimal and noncontroversial constraint on any agent's having the power at a time *t* to actualize a state of affairs *p* that there be a possible world *W* just like ours prior to *t* such that at *t* in *W* someone actualizes *p*.[7] But, the argument continues, there is no such world in the case of (1). Nevertheless, (1) satisfies the condition laid down in (A), since it is easy enough to conceive of a possible world in which someone actualizes it. Such an agent might, for example, prevent Jones's coming into existence or arrange for him not to play basketball for a long time after his birth. So it is logically possible for some one to have the power to actualize (1), even though it is logically impossible that both (a) the world have the history it has had until now and (b) someone now have the power to actualize (1). Furthermore, there are any number of states of affairs which are like (1) in these respects. So any adequate account of omnipotence must be relativized to a time. In addition, these purely temporal restrictions on power may vary not only from moment to moment but also from possible world to possible world. And so an account of omnipotence should also be relativized to a possible world. Hence, our analysandum should be "S is omnipotent at t in W," and we should incorporate into our analysis the purely temporal restrictions on any agent's power.

This argument rests on two metaphysical presuppositions. The first is that states of affairs (and propositions) are tensed. We find this claim both natural and defensible, and so we accept it. (However, it may be possible for the friends of "tenseless" propositions to recast the argument in their own idiom.) One important consequence is that some logically contingent states of affairs may obtain at some times and not at others within the same possible world. For instance, the state of affairs of Jones's having played basketball does not obtain before Jones plays basketball for the first time but always obtains afterwards. Again, the state of affairs of its being the case that Jones will play basketball may obtain now, but it will not obtain after Jones plays basketball for the last time. Further, some states of affairs may first obtain, and then not obtain, and still later obtain again. An example is the present-tense state of affairs of Jones's (now) playing basketball.

The second metaphysical presupposition is that it is logically impossible that someone travel into the past. This claim, though eminently reasonable, has been challenged of late by several writers, who have asserted in effect that there are no purely temporal restrictions on any agent's power.[8] These philosophers would say that in the case alluded to above it is at least conceivable that someone now travel backwards two days into the past and find himself in a position to prevent Jones from playing basketball. Assuming that Jones has played basketball just this one time, our time traveler would have it within his power to actualize (1). If such a scenario is coherent, it may not be incompatible with our analysis of maximal power, since our third condition of adequacy is simply that an account of omnipotence should accommodate the (epistemic) possibility that there are purely temporal restrictions on the power of an omnipotent agent. We will satisfy this condition by claiming that an omnipotent agent should be expected to have the power at t in W to actualize p only if there is a world W^* such that (i) W^* shares the same history with W at t and (ii) at t in W^* someone actualizes p. Perhaps a proponent of the conceivability of time travel can find a plausible interpretation of the notion of two worlds sharing the same history that allows him to accept this third condition while maintaining that it adds no restrictions on power beyond those already embodied in our second condition of adequacy. (We will return shortly to the notion of sharing the same history.) On the other hand, it may be that any theory of time travel is incompatible with our suggestion for satisfying the third condition. If this is the case, then so much the worse for time travel.

Two points of clarification should be made here. First, we assume that it is logically possible for agents to actualize future-tense states of affairs. For instance, an agent may bring it about at t that Jones will be in Chicago within two hours or that Jones will be in Chicago two hours after t. (Below we will claim that an agent brings about a future-tense state of affairs by bringing it about that a given present-tense state of affairs will obtain at the appropriate future time. So someone brings it about at t that Jones will be in Chicago within two hours by bringing it about that the present-tense state of affairs of Jones's being in Chicago will obtain within two hours after t.) Some may even go so far as to say that where p is a present-tense state of affairs, it is not possible for any agent S to bring it about at t that p obtains at t. That is, S's actualizing p cannot be simultaneous with p's obtaining but must rather precede p's obtaining. If this is so, then every instance of actualization involves the actualization of a future-tense state of affairs. In any case, it is reasonable to expect that an agent who is omnipotent at t will have extensive control over what can happen at any time after t – subject to the restriction which will be set down by our fourth condition of adequacy discussed below.

Second, it should be noted that our third condition of adequacy does not by itself rule out the possibility that someone have the power to bring about (as opposed to alter) the past. This is a separate issue which, as noted above, falls under our second condition of adequacy. So, for example, if it is logically possible that someone now, given the history of our world, brings it about that Carter was elected president in 1976, then an omnipotent agent now has the power to actualize this past-tense state of affairs. Given that Carter was in fact elected in 1976, the argument presented at the beginning of this section does not by itself rule out such backward causation. Again, this is an issue that must be decided independently.

We claimed above that an omnipotent being should be expected to have the power at t in W to actualize p only if there is a world W^* such that (i) W^* shares the same history with W at t and (ii) at t in W^* someone actualizes p. But so far we have said nothing about what it is for two worlds to share the same history at a given time. Perhaps it is not fair to demand that one who gives an analysis provide an exact characterization of each concept used in that analysis, especially when those concepts are tolerably clear on their own. Nevertheless, in this case we feel obligated to say something more, since the concept in question is open to seemingly acceptable construals which would undermine the adequacy of our account of maximal power.

Consider, for instance, the following "natural" explication of sharing the same history:

(2)   W shares the same history with W* at t if and only if for any state of affairs p and time t* earlier than t, p obtains at t* in W if and only if p obtains at t* in W*.

Since we are assuming that states of affairs are tensed, if we take (2) together with the analogue of the law of bivalence for states of affairs, the net effect is that W can share the same history with W* at t only if W also shares the same present and future with W* at t, that is, only if W is identical with W*. For among the states of affairs that obtain at any time prior to t in W are future-tense states of affairs which specify exactly what will be true in W at and after t. Moreover, even if we deny that the law of bivalence holds for so-called "future contingent" states of affairs, so that no such state of affairs ever obtains, (2) will still be unacceptable. For on the most popular construal of the notion of a future contingent, a state of affairs is a future contingent at a given time only if it is future-tense and not causally necessary at that time. So even when we make an exception for future contingents, it still follows from (2) that W and W* share the same history at t only if they share at t what we might call their causally necessitated futures. Such a result is particularly unwelcome when one is trying to explicate maximal power, since it is generally conceded that an agent who is omnipotent at t has the power at t to bring about events whose occurrence is in some sense contrary to nature.[9]

Our own account of two worlds sharing the same history at a given time, which is Ockhamistic in inspiration, has been set out in detail in another place.[10] So we will simply outline it rather broadly here. The basic insight involved is that what is temporally independent – or, to use Chisholm's phrase, rooted in the present – at any given time can be specified in terms of the present-tense (or, as we prefer to say, immediate) states of affairs which obtain at that time. All nonimmediate, or temporally dependent, states of affairs that obtain at a time t obtain at t only in virtue of the fact that the appropriate immediate states of affairs did or will obtain at moments other than t. So, for instance, the nonimmediate state of affairs of Jones's having played basketball obtains now in virtue of the fact that the immediate state of affairs of Jones's playing basketball obtained at some past time. Likewise, the nonimmediate state of affairs of its being the case that Jones will play basketball obtains now in virtue of the fact that Jones's playing basketball will obtain at some future time. This is why it is reasonable to believe that an agent brings it about that Jones will play basketball only by bringing it about that Jones's playing basketball will obtain.

Our claim is that for any moment t in a world W there is a set k of immediate states of affairs which determines what obtains at t in a temporally independent way, that is, what obtains at t but does not obtain at t in virtue of what occurs at moments other than t. We call k the *submoment* of t in W and say that k obtains in W when and only when each of its members obtains in W. Then W and W^* share the same history at t if and only if they share all and only the same submoments, obtaining in exactly the same order, prior to t. Since no future-tense state of affairs is immediate or, consequently, a member of any submoment, it follows that W and W^* may share the same history at t even if their futures are radically diverse at t – and this diversity may extend even to their laws of nature at and after t or to events contrary to the laws of nature that they share at or after t.

Given this general picture, the most pressing task is to provide a plausible characterization of the distinction between immediate and nonimmediate states of affairs. However, our account of this distinction is much too complicated to be presented in passing here. Since it has been worked out in sufficient detail elsewhere, we will simply note one result which will become relevant below. As far as we can tell, this is the only consequence of what we say about the purely temporal restrictions on power that may prove troublesome for our claim that even a divine being may have maximal power.

According to our explication of immediacy, states of affairs involving present-tense propositional attitudes directed at future-tense propositions, for example,

(3) Jones's believing that Smith will arrive at 2:00 P.M.,

and

(4) Jones's promising that Smith will receive a gift,

are immediate unless they entail the future-tense propositions which they involve.[11] On the other hand, if these entailments do hold, then such states of affairs are nonimmediate and hence not members of any submoment. But now consider the following states of affairs:

(5) God's believing that Smith will be saved,

and

(6) God's promising that Smith will be saved.

Since (5) and (6) both entail that Smith will be saved, each is on our account nonimmediate and hence not eligible for membership in a submoment. This is a welcome result in the case of (5), since it enables us to reconcile divine foreknowledge with human freedom. In short, even if (5) has already obtained, there may still be a world W such that (i) W shares the same history with our world at the present moment and yet

(ii) Smith is never saved in W. So even if it has already been true that God believes that Smith will be saved, Smith may still have it within his power to bring it about that he will never be saved. However, this same result is somewhat more troublesome in the case of (6).[12]

4. Some might suspect that what we have already said is sufficient for explicating maximal power. For at this point we have the resources to formulate the following analysis:

> (B) S is omnipotent at t in W if and only if for any state of affairs p, if there is a world W^* such that
> (i) W^* shares the same history with W at t, and
> (ii) at t in W^* someone actualizes p,
> then S has the power at t in W to actualize p.

Though this analysis is surely appealing, we believe that it is nonetheless inaccurate. Its insufficiency can be traced to one primary deficiency: such an analysis fails to take account of the way in which the free actions (and dispositions to free action) of other beings would necessarily limit the power of any omnipotent being. Let us now show how this limitation arises.

As noted above in our discussion of actualization, there seems to be good reason to think that the libertarian analysis of freedom is correct. If so, it follows that not even an omnipotent being can causally determine the free actions of another agent. This fact, of course, was what accounted for the distinction between strong and weak actualization, a distinction which allows that a being can bring about a state of affairs in two distinct ways.

However, if libertarianism is true, it has a second and equally significant impact on the analysis of omnipotence. To see this, let us imagine the following situation. Suppose that at a time t a non-omnipotent being named Jones is free with respect to writing a letter to his wife. In that case Jones has the power at t to actualize

> (7) Jones's freely deciding at t to write a letter to his wife,

and he also has the power at t to actualize

> (8) Jones's freely deciding at t to refrain from writing a letter to his wife.

From this it follows that there is a world W, sharing the same history with our world at t, such that at t in W someone (viz., Jones) actualizes (7); and it also follows that there is a world W^*, sharing the same history with our world at t, such that at t in W^* someone (viz., Jones) actualizes (8). So given (B), any agent who is omnipotent at t in our world must have at t both the power to actualize (7) and the power to actualize (8).

However, on the assumption that libertarianism is true it is fairly easy to show that no one distinct from Jones – not even an omnipotent agent – *can* have at *t* both the power to actualize (7) and the power to actualize (8). Let C stand for the circumstances in which Jones finds himself at *t*. If libertarianism is true, then C includes the fact that there is a temporal interval beginning before *t* and including *t*, in which there is no causally sufficient condition either for Jones's deciding at *t* to write the letter or for his deciding at *t* not to write the letter. But now consider the following counterfactual:[13]

> (9) If Jones were in C at *t*, he would freely decide at *t* to refrain from writing a letter to his wife.

Like any proposition, (9) is either true or false. Furthermore, since (9) tells us what Jones would do if left free in a certain situation, no one other than Jones can simply decide to make (9) true or false, for no one other than Jones can determine how Jones would *freely* act. Therefore, not even an omnipotent being can decide by himself to make (9) true or false; its truth-value is something he is powerless to affect.

The consequence of this inescapable powerlessness is that, regardless of whether (9) is true or false, there will be a state of affairs which, despite meeting the conditions set down in (B), cannot be actualized at *t* by any being other than Jones – even if that being is omnipotent at *t*. For suppose (9) is true. In that case, even an agent who is omnipotent at *t* does not have the power at *t* to actualize (7). He cannot, of course, strongly actualize (7), for he cannot causally determine Jones's acting freely in a certain way. But neither can he weakly actualize (7).

He can, perhaps, arrange things so that Jones is in C at *t*. But if he does so arrange things, then (9) tells us that Jones will freely refrain from writing the letter and thereby actualize (8) rather than (7). On the other hand, if (9) is false, then our omnipotent agent cannot at *t* weakly actualize (8). The most he can do in an attempt to bring about (8) is to bring it about that Jones is in C at *t*. But if (9) is false, then it is *not* the case that if Jones were in C at *t*, he would strongly actualize (8). And no one weakly actualizes (8) unless Jones strongly actualizes it. So if (9) is in fact false, then not even an omnipotent agent has the power at *t* to actualize (8).[14]

Therefore, whether or not (9) is true, there will be some state of affairs satisfying the conditions specified in (B) which even an omnipotent agent is incapable of actualizing. And since this inability results solely from the *logically necessary* truth that one being cannot causally determine how another will freely act, it should not be viewed (as [B] does view it) as a kind of inability which disqualifies an agent from ranking as omnipotent.

It follows, then, that an adequate analysis of omnipotence must acknowledge the logically inescapable limitations which counterfactuals such as (9) would place on an omnipotent agent. Now it should be obvious that there are many counterfactuals which, like (9), tell us how beings would freely act. In fact, since there are presumably an infinite number of circumstances in which a being can find himself, there will be an infinite number of such counterfactuals for any free agent. Nor can we limit our consideration exclusively to *actual* free beings. For though an omnipotent agent might well have the power to create free beings who are not now actual, he would nonetheless be limited by the counterfactuals relating to the free actions of these beings as well. Hence, our analysis of omnipotence must recognize the importance of counterfactuals of freedom regarding not only *actual* beings but *possible* beings as well. If we believe that, strictly speaking, there are no possible but non-actual beings, we can make this last point by saying that the relevant counterfactuals relate not to individuals but to *individual essences*, where P is an individual essence if and only if P is a property which is such that (i) in some possible world there is an individual x who has P essentially and (ii) there is no possible world in which there exists an individual distinct from x who has P.[15] An individual x will thus be said to be an *instantiation* of individual essence P just in case x has P.

Now suppose we call a complete set of such counterfactuals of freedom a *world-type*. If the law of conditional excluded middle were true – that is, if it were the case that for any propositions p and q, either p counterfactually implies q or p counterfactually implies the negation of q – then a world-type could be defined as a set of counterfactuals indicating, for every individual essence and every possible set of circumstances and times in which it could be instantiated and left free, how an instantiation of that essence would freely act if placed in those circumstances.

However, many philosophers reject the law of conditional excluded middle, for they feel there are at least some cases in which p counterfactually implies neither q nor its negation.[16] Hence, it would probably be wiser for us to provide a more general definition of a world-type which does not presuppose the truth of this law. Let us say, then, that a world-type is a set which is such that for any *counterfactual of freedom* – that is, any proposition which can be expressed by a sentence of the form "If individual essence P were instantiated in circumstances C at time t and its instantiation were left free with respect to action A, the instantiation of P would freely do A" – either that counterfactual or its negation is a member of the set.

(To obviate certain esoteric technical problems, we might also stipulate that for any two members of the set, the conjunction of those two members is a member of the set as well.) Let us also say that a world-type is *true* just in case every proposition which is a member of it is true. (Since we are assuming an exact isomorphism between propositions and states of affairs, we may take a world-type to be, alternatively, a set of counterfactual states of affairs.)

Now any free being will have some say in determining which world-type is true. For example, since Jones is free to decide whether or not to write that letter to his wife, it is up to him whether the true world-type includes (9) or its negation. However, the vast majority of the counter-factuals which go to make up a world-type relate to beings other than Jones, and Jones, of course, is powerless to make such counterfactuals true or false. So for any free agent x there will be a set of all and only those true counterfactuals of freedom (or true negations of such counterfactuals) over whose truth-value x has no control. Since such a set will clearly be a subset of the true world-type and will be characteristic only of x, let us refer to it as the *world-type-for-x*.[17]

So it is a necessary truth that every being is in a sense simply presented with a set of counterfactuals whose truth-values he is powerless to control. That is, for any agent x the world-type-for-x will remain true regardless of what x does. So it is logically impossible for x to bring about any state of affairs which is inconsistent with the truth of the world-type-for-x with which he happens to be con-fronted. That is, it is logically impossible for him to bring about any state of affairs which does not obtain in any world in which that world-type-for-x is true. And since it is also logically impossible for any agent to escape this type of limitation, we cannot allow such a limitation of power to disqualify a being from ranking as omnipo-tent. Hence, if we allow "Lx" to stand for the true world-type-for-x, then x should not be required, in order to rank as omnipotent, to possess the power to actualize any state of affairs that does not obtain in any world in which Lx is true. We can consider this as our fourth condition for an adequate analysis of omnipotence.

So the power of any being x will necessarily be limited by the set of counterfactuals of freedom which constitute the true world-type-for-x. Moreover, since these counterfactuals do relate to the *free* actions of agents, none of them will be logically necessary truths. Even if (9) is true in the actual world, it could not be a necessary truth, for Jones could not be free regarding letter writing if there were no world in which he does decide to write in the circumstances in question. So though the true world-type-for-x (where x is distinct from Jones) in our world may include (9), there are other worlds in which the true world-type-for-x includes the negation of (9). Hence, different world-types-for-x may be true in different worlds. And this gives further support to the claim, made above, that an analysis of omnipotence must be relativized to a possible world.[18]

5. If our first four conditions of adequacy were pedantically specific, our fifth and final condition is refreshingly vague. Simply stated, it is that no being should be considered omnipotent if he lacks the kind of power which it is clear an omnipotent agent ought to possess. Such a requirement might appear redundant at this point. However, it is actually needed to rule out an analysis like the following, which satisfies our first four conditions:

(C) S is omnipotent at t in W if and only if for any state of affairs p and world-type-for-S Ls such that p is not a member of Ls, if there is a world W^* such that
(i) Ls is true in both W and W^*, and
(ii) W^* shares the same history with W at t, and
(iii) at t in W^* S actualizes p,
then S has the power at t in W to actualize p.[19]

Instead of furnishing us with an analysis of absolute maximal power, the right-hand side of (C) merely provides an analysis of the maximal amount of power that can be had at t in W by *any being with S's nature*. As such, it may be satisfied by a being obviously lacking omnipotence, for example, the infamous Mr. McEar. To avoid this result we will satisfy our fifth condition by insisting that to count as omnipotent, a being should have the maximal amount of power consistent with our first four conditions.[20]

II

Though we are aware of no previously offered analysis which satisfies each of these five conditions, it seems to us that an acceptable analysis of omnipotence can be formulated. For consider:

(D) S is omnipotent at t in W if and only if for any state of affairs p and world-type-for-S Ls such that p is not a member of Ls, if there is a world W^* such that
(i) Ls is true in both W and W^*, and
(ii) W^* shares the same history with W at t, and
(iii) at t in W^* someone actualizes p,
then S has the power at t in W to actualize p.

(D) appears to satisfy each of our desiderata. It is stated in terms of actualizing states of affairs and does not presuppose that an omnipotent being would have to strongly actualize every state of affairs he brings about; in other words, it leaves a place for weak actualization. The inability of even an omnipotent being to actualize necessarily unactualizable states of affairs is acknowledged by (iii), while his inability to change the past is recognized by (ii) and (iii) together. Furthermore, by employing the notion of a world-type-for-*S*, (D) satisfies our fourth condition. And, finally, (D) requires that an agent who is omnipotent at *t* in *W* have the power to actualize *any* state of affairs (other than a member of *Ls*) which *any* agent actualizes at *t* in *any* world satisfying conditions (i) and (ii). Consequently, it seems to us that (D) does provide a philosophically adequate analysis of maximal power.

[. . .]

Again, take the following state of affairs:

(11) Its being the case that a completely uncaused event will occur.

Does (D) require that Sam have the power at *t* to actualize (11)? If one can actualize (11) only by causing the event in question, then (D) does not require that Sam be able to actualize (11). For in that case it is logically impossible for anyone to actualize (11), even if (11) is a logically contingent state of affairs. On the other hand, if (11) is possibly actualized by someone, then Sam must have the power at *t* to actualize it. In neither case is there a paradoxical result.

But what of this state of affairs:

(12) Someone is actualizing *p*, and Sam, though omnipotent, is not actualizing *p*,

where *p* is a state of affairs which even nonomnipotent agents can normally actualize? Must Sam have the power at *t* to bring it about that (12) will obtain? One might have doubts about whether it is logically possible for any agent to actualize (12). However, anyone who holds a fairly liberal position with respect to the diffusiveness of power might plausibly contend that it is logically possible. For instance, a nonomnipotent being could bring it about at *t* that (12) will obtain at *t** by bringing it about that he will be actualizing *p* at *t**, when in fact it is true that Sam will not be actualizing *p* at *t**. But then, by the same token, it appears that Sam too may have the power at *t* to bring it about that (12) will obtain at *t**. Sam would do this by bringing it about that he will not be actualizing *p* at *t**, when in fact it is true that someone else will be actualizing *p* at *t**.

Of course, it is plausible to think that if Sam is an essentially divine (i.e., eternally omnipotent, omniscient, and provident) being, then he weakly or strongly actualizes at any time *t* every state of affairs (other than a member of the true world-type-for-Sam) which *anyone* actualizes at *t*. In that case Sam would never have the power to bring it about that (12) will obtain. But neither would any other agent ever have this power in any world containing an essentially divine being. So (D) would not in this case require that Sam have the power at t to bring it about that (12) will obtain. In short, (12) seems to present no serious problem for our analysis of omnipotence. Perhaps there are other states of affairs which would present a problem, but we have not been able to think of any.

Furthermore, our analysis has not been "corrupted" by theological considerations. Indeed, (D) appears to be quite neutral with regard to what additional properties an omnipotent being might conceivably have. Given (D), there is no obvious conceptual requirement that an omnipotent agent be eternal, necessary, essentially omnipotent, uniquely omnipotent, omniscient, or morally impeccable – a being could conceivably lack any or all of these attributes at a time t in a world W and yet still be omnipotent at t in W. Of course, for all that (D) tells us, an omnipotent being could equally well possess any or all of these attributes (leaving open for now the question of moral impeccability). In short, it appears that (D) neither requires nor forbids an omnipotent being to possess the theologically significant properties mentioned above and thus does exhibit the kind of independence from religious matters which we would presumably prefer our analysis to exhibit.

NOTES

1. To the best of our knowledge, McEar makes his first contemporary appearance in Alvin Plantinga's *God and Other Minds* (Ithaca, 1967), pp. 168–73.
2. See Alvin Plantinga, *The Nature of Necessity* (Oxford, 1974), pp. 172–73.
3. Plantinga's discussion of weak actualization is in the place cited in note 2. Chisholm's discussion occurs in *Person and Object* (LaSalle, Ill., 1976), pp. 67–69. (Chisholm takes as basic the concept of causally contributing to a state of affairs rather than the notion of actualizing a state of affairs.) It is no mean feat to formulate an exact analysis of weak actualization, but an intuitive grasp of this notion will suffice for our purposes in this paper.
4. For some analyses of omnipotence *not* stated in terms of actualizing states of affairs, see Richard Francks, "Omniscience, Omnipotence and Pantheism," *Philosophy* 54 (1979): 395–99; Jerome Gellman, "The Paradox of Omnipotence, and Perfection," *Sophia* 14 (1975): 31–39; and (though less explicitly) J. L. Mackie, "Evil and Omnipotence," *Mind* 64 (1955): 200–12.
5. We say "at least some," since those who espouse an Ockhamistic response to the problem of future contingents might want to insist that we can have the power to actualize certain "future-infected" past-tense states of affairs. See Alfred J. Freddoso, "Accidental Necessity and Power over the Past," *Pacific Philosophical Quarterly* 63 (1982): 54–68.
6. Despite what we have said, it may be the case that Descartes is an offender rather than just a trivializer of our second condition. See Harry Frankfurt, "Descartes on the Creation of the Eternal Truths," *Philosophical Review* 86 (1977): 36–57.
7. This condition on power, despite first appearances, is consistent even with compatibilism. The compatibilist would, however, deny the libertarian claim that we can add the further condition that W and our world continue to share the same laws of nature (with no violations) at t itself.

8. See, for instance, Jack W. Meiland, "A Two-Dimensional Passage Model of Time for Time Travel," *Philosophical Studies* 26 (1974): 153–73; and David Lewis, "The Paradoxes of Time Travel," *American Philosophical Quarterly* 13 (1976): 145–52.

9. For a dissenting view cf. Dennis M. Ahern, "Miracles and Physical Impossibility," *Canadian Journal of Philosophy* 7 (1977): 71–79. Our own inclination, on the other hand, is to believe that laws of nature specify the causal powers or dispositions of natural substances. Hence, such a law, e.g., that potassium has by nature a disposition to ignite when exposed to oxygen, might remain true even when the manifestation of the disposition in question is prevented solely by the action of a supernatural agent.

10. See Alfred J. Freddoso, "Accidental Necessity and Logical Determinism," *Journal of Philosophy* 80 (1983): 257–78. This paper argues for our account of sharing the same history on purely philosophical grounds rather than on the theological grounds suggested below.

11. A state of affairs p may be said to entail a proposition q just in case it is logically impossible that p obtains and q does not. And p may be said to involve q just in case p is necessarily such that whoever conceives it conceives q.

12. Many recent philosophers have failed to recognize explicitly that any being's power is necessarily limited to states of affairs which are "temporally contingent." In addition to Francks, Gellman, and Mackie, see George Mavrodes, "Defining Omnipotence," *Philosophical Studies* 32 (1977): 191–202; Nelson Pike, "Omnipotence and God's Ability to Sin" *American Philosophical Quarterly* 6 (1969): 208–216; and Richard Purtill, *Thinking about Religion* (Englewood Cliffs, N.J., 1978), p. 31.

13. Throughout this essay we shall follow David Lewis's practice of not presupposing that the term "counterfactual" is to be applied only to conditionals with false antecedents. See David Lewis, *Counterfactuals* (Cambridge, Mass., 1973), p. 3.

14. The argument here is little more than a variant of Alvin Plantinga's argument against the thesis that God must have the ability to actualize any possible world. See Plantinga, *Nature of Necessity*, pp. 180–84.

15. The definition of an individual essence is taken from Plantinga, *Nature of Necessity*, p. 72.

16. For a discussion of conditional excluded middle see Lewis, *Counterfactuals*, pp. 79–82. We wish to note in passing, however, that even if the law of conditional excluded middle is false, there may be a weaker analogue of that law which is true and would be sufficient for our present purposes if we chose to invoke it. For the antecedents of the counterfactual conditionals which concern us here are all of the form "Individual essence P is instantiated in circumstances C at time t, and P's instantiation is left free with respect to action A." Now suppose we stipulate that the substituend for "C" must be a complete description of the past at t along with a clause specifying that the same laws of nature continue to hold at t. In that case there seems to be good reason to believe that where p is a proposition expressed by a sentence of *this* form, then for any proposition q, either p counterfactually implies q or p counterfactually implies the negation of q. However, a complete defence of this position is impossible here, and so we will proceed on the assumption that there is no acceptable version of the law of conditional excluded middle.

17. The relationship between the world-type-for-God and divine freedom is discussed at length in Thomas P. Flint, "The Problem of Divine Freedom," *American Philosophical Quarterly* 20 (1983). One terminological point suggested there might also be noted in passing here: God's knowledge of the world-type-for-God is identical with what is generally referred to as God's *middle knowledge*. The Molinist thesis that God has middle knowledge of contingent propositions whose truth-values he cannot control is hotly contested in traditional theological discussions of grace, providence, and predestination. We cannot pursue the matter here but simply wish to note our belief that it is only by adopting some version of Molinism that one can preserve a

suitably strong understanding of both (a) the doctrine of divine providence and (b) the thesis that human beings are free.

18. Among authors discussed previously, Francks, Gellman, Mackie, Pike, and Purtill all fail to satisfy this fourth condition. In addition see Gary Rosenkrantz and Joshua Hoffman, "What an Omnipotent Agent Can Do," *International Journal for Philosophy of Religion* 11 (1980): 1–19; James Ross, *Philosophical Theology* (Indianapolis, 1969), p. 221; and Douglas Walton, "Some Theorems of Fitch on Omnipotence," *Sophia* 15 (1976): 20–27.

19. The stipulation that p not be a member of Ls is required if we assume that by their free actions agents actualize the corresponding counterfactuals of freedom. In the example used above, this assumption would amount to the claim that by actualizing (8) Jones also actualizes (9). If, on the other hand, we deny that a counterfactual of freedom can properly be said to be actualized by anyone, then the stipulation in question is, though superfluous, completely harmless. So we have added it just to be safe.

20. Despite Richard Swinburne's protestations to the contrary, the conceivability of McEar disqualifies his analysis. See Richard Swinburne, "Omnipotence," *American Philosophical Quarterly* 10 (1973): 231–37. For much the same reason an analysis offered tentatively by Plantinga must also be deemed unacceptable. On this analysis a being S is viewed as omnipotent at time t in world W if and only if (1) there are states of affairs S can strongly actualize at t, and (2) for any state of affairs p such that there is a possible world which shares the initial world-segment prior to t with W and in which S at t strongly actualizes p, S can at t strongly actualize p.

GOODNESS
3.6

'WHAT EUTHYPHRO
SHOULD HAVE SAID'

William P. Alston

I must confess that my title is just a 'come-on'. I am not going to discuss the specific Euthyphro problem, whether an act is pious because it is loved by the gods or is loved by the gods because it is pious. I shall rather be discussing the divine-command-ethics analogue of this question, at a first approximation, whether God commands us to love one another because that is right (our moral obligation, what we ought to do morally) or whether that is right because God commands us to do it. Hence I shall not really be trying to determine what Euthyphro should have said. What I shall do is to consider what view of God and human morality a divine command theorist should adopt if she is to be in the best position to deal with this dilemma. I lack at least the time to establish those views; I shall have to content myself with exhibiting them as not unreasonable, plausible and coherent, and with showing how they enable the divine command theorist to deal with certain difficulties involved in the above dilemma.

When I embarked on this project I had little real sympathy for divine command theory. The subject interested me because of the way in which thinking about the problems involved forces us to come to grips with basic questions about the nature of God and our relations with him. However, in the course of the enterprise I have warmed to the topic, and now I think there might really be something to a divine command ethics. At least the considerations I shall be presenting have led to a much more positive assessment of its viability than I had previously.

William P. Alston, 'What Euthyphro Should Have Said' (not previously published).

The form of divine command theory I shall be discussing is the one presented in Robert Adams's latest paper on the subject, 'Divine Command Metaethics Modified Again'.[1] This is not a view as to what words like 'right' and 'ought' mean. Nor is it a view as to what our concepts of moral obligation, rightness and wrongness amount to. It is rather the claim that divine commands are constitutive of the moral status of actions. As Adams puts it, 'ethical wrongness *is* (i.e., is identical with) the property of being contrary to the commands of a loving God'.[2] Hence such a view is immune to the objection that many persons, at least, don't mean 'is contrary to a command of God' by 'is morally wrong' just as the view that water is H_2O is immune to the objection that many people do not mean 'H_2O' by 'water'. I intend my discussion to be applicable to any version of this 'objective constitution' sort. It could just as well be an 'ultimate *criterion* of moral obligation' view or a view as to that on which moral obligation *supervenes*. I shall understand 'constitutive' to range over all these variants. Thus I can state the version to be considered in the following simple form:

1. Divine commands are constitutive of moral obligation.

Let me say a further word as to how (1), or the range of theories it encapsulates, is to be understood, though I shall only have time to scratch the surface. First, there is a variety of terms that could be, and have been, used to specify what it is that divine commands are held to constitute. These include 'right', 'wrong', 'ought', 'obligation' and 'duty'. For reasons that will emerge in the course of the paper, I prefer to concentrate on '(morally) ought'. I have used the term 'moral obligation' in (1) because it makes possible a more succinct formulation, but whenever in the sequel I speak of 'moral obligation' I do not, unless the reader is warned to the contrary, mean to be trading on any maximally distinctive features of the meaning of that term. I will rather be understanding 'S has a moral obligation to do A' as simply an alternative formulation for 'S morally ought to do A'. I shall often omit the qualifier 'morally' when the context makes it clear what is intended. Second, should we think of each particular obligation of a particular agent in a particular situation as constituted by a separate divine command, or should we think of general divine commands (as in the Ten Commandments) constituting general obligations, from which particular obligations follow? No doubt, God does command particular people to do particular things in particular situations; but this is presumably the exception rather than the rule. Therefore in this paper we shall have our eye on the idea that general divine commands are constitutive of general obligations or, if you like, of the truth or validity of general principles of obligation.

Now let's return to the Euthyphro-like dilemma. Both horns have often been thought to be unacceptable for the theist; so that the dilemma is not just an objection to divine command ethics, but an allegedly fatal difficulty for any theism. It is the first horn, of course, to which divine command theory drives us. (We ought to do A because God commands us to.) But just what is supposed to be unacceptable about saying that we are obliged to love one another because God commands us to? I am going to focus on two closely interrelated difficulties that seem to me the thorniest.

A. This makes divine commands, and hence morality, arbitrary. Anything that God should decide to command would thereby be obligatory. If God should command us to gratuitously inflict pain on each other we would thereby be obliged to do so. The theory requires that divine commands be arbitrary because it blocks off any moral reason for them. God can't command us to do A because that it is what is morally right; for it doesn't become morally right until he commands it.

B. This horn leaves us without any adequate way of construing the goodness of God. No doubt, it leaves us free to take God to be metaphysically good, realising the fullness of being and all that; but it forecloses any conception of God as morally good, the sort of goodness that is cashed out in being loving, just and merciful. For since the standards of moral goodness are set by divine commands, to say that God is morally good is just to say that he obeys his own commands. And even if it makes any sense to think of God as obeying commands that he has given himself, that is not at all what we are looking for in thinking of God as supremely morally good. We aren't just thinking that God practises what he preaches, whatever that might be.

These objections are intimately interrelated. If we could answer the second by showing how the theory leaves room for an acceptable account of the goodness of God, we could answer the first. For if God is good in the right way, especially if God is essentially good, then there will be nothing arbitrary about his commands; indeed it will be metaphysically necessary that he issue those commands for the best.

In the most general terms it is clear what the divine command theorist's strategy should be. He must fence in the area constituted by divine commands so that the divine nature and activity fall outside that area. That will leave him free to construe divine goodness in some other way, so that the divine goodness can be a basis for God issuing commands to us in one way rather than another. The simplest way of doing this is to restrict (1) so that it applies only to human, or, more liberally, creaturely, obligation. Then something else can constitute moral rightness for divine actions. This move should be attractive to one who supposes that what gives a divine command its morality-constituting force is solely God's metaphysical status in the scheme of things. God is our creator and sustainer, without whose continual exercise of creative activity we would lapse into nothingness. If God's commands are morally binding on us solely because he stands in that relation to us, it follows that they are not morally binding on himself; and so if there are moral facts involving God they will have to be otherwise constituted. But, apart from objections to thinking of the moral authority of God exclusively in terms of power and status, there seems to be more commonality than this position allows between divine and human goodness. When we are enjoined to love one another as our Father in heaven loves us, it seems to be presupposed that, even though our love can be at best but a pale imitation of divine love, what makes it good for us to love is not wholly different from what makes it good for God to love.[3]

However (1) implies that divine moral goodness is a matter of obeying divine commands only if moral obligation attaches to God; and I take it that the divine command theorist's best move is to deny just this. If the kind(s) of moral status that are engendered by divine commands are attributable only to creatures, then no puzzles can arise over the constitution of divine morality by divine commands. If this move is to work it will have to leave a suitable kind of moral status open for God. I shall now elaborate this suggestion.

Let's consider the family of moral terms that most centrally includes 'ought', 'duty' and 'obligation'. As I have already made explicit, I am taking the divine command theorist to suppose that it is facts expressible in such terms that are constituted by divine commands. Now if it is impossible for God to have duties or obligations, if it cannot ever be true that God ought to do something or other, then divine commands can be constitutive of these sorts of moral facts, for human beings and perhaps other creatures, while leaving other sorts of facts that are constitutive of divine moral goodness to be otherwise constituted. What reasons are there to suppose this to be so?

[. . .]

An easy way out would be to let Kant provide our argument.

> [I]f the will is not of itself in complete accord with reason (the actual case of men), then the actions which are recognized as objectively necessary are subjectively contingent, and the determination of such a will according to objective laws is constraint.
>
> The conception of an objective principle, so far as it constrains a will, is a command (of reason), and the formula of this command is called an *imperative*.
>
> All imperatives are expressed by an 'ought' and thereby indicate the relation of an objective law of reason to a will which is not in its subjective constitution necessarily determined by this law. This relation is that of constraint. Imperatives say that it would be good to do or to refrain from doing something, but they say it to a will which does not always do something simply because it is presented as a good thing to do.
>
> A perfectly good will, therefore, would be equally subject to objective laws (of the good), but it could not be conceived as constrained by them to act in accord with them, because, according to its own subjective

constitution, it can be determined to act only through the conception of the good. Thus no imperatives hold for the divine will or, more generally, for a holy will. The 'ought' is here out of place, for the volition of itself is necessarily in unison with the law. Therefore imperatives are only formulas expressing the relation of objective laws of volition in general to the subjective imperfection of the will of this or that rational being, e.g., the human will.[4]

It will come as no surprise to you to learn that I feel that Kant is on the right track here. But his argument leaves something to be desired. A sufficiently canny opponent would not give him the assumption that 'ought' expresses an imperative for something with the force of an imperative. Given that assumption the conclusion follows right away, for surely nothing like an imperative can be addressed to a holy will. But the opponent holds that even if nothing with imperative force can be appropriately addressed to God, it still remains true that God ought to do certain things rather than others. Hence the opponent is not prepared to admit that 'God ought to do A' is just some kind of imperative. In fact, once we spell out Kant's argument it turns out to be a variant of the inappropriateness argument we have already rejected. (Imperatives cannot appropriately be addressed to God. Therefore it cannot be true that God ought to do so-and-so.) So more needs to be said.

Let's grant that 'ought' is not merely used to express imperatives, and that there are objective facts of the form 'S ought to do A'. To determine whether there are any such facts where S is God, we have to be more explicit as to just what sort of facts these are. Let's put the problem this way. In thinking of God as perfectly good, with respect to his actions as well as otherwise, we are thinking that it is a good thing, indeed a supremely good thing, that God acts as he does. What is at issue is that, in addition to its being a good thing that he acts as he does, it is also true that this is the way in which he ought to act. What does the latter add to the former? If it adds nothing there can be no objection to speaking of how God ought to act. But there is clearly a difference. It would be a good thing if I were to learn Sanskrit, for it would represent an actualisation of one of my (beneficient) potentialities. But I have no obligation to learn Sanskrit, nor is it true that I ought to do so. So what is missing here?

Without suggesting that this is the whole story, one thing that is required for the truth of an 'ought' statement is this. There are general principles, laws, or rules that lay down conditions under which an action of a certain sort is required, permitted, or forbidden. Call them 'practical rules (principles)'. Practical principles are in force, in a non-degenerate way, with respect to a given population of agents only when there is at least a possibility of their playing a governing or regulative function; and this means only when there is a possibility of agents in that population violating them. Given that possibility, behavior can be guided, monitored, controlled, corrected, criticised, praised, blamed, punished, or rewarded on the basis of the principles. There will be social mechanisms for inculcating and enforcing the rules, positive and negative sanctions that encourage compliance and discourage violation. Psychologically, the principles will be internalised in higher level control mechanisms that monitor behaviour and behavioural tendencies and bring motivational forces to bear in the direction of compliance and away from violation. There can be something like the Freudian distinction of id, ego, and superego within each agent in the population. I take it that terms like 'ought', 'duty' and 'obligation' acquire a use only against this kind of background, that their application presupposes that practical principles are playing, or at least can play, a regulative role, socially and/or psychologically. And this is at least an essential part of what is added when we move from saying that it would be a good thing for S to do A to saying that S ought to do A.

If I had time I would point out a number of ways in which these connections show themselves. Since time is short I will make only the following point. In games and other forms of social intercourse we bother to lay down rules and requirements only where we think there is a significant chance of people acting in ways other than those we wish to encourage. In football there is a rule against a potential pass receiver stepping out of bounds and then returning to catch a pass; but there is no rule requiring players to try to win. A general failure to try to win would be destructive of the purposes of the game, but we feel that there is not enough of a chance of that to make it worthwhile to legislate against it. Rules of etiquette govern the utensils with which a given operation of eating is performed, but no rule of etiquette lays it down that food is to be placed in the mouth. And it is only where there are rules in force that we are inclined to speak of what participants ought to do. One should use a knife to cut meat; but not 'one should put one's food in one's mouth'.[5]

Instead of arguing, as I have just been doing, that a regulative role of practical principles is presupposed in the use of 'ought', I could, as Kant does, exploit the fact that practical principles themselves, and more specifically the sub-class that can be called moral principles, are naturally expressed in terms of 'ought', and argue more directly for the inapplicability of moral principles to God.[6] Under what conditions does the general moral principle that one ought to take account of the needs of others apply to an agent, as well as the evaluative principle that it is a good thing for one to take account of the needs of others? For reasons of the sort we have been giving, it seems that such a principle has force, relative to an agent or group of agents, only where it has, or can have, a role in governing, directing, guiding the conduct of those agents. Where it is necessary that S will act in manner A what sense is there in supposing that the general principle, one ought to do A, has any application to S? Here there is no foothold for the 'ought'; there is nothing to make the ought-principle true rather than, or in addition to, a factual statement that S will (necessarily) act in this way. 'Law' or 'principles' have here a descriptive rather that a regulative role. That is, the closest we can get to a moral law requiring God to love others is the modal factual statement that God necessarily loves whatever others there are.

Eleonore Stump has urged, in conversation, that if God should break a promise then he would be doing something he ought not to do; and this implies that 'ought' does have application to God. My reply is that if God should do something that is forbidden by a valid and applicable moral principle (and the example assumes that breaking a promise on the part of God would be that), this would show that he does have tendencies to act in contravention of moral principles and so 'ought' would be applicable to him because of that. In other words, Stump's argument shows only that 'ought' would be applicable to God under certain counterfactual conditions (indeed counterpossible conditions if God is essentially perfectly good), not that 'ought' is applicable to him as things are.

But what about 'right' and 'wrong'? Is it correct to say that God acts rightly even if we can't say that he acts as he ought? A. C. Ewing, in the passage referred to in note 4, endorses that position. Nothing in this paper hangs on how we decide that issue, but I am inclined to think that, as 'right' is most centrally used in moral contexts, it is tied to terms of the 'ought' family and borrows its distinctive force from them. In asking what is the right thing for me to do in this situation. I am, I think, asking what I ought to do in this situation. Ewing and others hold the view that 'right' in moral contexts means something like 'fitting' or 'appropriate' (in a certain specific way) and hence does not carry the force of 'required', 'bound', 'culpable if not', that is distinctive of 'ought' and 'obligation'. I am not inclined to agree, but it is of no moment for the present problem.

If this suffices to make plausible the view that terms of the 'ought' family apply only where there is at least the possibility of contravention, and that is all I am aspiring to here, we can apply the point to our Euthyphro problem. The divine command theorist can answer the two objections under consideration as follows. Divine commands are constitutive of facts of the form 'S morally ought to do A'. Since no such facts apply to God, we don't have to think of the goodness of God, or any aspect thereof, as consisting of his compliance with his own commands, as consisting in his doing what He ought to do as determined by his commands. If we want to say that moral goodness can be attributed to a being only if that being is subject to the moral ought, his moral obligations and the like, then we won't say that God is, strictly speaking, morally good. But God can still be called good by virtue of his lovingness, justice and mercy, qualities that are moral virtues in a being subject to the moral ought. In the language of supervenience, part of God's goodness is supervenient on characteristics that are the foundation of moral goodness in a being with contrary tendencies. Since I can't see that anything of substance hangs on it, I will continue to speak of God's moral goodness, remembering that this will be different from human moral goodness, apart from differences in degree, in the ways we have been emphasising, even when supervenient on what are generically the same action tendencies.[7]

Since divine command theory does not rule out a satisfactory construal of the moral goodness of God, it enables us to escape the arbitrariness objection also. So far from being arbitrary, God's commands to us are an expression of his perfect goodness. Since he is perfectly good by nature, it is impossible that God should command us to act in ways that are not for the best. What if God should command us to sacrifice everything for the acquisition of power? (We are assuming that this is not for the best.) Would it thereby be our moral obligation? The answer to this depends on how it is best to handle subjunctive conditionals with impossible antecedents. But whatever our logic of conditionals it is not a substantive difficulty just because there is no possibility of the truth of the antecedent.

To help nail down this point, let's consider another form of the arbitrariness objection, that on the divine command theory God could have no reason, or at least no adequate moral reason, for issuing the commands he does issue. Now if it is ruled that the only thing that counts as a moral reason for issuing a command to do A is that the addressee morally ought to do A or has a moral duty or obligation to do A, then God cannot have a moral reason for his commands. Since the addressees have a moral obligation to do A only by virtue of the fact that the command to do A is addressed to them by God, this is not a fact, obtaining independently of the command, that God could take as a reason for issuing the command. I have already indicated that I don't want to get into an argument over the boundaries of 'moral', and so I won't contest this point, even though I think that the term 'moral reason' is correctly applied to facts of other sorts, for example, that an act would be a repaying of a kindness or that it is a good thing to behave in a certain way. But however we decide to use the term 'moral', the fact remains that God can have an adequate reason for issuing the commands he issues, namely, that it is best for us to behave as he commands us to behave. In other words, his commands can be constitutive of moral obligation for us, even though there are objective facts about what is good or best that obtain independently of divine commands.

If what I have been saying is correct, a divine command theorist can avoid being impaled on the first horn of the dilemma, at least so far as the dangers of that horn stem from the two difficulties we have been discussing. But perhaps he has escaped the first horn only to be impaled on the second. We evaded our two objections by taking divine goodness, including the goodness of divine actions and action tendencies, not to be constituted by conformity to divine commands, but rather to be a fact logically prior to any divine commanding activity. And the same considerations that led to this position will equally constrain us to take divine goodness to be independent of all divine volition or voluntary activity. For if God's being good is a matter of God's carrying out what he wills for whatever divine willings, then the arbitrariness objection applies in full force; and divine goodness becomes trivialised as 'God carries out his volitions, whatever they are'. But doesn't that leave us exposed to the second horn? We are not confronted with that horn in the original form, 'God commands us to love our neighbours because that is what we ought to do', but with a closely analogous form, 'God commands us to love our neighbour because it is good that we should do so'. And that possesses the sort of feature deemed repellent to theism just as much as the first form, namely, that it makes the goodness of states of affairs independent of the divine will, thereby subjecting God to valuational facts that are what they are independent of him. It thereby contradicts the absolute sovereignty of God; it implies that there are realities other than himself that do not owe their being to his creative activity. If it is true, independently of God's will, that loving communion is a supreme good, and that forgiveness is better than resentment, then God is subject to these truths. He must conform himself to them and so is not absolutely sovereign.

One way of meeting this objection is to assimilate evaluative principles to logical truths. If evaluative principles are logically necessary, then God's 'subjection' to these principles is just a special case of his 'subjection' to logical truths, something that is acknowledged on almost all hands.

However, I am going to suggest a more radical response. The difficulty with this horn is generally stated, and as I just stated it, in terms of a Platonic conception of the objectivity of goodness and other normative and evaluative statuses. If it is an objective fact that X is good, this is because there are objectively true general principles that specify the conditions under which something is good (the features on which goodness supervenes) and X satisfies (enough of) these conditions. To go back to the Euthyphro:

> Soc. Remember that I did not ask you to give me two or three examples of piety, but to explain the general idea which makes all pious things to be pious . . . Tell me what is the nature of this idea, and then I shall have a standard to which I may look, and by which I may measure actions, whether yours or those of anyone else, and then I shall be able to say that such and such an action is pious, such another impious. (6)

What is ultimate here is the truth of the general principles; any particular example of goodness has that status only because it conforms to the general 'Idea'. And the general principles, or the fact(s) that make them true, are thought to have the kind of being attributed by Plato to the Ideas; hence they have a reality independent of God. Or else desperate and, I believe, unsuccessful attempts are made to show that they can play the role just specified even though their ontological locus is somehow the mind of God.

I want to suggest, by contrast, that we can think of God himself, the individual being, as the supreme standard of goodness. God plays the role in evaluation that is more usually assigned, by objectivists about value, to Platonic Ideas or principles. Lovingness is good (a good-making feature, that on which goodness is supervenient) not because of the Platonic existence of a general principle or fact to the effect that lovingness is good, but because God, the supreme standard of goodness, is loving. Goodness supervenes on every feature of God, not because some general principles are true but just because they are features of God. Of course, we can have general principles, for example, lovingness is good. For this principle is not ultimate; it, or the general fact that makes it true, does not enjoy some Platonic ontological status; rather it is true just because the property it specifies as sufficient for goodness is a property of God.

It may be useful to distinguish (a) 'Platonic' predicates, the criterion for the application of which is a general 'essence' or 'Idea' that can be specified in purely general terms, and (b) 'particularistic' predicates, the criterion for the application of which makes essential reference to one or more individuals. Geometrical terms like 'triangle' have traditionally been taken as paradigms of the former. There seem to be rather different sub-classes of the latter type. It is plausible to suggest, for example, that biological kind terms, like 'dog' are applied not on the basis of a list of defining properties but on the basis of similarity to certain standard examples. The same sort of thing can be suggested with respect to 'family resemblance' terms like 'game' or 'religion'. A sub-type closer to our present concern is the much discussed 'meter'. Let's say that what makes a certain length a meter is its equality to a standard meter stick kept in Paris. What makes this table a meter in length is not its conformity to a Platonic essence but its conformity to a concretely existing individual. Similarly, on my present suggestion, what most ultimately makes an act of love a good thing is not its conformity to some general principle but its conformity to, or imitation of, God, who is both the ultimate source of the existence of things and the supreme standard by reference to which they are to be assessed.

Note that on this view we are not debarred from saying what is supremely good about God. God is not good, *qua* bare particular or undifferentiated thisness. God is good by virtue of being loving, just, merciful and so on. Where this view differs from its alternative is in the answer to the question, 'By virtue of what are these features of God good-making features?' The answer given by this view is: 'By virtue of being features of God.'

It may help further to appreciate the difference of this view from the more usual valuations of objectivism if we contrast the ways in which these views will understand God's supremely good activity. On a Platonic view God will 'consult' the objective principles of goodness, whether they are 'located' in his intellect or in a more authentically Platonic realm, and see to it that his actions conform thereto. On my particularist view God will simply act as he is inclined to act, will simply act in accordance with his character, and that will necessarily be for the best. No preliminary stage of checking the relevant principles is required.

[. . .]

I will briefly consider two objections to my valuational particularism. First, it may seem that it is infected with the arbitrariness we have been concerned to avoid. Isn't it arbitrary to take some particular individual, even the supreme individual, as the standard of goodness, regardless of whether this individual conforms to general principles of goodness or not? To put it another way, if we want to know what is good about a certain action or human being, or if we want to know why that action or human being is good, does it throw any light on the matter to pick out some other individual being and say that the first is good because it is like the second? That is not advancing the inquiry. But this objection amounts to no more than an expression of Platonist predilections. One may as well ask: 'How can it be an answer to the question "Why is this table a meter long?" to cite its coincidence with the standard meter stick?' There just are some concepts that work that way. My suggestion is that goodness is one of those concepts, and it is no objection to this suggestion to aver that no concept can work in that way.

Here is another way of responding to the objection. Whether we are Platonist or particularist, there will be some stopping place in the search for explanation. An answer to the question, 'What is good about?' will, sooner or later, cite certain good-making characteristics. We can then ask why we should suppose that good supervenes on those characteristics. In answer either a general principle or an individual paradigm is cited. But whichever it is, that is the end of the line. (We can, of course, ask why we should suppose that this principle is true or that this individual is a paradigm; but that is another inquiry.) On both views something is taken as ultimate, behind which we cannot go, in the sense of finding some explanation of the fact that it is constitutive of goodness. I would invite one who finds the invocation of God as the supreme standard arbitrary, to explain why it is more arbitrary than the invocation of a supreme general principle. Perhaps it is because it seems self-evident to him that the principle is true. But it seems self-evident to some that God is the supreme standard. And just as my opponent will explain the lack of self-evidence to some people of this general principle by saying that they have not considered it sufficiently, in an impartial frame of mind or whatever, so the theistic particularist will maintain that those who don't acknowledge God as the supreme standard are insufficiently acquainted with God, or have not sufficiently considered the matter.

Secondly, it may be objected that, on theistic particularism, in order to have any knowledge of what is good we would have to know quite a bit about God. But many people who know little or nothing about God know quite a bit about what is good. The answer to this is that the view does not have the alleged epistemological implications. It does have some epistemological implications. It implies that knowing about the nature of God puts us in an ideal position to make evaluative judgements. But it does not imply that explicit knowledge of God is the only sound basis for such judgements. The particularist is free to recognise that God, being the source of our being and governor of the universe as well as the standard of value, has so constructed us and our environment that we are led to form sound value judgements under various circumstances without tracing them back to the ultimate standard. Analogously, we are so constructed and so situated as to be able to form true and useful opinions about water, without getting so far as to discern its ultimate chemical or physical constitution.

As a final note on particularism, I should like to point out its connection with certain familiar themes, both Christian and otherwise. It is a truism of what we might call evaluational development (of which moral development is a species) that we come to recognise and appreciate good-making properties more often through acquaintance with specially striking exemplifications than through being explicitly instructed in general principles. We acquire standards in art, music and literature, through becoming intimately familiar with great works in those media; with that background we are often able to make confident judgements on newly encountered works without being able to formulate general principles on which we are relying. Our effective internalisation of moral standards is more often due to our interaction with suitable role models than to reflecting on general moral maxims. The specifically Christian version of this is that we come to learn the supreme value of love, forgiveness, self-sacrifice and so on, by seeing these qualities exemplified in the life of Christ, rather than by an intellectual intuition of Platonic Forms. I do not mean to identify these points about our access to the good with the particularist theory as to what it is that ultimately makes certain things good. They are clearly distinguishable matters. But I do suggest that a full realisation of how much we rely on paradigms in developing and shaping our capacities to recognise goodness will render us disposed to take seriously the suggestion that the supreme standard of goodness is an individual paradigm.

Now for the final hurdle; not the last hurdle with which the divine command theorist will ever be confronted, I fear, but the last one to be considered in this paper. According to the position I have been developing for the divine command theorist, God is himself the supreme standard of goodness. Why then are divine commands needed to provide an objective grounding for human morality? Why doesn't the nature of God suffice for that? Why can't we say that what I ought to do is determined by what would be the closest or most appropriate imitation of the divine nature for a creature with my nature and in my circumstances? To put it crudely, why isn't the answer to 'What ought I do about this?' sufficiently given by 'Do what God would do if God were a human being in this situation'. In fact, Christians are specially well placed to employ this 'crude' form of the view, since we hold that God is, or has been, a human being; hence we can say that what I ought to do in this situation is determined by what Christ would have done even if what I ought to do is only some approximation thereto. It is clear, in any event, that one who takes God to be the supreme standard of value must hold that our actions, our characters, or anything else in the world are good to the extent that they imitate or approximate the being of God in whatever way is appropriate to their position in creation. Since we are already in possession of these resources, why don't they suffice to give us the basis of morality? Why do we need to invoke divine commandments for this purpose? No doubt, divine commands would still have a role to play – to communicate to us what we ought to do when we might otherwise be ignorant of this, to impress this on our minds, to render it unmistakably clothed with divine majesty, and so on. But divine commands would not be needed to play a constitutive role.

We have already developed the chief tool needed for an answer to this difficulty, namely, the basic distinction between goodness and obligation, on which our account of divine goodness was based. If the divine command theorist embraces the positions I have been developing for him he will have to acknowledge that the goodness, including moral goodness, of actions, persons, traits of character, or anything else, is most basically constituted by its degree of conformity to the divine being. That is all that is required to make it a good thing that I develop my talents, or lend aid to those in need. But what about obligation, duty, or the moral ought? By virtue of what do I have an obligation to develop my talents or act in a loving manner, even admitting that this would be a good thing for me to do? By virtue of what am I required or bound to act in these ways? By virtue of what would I be culpable, guilty, blameworthy, reprehensible for failing so to act? If and only if some basis for all this is needed over and above the goodness of these modes of behaviour, can one who recognises God as the supreme standard of goodness take divine commands to be constitutive of moral obligation. And so our crucial question becomes: is it possible for A to be a good, even the best, thing for me to do, without my being obligated or required to do it, without my being culpable or blameworthy for failing to do it?

When we consider this question in its full generality we only need ask it to see that the answer is in the affirmative. First, though not directly germane to this issue, it is worth reminding ourselves that it can be good thing for a state of affairs to be realised without my having an obligation to do what I can to bring it about. It is, no doubt, a good thing that the children of a certain small Siberian village should have piano lessons, but surely I have no obligation to see to this. However, the specific question with which we are confronted is whether the fact that it would be a good thing for me to do A entails that it is my obligation to do A, that I morally ought to do A; and again the answer is obviously negative. Most obviously, various incompatible lines of action can all be good ones for me to pursue, but I can hardly be obligated to pursue them all. This afternoon it would be a good thing for me to finish this paper, to go out cross-country skiing, and to finish a novel I am reading; but time does not permit me to do more than one. Since ought implies can, it cannot be true that

I ought to do everything it would be good for me to do. But even apart from competition between incompatible goods we get the same conclusion. It would be a very good thing for me to spend the afternoon practising the cello, both because it would be enjoyable and because it would be a development of my talents and would contribute toward putting me in a better position to give pleasure to others. But, assuming I have made no promises or assumed no obligations on the subject, I am clearly not obligated to do this; nor, apart from any special restrictions on the term 'obligation', is it true that I ought to do it. This last example is representative of a large class of 'optional' or 'gratuitous' desiderata that I am free to pursue or not as I choose, without any blame or guilt attaching to either choice.

However it may be said that I have achieved this result by restricting myself to nonmoral goods; and that if we consider the specifically moral goodness of actions, we will see that an action cannot be morally good, or at least cannot be morally the best thing for me to do in a given situation, without its being true that I morally ought to do it. To evaluate this claim we will first have to consider what is involved in an action's being morally good. One possibility is that an action can be called morally good when it is something I morally ought to do. In that case my opponent's claim would have to be accepted, but only because obligation is already built into that from which it is alleged to follow. And the question of what is required to make it true that I morally ought to do A would remain unanswered. Second, a widely accepted view is that an action is morally good if it is done from a morally good motive. Or, third, an action might be said to be morally good if it is desirable, commendable, satisfactory that it should be done, from 'the moral point of view', from the standpoint of the ends that the institution of morality is designed to achieve, whether this be social harmony, the maximisation of human welfare, the enlargement of human sympathies, or whatever. Suppose we take the notion in either this second or third way. Then I think we can see that an action can be morally a good thing for me to do, even the best thing for me to do, without my being bound or required to do it, without my rightly incurring reproach or blame in case I don't. All that is needed to establish this is the phenomenon of supererogation. If there are actions that it is good morally, even supremely good morally, for agents to perform, and that go beyond anything that could reasonably be considered their duty, obligation, or moral requirement, then the case is closed. And surely there are such. It would be a supremely fine and noble thing for me to sell all that I have and give it to the poor (assuming that this is done in a prudent way so that most of it does not wind up in the hands of dishonest bureaucrats taking their rake-off), or to throw up my comfortable way of life and use my time and energy to care for the destitute in Calcutta; but surely I am not required or obligated to do this; it is not true that I morally ought to do it. (I am not saying that I could not be morally obligated to take one of these lines of actions; if I had promised to do so, or if God had commanded me to do so, I would be obligated. I am saying rather that the mere fact that it would be a supremely good thing, morally, for me to act in this way is not enough by itself to entail that I have an obligation to do it.) Thus it is one thing for it to be a good or the best thing, even morally, for me to do A, and another thing for me to be obligated or required to do A.

Thus there is a question about the basis of moral obligation, over and above the question about the basis of goodness that is answered by reference to the divine being. Of course there is such a question only if there are objective facts of moral requiredness that are constituted in some way or other. And this may be, and has been, denied. Our sense of its being absolutely incumbent on us to act in certain ways – however we feel about it, whatever our preferences, whatever the bearing on our welfare – may be deemed to be merely a not wholly fortunate internalisation of parental voices, or a projection of hostile impulses, or the result of diabolically clever social exploitation. But in this paper we are proceeding on the assumption of the objectivity of value and obligation. And given that assumption, what we have just indicated is that there is a constitutive job left for divine commands in the moral sphere, namely, the constitution of our moral obligations, what we ought to do morally. This role is there to be filled even if goodness, including moral goodness, is constituted independently.

To be sure, I have not shown, or even argued, that divine commands are or can be constitutive of moral obligation. I have merely aspired to set out in this paper a way of construing God, morality and value that leaves open the possibility that divine commands should do so. To go beyond that is a task for another occasion.[8]

NOTES

1. Robert Adams, 'Divine Command Metaethics Modified Again', *Journal of Religious Ethics*, Vol. 7, no. 1 (1979), pp. 71–9.
2. Adams, 'Divine Command Metaethics', p. 76.
3. It would be even more unproductive to cite differences between the *content* of divine and human moral goodness. No doubt, there are numerous and important differences. Divine virtues do not include obedience to God, temperance in eating, and refraining from coveting one's neighbor's wife. But as the last sentence in the text indicates, there is overlap too. Furthermore, even if there were no overlap in content it would still remain a further question whether that by virtue of which X is morally good is the same for God and man.
4. Immanuel Kant, *Foundations of the Metaphysics of Morals*, tr. Lewis White Beck (New York: Liberal Arts Press, 1959), pp. 29–31. For a couple of other endorsements of this position see A. C. Ewing, *The Definition of Good* (London; Routledge & Kegan Paul, 1948), p. 123; and Geoffrey J. Warnock, *The Object of Morality* (London: Methuen & Co. Ltd., 1971), p. 14.
5. I could greatly extend the range of these examples by pointing out that we apply neither rules nor terms of the ought-family to matters outside our voluntary control. There is no rule in football forbidding a player to fly through the air with the ball, nor is there a rule of etiquette requiring a diner to secrete gastric juices. And here too the absence of 'ought' goes along with the absence of rules. But it might be thought that in these cases this is to be explained by the absence of freedom rather than by the absence

of contrary tendencies, and hence these cases do not unambiguously support my present thesis.

6. This applies most directly to principles *requiring* actions, but interdictions can be expressed in terms of 'ought not' and permissions in terms of 'not ought not'.

7. This point is well developed in Thomas V. Morris, 'Duty and Divine Goodness,' *American Philosophical Quarterly* Vol. 21, no. 3 (July, 1984).

8. This paper has profited greatly from discussions with Robert Adams, Jonathan Bennett, Norman Kretzmann, John Robertson, Eleonore Stump, and Stewart Thau.

SUGGESTED READING

GENERAL

Kenny, Anthony (1979), *The God of the Philosophers*, Oxford: Clarendon Press.
Wierenga, Edward (1989), *The Nature of God*, Cornell Studies in the Philosophy of Religion, New York: Cornell University Press.

NECESSITY

Adams, Robert (1983), 'Has It Been Proved That All Real Existence Is Contingent?' *American Philosophical Quarterly*, 8: pp. 284–91.
Adams, Robert (1983), 'Divine Necessity', *Journal of Philosophy*, 80: pp. 741–52.
Plantinga, Alvin (1974), *The Nature of Necessity*, Clarendon Library of Logic and Philosophy, Oxford: Clarendon Press.

ETERNITY

Craig, William Lane (2001), *God, Time, and Eternity: The Coherence of Theism II: Eternity*, Dordrecht: Kluwer Academic Publishers.
Ganssle, Gregory E. and David M. Woodruff (eds) (2001), *God and Time*, New York: Oxford University Press.
Leftow, Brian (1991), *Time and Eternity*, Cornell Studies in the Philosophy of Religion, Ithaca, NY: Cornell University Press.
Yates, John C. (1990), *The Timelessness of God*, Lanham, MD: University Press of America.

OMNISCIENCE

Craig, William Lane (1990), *Divine Foreknowledge and Human Freedom: The Coherence of Theism I: Omniscience*, Brill's Studies in Intellectual History 19, Leiden: E. J. Brill.

Fisher, John Martin (ed.) (1989), *God, Foreknowledge, and Freedom*, Stanford Series in Philosophy, Stanford, CA: Stanford University Press.

Kvanvig, Jonathan L. (1986), *The Possibility of an All-Knowing God*, New York: St. Martin's Press.

Prior, A. N. (1968), 'The Formalities of Omniscience,' in *Papers on Time and Tense*, Oxford: Clarendon Press, 1968, pp. 26–44.

OMNIPOTENCE

Frankfurt, Harry (1964), 'The Logic of Omnipotence', *Philosophical Review*, 73: pp. 262–3.

Plantinga, Alvin (1967), *God and Other Minds*, Ithaca, NY: Cornell University Press, pp. 168–73.

Plantinga, Alvin (1980), *Does God Have a Nature?*, Milwaukee: Marquette, University Press. pp. 92–140.

Quinn, Philip L. and Charles Taliaferro (eds) (1997), *A Companion to Philosophy of Religion*, Oxford: Blackwell, s.v. 'Necessity', by William E. Mann.

GOODNESS

Helm, Paul (ed.) (1981), *Divine Commands and Morality*, Oxford: Oxford University Press.

Idziak, Janine M. (ed.) (1980), *Divine Command Morality: Historical and Contemporary Readings*, Lewiston, NY: Edwin Mellen Press.

Morris, Thomas V. (1987), *Anselmian Explorations*, Notre Dame, In: University of Notre Dame Press.

Nielsen, Kai (1973), *Ethics without God*, London: Pemberton Books.

Quinn, Philip L. (1978), *Divine Commands and Moral Requirements*, Oxford: Clarendon Press.

PART IV
THE PROBLEM OF EVIL

THE PROBLEM OF EVIL: INTRODUCTION

Timothy O'Connor

'Why is light given to those in misery, and life to the bitter of soul . . .' cried out Job – and with good reason: in a short period, he had witnessed the apparently senseless obliteration of his fortune and the death of his children, and his own body was wracked with pain. In this response to calamitous misery, Job is not alone. Indeed, in all cultures in which belief in a personal and caring Creator is prevalent, most people at one time or another have pondered the simple question, Why? Why would a perfectly loving and all-powerful God choose to create a world filled with seemingly unjust and pointless suffering of his creatures? All of us hear of horrific atrocities inflicted on defenceless and innocent fellow human beings; of equally horrific consequences visited on people and animals through natural disasters; of even cruel ironies, whereby a parent unintentionally participates in grievous harm to or death of a beloved child.

Reading unsparing accounts of these events produces profound distress in any morally sound human being. (An especially moving example comes from the pen of a believer, the great Russian novelist Fyodor Dostoevsky, in his oft-anthologised chapter 'Rebellion' from *The Brothers Karamazov*.) In religious persons, these faithful depictions of the worst moments in human life produce strong emotions, colouring one's perception of God's character and purpose. We at times begin to doubt the manner of His concern for our welfare or to mistrust his purposes. Or we may simply cease to draw comfort from our belief in his providence, deeming his care over our lives to be, apparently, consistent with our experiencing the cruelest of fates. In non-religious persons (and in some religious persons, too), steadily gazing on the depth of human and animal suffering also produces a tendency towards disbelief. How often do we hear it said. 'I simply cannot believe that a loving and merciful God would create a world such as this'?

What role does or can careful philosophical reflection play in fostering or diminishing these kinds of reactions to evil? The verdict is at best mixed, it seems, and varies a great deal, depending on the individual and circumstance. Certainly, it is of little value to one in the midst of intense personal suffering. People suffering at the hands of a merciless tormentor, or convulsed with grief at the untimely loss of a young child, are not in need of a book of philosophical ruminations on why God's existence and goodness may be compatible with their pain. Clearly, they are far better served by the practical care and prayers of their community.

Philosophy's usefulness in this matter is best located elsewhere. Unbelievers and wavering believers alike often claim or imply that the gruesome facts of suffering provide unmistakable, objective evidence – indeed, overwhelming evidence – that an all-powerful and perfectly loving God does not exist. And this is a claim that philosophy can shed some light on. For philosophy at its best insists that whenever ones takes an acknowledged truth A to provide reason for accepting some further, contentious claim B, one should try to formulate explicitly an argument that clarifies the alleged link from A to B, so that it can be subjected to careful scrutiny. That is, one spells out all relevant claims that one is presupposing and determines whether those premises can be shown to support what one is concluding, where 'support' consists in logically entailing the truth or at least high probability of that conclusion. To the casual reasoner, this can seem tedious, a belabouring of the obvious. ('Isn't it just obvious to anyone whose mind is not clouded by religious zeal that no loving God would create this?' – said with a sweeping gesture of one's hand.) But the history of philosophy is littered with plausible-sounding arguments for all manner of conclusions that careful examination shows to be defective in one of two basic ways: either one or more of the premises presupposed are reasonably doubted (that is, the evidence was less strong than it seemed at first) or the conclusion simply does not follow (that is, there was a subtle error in reasoning from the evidence). It would be extremely rash to base one's answer to so momentous a question as the existence of God on an argument that one has never fully spelt out, much less subjected to critical scrutiny.

The philosopher's task, then, is to see whether the facts of suffering, which induce a range of powerful religious reactions involving belief, emotion and motivation, also provide the basis for a cogent argument from evil to the non-existence of God – an argument that should persuade the reasonable person who considers it carefully. As we shall see, there are several such arguments worth considering, posing distinctive issues. In what follows, I shall briefly develop the best such arguments and then describe the responses to them put forth by some contemporary Christian philosophers.

THE LOGICAL ARGUMENT FROM EVIL

The oldest form of argument from evil is also the boldest, suggesting that a very simple line of thought demonstrates the impossibility of God's creating a world containing any evil whatsoever. Its basic form goes back to the ancient Greek Epicurus and was famously restated in a forceful way by the eloquent eighteenth-century Scottish philosopher and fierce critic of Christianity, David Hume, in his *Dialogues Concerning Natural Religion*: 'Is He willing to prevent evil, but not able? then He is impotent. Is He able, but not willing? then He is malevolent. Is He both able and willing? whence then is evil?' To put this argument in a form most useful for evaluation, we shall have to sacrifice some of the beauty of its prose. It is clear that Hume means to identify an inconsistency in there being evil in a world created by an omnipotent God. We might put his reasoning thus:

1. If God exists and is perfectly good, then He will prevent as much evil as He can.
2. If God exists and is omnipotent (and omniscient), then He can prevent any evil from occurring.
3. There is evil.

Conclusion: God does not exist, or He is not omnipotent and omniscient, or He is not perfectly good.

A couple of brief remarks: I inserted the phrase 'and omniscient', since one might object to Hume's own formulation that were God's knowledge deficient in some way, He might not realise that using His power in a certain way would result in evil. This is a little persnickety, since nearly all theists assume that God is omniscient (though they may disagree about the scope of what is to be known). But it is wise to get into the habit of placing all that one is assuming in an argument out on the table, since it sometimes happens that one may either discover reason to question the assumption or come to see that its consequences are less clear than one had thought. Similarly, I worded the conclusion as I did, rather than as simply 'God does not exist', since without an explicit definition of 'God', one could respond to the reasoning by weakening one's notion of God, rather than embracing outright atheism. Traditional Christians will be loathe to do that, however, and so will view the qualified conclusion as tantamount to an assertion of atheism.

Note that the conclusion really does follow from the premises. So if we deny the conclusion, we must likewise deny one or more of the premises. Alvin Plantinga, a prominent Christian philosopher, directs our attention to premise (1): if God exists and is perfectly good, then He will prevent as much evil as He can. Think for a moment about the policies (imperfectly) followed by good-willed human beings toward those they care about. Do they always try to eliminate every 'evil' – every form of pain or suffering, every circumstance that, considered in and of itself, is a bad thing? Clearly not. As a parent, for example, I take my children to the doctor at the appointed time to receive vaccination shots. In doing so, I am purposefully permitting them to experience pain that I could easily prevent. Yet this does not reflect poorly on me. Why? – Because I know that while the momentary pain of the shot is, in and of itself, a bad thing, it is greatly outweighed by the good that I can help to bring about only by having them undergo it. There is no painless form of vaccination available to me, and I cannot discern the future, permitting me to know whether my child would happen to escape the disease even without the vaccination. Given my circumstances, the best thing to do overall is to require the vaccination, despite my child's protests.

The argument above does not explicitly consider this kind of point in relation to God and the permission of evil. Hume might well suppose that such a consideration is clearly irrelevant in the special case of omnipotence, but, as I emphasised, it is best to be very explicit about what we are committed to believing when we advance an argument. So we might reformulate the argument as follows:

1. If God exists and is perfectly good, then He will prevent as much evil as He can without either bringing about a greater evil or preventing a good that outweighs the evil in question.
2. If God exists and is both omnipotent and omniscient, then He can prevent any evil from occurring without either bringing about a greater evil or preventing a good that outweighs the evil in question.
3. There is evil.

Conclusion: God does not exist, or He is not both omnipotent and omniscient, or He is not perfectly good.

Again, it is evident that the form of reasoning here is valid. Furthermore, premiss (1) now looks very plausible. To deny it seems to commit one to the idea that perfect goodness might permit entirely pointless evil, and this seems hard to credit. Certainly it is not suggested by analogy with human goodness. So let us provisionally suppose that it is true. And (3) is both obvious and integral to Christian theology.

That leaves premiss (2) as the remaining point of attack for those of us who reject the conclusion. At first sight, it looks unassailable. Perfect power, it seems, cannot be forced into the inevitable trade-offs facing more limited beings (as when I am forced to permit the pain of a shot to achieve the greater good of immunisation). However, as Plantinga points out, this overlooks the possibility that some goods that a perfectly good God might wish to bring about might strictly require that God not directly guarantee certain outcomes and indeed require that He permit the possibility of evil upshots from those goods. Human freedom may be just such a good. It appears to be an open question whether God might (correctly) see great value in the good of creatures engaging in freely chosen responses of love to Him and to one another. And it appears that for such responses to be truly free, He cannot so act as to guarantee that they will use that choice wisely. (After all, a computer scientist who designs a robot, however sophisticated, to 'respond' with affirmations of affection and devotion to his human creator would strike us as deluded – and pathetic to boot.) If, contrary to His wishes, free creatures choose to spurn God's overtures and, indeed, to act in malice towards one another, the resulting evil is not to His discredit, but theirs.

So creating free creatures entails some risk, even for an omnipotent Creator. Or does it? One astute atheist, the late John Mackie, argued that even if God greatly valued free creaturely response, He would have perfect knowledge prior to creation of how any freedom-enriched possible creation (what I will call a 'freedom world') would play out. Given such knowledge, He could carefully select from among the many possibilities a suitably good one in which everyone happened to choose the good at all times. Then He could have a world with free choices that is also free of the evil consequences of the misuse of freedom. So, says Mackie, we are back to thinking that premiss (2) is highly plausible. Whatever goods an unlimited God might pursue, including the good of freedom, it is possible for Him to choose a world achieving those goods without being forced to risk its being marred by freely-chosen evil.

The issues become more subtle at this point. One might well question the assumption that even omniscience allows God to know what would be freely chosen in any possible circumstance. It is not clear that there is even a fact of the matter as to what I would have freely chosen to do had God placed me in a very different world. (And if there is no fact to be known, that even a perfect knower cannot know it.) Bear in mind that if my choice is to be free, my character cannot guarantee that I would make a particular choice. Otherwise, we would be led to say that our computer scientist could program his robot to freely express unfailing devotion to its creator. Just program it so that its 'character' is such that it wants to do so and has no competing desire whatsoever. But this seems a thin form of freedom indeed. Perfect knowledge would certainly know the range of possible choices consistent with my character and would further know how likely it is that I would choose in any particular fashion. But perhaps the facts run out at this point: relative likelihood of choosing in certain ways rather than others. If we accept this view, then we can say that while God might be careful to create a freedom world that is highly conducive to creatures always choosing the good, He still would be running a risk. His power and knowledge do not rule out the possibility that evil will result, and so premiss (2) is at least doubtful.

However, some theists do think that God has complete knowledge of how things would go (and not just how they might go) with respect to any creaturely free choice. Such putative knowledge is sometimes termed 'middle knowledge'. The reader is directed to the section essay, Craig, 'Coherence of Theism,' in this volume for further argument on whether omniscience includes middle knowledge. Alvin Plantinga is among those who affirm the view. He argues that even so, there is still reason to doubt premiss (2) of the revised argument above. For suppose that God was committed to creating a freedom world that passes some threshold level, T, of on-balance goodness. And note that the presence of freedom means that, were God to choose a world W_1, God would not directly bring about everything that happens in W_1. He creates all the stuff, including the free creatures, determines the laws that govern how much of it works, and so on. But some of the details are filled in by those creatures. Let us call all the facts about W_1 that would ultimately be fully determined by God 'W-minus'. Notice that there is more than one completion to W-minus. W_1 is one of those, but so are many other possibilities where the free choices and their consequences go differently. However, God knows which completion would occur, as it happens, if He were to bring about W-minus (W_1, let us say, and not the equally possible W_2). Now consider: suppose W_1 is worse than W_2. It involves misuse of freedom while such misuse is absent from W_2 altogether. God would clearly prefer W_2 to W_1. But He is powerless to bring it about! It is a freedom world, a real possibility, that He may well value. But surely it could be that were He to do his part and directly achieve W-minus, the free creatures would fail to do theirs.

Knowing this, He might well choose to move on and consider other scenarios. (I speak anthropomorphically here, of course.) He considers W^*-minus, $W@$-minus, and so on, each of which has at least one possible completion by its free creatures where they always do the right thing. Now maybe, Plantinga proposes, just maybe, for every creation scenario meeting the threshold level T which God requires, even though it is possible that all its creatures would always use their freedom well, were God to go ahead and do His part in bringing about the part He directly controls, somewhere in some way some hapless creature would mess things up by misusing his freedom, with evil consequences as a result. If this worst-case scenario is so much as possible, then God's middle knowledge could have Him resigned to the fact that none of the T-level world possibilities that are free from evil are achievable! It all depends on the facts about how creatures would in fact decide in various scenarios God might contemplate, and these are facts that God cannot predetermine (on pain of negating the creatures' freedom) but can only discover. If it is possible that these facts might happen to line up in a way that frustrates the purpose of a sufficiently valuable, yet blemish-free world, then the argument's second premise is not true. Since none of us seems in a position to say whether the situation Plantinga envisions is not possible (not being able to contemplate infinitely-detailed world descriptions), we have reason to doubt premiss (2). But that is enough to render it unsuccessful as a compelling argument for its conclusion.

THREE EVIDENTIAL ARGUMENTS FROM EVIL

Note that premiss (2) was called into question by the possibility that God might inevitably be required to accept some evil in any creation of sufficiently high value, where this will plausibly include creaturely freedom. Looked at in one way, asserting that possibility is saying a lot less than it sounds. For possibility is a long way from plausibility; moreover, even if we could show that this particular possibility is plausibly true, the evil required for freedom's sake may well be insignificant. (My having a minor ache in the little toe on my left foot might do the trick, for example, given only the line of argument by Plantinga that we have summarised until this point.) But no one has trivial evils in mind when wondering at God's purposes in creating the world we in fact see around us. That is, it is not just the existence of any blemish at all, no matter how insignificant, that tempts such persons to atheism, but significant particular evils that appear pointless, or the sheer amount of evil, or certain horrific kinds of evil. The logical argument from evil was worth exploring, since it held out the promise of a neat and clean demonstration of the incompatibility of God and any evil whatsoever, without our having to consider the messy and hard details of how evil and goodness are to be measured and how they balance out in this world. But it may be that a more powerful argument, though also more complicated, can be developed by incorporating into the argument the most disturbing facts of evil as they are actually manifested.

Here are three parallel arguments that focus on different aspects of the observable evil in our world:

This-Particular-Evil Argument
1. There is no reason that would justify God's permitting some particular evil _____ to occur. (Fill in the blank with an apparently pointless evil, one that seems not to serve any greater purpose.)
2. If God exists, there must be such a reason.

So, God does not exist.

This-Amount-of-Evil Argument
1. There is no reason that would justify God's permitting so much evil to occur.
2. If God exists, there must be such a reason.

So, God does not exist.

This-Kind-of-Evil Argument
1. There is no reason that would justify God's permitting certain horrendous kinds of evil to occur.

(For example, children being ruthlessly tortured and murdered.)

2. If God exists, there must be such a reason.

So, God does not exist.

These arguments are sometimes termed 'evidential', rather than 'logical', because they do not purport to show that mere reflection on the very concept of God can directly show (by a 'logical analysis') the impossibility of God's permitting something that is uncontroversially the case (evil exists). Instead, they consider the way evil is manifested and try to show that it constitutes powerful evidence for the non-existence of an adequate moral justification for an omnipotent being's permitting it to occur. (We could make an analogy to a trial lawyer's attempt to show that, given certain facts, the jury should conclude that the defendant's action could not possibly have been motivated by any legally adequate justification.)

There is reason to think the first argument is less plausible than the second two. For, as Peter van Inwagen has pointed out, we can well imagine that a perfectly good and just God might act under a general policy that allows certain kinds or amounts of evil which serve some greater purpose, without having any reason for particular instances of it. (The occurrence of widely known evils might help people to realise the hideousness of life without God, for example, but it may not matter that I suffer such an evil.) But surely a good God could not act on a policy that did not have any specific reason for allowing horrific forms of evil or roughly the amount of evil that we observe. If His purposes could be accomplished through much less evil, or much less intense evils, then surely He would be callous not to choose such alternatives. Note also that we could soften the arguments by inserting the word 'probably' before the first premiss and the conclusion of each of the arguments. The conclusion then becomes a bit weaker, but it is still significant. (If I am persuaded that God's existence is very unlikely, this may make my continued belief irrational; it certainly will affect the strength of my conviction.) Doing so has the advantage that the first premiss claims less, and so is more easily believed. Let us bear this possible qualification in mind as we briefly review some responses to such arguments.

Christian Responses to Evidential Arguments

Theodicies

I shall be considering two broad sorts of response to evidential arguments from evil like the ones I noted in the previous section. The first of these types is the most ambitious. It actually represents a large family of different strategies, only a few of which will be considered here. These strategies aim to sketch a reason, or set of reasons, that a perfectly good and just God might have for

THE PROBLEM OF EVIL: INTRODUCTION

permitting the amounts and kinds of evil that we observe. (Hence, the term 'theodicy', which denotes an attempt to justify God's ways before human criticism.) They do not presume to give the actual reasons that motivated God in His creation act but rather suggest reasons that, plausibly, He might have had, consistent with His goodness and power. More exactly, they need claim only that we do not have good reason to think that they are not adequate reasons for a perfect God. After all, it is the objector who purports to give an argument that shows us otherwise; if we give reason seriously to doubt one of the argument's key claims, then we have nullified the argument. We need not go so far as to prove that the premiss is wrong.

These responses often draw on Christian theological claims. This is entirely appropriate in this context, provided they are not clearly at odds with well-established empirical facts. For the theist is not here defending the truth of his theism or of his specifically Christian belief. Instead, he is merely rebutting an argument that purports to show an inconsistency of certain indisputable facts with his religious beliefs, and these include any theological beliefs that the theist may see as helping to undercut arguments from evil.

An atheist who objects to this procedure on the grounds, say, that Christian claims about God's actions and purposes in human history are somehow unlikely 'in the light of scientific advance', or some such thing, is really declining the opportunity to show that the facts of suffering provide independent evidence for God's non-existence. He is alleging instead the availability of a more complicated argument, one that has the argument from evil as a component, dependent on other components. (First show that God, if He exists, evidently is not guided by certain purposes involving His direct intervention in human history. Then show that lacking such resources, there can be no reason for Him to permit so much evil, or certain horrific kinds of evil.) But whatever the merits of such a strategy, there is no reason for the objector not to consider also whether the facts of evil are independent grounds for atheism, as we are doing here. One can grant someone a claim just for the sake of argument and try to show that, even if it were so, his position is problematic. That is the natural form for an argument from evil to take from someone who thinks there are other, independent reasons for doubting Christian beliefs.

One final caveat: as C. S. Lewis emphasized in *The Problem of Pain*, the kinds of reasons one is likely to consider here will depend on what one takes the ultimate good for human beings to be. And this question is not independent of one's religious beliefs. It is plausible for theists to suppose, and is in fact taught by Judaism and Christianity, that the good for human beings is principally a matter of union with God, which in part involves our leading lives in accordance with his plans. One who advances an argument from evil for atheism must take this into account. He may well have to consider suggestions of divine purpose behind evil that are at odds with what many atheists take to be the good for human beings. Since it is an argument for atheism, it cannot presuppose anything that is inconsistent with a plausible way for a theist to see things. (If the theist already believed something more clearly inconsistent with his theism, he would not need to consider an argument from evil.)

There are a variety of strategies pursued in developing plausible theodicies. Here I can only note in broad strokes several themes in popular and scholarly thought, some of which are developed in our readings. Note that these strategies need not, and generally are not, advanced as individually sufficient responses to evidential arguments.

Earthly Punishment and the Afterlife
Christians, at least in the West, are apt to begin a discussion of evil by pointing to the Fall of humanity and God's righteous decree of death as the penalty for sin. Similarly, Christian doctrine concerning the afterlife has obvious relevance to theodicy. For those whose lives have been filled with deep pain – and some of these are very short lives, with little of the adult attitudes and goods described below – this life is not the final word. Likewise, for those who have experienced relative comfort despite great and persistent wickedness.

Seeing the Folly Of Sin
Following a traditional Christian theme also developed of late by C. S. Lewis, van Inwagen in his essay for this volume suggests that one purpose God might have in permitting truly horrific evils to occur is that perhaps only in this way can human beings be prodded to see the depths of our own sinfulness, causing us to turn from our prideful rebellion and recognise that our happiness can be found only in union with God and His purposes for us.

Big Picture
It is sometimes said that evil seems incomprehensible to us only because we lack God's overall view, in which evil contributes to the beautiful perfection of Creation as a whole. One common analogy is to the presence of an ugly note that nonetheless enhances the overall quality of a complex symphony. Another likens the world to a patchwork quilt, full of knots and hanging threads on the underside (our view), yet forming a beautiful mosaic when viewed from the intended side (God's view).

Soul-Making
The idea here is that certain valuable moral qualities cannot be automatically conferred in creation but must be acquired in the face of evil. Only in the face of real adversity, for example, can one learn to be heroic. Heroism, patience, temperance and other qualities are most valuable where one has acquired them through struggle, in the face of the real possibility of embracing their opposing vices.

Deeper Goods and Their Inevitable Risks

Richard Swinburne suggests that we should consider certain purely natural goods for human beings that go deeper than the obvious goods of pleasure and contentment. In particular, there are the goods of having some degree of responsibility for ourselves, others and the world, and the 'receiving-end' goods of being valuable, of use to ourselves and each other. It is a benefit to me, for example, that I should have significant responsibility in shaping the development of my children. But this carries the risk that I will abuse this responsibility by inflicting harm upon them. Similarly, he suggests, it is a good for my children that they be of such use to me. (This is not to say that they should not also have the good of having responsibility for the fate of another.) Even if I abuse them, they retain this good. It is their good fortune, however small, that the suffering is not random, but at least serves this purpose. Swinburne hastens to add that there are limits to how much evil God might justly allow one to suffer in this way and points to the built-in limits of capacity for suffering at a time and, through death, over time.

The challenge for the theodicist is to weave together these sorts of themes into a narrative that justifies significant doubt about the 'There is no reason . . .' premisses in the evidential arguments. Assessing the prospects for theodicy is beyond the scope of this introduction. However, to aid the reader who wishes to evaluate a developed theodicy or construct one of his own, I will note certain points that are often made in response to one or more of the above themes.

1. Horrific evils must not be gratuitous. Any indirect value to which they may lead must not be achievable without them.
2. The distribution of pain and suffering must ultimately be just. This is especially pressing, perhaps, in regards to horrific evils.
3. Grave evils cannot be morally justified by their service of aesthetic or other non-moral value.
4. For specific goods to individuals, such as freedom, responsibility and participation in the development of one's own character, we should carefully consider how much evil has to be permitted to accomplish those ends. We should also recognise that the effects on character of grave suffering are often bad, in ways not clearly within the agent's control. (Consider the profound psychological damage that often results from traumatic experiences.) Finally, freedom and responsibility come in degrees. Analogy to the policies of wise human parents might lead one to expect that God would give humans less control over their own fates and those of others – or initially limited control to any given individual, to be increased only as they come to show wisdom and maturity in its use.

Finally, I note that some argue that Christian theology puts one significant constraint on any theodicy pursued by a Christian. (See the work by Marilyn

Adams and the essay by Eleonore Stump in the readings.) In Christianity, the dignity and value of human persons is strongly emphasised. This is generally taken to entail that persons are not to be used as mere means to some greater ends. And so it would seem that any reasons God might have for allowing us to suffer great pain must include their meaningfulness to the one who suffers them. (Thus we see Swinburne attempting to identify a value even to an abused child of his being useful to his abuser. But perhaps the suggested constraint is too strong. Perhaps, as Plantinga (2000) suggests, we should say only that, under God's providence, a person who suffers great evil would benefit from it or at least affirm its appropriateness, were his moral cognitive capacities and his will working properly, undistorted by sin.)

A Sceptical Solution

Many thoughtful people, including some Christians, believe the prospects for an adequate, many stranded theodicy are dim. They think that while these considerations certainly go a long way towards making sense of there being some significant amount and kinds of evil in our world, they do not nearly account for the staggering amount we actually see or the most horrific evils we know about. Suppose for argument's sake that they judge rightly. Would that mean checkmate against the theist? Much recent writing by Christian philosophers attempts to justify a negative answer to this question.

Let us focus on just one of our arguments. (The reader should persuade himself that what I shall go on to say will apply equally well to the other arguments.) Here again is the 'This-Kind-of-Evil' Argument:

1. There is no reason that would justify God's permitting certain horrendous kinds of evil to occur.
2. If God exists, there must be such a reason.

So God does not exist.

As Stephen Wykstra and others point out, there is a hidden assumption behind the typical acceptance of premiss (1). Wykstra terms it a 'noseeum inference', which, in its general and folksy form, is simply, 'If we don't see 'um, they ain't there'. That is to say, one tries to observe something and upon failing infers that what one seeks is simply not there. In our present context, we are searching the 'space' of morally permissible divine reasons. Theologians have not uncovered, we are supposing, a fully adequate reason that would justify God. Defenders of the argument infer that there is no reason.

A crucial question is whether and when noseeum inferences are justified. A plausible answer is: when, and only when, it is quite likely that we would see our target if it were there. When Frances looks in her fridge for her favourite drink and does not see it, it is reasonable for her to conclude it is not there, since if it were she very likely would have seen it. (We need not suppose that she certainly would have seen it, just that she very probably would have.) But when she looks into the stars above from her home in Seattle and does not see the Big Dipper, she should not conclude that it is not there, since she is not particularly likely to see it from a cloudy urban location. Likewise, were she to search her backyard for small bugs from her kitchen window.

What should we say about our fruitless search of the 'space of reasons' for an adequate reason for God's permission of evils as horrific as the torture and murder of young children? In his essay, William Alston argues that this case is much more like the search for bugs in the backyard from a distance than it is like the search for a drink in the fridge. (That is, the noseeum inference is out of place here.) He bases this judgement on the fact that our minds are so much less sophisticated than that of an omniscient being. So we cannot say whether there might be (1) reasons that are too complex for us to grasp (compare a novice's take on a chess grandmaster's strategy), or even (2) goods that we cannot contemplate or have yet to discover, reasons and goods which an omniscient being would recognise and which would motivate a course of action rather different from any we ourselves might devise. Moreover, we are not in a position to judge how likely it is that such reasons and goods exist. (The point is not merely that we cannot completely rule it out, but that our cognitive deficiencies preclude our assigning any probability to the matter at all.) If this is so, we should draw no conclusions from our inability to discern a justifiable reason for certain evils in this world. In particular, we should not infer the truth, or even probable truth, of premiss (1) in the above argument.

The reason I termed this a 'sceptical solution' is that it seeks to motivate a strong measure of scepticism regarding our ability to get an adequate grasp on the purposes that would motivate an all-knowing, almighty and perfectly good Creator.[1] The reader should consider carefully the degree of scepticism that it does and does not encourage. No Christian should suppose that we are completely unable to discern any of the true goods for human beings.[2] As the philosopher and critic of Christianity John Stuart Mill argued long ago, total scepticism about what divine goodness entails seems to make empty our affirmation of the goodness of God. We do take ourselves to see, for example, that God's permission of great evil in our lives must potentially serve some benefit to those who undergo the sufferings (even if only in the afterlife), and not just be means for goods to others around us. Here the lives and testimonies of heroic saints are important, as Stump emphasises.[3] When people who have suffered much testify to experiencing great joy in God despite their pain, our conviction that there are great goods that can be achieved through suffering rightly increases. Likewise, with a bit more imagination, we are better able to imagine that such joys may also await those, such as the innocent children, who were not granted them in this life.

NOTES

1. Assignment for the reader: various forms of argument from design for theism seem to assume that we can reasonably discern certain features that a purposive Creator would likely value in His handiwork—specifically, that it would be conducive to the development and sustenance of living, conscious and intelligent beings. Does scepticism about our ability to discern the full range of considerations that might make a world with vast amounts of evil morally acceptable undercut the design argument's assumption? (Can one formulate a principled way of characterising the appropriate scope of scepticism that does not have this implication?)

2. Consider the many scriptural texts with a contrary thrust. One example is Rom. 2:15: '[the Gentiles] show that the requirements of the law are written on their hearts, their consciences also bearing witness'.

3. Dostoyevsky appears to be making this point in *The Brothers Karamazov*. Early in the novel, the sceptical Ivan powerfully advances the case for atheism from horrific evils. But near the end, the saintly Father Zossima discusses his pain-filled life and how he has come to see great value in it as he has drawn closer to God.

'THE PROBLEM OF EVIL AND SOME VARIETIES OF ATHEISM'

William L. Rowe

This paper is concerned with three interrelated questions. The first is: Is there an argument for atheism based on the existence of evil that may rationally justify someone in being an atheist? To this first question I give an affirmative answer and try to support that answer by setting forth a strong argument for atheism based on the existence of evil.[1] The second question is: How can the theist best defend his position against the argument for atheism based on the existence of evil? In response to this question I try to describe what may be an adequate rational defence for theism against any argument for atheism based on the existence of evil. The final question is: What position should the informed atheist take concerning the rationality of theistic belief? Three different answers an atheist may give to this question serve to distinguish three varieties of atheism: unfriendly atheism, indifferent atheism, and friendly atheism. In the final part of the paper I discuss and defend the position of friendly atheism.

Before we consider the argument from evil, we need to distinguish a narrow and a broad sense of the terms "theist," "atheist," and "agnostic." By a "theist" in the narrow sense I mean someone who believes in the existence of an omnipotent, omniscient, eternal, supremely good being who created the world. By a "theist" in the broad sense I mean someone who believes in the existence of some sort of divine being or divine reality. To be a theist in the narrow sense is also to be a theist in the broad sense, but one may be a theist in the broad sense—as was Paul Tillich—without believing that there is a

William L. Rowe, 'The Problem of Evil and Some Varieties of Atheism', *American Philosophical Quarterly*, 16, 4 (October 1979), pp. 335–41.

supremely good, omnipotent, omniscient, eternal being who created the world. Similar distinctions must be made between a narrow and a broad sense of the terms "atheist" and "agnostic." To be an atheist in the broad sense is to deny the existence of any sort of divine being or divine reality. Tillich was not an atheist in the broad sense. But he was an atheist in the narrow sense, for he denied that there exists a divine being that is all-knowing, all-powerful and perfectly good. In this paper I will be using the terms "theism," "theist," "atheism," "atheist," "agnosticism," and "agnostic" in the narrow sense, not in the broad sense.

I

In developing the argument for atheism based on the existence of evil, it will be useful to focus on some particular evil that our world contains in considerable abundance. Intense human and animal suffering, for example, occurs daily and in great plenitude in our world. Such intense suffering is a clear case of evil. Of course, if the intense suffering leads to some greater good, a good we could not have obtained without undergoing the suffering in question, we might conclude that the suffering is justified, but it remains an evil nevertheless. For we must not confuse the intense suffering in and of itself with the good things to which it sometimes leads or of which it may be a necessary part. Intense human or animal suffering is in itself bad, an evil, even though it may sometimes be justified by virtue of being a part of, or leading to, some good which is unobtainable without it. What is evil in itself may sometimes be good as a means because it leads to something that is good in itself. In such a case, while remaining an evil in itself, the intense human or animal suffering is, nevertheless, an evil which someone might be morally justified in permitting.

Taking human and animal suffering as a clear instance of evil which occurs with great frequency in our world, the argument for atheism based on evil can be stated as follows:

1. There exist instances of intense suffering which an omnipotent, omniscient being could have prevented without thereby losing some greater good or permitting some evil equally bad or worse.[2]
2. An omniscient, wholly good being would prevent the occurrence of any intense suffering it could, unless it could not do so without thereby losing some greater good or permitting some evil equally bad or worse.
3. There does not exist an omnipotent, omniscient, wholly good being.

What are we to say about this argument for atheism, an argument based on the profusion of one sort of evil in our world? The argument is valid; therefore, if we have rational grounds for accepting its premises, to that extent we have rational grounds for accepting atheism. Do we, however, have rational grounds for accepting the premises of this argument?

Let's begin with the second premise. Let s_1 be an instance of intense human or animal suffering which an omniscient, wholly good being could prevent. We will also suppose that things are such that s_1 will occur unless prevented by the omniscient, wholly good (OG) being. We might be interested in determining what would be a *sufficient* condition of OG failing to prevent s_1. But, for our purpose here, we need only try to state a *necessary* condition for OG failing to prevent s_1. That condition, so it seems to me, is this:

> *Either* (i) there is some greater good, G, such that G is obtainable by OG only if OG permits s_1,[3]
>
> or (ii) there is some greater good, G, such that G is obtainable by OG only if OG permits either s_1 or some evil equally bad or worse,
>
> or (iii) s_1 is such that it is preventable by OG only if OG permits some evil equally bad or worse.

It is important to recognize that (iii) is not included in (i). For losing a good greater than s_1 is not the same as permitting an evil greater than s_1. And this because the *absence* of a good state of affairs need not itself be an evil state of affairs. It is also important to recognize that s_1 might be such that it is preventable by OG *without* losing G (so condition [i] is not satisfied) but also such that if OG did prevent it, G would be lost *unless* OG permitted some evil equal to or worse than s_1. If this were so, it does not seem correct to require that OG prevent s_1. Thus, condition (ii) takes into account an important possibility not encompassed in condition (i).

Is it true that if an omniscient, wholly good being permits the occurrence of some intense suffering it could have prevented, then either (i) or (ii) or (iii) obtains? It seems to me that it is true. But if it is true then so is premise (2) of the argument for atheism. For that premise merely states in more compact form what we have suggested must be true if an omniscient, wholly good being fails to prevent some intense suffering it could prevent. Premise (2) says that an omniscient, wholly good being would prevent the occurrence of any intense suffering it could, unless it could not do so without thereby losing some greater good or permitting some evil equally bad or worse. This premise (or something not too distant from it) is, I think, held in common by many atheists and nontheists. Of course, there may be disagreement about whether something is good, and whether, if it is good, one would be morally justified in permitting some intense suffering to occur in order to obtain it. Someone might hold, for example, that no good is great enough to justify permitting an innocent child to suffer terribly.[4] Again, someone might hold that the mere fact that a given good outweighs some suffering and would be loss if the suffering were prevented, is not a morally sufficient reason for permitting the suffering. But to hold either of these views is not to deny (2). For (2) claims only that *if* an omniscient, wholly good being permits intense suffering *then* either there is some greater good that would have been lost, or some equally bad or worse evil that would have occurred, had the intense suffering been prevented. (2) does not purport to describe what might be a *sufficient* condition for an omniscient, wholly good being to permit intense suffering, only what is a *necessary* condition. So stated, (2) seems to express a belief that accords with our basic moral principles, principles shared by both theists and nontheists. If we are to fault the argument for atheism, therefore, it seems we must find some fault with its first premise.

Suppose in some distant forest lightning strikes a dead tree, resulting in a forest fire. In the fire a fawn is trapped, horribly burned, and lies in terrible agony for several days before death relieves its suffering. So far as we can see, the fawn's intense suffering is pointless. For there does not appear to be any greater good such that the prevention of the fawn's suffering would require either the loss of that good or the occurrence of an evil equally bad or worse. Nor does there seem to be any equally bad or worse evil so connected to the fawn's suffering that it would have had to occur had the fawn's suffering been prevented. Could an omnipotent, omniscient being have prevented the fawn's apparently pointless suffering? The answer is obvious, as even the theist will insist. An omnipotent, omniscient being could have easily prevented the fawn from being horribly burned, or, given the burning, could have spared the fawn the intense suffering by quickly ending its life, rather than allowing the fawn to lie in terrible agony for several days. Since the fawn's intense suffering was preventable and, so far as we can see, pointless, doesn't it appear that premise (1) of the argument is true, that there do exist instances of intense suffering which an omnipotent, omniscient being could have prevented without thereby losing some greater good or permitting some evil equally bad or worse?

It must be acknowledged that the case of the fawn's apparently pointless suffering does not *prove* that (1) is true. For even though we cannot see how the fawn's suffering is required to obtain some greater good (or to prevent some equally bad or worse evil), it hardly follows that it is not so required. After all, we are often surprised by how things we thought to be unconnected turn out to be intimately connected. Perhaps, for all we know, there is some familiar good outweighing the fawn's suffering to which that suffering is connected in a way we do not see. Furthermore, there may well be unfamiliar goods, goods we haven't dreamed of, to which the lawn's suffering is inextricably connected. Indeed, it would seem to require something like omniscience on our part before we could lay claim to *knowing* that there is no greater good connected to the fawn's suffering in such a manner than an omnipotent, omniscient being could not have achieved that good without permitting that suffering or some evil equally bad or worse. So the case of the fawn's suffering surely does not enable us to *establish* the truth of (1).

The truth is that we are not in a position to prove that (1) is true. We cannot know with certainty that instances of suffering of the sort described in (1) do occur in our world. But it is one thing to *know* or *prove* that (1) is true and quite another thing to have *rational grounds* for believing (1) to be true. We are often in the position where in the light of our experience and knowledge it is rational to believe that a certain statement is true, even though we are not in a position to prove or to know with certainty that the statement is true. In the light of our past experience and knowledge it is, for example, very reasonable to believe that neither senators Barry Goldwater nor George McGovern will ever be elected President of the United States, but we are scarcely in the position of knowing with certainty that neither will ever be elected President. So, too, with (1), although we cannot know with certainty that it is true, it perhaps can be rationally supported, shown to be a rational belief.

Consider again the case of the fawn's suffering. Is it reasonable to believe that there is some greater good so intimately connected to that suffering that even an omnipotent, omniscient being could not have obtained that good without permitting that suffering or some evil at least as bad? It certainly does not appear reasonable to believe this. Nor does it seem reasonable to believe that there is some evil at least as bad as the fawn's suffering such that an omnipotent being simply could not have prevented it without permitting the fawn's suffering. But even if it should somehow be reasonable to believe either of these things of the fawn's suffering, we must then ask whether it is reasonable to believe either of these things of *all* the instances of seemingly pointless human and animal suffering that occur daily in our world. And surely the answer to this more general question must be no. It seems quite unlikely that *all* the instances of intense suffering occurring daily in our world are intimately related to the occurrence of greater goods or the prevention of evils at least as bad; and even more unlikely, should they somehow all be so related, that an omnipotent, omniscient being could not have achieved at least some of those goods (or prevented some of those evils) without permitting the instances of intense suffering that are supposedly related to them. In the light of our experience and knowledge of the variety and scale of human and animal suffering in our world, the idea that none of this suffering could have been prevented by an omnipotent being without thereby losing a greater good or permitting an evil at least as bad seems an extraordinary absurd idea, quite beyond our belief. It seems then that although we cannot *prove* that (I) is true, it is, nevertheless, altogether *reasonable* to believe that (1) is true, that (1) is a *rational* belief.[5]

Returning now to our argument for atheism, we've seen that the second premise expresses a basic belief common to many theists and nontheists. We've also seen that our experience and knowledge of the variety and profusion of suffering in our world provides *rational support* for the first premise. Seeing that the conclusion, "There does not exist an omnipotent, omniscient, wholly good being" follows from these two premises, it does seem that we have *rational support* for atheism, that it is reasonable for us to believe that the theistic God does not exist.

II

Can theism be rationally defended against the argument for atheism we have just examined? If it can, how might the theist best respond to that argument? Since the argument from (1) and (2) to (3) is valid, and since the theist, no less than the nontheist, is more than likely committed to (2), it's clear that the theist can reject this atheistic argument only by rejecting its first premise, the premise that states that there are instances of intense suffering which an omnipotent, omniscient being could have prevented without thereby losing some greater good or permitting some evil equally bad or worse. How, then, can the theist best respond to this premise and the considerations advanced in its support?

There are basically three responses a theist can make. First, he might argue not that (1) is false or probably false, but only that the reasoning given in support of it is in some way *defective*. He may do this either by arguing that the reasons given in support of (1) are *in themselves* insufficient to justify accepting (1), or by arguing that there are other things we know which, when taken in conjunction with these reasons, do not justify us in accepting (1). I suppose some theists would be content with this rather modest response to the basic argument for atheism. But given the validity of the basic argument and the theist's likely acceptance of (2), he is thereby committed to the view that (1) is false, not just that we have no good reasons for accepting (1) as true. The second two responses are aimed at showing that it is reasonable to believe that (1) is false. Since the theist is committed to this view I shall focus the discussion on these two attempts, attempts which we can distinguish as "the direct attack" and "the indirect attack."

By a direct attack, I mean an attempt to reject (1) by pointing out goods, for example, to which suffering may well be connected, goods which an omnipotent, omniscient being could not achieve without permitting suffering. It is doubtful, however, that the direct attack can succeed. The theist may point out that some suffering leads to moral and spiritual development impossible without suffering. But it's reasonably clear that suffering often occurs in a degree far beyond what is required for character development. The theist may say that some suffering results from free choices of human beings and might be preventable only by preventing some measure of human freedom. But, again, it's clear that much intense suffering occurs not as a result of human free choices. The general difficulty with this direct attack on premise (1) is twofold. First, it cannot succeed, for the theist does not know what greater goods might be served, or evils prevented, by each instance of intense human or animal suffering. Second, the theist's own religious tradition usually maintains that in this life it is not given to us to know God's purpose in allowing particular instances of suffering. Hence, the direct attack against premise (1) cannot succeed and violates basic beliefs associated with theism.

The best procedure for the theist to follow in rejecting premise (1) is the indirect procedure. This procedure I shall call "the G. E. Moore shift," so-called in honor of the twentieth-century philosopher, G. E. Moore, who used it to great effect in dealing with the arguments of the skeptics. Skeptical philosophers such as David Hume have advanced ingenious arguments to prove that no one can know of the existence of any material object. The premises of their arguments employ plausible principles, principles which many philosophers have tried to reject directly, but only with questionable success. Moore's procedure was altogether different. Instead of arguing directly against the premises of the skeptic's arguments, he simply noted that the premises implied, for example, that he (Moore) did not know of the existence of a pencil. Moore then proceeded indirectly against the skeptic's premises by arguing:

> I do know that this pencil exists.
> If the skeptic's principles are correct I cannot know of the existence of this pencil.

∴ The skeptic's principles (at least one) must be incorrect.

Moore then noted that his argument is just as valid as the skeptic's, that both of their arguments contain the premise "If the skeptic's principles are correct Moore cannot know of the existence of this pencil," and concluded that the only way to choose between the two arguments (Moore's and the skeptic's) is by deciding which of the first premises it is more rational to believe—Moore's premise "I do know that this pencil exists" or the skeptic's premise asserting that his skeptical principles are correct. Moore concluded that his own first premise was the more rational of the two.[6]

Before we see how the theist may apply the G. E. Moore shift to the basic argument for atheism, we should note the general strategy of the shift. We're given an argument: p, q, therefore, r. Instead of arguing directly against p, another argument is constructed—not-r, q, therefore, not-p—which begins with the denial of the conclusion of the first argument, keeps its second premise, and ends with the denial of the first premise as its conclusion. Compare, for example, these two:

I. p	II. not-r
q	q
r	not-p

It is a truth of logic that if I is valid II must be valid as well. Since the arguments are the same so far as the second premise is concerned, any choice between them must concern their respective first premises. To argue against the first premise (*p*) by constructing the counter argument II is to employ the G. E. Moore shift.

Applying the G. E. Moore shift against the first premise of the basic argument for atheism, the theist can argue as follows:

not-3. There exists an omnipotent, omniscient, wholly good being.
   2. An omniscient, wholly good being would prevent the occurrence of any intense suffering it could, unless it could not do so without thereby losing some greater good or permitting some evil equally bad or worse. therefore,
not-1. It is not the case that there exist instances of intense suffering which an omnipotent, omniscient being could have prevented without thereby losing some greater good or permitting some evil equally bad or worse.

We now have two arguments: the basic argument for atheism from (1) and (2) to (3), and the theist's best response, the argument from (not-3) and (2) to (not-1). What the theist then says about (1) is that he has rational grounds for believing in the existence of the theistic God (not-3), accepts (2) as true, and sees that (not-1) follows from (not-3) and (2). He concludes, therefore, that he has rational grounds for rejecting (1). Having rational grounds for rejecting (1), the theist concludes that the basic argument for atheism is mistaken.

III

We've had a look at a forceful argument for atheism and what seems to be the theist's best response to that argument. If one is persuaded by the argument for atheism, as I find myself to be, how might one best view the position of the theist? Of course, he will view the theist as having a false belief, just as the theist will view the atheist as having a false belief. But what position should the atheist take concerning the *rationality* of the theist's belief? There are three major positions an atheist might take, positions which we may think of as some varieties of atheism. First, the atheist may believe that no one is rationally justified in believing that the theistic God exists. Let us call this position "unfriendly atheism." Second, the atheist may hold no belief concerning whether any theist is or isn't rationally justified in believing that the theistic God exists. Let us call this view "indifferent atheism." Finally, the atheist may believe that some theists are rationally justified in believing that the theistic God exists. This view we shall call "friendly atheism." In this final part of the paper I propose to discuss and defend the position of friendly atheism.

If no one can be rationally justified in believing a false proposition then friendly atheism is a paradoxical, if not incoherent position. But surely the truth of a belief is not a necessary condition of someone's being rationally justified in having that belief. So in holding that someone is rationally justified in believing that the theistic God exists, the friendly atheist is not committed to thinking that the theist has a true belief. What he is committed to is that the theist has rational grounds for his belief, a belief the atheist rejects and is convinced he is rationally justified in rejecting. But is this possible? Can someone, like our friendly atheist, hold a belief, be convinced that he is rationally justified in holding that belief, and yet believe that someone else is equally justified in believing the opposite? Surely this is possible. Suppose your friends see you off on a flight to Hawaii. Hours after take-off they learn that your plane has gone down at sea. After a twenty-four hour search, no survivors have been found. Under these circumstances they are rationally justified in believing that you have perished. But it is hardly rational for you to believe this, as you bob up and down in your life vest, wondering why the search planes have failed to spot you. Indeed, to amuse yourself while awaiting your fate, you might very well reflect on the fact that your friends are rationally justified in believing that you are now dead, a proposition you disbelieve and are rationally justified in disbelieving. So, too, perhaps an atheist may be rationally justified in his atheistic belief and yet hold that some theists are rationally justified in believing just the opposite of what he believes.

What sort of grounds might a theist have for believing that God exists? Well, he might endeavor to justify his belief by appealing to one or more of the traditional arguments: Ontological, Cosmological, Teleological, Moral, etc. Second, he might appeal to certain aspects of religious experience, perhaps even his own religious experience. Third, he might try to justify theism as a plausible theory in terms of which we can account for a variety of phenomena. Although an atheist must hold that the theistic God does not exist, can he not also believe, and be justified in so believing, that some of these "justifications of theism" do actually rationally justify some theists in their belief that there exists a supremely good, omnipotent, omniscient being? It seems to me that he can.

If we think of the long history of theistic belief and the special situations in which people are sometimes placed, it is perhaps as absurd to think that no one was ever nationally justified in believing that the theistic God exists as it is to think that no one was ever justified in believing that human beings would never walk on the moon. But in suggesting that friendly atheism is preferable to unfriendly atheism, I don't mean to rest the case on what some human beings might reasonably have believed in the eleventh or thirteenth century. The more interesting question is whether some people in modern society, people who are aware of the usual grounds for belief and disbelief and are acquainted to some degree with modern science, are yet rationally justified in accepting theism. Friendly atheism is a significant position only if it answers this question in the affirmative.

It is not difficult for an atheist to be friendly when he has reason to believe that the theist could not reasonably be expected to be acquainted with the grounds for disbelief that he (the atheist) possesses. For then the atheist may take the view that some theists are rationally justified in holding to theism, but would not be so were they to be acquainted with the grounds for disbelief—those grounds being sufficient to tip the scale in favor of atheism when balanced against the reasons the theist has in support of his belief.

Friendly atheism becomes paradoxical, however, when the atheist contemplates believing that the theist has all the grounds for atheism that he, the atheist, has, and yet is rationally justified in maintaining his theistic belief. But even so excessively friendly a view as this perhaps can be held by the atheist if he also has some reason to think that the grounds for theism are not as telling as the theist is justified in taking them to be.[7]

In this paper I've presented what I take to be a strong argument for atheism, pointed out what I think is the theist's best response to that argument, distinguished three positions an atheist might take concerning the rationality of theistic belief, and made some remarks in defence of the position called "friendly atheism." I'm aware that the central points of the paper are not likely to be warmly received by many philosophers. Philosophers who are atheists tend to be tough minded—holding that there are no good reasons for supposing that theism is true. And theists tend either to reject the view that the existence of evil provides rational grounds for atheism or to hold that religious belief has nothing to do with reason and evidence at all. But such is the way of philosophy.[8]

NOTES

1. Some philosophers have contended that the existence of evil is *logically inconsistent* with the existence of the theistic God. No one, I think, has succeeded in establishing such an extravagant claim. Indeed, granted incompatibilism, there is a fairly compelling argument for the view that the existence of evil is logically consistent with the existence of the theistic God. (For a lucid statement of this argument see Alvin Plantinga, *God, Freedom, and Evil* (New York, 1974), pp. 29–59.) There remains, however, what we may call the *evidential* form—as opposed to the *logical* form—of the problem of evil: the view that the variety and profusion of evil in our world, although perhaps not logically inconsistent with the existence of the theistic God, provides, nevertheless, *rational support* for atheism. In this paper I shall be concerned solely with the evidential form of the problem, the form of the problem which, I think, presents a rather severe difficulty for theism.
2. If there is some good, G, greater than any evil, (1) will be false for the trivial reason that no matter what evil, E, we pick the conjunctive good state of affairs consisting of G and E will outweigh E and be such that an omnipotent being could not obtain it without permitting E. (See Alvin Plantinga, *God and Other Minds* [Ithaca, 1967], p. 167.) To avoid this objection we may insert "unreplaceable" into our premiss (1) and (2) between "some" and "greater." If E isn't required for G, and G is better than G plus E, then the good conjunctive state of affairs composed of G and E would be *replaceable* by the greater good of G alone. For the sake of simplicity, however, I will ignore this complication both in the formulation and discussion of premiss (1) and (2).

3. Three clarifying points need to be made in connection with (i). First, by "good" I don't mean to exclude the fulfillment of certain moral principles. Perhaps preventing s_1 would preclude certain actions prescribed by the principles of justice. I shall allow that the satisfaction of certain principles of justice may be a good that outweighs the evil of s_1. Second, even though (i) may suggest it, I don't mean to limit the good in question to something that would *follow in time* the occurrence of s_1. And, finally, we should perhaps not fault OG if the good G, that would be lost were s_1 prevented, is not actually greater than s_1, but merely such that allowing s_1 and G, as opposed to preventing s_1 and thereby losing G, would not alter the balance between good and evil. For reasons of simplicity, I have left this point out in stating (i), with the result that (i) is perhaps a bit stronger than it should be.

4. See Ivan's speech in Book V, Chapter IV of *The Brothers Karamazov*.

5. One might object that the conclusion of this paragraph is stronger than the reasons give warrant. For it is one thing to argue that it is unreasonable to think that (1) is false and another thing to conclude that we are therefore justified in accepting (1) as true. There are propositions such that believing them is much more reasonable than disbelieving them, and yet are such that *withholding judgment* about them is more reasonable than believing them. To take an example of Chisholm's: it is more reasonable to believe that the Pope will be in Rome (on some arbitrarily picked future date) than to believe that he won't; but it is perhaps more reasonable to suspend judgment on the question of the Pope's whereabouts on that particular date, than to believe that he will be in Rome. Thus, it might be objected, that while we've shown that believing (1) is more reasonable than disbelieving (1), we haven't shown that believing (1) is more reasonable than withholding belief. My answer to this objection is that there are things we know which render (1) probable to the degree that it is more reasonable to believe (1) than to suspend judgment on (1). What are these things we know? First, I think, is the fact that there is an enormous variety and profusion of intense human and animal suffering in our world. Second is the fact that much of this suffering seems quite unrelated to any greater goods (or the absence of equal or greater evils) that might justify it. And, finally, there is the fact that such suffering as is related to greater goods (or the absence of equal or greater evils) does not, in many cases, seem so intimately related as to require its permission by an omnipotent being bent on securing those goods (the absence of those evils). These facts, I am claiming, make it more reasonable to accept (1) than to withhold judgment on (1).

6. See, for example, the two chapters on Hume in G. E. Moore, *Some Main Problems of Philosophy* (London, 1953).

7. Suppose that I add a long sum of numbers three times and get result x. I inform you of this so that you have pretty much the same evidence I have for the claim that the sum of the numbers is x. You then use your calculator twice over and arrive at result y. You, then, are justified in believing that the sum of the numbers is *not* x. However, knowing that your calculator has been damaged and is therefore unreliable, and that you have no reason to think that it is damaged, I may reasonably believe not only that the sum of the numbers is x, but also that you are justified in believing that the sum is not x. Here is a case, then, where you have all of my evidence for p, and yet I can reasonably believe that you are justified in believing not-p—for I have reason to believe that your grounds for not-p are not as telling as you are justified in taking them to be.

8. I am indebted to my colleagues at Purdue University, particularly to Ted Ulrich and Lilly Russow, and to philosophers at The University of Nebraska, Indiana State University, and The University of Wisconsin at Milwaukee for helpful criticisms of earlier versions of this paper.

4.2

'PAIN AND PLEASURE: AN EVIDENTIAL PROBLEM FOR THEISTS'

Paul Draper

I. The Nature of the Problem

I will argue in this paper that our knowledge about pain and pleasure creates an epistemic problem for theists. The problem is not that some propositions about pain and pleasure can be shown to be both true and logically inconsistent with theism. Rather, the problem is evidential. A statement reporting the observations and testimony upon which our knowledge about pain and pleasure is based bears a certain significant negative evidential relation to theism.[1] And because of this, we have a prima facie good epistemic reason to reject theism—that is, a reason that is sufficient for rejecting theism unless overridden by other reasons for not rejecting theism.

By "theism" I mean the following statement:

> There exists an omnipotent, omniscient, and morally perfect person who created the Universe.

I will use the word "God" as a title rather than as a proper name, and I will stipulate that necessary and sufficient conditions for bearing this title are that one be an omnipotent, omniscient, and morally perfect person who created the Universe. Given this (probably technical) use of the term "God," theism is the statement that God exists.

Some philosophers believe that the evils we find in the world create an evidential problem for theists because theism fails to explain these evils (or

Paul Draper, 'Pain and Pleasure: An Evidential Problem for Theists', Noûs, 23 (1989), pp. 331–50.

most of what we know about them). (See, for example, Hareind Madden 1968.) This position is attractive. It seems to reflect the intuitions of a great many people who have regarded evil as an epistemic problem for theists. After all, the most common way of stating the problem of evil is to ask a why question like "if God exists, then why is there so much evil in the world?" And such questions are either genuine or rhetorical requests for explanation. Moreover, the relevance of theodicies to this alleged problem of evil is quite clear, since a theodicy can very naturally be understood as an attempt to explain certain evils or facts about evil in terms of theism.

But other philosophers who agree that theism fails to explain most of the evils we find in the world deny that this creates an epistemic problem for theists—that is, they deny that this explanatory failure is a prima facie good reason to reject theism. This disagreement has led to a debate over how much evil, if any, theism needs to explain to avoid disconfirmation. (See, for example, Yandell 1969a and 1969b, Kane 1970, Mavrodes 1970, pp. 90–111, Ahern 1971, Hare 1972, and Yandell 1972.)* What the members of both sides of this debate have failed to recognize is that one cannot determine what facts about evil theism needs to explain or how well it needs to explain them without considering alternatives to theism. The important question, a question that David Hume asked (1980, Part XI, pp. 74–75) but that most contemporary philosophers of religion have ignored, is whether or not any serious hypothesis that is logically inconsistent with theism explains some significant set of facts about evil or about good and evil much better than theism does.

I will argue for an affirmative answer to this question. Specifically, I will compare theism to the following alternative, which I will call "the Hypothesis of Indifference" ("HI" for short):

> HI: neither the nature nor the condition of sentient beings on earth is the result of benevolent or malevolent actions performed by nonhuman persons.

Unlike theism, HI does not entail that supernatural beings exist and so is consistent with naturalism. But HI is also consistent with the existence of supernatural beings. What makes HI inconsistent with theism is that it entails that, if supernatural beings do exist, then no action performed by them is motivated by a direct concern for our well-being. Now let "O" stand for a statement reporting both the observations one has made of humans and animals experiencing pain or pleasure and the testimony one has encountered concerning the observations others have made of sentient beings experiencing pain or pleasure. By "pain" I mean physical or mental suffering of any sort. I will argue that the pain and pleasure in our world create an epistemic problem for theists by arguing that:

---

* See references at the end of this article.

C: HI explains the facts O reports much better than theism does.

One problem with this formulation of C is that the verb "to explain" has a number of distinct but easily confused meanings. For my purposes here, it will suffice to point out that in some instances the claim that one hypothesis explains some observation report much better than another is equivalent in meaning, or at least bears a close conceptual connection, to the claim that the truth of that observation report is much less surprising on the first hypothesis than it is on the second. Since I suspect that it is only in these instances that comparisons of explanatory power support comparisons of probability, I will reformulate C as the claim that the facts O reports are much more surprising on theism than they are on HI, or, more precisely, that the antecedent probability of O is much greater on the assumption that HI is true than on the assumption that theism is true. By the "antecedent" probability of O, I mean O's probability, independent of (rather than temporally prior to) the observations and testimony it reports. So my reformulation of C is best expressed as follows:

> C: independent of the observations and testimony O reports, O is much more probable on the assumption that HI is true than on the assumption that theism is true.

For the sake of brevity, I will use $P(x/y)$ to represent the probability of the statement x, *independent of the observations and testimony O reports*, on the assumption that the statement y is true. Using this notation, I can abbreviate C in the following way:

> C: $P(O/HI)$ is much greater than $P(O/theism)$.

One last elucidatory remark about C. The probabilities employed in C are epistemic ones rather than, for example, statistical, physical, or logical probabilities.[2] Thus, they can vary from person to person and from time to time, since different persons can be in different epistemic situations at the same time and the same person can be in different epistemic situations at different times. For example, suppose that six hands of poker are dealt. Then the epistemic probability that one hand includes four aces will be different for those players who inspect their hands and find no aces and those players who inspect their hands and discover one or more aces. And the epistemic probability for any of the six players that one hand includes four aces will be different before inspecting his or her hand than after inspecting it.

Now suppose that I succeed in showing that C is true (relative to my own and my readers' epistemic situations). Then the truth of C is (for us) a prima facie good (epistemic) reason to believe that theism is less probable than HI. Thus, since the denial of theism is obviously entailed by HI and so is at least as probable as HI, the truth of C is a prima facie good reason to believe that theism is less probable than not. And since it is epistemically irrational to believe both that theism is true and that it is less probable than not, the truth of C is also a prima facie good reason to reject (i.e., to cease or refrain from believing) theism.

In Section II, I will argue that C is true. However, my argument will depend on the assumption that theodicies do not significantly raise P(O/theism). In Section III, I will defend this assumption. And in Section IV, I will discuss the significance of C's truth.

II. THE BIOLOGICAL UTILITY OF PAIN AND PLEASURE

The claim that P(O/HI) is much greater than P(O/theism) is by no means obviously true. The fact that O reports observations and testimony about pleasure as well as pain should make this clear. So an argument for this claim is needed. I will argue that it is the biological role played by both pain and pleasure in goal-directed organic systems that renders this claim true. In order to explain precisely why this is so, I will need to introduce a concept of "biological usefulness."

Though no one doubts that organic systems are goal-directed in some objective sense, it is by no means easy to provide a precise analysis of this kind of goal-directedness. As a first approximation, we may say that a system S is "goal-directed" just in case from some property G that S has exhibited or will exhibit, a broad range of potential environmental changes are such that: (i) if they occurred at a time when S is exhibiting G and no compensating changes took place in the parts of S, then S would cease to exhibit G and never exhibit G again, and (ii) if they occurred at a time when S is exhibiting G, then compensating changes would take place in the parts of S, resulting in either S's continuing to exhibit G or in S's exhibiting G once again. (Cf. Boorse 1976 and Ruse 1973.) Notice that to be goal-directed in this sense does not entail direction to the conscious end of some intelligent being. Notice also that the organic world is made up of complex and interdependent goal-directed systems, including ecosystems, populations of organisms, organisms, parts of organisms, parts of parts of organisms, and so on.

I will call the goals to which organic systems are directed in this sense their "biological goals." And I will say that a part of some goal-directed organic system S is "biologically useful" just in case (i) it causally contributes to one of S's biological goals (or to one of the biological goals of some other goal-directed organic system of which it is a part), and (ii) its doing so is not biologically accidental. (It is in virtue of clause ii that, for example, a nonfatal heart attack that prevents a person from committing suicide cannot be called biologically useful.) Notice that much of the pain and pleasure in the world is biologically useful in this sense. Consider, for example, the pain my cat Hector felt when he jumped on top of a hot oven door. Hector's quick response to this pain enabled him to avoid serious injury, and he now flees whenever an oven door is opened. Hector's pain in this case, like much of the pain reported by O, was biologically useful. For it causally contributed to two central biological goals of individual organisms, namely, survival and reproduction, and its doing so was plainly not accidental from a biological point of view. Of course, there is also much pain and pleasure in our world that is not biologically useful: for instance, masochistic pleasure and pain resulting from burns that ultimately prove fatal. (I will sometimes call this kind of pain and pleasure "biologically gratuitous.")

This notion of biological utility enables me to introduce a statement logically equivalent to O that will help me show that C is true. Let "O1," "O2," and "O3" stand for statements respectively reporting the facts O reports about:

(1) moral agents experiencing pain or pleasure that we know to be biologically useful,
(2) sentient beings that are not moral agents experiencing pain, or pleasure that we know to be biologically useful, and
(3) sentient beings experiencing pain or pleasure that we do not know to be biologically useful.

Since O is obviously logically equivalent to the conjunction of O1, O2, and O3, it follows that, for any hypothesis h:

$$P(O/h)=P(O1 \text{ \& } O2 \text{ \& } O3/h)$$

But the following theorem of the mathematical calculus of probability holds for epistemic probability:

$$P(O1 \text{ \& } O2 \text{ \& } O3/h)=P(O1/h) \times P(O2/h \text{ \& } O1) \times P(O3/h \text{ \& } O1 \text{ \& } O2).[3]$$

Thus, C is true—P(O/HI) is much greater than P(O/theism)—just in case:

A: $P(O1/HI) \times P(O2/HI \text{ \& } O1) \times P(O3/HI \text{ \& } O1 \text{ \& } O2)$

is much greater than

B: $P(O1/theism) \times P(O2/theism \text{ \& } O1) \times P(O3/theism \text{ \& } O1 \text{ \& } O2).$

I will argue that A is much greater than B by arguing that each of the multiplicands of A is either greater or much greater than the corresponding multiplicand of B. As I will explain in Section III, my arguments will assume that theodicies do not significantly raise P(O/theism).

Let us begin with O1, which reports those facts reported by O about humans (who are moral agents) experiencing pain or pleasure that we know to be biologically useful. We know antecedently—that is, we know independent of the observations and testimony O reports—that humans are goal-directed organic systems, composed of parts that systematically contribute to the biological goals of these systems. This seems to give us reason to expect that human pain and pleasure, if they exist, will also systematically contribute to these goals. (And this is, of course, precisely what O1 reports.) But notice that pain and pleasure are in one respect strikingly dissimilar to other parts of organic systems: they have intrinsic moral value. Pain is intrinsically bad, and pleasure is intrinsically good. Does this difference substantially decrease the amount of support that our antecedent knowledge about humans gives to the "prediction" that pain and pleasure, if they exist, will systematically contribute to biological goals? I submit that it does if we assume that theism is true, but does not if we assume that HI is true. It is this difference between HI and theism that makes P(O1/HI) much greater than P(O1/theism).

Allow me to explain. HI entails that, if pain and pleasure exist, then they are not the result of malevolent or benevolent actions performed by nonhuman persons. So on HI, the moral difference between pain and pleasure and other parts of organic systems gives us no antecedent reason to believe that pain and pleasure will not play the same biological role that other parts of organic systems play. Indeed, a biological explanation of pain and pleasure is just the sort of explanation that one would expect on HI. But theism entails that God is responsible for the existence of any pain and pleasure in the world. Since God is morally perfect, He would have good moral reasons for producing pleasure even if it is never biologically useful, and He would not permit pain unless He had, not just a biological reason, but also a morally sufficient reason to do so. And since God is omnipotent and omniscient, He could create goal-directed organic systems (including humans) without biologically useful pain and pleasure. So theism entails both that God does not need biologically useful pain and pleasure to produce human goal-directed organic systems and that, if human pain and pleasure exist, then God had good moral reasons for producing them, reasons that, for all we know antecedently, might very well be inconsistent with pain and pleasure systematically contributing to the biological goals of human organisms. Therefore, we would have much less reason on theism than on HI to be surprised if it turned out that human pain and pleasure differed from other parts of organic systems by not systematically contributing to the biological goals of those systems. Hence, since O1 reports that the pain and pleasure experienced by humans (who are moral agents) do contribute in this way, P(O1/HI) is much greater than P(O1/theism).

One might object that from theism and our antecedent knowledge that goal-directed organic systems exist, we can infer that the biological functions of the parts of those systems are themselves morally worthwhile, which gives us reason on theism that we do not have on HI to expect pain and pleasure to have biological functions. It might be thought that this counterbalances the reasons offered above for concluding that O1 is antecedently much more likely given HI than it is given theism.[4] Now we obviously cannot infer from theism and our antecedent knowledge that the greater the number of functioning parts in an organic system, the more valuable the system. We might be able to infer that organic systems are valuable and that the parts of these systems that have biological functions are valuable because the systems could not exist without functioning parts. But this does not imply that we have as much or even close to as much reason on theism as on HI to expect pain and pleasure to have biological functions. For an omnipotent and omniscient being could produce such systems without biologically useful pain and pleasure. Thus, since a morally perfect being would try to accomplish its goals with as little pain as possible, the value of organic systems gives us no reason on theism to expect pain to have biological functions. And since pleasure has intrinsic value and so is worth producing whether or not it furthers some other goal, the value of organic systems gives us very little reason on theism to expect pleasure to have biological functions.

O2 reports the observations and testimony reported by O about sentient beings that are not moral agents (e.g., young human children and nonhuman animals) experiencing pain or pleasure that we know to be biologically useful. Independent of the observations and testimony O reports, we know that some sentient beings that are not moral agents are biologically very similar to moral agents. Since O1 implies that moral agents experience biologically useful pain and pleasure, this knowledge makes it antecedently likely on H1 and O1 that some sentient beings that are not moral agents will also experience biologically useful pain and pleasure. Now at first glance, one might think that this knowledge makes the existence of such pain and pleasure just as likely on theism & O1. After all, from the assumption that theism & O1 are both true, it follows that God has good moral reasons for permitting biologically useful pain. But there is an important difference between the biologically useful pain that O1 reports and the biologically useful pain that O2 reports. Given theism & O1, we have reasons to believe that God permits the pain O1 reports because it plays some sort of (presently indiscernible) moral role in the lives of the humans that experience it. But the pain O2 reports cannot play such a role, since the subjects of it are not moral agents. This difference is plainly not relevant on HI & O1, but it gives us some reason on theism & O1 to expect that the good moral reasons God has for permitting moral agents to experience pain do not apply to animals that are not moral agents, and hence some reason to believe that God will not permit such beings to experience pain. So P(O2/HI & O1) is somewhat greater than P(O2/theism & O1).

O3 reports facts about sentient beings experiencing pain or pleasure that we do not know to be biologically useful. This includes much pain and pleasure that we know to be biologically gratuitous, as well as some that is not known to be useful and is also not known to be gratuitous. I will give a two-part argument for the conclusion that P(O3/HI & O1 & O2) is much greater than P(O3/theism & O1 & O2).

First, we obviously have much more reason on theism & O1 & O2 than we have on HI & O1 & O2 to expect sentient beings (especially nonhuman animals) to be happy—in any case much more happy than they would be if their pleasure were limited to that reported by O1 and O2. Instead, when the facts O3 reports are added to those reported by O1 and O2, we find that many humans and animals experience prolonged and intense suffering and a much greater number are far from happy. In addition, we have more reason on theism & O1 & O2 than on HI & O1 & O2 to expect to discover a close connection between certain moral goods (e.g., justice and virtue) and biologically gratuitous pain and pleasure, but we discover no such connection.

Second, we have, antecedently, much more reason on HI & O1 & O2 than on theism & O1 & O2 to believe that the fundamental role of pain and pleasure in our world is a biological one and that the presence of biologically gratuitous pain and pleasure is epiphenomenal, a biological accident resulting from nature's or an indifferent creator's failure to "fine-tune" organic systems. And this is undeniably supported (though not entailed) by what O3 reports. To demonstrate this, a couple of definitions are needed. First, by "pathological" pain or pleasure, I mean pain or pleasure that results from the failure of some organic system to function properly. For example, pain caused by terminal cancer and sadistic pleasure are pathological in this sense. And second, by "biologically appropriate" pain or pleasure, I mean pain or pleasure that occurs in a situation which is such that it is biologically useful that pain or pleasure is felt in situations of this sort. For instance, the pain felt by a person killed in a fire is not biologically useful, but it is biologically appropriate because it is biologically useful that humans feel pain when they come in contact with fire. Clearly much of the pain and pleasure reported by O3 is either pathological or biologically appropriate, and very little is known to be both non-pathological and biologically inappropriate.[5] And this is exactly what one would expect if pain and pleasure are fundamentally biological rather than moral phenomena, and so is much more to be expected on HI & O1 & O2 than on theism & O1 & O2.

Therefore, assuming that theodicies do not significantly raise P(O/theism), the first and third multiplicands of A are much greater than the first and third multiplicands of B, and the second multiplicand of A is greater than the second multiplicand of B. And this implies that P(O/HI) is much greater than P(O/theism).

III. THE MORAL VALUE OF PAIN AND PLEASURE

In addition to their biological roles, pain and pleasure also play various moral roles in our world. By appealing to these roles, the theist might hope to explain some of the facts O reports in terms of theism, and thereby render O less surprising on theism than it is initially. This would seem to be the theist's most promising strategy for undermining the argument for C given above. Theodicies can be treated as attempts to carry out such a strategy.[6] While few would deny that most theodicies are rather obvious failures, it is widely thought that plausible theistic explanations of suffering can be constructed by appealing to the intrinsic or instrumental moral value of free will. So it is necessary to determine what effect such theodicies have on P(O/theism). Additionally, it is important to evaluate the increasingly popular position that evidential arguments from evil against theism fail because the disproportion between omniscience and human knowledge makes it quite likely, on the assumption that God exists, that humans would not understand why God permits evil. (For a defence of this position, see Wykstra 1984.)

A. Evaluating Theodicies

Explaining some phenomenon in terms of a statement usually involves adding other statements to that statement. This is certainly true in the case of theodicies, which typically add to the claim that God exists the claims that God has a certain goal, that even God must produce or permit certain evils in order to accomplish that goal, and that accomplishing the goal is, from a moral point of view, worth the evils. I will say that a statement h* is an "expansion" of a statement h just in case h* is known to entail h. (Notice that h* can be an expansion of h even if it is logically equivalent to h.) The effect of a theodicy on P(O/theism) can be assessed by identifying an appropriate expansion T_n of theism that the theodicy employs and then using the following principle to evaluate P(O/theism) (cf. Adams 1985, appendix, p. 252): P(O/theism)=(P(T_n/theism) × P(O/T_n))+(P($\sim T_n$/theism) × P(O/theism & $\sim T_n$)).[7]

I will call this principle the "Weighted Average Principle" ("WAP" for short) because it identifies one probability with a probability weighted average of two others. Roughly, WAP tells us that P(O/theism) is the average of P(O/T_n and P(O/theism & $\sim T_n$). This average, however, is a probability weighted average, the weights of which are P(T_n/theism), and P($\sim T_n$/theism). The higher P(T_n/theism), the closer P(O/theism) will be to P(O/T_n). And the lower P(T_n/theism), the closer P(O/theism) will be to P(O/theism & $\sim T_n$).

WAP clarifies the relationship between theodicies and the argument for C I gave in Section II. For example, suppose that, for some expansion T_n of theism that a certain theodicy employs, P(T_n/theism) is high. My argument for C in Section II ignores this theodicy and so in effect equates P(O/theism) with P(O/theism & $\sim T_n$). Since P(T_n/theism) is high, WAP tells us that P(O/theism) is actually closer to P(O/T_n) than to P(O/theism & $\sim T_n$) (assuming that these are not the same). To successfully defend my assumption in Section II that this theodicy does not significantly raise P(O/theism), I would need to show that P(O/T_n) is not significantly greater than P(O/theism & $\sim T_n$). In other words, I would need to show that, independent of the observations and testimony O reports, we have little or no more reason on T_n than we have on theism & $\sim T_n$ to believe that O is true.

B. Free Will and the Advancement of Morality

Most free will theodicies appeal to a certain sort of moral freedom, which I will call "freedom*." An action is free* only if (i) it is free in an imcompatibilist sense—that is, in a sense incompatible with its being determined by antecedent conditions outside the agent's control—and (ii) if it is morally right, then at least an alternative action that is open in an incompatibilist sense to the agent is such that it would be morally wrong for the agent to perform that alternative action. This concept of freedom is used to give the following theistic explanation of immorality. Freedom* has great value (either because morally right actions that are freely* performed or are more valuable than right actions that are not freely* performed or because, following Hick 1966, moral virtue that is acquired by freely* performing right actions is more valuable than moral virtue that is not freely* acquired). For this reason, God endows humans with freedom. However, since it is logically impossible to force a person to freely* perform a right action instead of a wrong one, God cannot give humans freedom* and ensure that humans will never perform morally wrong actions.

Unfortunately, humans sometimes abuse their freedom* by performing wrong actions. Nevertheless, God is justified in giving humans freedom* because a world in which humans freely* perform both right and wrong actions is (provided that the balance of right over wrong actions or of morally good humans over morally bad humans is sufficiently favorable) better than a world in which immorality is prevented by withholding freedom* from humans.

Notice that, so far, we have no explanation of the existence of pain. For there are morally right actions and morally wrong actions that do not entail the existence of pain. Wrong actions of this sort include some instances of breaking promises, killing, attempting to cause pain, and depriving someone of pleasure. So God could have given humans freedom* without permitting pain. The first version of the free will theodicy that I will evaluate adds to the above explanation of immorality the proposal that God permits pain in order to advance morality. This proposal can be spelled out in the following way. God wants humans to freely* perform right actions instead of wrong ones. Of course, as mentioned above, He cannot force humans to freely* perform only morally right actions, but He would have some control over the balance of right over wrong actions because even free* choices can be influenced and because God would know what free* choices humans would make (or would be likely to make)[8] in various situations. In particular, God might use pain to influence humans to freely* perform right actions instead of wrong ones.

Also, some right actions entail the existence of pain, and God might know prior to creating humans that some or all humans would perform (or would be likely to perform) these right actions if given the chance. Therefore, God might use pain to obtain a more favorable balance of freely* performed right actions over wrong actions.

This version of the free will theodicy employs the following expansion of theism:

> T_1: God exists, and one of His final ends is a favorable balance of freely* performed right actions over wrong actions.[9]

I doubt that a consensus could ever be reached about $P(T_1/\text{theism})$. For T_1 presupposes several very controversial metaphysical and ethical positions. For example, it presupposes that the concept of "freedom*" is coherent, that humans have freedom*, and that freedom* is of great value. Since I obviously do not have the space here to discuss how plausible these claims are, I will assume for the sake of argument that $P(T_1/\text{theism})$ is high.

I will argue, however, that $P(O/T_1)$ is not significantly higher than $P(O/\text{theism} \& \sim T_1)$. This implies that, even if $P(T_1/\text{theism})$ is high, our first version of the free will theodicy does not significantly increase $P(O/\text{theism})$. If, as I will assume, it is, morally permissible for God to use pain to advance morality, then we have reason on T_1 that we do not have on theism $\& \sim T_1$ to expect that the world will contain both pain that influences humans to perform morally right action and pain that is logically necessary for some of the right actions humans perform. Since O reports the existence of pain of both these sorts, we have a predictive success for the theodicy. But O also reports both that pain often influences humans to perform morally wrong actions and that pain is logically necessary for many of the wrong actions humans perform. And we have reason on T_1 that we do not have on theism $\& \sim T_1$ to be surprised by these facts. Furthermore, the observations and testimony O reports provide strong evidence that the world does not presently contain a very impressive balance of right over wrong actions performed by humans and that this is due in part both to a variety of demoralizing conditions like illness, poverty and ignorance, and to the absence of conditions that tend to promote morality. All of this is even more surprising on T_1 than on theism $\& \sim T_1$ (Cf. Adams 1985, pp. 250–251.) So T_1's "predictive" advantages are counterbalanced by several serious "predictive" disadvantages, and for this reason $P(O/T_1)$ is not significantly greater than $P(O/\text{theism} \& \sim T_1)$.

C. Free Will and Responsibility

Some free will theodicists claim that God gives humans freedom* to bring about suffering (either by producing it or by failing to prevent it) in order to increase the responsibility humans have for their own well-being and the well-being of others and thereby increase the importance of the moral decisions humans make. By an "important" moral decision, these theodicists mean a decision upon which the presence or absence of something of great positive or negative value depends. The key value judgment here is that, all else held equal, the more important the moral decisions we are free* to make, the more valuable our freedom* is. By not preventing us from freely* bringing about evils, including serious ones, God increases our control over how valuable the world is and thereby increases the value of our freedom*. This theodicy employs the following expansion of theism:

> T_2: God exists, and one of His final ends is for humans to have the freedom* to make very important moral decisions.

I will assume, once again, that $P(T_2/\text{theism})$ is high, and I will argue that this second version of the free-will theodicy does not significantly raise $P(O/\text{theism})$ by arguing that $P(O/T_2)$ is not significantly greater than $P(O/\text{theism} \ \& \ \sim T_2)$.

I will begin by arguing that Richard Swinburne (1979, Ch. 11) fails in his attempt to extend this theodicy so that it accounts for pain for which humans are not morally responsible. (I will call this sort of pain "amoral pain.") Swinburne believes that free will theodicies that employ T_2 can account for such pain because (i) they explain why God gives humans the freedom* to bring about suffering and (ii) amoral pain is necessary if humans are to have genuine freedom* to bring about suffering. Swinburne defends (ii) in the following way. Freedom* to bring about suffering requires the knowledge of how to bring about suffering. And humans can obtain such knowledge in only one of two ways: either by God telling them how to bring about suffering or by experiencing how this is done. Unfortunately, if God told humans how to bring about suffering, then humans would know that God exists, and hence would have little temptation to do evil and so no genuine freedom* to bring about suffering. So for humans to have such freedom, they must learn by experience how to bring about suffering, and hence must learn this either by observing suffering for which no human is morally responsible or by observing suffering brought about by other humans. But for any particular kind of suffering, there must have been a first time when a human knew how to bring it about despite never having observed suffering of that kind brought about by a human. Hence, if humans are to learn by experience how to bring about suffering, then amoral pain must exist. Therefore, such suffering is necessary for humans to have the freedom* to bring about suffering.

I will make three comments about this argument for (ii). First, even if it is sound, it obviously does not provide an adequate theistic account of amoral pain from which humans gain no new knowledge about how to produce or prevent suffering. Second, even if it is sound, it does not provide an adequate theistic explanation of most of the amoral pain that does give humans new knowledge of this sort. For an omnipotent and omniscient being could have greatly decreased the variety of ways in which humans know how to harm others, and so greatly decreased the amount of amoral pain needed for this knowledge, without decreasing the amount of harm humans can do to others and so without decreasing the amount of control that humans have over the well-being of others. Third, and most importantly, the argument is not sound. As Stump 1983 and Moser 1984 have observed, God could, without permitting amoral pain, give humans the knowledge of how to bring about suffering without revealing His existence and so without undermining human freedom*. For example, as Stump (pp. 52–53) has pointed out, humans might regularly have vivid, message-laden dreams and learn of their reliability, and yet not be compelled to believe in God.

So if this second version of the free will theodicy raises P(O/theism) at all, it is because we have reason on T_2 that we do not have on theism & $\sim T_2$ to expect the existence of pain for which humans are morally responsible. Now, giving humans the freedom* to bring about intense suffering is certainly one way (though not the only way) of giving humans the freedom* to make important moral decisions. So assuming that there is no better way,[10] we have some reason on T_2 to expect humans to have such freedom*, and so reason on T_2 to expect the existence of pain for which humans are morally responsible. But even granting all this, it can be shown that $P(O/T_2)$ is not significantly greater than $P(O/\text{theism} \ \& \ \sim T_2)$ by showing that other facts O reports are even more surprising on T_2 than they are on theism & $\sim T_2$.

An analogy between God and a good parent will be useful here. Ironically, such an analogy is often used to defend this sort of theodicy. For example, Swinburne (1979) responds to the objection that God should not give humans the freedom* to seriously harm others by asserting that the objector is asking that God "make a toy-world, a world where [our choices] matter, but not very much" (p. 219). Such a God "would be like the over-protective parent who will not let his child out of sight for a moment" (p. 220). But Swinburne neglects to ask whether or not humans are worthy of the freedom* to seriously harm others. A good parent gradually increases a child's responsibility as the child becomes capable of handling greater responsibility. Children who are unworthy of a certain responsibility are not benefited by parents who give them that responsibility. On the assumption that T_2 is true, one would expect that God would behave like a good parent, giving humans great responsibility only when we are worthy of it. I am not claiming that on T_2 one would expect God to impose a good moral character on humans before He gives them serious responsibilities. Nor am I claiming that creatures who are worthy of great responsibility would never abuse that responsibility. Rather, I am claiming that on T_2 one would expect God to give all or some humans less responsibility—and in particular no ability to do serious evils—until they freely* developed the strength of character that would make them worthy of greater responsibility. And if at some point humans become worthy of and are given great responsibility but nevertheless abuse this responsibility to such an extent that they are no longer worthy of it, then one would on T_2 expect God, like a good parent, to decrease the amount of responsibility humans have until they are worthy of a second chance.

But O conflicts with all of these expectations. Many humans are plainly not worthy of the freedom* to do serious evils. Nor is the human race making any significant amount of moral progress. If God exists, then for centuries He has been allowing his children to torment, torture, and kill each other. Thus, even if they were once worthy of great responsibility, they no longer are, and hence are not benefited by having such responsibility. So like T_1 T_2's predictive advantages are counterbalanced by several serious predictive disadvantages. Therefore, $P(O/T_2)$ is not significantly greater than $P(O/\text{theism} \ \& \sim T_2)$, and hence this second version of the free will theodicy fails to significantly raise $P(O/\text{theism})$.

D. The "Infinite Intellect Defence"

Some philosophers think that "evidential arguments from evil" can be refuted by pointing out that since God's knowledge about good and evil is limitless, it is not all that surprising that He produces or permits evils for reasons that are unknown to humans. The expansion of theism suggested here is the following:

> T_3: God exists and has a vast amount of knowledge about good and evil and how they are related that humans do not have.

Since $P(T_3/\text{theism})=\text{one}$, $P(O/\text{theism})=P(O/T_3)$. But this does not reveal any defect in my argument for C. For antecedently—that is, independent of the observations and testimony O reports—we have no reason to think that God's additional knowledge concerning good and evil is such that He would permit any of the facts O reports to obtain. Of course, an omnipotent and omniscient being might, for all we know antecedently, have moral reasons unknown to us to permit the evil reported by O. But it is also the case that such a being might, for all we know antecedently, have moral reasons unknown to us to prevent this evil. Indeed, we have no more reason antecedently to believe that such a being would know of some great good unknown to us whose existence entails the existence of the pain O reports than we have reason to believe that such a being would know of some great good unknown to us whose existence entails the nonexistence of the pain or the pleasure O reports. And an omnipotent and omniscient being might very well know of means, far too complicated for humans to understand, by which He could obtain certain goods without the evil O reports. Of course, *given the facts O reports*, we have some reason on T_3 to expect that humans will be unable to produce a plausible theistic explanation of those facts. But HI gives us even more reason to expect this. So human ignorance does not solve the theist's evidential problems.

Hence, none of the theodicies we have considered significantly raises P(O/theism). Therefore, relative to the espistemic situations of those of us who are unable to think of some other much more successful theodicy (i.e., all of us, I suspect), C is true: P(O/HI) is much greater than P(O/theism).

IV. THE SIGNIFICANCE OF THE PROBLEM

In *The Origin of Species*, Charles Darwin argued that his theory of the evolution of species by means of natural selection explains numerous facts (e.g., the geographical distribution of species and the existence of atrophied organs in animals) much better than the alternative hypothesis, that each species of plant and animal was independently created by God. (Let us call this latter hypothesis "special creationism.") Darwin's results were significant partly because special creationists at Darwin's time did not have nor were they able to obtain any evidence favoring special creationism over evolutionary theory that outweighed or at least offset Darwin's evidence favoring evolutionary theory over special creationism. For this reason, many theists, while continuing to believe in creationism, which is consistent with Darwin's theory, rejected special creationism. And those theists who were familiar with Darwin's arguments and yet remained special creationists did so at a cost: their belief in special creationism was no longer an epistemically rational one.

Similarly, how significant my results are depends, in part, on how many theists have or could obtain propositional or nonpropositional evidence favoring theism over HI that offsets the propositional evidence, provided by my argument for C, favoring HI over theism.[11] Any theist confronted with my argument for C who lacks such evidence and is unable to obtain it cannot rationally continue to believe that theism is true. It is beyond the scope of this paper to determine how many theists would be in such a position. But I will make four sets of comments that I hope indicate how difficult a theist's search for the needed evidence might be.

First, I do not see how it could be shown that HI is an ad hoc hypothesis or that theism is *intrinsically* more probable than HI. For HI is consistent with a wide variety of both naturalistic and supernaturalistic hypotheses, and it has no positive ontological commitments. Theism, on the other hand, is a very specific supernaturalistic claim with a very strong ontological commitment. Indeed, such differences between theism and HI might very well provide additional evidence favoring HI over theism.

Second, traditional and contemporary arguments for theism are far from compelling—that is, they are far from being so persuasive as to coerce the acceptance of all or even most rational theists. Thus, even if some such arguments were sound, most theists, including many philosophically sophisticated ones, would not recognize this, and hence the argument would not provide them with evidence favoring theism over HI. (The evidence would exist, but they would not *have* it.)

Third, many traditional and contemporary arguments for theism, including many versions of the cosmological argument, the teleological argument, and the argument from consciousness, may not solve the theist's problem even if they are sound and recognized by the theist to be so. For they at most purport to show that an omnipotent and omniscient being exists—not that the being is morally perfect. Suppose then that some such argument is sound. My argument for C would work just as well if HI were replaced with the following hypothesis, which I will call "the Indifferent Deity Hypothesis":

> There exists an omnipotent and omniscient person who created the Universe and who has no intrinsic concern about the pain or pleasure of other beings.

Like theism, this hypothesis entails that an omnipotent and omniscient being exists. So establishing that such a being exists would help the theist only if the theist also has strong evidence favoring theism over the Indifferent Deity Hypothesis.[12]

Finally, religious experiences of the kind appealed to by "Reformed Epistemologists" like Alvin Plantinga (1983) are ambiguous with respect to the moral attributes of the creator. While Plantinga is correct in claiming that theists typically do feel inclined in certain circumstances (e.g., "when life is sweet and satisfying") to think that the creator is morally good, sensitive theists also feel inclined in other circumstances—namely, when they experience poignant evil—to believe that the creator is indifferent to their good or to the good of others. And many atheists have very powerful experiences in which they seem to be aware of the ultimate indifference of *nature*. These experiences are very common and are very similar phenomenologically to the experiences Plantinga mentions. Moreover, C implies that these "experiences of indifference" are better corroborated than the "theistic experiences" to which Plantinga appeals. Thus, even if Plantinga is correct in thinking that theistic experiences confer prima facie justification on the theist's belief in God, experiences of indifference defeat this justification. Therefore, theistic experiences do not provide nonpropositional evidence that favors theism over HI, or at least none that outweighs the propositional evidence favoring HI over theism provided by my argument for C.[13]

NOTES

This essay originally appeared in *Noûs*, volume 23 (1989). Reprinted by permission of Blackwell Publishers.
1. I agree with most philosophers of religion that theists face no serious logical problem of evil. This chapter challenges the increasingly popular view, defended recently by Pargetter (1976), Plantinga (1979), and Reichenbach (1980), that theists face no serious evidential problem of evil.
2. The concept of epistemic probability is an ordinary concept of probability for which

no adequate philosophical analysis has, in my opinion, been proposed. As a first approximation, however, perhaps the following analysis will do: Relative to K, p is epistemically more probable than q, where K is an epistemic situation and p and q are propositions, just in case any fully rational person in K would have a higher degree of belief in p than in q.

3. One difficulty with the claim that this theorem of the probability calculus is true for epistemic probability is that, since multiplication and addition can only be performed on numbers, it follows that the theorem presupposes that probabilities have numerical values. But most epistemic probabilities have only comparative values. This difficulty can be overcome by interpreting the claim that this theorem is true for epistemic probability as the claim that (i) if each of the probabilities in the theorem have numerical values, then the theorem states the numerical relationships which hold between them, and (ii) if at least one probability in the theorem does not have a numerical value, then all statements of comparative probability entailed by that theorem are true. My reason for believing that this theorem is true for epistemic probability in this sense is that I can find no counterexample to it. I do not place a lot of emphasis on the mere fact that it is a theorem of the probability calculus. For I do not believe that all theorems of the probability calculus are true for epistemic probability.

4. I am grateful to a *Noûs* referee for this objection.

5. Even the enjoyment of perceiving beauty may be biologically appropriate. For our enjoyment of clear perception is plausibly thought to be biologically useful, and Guy Sircello (1975, pp. 129–134) gives a very interesting argument for the conclusion that perceiving beauty is a special case of clear perception.

6. The term "theodicy" is often defined as "an attempt to state what God's actual reason for permitting evil is." This definition implies that in order to show that some theodicy is successful, one must show that God exists. I prefer a definition of "theodicy" that avoids this implication. By a "theodicy" I mean an attempt to give a plausible theistic explanation of some fact about evil.

7. More generally, it follows from the probability calculus that $P(O/\text{theism}) = (P(T_n/\text{theism}) \times P(O/\text{theism} \& T_n)) + (P(\sim T_n/\text{theism}) \times P(O/\text{theism} \& \sim T_n))$. WAP replaces $P(O/\text{theism} \& T_n)$ with $P(O/T_n)$ because T_n is an expansion of theism and hence is known to be logically equivalent to theism $\& T_n$.

8. Robert Adams (1977) argues that God, despite being omniscient, would not know what free* choice a particular human would make in a certain situation prior to deciding both to place that human in that situation and to allow him to make that choice. Adams also argues, however, that God would have prior knowledge of what free* choices humans would be likely to make in various situations.

9. A slightly different version of this theodicy employs the following expansion of theism:

T_1*. God exists, and one of His final ends is a favorable balance of morally good humans whose moral goodness was freely* acquired over morally bad humans.

I suspect that $P(T_1*/\text{theism})$ is greater than $P(T_1/\text{theism})$ because God would be more likely to be concerned about persons than about actions. However, I need not evaluate T_1* separately because I will assume that $P(T_1/\text{theism})$ is high and my arguments concerning $P(O/T_1)$ would work just as well if T_1 were replaced with T_1*.

10. One might challenge this assumption and thereby attack theodicies that employ T_2 in the following way. Choosing whether or not to produce a large amount of pleasure is, all else held equal, a more important moral decision than choosing whether or not to produce a small amount of pain. Hence, it would seem that by increasing our capacity to produce or prevent pleasure, God could give us the power to make moral decisions about pleasure that are as important as any that we now make concerning pain. It is antecedently likely that such a world would be a better world than one in which humans have the ability to cause others to suffer. Therefore, it is antecedently unlikely that God would use pain to accomplish His goal of giving humans important moral choices.

11. One way of attempting to show that such evidence exists would be to (i) identify an appropriate body of evidence (call it O*) that is broader than O (e.g., a statement reporting the relevant observations and testimony, not just about pain and pleasure but about all intrinsic goods and evils) and then (ii) attempt to show that independent of the observations and testimony O* reports, O* is at least as likely on theism as it is on HI.

12. Swinburne (1979, chap. 5) argues that quasi-theistic hypotheses like the Indifferent Deity Hypothesis are intrinsically much less probable than theism. I do not believe his argument is sound, but, if it were, then strong evidence favoring theism over the Indifferent Diety Hypothesis would be available.

13. For criticisms of previous versions of this chapter, I am grateful to Gary Gutting, C. Stephen Layman, Nelson Pike, Alvin Plantinga, Philip L. Quinn, and an anonymous *Noûs* referee.

References

Adams, Robert M. "Middle Knowledge and the Problem of Evil," *American Philosophical Quarterly* 14 (1977): 109–17.

—. "Plantinga on the Problem of Evil," in *Alvin Plantinga*, ed. James E. Tomberlin and Peter van Inwagen. Dordrecht: Reidel, 1985: 225–55.

Ahern, M. B. *The Problem of Evil*. London: Routledge and Kegan Paul, 1971.

Boorse, Christopher, "Wright on Functions," *Philosophical Review* 85 (1976): 70–86.

Hare, Peter H., and Edward H. Madden. *Evil and the Concept of God*. Springfield: Charles C. Thomas, 1968.

—. "Evil and Inconclusiveness," *Sophia* (Australia) 11 (1972): 8–12.

Hick, John. *Evil and the God of Love*. New York: Harper & Row, 1966.

Hume, David. *Dialogues concerning Natural Religion*, ed. Richard Popkin. Indianapolis: Hackett, 1980.

Kane, Stanley. "Theism and Evil," *Sophia* (Australia) 9 (1970): 14–21.

Mavrodes, George I. *Belief in God: A Study in the Epistemology of Religion*. New York: Random House, 1970.

Moser, Paul K. "Natural Evil and the Free Will Defence," *International Journal for Philosophy of Religion* 15 (1984): 49–56.

Pargetter, Robert. "Evil is Evidence against the Existence of God," *Mind* 85 (1976): 242–45.

Plantinga, Alvin. "The Probabilistic Argument from Evil," *Philosophical Studies* 35 (1979): 1–53.

—. "Reason and Belief in God," in *Faith and Rationality: Reason and Belief in God*, ed. Alvin Plantinga and Nicholas Wolterstorff. Notre Dame: University of Notre Dame Press, 1983; 16–93.

Reichenbach, Bruce. "The Inductive Argument from Evil," *American Philosophical Quarterly* 17 (1980); 221–27.

Ruse, Michael. *The Philosophy of Biology*. London: Hutchingson, 1973.

Sircello, Guy. *A New Theory of Beauty*. Princeton: Princeton University Press, 1975.

Stump, Eleonore. "Knowledge, Freedom and the Problem of Evil," *International Journal for the Philosophy of Religion* 14 (1983): 49–58.

Swinburne, Richard. *The Existence of God*. Oxford: Clarendon Press, 1979.

Wykstra, Steven. "The Humean Obstacle to Evidential Arguments from Suffering: On Avoiding the Evils of 'Appearance'," *International Journal for the Philosophy of Religion*, 16 (1984): 73–93.

Yandell, Keith E. "Ethics, Evils, and Theism," *Sophia* 8 (1969a): 18–28.

—."A Premature Farewell to Theism," *Religious Studies* 5 (1969b): 251–55.

—. 'Theism and Evil: A Reply," *Sophia* 11 (1972): 1–7.

4.3

'SOME (TEMPORARILY) FINAL THOUGHTS ON EVIDENTIAL ARGUMENTS FROM EVIL'

William P. Alston

I

I have been assigned the unenviable job of "clean-up hitter." The baseball metaphor, though of obvious application, can be misleading in more than one way. So far from aiming to bring the previous batters home (to their intended destination), my efforts will be much more often directed to stranding them on the base paths. Moreover, the targets of my discussion are largely drawn from the opposing team, the members of which are bending their efforts to keeping me from making solid contact with the ball. Perhaps a more felicitous term for the assignment would be "groundskeeper." My assignment is to restore the playing field to its pristine state after the depredations wrought by my predecessors.

Extricating myself from these athletic metaphors, it goes without saying that any "final word" on this topic is final only until the next round of comment and countercomment. My aim in this essay is to draw some of the threads of recent discussion into the fabric I am inclined to weave. No doubt, many of my colleagues would discern a different pattern. More specifically, I will offer some second thoughts on an earlier essay of mine (Alston 1991: see n. 5), then seek to do a better job of bringing out what I take to be the fatal weakness in evidential atheological arguments from evil.

William P. Alston, 'Some (Temporarily) Final Thoughts on Evidential Arguments from Evil', in D. Howard-Snyder (ed.), *The Evidential Argument from Evil* (Bloomington, IN: Indiana University Press, 1996), pp. 311–32.

II

The main reason why my 1991 essay is not more successful is that I was trying to do two quite different things that did not smoothly blend into a unified presentation. First, I wanted to neutralize the arguments of Rowe and Russell, arguments based on particularly refractory cases of evil. Second, I wanted to use various theodicies for a purpose for which they were not intended, viz., as a source of *possibilities* for God's purpose in permitting various evils, possibilities that, so I claimed, we cannot be in an epistemic position to dismiss. I endeavored to use the second project as a way of carrying out the first. But this turned out not to be a very effective way of dismantling their arguments. Indeed, I candidly acknowledge in the essay that from the theodicies I consider we can glean at most some unexcludable possibilities for part of God's reasons for allowing the particular cases of evil they focus on. I appeal to the live possibility of divine reasons unenvisaged by us to take up the slack, and I still think it is sufficient to take up whatever slack there is, including 100 percent if needed. But I now prefer to drop the rehearsal of theodicies and criticize the Rowe-Russell arguments in a somewhat different way.

III

As already indicated, I want to do a better job of bringing out the ineffectiveness of arguments that start from our inability to discern a sufficient reason God might have for permitting certain evils. But since I will be concentrating on versions of the argument Rowe has already published, I should first explain why I do not abandon that project and concentrate instead on the somewhat different Bayesian argument he presents in "The Evidential Argument from Evil: A Second Look" (1996). Rowe's stated motivation for this replacement concerns his disenchantment with the enumerative induction from (P) "No good we know of justifies an omnipotent, omniscient, perfectly good being in permitting E1 and E2 (the sufferings of Bambi and Sue)" to (Q) "No good at all justifies an omnipotent, omniscient, perfectly good being in permitting E1 and E2." He now holds that though this induction increases the antecedent probability of Q, it does not, as it stands, make Q more likely than not.[1] The new argument aims to show both that P, together with background evidence, renders Q more likely than not, and that P, with background evidence, renders theism less likely than not. If the latter succeeds, we can bypass Q altogether in the argument against theism from P. Before turning to the issues I will discuss in detail I will briefly indicate why I do not find this new argument convincing.

Like most Bayesian arguments directed to controversial philosophical positions, Rowe's relies on questionable probability assignments. The assignments I am inclined to question are the following:

1. Pr (G(theism)/k(background evidence))=.5.
2. Pr (P/not-G & k)=1.
3. Pr (P/G & k)=.5.

Though 1 is controversial, I don't choose to rest my case, even in part, on contesting it. I will focus on 2 and 3.

My point about 2 is not that the assignment is unjustified, *as Rowe construes the propositions involved*. My objection is to one of the construals. Rowe's basis for 2 is that P is entailed by not-G. Consider how P must be understood if this entailment is to hold. P is the denial of some proposition, and if it is to be entailed by not-G, that proposition has to be committed to G. Rowe spells out not-P as a conjunction.

> I. God exists, and some good known to us justifies him in permitting E1 and E2.

The denial of this conjunction, P, is a disjunction of the negations of the conjuncts.

> II. Either God does not exist, or no good known to us justifies God in permitting E1 and E2.

So construed, Rowe is clearly right in judging that not-G entails P.

But although II allows Rowe to make probability assignment 2, which is crucial for his argument, it is untenable on other grounds. The first thing to note is that II is compatible with:

> III. There are known goods that *would* be sufficient to justify God in permitting E1 and E2 if God should exist.

II is compatible with III since the truth of the first disjunct would be sufficient for II's truth.[2] If God does not exist, II is thereby true, and would still be true even if there are known goods that *would* justify God in permitting E1 and E2. But then an argument for not-G from P, on this reading of P, that is, on II, is *not* an argument from evil, at least not an argument from evil of the sort Rowe presumably means to be giving, at least not an argument of the sort he has given in the past. For the basis of *that* sort of argument is the contention that no known goods would justify God in permitting E1 and E2. Thus when P is construed such that it is compatible with the denial of that basis, something has gone seriously amiss with the enterprise.

But what if Rowe denies that the sort of argument he intends to be giving now is one that essentially depends on the denial of III? The trouble with that is that the support he actually gives for P runs as follows:

The main reason to believe P is this. When we reflect on some good we know of we can see that it is very likely, if not certain, that the good in question *either* is not good enough to justify God in permitting E1 or E2 *or* is such that an omnipotent, omniscient being could realize it (or some greater good) without having to permit E1 or E2.

What these considerations directly support is not-III, and hence Rowe can hardly claim that his argument does not depend on not-III. Moreover, if he is to claim that these considerations establish P, as presently construed, that is, as II, he owes us an argument that P follows from, or at least is strongly supported by, not-III.

Mark Brown pointed out to me that Rowe might attempt to justify the derivation as follows. A denial of III as just formulated would read:

IV. There are no known goods that *would* be sufficient to justify God in permitting E1 and E2 if God should exist.

Let's say that this is equivalent to the following subjunctive conditional:

V. If God should exist, there are no known goods that would be sufficient to justify Him in permitting E1 and E2.

Let's further take V to entail the material conditional:

VI. If God exists, there are no known goods that would be sufficient to justify Him in permitting E1 and E2.

And this is equivalent to the disjunction:

VII. Either God does not exist, or there are no known goods that would be sufficient to justify Him in permitting E1 and E2.

And if we make the existential commitment of the second disjunct explicit, this is Rowe's P on the present interpretation, that is, II.

The weak point in this argument is the claim that IV is equivalent to V or to any other subjunctive conditional. IV makes a categorical statement as to the nonexistence of anything of a certain sort in the actual world. It does not make this nonexistence contingent on the holding of some condition (God's existence) that, so far as it says, may or may not hold. Thus the derivation of P (on the present interpretation) from not-III never really gets started.[3]

The third assignment—$\Pr (P/G \;\&\; k) = .5$—damages the argument for another reason: it is question begging. Some, like Wykstra, will object that .5 is much too low a value, since they hold that theism leads us to expect that many of God's reasons for permitting evil will not be apparent to us.[4] But I think we are in no position to make any such probability assignment, even a rough, approximate one. As I argued in "The Inductive Argument from Evil and the Human Cognitive Condition,"[5] and as I hope to clarify below, we are in no position to judge whether among the goods known to us there are any that figure in a justifying reason God has (would have) for permitting one or another evil. Since this is at least one of the positions that Rowe must discredit if his argument is to be cogent, I regard any assignment of a probability to (P/ G & k) to beg the question against one of the major opposing positions. Since I can't go along with two of the three antecedent conditional probability assignments that are crucial to Rowe's Bayesian argument, I find it unsuccessful. That throws me back to a consideration of the simpler argument that, to put it roughly, moves from what we can discern of possible sufficient divine reasons for permitting certain evils to a conclusion as to whether there are such reasons.[6]

IV

In Rowe's essay "The Problem of Evil and Some Varieties of Atheism,"[7] the first premise of the argument is:

1. There exist instances of intense suffering which an omnipotent, omniscient being could have prevented without thereby losing some greater good or permitting some evil equally bad or worse.

Rowe then argues for 1 by maintaining that there are instances of suffering that, so far as we can see, satisfy 1, for example, the fawn (which I call "Bambi") trapped in a forest fire. From "Evil and Theodicy"[8] on, he uses what he considers a more discriminating formulation, distinguishing goods known to us from all others. Simplifying by taking the avoidance of a greater evil as special case of realizing a greater good, he argues for the functional equivalent of premise 1 in the previous argument as follows:

P. No good state of affairs we know of is such that an omnipotent, omniscient being's obtaining it would morally justify that being's permitting E1 or E2.

Therefore:

Q. No good state of affairs is such that an omnipotent, omniscient being's obtaining it would morally justify that being in permitting E1 or E2.

Rowe's argument for P is pretty much the same as before. The inference of Q from P is presented as a run-of-the-mill enumerative induction.

Although Rowe 1988 looks superior since it more finely discriminates aspects of the problem, it has led him to slight crucial problems. Moreover, Rowe 1979 provides a better starting point for the argument. Let me explain why.

The main trouble with Rowe 1988 is that it encourages the false belief that the only movement from the known to the unknown required by the argument is that involved in taking goods we know about as a representative sample of all goods (representative at least for their capacity to provide justifying reasons for permitting the evils on which Rowe concentrates). It encourages the supposition that we can tell whether *known goods* could provide God with a justifying reason for permitting certain evils. It is goods that fall beyond our ken that are a problem. But in fact there are two areas in which it is important to distinguish between what we know and what we do not know. By Rowe's lights, for God to be justified in permitting an evil there must be a sufficiently great good for the sake of which God permits it, *and it must be the case that that good could not have been realized without permitting that evil.* In looking for possible divine reasons for permitting evil, we must not only consider what candidate goods are out there, but also *what the conditions of realization of those goods are*, conditions that even Omnipotence would have to respect. And since there are both these aspects to the problem, we have to consider what we do and do not know about the conditions of realization of goods as well as about what goods there are. If we can't see any justifying reasons for God to permit Bambi's suffering, we have to consider not only whether there are goods we are not aware of that might figure in such reasons, but also whether there are conditions of realization of goods of which we are ignorant, conditions of realization *both of goods we are not cognizant of and of goods we are cognizant of*. Under the second heading, we have to consider whether some good we do have some conception of—eternal blessedness in heaven, for example—has, unbeknownst to us, some kind of suffering or God's permission thereof as a necessary precondition. This consideration is as crucial to the problem as considering whether there may be goods, undreamed of by us, that play a justifying role.[9]

Because there is just as big a problem in moving from known interconnections to all interconnections as there is in moving from known goods to all goods, the argument can be more fruitfully addressed in something more like its 1979 form. Rowe's empirical base can be put as follows: As far as he can see, on careful reflection, there is no known good, that is, anything we can envisage that we can see to be good, such that it is true both that (a) God could not realize it without permitting Bambi's or Sue's suffering, and (b) it is of such magnitude that God could reasonably take its realization to outweigh (or neutralize) the disvalue of Bambi's or Sue's suffering.[10] The crucial problem is that of moving from "so far as one can see no good satisfies both (a) and (b)" to the conclusion that "no good satisfies both (a) and (b)." This requires us not only to consider the possibility that some good that is totally outside our ken satisfies both (a) and (b), but also the possibility that some good we can envisage satisfies both conditions, even though we cannot see that it does.

I concede that Rowe is not idiosyncratic in failing to "see," with respect to any envisaged good, that it satisfies both (a) and (b). If I thought that this failure was due to a lack on his part, and that others can see what he cannot, I would not view the problem as basically a matter of whether we can infer "It isn't there" from "We can't see it." I agree that we cannot discern any sufficient divine reason for permitting Bambi's and Sue's suffering.

V

Now I come to the basic claim of this chapter. Given that we cannot see, of any divine reason we can envisage, that this reason would justify God in permitting Bambi's or Sue's suffering, does this justify us in supposing that there is no divine reason that would justify such a permission? Are we warranted in making this step from "I can't see any" to "There isn't any"? My contention is that we are not.

My reasons for believing this are not original. They have to do with our cognitive powers, vis-à-vis the reasons an omnipotent, omniscient, perfectly good being might have for His decisions and actions. I simply hope to bring out more clearly and in more detail than heretofore the basic lines of this insight, while avoiding distracting side issues.

Think of the matter in this way. We are considering whether the fact that we cannot see what sufficient justifying reason an omniscient, omnipotent being might have for doing something provides strong support for the supposition that no such reason is available for that being. I think the absurdity of the claim that it does provide strong support is evident on the face of it. But perhaps a series of analogues will make the matter clearer for those who disagree. There are various distinguishable aspects of the situation with which we are concerned here. We can find analogues for each of these aspects, analogues in which it is, I hope, obvious that we are not justified in the inference in question.

A. The most salient feature of the inference from "I can't see any sufficient reason for God to permit this evil" to "There is no sufficient reason for God to permit this evil" is that we are taking the insights attainable by finite, fallible human beings as an adequate indication of what is available in the way of reasons to an omniscient, omnipotent being. This aspect of the matter has not escaped the attention of critics of the argument. Ahern points out that our knowledge of the good and evils in the world and of the interconnections between things is very limited. Fitzpatrick adduces the deficiencies in our grasp of the divine nature. Wykstra and Plantinga point out that our cognitive capacities are much more inferior to God's than is a small child's to his parents.[11] I find these remarks to be generally well taken, though I am not sure that the limitations of our grasp of the divine nature is directly relevant to the issue. My version will be most similar to Wykstra's approach, but I will steer clear of his small child analogy, because, though I find it apt, it is also disanalogous in ways that leave loopholes for the opponent, as Rowe (1996). points out.

Suppose I am confronted with the activity or the productions of a master in a field in which I have no expertise. This may involve a scientific theory or experiment, a painting, a musical composition, an architectural design, or a chess move. I look at a theory of quantum phenomena and fail to see any reason for the author to draw the conclusions he draws. Does that entitle me to suppose that he has no sufficient reason for his conclusions? It certainly doesn't if I lack the requisite expertise. How could I expect to discern his reasons if I am too ignorant of the subject to follow what is going on? The same point is to be made of the following situations: (1) Lacking any training in or appreciation of painting, I fail to see why Veronese organized the figures in a certain painting as he did. Does that give me the right to conclude that he had no sufficient reason for doing so? (2) Being in the same position with respect to music, I fail to see any reason for Mozart to develop a theme as he did. Ditto. (3) Having only the sketchiest grasp of chess, I fail to see any reason for Karpov to have made the move he did at a certain point in a game. Does that entitle me to conclude that he had no good reason for making that move?

I take it that it will be beyond controversy that the answer to each of these questions is a resounding no. And why shouldn't the same response be made to the inference from "I can't see any sufficient reason for God to permit the sufferings of Bambi and Sue" to "God has no sufficient reason to do so"? Here too a judgment is made in the absence of any reason to suppose one has a sufficient grasp of the range of possible reasons open to the other party. Surely our purchase on what reasons God might have for His actions is as inadequate as the grasp of the judger in the other cases. Surely an omniscient, omnipotent being is further removed from any of us in this respect than a brilliant physicist is from one innocent of physics, or a Mozart is from one innocent of music, or Karpov is from a neophyte. Surely the extent to which God can envisage reasons for permitting a given state of affairs exceeds our ability to do so by *at least as much* as Einstein's ability to discern the reason for a physical theory exceeds the ability of one ignorant of physics.

B. The above analogies were maximally similar to the target situation. They, like the latter, involved judgments concerning the reasons someone else might have for a line of action. As such they are well suited for bringing out a crucial feature of our target case—the incapacity of the judge to make a sound judgment. But less close analogies can bring out other aspects of the situation. Another prominent feature of our central case is that it involves trying to determine whether there is a so-and-so in a territory the extent and composition of which is largely unknown to us. Or at least it is a territory such that we have no way of knowing the extent to which its constituents are unknown to us. How can we possibly think that we have a reliable internal map of the diversity of considerations (even limiting this to values and the conditions of their realization) that are available to an omniscient being? Given what we know of our limitations—the variety of questions we don't know how to answer, the possibilities we can't exclude of realms of being to which we have no access, our ignorance even of many of the details of human history, and so on—how can we suppose that we are in a position to estimate the extent to which the possibilities we can envisage for divine reasons for permitting evils even come close to exhausting the possibilities open to an omniscient being? It is surely the better part of wisdom to acknowledge that we are groping in the dark in assessing the extent to which we can survey the whole field.

And now for the analogies. This is like going from "We haven't found any signs of life elsewhere in the universe" to "There isn't life elsewhere in the universe." It is like someone who is culturally and geographically isolated going from "As far as I have been able to tell, there is nothing on earth beyond this forest" to "There is nothing on earth beyond this forest." Or, to get a bit more sophisticated, it is like someone who reasons "We are unable to discern anything beyond the temporal bounds of our universe," where those bounds are the Big Bang and the final collapse, to "There is nothing beyond the temporal bounds of our universe."

These examples involve a "territory" in the literal sense of a spatial or a temporal "region." But there are analogous cases in which the "territory" is of a more conceptual sort. Can we anticipate future intellectual or artistic developments? No, at least not in any detail; for if they were predicted in detail, they would already have occurred and would not be future. Even very unspecific predictions are risky at best and often turn out to be incorrect. Consider the eighteenth-century confidence that all that remained for physics to do was to tidy up and extend Newtonian mechanics and Comte's example of a useless metaphysical speculation in science—the chemical composition of the stars! Who in the late nineteenth century could have foreseen the development of atonal music, not to mention the still weirder developments that have been assaulting our ears in this century. Our inability to survey the "space" of possible future developments and segregate them into the more or less likely subverts any attempt to argue from "So far as I can see there will not be such-and-such a type of development" to "There will not be any such development." Again, can there be intelligent beings with some non-hydro-carbon-based chemistry? We don't have a clue as to how to assess the possibilities and probabilities here. The fact that we don't see how non-hydrocarbon-based animal life is possible is little ground to suppose that it is not possible. These cases are closely analogous to our situation with respect to determining whether God has a justifying reason for permitting Bambi's or Sue's suffering, on the basis of our inability to ascertain such a reason. Here too we are in no position to map the "territory" of possible reasons. We lack the resources to determine the extent to which the possibilities we can envisage and understand exhaust the field, and to determine the extent, variety, and detailed constitution of the terra incognita.

These analogies warn us not to make our cognitive limitations a recipe for what there is. If we are unable to map the territory within which to look for something, we are correspondingly unable to infer from our inability to find something that there isn't one there. It will be instructive to look at Bruce Russell's objection to this position:

> the view that there are reasons beyond our ken that would justify God, if he exists, in allowing all the suffering we see [is] like the view that there are blue crows beyond our powers of observation. Once we have conducted the relevant search for crows (looking all over the world in different seasons and at crows at different stages of maturity), we are justified in virtue of that search in believing there are no crows beyond our powers of observation which are relatively different from the crows we've seen . . . Similarly, once we've conducted the relevant search for moral reasons to justify allowing the relevant suffering (thinking hard about how allowing the suffering would be needed to realize sufficiently weighty goods, reading and talking to others who have thought about the same problem), we are justified in believing that there are no morally sufficient reasons for allowing that suffering.[12]

The crow search is crucially different from the divine reasons search in just the respect brought out by this second set of analogies. The territory of the search is well mapped. Furthermore, we know that, by the nature of the beast, a crow is open to sensory observation, given suitable conditions. Hence, given a careful enough search, we can be amply justified in supposing that there are no blue crows. But the search for divine reasons differs in just these respects. We have no idea how to map the relevant territory—what its boundaries are and what variety it contains. Nor can we be assured that the cognitive powers we possess are sufficient for detecting the quarry if it exists. Hence, contrary to what Russell intended, the crow case nicely displays the defect of the inference in question.

In Alston 1991, I presented some considerations that were designed to indicate the rationality of supposing that there is an indefinitely large realm of facts, evaluative and otherwise, that lie beyond our ken. The pervasive phenomenon of human intellectual progress shows that at any given time in the past there were many things not known or even conceived that came to be conceived and known at a later stage. The induction is obvious. It would be highly irrational to suppose that we have reached the limit of this process and have ascertained everything there is to be learned. This creates a presumption that with respect to values, as well as their conditions of realization, there is much that lies beyond our present grasp.

Several critics have found fault with this line of reasoning, but they have generally misread the argument. Here is an example from Richard Gale's essay:

> What Alston [is] doing is likening morality to a "natural kind"—a kind of entity possessed of an essential nature that is to be unearthed by scientific inquiry, there being some analogous method of inquiry into the inner, hidden nature of morality to that employed in science. But morality is a paradigm of a nonnatural kind, one whose "nature," that is, basic principles and rules, is completely on the surface, patently obvious to the gaze of all participants in the moral language game. A hidden morality is no morality.[13] *Pace* Alston, there is no "history of the apprehension of values . . . parallel to the history" of scientific discovery.[14]

The misreading here comes from supposing that the intellectual progress to which I appeal is entirely or mostly a matter of discovering the essential nature of some natural kind. But if one will go back to the relevant passage of Alston 1991, one will see that my main emphasis was on advances—getting into a position to conceptualize aspects of the world that were previously hidden from us, rather than discovering the inner nature of a kind of thing with which we were already familiar. Indeed, my initial examples, omitted from Gale's quotation, were of conceptual developments in philosophy. My argument was not specially concerned with scientific advances.

But leaving aside issues of Alstonian exegesis, I cannot agree that this appeal to "moral language games" scotches the idea of moral progress, much less progress in the apprehension of values generally. Let's agree that membership in a moral community requires the internalization of certain basic moral rules, principles, and concepts. But that does not preclude the realization of new principles and values, any more than the fact that membership in a scientific community requires the internalization of certain concepts, "paradigms," methods, etc. precludes new scientific discoveries. A language game approach fails to support Gale's ironclad moral conservatism.

I have been arguing that we are not in a position to assert that there are no sufficient justifying reasons for God to permit Bambi's and Sue's suffering. I have not argued that we cannot discern such reasons, but rather that we should not expect to be able to discern such reasons if they exist. (I have not argued that it is *impossible* for us to discern God's reasons, only that our failure to do so is no indication of their nonexistence). I take seriously the possibility that God would not make us privy to His reasons for permitting a particular case of suffering, would not even communicate those reasons to the sufferer herself.[15] And theism has been attacked on just this point. Some argue that it is incompatible with the goodness of God to leave us in ignorance as to why He permits us to suffer.[16] Surely, these people say, a loving Father would explain to His children why He is allowing them to undergo their suffering if He could. And since God is omnipotent and omniscient, He could certainly do so. My response to this is that our ignorance of God's reasons for permitting our sufferings is just one more instance of evil the reason for permitting which we cannot see. Hence the present objection simply amounts to saying that my position implies that there is a certain kind of evil God's reason for permitting which we cannot discern. But of course! That's not an objection; it's a restatement of the common starting point from which my opponents and I go in opposite directions.

Russell maintains that if "after failing to find sufficiently weighty moral reasons to justify God's allowing [Sue's suffering] we are *not* justified in believing there are none" "it will follow that we are also not justified in believing that some human being who could easily have stopped the heinous crime did something wrong in failing to intervene." An obvious retort, as Russell notes, is that "we cannot expect to discern *God's* reasons (his motives) for allowing the murder, but can expect to discern *the onlooker's*." But he holds that this "has no bearing on the question at issue. The question at issue is whether we must be unable to judge that there are no *justifying* reasons for human nonintervention if we are unable to judge that there are none for divine nonintervention. I have argued that we must". The argument is that if God could have justifying reason for allowing the brutality, so could the human onlooker, for that same reason could justify both noninterventions. But this badly misconstrues moral justification. Whether I am morally justified in doing something is not a function of whether there are objective facts that could be used by *someone* as a morally good reason for doing it. It is rather a function of whether *I* have such a morally good reason for doing it. And it is quite possible (highly likely, I would say) that God should have such a reason that no human being could have—either because we are incapable of grasping the reason or because the reason concerns features of God's relation to the situation that we cannot share.

This completes my case for the thesis that the fact that we are unable to see any justifying reason for God to permit Bambi's or Sue's suffering gives us no reason of any weight to suppose that God has, or would have if He existed, no justifying reason for these permissions. Being unable to estimate the extent to which what we can discern exhausts the possibilities, we are in no position to suppose that our inability to find a justifying divine reason is a sufficient ground for supposing there is none. We are in the kind of situation illustrated by the analogues I have set out.[17]

I would like to stress that my argument is neither based on, nor does it issue in, a generalized skepticism. For that matter, it is not based on, nor does it support, a general theological skepticism. It is compatible with our knowing quite a bit about the divine nature, activities, purposes, and relations with humanity. The conclusion of the argument is only that we are unable to form sound judgments on whether there are justifying reasons for God's permitting certain evils. Indeed, it is crucial to my argument to contrast our cognitive situation vis-à-vis divine reasons for evil with our cognitive situation vis-à-vis many other things, highlighting the unfavorable state of the former by contrast with our epistemically favorable condition in the latter. I make this point because more than one critic of Alston 1991 has made it a reproach to my position that it leads to general skepticism.

VI

I will now apply the contentions of section V to Rowe's arguments for atheism. In Rowe 1979 the "evidential" premise was:

1. There exist instances of intense suffering which an omnipotent, omniscient being could have prevented without thereby losing some greater good or permitting some evil equally bad or worse.

The above considerations subvert Rowe's argument for 1: "Since the fawn's intense suffering was preventable [by God] and, so far as we can see, pointless, doesn't it appear that premise (1) of the argument is true . . . ?" They are designed to show that the fact that we are unable, even on the most careful reflection, to discern any point to the fawn's suffering (i.e., any good reason God would have for allowing it) does not justify the claim that it has no point.

The application to the 1988 argument is more complicated. In Rowe 1988 the argument is set up as follows.

P. No good state of affairs we know of is such that an omnipotent, omniscient being's obtaining it would morally justify that being's permitting E1 or E2.

Therefore:

Q. No good state of affairs is such that an omnipotent, omniscient being's obtaining it would morally justify that being in permitting E1 or E2.

From Q we infer that no such being exists, since there would be no suffering that this being is not morally justified in permitting.

This structuring of the argument, I have argued, gives the false impression that the main problem is one of generalizing to all goods from known goods, whereas the main problem is not that but rather the inference from "We cannot discern any way in which God would be morally justified in permitting E1 or E2" to "There is no such way." When we apply my objections to this latter inference to the 1988 version of Rowe's argument, we get the following:

First, my objection hits at Rowe's case for P itself. That case is substantially equivalent to his case for 1 in Rowe 1979. To repeat once more his new summary statement:

> When we reflect on some good we know of we can see that it is very likely, if not certain, that the good in question *either* is not good enough to justify God in permitting E1 or E2 *or* is such that an omnipotent, omniscient being could realize it (or some greater good) without having to permit E1 or E2.

This support for P does not explicitly involve an inference from "I can't see any way in which this good would justify God in permitting E1 or E2" to "This good does not justify God in permitting E1 or E2." Indeed, Rowe 1988 explicitly disavows any reliance on such an inference:

> I don't mean simply that we can't see how some good we know about (say, my enjoyment on smelling a good cigar) would justify an omnipotent being's permitting E1 or E2. I mean that we can see how such a good would not justify an omnipotent being's permitting E1 or E2.

Here Rowe denies that he is moving from "Can't see" to "Isn't." Still, that inference is implicit. In claiming that for any good we can envisage he can see that realizing that good would not morally justify God in permitting E1 or E2, he is relying on what he can "see," on careful reflection, to be all the relevant considerations. Hence, if he is unwarranted in moving from that to "The obtaining of no such good would justify God in permitting E1 or E2," his case for P is without force. So if I have subverted that move, I have subverted Rowe's case for P.

One might think that my objections to this last inference do not have the force I was claiming for them in section V, when, as here, the discussion is restricted to goods we can envisage. For in those cases are we not in a position to judge whether the realization of any such good would justify God in permitting certain cases of evil, even if we are not in such a position vis-à-vis goods generally?

In a word, "no," for two reasons. The first reason has to do with our "knowledge" of the goods. Rowe rightly says that he does "not mean to limit us to goods that we know to have occurred" or "to those goods and goods that we know will occur in the future. I mean to include goods that we have some grasp of, even though we have no knowledge at all that they have occurred or ever will occur." Moreover, Rowe is thinking of good-types rather than good-tokens. For when he considers a good that, so far as he knows, never has occurred and never will occur, he cannot be directing his thought to some particular token. Finally, he does not require any particular degree of adequacy of grasp of the good in question. He says that he will include "experiencing complete felicity in the everlasting presence of God" as a known good, "even though we don't have a very clear grasp of what this great good involves."

These clarifications imply that a good's being "known" does not necessarily put us in a favorable position to assess its magnitude and hence does not necessarily put us in a favorable position to say whether its obtaining would justify God's permitting a certain evil (assuming it could not be realized by God without His permitting that evil). Note that when Rowe contends, with respect to specific goods, that they are not of sufficient worth for their realization to justify permitting Bambi's or Sue's suffering, he always picks good-types with many tokens of which he is familiar, for example, his enjoyment of smelling a good cigar or Sue's pleasure upon receiving some toys. Surely we are not in nearly as good a position to assess the degree of value of goods we have never experienced as we are with those we have experienced. This point clearly applies to "experiencing complete felicity in the everlasting presence of God," where "we don't have a clear grasp of what this great good involves." Although, as this example suggests, deficiencies in our grasp of the details of a good tend to go along with lack of experience of tokens, we have more of a grasp of some unexperienced goods than of others, just because some unexperienced goods have a stronger analogy with experienced ones. I have a much better grasp of the good of writing great poetry than I do of complete fulfillment of my nature, even though I have experienced neither. To sum up, when we consider unexperienced goods of which we have only a minimal grasp—and it may be that the livest candidates for goods the realization of which would justify God in permitting suffering all fall within this class—we are in a bad position to determine whether the magnitude of the good is such as to make it worthwhile for God to permit a certain evil in order to make its realization possible.[19]

However, the main bar to our being justified in accepting P (and this is the second reason) has to do with the state of our knowledge of the conditions of realization for various goods. Here the extent of our grasp of one or another good is very important. We have a pretty good handle on the conditions under which Rowe's favorite—the enjoyment of smelling a good cigar—would be realized. But when it comes to *experiencing complete felicity in the eternal presence of God*, we have clearly gotten out of our depth. Perhaps we can make a stab at enumerating states of character that would fit someone for this and those that would interfere with it, but for all we know there are other conditions for this supreme fulfillment of which we have little or no idea. And what about the states of character just alluded to, for example, pride and humility? We undoubtedly have some idea as to social influences, interpersonal interactions, lines of conduct, regimens, etc., that are conducive to one or the other. But our understanding of all this is fragmentary, being largely limited to natural, this-worldly factors, in contrast to supernatural influences that might be involved in God's plans, such as the sanctifying activity of the Holy Spirit. I am not trying to show that there *are* conditions of realization that are unknown to us. On the contrary. By mentioning such putative possibilities, I mean to indicate that we are not in a position to determine the extent to which there are such additional conditions and what they are. Hence we are in no position to assert, with respect to a given good that is not disqualified by a low degree of value, that a certain kind of suffering is not required for the realization of that good.

We are frequently reminded that the attainment of a particular good justifies God's permission of a certain evil only if an omnipotent being could not realize that state of affairs without permitting that evil or some evil just as bad or worse. And that is a stringent requirement indeed. But this is to take too piecemeal an approach. Suppose God permits certain evils to befall Sam because He sees those evils are needed to turn Sam in the direction of spiritual development, which in turn is required for the supreme consummation of eternal loving communion with Himself. Presumably God could realize this last end without these prerequisites. He could bring it about by fiat that Sam is in that condition. Does that show that the reason for permitting those evils is not justifying? No. For it may be that if God were to confer the beatific vision by arbitrary fiat, rather than as the outcome of a "natural"[20] course of development, that would militate against other features of the divine master plan. For example, it might violate regularities that are needed for some other purpose.[21] Hence, even if God could achieve the particular good without permitting this evil, or some evil equally bad or worse, doing so might involve too much a sacrifice elsewhere in the scheme. It may be that if we specify the justifying good in global enough terms, it would include everything that is relevant to the case. Thus, with respect to this case we could specify the good in question not just as Sam's enjoying eternal loving communion with God but as Sam's attaining this *in a certain way*. But if we were to beef up the specification so that it includes everything relevant, it might be too comprehensive for us to comprehend. When we are at the level of the specific, limited sorts of good Rowe and others mention, the point made in this paragraph holds.

Thus, when we consider what we justifiably believe about "known" goods, there are two factors that can prevent us from justifiably accepting P. First, our grasp of the nature of the good may not be sufficient for us to assess it properly for degree and kind of value. Second, our grasp of the conditions of its realization may not be sufficient for us to say with justified confidence that God could have realized that good without permitting the evil in question and without making too much of a sacrifice of good (or prevention of evil) elsewhere in the scheme.

So much for P. Now since, on my view, the crucial inference is from "We can't find a reason" to "There isn't one," rather than from "No known goods constitute a reason" to "No goods constitute a reason," the burden no longer rests on an enumerative induction from known goods to all goods; hence questions of representativeness of samples and the like no longer bulk large.

Indeed, as I construe the argument there is no way of structuring it so that the distinction between known and unknown goods plays an important part. The most we can do with that distinction is the following: The consideration of known goods, I have urged, leaves us with unelimated possibilities for a sufficient justifying reason for God's permitting some evil. When we then consider the idea that there may be values that are currently not even conceived or envisaged by us, that simply widens the gap between "We can't discern a sufficient divine justifying reason for permitting the evil" and "There is no such reason." For since we cannot be justified in denying that there are values we have not discerned, and since if any of those values should provide God with a justifying reason for permitting a certain evil we would not be able to discern it, that gives us an additional reason for supposing that "We can't discern a reason" does not provide strong support for "There is no such reason."

But even though the known-unknown good distinction can play no major role in the discussion, I still want to maintain, as I did rather briefly in Alston 1991, that, as the argument is set up in Rowe 1988, the enumerative induction from P to Q is weak. Rowe claimed that "we are justified in making this inference in the same way we are justified in making the many inferences we constantly make from the known to the unknown . . . If I encounter a fair number of pit bulls and all of them are vicious, I have reason to believe that all pit bulls are vicious."

In Alston 1991 I take up this example to make the point that we have general reasons for thinking that marked temperamental features are breed specific in dogs. Hence if all or most of the members of a given breed we have observed display a certain temperament, we are on solid ground in taking our sample to be representative of the breed in this regard. I contrasted this with Rowe's generalization from known goods to all goods by making the same kind of point I have been making in this chapter concerning our inability to "map" the relevant "territory": "We have no way of drawing boundaries around the total class of goods; we are unable to anticipate what may lie in its so-far-unknown sub-class." Thus we are not in the kind of position for generalizing from a sample that we are in when making an inductive generalization about temperamental features of a breed of dogs from a proper sample of that breed.

Unfortunately, my formulation there, though ambiguous on this point, could well be interpreted as claiming that anyone making an inductive generalization has to *justifiably believe* that his sample is representative in the relevant respect in order to be justified in making the inductive generalization and hence in believing the conclusion on the basis of that induction.[22] Such a strong higher-level requirement would not be satisfied by most inductive conclusions we ordinarily judge to be sound. For most (relatively naive) inducers are innocent of any justified beliefs about representativeness of samples, innocent, in fact, of any such beliefs at all. Hence I am anxious to avoid holding individual inducers responsible for having sufficient justification for a higher-level belief about the representativeness of their samples.

Well, then, exactly what am I requiring for a sound inductive inference? I can take the consideration of this question as an opportunity to be more explicit as to what I claim Rowe, or anyone else, lacks in inferring "God would have no sufficient reason for permitting E1 and E2" from "I can see no sufficient reason for permitting E1 and E2." I have spoken in terms of our (anyone's) not being in a "position" to take our inability to see any such reason as a sufficient basis for supposing there is no such reason. But what is it to be in a "position" to do this? Just what is it, in my view, that we lack and that we must have in order to be justified in affirming "There is no such reason"?

Going back to my "territory" metaphor, we can distinguish a more subjective and a more objective sense in which there might be an adequate "mapping" of the territory, one that must "be there" if we can warrantedly take our inability to find something as a good reason for supposing it isn't there. The more subjective sense is the one I have just rejected—the subject's being justified in beliefs about the territory that imply that one's inference basis is sufficiently representative of that territory. The most objective sense is this: one's sample being in fact representative of the territory, whether one knows this, justifiably believes it, or believes it at all. That isn't the sense I want either. To condemn my opponent on those grounds would be to claim that in fact what we can discern about these matters is not a fair representation of what is there. And, of course, I don't want to claim that, for I have argued that we are in no position to determine whether or not that is the case.

So how is my position to be understood? The preceding paragraph naturally suggests that what I need is something between the subjective and objective extremes; and that is where I shall look. The clue to the via media lies in the social dimension of knowledge. When I say that *we* are in no position to suppose that what we can discern is an adequate guide to what God can discern, the plural form of the first-person pronoun is no mere *façon de parler*. What it takes for *me* to be in a position to make that inference is that there are, in the larger community with which I am at least potentially in effective contact, persons who have sufficient reason to think that what we can discern of justifying reasons is an adequate guide to what justifying reasons God has available to Him. In another version of this general idea, *this is known* (within my community), even if I personally do not have that knowledge. The social availability of a justification for supposing my sample to be representative is something that is objective vis-à-vis me and any other individual cognitive subject, though, since it is a fact about human knowledge of (justified belief about) the world, rather than a fact about that world itself, it is not as severely objective as the second alternative I rejected earlier. By this device I am enabled to steer between the Scylla of requiring higher level knowledge of each believer and the Charybdis of making assumptions about the real state of affairs with respect to the human and divine situation vis-à-vis justifying reasons. Each of us is in no position to infer "God has no reason" from "We can't see any reason that He has," just because none of us is justified in supposing that our insights into these matters are a sufficient guide to the way it is with God.[23]

This completes my current criticism of the view that from the fact that, so far as we can see, there are no justifying reasons for God to permit Bambi's or Sue's suffering, we may reasonably conclude that there are no such reasons.

VII

Finally, I want to say something about the explanatory argument developed by Paul Draper.[24] Draper considers an hypothesis that is an alternative to theism, viz., the "Hypothesis of Indifference" (HI):

> HI: Neither the nature nor the condition of sentient beings on earth is the result of benevolent or malevolent actions performed by nonhuman persons.

He then argues that HI explains O (the facts about the distribution of pain and pleasure in the world)[25] much better than theism. And from this he infers that we have a prima facie good reason to believe that theism is less probable than HI. We could also mount an argument of this general sort in which the explanandum is the fact that we can't discern any sufficient justifying reason for God's permitting certain cases of suffering, rather than O.

Elsewhere, Draper takes me to task for supposing that my claim that we are unable to determine whether God would have a justifying reason to permit certain evils implies that "all probabilistic arguments from evil fail." He points out correctly that this thesis does not tell at all against explanatory arguments like his, for such arguments do not depend on supposing that "it is unlikely that an omnipotent and omniscient being would have a morally sufficient reason to permit certain evils." It is true that in Alston 1991 I use the terms *inductive*, *empirical*, and *probabilistic* indifferently to characterize the kind of argument I am criticizing, and then at the end of the essay talk as if the considerations adduced there dispose of all such arguments. This was sloppy of me. I never meant to be discussing explanatory arguments, even by implication, though I can see how my words might lead someone to think so.

But what about explanatory arguments like Draper's? Draper takes it that the fact that HI explains O much better than theism tells significantly against theism. But, as Plantinga points out, this depends on the relevance of this explanatory task to the evaluation of theism, and that is a complicated matter. Here I shall pursue some other issues.

First, does Draper really succeed in comparing two *explanations* of O? Just what are these alleged explanations? The only thing he does to identify them is to say that they are provided by theism and HI respectively. But that does not suffice to specify any particular explanations. This can be seen by noting that the following are two different explanations of O:

1. God permits O to be the case so that human beings will have a chance to develop good moral characters.
2. God permits O to be the case so that the creation may exhibit as much variety as possible.

These are both theistic explanations of O, but they are by no means the same explanation. Thus merely citing theism, that is stating that O is due to God, does not suffice to *explain* O. At most, it indicates where we are to look for an explanation but without actually providing an explanation of that sort. It only says that the explanation is of some theistic sort.

The same point is to be made vis-à-vis the alleged explanation by HI. HI merely stipulates that O is not due to the actions of nonhuman persons. That obviously leaves a tremendous field of possibilities open. Until the field is considerably narrowed down, we don't have any particular explanation of O. Is O due to blind chance, to the inevitable workings of mechanical forces, to some Bergsonian élan vital, or what? Simply to invoke HI is to tell us one kind of thing that is not involved. It is to rule out one large class of explanations, including those that count as theistic. But an innumerable throng is left.

Draper may insist that he has indeed specified two explanations. It is just that he has not spelled them out completely. Many things we count as explanations leave loose ends dangling. We explain an instance of corrosion by citing the presence of an acid, without spelling out the chemical laws involved. We explain the bridge's collapse by citing an abnormal load without specifying the magnitude of the load or saying how much the bridge is capable of supporting. Why don't Draper's explanations exemplify the same kind of incompleteness?

The answer is that there is a difference between an incomplete explanation and no explanation at all. A genuine explanation throws light on the explanandum; it enables us to see why it happened or was brought into being. The incomplete explanations just cited do that. They genuinely throw light on why the thing in question happened. But neither theism nor HI throws light in the same way on the fact that O obtains. They merely tell us, in the case of theism, the kind of being that is ultimately responsible and, in the case of HI, the kind of being that is not ultimately responsible. This would be like saying of the growth of plants that it is due to the sun, without saying what it is about the sun and its activity that brings this about. It would be like saying of certain administrative arrangements that they were instituted by Mr. Carter without saying anything about why he did so or for what purpose. And as for HI, we don't get even that much. The "HI explanation" is like saying of those administrative arrangements that they were not instituted by Mr. Carter, and letting it go at that.

So if Draper wants to maintain that theism suffers epistemically because some other explanation of O is markedly superior to a theistic explanation, he will have to give us a theistic and a nontheistic explanation to work with. Otherwise, he is just beating the air to no purpose.

But perhaps it is a mistake to think that Draper seriously means to be talking about explanation. In Draper 1989, after formulating "C: HI explains the facts O reports much better than theism does," Draper goes on to explain his use of "explain" as follows:

> I will reformulate C as the claim that the facts O reports are much more surprising on theism than they are on HI, or, more precisely, that the antecedent probability of O is much greater on the assumption that HI is true than on the assumption that theism is true. By the "antecedent" probability of O, I mean O's probability independent of (rather than temporally prior to) the observations and testimony it reports.

He further lays it down that "The probabilities employed in C are epistemic ones rather than, for example, statistical, physical, or logical probabilities." And in a note to this statement he writes:

> The concept of epistemic probability is an ordinary concept of probability for which no adequate philosophical analysis has, in my opinion, been proposed. As a first approximation, however, perhaps the following analysis will do:
>> Relative to K, p is epistemically more probable than q, where K is an epistemic situation and p and q are propositions, just in case any fully rational person in K would have a higher degree of belief in p than in q.

The reason this indicates that Draper is not seriously concerned with explanation is that there is no sense of *explain* in which "P explains x better than Q" *means* "The antecedent probability of x is greater on P than on Q." First of all, there are many cases of epistemic probability in which there is no explanatory relation at all. Consider inductive generalization. The antecedent probability of "This specimen of copper melted at 327 degrees C" is greater on "Copper always melts at 327 degrees C" than on "Copper sometimes melts at 327 degrees C." But neither of the latter goes any way at all toward explaining the fact that this specimen of copper melted at 327 degrees C. And going the other way, "Copper always melts at 327 degrees C" has a higher probability on "All observed samples of copper melted at 327 degrees C" than on "Half of the observed samples of copper melted at 327 degrees C." And even more obviously the behavior of the observed samples contributes nothing to the explanation of the general fact. To take another kind of example, the probability of "Robinson shot the victim" is greater on "Potter (an eminently respectable citizen with no self-interest in the matter) testified that he saw Robinson shoot the victim" than on "Wheelwright (a convicted criminal who is trying to get the best plea bargain) testified that he saw Robinson shoot the victim." But in neither case does the testimony do anything to explain the fact that Robinson shot the victim. This point could be illustrated by many other sorts of cases.

Secondly, comparative goodness of explanations doesn't always hang on the comparison of antecedent probability of the explanandum on the explanans. Sometimes it hangs on how well the explanans fits in with the rest of our knowledge, whether the fact cited by the explanans actually obtains, comparative simplicity of the rivals, and many other things. Thus the failure of my amplifier has at least as great a probability on the hypothesis of gremlins as on the hypothesis of a defective transistor. But we would prefer the latter explanation for the first two reasons just mentioned.

The moral of this is that one can't define *explain* in any way that strikes one's fancy. The term *explain* is certainly not perfectly precise; nor does it have only one meaning. But there are limits to its correct use. And Draper, I fear, has not identified even one meaning of "P explains x better than Q." At most, he has identified one factor that contributes to explanatory superiority.

This suggests that we should forget about explanation and take Draper to be concerned only with epistemic probability. How does the argument stack up in that case? Not very well. Draper supposes that whenever a set of facts, F, has a higher "antecedent probability" on q than on p, where q is inconsistent with p and is a "serious" hypothesis, then we have a prima facie good (epistemic) reason to reject q.[26] For counter examples to this claim, seem Plantinga's "On Being Evidentially Challenged" (in Howard-Snyder, ed., 1996).[27]

NOTES

1. William L. Rowe, "William Alston on the Problem of Evil," in *The Rationality of Belief and the Plurality of Faiths*, ed. Thomas D. Senor (Ithaca: Cornell University Press, 1994).
2. In note 8, ibid., Rowe contrasts his construal of P with not-III (in a slightly different wording) and explicitly disavows the latter as his understanding of P.
3. I am indebted to Rowe for pointing out some mistakes in two earlier attempts to say what is wrong with his present reading of P.
4. This is not quite accurate. As I will stress later, the category of justifying goods known to us is by no means identical to the category of justifying *reasons* known by us.
5. *Philosophical Perspectives* 5 (1991). Hereafter I will refer to this article as "Alston 1991."
6. One would like to determine just how this new argument of Rowe's is related to his earlier inductive argument from P to Q. For example, one would like to know whether the soundness of that induction is somehow presupposed in this Bayesian argument. To go into the matter thoroughly would be a major undertaking for which there is no room in this chapter. I will just point out that my objection to a probability assignment for P/G & k is closely related to my objections to supposing

that our inability to see a sufficient reason for God's permitting E1 and E2 provides no substantial basis for supposing that there is no such reason.

7. *American Philosophical Quarterly* 16 (1979); chapter 4.1 in this volume. Hereafter I refer to this article as "Rowe 1979."

8. *Philosophical Topics* 16 (1988). Hereafter I refer to this article as "Rowe 1988."

9. I am far from suggesting that Rowe is unaware of this. On the contrary, in presenting his case for P (for 1 in Rowe 1979), he often proceeds by attending to both facets of the question as to whether any known goods would provide God with a sufficient justifying reason for permitting, e.g., Bambi's suffering. In the passage I have quoted in which Rowe presents his case for P, he addresses himself to both facets of the problem. Nor is this a recent reform on his part. See Rowe 1988, 120–21, and Rowe 1979. Indeed, in the latter passage Rowe focuses exclusively on the conditions of realization rather than on the nature of the good. So if Rowe consistently exhibits awareness of both aspects of the problem, why am I making such a big deal out of this? Because the way his argument is structured from 1988 on inevitably focuses on the inference from known goods to all goods, and tends to divert us from the need to consider what we know about the conditions of realization. For example, in his later 1996 essay, he asks, "Under what conditions would P be true?" He mentions two conditions: (1) "the nonoccurrence of the known good (supposing there is just one) whose occurrence would justify God in permitting E1 or E2"; (2) "the nonexistence of God." Nothing is said about the conditions of realization of the good. True, Rowe does not claim that this list is exhaustive, but it is significant that he omits the crucial condition that his structuring of the argument tends to de-emphasize. Again, while Rowe has been quite concerned to defend his inference from "no known goods justify the permission" to "no goods justify the permission," he exhibits no such concern for the equally problematic inference from "our knowledge of interconnections does not indicate that the permission of E1 or E2 would be necessary for God to realize some sufficiently great good" to "there are no such interconnections."

10. I have represented Rowe's empirical base more modestly than he does. I have presented that base as "No good satisfies (a) and (b), so far as he can tell on careful reflection." But what he maintains is that on reflection "we can see [of any good we can envisage] that it is very likely, if not certain, that the good in question either is not good enough to justify God in permitting E1 or E2 or is such that an omnipotent, omniscient being could realize it (or some greater good) without having to permit E1 or E2" (1996; see also Rowe 1988, 120). Where I specify Rowe's starting point as a statement about what is the case *so far as he can see*, he claims that it is reasonable to believe that this is the case, that on reflection he can see it as "very likely, if not certain." I do not accept these more ambitious claims. In contesting them, I shall push the discussion back to what I take to lie behind them, viz., that no known goods satisfy both (a) and (b), so far as he can see on careful reflection. Rowe, I am supposing, takes this to adequately support the claim that no known good satisfies both (a) and (b). It is this inference that I will assess.

11. M. B. Ahern, *The Problem of Evil* (London: Routledge and Kegan Paul, 1971), 54–55, 57, 72–73; F. J. Fitzpatrick, "The Onus of Proof in Arguments about the Problem of Evil," *Religious Studies* 17 (1981): 25–28; Stephen J. Wykstra, "The Humean Obstacle to Evidential Arguments from Suffering: On Avoiding the Evils of 'Appearance,'" *International Journal for Philosophy of Religion* 16 (1984): 88.

12. "Defenceless," in *The Evidential Argument from Evil*, ed. Daniel Howard-Snyder (Bloomington: Indiana University Press, 1996), 197.

13. Gale, as well as the others I am about to discuss on this topic, lump all consideration of values under the rubrics of "morality," "moral philosophy," "moral values," "morally significant values," and the like. They all seem to suppose that any value (or disvalue) that can have a bearing on moral decisions, i.e., any value, is properly termed "moral." That seems to me, at best, infelicitous. I prefer to use *moral* in a more discriminating fashion. But to avoid confusion I will go along with my

opponents on this point and pretend that the topic of values generally can be treated as part of morality.

14. "Some Difficulties in Theistic Treatments of Evil", in *The Evidential Argument from Evil*, ed. Howard-Snyder, 210.

15. Note that, unlike Wykstra, I do not argue that there is an antecedent probability that many of God's reasons for permitting evil would be hidden from us. I see no general theological or other reasons for expecting this. It is just that, along with Rowe, I hold that in many cases of evil we do not, in fact, see what reasons would justify God in permitting them. Hence, if God exists, His reasons for these permissions are in fact hidden from us.

16. Rowe (1996) and Gale (1996).

17. Let me emphasize that the analogues are not presented as an argument for my thesis. They do not *show* that the discernment-of-divine-reasons case is analogous to them in the relevant respects. I did not present them to do that job. Rather, they are designed to help us see the features of the divine reasons case to which they are analogous.

18. "The Evidential Argument from Evil: A Second Look," in *The Evidential Argument from Evil*, ed. Howard-Snyder.

19. Another complexity here is that whether it is worth enduring the suffering to achieve the good depends not just on the general type to which the good belongs but also on the degree of it, where it is something that admits of degrees, as "felicity" does. To give Rowe the benefit of the doubt, let's assume that he is playing fair with the theist by considering in each case the maximum degree of the good.

20. That is, in accord with the natural potentialities and capacities of the subject, without violating the subject's nature.

21. If I were attempting to lay out a plausible scenario for the divine master plan, this last suggestion would be woefully deficient. But I am only concerned here to indicate abstract possibilities in order to suggest that we are not in a position to tell whether they are realized in some form of other; I am not concerned to spell out the details of a particular possible realization.

22. See, e.g., Daniel Howard-Snyder, "Inscrutable Evil and the Silence of God," doctoral dissertation, Syracuse University, 1992, §20. To make this supposition would be tantamount to requiring S's being justified in believing that *S is justified in believing that p* for it to be the case that S is justified in believing that p, and thus to fall into the sort of "level confusion" against which I have been repeatedly warned by confreres. See Alston, "Level Confusions in Epistemology," *Epistemic Justification* (Ithaca: Cornell University Press, 1989).

23. The immediate inspiration for this move is the notion of a belief's being "objectively evidence essential" in Stephen Wykstra, "Toward a Sensible Evidentialism: On the Notion of 'Needing Evidence,'" in *Philosophy of Religion*, ed. William Rowe and William Wainwright (New York: Harcourt Brace Jovanovich, 1989). A more remote inspiration is the emphasis on a social "division of labor" in Hilary Putnam, "The Meaning of 'Meaning,'" in *Language, Mind, and Knowledge*, ed. K. Gunderson (Minneapolis: University of Minnesota Press, 1975).

24. Paul Draper, "Pain and Pleasure: An Evidential Problem for Theists," *Noûs* 23 (1989). Hereafter I shall refer to this article as "Draper 1989."

25. O is "a statement reporting both the observations one has made of humans and animals experiencing pain or pleasure and the testimony one has encountered concerning the observations others have made of sentient beings experiencing pain or pleasure."

26. I'm not sure just what it takes for an hypothesis to be "serious," but let's say that it requires at least that the hypothesis not be known to be false and that in the epistemic situation in question it seems to be a live possibility.

27. For comments on and discussion of various parts of this chapter, I thank Mark Brown, Paul Draper, Daniel Howard-Snyder, and William Rowe.

'THE MAGNITUDE, DURATION, AND DISTRIBUTION OF EVIL: A THEODICY'

Peter van Inwagen

In his work on the problem of evil, Alvin Plantinga has made a useful distinction between "giving a theodicy" and "giving a defence." To give a theodicy is to "answer in some detail the question 'What is the source of the evil we find, and why does God permit it?' "[1] To give a defence is to construct a story according to which both God and evil exist and to attempt to show that this story is "possible in the broadly logical sense."[2] The purpose of giving a theodicy is "to justify the ways of God to men." The purpose of giving a defence is, in the first instance, to show that the co-existence of God and evil is possible. (In the first instance. But one might have further projects in mind—such as the project of showing that the existence of God is not improbable on some body of evidence that includes a description of the amounts and kinds of evil that actually exist.)

Plantinga is rather down on theodicies. I have heard him say that to give a theodicy is "presumptuous." I propose, nevertheless, to offer a theodicy. I propose to explain God's ways—or at least to offer a partial and speculative explanation of those ways. I am sufficiently sensitive to the merits of Plantinga's charge of presumption, however, to wish to say something in response to it. I will make three points.

(1) I do not claim that the theodicy I shall offer is *comprehensive*. That is, while I shall ascribe to God certain reasons for allowing evil to exist, I do not claim to give *all* of His reasons, or even to claim that

Peter van Inwagen, 'The Magnitude, Duration, and Distribution of Evil: A Theodicy', *Philosophical Topics*, 16, 2 (Fall 1988), pp. 161–87.

the reasons I shall give are His most important reasons. For all I know, God has reasons for allowing evil to exist that no human being could understand; perhaps, indeed, He has hundreds of perfectly good reasons that no *possible* creature could understand. What I claim for the theodicy presented in this essay is this: it alleges a reason, or an interconnected set of reasons, that God has for allowing evil—of the amounts and kinds we observe—to come to be and to continue; if these were the only reasons God had for permitting evil, they would by themselves justify this permission.

(2) The theodicy I shall present is not in any large part my own invention. I do not claim to be the first human being in history to have fathomed God's purposes. Nor do I claim to be the recipient of a special revelation from God: I do not claim to be a prophet whom God has charged with the task of disseminating an explanation of His ways. The method of this paper is simply philosophical reflection on the data of Christian revelation—or, more exactly, on what one tradition holds (in my view, correctly) to be the data of Christian revelation. (Those who do not share my allegiance to these data may wish to regard this paper as providing one more defence, in Plantinga's sense.)

(3) Insofar as anything in this paper is original, it is speculative. I do not claim that what is unique to this paper has any authority over those who accept the data of Christian revelation referred to above. But I claim more for these speculations than that they are "possible in the broadly logical sense." I offer them as consonant with and a plausible elaboration of the data of Christian revelation. (This, by the way, could not be claimed for them if they contained any element that was improbable on the known facts of science and history. I therefore explicitly claim that no proposition contained in the theodicy presented in this paper is improbable on the whole set of propositions endorsed by the special sciences.) One might object that someone who offers a theodicy in such a tentative fashion as this is not really "giving a theodicy" in Plantinga's sense. To "give a theodicy," one might argue, is to represent oneself as *knowing* that every proposition one puts forward is true. Perhaps there is some justice in this protest. If so, however, there is certainly *room* for the kind of thing I propose to do. There seems to be no reason to require that everyone who tells a story about God and evil must either claim to know this story to be true, or else claim only that it is possible in the broadly logical sense. And I think that if one does put forward an admittedly speculative, but (or so one believes) plausible account of God's reasons for allowing the existence of evil, one is not abusing language if one describes one's offering as a theodicy.

These three points, it seems to me, are sufficient to disarm the charge of presumption.

I

It is generally, but not universally, conceded by Christians that the existence of evil has something to do with free will. The theodicy I shall present is of the "free will" type. That is to say, it proceeds by extending and elaborating the following story:

> God made the world and it was very good. An important part of its goodness was that it contained creatures made in His own image—that is, created beings capable of understanding (to some degree) their own nature and their place in the scheme of things entire; creatures, more-over, that were fit to be loved by God and to love Him in return and to love one another. But love implies freedom: for A to love B is for A freely to choose to be united to B in a certain way.[3] Now even an omnipotent being cannot *insure* that some other being *freely* choose x over y. For God to create beings capable of loving Him, therefore, it was necessary for Him to take a risk: to risk the possibility that the beings He created would freely choose to withhold their love from Him.
>
> To love God and to desire to submit to His will are very closely related—at least as closely as the love of one's offspring and the desire to nurture and protect and raise them. God's free creatures—or some of them—instead of loving Him and submitting to His will, chose to turn away from Him and "to follow instead the devices and desires of their own hearts." It was thus that evil entered the world. A husband and father who turns away from his wife and children and suppresses his natural desire to live with and to love and protect them, and chooses instead to indulge a desire for fame or sexual adventure or "self-realization," turns himself into something unnatural and harmful. Like-wise, a creature who turns away from God turns himself into something unnatural and harmful. Having turned away from God, His creatures laid violent hands on the created world. They snatched it out of His grasp, and turned it to their own purposes. We are now living with the catastrophic consequences of that act.

This is the beginning of our theodicy. At its heart is what is a familiar "move" in discussions of the problem of evil, the insistence that even an omnipotent being cannot insure that someone *freely* do one thing rather than some contemplated alternative. Some philosophers have said that the proposition

> An omnipotent being cannot insure that a creature who has a free choice between x and y choose x rather than y

is false—and, of course, necessarily false, for, owing to its modal character, this proposition is necessarily false if it is false at all. The issues raised by this contention have been extensively debated, and I have nothing new to say about them. I shall simply assume that this proposition is true.

I proceed now to elaborate the above very sketchy narrative of the origin of evil. It is obvious that this must be done. As it stands, the narrative accounts for the existence of only, as we might say, "some evil or other." It says nothing about evil of the kinds or in the amounts we actually observe, or anything about its duration—thousands upon thousands of years—or anything about the fact that its worst effects are distributed apparently at random and certainly without regard for desert. I shall elaborate this narrative with certain propositions drawn from Christian theology. All Christian theologians who could lay any claim to the titles "orthodox," "Catholic," or "traditional" would accept the following theses:

— *All* evil is the result of the primordial act of turning away from God; there is no source of evil other than creaturely rebellion.
— The creatures who committed the initial act of rebellion received sufficient warning that their act would lead to disaster. While they may have been unlike us in many ways, they were not children and were at least as intelligent as we; they fully understood the warning and the wisdom and authority of its Source.
— Among the creatures who rebelled were an entire generation of human beings, all of the human beings who were alive at some particular moment. [In my view, it was the *first* generation of human beings. But I shall not build this into our theodicy because (a) it is not necessary, and (b) to argue that the proposition that there *was* a first generation of human beings is compatible with what we know about our evolutionary history would require a lengthy digression. The digression would involve the removal of two sorts of misunderstanding: misunderstandings about what it would be for there to be a first generation of human beings, and misunderstandings about what scientific study of the evolutionary history of our species has actually shown.] Before this rebellion, there was no evil—or at any rate none that affected human beings.[4]
— In turning away from God, our ancestors ruined themselves; they became unable to turn back to Him of their own power, as someone who ignores a warning not to go too near the edge of a pit may fall into it, injure himself, and be unable to climb out. Thus, the act of rebellion, or its immediate consequences, may be called "the Fall."
— Their ruin was in some way inherited by all of their descendants. [This does not necessarily mean that their genes were altered by the Fall. I believe that it is possible to construct models of the Fall according to which its hereditary aspect is due to the effects of

unaltered genes operating under conditions for which they were not "designed"—namely, conditions attendant upon separation from God. But I will not argue for this here.] Thus, evil is a persisting and—by any natural means—unalterable fact of history.[5]

— God has not left His creatures to their misery—not, at any rate, His human creatures. He has inaugurated a plan whose workings will one day eventuate in the Atonement (at-one-ment) of His human creatures with Himself. (Or, at least, the Atonement of some of His human creatures with Himself. It may be that some of His creatures will, by their own free choice, resist Atonement forever.) In order to achieve Atonement with God, a ruined creature must turn to God and ask for His help and accept that help. The undoing of creaturely ruin must be a cooperative endeavor. The creature cannot accomplish it for himself, and even an omnipotent being cannot effect the required sort of regeneration of a creature if the creature refuses to be regenerate. Any aspect of the creatures' environment that would tend to discourage them from turning to Him and asking for His help would therefore be an obstacle to the completion of His plan.[6]

— Every human being has an eternal future (and, therefore, the human species has an eternal future). We are now living, and have been living, throughout the archaeologically accessible past, within a temporary aberration in human history, an aberration that is a finite part of an eternal whole. When God's plan of Atonement comes to fruition, there will never again be undeserved suffering or any other sort of evil. The "age of evil" will eventually be remembered as a sort of transient "flicker" at the very beginning of human history.

I have said that I have drawn these points from Christian theology. But I have stated them so abstractly that, I think, at least some Jews and Muslims would agree with most of them. (The major point of disagreement would probably be over my inclusion among them of the doctrine of Original Sin; that is, the doctrine of hereditary ruin.) Now the body of Christian theology deals with what we may call—from our present vantage-point of lofty abstraction—the *details* of (what Christians believe to be) God's plan of Atonement. But in the present essay I shall hardly mention such matters as God's calling of Israel to be His people, the giving of the Law, the Incarnation, the ministry of Jesus, the institution of the Eucharist, the Crucifixion, the Resurrection, the Ascension, the Descent of the Holy Spirit, or the one, holy, Catholic, and Apostolic Church. It will be enough for my purposes to include in my theodicy the proposition that God has *some* plan of Atonement and that it will someday succeed in reuniting to Him all who choose to be reunited.

I added the above flesh to the skeleton provided by the standard "free-will" account of the origin of evil because it was clear that that skeleton was no theodicy. The skeleton, however, will require more flesh than this. We have still not got a finished theodicy. If we claimed that we had, a sceptic might, quite properly, respond along the following lines.

"God, you say, has set in motion a plan of Atonement. But why is it taking so long for His plan to work out? It's all very well to tell a tale that represents 'the age of evil' as a 'transient flicker at the very beginning of human history.' But every finite period is a mere flicker in Eternity. Nothing has been said to challenge the obvious proposition that God would not allow 'the age of evil' to go on any longer than necessary. Why, then, is 'this long' necessary?

"And why is there so *much* evil at any given time? Evil may be, as you say, the result of the creaturely abuse of free will. But the amount of evil could have been far less. For example, God, without in any way diminishing Cain's free will, could have warned Abel not to turn his back on him. If the implied general policy had been put into effect, a vast amount of evil would have been avoided.

"And why does God allow evil to be so unfairly distributed? Why is it so often the innocent—small children, for example—who suffer? Why is it so often the wicked who prosper?

"And what about 'physical' or 'natural' evil? How can the effects of the Bubonic Plague or the Lisbon earthquake be a result of creaturely free will?

"To roll all of these questions into one, Why has it been for thousands and thousands of years that enormous numbers of uncomprehending children have died as a result of epidemic disease and famine and natural disaster—while many a tyrant has died in bed? How could evil of such types and quantity and duration and distribution be necessary to God's plan of Atonement? Or, if all this evil is *not* necessary to God's plan, why does He not eliminate most of it, and make do with that residue of evil that is really necessary?"

II

I will continue to flesh out our skeletal theodicy by attending to the questions posed by our imaginary sceptic. I will address the last of them first.

The question presupposes that if there are evils that are not required by God's plan of Atonement, then there is such a thing as "that residue of evil that is really necessary," the minimum of evil that is required for God's plan to succeed. But this is not a very plausible thesis. It is not very plausible to suppose that there is a way in which evil could be distributed such that (i) that distribution of evil would serve God's purposes as well as any distribution could and (ii) God's purposes would be less well served by *any* distribution involving less evil. (One might as well suppose that if God's purposes require an impressively tall prophet to appear at a certain place and time, there is a minimum height such a prophet could have.) But if there is no minimum of evil that would serve God's purposes, then one cannot argue that God is unjust or cruel for not "getting by with less evil"—any more than one can argue that a law that fines motorists $25.00 for illegal parking is unjust or cruel owing to the fact that a fine of $24.99 would have an identical deterrent effect. The same point can be made in relation to time. If there is a purpose that is served by allowing "the age of evil" to have a certain duration, doubtless the same purpose would be served if the age of evil were cut short by a day or a year or even a century. But we would not call a judge unjust or cruel for imposing on a criminal a sentence of ten years on the ground—doubtless *true*—that a sentence of ten years less a day would have served as well whatever end the sentence was designed to serve. It is obvious that if, for any amount of evil that would have served God's purposes, slightly less evil would have served His purposes just as well—a very plausible assumption—then the principle that God should have got by with less evil, if less would have served, entails the (*ex hypothesi* false) conclusion that God should have got by with no evil at all. It may be a difficult problem in philosophical logic correctly to diagnose the defect in illegitimate *sorites* arguments, but it is certainly evident that such a defect exists.

The important things to recognize about these two points are, first, that they are valid and that to ignore them is to court confusion, and, secondly, that, valid though they be, they do not really meet the essence of the difficulty perceived by the sceptic, the difficulty that prompts him to ask, Why so much?, Why so long? To revert to our legal and judicial analogy, there may be no minimum appropriate fine for illegal parking, but (most of us would agree) if a fine of $25.00 would serve whatever purposes a fine for illegal parking is supposed to serve—deterrence, presumably—then it would be wrong to set the fine at five thousand dollars. Similarly, if an "age of evil" of twenty years' duration, an age during which there were a few dozen broken bones and a score or so of very bad cases of influenza, would have served God's ends as well as the actual evil of human history serves them, then the enormity of His achieving these same ends by allowing the existence of "actual evil" passes all possibility of adequate description.

What the theodicist must do, given the facts of history, is to say what contribution—what essential contribution—to God's plan of Atonement is made by the facts about the types, magnitude, duration, and distribution of evil that are made known to us by historians and journalists (not to mention our own experience).

It will be useful to divide this problem facing the theodicist—and why not call it simply the problem of evil?—into several sub-problems. One division of the problem of evil is well known: the division of the problem into "the problem of moral evil" and "the problem of natural evil." A second division, one that will be particularly useful in our project of fleshing out our skeletal theodicy so as to meet the questions of the imaginary sceptic, cuts across the first. It divides the problem into three:

— the problem of the magnitude of evil
— the problem of the duration of evil
— the problem of the distribution of evil.

III

I assume that we already have an adequate answer to the problem of moral evil. I am not much interested in treating the problem of natural evil; my main interest in the present paper is the sub-problems generated by the second division. I shall, accordingly, treat the problem of natural evil in a rather perfunctory way. I shall suggest the broadest outlines of a solution, and leave the details for another time—or another writer. (But some of the things said in the course of our later discussion of the distribution problem will have some relevance to questions about the role in God's plan of natural evil.)

Natural evil is often cited as a special problem for those who say that evil entered the world through the creaturely abuse of free will, since tornadoes and earthquakes are obviously not caused by the acts—free or unfree—of human beings. The evil that results from tornadoes and earthquakes must nevertheless be treated in any theodicy of the "free will" type as somehow stemming from creaturely free will. One notorious way of doing this is to postulate that tornadoes and earthquakes are caused by malevolent non-human creatures. Another way (the way I shall take) proceeds from the observation that it is not earthquakes and tornadoes *per se* that are evil, but rather the suffering and death that they cause. Consider the following tale.

"Earthquakes all occur in one particular region called Earthquake Country, a region that was uninhabited (because everyone knew about the earthquakes and had no reason to go there) until twenty years ago. At that time, gold was discovered on the borders of Earthquake Country and the geological indications were that there was much more inside. Motivated solely by a desire to get rich, many people—people by no means in want—moved to Earthquake Country to prospect for gold. Many took their families with them. Some of them got rich, but many of them were killed or maimed by earthquakes."

This tale may not be true, but it demonstrates that earthquakes need not be caused by the actions of creatures for the suffering and death caused by earthquakes to be a result of the actions of those creatures.

Our theodicy, as we have so far stated it, entails that at one time—before the Fall—our ancestors lived in a world without evil. This, I suppose, entails that they were not subject to the baleful effects of earthquakes and tornadoes. But why not? Well, for the purposes of a *perfunctory* treatment of the problem of natural evil, we need assume only that there was *some* reason for this, a reason that became inoperative when our ancestors separated themselves from God. We *might* suppose, for example, that the old tradition (it is without Biblical warrant) that Adam and Eve possessed "preternatural powers" is substantially correct, and that these powers included certain cognitive powers; we might suppose that our unfallen ancestors knew (and pretty far in advance) whether an earthquake or tornado would strike a particular spot—and when. And we might suppose that their being able to know such things depended on their union with God and was lost as a natural consequence of their separating themselves from God. We must remember that, according to Christianity, human beings were designed for union with God, in the same sense as that in which they are designed to live in community with one another and to use language. A "feral child" is a ruined human being—though he is no less our brother than is Homer or Leonardo—and his ruin entails a grave diminution of his cognitive powers. According to Christianity, we have all been ruined by our separation from God, just as the feral child has been ruined by his separation from the human community. (The feral child's ruin is thus a ruin within a ruin, a second, individual ruin of an already ruined common human nature.) And the ruin of human nature consequent on our separation from God may have involved a grave diminution of our cognitive powers. According to the "just-so story" I am telling,[7] we were designed by God to be able to protect ourselves from earthquakes and tornadoes—if you think that it would be possible to design a planet, and a universe to contain it, that was both capable of supporting human life and contained no earthquakes or tornadoes, I can only point out that you have never tried[8]—and that the loss of this power is as natural a consequence of our ancestors' separation from God as is the loss of the capacity to acquire language a natural consequence of the feral child's separation from the human community. (Expansion of this just-so story to cover tigers and droughts and epidemic disease and so on is left as an exercise for the reader.) Doubtless we could tell many tales of speculative theological fiction having the feature that our being subject to the destructive forces of nature is ultimately a consequence of the creaturely abuse of free will. For our purposes, as I have said, it will suffice to assume that one of the tales that fits this abstract description is true.

This is all I have to say about natural evil, but I wish to remind the reader that if all human beings were wise and good, our sufferings would be vastly less than they are; and it is probably not true that we should be much better off for a complete elimination of natural evil. Doubtless there would be human beings more than willing to take up the slack. Our ancestral ruin is *primarily* a moral, as opposed to a cognitive, ruin. But ruins we are. If two explorers—who have never seen such a thing—come upon a ruined temple in the jungle, and if one of them thinks that it is a natural geological formation and the other that it is a building that is just as it was designed to be, neither will understand its shape. From the Christian point of view, it is impossible for one to understand humanity if one thinks of a human being as either a product of natural forces behind which there is no Mind or as the work that a Mind intended to produce. Both naturalism and deism (Christianity holds) go wrong about our nature right at the outset, and neither can yield an understanding of that nature.

We thus have some basis for understanding both "moral" and "natural" evil. (In a sense, the theodicy I am proposing entails that there is no fundamental distinction between them: natural evil is a special category of moral evil.) That is, we have a basis for understanding why God would allow such things to come to be. (This is a very abstract statement. Remember, we have not yet said anything about the magnitude, duration, or distribution of either sort of evil.) We may, to sum up, add the following statement to our theodicy.

> Our unfallen ancestors were somehow able to protect themselves from earthquakes and tornadoes and wild beasts and disease and so on. This ability depended on their union with God, and was lost when they separated themselves from Him.

I now turn to my primary interests in offering a theodicy: The magnitude, duration, and distribution of evil.

IV

"Our ancestors turned away from God and ruined themselves both morally and intellectually—and thus they began to harm one another and they lost their aboriginal power to protect themselves from the potentially destructive forces of non-human nature. This condition—their wickedness and help-lessness—has persisted through all the generations, being somehow heredi-tary. But God has set a chain of events in motion that will eventually bring this state of affairs to an end."

The theodicist who wishes to add to this story elements that will account for evil as we actually find it must consider the questions about the magnitude, duration, and distribution of evil that we have put into the mouth of our imaginary sceptic. It will aid my order of exposition—and not, I think, unfairly modify the sceptic's case—if we recast the sceptic's three questions as four questions. The first and third have to do with the duration of evil, the second with its magnitude, and the fourth with its distribution.

> Question 1. Why didn't God immediately restore His fallen creatures to their original union with Him?
>
> Question 2. Why doesn't God protect His fallen creatures from the worst effects of their separation from Him: the horrible pain and suffering?
>
> Question 3. Why has God allowed "the age of evil" to persist for thousands and thousands of years?
>
> Question 4. Why do the innocent suffer and the wicked prosper?

Question 1

What would doing that actually have involved? Suppose that two brothers quarrel. Suppose that the quarrel becomes violent and then bitter and that finally they come to hate each other. Suppose that their mother prays to God that He restore their mutual love—and not by any gradual process, but immediately, right on the spot. What is she asking God to do? I can think of only one thing: to grant her request, God would have to wipe away all memory of everything that had happened between them since just before the moment they quarreled. Any philosopher worth his salt will probably be able to think of several grave conceptual difficulties that would attend this plan, but (assuming they could be overcome by omnipotence) God would not do such a thing, because, as Descartes has pointed out, God is not a deceiver, and such an act would constitute a grave deception about the facts of history. (I have no memory of a violent, bitter quarrel with Eleonore Stump, and thus my memory represents the past to me as containing no such quarrel. I have the best epistemic warrant for believing that no such quarrel has ever occurred. If she and I *have* so quarreled and if God has "deleted" my memories of it—and has somehow rendered the resulting set of memories coherent—then He has deceived me about the past.) I cannot see how God could simply, by sheer fiat, immediately have restored fallen humanity other than by a similar grave deception. And, we may add, if He did, what would happen next? What would prevent the Fall from immediately recurring?

V

Question 2

Consider the parable of the Prodigal Son. (Those whose memory of this story is dim will find it in the Gospel according to St. Luke, 15:11–32.) Suppose the father of the Prodigal had foreseen the probable effects of his son's rash use of his patrimony, and had hired actors to represent themselves as gamblers and deliberately to lose substantial sums to the Prodigal; and suppose that he had further arranged for his agents to bribe prostitutes to tell the Prodigal that they had fallen in love with him and wanted to give him all their earnings (following which declaration they are to pass on to him monies provided by his father); and suppose that the father's agents, on his instructions, had followed the Prodigal about in secret to protect him from the dangers attendant on the night life of the ancient Middle East.

What would have been the effects of this fatherly solicitude? Certainly the son could have continued to squander his substance indefinitely and with impunity. But here the word impunity must be understood in a rather superficial sense: for the son will be living a life of illusion (and that is a misfortune), and it is hard to see what could ever induce him to consider returning to his father (and I am inclined to think that that would also be a misfortune).

This modification of the story of the Prodigal Son suggests why it is that God does not simply "cancel"—by an almost continuous series of miracles—the pain and suffering that our separation of ourselves from Him has led to. First, if He did so, He would be, no less than in the case of the deleted memories, a deceiver. If He did so, we should be living in a world of illusion. Our lives would be invisibly "propped up" by God, but we should—justifiably—think that we were living successfully simply by the exercise of our native powers. This, it seems to me, would reduce our existence to something worse than meaningless: We should be, every one of us, *comic* figures. (If there were a novel whose plot was the "revised" life of the Prodigal Son sketched above, he could not be its hero or even a sympathetic character. The novel would be a low comedy and he would be the butt of the joke.) Now illusion of this sort is a bad thing in itself, but it would have consequences even worse than its intrinsic badness. If God did what is proposed, we should all be satisfied with our existence—or at least a lot closer to being satisfied than most of us are now. And if we are satisfied with our existence, why should we even consider turning to God and asking for His help? An essential and important component of God's plan of Atonement—this constitutes an addition to our theodicy—is to make us *dissatisfied* with our state of separation from Him; and not by miraculously altering our values or by subjecting us to illusion or by causing us suffering that has no natural connection with our separation, but simply by allowing us to "live with" the natural consequences of this separation, and by making it as difficult as possible for us to delude ourselves about the kind of world we live in: a hideous world, much of whose hideousness is quite plainly traceable to the inability of human beings to govern themselves or to order their own lives. Let us expand our theodicy:

> An essential part of God's plan of Atonement for separated humanity is for human beings to perceive that a natural consequence of human beings' attempting to order their own lives is a hideous world—a world that is hideous not only by His standards, but by the very standards they themselves accept.

Why is it important for human beings to perceive the hideousness of the world? Well, first, because that's how things are. That's what "man on his own" *means*. Look at the world around you—the world of violence, starvation, hatred, the world of the death camps and the Gulag and (quite possibly) thermonuclear or ecological catastrophe. (These are not the worst features of separated human life in the eyes of God, for these are all finite evils, and He can see quite plainly that each of us daily risks an infinite evil, the loss of the end for which he was made. But they really are hideous and they are recognizable as hideous by almost everyone, no matter what his beliefs and values may be.) These are natural effects of our living to ourselves, just as a literally feral existence is a natural effect of an infant's separation from the human community.

People who do not believe in God do not, of course, see our living to ourselves as a result of a prehistoric separation from God. But they can be aware—and it is a part of God's plan of Atonement that they *should* be aware—that something is pretty wrong and that this wrongness is a consequence of the intrinsic inability of human beings to devise a manner of life that is anything but hideous. (They *can* be aware. Few are. Part of the reason is that various myths[9] have been invented[10] for the purpose of obscuring the intrinsic incapacity of human beings to live successfully even by their own standards. The myths of Enlightenment, Progress, and the Revolution are the most prominent of these. Such myths in the end refute themselves by leading to ever deeper human misery; but, unfortunately, only in the end.) The broad psychological outlines of this feature of the plan that our theodicy ascribes to God are not hard to fathom. The realization that undirected human life is bound to be a failure even in secular terms may possibly set people to wondering whether there may not be some direction somewhere. But people who still think that the obvious hideousness of our world is caused by some accidental feature of human life—superstition, technological backwardness, primitive economic organization—, one that we shall presently get round to altering, are probably not going even to consider turning to God. It is a commonplace that religious belief is more common in South America and the Middle East and Africa than in the English-speaking countries and Western Europe. One possible explanation of this fact is that miserable and uneducated people turn to religious institutions as a man with a painful and incurable illness turns to quacks (and he is all the more likely to fall prey to quacks if he is uneducated). Here is another possible explanation. In the relatively prosperous and well-ordered West, people—middle-class people, anyway—are subject to an illusion about human nature and the conditions of human life. Although the prosperity and order in their lives is due to a special, fragile, and transient set of circumstances, they foolishly regard the kind of life they lead as the sort of thing human nature can be trusted to produce. The "wretched of the earth," on the other hand, see human nature as it really is. Many of them may be uneducated, in the sense of lacking the cognitive skills necessary to construct and operate a machine-based civilization, but they are far better educated than middle-class Europeans and Americans as regards the most general and important features of human nature. If an analogy involving medical quackery is wanted, we may say that a typical "post-religious" American or European is like a desperately sick man who has got his hands on some temporary panacea and who, as a consequence, has decided that the doctors who attempted to impress upon him the gravity of his condition are all quacks.

God's refusal to "cancel" the suffering that is a natural consequence of the

Fall by providing separated humanity with a vast set of miraculous and invisible props can (according to the theodicy I propose) be understood on the model of a doctor who refuses to prescribe a pain-killer (say, for angina), on the ground that he knows that his patient will curtail some beloved but self-destructive activity—long-distance running, say—only if the patient continues to experience the pain that his condition signals. Now this sort of behavior on the part of a *doctor* may well be morally objectionable. The doctor is the patient's fellow adult and fellow citizen, and, or so it can plausibly be argued, it would be presumptuous of him to act in such a paternalistic way. One might even say that in so acting the doctor would be "playing God." But we can hardly accuse *God* of playing God. God is justifiably paternalistic because He is our Father and because He is perfect in knowledge and wisdom and because, or so I would argue, He has certain rights over us. These rights, as I see it, derive from the following facts: He made up the very idea of there being creatures like us out of the thought of His own mind, and He made us out of nothing to meet the specifications contained in that idea; everything we have—including the intellectual and moral faculties by means of which we make judgments about paternalism—we have received from Him; He made us for a certain purpose (to glorify Him and to enjoy Him forever) and we threaten to prevent that purpose from being fulfilled.

I have suggested that the initial stage of God's plan of Atonement essentially involves His separated creatures' being aware of the hideousness of their condition and of its being a natural result of their attempting to order their own lives. I would also suggest that the *outcome* of His plan of Atonement, the unending union of creatures with Himself, will essentially involve the *memory* of that hideousness. A student of mine, a Christian, once told me of a professor of philosophy who had questioned him somewhat as follows. "You Christians believe that in the beginning man was in Paradise, and that in the end man will be in Heaven. In each of these states, man is in perfect union with God. So what is the difference between Paradise and Heaven? By abusing his free will, you say, man lost Paradise. And, you say, Heaven will be forever. But how can you know that man, having attained Heaven, won't proceed to lose it again by abuse of his free will?" There is a very simple answer to this question. The human beings in Heaven (that is, those whom God has rescued and restored to union with Himself; 'Heaven' is not the name of a place but of a condition) will know what it's like to be separated from God. They will remember the hideousness of their lives before the restoration of their union with God, and their continuing in their restored state will be no more puzzling than the refusal of the restored Prodigal Son to leave his father's house a second time. (Christian theologians have generally held that the inhabitants of Heaven—unlike the inhabitants of Paradise—are *unable* to sin. If the considerations of the present paragraph are combined with the theses on the nature of free will that I have argued for in my paper "When Is the Will Free?,"[11] it is easy to see why this should be so.) Theologians have also held that the happiness of those in Heaven will essentially involve, will perhaps be identical with, an immediate, intuitive knowledge of God, generally called the Beatific Vision. We might speculate that this Vision will have as a component an awareness of God's opposite, an awareness best revealed in the memory of separation from Him. Reflection on reunited lovers or returned exiles suggests why this might be the case.

Let us formally add these ideas to our theodicy:

> The perception by human beings of their incapacity to "live to themselves" is essential to God's plan of Atonement because, first, without this perception few if any human beings would consider turning to God. (If, therefore, God were miraculously to "cancel" the natural consequences of separation from Himself, He would not only be a deceiver but would remove the only motivation fallen human beings have for turning to Him.) And because, secondly, memory of the hideousness of separated human life will be an important, perhaps an essential, component of the final state of restored humanity. Among the natural consequences of separation from God is the vast quantity of pain and suffering that we observe.

VI

Question 3

I am uncertain about what to say about the duration of the "age of evil." I suggest some speculations that seem to me to be plausible.

— Perhaps God wants the final community of those in union with Him to be rather *large*. (Couldn't God allow an increase in the human population to occur *after* His plan of Atonement has been completed? Well, there is certainly the point to be considered that people born after the completion of God's plan would not remember the "age of evil" and thus would be just as liable to sin as their remote ancestors in Paradise; and it might be, as I have speculated, that memory of a world separated form God will be an essential part of the final condition of restored humanity.)

— Perhaps God wants the final community of those in union with Him to be rather *diverse*. It seems plausible to suppose that if God had brought the age of evil to an end in, say, 1000 A.D., the final human community would have been very unlike what it would be if He brought that age to an end tomorrow. In the latter case the final community would contain men and women whose cast of mind and world-view were radically unlike those of the members of any earlier age or culture. One might speculate that the members of a community composed of people born in diverse periods and cultures would be able to perceive and to communicate to one another aspects of the Divine Nature that the members of a community of less heterogeneous cultural origins would have been blind to.

— Various important stages in God's plan of Atonement may require particular levels of social and cultural development. The unhappy first generation of separated human beings must have been in a truly miserable state, having lost the smoothly functioning behavioral instincts of their purely animal ancestors, but without the learned social organization, custom and tradition by which human beings— as we know them—maintain themselves in an environment indifferent to their welfare. (Perhaps they were even without an actual language: a population of feral children, as it were. I suppose no one claims to know what would happen to a closed population of feral children over many generations?) Or even if they were never wholly without a culture and social organization, we can hardly suppose them to have had anything but a tribal culture. It may well be that God's plan of Atonement requires that at certain points in history some people belong to a more "advanced" culture than a tribal culture. If we consider the Christian account of God's plan of Atonement, for example, we shall see that it is evident that the ministry of Jesus (an essential part of God's plan) could not have taken place in a culture much different from that of first-century Palestine; certainly it could not have taken place in a tribal culture, or in a "normal" culture of the ancient Mediterranean world, a pagan polytheism. A "specialized" culture like that of ancient Judaism cannot appear overnight. Even if one does not believe the Biblical account of God's long interaction with Israel, one must grant that the Hebrew culture of two thousand years ago embodied a long history. (God doubtless had the power to "raise up children for Abraham from these stones," but if He had exercised that power He would have been a deceiver; vivid and detailed memories of the long history of their people were an essential part of the reaction of Jesus' Hebrew audience to His preaching.) And, of course, the rapid and accurate spread of the news about Jesus (also an essential part of God's plan, according to Christians) could hardly have happened except within the setting of a vast, cosmopolitan empire.

— Creatures like ourselves, sunk deep in self-will, take a long time to respond to any sort of guidance, particularly if it appeals to considerations higher than power and wealth. It may be hard to kick against the goad, but it is certainly done.

Question 4

Let us not discuss cases of the suffering of the innocent that depend on human wickedness or folly or corrupt institutions. Let us instead examine cases in which there are no oppressors but only victims. These would seem to raise all of the difficulties for the theodicist that are raised by cases in which an oppressor is present, and to be amenable to a smaller class of solutions; they are not, for example, amenable to any solution that involves a concern for the ultimate spiritual welfare of the oppressor or respect for his free will or anything of that sort.

A young mother dies of leukemia. A school bus full of children is crushed by a landslide. A child is born without limbs. A wise and good man in the prime of life suffers brain damage and spends the remaining thirty years of his life in a coma. I do not know of a good general term for such events. Journalists often call them tragedies. But this word is properly applied only to events that are in some sense meaningful, and I know of no reason to think that such events *always* have a "meaning." I will call them *horrors*.

Why do horrors happen? I want to suggest that horrors happen for no reason at all, that when, for example, a child is born without limbs, the only answer to the question, "Why did that happen?" is "There is no reason or explanation; it just happened." Or, at any rate, I want to suggest that this is sometimes the case. (Whether some horrors are brought about by God for special purposes is a question I shall not attempt to answer.[12] If *some* horrors are brought about by God, and thus have a purpose and a meaning known to God but not to us, I have no opinion as to what percentage of the whole they might constitute.) But are not *all* events ordered by God, and must not *all* events therefore have some sort of meaning? Christians and other theists are, I believe, committed to the truth of the following proposition:

> God is the maker of all things, visible and invisible (other than Himself); He sustains all created things in existence from moment to moment, and continuously supplies them with their causal powers.

In a previous paper,[13] in which I presented an account of God's action in the world, I argued that this proposition is consistent with the proposition that there are events having the following feature: If one asks concerning one of these events, "Why did that happen?," the only answer to one's question is, "There is no reason or explanation for that event. God did not cause it to happen or intend it to happen. It is not a part of God's plan for the world or anyone else's plan for anything. It just happened, and that's all there is to say about it." (Let us say of such events that they are *due to chance*.) I will not reproduce my arguments. Interested readers may turn to the earlier paper, to which the present paper is a sequel (although I have tried to make it self-contained). Now to say that there is no answer to the question, Why did X occur? is not to say that there is no answer to such questions as Why did God allow X to occur? or Why did God not prevent X? I ended the earlier paper with these words:

> If what I have said is true, it yields a moral for students of the Problem of Evil: Do not attempt any solution to this problem that entails that every particular evil has a purpose, or that, with respect to every individual misfortune, or every devastating earthquake, or every disease, God has some special reason for allowing it. Concentrate rather on the problem of what sort of reasons a loving and providential God might have for allowing His creatures to live in a world in which many of the evils that happen to them happen to them for no reason at all.

I will now take my own advice and present my solution to this problem. God's reason for allowing His creatures to live in such a world is that their living in such a world is a natural consequence of their separation from Him. Consider again our earlier sketchy account of natural evil: in separating ourselves from God, we have somehow deprived ourselves of our primordial defences against such potentially destructive things as tigers and landslides and tornadoes. But if, by our rebellion and folly, we have allowed the destructive potential of these things to become actual, how shall we expect the effects of that actuality to be distributed? At random, surely? That is, with no correlation between these things and the innocence or wickedness of the people they impinge on— since the operations of these things in no way depend upon the moral qualities of the people they interact with? In fact, there is little correlation between the manner in which these things operate and *any* factor under human control (although civilization does what it can to try to induce correlations of this type).

Suppose that a certain man chooses, of his own free will, to stand at spot x at time t. His arrival at that place at that time converges with the arrival of an avalanche. Let us suppose that God did not miraculously cause the avalanche, and that He did not "move" the man to be at that place at that time. And let us also suppose that neither the man's arrival at x at t nor the avalanche's arrival at x at t was determined by the laws of nature and the state of the world, say, one hundred years earlier. (This is a plausible assumption on scientific grounds. Quantum mechanics has the following astounding consequence: Imagine a billiard table, one not subject to external influence other than constant, uniform gravitation, on which there are rolling perfectly spherical and perfectly elastic balls that—somehow —do not lose energy to the walls of the table in collision or to its surface in friction; the position of the balls a minute or so in the future is not even approximately determined by the laws of nature and the present physical state of the balls. This example strongly suggests that the precise moment at which an avalanche occurs is not determined a hundred years in advance.)

The man's death in the avalanche would seem to be in every sense due to chance, even though (the theist must suppose) God knew in advance that he would be killed by the avalanche and could have prevented it. In fact, the theist must suppose that, during the course of that event, God held all of the particles that composed the man and the moving mass of snow and ice in existence and continuously decreed the operation of the laws of nature by which those particles interacted with one another.

Why did God not miraculously save the man? We have seen the answer to this question already. He might very well have. Perhaps He sometimes does miraculously save people in such situations. But if He *always* did so, He would be a deceiver. If He always saved people about to be destroyed by a chance encounter with a violent phenomenon of nature, He would engender an illusion with the following propositional content:

> It is possible for human beings to live apart from God and not be subject to destruction by chance.

To live under this illusion would be a bad thing in itself, but, more importantly, it would have harmful effects. This illusion would be, as it were, a tributary of illusion feeding into a great river of illusion whose content was, "Human beings can live successfully in separation from God."

In our current state of separation from God, we are continually blundering into "lines of causation" (the descent of an avalanche; the evolution of the AIDS virus; the building up of tension along a geological fault) that perhaps have no purpose at all and certainly have no purpose in relation to us. (It is simply a part of the mechanics of nature that intrinsically harmless but potentially destructive things like avalanches or viruses or earthquakes should exist. As I remarked above, if you think that you can design a world that does not contain such things and which can also serve as a home for human beings, you have never tried. Such things are a part of God's design in the sense that the ticking sound made by a clock is a part of the watchmaker's design: not intended, necessitated by what *is* intended, foreseen, and allowed for. What is not in any sense a part of God's design is *this* avalanche, *this* virus, and *this* earthquake. These are—sometimes, at any rate—due to chance.) If we had never separated ourselves from God, we should have been able to avoid such blunders. No longer to be able to avoid them is a natural consequence of the Fall. It is as if God had had—for some purpose—to cover the earth with a certain number of deep pits. These pits (we may stipulate) were not dangerous, since they could easily be seen and avoided; but we frustrated God's Providence in this matter by deliberately making ourselves blind; and now we complain that some of us—quite often the good and wise and innocent—fall into the pits. God's response to this complaint, according to the theodicy I propose, is this: "You are the ones who made yourselves blind. If you make yourselves blind, some of you will fall into the pits, and moreover, *who* falls into a pit and *when* will be wholly a matter of chance. Goodness and wisdom and innocence have no bearing on this matter. That's part of what being blind means." Or, rather, this is what we might imagine God's response to be in our simple "world of pits." In the real world, we should have to picture God as saying something more complex, something like the following.

"Even I can't make a world that is suitable for human beings but which contains no phenomena that would harm human beings *if* they were in the wrong place at the wrong time. The reasons for this are complicated, but they turn on the fact that the molecular bonds that hold you human beings together must be weaker by many orders of magnitude than the disruptive potential of the surges of energy that must happen here and there in a structurally and nomologically coherent world complex enough to contain you. My Providence dealt with this fact by endowing you with the power never to be in the wrong place at the wrong time, a power you lost when you ruined yourselves by turning away from Me. That is why horrors happen to some of you: you simply blunder into things. If I were to protect you from the consequences of your blindness by guiding you away from potentially destructive phenomena by an unending series of miracles—and I remind you that for all you know I *sometimes* do guide you out of harm's way—I should be deceiving you about the meaning of your separation from Me and seriously weakening the only motivation you have for returning to Me."

We may add the following proposition to our theodicy:

> Among the natural consequences of the Fall is the following evil state of affairs: Horrors happen to people without any relation to desert. They happen simply as a matter of chance. It is a part of God's plan of Atonement that we realize that a natural consequence of our living to ourselves is our living in a world that has that feature.

This completes my presentation of the theodicy I propose.[14] I have fleshed out the well-known story about how evil entered the world through the abuse of the divine gift of free will; I have fleshed it out in such a way as to provide plausible—at any rate, I find them plausible—answers to four pointed questions about the magnitude, duration, and distribution of evil. But in a sense it is not possible effectively to present a theodicy in a single piece of work by one author. Various elements in any proposed theodicy are bound to be thought false or felt to be implausible by some people. An essential part of presenting a theodicy is meeting the objections of those who have difficulties with it, or perhaps refining it in the face of their objections. A theodicy is a dialectical enterprise. The present paper, therefore, is best regarded as the "opening move" in such an enterprise, rather than a finished product. In closing, I wish to answer one objection to the theodicy I have presented, an objection that has been raised in conversation and correspondence by Eleonore Stump. Professor Stump objects that the theodicy I have presented represents God as allowing people to suffer misfortunes that do not (even in the long run) benefit *them*. An example may make the point of this objection clear. Suppose that God allows a horrible, disfiguring accident to happen to Alice (a true accident, an event due entirely to chance, but one that God foresaw and could have prevented). And suppose that the only good that is brought out of this accident is embodied in the following state of affairs and certain of its remote consequences: The accident, together with an enormous number of similar horrors, causes various people to realize that one feature of a world in which human beings live to themselves is that in such a world horrors happen to people for no reason at all. But suppose that Alice herself did not need to realize this; suppose that she was already fully aware of this consequence of separation from God. And suppose that many of the people who do come to realize this partly as the result of Alice's accident manage (owing mainly to luck) to get through life without anything very bad happening to them. According to Stump, these suppositions—and it is pretty certain that there *are* cases like this if our theodicy is correct—represent God as violating the following moral principle:

> It is wrong to allow something bad to happen to X—without X's permission—in order to secure some benefit for others (and no benefit for X).

I do not find this principle particularly appealing—not as a *universal* moral principle, one that is supposed to apply with equal rigour to all possible moral agents in all possible circumstances. The circumstances in which it seems most doubtful are these: The agent is in a position of lawful authority over both X and the "others" and is responsible for their welfare (consider, for example, a mother and her children or the state and its citizens); the good to be gained by the "others" is considerably greater than the evil suffered by X; there is no way in which the good for the "others" can be achieved except by allowing the evil in question to happen to X or to someone else no more deserving of it than X; the agent knows these things to be true. By way of example, we might consider cases of quarantine or of the right of eminent domain. Is it not morally permissible for the state to restrict my freedom of movement and action if I am the carrier of a contagious disease, or to force me to move if my house stands in the way of a desperately needed irrigation canal (one that will not benefit *me* in any way)? It is not to the point to protest that these cases are not much like cases involving an omnipotent God, who can cure diseases or provide water by simple fiat. They are counterexamples to the above moral principle, and, therefore, that moral principle is false. What is required of anyone who alleges that the theodicy I have proposed represents God as violating some (correct) moral principle is a careful statement of that moral principle. When we have examined that carefully stated moral principle, and have satisfied ourselves that it is without counterexample, we can proceed with the argument.

NOTES

1. The characterization is Plantinga's. See his "Self-Profile," in *Alvin Plantinga*. James E. Tomberlin and Peter van Inwagen, eds. (Dordrecht: D. Reidel, 1985), p. 42.

2. The characterization is mine. The phrase "possible in the broadly logical sense," however, is Plantinga's. See, e.g., *The Nature of Necessity* (Oxford: Clarendon Press, 1974), p. 2.

3. At any rate this is true for certain sorts of love (I concede that the world 'love' may sometimes refer to a mere feeling), and it is love of these sorts that is meant. Anyone who is doubtful that there are kinds of love that have this feature should meditate on Ruth 1:16–17 and the Anglican wedding vow:

   > And Ruth said, Entreat me not to leave thee, or to return from following after thee, for whither thou goest, I will go; and where thou lodgest, I will lodge: thy people shall be my people and thy God my God: Where thou diest, will I die, and there will I be buried.

   > I M. take thee N. to my wedded wife, to have and to hold from this day forward, for better for worse, for richer for poorer, in sickness and in health, to love and to cherish, till death us do part, according to God's holy ordinance; and thereto I plight thee my troth.

4. To allay the possible curiosity of some readers, I will mention that I regard the story of Adam and Eve in Genesis as a myth, in the sense that, in my view, it is not a story that has come down to us *via* a long historical chain of tellings and retellings that originated with the testimony of participants in the events it describes. In my view, the rebellion of creatures against God happened far too long ago for any historical memory of it to have survived to the present day. (There are not even any surviving stories of the last glaciation, and the rebellion of our species was certainly before that.) I believe, however, that the development of this myth in the ancient Middle East and its eventual literary embodiment in Genesis took place under the guidance of the Holy Spirit; and I believe that, within certain limits, Genesis can be used as a guide to what actually happened. The key to observing these limits is to concentrate on the spiritually relevant features of the story, and to remember that the Bible is addressed equally to the people of all epochs and cultures and that a story of those remote events that satisfied modern standards of historical accuracy would probably have to involve concepts and facts that would render it inaccessible to the people of most epochs and cultures.

5. This is not a popular view among theologians just at present. The following passage by the late Lord Ramsey is typical: The acceptance by Christian teachers of . . . the findings of evolutionary biology . . . [has] radically altered . . . the doctrine of the creation and fall of man . . . [T]here is a radical reappraisal of the fall of man, so radical that the use of the word 'fall' is questionable. No longer is it thought that mankind's first parents collapsed from a state of innocence bringing pain and death as a punishment. (Michael Ramsey, *Jesus and the Living Past* (Oxford: Oxford University Press, 1980), pp. 20–21).

   If these words were simply a description of the reaction of nerveless academic theologians, carried about with every wind of doctrine, to what they believe to be the findings of evolutionary biology, they would, unfortunately, be unobjectionable. But what they are in fact is a statement of the way theologians *ought* to react to the findings of evolutionary biology. To this statement I can only say (borrowing from Russell) that I should not believe such a thing if it were told to me by the Archbishops of Canterbury *and* York. What one does not find in the writings of theologians like Lord Ramsey is a clear statement of what they take the "findings of evolutionary biology" to be, and an argument to show that acceptance of these "findings" requires a radical alteration of the doctrine of the Fall. But my strong feelings on this matter should not be allowed to give the impression that I think that the theodicy I present in this paper could not possibly be modified to accommodate a "radically revised doctrine of the fall." I leave that an open question, one to be investigated when it becomes clear that there is some reason to attempt such a revision.

6. These words are consistent with the heretical doctrine called semi-Pelagianism (i.e., the doctrine that the ruin of those creatures who separated themselves from God was not so complete as to deprive them of the power of turning to Him and asking for His help), but they by no means entail it.

7. I have borrowed this use of "just-so story" from Daniel Dennett. (See his *Elbow Room: The Varieties of Free Will Worth Wanting* (The M.I.T. Press: Cambridge, Mass., [1980] p. 38.)) Dennett's just-so stories are tales told to illustrate possibility, tales told against a background that may be described as the standard model of evolution. My just-so story is of a similar sort, but the "background" is provided by what I have described as "the data of Christian revelation."

8. Before you try, you should read "Logical Possibility" by George Seddon (*Mind*, LXXXI [1972] pp. 481–494). See also my discussion of possibility and consistency in "Ontological Arguments," *Nous* 11 (1977), pp. 375–395, pp. 382–386 in particular, and my review of Richard Swinburne's *The Coherence of Theism* (*Philosophical Review*, LXXXVII [1979] pp. 668–672).

9. 2 Timothy 4:3–4.

10. Ephesians 6:12.

11. To appear in *Philosophical Perspectives*, Vol. 4. I owe this point to Eleonore Stump.

12. I shall not attempt to answer it because I do not think that there is any way to get a purely philosophical grip on it. Any useful discussion of this question must presuppose an agreed-upon deposit of divine revelation, of God's statements to us about His purposes. The relevant Biblical texts are very numerous. (Many of them, obviously, are contained in the book of Job.) Two important texts, which I choose almost at random, are Jeremiah 45:1–5 and John 9:1–3.

13. "The Place of Chance in a World Sustained by God," in *Divine and Human Action: Essays on the Metaphysics of Theism*, Thomas V. Morris, ed. (Ithaca: Cornell University Press, 1988).

14. It is often contended that a theodicy is a mere intellectual exercise; that the theodicist has nothing to say that would profit or comfort or even interest a religious believer who was undergoing, or watching a loved one undergo, terrible suffering, and who cried out to God for an explanation. The usual response to this contention is rather defensive: A distinction is made between intellectual and pastoral concerns and it is declared that a theodicy purports to be a solution only to the intellectual problems that human suffering raises for the theist. I believe, however, that there is a closer connection between intellectual and pastoral concerns than this response suggests. One is certainly asking too much of a work of theodicy if one demands that it should be capable of being read with profit by someone in terrible pain or distress. But one is not asking too much of a work of theodicy if one demands that it should be capable of being read with profit by someone whose vocation it is to minister to those in terrible pain or distress. By way of illustration, I should like to quote, with the writer's permission a paragraph from a letter I have received (concerning the paper cited in note 13, above) from Dr. Stephen S. Bilynskyj, who is both a trained philosopher and the Lead Pastor of the First Evangelical Covenant Church of Lincoln, Nebraska: "As a pastor, I believe that some sort of view of providence which allows for genuine chance is essential in counseling those facing what I often call the "practical problem of evil." A grieving person needs to be able to trust in God's direction of her life and the world, without having to make God directly responsible for every event that occurs. The message of the Gospel is not, I believe, that everything that occurs has some purpose. Rather, it is that God's power is able to use and transform any event through the grace of Jesus Christ. Thus a person may

cease a fruitless search for reasons for what happens, and seek the strength that God offers to live with what happens. Such an approach is very different from simply assuming, fideistically, that there must be reasons for every event, but we are incapable of knowing them." In addition to illustrating the point I wished to make, this paragraph raises an important further point. Dr. Bilynskyi's words suggest that God will at least sometimes use the sufferings that come to us—whether they come by chance or by providential design—not only for the general spiritual benefit of separated humanity, but for the individual spiritual benefit of the sufferer himself (at least if the sufferer submits to God's will and cooperates). I myself believe this, as, I suppose, do all Christians. I have not, however, incorporated this thesis into the theodiey I have presented. There are three reasons for this. First, a plausible discussion of the spiritual benefits of suffering would require a far longer paper than this one and it would radically alter the character of the paper: it would necessitate a paper that contained a great deal more specifically Christian soteriology than the present paper. Secondly, I think that the theodicy I have presented gives, as it stands, an *adequate* explanation of the magnitude, duration, and distribution of suffering and other sorts of evil; I do not claim to have presented a complete account of the use God makes of evil. Thirdly, and most importantly, I see no reason whatever to believe that God does make use of *every* instance of suffering in a way that benefits the sufferer. And if there are any cases of suffering that do not benefit the sufferer, these are the "hard" cases and are therefore the ones that a theodicy (especially one that makes no claim to completeness) should concentrate on. If, however, anyone wishes to add to the theodicy I have presented the thesis that in at least some cases, *perhaps* in all cases, God uses suffering to bring important spiritual benefits to the sufferer himself, I shall certainly regard that as a "friendly amend-ment."

While we are on the subject of pastoral concern, I will briefly mention one other objection that has been made to the theodicy I have given, an objection that I think is best classified as "pastoral." A friend has told me that I have represented God as a lofty Benthamite deity who coldly uses suffering as a tool with which to manipulate His creatures (albeit for their own good). I don't see it. I will leave aside the point that as a Christian I believe that God is Himself a human being and was once tortured to death (a peculiar kind of loftiness). I will only record my conviction—a conviction that seems to me to be in no sort of tension with the theodicy presented in the text—that when we no longer see through a glass darkly, when we know as we are known, when God's sorrows are made manifest to us, we shall see that *we* have never felt anything that we could, without shame, describe as sorrow.

4.5

'THE PROBLEM OF EVIL'

Eleonore Stump

INTRODUCTION

The problem of evil traditionally has been understood as an apparent inconsistency in theistic beliefs.[1] Orthodox believers of all three major monotheisms, Judaism, Christianity, and Islam, are committed to the truth of the following claims about God:

(1) God is omnipotent;
(2) God is omniscient;
(3) God is perfectly good.

Reasonable people of all persuasions are also committed to this claim:

(4) There is evil in the world;

and many theists in particular are bound to maintain the truth of (4) in virtue of their various doctrines of the afterlife or the injunctions of their religion against evil. The view that (1)–(4) are logically incompatible has become associated with Hume in virtue of Philo's position in the *Dialogues Concerning Natural Religion*, though many other philosophers have maintained it,[2] including in recent years J. L. Mackie[3] and H. J. McCloskey.[4] As other philosophers have pointed out, however, Philo's view that there is a logical inconsistency in (1)–(4) alone is mistaken.[5] To show such an

Eleonore Stump, 'The Problem of Evil', *Faith and Philosophy*, 2, 4 (October 1985), pp. 392–423.

inconsistency, one would need at least to demonstrate that this claim must be true:

> (5) There is no morally sufficient reason for God to allow instances of evil.

Since Hume, there have been attempts to solve the problem of evil by attacking or reinterpreting one of the first four assumptions. Mill, for example, suggested a radical weakening of (1) and (2),[6] and according to Mill, Mansel reinterpreted (3) in such a way as almost to make (4) follow from it, by in effect claiming that God's goodness might include attributes which we consider evil by human standards.[7] But, for reasons which I think are obvious, theists have generally been unwilling to avail themselves of such solutions; and most attempts at solving the problem, especially recently, have concentrated on strategies for rejecting (5). Some of these attempted rejections of (5) make significant contributions to our understanding of the problem, but none of them, I think, ultimately constitutes a successful solution of the problem. In this paper, I will briefly review what seem to me three of the most promising discussions of the problem of evil and then develop in detail a different solution of my own by presenting and defending a morally sufficient reason for God to allow instances of evil.

I

Plantinga's presentation of the free will defence is a landmark in contemporary discussions of the problem of evil. As Plantinga expounds it,[8] the free will defence rests on these two philosophical claims, which it adds to the theological assumptions (1)–(3):

> (6) Human beings have free will;

and

> (7) Possession of free will and use of it to do more good than evil is a good of such value that it outweighs all the evil in the world.

Plantinga uses these assumptions to argue that a morally sufficient reason for God to permit evil is possible: the value of man's possession and use of free will is a possible reason for God's permitting moral evil, which is evil caused by man. The value of the fallen angels' possession of free will is a possible reason for God's permitting natural evil, evil which is not caused by human free choice but which (Plantinga suggests) could be attributed to the freely chosen actions of fallen angels. As long as it is possible that there be a morally sufficient reason for God to allow evil, regardless of whether or not that possibility is actualized, the existence of evil is not logically incompatible with the existence of a good God.

Plantinga's work has generated considerable discussion, which cannot be effectively summarized here.[9] But for my purposes perhaps the most interesting criticism is the objection that even if we grant Plantinga's free will defence everything it wants and needs, what results does not seem to be even a candidate for a morally sufficient reason justifying God's permitting instances of evil. In "The Irrelevance of the Free Will Defence",[10] Steven Boer has argued that nothing in the grant of free will to creatures entails that creatures always be able successfully to inflict the harm which they have willed. It is possible that God allow his creatures to be free with respect to their willing and yet prevent by natural or supernatural means the suffering which their evil will and actions aim at. Thus, for example, God could allow Smith to will to murder Jones and to act on that will by hiring killers to shoot Jones, and at the same time God could warn Jones of Smith's intentions in time for Jones to run away and hide until Smith's wrath had subsided. By warning Jones God would prevent the evil of Jones' murder without interfering with Smith's exercise of free will. Many critics of Plantinga's position are bothered by the fact that they cannot seriously entertain the notion that Plantinga's possible sufficient reason for evil might actually obtain. The thought that all natural evil might be caused by fallen angels seems to many a particularly implausible view. This criticism does not especially worry Plantinga, however, because his purpose was to show not what God's reason for allowing evil is but rather just that there could be such a reason; and this is all he needs to show in order to refute those who think that the existence of God is logically incompatible with the existence of evil. Plantinga's strategy is similar in his arguments against those who hold the weaker view that the existence of evil renders it *improbable* that God exist.[11] He does not attempt a justification for God's allowing evil which would diminish the critic's sense of the improbability of God's existence. Rather he argues that the critic has not made his case. Judgments of a claim's probability are relative to a knower's whole set of beliefs. But a theist's set of beliefs includes the belief that God exists, so that atheists' assessments of the probability of God's existence given the existence of evil will not be the same as theists'. Therefore, the atheist critic's argument that God's existence is improbable is not telling against theism.

The problem with Plantinga's general strategy for the defence of theism against arguments from evil is that it leaves the presence of evil in the actual world mysterious. Plantinga's tendency is to show the weaknesses inherent in arguments from evil, not to provide a theodicy, and so it yields no explanation for why we in this world suffer from evil if our world is governed by a good God. No doubt many people, including Plantinga, would not find this result problematic. In fact, in a recent paper Steven Wykstra has argued that given the limitlessness of God's intellect and the finitude of ours, the mysteriousness of evil in our world is just what we might expect;[12] it is reasonable to suppose that we cannot understand why an omniscient and omnipotent entity does what he does. I think that there is some plausibility in Wykstra's thesis; and if all efforts at theodicy fail utterly, no doubt theists will be glad of arguments like Wykstra's and content with strategies like Plantinga's. The problem with such arguments and strategies, to put it crudely, is that they leave people on both sides of the issue unsatisfied. The atheist is inclined to claim, as William Rowe does in a recent paper,[13] that it is apparent there is *no* justifying or overriding good for some evils that occur in the world. To tell such an atheist that he hasn't succeeded in undermining theists' beliefs in the existence of such a good although they don't know what it is, or that his inability to see such a good is just what theists would expect, is likely to strike him as less than a powerful response. As for the theist struggling with the problem of evil, even if he entertains no anxieties about the rationality of his theistic belief in consequence of the existence of evil, he may well still be weakened in his religious belief by the consideration that the deity in whom he is to place his *trust* seems to act in ways which are unintelligible to him at best and apparently evil at worst. So, if it is at all possible to do so, it seems worth trying to construct a more positive explanation for the compatibility of God and evil; and such an explanation is in fact what we find in the work of Swinburne and Hick.

Swinburne's recently published solution to the problem of evil involves in effect an alteration of (7). What we value about free will, according to Swinburne, is not merely our possession of it or the balance of moral good over moral evil which it produces but rather our ability to exercise it in significant ways in the "choice of destiny and responsibility."[14] Without significant exercise of free will, Swinburne argues, we would live like God's pets, inhabiting a toy world in which God would reserve to himself all the important decisions.[15] To accommodate Swinburne's view, then, we ought to reformulate Plantinga's (7) as

> (7′) Significant exercise of free will with a choice of destiny, with "the opportunity to bring about serious evils or prevent their occurrence,"[16] is of such great value that it outweighs all the evil in the world.

Swinburne builds his own solution to the problem of evil on (7′). The morally sufficient reason for God's allowing instances of evil is that the significant exercise of human free will is worth the evil it involves. Moral evil is readily explicable on this view: God does not prevent human beings from accomplishing the ends of their evil wills, because to do so consistently would be to deprive them of the significant exercise of their free wills and reduce them to the status of pets. But natural evil, evil not caused by human choices, is harder to explain. Swinburne tries to justify it by claiming that natural evil is necessary for a certain sort of knowledge, which is itself necessary for significant exercise of free will, so that God could not take away instances of natural evil without also taking away the significant exercise of human free will. The connection between natural evil and free will Swinburne explains in this way. We could not know the consequences of our choices, according to

Swinburne, without the existence of natural evil. Unless someone died accidentally of cyanide poisoning, for example, or unless people died of rabies, we would not have the significant choice of trying to prevent cyanide poisoning or rabies. Similarly, if there were no earthquakes, we would not have the choice of building or refusing to build cities on fault lines, of helping or refusing to help earthquake victims.[17]

The weakest part of this solution to the problem of evil seems to me to be its attempted justification of natural evil.[18] Contrary to Swinburne, I think that the knowledge Swinburne values does not require natural evils; it can be acquired in a number of other ways. In particular, for example, God could inform men, directly or indirectly, of the consequences of their choices, and it is clear from various Biblical stories that God could do so without infringing the human freedom which Swinburne is concerned to safeguard.[19] Furthermore, the particular knowledge gained from the occurrence of natural evil and the choices it provides is valuable, Swinburne seems to argue, simply because free will can consequently be exercised in serious choices. But the world would contain ample opportunity for significant exercise of free will even without natural evil. Belsen and Hiroshima were the results of significant exercises of free will, and those free choices would have been possible even if the world contained no birth defects, cancer, tornadoes, or drought. So I think Swinburne's solution cannot justify the natural evils of this world even if his case concerning moral evil is convincing.

Hick's solution to the problem of evil, like Swinburne's, consists in effect in an alteration of (7); and though Hick's work was published before Swinburne's, it can be conveniently thought of as providing a complicated addition to the formulation of (7) underlying Swinburne's solution.[20] On Hick's view, (7) should be reformulated in this way:

> (7″) Significant exercise of free will in the enterprise of soul-making is of such great value that it outweighs all the evil in the world.

Soul-making, on Hick's view, is the process by which human beings develop certain traits of character, such as patience, courage, and compassion, as a result of struggling with evils. Those who successfully complete this process will be admitted to the kingdom of God, in which there is no evil. The evil in the world is logically necessary for soul-making and so cannot be prevented if the process of soul-making is to be preserved.

Hick's solution to the problem of evil has received a great deal of attention in the literature,[21] but the most effective criticism of it, I think, is Stanley Kane's.[22] He argues that the traits of character so valued by Hick in fact do not require the existence of evil for their development or display:

> Courage and fortitude, for instance, could manifest themselves as the persistence, steadfastness, and perseverance it takes to accomplish well

any difficult or demanding long-range task—the writing of a doctoral dissertation, for example, or training for and competing in the Olympic Games . . . Compassion could be evidenced in the sympathy and fellow-feeling that a person could show for someone engaged in one of these long-range enterprises . . . It is hard to see why a man or a woman cannot develop just as much patience, fortitude and strength of character in helping his or her spouse complete a doctoral dissertation as in caring for a sick child through a long and serious illness. It is hard to see why people cannot learn just as much of the spirit of help and coopera-tion by teaming together to win an athletic championship as by coming together to rescue a town leveled by a tornado or inundated by a flood.[23]

Even apart from this objection, Kane argues, Hick's solution is vitiated by an absurdity in the general scheme he postulates. According to Hick, evil is justified by man's acquisition of intrinsically valuable character traits which require the existence of evil for their development and display. Those who develop these character traits will be admitted to heaven where there is no evil and where, consequently, it is impossible to manifest the character traits they have acquired. But this is senseless, Kane maintains. On Hick's view, all the evils in the world are justified as a means of developing traits of character which it will be impossible to maintain thereafter in heaven, the reward for having developed such character traits. Why should we value a process which results in a character which cannot then be manifested? And if it is the possession rather than the manifestation of these character traits which is valued, so that what is wanted is a certain disposition, which can be had in heaven even in the absence of evil, then it is not clear why God could not have imparted the disposition without the evil or why evil in the world is justified by the acquisition of such dispositions.[24] I think Hick has no good answers to these questions.[25]

II

No doubt there are other ingenious ways of altering (7), but the many objections to the carefully worked-out solutions by Plantinga, Swinburne, and Hick suggest that (6) and a version of (7) by themselves are an insufficient foundation for a satisfactory solution to the problem of evil. Reflection on the nature of the problem seems to me to confirm this suggestion. The problem of evil is generally presented as some sort of inconsistency in theistic beliefs, and (1)–(4) present the relevant theistic assumptions. And yet *mere* theists are relatively rare in the history of religion. Most people who accept (1)–(4) are Jews or Christians or Muslims. If we are going to claim that *their* beliefs are somehow inconsistent, we need to look at a more complete set of Jewish or Muslim or Christian beliefs concerning God's goodness and evil in the world, not just at that limited subset of such beliefs which are common to all three religions, because what *appears* inconsistent if we take a partial sampling of beliefs may in fact look consistent when set in the context of a more complete set of beliefs. I do not of course mean to suggest that an inconsistent set of propositions could become consistent if we add more propositions to it. My point is simple and commonsensical: that the appearance of inconsistency in a set of beliefs may arise from our interpretation of those beliefs, and our reinterpretation of them in light of a larger system of beliefs to which they belong may dispel the appearance of inconsistency.[26] A more promising foundation for a solution to the problem of evil, then, might be found if we consider a broader range of beliefs concerning the relations of God to evil in the world, which are specific to a particular monotheism.

Furthermore, attempted solutions to the problem of evil based solely on a few theistic assumptions common to the major monotheisms are likely themselves to be incompatible with Jewish or Christian or Islamic beliefs. Swinburne's attempted solution, for example, seems incompatible with traditional Christian beliefs about heaven. On Swinburne's account, we are more like pets than humans unless we have significant exercise of our free will, and natural evil is necessary for such a significant exercise. But there is no natural evil in heaven and so, according to Swinburne's position, no significant exercise of free will either. Hence, on Swinburne's account, persons in heaven are not perfected in virtue of their translation to heaven, as Christian doctrine has traditionally claimed, but rather diminished in status. Thoughtful Christians troubled by the problem of evil, then, are not likely to be reassured by Swinburne's solution.

For these reasons, in what follows I will focus on one particular monotheism, namely, Christianity; I do not know enough about Judaism or Islam to present a discussion of the problem of evil in the context of those religions. In fact, my account will not deal even with all varieties of Christian belief. Because my account will depend on a number of assumptions, such as that man has free will, it will present a solution to the problem of evil applicable only to those versions of Christianity which accept those assumptions. Christians who reject a belief in free will, for example, will also reject my attempt at a solution to the problem of evil.

Besides (1)–(4), there are three Christian beliefs that seem to me especially relevant to the problem of evil. They are these:

(8) Adam fell.
(9) Natural evil entered the world as a result of Adam's fall.
(10) After death, depending on their state at the time of their death, either (a) human beings go to heaven or (b) they go to hell.[27]

It is clear that these beliefs themselves raise a host of problems, partly because they seem implausible or just plain false and partly because they seem to raise the problem of evil again in their own right. In this section I will consider worries raised by these beliefs themselves; in the next section I will argue that these three beliefs together with a new formulation of (7) provide a basis for a Christian solution to the problem of evil for those varieties of Christian belief which accept (1)–(4) and (6)–(10). The applicability of this solution to monotheisms other than Christianity depends on whether they accept these beliefs.

It would, of course, make a difference to my solution if any of the beliefs added in (8)–(10) could be *demonstrated* to be false, and so I will devote this section of the paper primarily to arguing that though (8)–(10) are controversial and *seem* false to many people, they are not *demonstrably* false. The fact that the problem of evil is raised again by (8)–(10) in conjunction with (1)–(3) is also worrisome. If a solution to the problem of evil relies on (8)–(10) and (8)–(10) themselves raise the problem, the problem is not solved but simply pushed back a stage. If (8)–(10) are to serve as the basis for an effective solution, the appearance they give of being inconsistent with the existence of a good God must be dispelled; attempting to do so is my other main concern in this section. If I can show that these beliefs are not demonstrably false and are not themselves incompatible with belief in a good God, which is all I want to do in this section, it will then be possible for me in the next section to use (8)–(10) in my attempted solution to the problem of evil.

The Christian belief summarized as (10) appears to raise the problem of evil because it gives rise to questions such as these:

(Q1) If an omnipotent God could bring it about that all human beings be in heaven and if a good God would want no human beings in hell, wouldn't a good, omnipotent God bring it about that all human beings be in heaven?

(Q2) Even if an omnipotent God does not bring it about that all human beings be in heaven, how could a good omnipotent God allow any human beings to suffer torment in hell?

(Q3) How could a good, just God decree that some human beings suffer torment for an infinite time for evils done during a finite human lifetime?

(Q4) Wouldn't a good God give all those in hell "a second chance," thereby ensuring that all human beings, or virtually all, be brought to heaven?

No doubt (10) raises more questions concerning God's goodness, but these are the ones most commonly raised by philosophers and other reflective people concerned with these issues.[28] I cannot do justice to these difficult questions in this paper; but without destroying the usefulness of (10) in my solution to the problem of evil, I can do enough, I think, to show that (10) can be interpreted in a way which significantly diminishes or dispells the appearance that it is incompatible with God's goodness.

To begin with, on Christian doctrine heaven should be understood not as some place with gates of pearl and streets of gold but rather as a spiritual state of union with God; and union with God should be understood to involve as a necessary (but not sufficient) condition the state of freely willing only what is in accordance with the will of God. This understanding of heaven, which is traditional in the history of Christian thought,[29] goes some way towards answering (Q1). If, as I think and as has been well argued elsewhere,[30] it is not logically possible for God to make human beings do anything freely, and if heaven is as I have described it, then it is not within God's power to insure that all human beings will be in heaven, because it is not within his power to determine what they freely will.

An answer to (Q2) also can be sketched by looking more closely at the Christian doctrine being questioned. Hell is commonly regarded as God's torture chamber, and it is considered fearsome because of the unending physical torments imposed by God on those sent there. This is, of course, a conception of hell which has been promoted by various popular preachers and has its roots in biblical Christianity; passages such as Matt. 25:41–46 and Luke 16:19–26 have been cited in support of it. And yet even a cursory look at traditional Christian writings shows that this is a crude and simplistic account of the doctrine of hell. For example, Dante, who has given perhaps the most famous Christian description of hell, includes as part of hell something like what Socrates was hoping for as other-worldly bliss:[31] a beautiful, bright place with green meadows and gentle streams in which the noblest and wisest of the ancients discuss philosophy.[32] This is part of Limbo, and on Dante's view it is in hell and fearsome. What makes Limbo awful is not physical tortures or spiritual torments, of which there are none, but rather the fact that the people there are separated from union with God and will always be so; and for Dante, I think, that is the fundamental awfulness of all the rest of the hell, too.

Dante, of course, has also given us some of our most graphic images of hellish tortures, but there is something odd about the tortures in Dante's hell. Dante portrays Ulysses as perpetually in the process of being consumed by fire, and yet he also has Ulysses deliver a long and elaborate speech; Farinata is being tortured in a burning iron tomb but he engages in a proud and leisurely conversation with Dante the traveler. In short, although Dante is the source for some of the most frightful representations of hell's punishments, he does not represent the people in hell as suffering from those punishments in the way human beings ordinarily would suffer them; no man who was on fire and had been so for some time would be capable of the calm, lengthy speech Ulysses makes. One might, of course, suppose that putting such speeches into the mouths of the tortured damned is just a poetic device for Dante; but such a supposition seems implausible to me for several reasons. To state just one, I think it highly unlikely that Dante meant to portray hell as a place where people are being literally burned by real fire because none of the persons in

Dante's hell other than Dante the traveler is embodied, and it is improbable that Dante believed fire could burn souls in the way it burns bodies. Rather Dante's idea of hell, which strikes me as philosophically and theologically interesting, seems to have been that the pains a person such as Ulysses suffers are not so much an externally imposed physical punishment as they are an external manifestation of a person's inner state, resulting from that person's previous and current free choices. Thus, on Dante's view, if I understand it correctly, the torments of hell are not physical pains which God has chosen to add to the burden of hell's inhabitants but the natural psychological state of those who have habitually made bad choices and whose will is not conformable to the divine will.

On Dante's view, then, the essence of Hell consists in the absence of union with God, a condition entailed by a person's psychological state which is a result of that person's free choices and which is naturally painful. (By a naturally painful psychological state I mean that human beings, in consequence of the nature they have, experience the state in question as painful; it is open to God to produce that state in people without the pain but only at the cost of altering their nature. Humiliation and grief seem to me examples of naturally painful psychological states.) On this view of hell which I have been attributing to Dante, an answer to (Q2) might go along these lines. Everlasting life in hell is the ultimate evil which can befall a person in this world; but the torments of hell are the natural conditions of some persons, and God can spare such persons those pains only by depriving them of their nature or their existence. And it is arguable that, of the alternatives open to God, maintaining such persons in existence and as human is the best.[33]

I am not arguing that this view of hell is the only one or even necessarily the right one for Christians to have; nor have I presented any argument for the account of human psychology on which this view is based. What I am claiming is that the view described here, which I will call the Dantean view, has a place in traditional Christian theology and that a philosophical case could be made for it. For present purposes I will take the Dantean view as the Christian view of Hell, and I will take (10b) and all other talk of hell in this paper as referring to hell in the Dantean sense. Of the various views of hell I know, the Dantean view seems to me the one most likely to be philosophically defensible, and it is entirely adequate for the solution to the problem of evil I will develop. But the Dantean view is a comparatively mild view of hell. Many Christian thinkers have believed God imposed terrible physical torments on those in hell as punishment for their sins in addition to their natural psychological pains. This is a much stronger view of hell than the Dantean view, and it raises a host of problems. The strong version of (10b), for example, raises the problem of evil in a way that can be settled only by considering whether retributive punishment is morally justifiable, what criteria we use to determine the degree of punishment appropriate to a crime, what the nature of the crimes punished in hell is, and many other questions, which plainly require lengthy treatment and cannot be dealt with in passing in this paper. If hell understood in this strong sense as including retributive punishment can be shown consistent with the existence of a good God, then my solution will be compatible with that strong interpretation; nothing in my solution rules out the strong version of hell if such a hell can be shown to be founded on justice and love, as Dante claimed for his version of hell.[34] On the other hand, if hell on the strong interpretation cannot be shown consistent with God's goodness, my solution will still hold; but there will be a dilemma for Christian belief: either to give up the strong interpretation of hell or to accept it and with it a version of the problem of evil which is insoluble by rational means.

The answer to (Q2), then, is also the answer to (Q3): on the Dantean view, hell is the natural state and, even understood as unending, it is arguably the best possible state of those whose free wills are not in conformity with the divine will, on the assumption that continued existence as a human being even with pain is more valuable than the absence of that pain at the cost of one's existence or human nature.

As for (Q4), I do not think it poses much of a problem. It seems reasonable to suppose and it is traditional Christian doctrine,[35] that God always wills the good for its own sake. So to will in accordance with God's will, a man must also will the good for its own sake. The assumption behind (Q4) is that anyone who has once had a taste of hell would henceforth do whatever he had to do to avoid hell. But then such a person would be willing the good not for its own sake but for the sake of avoiding hell. Such a person's will would thus not be in conformity with God's will, and so it would not be possible for God to bring it about that such a person participate in the union with God which is essential to life in heaven.[36]

The Christian belief in the fall of Adam, expressed in (8), has been interpreted in many ways.[37] Some (but not all) of these interpretations are incompatible with the theory of evolution; and if the current theory of evolution is provably true, such interpretations can be shown to be false and so cannot be used in any effective attempt to solve the problem of evil. My solution, however, will rely on only a few elements which are common to many interpretations of (8) and not incompatible with the theory of evolution, namely, that

(8′) (a) at some time in the past as a result of their own choices human beings altered their nature for the worse,
     (b) the alteration involved what we perceive and describe as a change in the nature of human free will,[38]

and

     (c) the changed nature of the will was inheritable.

(8′) is compatible with the denial (as well as with the affirmation) that there once was a particular man named Adam who fell from a better to a worse state in consequence of a bad choice, but for the sake of convenience I will continue to refer to the events described in (8') as 'Adam's fall'. Nothing in the theory of evolution entails the falsity of any part of (8'), and (8') is compatible with any number of interpretations of (8).

Of course, the fact that the theory of evolution does not entail the falsity of (8) understood as (8') does not rule out the possibility that (8) is demonstrably false for some other reason. The historical claim of (8'a) will strike many people as implausible, unsupported by evidence, the product of neurotic psychological forces, and so on. But although such reactions show that (8') is controversial, they are of course not sufficient to show that (8') is false. A more promising line of attack on (8') involves (8'b) or (8'c). What a change in the nature of the will is supposed to be is unclear, but any sensible account of such a change would, it seems, have to be incompatible with the notion that such a change in the will is inheritable. A reply to this objection requires a closer examination of the traditional Christian understanding of the will and its post-fall alteration.

One of the classic expositions of this understanding is that given by Anselm.[39] Anselm's theory of the will is very different from most contemporary accounts,[40] and I cannot do it justice in this paper. I want to present just enough of the theory to show the difference it makes to an evaluation of (8). According to Anselm, human beings originally had wills disposed to will as they ought to will and an ability to preserve that disposition. This ability is what Anselm calls free will. On Anselm's view, free will is a strength. The capacity for either getting sick or staying healthy, Anselm would say, is not a strength, only the capacity to stay healthy is. Similarly, Anselm maintains that the ability to will what one ought to will or what one ought not to will is not a strength and cannot count as free will: only the ability to will what one ought to will is a strength and it alone is free will. Human beings in their pre-fall state could do evil because as finite beings they could be less than they had the strength to be. They could fail to use their strength to preserve the uprightness of their wills and so fall into evil. Adam's fall consists in such a failure. In consequence of past failure of this sort, human beings have lost their initial disposition to will what they ought to will and acquired instead a disposition to will what they ought not to will. This acquired disposition consists primarily of an inclination to will one's own power or pleasure in preference to greater goods,[41] it was and is inheritable. Although human beings still have some sort of ability to do good after the fall, because of the disposition of their will they find it very difficult (but not impossible) to resist evil. To this extent, then, their free will (in Anselm's sense of 'free will') is diminished.

The notion of a disposition of the will which is operative in this account needs to be understood in light of Anselm's unusual definition of free will. A free will is a will disposed to will the good and able to maintain such a disposition. In Aquinas's development of Anselm's account, recognition of what is good is the job of reason; and the righteous disposition of free will is a function of a right relationship among reason, the will, and desire.[42] For the will to be free, desire must be subject to reason, and reason must guide both the will and desire to what really is good. The post-fall disposition of the will is the result of a disordered relationship among these three. Desire is not subject to reason; often enough it governs reason instead. And rather than being guided by reason, the will tends to be moved by irrational desire, so that it wills an apparent or partial good rather than what is really or wholly good. This disordered relationship among reason, the will, and desire on Aquinas's view constitutes the change in the will produced by Adam's fall.[43] The original inclination of the will to will the good proposed by reason has been lost and replaced by an inclination to will what is sought as good by the appetites. These inclinations are inclinations of the will itself, not external constraints on the will; and they are only inclinations or tendencies, not necessitated willing. Post-fall evil is voluntary, not compelled. On the other hand, this account lends plausibility to the claim that the altered disposition of the will is inheritable. What is said to be inherited is not a certain set of acts of will or a specific habit of willing but rather a weakened influence of reason and strengthened influence of appetite on the will, a loss of the will's natural inclination to follow reason. There is nothing obviously incoherent, as far as I can see, in supposing this change in the relationship of reason, will, and desire to be inheritable.

(8) also raises the problem of evil in two ways which must be briefly considered here:

(Q5) In view of all the subsequent evil occasioned by Adam's fall, shouldn't a good God have destroyed the human race immediately after Adam's fall?

(Q6) Couldn't God have prevented the human race from inheriting this evil inclination of will after Adam's fall, by some miraculous intervention in human history if necessary?

The answer to (Q5), I think, is that 'ending is better than mending' is not a principle appropriate to Christianity. On Christian doctrine, persons once created are everlasting and infinitely valuable; if they become defective, it is up to a good God not to eliminate them but to fix them if he can. This view, of course, is not peculiar to Christianity. If a family has a child with a possibly terminal, genetically transmissible disease, it does not usually consider destroying the child, but instead puts the child and the rest of the family to a great deal of pain and trouble caring for the child and trying to alleviate or cure the disease.

(Q6) is harder to deal with. Without destroying any of his creatures, God could have prevented the transmission of a defective free will in any number of ways. He could have prevented procreation on the part of the defective people, for example, or he could miraculously have prevented the transmissible defect from actually being transmitted. But I think there are two things to be said against these alternatives. In the first place they constitute in effect the abrogation of God's first creation; they put an end to the first human beings God produced. If God were then to replace these human beings by others and they also corrupted their wills, God would then presumably replace them also, and so on, in what appears to be a series of frustrations and defeats inappropriate to a deity. It seems to me arguable that there is more power and dignity and also more love and care in restoring fallen humanity to a good state than in ending and replacing it. Secondly, Swinburne seems to me right in maintaining that what makes God's human creatures persons rather than pets is the ability to exercise their free will in serious choices. If God immediately removed or prevented the consequences of any free choice eventuating in major evil, his creatures would not have that significant exercise of free will and would thus not be persons.

As for (9), it can be read in either of these two ways:

(9') There were no diseases, tornadoes, droughts, etc. in the world until Adam's fall; or
(9") no person suffered from diseases, tornadoes, droughts, etc. until Adam's fall.

The weaker assumption, of course, is (9"), and it is all I need for my purposes here. The ways in which an omnipotent God might have brought about (9") are limited only by one's imagination, and there is no need to specify any one of them here.

In this brief account of (8), (9), and (10), I cannot hope to have given either an adequate presentation of these doctrines or a sufficient answer to the questions they raise. But my sketchy treatment indicates, I think, both that none of these three beliefs is demonstrably false and that there are some reasonable arguments against the charges that (8) and (10) are themselves incompatible with God's goodness. Those results are enough to enable me to use (8)–(10) in an attempt to show how on Christian beliefs the existence of evil is compatible with the existence of an omnipotent, omniscient, perfectly good God.

III

According to the Christian beliefs summarized as (8), (9), and (10), all human beings since Adam's fall have been defective in their free wills, so that they have a powerful inclination to will what they ought not to will, to will their own power or pleasure in preference to greater goods. It is not possible for human beings in that condition to go to heaven, which consists in union with God; and hell understood in Dantean terms is arguably the best alternative to annihilation. A good God will want to fix such persons, to save them from hell and bring them to heaven; and as the creator of these persons, God surely bears some responsibility for fixing and saving them if he can. How is he to do so?

It seems to me clear that he cannot fix the defect by using his omnipotence to remove it miraculously. The defect is a defect in *free* will, and it consists in a person's generally failing to will what he ought to will. To remove this defect miraculously would be to force a person's free will to be other than it is; it would consist in causing a person to will freely what he ought to will. But it is logically impossible for anyone to make a person freely will something, and therefore even God in his omnipotence cannot directly and miraculously remove the defect in free will, without destroying the very freedom of the will he wants to fix.

Someone might object here that if the defect in the will is inheritable without prejudice to the freedom of the will, then it is also removable without detriment to the freedom of the will; and if it destroys freedom to have God remove the defect, then it also destroys freedom to have the defect inherited. This objection, I think, is based on a mistaken picture of the inheritance of the defect. If the traditional doctrine were that after the time of Adam's fall, human beings whose wills were in a pre-fall state suddenly acquired fallen, defective wills, then this objection would be sound. And perhaps the use of the word 'inheritance,' with its suggestions of one individual suddenly receiving something from another, invites such a picture. But in fact the doctrine of Adam's fall makes it clear that in the transmission of the defect there is no change of will on the part of post-fallen men. What the doctrine specifies is that individuals conceived and born after Adam's fall have defective wills from the very beginning of their existence. There is no change of will in this process; rather the process consists in the generation of persons whose free wills from birth are strongly inclined to certain sorts of evil actions. If God were to destroy such post-fall persons and generate new ones with non-defective wills (as I have argued he should not), he would not be violating the free wills of the new persons by so creating them any more than he violated Adam's free will when he created Adam in his pre-fall state. But if God intervenes to remove the defect in the wills of post-fall persons, he brings about a *change* in their wills; and this, I think, he cannot do if their wills are to remain free.[44]

If God cannot by his omnipotence directly fix the defect in free will, it seems that human beings must fix it themselves. Self-repair is a common feature of the natural world, but I do not think self-repair is possible for a person with post-fall free will. People, of course, do sometimes reform their lives and change their habits; but one necessary condition for their doing so is that, for whatever purpose or motive, they will something different from what they previously willed. Analogously, to reform the will requires willing something different from what one previously willed; that is, it requires a change of will. But how to change the will is the problem in the first place. If we want to know whether a man himself can fix a defect in his will, whether he himself can somehow remove his tendency to will what he ought not to will, it is no help to be told that of course he can if he just wills to change his will. We know that a man *can* change his will for the better; otherwise his will would not be free. The problem with a defect in the will is not that there is an inability to will what one ought to will because of some external restraint on the will, but that one does not and will not will what one ought to will because the will itself is bent towards evil. Consequently, changing the will is the end for which we are seeking the means; if one were *willing* to change one's will by willing what one ought to will, there would be no problem of a defect in the will.[45] Self-repair, then, is no more a solution to the problem of a defective will than is God's miraculous intervention.[46]

If God cannot and human beings will not fix the defect in their wills, what possible cure is there? Christianity suggests what seems to me the only remaining alternative. Let a person will that God fix his defective will. In that case, God's alteration of the will is something the person has freely chosen, and God can then alter that person's will without destroying its freedom. It is a fact well-attested in religious literature that people who find it next to impossible to will what (they believe) they ought to will may none-theless find it in themselves to will that God alter their wills. Perhaps two of the most famous examples are the sonnet of John Donne in which he prays for God to overwhelm him so that he will be chaste[47] and Augustine's prayers that God give him continence.[48] The traditional formulation of the crucial necessary condition for a person's being a Christian (variously interpreted by Protestants and Catholics) is that he wills God to save him from his sin; and this condition is, I think, logically (and perhaps also psychologically) equiva-lent to a person's willing that God fix his will. Willing to have God save one from one's sin is willing to have God bring one to a state in which one is free from sin, and that state depends essentially on a will which wills what it ought to will.

What role God plays in man's coming to will that God fix his will is controversial in the history of Christian thought. Some Protestant theologians have argued that God bears sole responsibility for such willing; Pelagius apparently argued that all the responsibility belongs to man. The first of these positions seems to me to have difficulties roughly analogous to those raised above by the suggestion that God might miraculously fix man's will, and the difficulties in the second are like those in the suggestion that a man himself might fix his own will. Perhaps the correct view here too consists in postulating a cooperative divine and human effort. Perhaps Socrates' way with those he encountered can serve as a model. When Socrates pursued a man with wit and care and passion for the truth, that man sometimes converted to philosophy and became Socrates' disciple. Such a man converted freely, so that it is false to say Socrates *caused* his conversion; and yet, on the other hand, it would be ridiculous to say in consequence that the man bears sole responsibility for his conversion. The responsibility and the credit for the conversion belong to Socrates, whose effort and ingenuity were necessary conditions of the conversion. That they were not sufficient conditions, however, and that the man nonetheless freely willed his conversion is clear from the cases of men such as Alcibiades, whom Socrates sought but did not succeed in converting. Without rashly trying to adjudicate in a paragraph an old and complicated controversy, I think that something along those lines can also be said of the process by which a man comes to will God's help. God's efforts on behalf of Augustine are the necessary condition of Augustine's conversion, and the credit for his conversion belongs to God; but God's efforts are not a sufficient condition, and so Augustine's free will is not impugned. Or, as Anselm says with regard to the fall of the angels, "although the good angel received perseverance [in willing what he ought to will] because God gave it, it is not the case that the evil angel did not receive it because God did not give it. But rather, God did not give it because Satan did not receive it, and he did not receive it because he was unwilling to receive it."[49]

At any rate, if a man does will that God fix his will or save him from his sins, then I think that God can do so without detriment to free will, provided that he does so only to the extent to which the man freely wills that God do so. There is in principle no reason why a person could not will at once that God fix the whole defect of his will; but in general, perhaps because of the extent of the defect in the will, people seem to turn from their own evil in a series of small-scale reforms. In Book VIII, chapter VII, of the *Confessions*, Augustine describes himself as praying that God give him chastity and making the private reservation 'but not yet.' If God were immediately to give Augustine chastity in such a case, he would in fact be doing so against Augustine's will. And so, in general, God's fixing the will seems to be a lengthy process, in which a little willing produces a little fixing, which in turn promotes more willing of more fixing. On Christian doctrine, this is the process of sanctification, which is not finally completed until after death when it culminates "in the twinkling of an eye" in the last changes which unite the sanctified person with God.[50]

The fixing of a defective free will by a person's freely willing that God fix his will is, I think, the foundation of a Christian solution to the problem of evil. What sort of world is most conducive to bringing about both the initial human willing of help and also the subsequent process of sanctification? To answer that question, we need to consider the psychological state of a person who wills God's help. Apart from the obvious theological beliefs, such a person must also hold that he tends to do what he ought not to do and does so because he himself wills what he ought not to will, and he must want not to be in such a condition. He must, in other words, have both a humbling recognition of himself as evil and a desire for a better state. So things that contribute to a person's humbling, to his awareness of his own evil, and to his unhappiness with his present state contribute to his willing God's help.

I think that both moral and natural evil make such a contribution. The unprevented gross moral evils in the course of human history show us something about the nature of man, and our own successful carrying out of our no doubt smaller-scaled evil wills shows us that we are undeniably members of the species. Natural evil—the pain of disease, the intermittent and unpredictable destruction of natural disasters, the decay of old age, the imminence of death—takes away a person's satisfaction with himself. It tends to humble him, show him his frailty, make him reflect on the transience of temporal goods, and turn his affections towards other-worldly things, away from the things of this world. No amount of moral or natural evil, of course, can *guarantee* that a man will seek God's help. If it could, the willing it produced would not be free. But evil of this sort is the best hope, I think, and maybe the only effective means, for bringing men to such a state.

That natural evil and moral evil, the successful carrying out of evil human wills, serve to make men recognize their own evils, become dissatisfied with things of this world, and turn to God is a controversial claim; and it is clear that a compelling argument for or against it would be very difficult to construct. To produce such an argument we would need a representative sample, whatever that might be, of natural and moral evil. Then we would need to examine that sample case by case to determine the effect of the evil in each case on the human beings who suffered or perpetrated it. To determine the effect we would have to know the psychological and moral state of these people both before and after the evil at issue (since the effect would consist in some alteration of a previous state); and we would have to chart their state for the rest of their lives after that evil because, like the effect of carcinogens, the effect of the experience of evil may take many years to manifest itself. Even with the help of a team of psychologists and sociologists, then, it would be hard to collect the data necessary to make a good argument for or against this claim. Hence, I am unable to present a cogent argument for one of the main claims of this paper, not because of the improbability of the claim but because of the nature of the data an argument for the claim requires; and perhaps it should just be categorized as one more Christian belief and added as (11) to the list of (8), (9), and (10) as a traditionally held, not demonstrably false Christian belief.[51] Still, there is *some* historical evidence for it in the fact that Christianity has tended to flourish among the oppressed and decline among the comfortable, and perhaps the best evidence comes from the raising of children. The phrase 'spoiling a child' is ambiguous in current parlance between 'turning a child into a unpleasant person' and 'giving a child everything he wants,' and the ambiguity reflects a truth about human nature. The pains, the hardships, the struggles which children encounter tend to make them better people. Of course, such experiences do not invariably make children better; children, like adults, are also sometimes made worse by their troubles. But that fact would be a counter-example to the general claim about the function of evil in the world only in case it maintained that evil was *guaranteed* to make people better; and that is something this claim could not include and still be compatible with Christianity as long as Christianity is committed to the view that human beings have free will.

Someone may object here that the suffering of children is just what this attempted solution to the problem of evil cannot explain. In *The Brothers Karamazov*, Dostoevsky provides the most eloquent presentation this objection is likely ever to get, concluding with Ivan's passionate insistence (implicit in a question addressed to Alyosha) that even if the whole world could be saved for eternal bliss by the torture of one innocent child, allowing the torture of that child for that purpose would be horribly wrong. I am in sympathy with the attitude Dostoevsky has Ivan express and in agreement with Ivan's conclusion. The suffering of children is in my view unquestionably the instance of evil most difficult for the problem of evil, and there is something almost indecent about any move resembling an attempt to explain it away. The suffering of children is a terrible thing, and to try to see it otherwise is to betray one's humanity. Any attempt to solve the problem of evil must try to provide some understanding of the suffering of children, but it must not lessen our pain over that suffering if it is not to become something monstrous and inhumane.

With considerable diffidence, then, I want to suggest that Christian doctrine is committed to the claim that a child's suffering is outweighed by the good for the child which can result from that suffering. This is a brave (or foolhardy) thing to say, and the risk inherent in it is only sharpened when one applies it to cases in which infants suffer, for example, or in which children die in their suffering. Perhaps the decent thing to do here is simply to sketch some considerations which may shed light on these hard cases. To begin with, it is important to remember that on Christian doctrine death is not the ultimate evil or even the ultimate end, but rather a transition between one form of life and another. From a Christian point of view, the thing to be avoided at all costs is not dying, but dying badly; what concerns the Christian about death is not that it occurs but that the timing and mode of death be such as to constitute the best means of ensuring that state of soul which will bring a person to eternal union with God. If children who die in their suffering thereby move from the precarious and frequently painful existence of this world to a permanently blissful existence in the other world and if their suffering was among part of the necessary means to effect that change, their suffering is justified. I am not trying to say here that the suffering which a child or any other person experiences is the only way in which that person could be brought to God. Rather, I am trying to avoid constructing the sort of explanation for evil which requires telling the sufferer that God lets him suffer just for the sake of some abstract general good for mankind. Perhaps it is true that such a general good—the significant freedom of created persons, for example—is the ultimate end for the sake of which God permits evil. It seems to me nonetheless that a perfectly good entity who was also omniscient and omnipotent must govern the evil resulting from the misuse of that significant freedom in such a way that the sufferings of any particular person are outweighed by the good which the suffering produces *for that person*; otherwise, we might justifiably expect a good God somehow to prevent that *particular suffering*, either by intervening (in one way or another) to protect the victim, while still allowing the perpetrator his freedom, or by curtailing freedom in some select cases.[52] And since on Christian doctrine the ultimate good for persons is union with God, the suffering of any person will be justified if it brings that person nearer to the ultimate good in a way he could not have been without the suffering. I think that Christianity must take some such approach to the suffering or death of children; and perhaps something analogous can be said in connection with the hardest case of all, the suffering of infants. Psychologists tell us that the first year of a child's life is tremendously important in molding the personality and character. For some persons the molding of the personality produced by suffering in infancy may be the best means of insuring a character capable of coming to God.[53]

In all these hard cases, the difficulty of formulating a Christian position which does not appear either implausible or inhuman will be diminished if we have clearly in mind the view of man Christianity starts with. On Christian doctrine, all human beings are suffering from the spiritual equivalent of a terminal disease; they have a defect in the will which if not corrected will cost them life in heaven and consign them to a living death in hell. Now suppose that we are the parents of a child with a terminal brain disease, which includes among its symptoms the child's rejecting the notion that he is sick and refusing to cooperate in any treatments. The doctors tell us that there are treatments which may well cure the child completely, but they hurt and their success is not guaranteed. Would we not choose to subject the child to the treatments, even if they were very painful? The child's suffering would be a terrible thing; we would and we should be grieved at it. But we would nonetheless be glad of the treatments and hope of a cure. And yet this example is only a pale reflection of what Christianity claims to be the case for all human beings, where the loss inflicted by the disease and the benefits of its cure are infinitely greater. If moral and natural evil contain an essential ingredient of a possible cure, surely the cure is worth the suffering such evil entails.

It might seem to some people that if this is God's plan, it is a tragic failure because the amount of evil in the world produces so few cures. The vast majority of people in the world are not Christians or theists of any kind; and even among those who are Christian many die in serious unrepented evil. But this complaint rests on an assumption for which we have no evidence, namely, that the majority of people end in hell. That even an evil-doer who dies a sudden, unexpected death may not die impenitent is shown vividly by Dante:

> I am Buonconte . . . wounded in the throat, flying on foot and bloodying
> the plain [I came]. There I lost my sight and speech. I ended on the name

413

of Mary, and there I fell, and my flesh remained alone . . . The Angel of God took me, and he from Hell cried, 'O you from Heaven, why do you rob me? You carry off with you the eternal part of him for one little tear which takes him from me'.[54]

As for those who live and die without the religious knowledge necessary for redemption from evil, it is not incompatible with Christian doctrine to speculate that in the process of their dying God acquaints them with what they need to know and offers them a last chance to choose.[55] Such a speculation might seem to vitiate the justification for evil which I have been developing in this paper, because if the whole process of redemption can be begun and completed in a person's dying hour, why do we need evil in the world? But this is a mistaken objection, because surely in any sort of deathbed repentance the sufferings of the dying person will have had a significant effect on that person's character and consequently on the choices he makes on his deathbed. So as long as some such speculation is not incompatible with Christian doctrine, it is not at all clear that the majority of people end in hell. And without that assumption the complaint that God's plan for the use of evil is a failure is altogether unwarranted.

Someone might also object here that this solution to the problem of evil prohibits us from any attempt to relieve human suffering and in fact suggests that we ought to promote it, as the means of man's salvation. Such an objection is mistaken, I think, and rests on an invalid inference. Because God can use suffering to cure an evil will, it does not follow that we can do so also. God can see into the minds and hearts of human beings and determine what sort and amount of suffering is likely to produce the best results; we cannot. (Our inability to do so is in fact one of the things which make it so difficult to discuss cases of infant suffering, for example.) Furthermore, God as parent creator has a right to, and a responsibility for, painful correction of his creatures, which we as sibling creatures do not have. Therefore, since all human suffering is *prima facie* evil, and since we do not know with any high degree of probability how much (if any) of it is likely to result in good to any particular sufferer on any particular occasion, it is reasonable for us to eliminate the suffering as much as we can. At any rate, the attempt to eliminate suffering is likely to be beneficial to our characters, and passivity in the face of others' suffering will have no such good effects.[56]

IV

The solution to the problem of evil I have been developing will be clarified further by being applied to an individual instance of evil. The instance I want to consider is the Old Testament story of Cain and Abel.[57] For my purposes here, this biblical story of an instance of evil has several advantages over a description of an instance of evil drawn from such sources as the newspapers.

The biblical story contains a description of God's intervention or lack of intervention in human history, and it includes an account of the inner thoughts and motivations of the principal characters. To the extent to which Christians are committed to accepting the Bible as the revealed word of God, to that extent they are committed to accepting this story as veridical also; and that fact obviously contributes to the use I want to make of the story. Finally, although the story of Cain and Abel is regularly taken by Christians as a paradigmatically moral and religious story, suitable for the edification of children, the incidents related in the story are such that a twentieth-century atheistic philosopher might have invented them as a showcase for the problem of evil.

Cain and Abel are two brothers who bring offerings to God.[58] Abel's offering is accepted, but Cain's is not—why, the story does not say.[59] In consequence, Cain is very angry at Abel. The story suggests that acceptance or rejection of the offerings is an (at least temporary) acceptance or rejection of the offerer; and Cain's anger at Abel apparently stems from jealousy over God's favoring Abel rather than Cain. Now there is something double-minded in Cain's anger and jealousy. Either God is right to reject Cain's offering—because there was something about it or about the person who brought it which made it objectively unacceptable—and in that case there are no grounds for anger; or God is wrong to reject Cain's offering—because it was a perfectly good offering brought in an altogether appropriate spirit—and in that case *God* is not good. And although one might then still be afraid of the consequences of incurring God's displeasure or resent those more favored by God, a single-minded belief that God's standards for accepting offerings are bad precludes jealousy towards those who are accepted. That Cain is angry and jealous indicates that he is double-minded about whether God is right to reject his offering.

Although he does reject Cain's offering, God does not leave Cain to himself in his double-minded anger. He comes to him and talks to him, asking Cain Socratic questions designed to get him to recognize and resolve his double-mindedness: "Why are you angry?"; "If you do well, will you not be accepted?" And God goes on to give Cain a warning, that he is in danger of sin. So God apparently anticipates Cain's attack on his brother, and he intervenes to warn Cain.

But Cain attacks and kills his brother. Abel, who has just been accepted by God and is evidently righteous, suffers violent and untimely death. When the killing is over, God speaks to Cain again, asking him more careful questions designed to lead him to confess his deed: first, "Where is Abel?", and then after the evasive response to that question, the stronger question "What have you done?" When Cain is obstinate in his evil, God punishes him by miraculously intervening in nature: the ground will be barren when Cain tills it, and apparently only when Cain tills it. Finally, we have the last piece of God's care for Cain in this story: Cain says his punishment is more than he can bear, and God comforts him by protecting him against being killed by other men, a danger Cain had understood to be part of his punishment.

Now consider God's actions in this story. In the first place, he punishes Cain for the murder of Abel, showing thereby that he regards the murder of Abel as bad and worthy of punishment. And yet he himself allowed the murder to take place, although obviously he could have prevented it. Any decent person who was present when Cain attacked his brother would have made some effort to rescue Abel; but God, who is always present everywhere and who even seems to anticipate Cain's attack, does nothing for Abel. On the other hand, consider what God does to or for Cain. He comes to him and warns him of the coming temptation. After the murder he returns to talk to Cain again, in a way designed to make Cain acknowledge his true state. When he imposes punishment, he does it in a way that seems to require a miracle. He banishes Cain from his land. And when Cain complains that his punishment is too much, God is merciful to him and guards him from being killed by other men. In short, God interferes in Cain's affairs to warn him; he talks to him earnestly to get him to see his true situation; he performs a miracle on his behalf; he sends him away from his own place; and he protects him from being murdered. Clearly, any *one* of these things done on Abel's behalf would have been enough to save him. But God does none of these things for *Abel*, the innocent, the accepted of God; he does them instead for *Cain*, a man whose offering was rejected and who is murderously angry at his brother. When it comes to righteous Abel, God simply stands by and watches him be killed. Why has such a story been allowed to stand as part of the canonical Scriptures?

On the solution to the problem of evil which I have been developing in this paper, if God is good and has a care for his creatures, his overriding concern must be to insure not that they live as long as possible or that they suffer as little pain as possible in this life but rather that they live in such a way as ultimately to bring them to union with God.

Abel presents God with no problems in this respect. He is apparently righteous at the time of his offering; and hence that is a safe, even a propitious, time for him to die, to make the transition from this life to the next. Given that he will die sometime, Abel's death at this time is if anything in Abel's interest; he dies at a time when he is accepted by God, and he enters into union with God. It is true that Abel dies prematurely and so is deprived of years of life. But on Christian doctrine, what he loses is years of a painful and spiritually perilous pilgrimage through this life, and what he gains is eternal bliss.[60]

Cain, on the other hand, is in trouble as regards both his current moral state and his prospects for the next life. If God were to rescue Abel by striking Cain with heart failure at the outset of Cain's attack on Abel, for example, Cain would die in mortal sin and so would go to hell, while righteous Abel would continue the morally dangerous journey of this life only to die later, perhaps in some less virtuous state. There are, of course, many other ways in which God could have stopped Cain and rescued Abel without going so far as killing

Cain. But perhaps stopping Cain even in those other ways would not have been good for Cain. Because God does not step in between Cain's willing and the successful realization of that willing, Cain is brought as forcefully as possible to a recognition of the depth of the evil he willed. And that forceful recognition is, I think, the most powerful means of bringing Cain to an acknowledgment of his own evil and a desire for help, which is a necessary condition for his salvation.

On the solution to the problem of evil which I have been developing here, then, God does not rescue Abel because contrary to appearances Abel is not in danger; and God's failure to rescue Abel, as well as all the other care for Cain recorded in the story, constitutes the best hope of a rescue for Cain, who is in danger, and not just of death but of a perpetual living death.

V

I think, then, that it is possible to produce a defensible solution to the problem of evil by relying both on the traditional theological and philosophical assumptions in (1)–(4) and (6), and on the specifically Christian doctrines in (8)–(10). Like other recent attempted solutions, this one also rests fundamentally on a revised version of (7), namely, this:

> (7''') Because it is a necessary condition for union with God, the significant exercise of free will employed by human beings in the process which is essential for their being saved from their own evil is of such great value that it outweighs all the evil of the world.

(7''') constitutes a morally sufficient reason for evil and so is a counter-example to (5), the claim that there is no morally sufficient reason for God to permit instances of evil. Like the positions of both Plantinga and Swinburne, this solution ties the justification for natural evils to free will, but in a way, I think, which does not raise the problem of evil all over again (as Plantinga's free will defence seems to do by leaving unjustified the successful acting on evil free will) and which shows a necessary connection between natural evil and the good that justifies it (as Swinburne's solution does not). Of the three solutions initially sketched in this paper, it is Hick's approach which my own solution most resembles; but the resemblance is only superficial. In reality, my solution is fundamentally different from Hick's both in its view of human beings and in its analysis of the function of evil, and so it escapes the basic criticisms of Hick's theodicy mentioned above. The changes in human beings which evil is said to produce on the solution I have developed here are logically necessary for union with God and life in heaven, as is not the case in Hick's account. And because of the particular nature of these changes, involving a fundamental change in the will, they could not be produced in any other way; unlike the changes which evil produces on Hick's view, these changes could not be brought about just by training for the Olympics or by writing a doctoral dissertation, for example.

Although I have argued against the solutions proposed by Plantinga, Swinburne, and Hick, I think that each of them makes an important contribution to a successful solution of the problem of evil; and what I find right in their work is, I think, compatible with the solution I have presented here. For example, there is a sense of

(7) The possession of free will and the use of it to do more good than evil is a good of such value that it outweighs all the evil in the world

which is true on Christian beliefs, I think, and compatible with my solution. On my solution, Christianity must assign an enormous value to free will, because the evil of Adam's fall and all subsequent moral and natural evil could have been prevented if human beings had never been given free will in the first place. But the good which free will produces and which outweighs subsequent evil should be understood, on my account, not just as morally good choices but rather as willing in accordance with the divine will and thus making possible union with God.

Furthermore, although I have argued for one particular good as the good which justifies moral and natural evil, nothing in my account rules out the possibility that either sort of evil may produce other goods as well. Thus I think Swinburne is right in his claim about the importance of our ability to act on our free will in significant ways. If our use of free will were restricted to trivial choices to prevent the possibility of our doing any major harm or if God always stepped in to remove the evil consequences of any bad act of will, I think Swinburne is right to claim we would be more like pets in God's dollhouse than like persons. So it seems to me that significant exercise of free will is a good which could only be produced by God's allowing evil and which therefore partially justifies the moral (but not the natural) evil in the world. On my account, however, what ultimately gives exercise of free will its main value is its necessary role in producing union with God; and it is this significant exercise of free will, a bent free will cooperating in its own cure, which I have argued outweighs all the evil in the world. So there is a sense of (7') too which is true on my solution.

I also think Hick is clearly right that some of the suffering produced by moral and natural evil results in character-building, so that some moral virtues are *another* good produced by evil. The problem with Hick's account is that the character-building he picks out to discuss could apparently be produced without any major moral or natural evil; hence the good produced by evil on Hick's account is not a good which can justify the evil in the world. But if we take character-building in the way I have described in my solution, not (like Hick) as an evolution from good to better, but as an alteration from a destructive psychological state to a life-giving one, then I think there is a reading of (7″) too which is true on Christian doctrine and compatible with my solution.

Finally, for the many other goods sometimes said to be produced by evil, such as punishment for sins or aesthetic completion of the whole canvas of creation, if any of these are in fact both good and produced by evil, I welcome them into my account. In (7‴) I have singled out one good produced by evil as the good which justifies all the evil in the world, but nothing in this claim rules out the possibility that evil produces various other lesser goods as well which may contribute to the justification of some sorts of evil.

In the brief exposition of this solution in this paper, I cannot hope to have given anything but a sketch and a preliminary defence of it; to do it justice and to consider carefully all the questions and objections it raises would require book-length treatment. For all its complexity, the story of Cain and Abel is the story of a simple instance of evil, which is easily dwarfed by any account of evil culled at random from today's newspapers; and I am under no illusions that by providing an explanation for the simple evil in the story of Cain and Abel I have given a sufficient and satisfying explanation of even the commonplace evils of ghetto violence, much less the almost unthinkable evils of Belsen or Hiroshima. What I would like to believe I have done is to have shown that with good will and careful attention to the details of the doctrines specific to a particular monotheism there is hope of a successful solution to the problem of evil along the lines developed here.[61]

NOTES

1. For a review of recent literature on the problem of evil, see Michael Peterson, "Recent Work on the Problem of Evil," *American Philosophical Quarterly* 20 (1983) 321–340.
2. Cf. Nelson Pike, "Hume on Evil," *Philosophical Review* 72 (1963) 180–181.
3. See "Evil and Omnipotence," *Mind* 64 (1955) 200–212.
4. "God and Evil," *Philosophical Quarterly* 10 (1960) 97–114.
5. Cf., e.g., Nelson Pike, op. cit.
6. Cf. John Stuart Mill, *Three Essays on Religion* (London: Longmans, Green and Co., 1875), pp. 176–190, 194.
7. John Stuart Mill, *An Examination of Sir William Hamilton's Philosophy* (London: Longmans, Green and Co., 1865), chap. 7.
8. Cf. Alvin Plantinga, "The Free Will Defence," in *Philosophy in America*, ed. Max Black (London: Allen and Unwin, 1965), pp. 204–220. A revised version of this paper is included in *God and Other Minds* (Ithaca, NY: Cornell University Press, 1967), pp. 131–155. Cf. also "Which Worlds Could God Have Created?" *Journal of Philosophy* 70 (1973) 539–552.
9. Among the most interesting criticisms of Plantinga are the following: Robert M. Adams, "Middle Knowledge and the Problem of Evil," *American Philosophical Quarterly* 14 (1977) 109–117; George Botterill, "Falsification and the Existence of God: A Discussion of Plantinga's Free Will Defence," *Philosophical Quarterly* 27 (1977) 114–134; Robert Burch, "Plantinga and Leibniz's Lapse," *Analysis* 39 (1979) 24–29; Nelson Pike, "Plantinga on Free Will and Evil," *Religious Studies* 15 (1979)

449–473; William Rowe, "God and Other Minds," *Nous* 3 (1969) 271–277; William Wainwright, "Christian Theism and the Free Will Defence: A Problem," *International Journal for the Philosophy of Religion* 6 (1975) 243–250; William Wainwright, "Freedom and Omnipotence," *Nous* 2 (1968) 293–301; and Peter Windt, "Plantinga's Unfortunate God," *Philosophical Studies* 24 (1973) 335–342.
10. *Analysis* (1975) 110–112.
11. See "The Probabilistic Argument from Evil," *Philosophical Studies* 35 (1979) 1–53.
12. Steven Wykstra, "The Humean Obstacle to Evidential Arguments from Suffering: On Avoiding the Evils of Appearance," forthcoming in *International Journal for the Philosophy of Religion*.
13. William Rowe, "The Empirical Argument from Evil," in *Rationality, Religious Belief, and Moral Commitment: New Essays in the Philosophy of Religion*, ed. R. Audi and W. Wainwright, Cornell University Press, forthcoming.
14. Richard Swinburne, *The Existence of God* (Oxford: Clarendon Press, 1979), pp. 200–224. See also "The Problem of Evil" in *Contemporary Philosophy of Religion*, ed. Steven M. Cahn and David Shatz (Oxford: Oxford University Press, 1982), pp. 3–19.
15. Richard Swinburne, *The Existence of God*, pp. 219–220.
16. *Ibid.*, p. 211.
17. *Ibid.*, especially pp. 206–208.
18. For a detailed criticism of Swinburne's solution, see my "Knowledge, Freedom, and the Problem of Evil," *International Journal for the Philosophy of Religion* 14 (1983) 49–58. See also David O'Connor, "Swinburne on Natural Evil," *Religious Studies* 19 (1983) 65–74.
19. Cf., e.g., I Sam. 23:9–11 and 30:7–8, Jeremiah 42:1–16, and Daniel 8–10.
20. John Hick, *Evil and the God of Love* (New York: Harper and Row, 1966).
21. See, e.g., L. T. Howe, "Leibniz on Evil," *Sophia* 10 (1971) 8–17; Roland Puccetti, "The Loving God—Some Observations on John Hick's *Evil and the God of Love*," *Religious Studies* 2 (1967) 255–268; and Illtyd Trethowan, "Dr. Hick and the Problem of Evil," *Journal of Theological Studies* 18 (1967) 407–416.
22. G. Stanley Kane, "The Failure of Soul-Making Theodicy," *International Journal for the Philosophy of Religion* 6 (1975) 1–22.
23. *Ibid.*, pp. 2–3.
24. *Ibid.*, pp.8ff.
25. For Hick's defence of his solutions against objections in the literature, see, for example, "God, Evil and Mystery," *Religious Studies* 3 (1968) 539–546; and "The Problem of Evil in the First and Last Things," *Journal of Theological Studies* 19 (1968) 591–602.
26. This sort of resolution of apparent inconsistencies can be found in contemporary scientific work. Earlier in this century, for example, biologists believed that cancers such as the Rous sarcoma could not be caused by a virus, because the Rous sarcoma was known to run in families and viral infections are not genetically transmissible. Given what was then known about cancer and viruses, the belief that a tendency to a certain cancer is inheritable seemed incompatible with the belief that cancer is virally caused. But in the broader context of current beliefs about the etiology of cancer, the beliefs which early in this century seemed inconsistent can be interpreted in such a way that they are compatible after all. We now believe that a cancer such as the Rous sarcoma is caused by a virus which acts on a certain inheritable genetic make-up, and so we have come to understand that cancer's being virally caused does not preclude the genes' having a role in the emergence of the disease.
27. For an example of this view in prominent Catholic and Protestant theologians, see, e.g., Thomas Aquinas, *Summa theologiae*, Ia–IIae, q. 87, q. 3, and John Calvin, *Institutes of the Christian Religion*, Bk. III, chap. xxiv, esp. section 6.
28. For recent discussions of some of these issues, see, e.g., Marilyn Adams, "Hell and the God of Justice," *Religious Studies* 11 (1975) 433–447, and "Divine Justice,

Divine Love, and the Life to Come," *Crux* vol. 13, no. 4 (1976–7) 12–28; and J. H. Hick, "The Problem of Evil in the First and Last Things," op. cit.; and Richard Swinburne, "A Theodicy of Heaven and Hell," in *The Existence and Nature of God*, ed. Alfred J. Freddoso (Notre Dame, Ind.: University of Notre Dame Press, 1983), pp. 37–54.

29. Cf., e.g., Thomas Aquinas, *Summa contra Gentiles*, Bk. III, chap. 37, 48, 51; and John Calvin, *Institutes of the Christian Religion*, Bk. III, chap. 25, sections 2 and 10.

30. See, e.g., Alvin Plantinga, *God and Other Minds* (Ithaca: Cornell University Press, 1967), pp. 132–148.

31. Cf. Plato, *Apology* 41a–c, *Phaedo* 63b–c, 108a–c, 109b–114c.

32. *Inferno*, Canto IV.

33. I have given the outline of such an argument in "Dante's Hell, Aquinas's Theory of Morality, and the Love of God," forthcoming. Frank Burch Brown has suggested to me that we in fact often make just the opposite evaluation, that people in the pain of some terminal illness frequently reject medical efforts to prolong their lives and insist that they prefer death to the continuation of such an existence. But such cases are disanalogous in important ways to the case of persons in hell. The pain of the terminally ill in such cases is usually great; the technology needed to prolong their lives often enough increases their pain; and what is purchased by that pain is only a very limited prolongation of life. It is not surprising that persons in such circumstances prefer death. But on the view of hell I'm attributing to Dante, the level of pains of the damned, however great, does not interfere with their ability to think and converse in a leisurely way; the prolongation of their existence does not depend on increasing their pain past that level; and their life is prolonged *indefinitely*. For the terminally ill, the choice is between great pain with death due soon, and greater pain with death due only slightly later. But for the persons in hell annihilation would put an end to an everlasting existence whose accompanying pain is compatible with reflective conversation. And so the fact that many terminally ill people prefer death sooner rather than later is no evidence that they would also prefer annihilation to life in hell.

34. *Ibid.*, Canto III.

35. See, e.g., Thomas Aquinas, *Summa theologiae*, Ia, q. 19, a. 2.

36. Someone might object here that a short experience of hell might provide the sort of information or insight which would make a crucial difference to a person's doing what he needs to do to be saved. For some consideration of a Christian position of those who lack the information they need in order to be redeemed, see the discussion of death-bed repentance in Section III.

37. For a brief historical review, see the entry on "Sin" in *A Religious Encyclopedia*, ed. Philip Schaff (New York: Funk and Wagnalls, 1891); for discussion of more contemporary approaches, see, e.g., "The Fall of Man," in *The New Catholic Encyclopedia* (New York: McGraw-Hill, 1967). Cf. also Thomas Aquinas, *Summa theologiae*, Ia IIae, q. 77, a. 4 and 5, q. 82, a. 3, and q. 83, a. 3; and John Calvin, *Institutes of the Christian Religion*, Bk. II, chap. 1, section 8.

38. Free will has, of course, been variously understood by both philosophers and theologians. Augustine, for example, defined free will as the power of choosing. On his view, Adam was free to choose either to sin or not to sin; fallen man is free to choose to sin but not free to choose not to sin. (Cf. *Enchiridion*, XXVII, XXX, and CV.) Aquinas took the will as a natural disposition to seek the good as apprehended by the intellect (cf. *Summa theologiae* Ia, q. 19, a. 1) and free will as the power of being inclined to various courses of action (*Summa theologiae*, Ia, q. 83, a. 1); in consequence of Adam's fall, on Aquinas's view, the will has become inordinately inclined to mutable good (*Summa theologiae*, Ia, q. 82, a. 3). Contemporary literature on the will is vast; perhaps a good place to begin (for a historical survey and a consideration of contemporary issues) is Brian O'Shaugnessy, *The Will: A Dual Aspect Theory* (Cambridge: Cambridge University Press, 1980). For some

recent discussions, especially helpful in this context, see Roderick Chisholm, "Free-
dom and Action," in Keith Lehrer (ed.), *Freedom and Determinism* (New York:
Random House, 1966), pp. 11–44; Harry Frankfurt, "Freedom of the Will and the
Concept of a Person," *Journal of Philosophy* 68 (1971) 5–20; Wright Neely,
"Freedom and Desire," *Philosophical Review* 83 (1974) 32–54; Peter Van Inwagen,
An Essay on Free Will (Oxford: Clarendon Press, 1983); Garry Watson, "Free
Agency," *Journal of Philosophy* 72 (1975) 205–220; and Susan Wolf, "Asymme-
trical Freedom," *Journal of Philosophy* 77 (1980) 151–166.

39. For a study of Anselm's position, see e.g., *Anselm of Canterbury: Truth, Freedom,
and Evil: Three Philosophical Dialogues*, ed. and tr. Jasper Hopkins and Herbert
Richardson (New York Harper and Row, 1967), pp. 26–44; Jasper Hopkins, *A
Companion to the Study of St. Anselm* (Minncapolis, Minn.: University of Minnesota Press, 1972), pp. 122–186; and G. Stanley Kane, *Anselm's Doctrine of Freedom
and the Will* (New York: Edwin Mellen Press, 1981).

40. Though it has some affinities with the views presented by Susan Wolf in a recent
paper; see the citation in note 38.

41. For a clear statement of this point, see Thomas Aquinas, *Summa theologiae*, Ia IIae,
q. 77, a. 4 and 5.

42. See, for example, *Summa theologiae* I, q. 82, articles 3–5 and q. 83, articles 1 and 3.

43. See, for example, *Summa theologiae* I–II, q. 82, articles 1 and 3.

44. Someone might also object that if post-fall persons inherit a disordered will, they are
not responsible for the evil they do and so should not be punished for it. But this
objection misunderstands the nature of the defect post-fall persons inherit. It is not
an external constraint on the will; it is a tendency within the will to will evil. A person
with post-fall will *can* will only right actions, but tends not to *want* to do so. Such a
person, who can will the right action in certain circumstances but who does not do so
because he does not want to, is generally held to be responsible for what he does.

45. I do not mean to suggest that changing one's character is accomplished by a single
act of will of any sort, only that a particular sort of act of will is a prerequisite for a
change of character.

46. This very sketchy discussion suggests a solution to the sort of quarrel engaged in by
Luther and Erasmus. Even the defective will is free, in the sense that it *can* will the
good; and to this extent it seems to me that Erasmus was right. But if this ability is
not exercised because, in virtue of a defect in the will, the will *does not* will the good,
then for practical as distinct from theological purposes Luther was right. Of himself,
man will not do what is right; to do so he must have external help. See Martin
Luther, *The Bondage of the Will*, tr. J. I. Packer and A. R. Johnston (London: James
Clarke & Co., Ltd., 1957); and Erasmus, *De Libero Arbitrio, Discourse on the
Freedom of the Will*, ed. and tr. Ernest F. Winter (New York, 1967).

47.   "Batter my heart, three-personed God; for You
   As yet but knock, breathe, shine, and seek to mend;
   That I may rise and stand, o'erthrow me, and bend
   Your force to break, blow, burn, and make me new.
   I, like an usurped town, to another due,
   Labor to admit You, but O, to no end;
   Reason, Your viceroy in me, me should defend,
   But is captived, and proves weak or untrue.
   Yet dearly I love You, and would be loved fain,
   But am betrothed unto Your enemy.
   Divorce me, untie, or break that knot again;
   Take me to You, imprison me, for I,
   Except You enthral me, never shall be free,
   Nor ever chaste, except you ravish me."

48. Augustine, *Confessions*, tr. Edward Pusey (New York: Macmillan Publishing Co.,
1961), Bk. viii, pp. 125, 130: "But I wretched, most wretched, in the very

commencement of my early youth, had begged chastity of Thee, and said, 'Give me chastity and continence, only not yet.' For I feared lest Thou shouldest hear me soon, and soon cure me of the disease of concupiscence, which I wished to have satisfied, rather than extinquished . . . [Now, however] I cast myself down I know not how, under a certain fig tree, giving full vent to my tears; and the floods of mine eyes gushed out an acceptable sacrifice to Thee . . . I sent up these sorrowful words: How long, how long, 'tomorrow, and tomorrow?' Why not now? Why not is there this hour an end to my uncleanness?"

49. Anselm, *The Fall of Satan*, tr. Jasper Hopkins and Herbert Richardson, op. cit., p. 157.

50. See, for example, the articles on sanctification in *The Encyclopedia of Religion and Ethics*, ed. James Hastings (New York: Charles Scribner's Sons, 1962), and in *A Theological Word Book of the Bible*, ed. Alan Richardson (New York: Macmillan Co., 1950), and the article on grace in *The Catholic Encyclopedia*, ed. Charles Herbermann *et al.* (New York: Robert Appleton Co., 1909).

51. That this is a claim Christians are committed to is clear from even a brief perusal of the Old Testament. The Old Testament prophetic books abound with statements such as these: "In vain have I smitten your children; they received no correction" (Jeremiah 2:30); "Oh Lord, . . . thou has stricken them, but they have not grieved; thou hast consumed them, but they have refused to receive correction" (Jeremiah 5:3); "The people turneth not unto him that smiteth them, neither do they seek the Lord of hosts" (Isaiah 9:13). Amos 4:6–11 is a particularly clear statement of this claim. The story of the blind man in John 9:1–38, which culminates in the blind man's expression of faith and worship, is an example of a New Testament story illustrating this claim.

52. For a Biblical story showing God protecting the victim while allowing the perpetrator the freedom to act on his evil will, cf., e.g., Daniel 3:8–25; a clear cut story showing God preventing suffering by curtailing the freedom of a human agent to act on his will is harder to find, but cf., e.g., Genesis 19:1–11, Genesis 22:11–12, and such stories of relief from oppression as Judges 6:11ff.

53. The death of infants has been variously handled in the history of Christian thought. It seems to me not so much a hard case as a borderline one. Like the suffering of animals, the death of infants is hard to account for in large part because we have an inadequate understanding of the nature of infants and animals. Do infants have free will? Do some of the more intelligent species of animals other than man have free will? If they do, maybe some version of the solution I am developing here applies to them also. As for creatures to whom no one would want to attribute free will, such as worms and snails, what sort of suffering do they undergo? Until we have a clearer account of the nature of infants and animals, it will not be clear what to say about the death of infants or the suffering of animals in connection with the problem of evil. For that reason, I leave both out of account here.

54. Dante, *Purgatorio*, V. 98–107; tr. Charles Singleton (Princeton, N.J.: Princeton University Press, 1973), p. 51.

55. For an interesting variation on such a speculation, see C. S. Lewis, *The Great Divorce* (N.Y.: MacMillan, 1946).

56. I have made no attempt in this section to discuss the connection, crucial for Christianity, between salvation from one's sins and the Incarnation and Resurrection of Christ. I intend to examine that connection in a forthcoming paper on the Atonement.

57. In what follows I am not concerned either to contribute to or to take account of contemporary biblical scholarship. I want to consider the story of Cain and Abel not as it contributes to our understanding of Israelite history, ancient Hebrew theology, the composition of the Old Testament, or anything else of the sort. I am interested in it as a story in the canonical Christian Scriptures; I am reading it in light of Christian doctrine to see what contributions it makes to Christian theology.

58. Literary analysis of the story suggests, however slightly, that the idea of bringing an offering was Cain's and that Abel was following Cain's lead: "And in process of time it came to pass that Cain brought of the fruit of the ground an offering to the Lord. And Abel, he also brought of the firstlings of his flock . . ." (Gen. 4:3–4). Furthermore, there is no suggestion that the offerings were anything but gifts of love. There is no hint that Cain is afraid of God or has a guilty conscience and wants to propitiate God or wants to lessen the post-fall alienation between him and God. On the contrary, when we find Cain talking to God later in the story, he speaks to him familiarly and without fear, and without surprise either, as if he were used to talking to God. These two suggestions taken together considerably increase the poignancy of the story. Among other things, they make the rejection of Cain's offering much harder for him to accept and for us to understand; they make more plausible the depth of the anger against Abel which the story attributes to Cain; and they suggest (again, however slightly) a loving relationship between Cain and God, in the context of which God's subsequent talking with Cain should be considered.

59. There is nothing in the story to suggest directly that there was anything wrong with Cain's offering. The story does say that Abel brought of the "firstlings" of his flock, suggesting that there was something specially reverent or respectful about his offerings; but the text says nothing to indicate that there was anything shabby or improper about Cain's offering. It seems to me that there is admirable artistry in the story's omitting to explain why Cain's offering was rejected. By doing so, it leaves its readers with the same choice Cain had: to believe either that God is good and Cain's offering was rightly rejected, or that Cain's offering was rejected arbitrarily and so unjustly by a God who is in consequence not good. The story, then, artfully forces its readers into Cain's shoes and faces them with Cain's temptation, the first recorded temptation after the fall, namely, the temptation to believe that God is not good.

60. As for the manner of Abel's death, we reasonably tend to assume that it was painful, but nothing in the story prohibits our believing that Abel died instantly, without pain. If we think that Abel in the story is spotlessly righteous, then, since the story gives us the option, it is more consistent to assume he died painlessly. On the other hand, if we are inclined to maintain that Abel's death was painful to some degree, then that pain is explicable as a last safeguard against pride and self-will for the first of the sons of Adam to die. There is also Adam and Eve's loss to be taken into account. On our ordinary unreflective-intuitions about this story, Adam and Eve suffer the loss of their son Abel, a loss for which they are apparently uncompensated. But as I have tried to show, on Christian doctrine the story is much more complicated. Once Cain becomes murderously angry at his brother, God has a choice only between evils for Adam and Eve. They can suffer the pain of the physical loss of their son Abel, or they can suffer the pain of having their son Cain spiritually lost. The arguments I have given for my solution to the problem of evil are also arguments for thinking that by choosing to let Abel die God picks the lesser of two evils for Adam and Eve also.

61. This paper has benefited substantially from comments by William Alston, Frank Burch Brown, Earle Coleman, Alvin Plantinga, Georgette Sinkler, Michael Smith, and Richard Swinburne. I am especially grateful to Norman Kretzmann for his numerous helpful suggestions, and I am indebted to John Crossett (died 1981), whose efforts on my behalf made this paper possible.

SUGGESTED READING

Adams, Marilyn McCord (1999), *Horrendous Evils and the Goodness of God*, Ithaca: Cornell University Press.

Hick, John (1975), *Evil and the God of Love*, rev. edn, New York: Harper & Row.

Howard-Snyder, Daniel (ed.) (1996), *The Evidential Argument from Evil*, Bloomington: Indiana, University Press. (This is an outstanding collection of cutting-edge but difficult work.)

Hume, David (1955), *Dialogues Concerning Natural Religion*, ed. H. D. Aiken, New York: Hafner Publishing.

Lewis, C. S. (1979), *The Problem of Pain*, New York: Macmillan.

Mackie, J. L. (1982), *The Miracle of Theism*, Oxford: Clarendon Press.

Plantinga, Alvin (2000), *Warranted Christian Belief*, New York: Oxford University Press. (See Ch. 14.)

Stump, Eleonore (1993), 'Aquinas on the Sufferings of Job', in E. Stump (ed.), *Reasoned Faith*, Ithaca: Cornell University Press, pp. 328–57.

Swinburne, Richard (1998), *Providence and the Problem of Evil*, Oxford: Clarendon Press.

PART V
THE SOUL AND LIFE EVERLASTING

THE SOUL AND LIFE EVERLASTING: INTRODUCTION

J. P. Moreland

Throughout history, Christianity has been interpreted as giving an affirmative answer to questions about the reality of the three great topics of Western philosophy, namely, God, the soul and life everlasting. For centuries, most Christian thinkers have believed in the souls of men and beasts, as it used to be put. Animals and humans are composed of an immaterial entity – a soul, a life principle, a ground of sentience – and a body. More specifically, a human person is a unity of two distinct entities – body and soul. The human soul, while not by nature immortal, is nevertheless capable of entering an intermediate disembodied state upon death, however incomplete and unnatural this state may be, and, eventually, of being reunited with a resurrected body.

Recently, several thinkers have disputed Christianity's association with dualism on the grounds that dualism is a Greek notion read into the Bible, that the Bible teaches a Hebraic holistic unity and not a Greek dualism, and that Christian hope for an afterlife rests on the resurrection of the body and not on the immortality of the soul. None of these assertions is persuasive.[1] Given that historic Christianity affirms the reality of an immaterial soul and life everlasting, the question remains whether these affirmations are true and defensible.[2]

THE SOUL

1. Property Dualism

Property dualism is the view that ostensibly mental properties are genuinely mental, and not physical, properties. It is hard to define a physical property, but if one takes it to be a property that may be adequately described in the language of physics, chemistry and neurophysiology, then the property dualist claims that mental properties are not physical. And if one adopts a property exemplification view of events (or a near cousin), then the property dualist also holds that individual mental events/states are genuinely mental and not physical.

At least three arguments have been proffered for property/event dualism. First, once one gets an accurate description of consciousness, it becomes clear that mental properties/events are not identical to physical properties/events. Mental states are characterised by their intrinsic, subjective, inner, private, qualitative feel, made present to a subject by first-person introspection. For example, a pain is a certain felt hurtfulness. Mental states cannot be intrinsically described by physical language, even if through study of the brain one can discover the causal/functional relations between mental and brain states.[3]

In general, mental states have some or all of the following features, none of which is a physical feature of anything: mental states like pains have an intrinsic, raw conscious feel. There is a 'what-it-is-like' to a pain. Most, if not all mental states have intentionality, that is, they are of or about things. Mental states are inner, private and known by first-person, direct introspection. Any way one has of knowing about a physical entity is available to everyone else, including ways of knowing about one's brain. But a subject has a way of knowing about his mental states not available to others – through introspection.

Mental states are constituted by self-presenting properties. One can be aware of the external, physical world only by means of one's mental states, but one need not be aware of one's mental states by means of anything else. For example, it is by way of a sensation of red that one is aware of an apple, but one is not aware of the sensation of red by way of another sensation. Mental states are necessarily owned, and, in fact, one's mental states could not have belonged to someone else. However, no physical state is necessarily owned, much less necessarily owned by a specific subject.

Some sensations are vague, for example, a sensation of an object may be fuzzy or vague, but no physical state is vague.[4] Some sensations are pleasurable or unpleasurable, but nothing physical has these properties. A cut in the knee is, strictly speaking, not unpleasurable. It is the pain event caused by the cut that is unpleasurable. Mental states can have the property of familiarity (e.g., when a desk looks familiar to someone), but familiarity is not a feature of a physical state.

Since mental states have these features and physical states do not, mental states are not identical to physical states. Some physicalists have responded by denying that consciousness has the features in question. For example, dualists have argued that thinking events are not spatially located even though the brain event associated with them is. Physicalists counter that thoughts are, after all, located in certain places of the brain. But there is no reason to accept this claim, since dualists can account for all the spatial factors in terms of the brain events causally related to thoughts. Moreover, through introspection subjects seem to know quite a bit about the features of their thoughts, and spatial location is not one of them. Similar responses are offered by dualists for physicalist claims about the other features of consciousness.

A second argument for property/event dualism is the Knowledge Argument, variously formulated by Thomas Nagel, Frank Jackson and Saul Kripke.[5] A standard presentation of the thought experiment has it that Mary, a brilliant scientist blind from birth, knows all the physical facts relevant to acts of perception. When she suddenly gains the ability to see, she gains knowledge of new facts. Since she knew all the physical facts before recovery of sight, and since she gains knowledge of new facts, these facts must not be physical facts and, moreover, given Mary's situation, they must be mental facts.

To appreciate the argument, it is necessary to focus on the nature of self-presenting properties and three kinds of knowledge. First, recall that a self-presenting property, such as being appeared to redly, presents both its intentional object and itself to the subject exemplifying it. Second, arguably, there are three forms of knowledge, irreducible to one another, though, of course, one form may be the epistemic ground for another:

1. knowledge by acquaintance: one has such knowledge when one is directly aware of something, for example, when someone sees an apple directly before him, he knows it by acquaintance. He does not need a concept of an apple or knowledge of how to use the word 'apple' to have knowledge by acquaintance of an apple.
2. propositional knowledge: this is knowledge that a proposition is true. For example, knowledge that 'the object there is an apple' requires having a concept of an apple and knowing that the object under consideration satisfies the concept.
3. know-how: this is the ability to do certain things, for example, to use apples for certain purposes.

Generally, knowledge by acquaintance provides grounds for propositional knowledge which, in turn, provides what is necessary to have genuine know-how. It is because one sees the apple that one knows that it is an apple, and it is in virtue of one's knowledge of apples that one has the skill to do things to or with them.

By way of application, Mary comes to exemplify the self-presenting mental property of being appeared to redly. In this way, Mary gains six new kinds of knowledge – she gains knowledge by acquaintance, propositional knowledge, and skill both with regard to the colour red and her sensation of red. Mary now knows by acquaintance what redness is. Upon further reflection and experience, she can now know things like *Necessarily, red is a colour*. She also gains skill about comparing or sorting objects on the basis of their colour, of how to arrange colour patterns that are most beautiful or natural to the eye, etc. Assuming a realist, and not a representative, dualist construal of secondary qualities, we may say that the three kinds of knowledge just listed are not themselves knowledge of mental facts but are forms of knowledge that can be gained only by way of mental states that exemplify the relevant self-presenting property.

Further, Mary gains knowledge about her sensation of red. She is now aware of having a sensation of red for the first time and can be aware of a specific sensation of red being pleasurable, vague, etc. She also has propositional knowledge about her sensations. She could know that a sensation of red is more like a sensation of green than it is like a sour taste. She can know that the way the apple appears to her now is vivid, pleasant, or like the way the orange appeared to her (namely, redly) yesterday in bad lighting. Finally, she has skill about her sensations. She can recall them to memory, re-image things in her mind, adjust her glasses until her sensations of colour are vivid, etc.

Physicalists David Papineau and Paul Churchland have offered slightly different versions of the most prominent physicalist rejoinder to this argument.[6] When Mary gains the ability to see red, she gains no knowledge of any new facts. Rather, she gains new abilities, new behavioural dispositions, new know-how, new ways to access the facts she already knew before gaining the ability to see. Before the experience, Mary knew all there was to know about the facts involved in what it is like to experience red. She could third-person imagine what it would be like for some other person to experience red. She could know what it is like to have an experience of red due to the fact that this is simply a physical state of the brain and Mary had mastered the relevant physical theory before gaining sight. But now she has a '*pre-linguistic representation* of redness', a first-person ability to image redness or recreate the experience of redness in her memory. She can re-identify her experience of red and classify it according to the type of experience it is by a new 'inner' power of introspection. Prior to the experience, she could merely recognise when someone else was experiencing red 'from the outside', that is, from observing the behaviours of others. Thus, the physicalist admits a duality of types of knowledge but not a duality of facts that are known.

For three reasons, this response is inadequate. First, it is simply not true that Mary gains a new way of knowing what she already knew instead of gaining knowledge of a new set of facts. Above, there is listed some of Mary's new factual knowledge, and it seems obvious that Mary failed to have this factual knowledge prior to gaining the ability to see.

Second, to be at all plausible, this physicalist rejoinder seems to presuppose a coarse-grained theory of properties according to which two properties are identical just in case they are either contingently or necessarily co-exemplified. This assumption allows the physicalist to identify the relevant property in the Knowledge Argument (being red, being an-appearing-of-red) with a property employed in physical theory isomorphic with it. But the coarse-grained theory is false. Being triangular and being trilateral are different properties even though necessarily co-exemplified, and the same may be said of various unexemplified or unexemplifiable properties.

Third, when Churchland and Papineau describe Mary's new know-how, they help themselves to a number of notions that clearly seem to be dualist ones. They are listed above: pre-linguistic representation, image, first-person introspection and so forth. These dualist notions are the real intuition pumps for the physicalist rejoinder. Remove the dualist language and replace it with notions that can be captured in physicalist language, and the physicalist response becomes implausible.

The third argument for property/event dualism is based on intentionality: some (perhaps all) mental states have intentionality. No physical state has intentionality. Therefore, (at least) some mental states are not physical. Intentionality is the 'ofness' or 'aboutness' of various mental states. Consider the following facts about intentionality:

1. When one represents a mental act to oneself, there are no sense data associated with it; this is not so with physical states and their relations.
2. Intentionality is completely unrestricted with regard to the kind of object it can hold as a term – anything whatever can have a mental act directed upon it, but physical relations only obtain for a narrow range of objects (e.g. magnetic fields only attract certain things.)
3. To grasp a mental act one must engage in a reflexive act of self-awareness, but no such reflexivity is required to grasp a physical relation.
4. For ordinary physical relations (e.g., x is to the left of y), x and y are identifiable objects irrespective of whether they have entered into that relation (ordinary physical relations are external); this is not so for intentional contents (e.g., one and the same belief cannot be about a frog and later about a house – the belief is what it is, at least partly, in virtue of what the belief is of).
5. For ordinary relations, each of the *relata* must exist in order for the relation to obtain (x and y must exist before one can be on top of the other); but intentionality can be of nonexistent things (e.g., one can think of Zeus).
6. Intentional states are intensional, but physical states are extensional.[7]

Many physicalists try to reduce intentionality to physical causal/functional relations. Dualists respond by offering thought experiments in which causal/functional relations are neither necessary nor sufficient for intentionality. Moreover, even if for every intentional state there were necessary and sufficient causal/functional conditions, this would show merely that the two were isomorphic, not identical.

2. Substance Dualism

Currently, there are three main forms of substance dualism being debated. First, there is Cartesian dualism, according to which the mind is a substance with the ultimate capacities for consciousness, and it is connected to its body by way of an external causal relation.[8] Second, there is Thomistic substance dualism, one important version of which takes the soul to be broader than the mind in containing not merely the capacities for consciousness but also those which ground biological life and functioning. On this view, the (human) soul diffuses, informs, unifies, animates and makes human the body. The body is not a physical substance but, rather, an ensouled physical structure such that, if it loses the soul, it is no longer a human body in a strict, philosophical sense.[9] According to the third form, a substantial immaterial self emerges from the functioning of the brain and nervous system, but once it emerges it exercises its own causal powers and continues to be sustained by God after death.[10]

At least five arguments have been offered in the recent literature for some form of substance dualism.

Argument 1
In acts of introspection, one is aware of: (1) one's self as an unextended centre of consciousness; (2) various capacities of thought, sensation, belief, desire and volition which one exercises and which are essential, internal aspects of the kind of thing one is; and (3) one's sensations as being such that there is no possible world in which they could exist and not be one's own. The best explanation for this fact is to take mental states to be modes of the self and mental properties to be kind-defining properties.

Argument 1 is actually two arguments that draw their force from what substance dualists claim people know about themselves from attending to themselves and their conscious states. Put more formally and in the first person, these two variants of an argument from introspection look like this: Variant One:

1. I am an unextended centre of consciousness (justified by introspection).
2. No physical object is an unextended centre of consciousness.
3. Therefore, I am not a physical object.
4. Either I am a physical object or an immaterial substance.
5. Therefore, I am an immaterial substance.

Variant Two:

1. My sensations (and other states of consciousness) are either externally or internally related to me.

2. If I am a physical object, then my sensations are externally related to me such that there is a possible world in which those sensations exist and are not so related to me.

3. There is no possible world in which my sensations exist without being mine (justified by introspection).

4. Therefore, I am not a physical object and my sensations are internally related to me.

5. If a sensation is internally related to me, then it is a mode of my self.

6. If an entity x is a mode of some entity y, then x is an inseparable entity dependent for its existence on y such that (1) x is modally distinct from and internally related to y and (2) x provides information about the nature of the thing y of which it is a mode.

7. Therefore, I am a thing whose nature is to have sensations (and other states of consciousness).

Stewart Goetz and Geoffrey Madell have advanced versions of argument 1.[11]

Argument 2

Personal identity at and through time is primitive and absolute. Moreover, counter-examples exist which show that the various bodily or psychological (e.g., memory) conditions proffered for personal identity are neither necessary nor sufficient. Put linguistically, talk about persons is not analysable into talk about their bodies or connected mental lives. Further, the primitive unity of consciousness cannot be accounted for if the self is a bodily or physical mereological compound. These facts are not innocuous but, rather, have important metaphysical implications. Substance dualism, according to which the soul is taken as a substance with an essence constituted by the potential for thought, belief, desire, sensation and volition is the best explanation of these facts. Different versions of this argument have been advanced by Richard Swinburne (see his selection to follow) and William Hasker.[12] Some non-reductive physicalists who advocate a material composition view of human persons have offered responses to some of these points.[13]

Argument 3

The indexicality of thought provides evidence for the truth of substance dualism. A complete, third-person physical description of the world will fail to capture the fact expressed by 'I am J. P. Moreland'. No amount of information non-indexically expressed captures the content conveyed by this assertion. The first-person indexical 'I' is irreducible and uneliminable, and this feature of 'I' is not innocuous, but rather is explained by claiming that 'I' refers to a non-physical entity – the substantial self with at least the power of self-awareness. Moreover, if mental predicates are added to the third-person descriptive language, this still fails to capture the state of affairs expressed by statements like 'I am thinking that P'. Finally, the system of indexical reference (e.g., 'I', 'here', 'there', 'this', 'that') must have a unifying centre that underlies it.[14] This unifying centre is the same entity referred to by 'I' in expressions like 'I am thinking that P', namely, the conscious substantial subject taken as a self-conscious, self-referring particular.[15] More formally:

1. Statements using the first-person indexical 'I' express facts about persons that cannot be expressed in statements without the first-person indexical.
2. If I am a physical object, then all the facts about me can be expressed in statements without the first-person indexical.
3. Therefore, I am not a physical object.
4. I am either a physical object or an immaterial substance.
5. Therefore, I am an immaterial substance.

Geoffrey Madell and H. D. Lewis have advocated this type of argument.[16]

Argument 4
Some have argued for substance dualism on the grounds that libertarian freedom is true, and either a necessary condition for libertarian freedom is substance dualism or the latter is the best explanation for the former. The argument may be put this way (using only the form in which substance dualism is a necessary condition for libertarian freedom):

1. Human beings exercise libertarian agency.
2. No material object (one which is such that all of its properties, parts and capacities are at least and only physical) can exercise libertarian agency.
3. Therefore, human beings are not material objects.[17]
4. Human beings are either material objects or immaterial substances.
5. Therefore, they are immaterial substances.

Substance dualist John Foster has employed this sort of argument.[18]

Argument 5
A modal argument for substance dualism has been advanced by Keith Yandell (see his selection) and Charles Taliaferro, and, while it comes in many forms, it may be fairly stated as follows:[19]

1. If x is identical to y, then whatever is true of x is true of y and vice versa.
2. I can strongly conceive of myself as existing disembodied or, indeed, without any physical particular existing.
3. If I can strongly conceive of some state of affairs S that S possibly obtains, then I have good grounds for believing of S that S is possible.

4. Therefore, I have good grounds for believing of myself that it is possible for me to exist and be disembodied.
5. If some entity x is such that it is possible for x to exist without y, then (1) x is not identical to y and (2) y is not essential to x.
6. My physical body is not such that it is possible for it to exist disembodied or without any physical particular existing.
7. Therefore, I have good grounds for believing of myself that I am not identical to a physical particular, including my physical body, and that no physical particular, including my physical body, is essential to me.

A parallel argument can be developed to show that possessing the ultimate capacities of sensation, thought, belief, desire and volition are essential to one's self.

3. Objections to Property/Substance Dualism

Various arguments have been raised against both property and substance dualism. Since these are advanced in the selection by Churchland and responded to in the articles by Foster and Yandell, only a few general points will be mentioned here. The objections fall into two classes: scientific problems and distinctively philosophical problems. In one way or another, the scientific objections imply that, while possible, scientific evidence makes dualism quite unlikely. But this is hard to substantiate. Reading the various arguments in philosophy of mind literature makes evident that science could not even formulate, much less resolve, most of the issues. For example, even if certain mental states are dependent upon specific regions of the brain (and there is evidence for dependency in the other direction as well), a dualist can explain the dependence as a form of correlation or causation, rather than as some sort of identity relation. It is not science per se, but philosophical or methodological naturalism, that is the main dualist opponent here, and dualists argue that naturalists beg important questions in their employment of science to justify physicalism.

Of the philosophical criticisms of dualism, two stand out: the problem of other minds and the problem of causal interaction. According to the first problem, dualism makes knowledge of other minds impossible or seriously problematic because, on a dualist construal, the mental states of other persons are always underdetermined by knowledge of the relevant physical facts about those persons, for example, brain states and body movements. Dualists respond in two ways. First, they claim that the underdetermination just mentioned is, in fact, a reality and it forms the basis for the Knowledge Argument and the dualist argument from first-person indexicals. So dualist underdetermination is a virtue and not a vice. Second, this physicalist argument takes scepticism too seriously by presupposing that if it is logically possible for some knowledge claim to be mistaken, then one cannot have knowledge or justified belief regarding the claim, at least not until the sceptic is refuted. So understood, the problem is not dualism, but scepticism in general. The dualist will argue that one can have knowledge or justified belief even if it is logically possible that one is mistaken and will offer a defeasible account of knowledge of other minds. Dualists Richard Swinburne and Alvin Plantinga have proffered, respectively, internalist and externalist accounts of knowledge of other minds adequate to rebut the physicalist challenge.[20]

Regarding the problem of causal interaction, it should be noted that Christian theism is a version of dualist interactionism regarding God himself. God, an immaterial spirit, is capable of causal interaction with the material world, and if God can part the Red Sea it is not clear why one cannot raise one's arm by willing it to be so. Moreover, as Yandell points out in his selection to follow, there is more justification for believing interaction takes place than for the various formulations of the principle that allegedly justifies the assertion that mind/body interaction is problematic.

4. Physicalist Alternatives to Dualism

To understand contemporary versions of physicalism, it is important to say a word about reduction. Currently, five different types of reduction are relevant to mind/body debates:

1. individual ontological reduction: one object (a macro-object like the person) is identified with another object (e.g., a physical simple or mereological compound such as the brain or body);
2. property ontological reduction: one property (heat) is identified with another property (mean kinetic energy);
3. linguistic reduction: one word or concept (pain) is defined as or analysed in terms of another word or concept (the tendency to grimace when stuck with a pin);
4. causal reduction: the causal activity of the reduced entity is entirely explained in terms of the causal activity of the reducing entity;
5. theoretical or explanatory reduction: one theory or law is reduced to another by biconditional bridge principles, usually associated with Nagel-type reductions. (Terms in the reduced theory are connected with terms in the reducing theory by way of biconditionals which serve as the grounds for identifying the properties expressed by the former terms with those expressed by the latter. For example, if one takes colour terms to be co-extensional with wavelength terms, then one can claim that colours are identical to wavelengths.)

Individual ontological reduction is affirmed by virtually all physicalists. Property reduction is affirmed by type identity physicalists and eschewed by token physicalists and eliminativists. There is a debate about whether or not functionalists accept property reduction (see below) but, apart from emergent supervenient physicalists (see below), all physicalists believe that in the actual world all the properties exemplified by persons are physical properties in some sense or another. Causal reduction is hotly disputed by physicalists. Part of the debate involves the causal closure of the physical and the reality of so-called top/down causation. It is safe to say that, currently, most physicalists follow Jaegwon Kim and John Searle and accept causal reduction. With the demise of philosophical behaviourism and positivist theories of meaning, linguistic reduction is no longer a main part of the debate. Finally, theoretical reduction is the main type of reduction employed in classifications of physicalism and, unless otherwise indicated, descriptions of reductive vs. non-reductive physicalism should be understood to employ it.

Currently, the main version of reductive physicalism is type identity physicalism. Type identity physicalists accept explanatory reduction and, on that basis, property ontological reduction. On this view, mental properties/types are identical to physical properties/types. Moreover, identity statements asserting the relevant identities are construed as contingent identity statements employing different yet co-referring expressions. The truth of these identity statements is an empirical discovery, and the statements are theoretical identities.

Two main objections seem decisive against type identity physicalism. First, it is just obvious that mental and physical properties are different from each other (see above), and physicalists have not met the burden of proof required to overturn these deeply ingrained intuitions. Physicalists respond that in other cases of identity (heat is mean kinetic energy), our intuitions about non-identity turned out to be wrong, and the same is true in the case of mental properties. But for two reasons, this response fails. For one thing, these other cases of alleged property identities are most likely cases of correlation of properties. Second, Kripke argued that we can easily explain why our intuitions were mistaken in the other cases but a similar insight does not appear in the case of mental properties.[21] Since there is a distinction between what heat is (mean kinetic energy) and how it appears to us (as being warm), our intuitions about non-identity confused appearance with reality. But since mental properties such as painfulness are identical to the way they appear, no such source of confusion is available. Thus, intuitions about their non-identity with physical properties remain justified.

The second difficulty with type identity theory is called the multiple realisation problem, though a more accurate label would be the multiple exemplification problem, since, according to dualists, mental properties are exemplified and not realised. In any case, it seem obvious that humans, dogs, Vulcans and a potentially infinite number of organisms with different physical type states can all be in pain and, thus, the mental kind, being painful, is not identical to a physical kind.

Largely in response to this last problem, a version of (allegedly) non-reductive physicalism – functionalism – has become the prominent current version of physicalism. Functionalists employ a topic-neutral description of mental properties/states in terms of bodily inputs, behavioural outputs and other mental state outputs. For example, a pain is whatever state is produced by pin sticks, etc., and which causes a tendency to grimace and desire pity. The state of desiring pity is, in turn, spelt out in terms of other mental states and bodily outputs. Mental properties are functional kinds. Machine functionalists characterise the various relations that constitute a functional state in terms of abstract computational, logical relations, and causal role functionalists spell them out in terms of causal relations. Either way, a mental property such as painfulness turns out to be the second-order property of having a property that plays the relevant functional role R.

Functionalism may also be characterised in terms of supervenience and realisation. There are different views of supervenience, but here is a standard formulation of (strong) property supervenience:

> (SS) Mental properties supervene on physical properties, in that necessarily any two things (in the same possible world or in different possible worlds with the same laws of nature) indiscernible in all physical properties are indiscernible in mental properties.

The realisation relation between mental property M and physical property P may be characterised in this way:

> (Rz) For some entity x, P realises M just in case x is M in virtue of x being P.

For the functionalist, P realises M just in case P has the property of satisfying functional role R in x. In this way, functionalism is a form of non-emergent, structural supervenience such that mental properties supervene on physical properties and the latter realise the former. More specifically, if P realises M, then M supervenes on P.

There are at least three serious difficulties with functionalism in its various formulations. First, there are problems regarding absent or inverted qualia. If a Vulcan realised the correct functional role for pain but exemplified the causal intermediary of being appeared to redly while feeling no hurtfulness at all, the functionalist will say the Vulcan is in pain. But it seems obvious that the Vulcan is experiencing the mental state of an appearing-of-red, and this supports property dualism. Qualia arguments turn on the observation that mental kinds are essentially characterised by their intrinsic properties and accidentally characterised by their extrinsic functional relations. Thus, property dualism correctly captures the essence of mental properties, and functionalism fails on this score.

Second, for two reasons, functionalism fails to account for first-person knowledge of one's own mental states by introspection. For one thing, on a functionalist interpretation, what makes a specific pain event a pain has nothing whatever to do with its intrinsic features. The individuation of mental kinds is entirely a matter of extrinsic relations to inputs from the environment and bodily and other mental outputs. The same brain event that realises pain in one possible world could realise any other mental state in a different world with a different functional context. Thus, there is no way for a subject to know what mental state he is having by being conscious of it. In fact, since bodily outputs are essential for placing the mental realiser in its mental kind, one would have to wait until he observed his own behaviour to see what mental state he was in.

Moreover, since one factor that constitutes a given mental state is its relationship to a further mental output, it is hard for a functionalist to avoid mental holism, roughly, the notion that a given mental state is individuated by its entire set of relations to all the other mental states in one's entire psychology. Even if the functionalist can delimit a subset of one's psychology to serve as the relevant *relata* (and this is doubtful) the problem still remains that one could not know what a given mental state is by attending to it without running through the entire set of internally related psychological states that constitute it. Phenomenologically, this is not how people know their own mental states, and, in any case, the functionalist notion that a mental state is constituted by both bodily outputs and other mental states makes problematic introspective knowledge of one's thoughts, sensations, etc. There can be no physics of money, and no amount of inspection of the intrinsic properties of a dollar bill will give any clue that it is money. Assignments of economic predicates are arbitrary as far as the intrinsic features of the realisers are concerned. The same may be said about awareness of and predicate assignments for the realisers of functionally characterised mental kinds.

Finally, there is no clear sense as to what the realisation relation is that is available to a strict physicalist. Realisation is not a relation that figures into chemistry and physics. Further, when physicalists characterise the realisation relation or realisers that stand in it in terms of paradigm cases, they select artifacts and appeal to mental notions such as intentions, values, goals and agent production in their characterisation.[22] If the objective is to characterise either realisation itself or what it is to be a realiser in non-mental terms, this will hardly do. Moreover, dualists claim that mental properties are not realised; rather, they are exemplified and thereby constitute that which grounds the unity of mental kinds.

Token physicalism is a hard view to classify. Fundamentally, it amounts to the claim that, even though there is no smooth property identity for mental types, every token mental event is identical to a physical event. Beyond that, things are not so clear. For some, token physicalism is not a distinct viewpoint; rather, it is part of the specification of a full-blown physicalist functionalism such that mental properties are functional types and physical events are the token realisers of those types. By contrast, Davidson's anomalous monism is a distinctive version of token physicalism. The view is analysed and criticised in the Foster selection. One central problem with the position is its depiction of mental events as bare particulars. However, in a more adequate property exemplification account of events, individual pain tokens have the property of being painful and necessarily so, but no pure physical event token has this property, much less necessarily so. Moreover, the unity of a class of mental tokens such as pains seems to reside in a property exemplified by and, thus, intrinsic to each member of the class, painfulness.

Finally, eliminative materialism is roughly the claim that mental terms get their meaning from their role in Folk Psychology, and, like Phlogiston theory, Folk Psychology will eventually be replaced with some neurophysiological theory. Thus, the various mental terms of Folk Psychology fail to refer to anything and should be eliminated. Some eliminative materialists apply the view to all mental states while others limit it to propositional states such as beliefs and thoughts.

Eliminative materialism has not garnered widespread acceptance. First, dualism is not primarily a theory, much less a replaceable one; rather, it is a descriptive report of the mental self and its states with which one is acquainted through introspection. Second, it simply seems implausible to say that no one has ever actually had a sensation or belief. Third, some have argued that, in effect, eliminative materialism is self-refuting in that it advocates the belief that there are no such things as beliefs. Some eliminative materialists have responded that self-refutation can be avoided because, while their view does in fact reject the existence of beliefs, it does allow for a physical replacement that plays the same role as beliefs and this replacement is what the theory advocates. But many critics remain sceptical of this response on the grounds that if an entity is found that actually plays the same role as a belief it will be a belief by another name. If it plays a different role, then self-refutation may be avoided only at the expense of proffering an inadequate revisionism.

Finally, a word should be said about supervenient physicalism. Emergent supervenience is the view that mental properties are distinctively new kinds of properties that in no way characterise the subvenient base. So understood, it is actually a form of property dualism. Structural supervenience is the view that mental properties are structural properties entirely constituted by the properties, relations, parts and events at the subvenient level. Functionalism is currently the most popular version of structural supervenience.

Taken by itself, supervenient physicalism is not a distinct viewpoint. Alone, it fails to capture property dependence and, instead, only expresses co-variance between mental and physical properties. So understood, it is consistent with substance dualism, type physicalism and epiphenomenalism. In fact, it allows for cases where A supervenes on B, yet B is in some sense dependent on *A*. Personhood supervenes on being human, but arguably this is a genus/species relation in which species are ontologically dependent on their genera for their existence and identity.

In order for supervenience to be adequate for at least minimal physicalism, it must be supplemented with two further principles:

1. The anti-Cartesian principle: there can be no purely mental beings (e.g., substantial souls) because nothing can have a mental property without having a physical property as well.
2. Mind–body dependence: what mental properties an entity has depend on and are determined by its physical properties.

By employing arguments already given above, property and substance dualists will reject (1) and (2). Moreover, since it is strictly a metaphysical thesis, there is no scientific evidence that could justify (1), so the authority of science cannot be claimed on its behalf. Regarding (2), there is scientific evidence for the dependency it expresses. But there is also scientific evidence that mental states causally effect brain states and, in any case, substance dualist arguments, for example, the modal argument and the argument from libertarian freedom, seek to undermine its justification.

Life Everlasting

Philosophers have been interested in two aspects of life after death: assessing the evidence for it and analysing problems with its intelligibility and coherence. The evidence for life after death falls into two categories: philosophical and historical/scientific. Near Death Experiences and the bodily resurrection of Jesus are two key examples of the latter category. Philosophical arguments divide into those that derive from theism and those that begin with the nature of the self. Arguments of the former sort appeal to things such as divine justice and love, as well as the fact that since human persons have high intrinsic value and God is a preserver of value, then God is a preserver of human persons. Arguments of the latter sort focus on the alleged simplicity of the self, along with its ability to act in ways that transcend dependence on bodily organs, for example, in exercises of free will and in abstract thought, as evidence that the self can exist independently of the body.

In general, it can be said that, given the truth of Christian theism, life everlasting is beyond reasonable doubt. But, granting that there may be some positive evidence for life after death that does not require assuming some form of theism, that evidence is far from conclusive. Thus, justification of an afterlife seems to be theistic dependent.

Regarding the intelligibility and coherence of life everlasting, most discussions have centred on epistemological and ontological issues involved in personal identity in a disembodied intermediate state or with respect to either a resurrected body or a resurrected person. In his selection, Stephen T. Davis discusses a number of these topics and clarifies and defends a substance dualist version of life everlasting that includes a disembodied intermediate state followed by a resurrection body.

NOTES

1. The resurrection of the body vs. the immortality of the soul is a false dichotomy, and biblical teaching about a disembodied intermediate state implies that the soul is immortal in the sense that once created it never ceases to be. Further, while the Bible does emphasise a functional holism of the human person, this is entirely consistent with an ontological dualism in which body and soul, though distinct, function in an integrated way. Finally, dualism is not a result of eisegesis of Scripture; for several reasons, it is the result of the best exegesis of the Bible, as most have seen throughout church history.

2. John Cooper, *Body, Soul, & Life Everlasting* (Grand Rapids, MI: Eerdmans, 1989); J. P. Moreland and Scott Rae, *Body & Soul* (Downer's Grove, IL: InterVarsity Press, 2000), ch. 1. The case for OT anthropological dualism rests on two lines of evidence. First, while admitting of a wide range of meanings, two key anthropological terms, *nephesh* (soul) and *ruach* (spirit), have clear cases where they mean an immaterial centre of thought, desire, emotion, a continuing locus of personal identity which departs at death, reunites with a resurrection body, and is that which God adds to the body to make a living person (Gen. 35:18; 1 Kings 17:21–33; Ezra 37; Ps. 146:4). In this sense, *nephesh* and *ruach* are used of disembodied spirits (angels) and of God himself. Even in cases where they are used in a synecdoche of part for whole, such figures of speech (e.g., 'all hands on deck') still presuppose the reality of the part. Second, *rephaim* is the OT term for the dead in Sheol and there are several contexts where it refers to disembodied persons there (Isa. 14:9–10, Ps. 88:10–12). OT affirmation of a disembodied intermediate state explains why it contains warnings about necromancy (communicating with the dead; cf. Deut. 18:11, 1 Sam. 28). In the NT, the evidence for some form of substance dualism is quite powerful. Death is referred to as a giving up of the soul (*psyche*) in Matt. 27:50 or spirit (*pneuma*) in Acts 5:10. The dead in the intermediate state are described as spirits/souls (Heb. 12:18–19, Rev. 6:9–11) prior to the resurrection of the body. Jesus himself distinguished the body and soul (Matt. 10:28), taught that the Patriarchs continued to be alive after their burial (Matt. 22:23–33), and promised the thief on the cross that he would be with Jesus in Paradise that very day (Luke 23:42–3). Paul affirmed a naked, i.e., disembodied intermediate state such that to be absent from the body was to be with the Lord (2 Cor. 5:1–10), and he believed that during a visionary experience he may well have been temporarily disembodied himself (2 Cor. 12:1–4).

3. There are at least five different kinds of mental states. A sensation is a state of awareness or sentience, e.g., a conscious awareness of sound. A thought is a mental content that can be expressed in an entire sentence and that only exists while it is being thought. Thoughts can be true or false, and they have intentionality. Some thoughts logically imply other thoughts. Some do not entail, but merely provide justification, for other thoughts. A belief is a person's view, accepted to varying degrees of strength, of how things really are. If a person has a belief (e.g., that it is raining), then that belief serves as the basis for the person's tendency or readiness to act as if the thing believed were really so (e.g., one gets an umbrella). Thus, beliefs are not dispositions to behave but are the grounds for such dispositions. At any given time, one can have many beliefs that are not currently being contemplated. A desire is a certain felt inclination to do, have, avoid, or experience certain things. Desires are either conscious or such that they can be made conscious through certain activities, e.g., through therapy. A volition or free choice is an exercise of active power, an endeavouring to do a certain thing, usually for the sake of some reason.

4. The supposed vagueness of quantum states prior to their measurement is irrelevant here for two reasons: (1) whatever else a sensation is, it is not a quantum state of some sort; and (2) quantum vagueness is, arguably, epistemological and not ontological.

5. Thomas Nagel, 'What Is It Like to be a Bat?' *Philosophical Review*, 83 (1974), pp. 435–50; Frank Jackson, 'Epiphenomenal Qualia', *Philosophical Quarterly*, 32 (1982), pp. 127–36; Saul Kripke, 'Naming and Necessity', in Donald Davidson and Gilbert Harman (eds), *Semantics of Natural Languages* (Dordrecht: D. Reidel, 1972), pp. 253–355. Subsequently, Jackson has raised doubts about the Knowledge Argument. See his 'What Mary Didn't Know', *Journal of Philosophy*, 83 (1986), pp. 291–5.

6. David Papineau, *Philosophical Naturalism* (Oxford: Blackwell, 1993), pp. 103–14; Paul M. Churchland, *Matter and Consciousness* (Cambridge, MA: MIT Press, 1984), pp. 33–4.

7. I set aside the modal aspects of physical states since modality is not a factor in the sorts of states employed in this argument.

8. See Richard Swinburne, *The Evolution of the Soul*, rev. edn (Oxford: Clarendon Press, 1997).

9. See Moreland and Rae, *Body & Soul*.

10. See William Hasker, *The Emergent Self* (Ithaca, NY: Cornell University Press, 1999).

11. Stewart Goetz, 'Modal Dualism', paper delivered at the Midwestern Meeting of the Society of Christian Philosophers, 9 March 1996; Geoffrey Madell, *The Identity of the Self* (Edinburgh: Edinburgh University Press, 1981; cf. Madell, *Mind & Materialism* (Edinburgh: Edinburgh University Press, 1988), pp. 103–25. Madell claims that argument 1 (and 2 and 3 below) support either a substantial, immaterial self or a view of the self in which it is taken to be an immaterial property of being a self. Madell opts for the latter. For a critique of Madell on this point, see J. P. Moreland, 'Madell's Rejection of a Substantial, Immaterial Self', *Philosophia Christi*, 1 (1999), pp. 111–14. Space forbids a defence of these arguments, but it may be useful to clarify certain notions central to them, e.g., 'being internally related to me', 'an external relation'. To begin with, let us take as primitive the notion of a constituent/whole relation. A constituent/whole relation obtains between two entities just in case one entity is in the other as a constituent. So understood, there are two main types of constituent/whole relations: the standard separable part/whole relation of mereology and the accidental or essential predication relation. When a whole has a part or an accidental or essential property, the part or property is a constituent in the whole. In the sense used here, when one entity is a constituent of a whole, it is internally related to that whole. By contrast, 'an external relation' in this context is one which relates one entity to another without the former becoming a constituent of the latter. Thus, 'to the left of' is an external relation in this sense. Next, it is important to clarify the notion of a mode. Here is a sufficient condition of some entity's being a mode of another entity. If, for some substance S and property P, S exemplifies P, then the state of affairs – S's exemplifying P (call it A) – is a mode of S. As such, the mode is dependent on S for its existence and is internally related to S. There is no possible world where A exists and S does not. Moreover, if at some time t, S exemplifies P, then at all times prior to t, S had the (first or higher order) potentiality to exemplify P. And part of what makes S the kind of substance it is, is its potentialities. Now the substance dualist argues that sensations (and other mental states) are modes of the substantial self. As such, they are constituted by kind-defining mental properties, and, thus, their possessors are members of mental kinds.

12. Swinburne, *Evolution of the Soul*, pp. 145–73; Hasker, *Emergent Self*, pp. 122–46.

13. Cf. Peter van Inwagen, *Material Beings* (Ithaca, NY: Cornell University Press, 1990), especially chs 2 and 9; Van Inwagen, 'Dualism and Materialism: Athens and Jerusalem?' *Faith and Philosophy*, 12 (1995), pp. 475–88; Lynn Rudder Baker, 'Need a Christian Be a Mind/Body Dualism?' *Faith and Philosophy*, 12 (1995),

pp. 489–504; Trenton Merricks, 'A New Objection to A Priori Arguments for Dualism', *American Philosophical Quarterly*, 31 (1994), pp. 81–5; Merricks, 'The Resurrection of the Body and the Life Everlasting', in Michael J. Murray (ed.), *Reason for the Hope Within* (Grand Rapids, MI: Eerdmans, 1999), pp. 261–86; Kevin J. Corcoran, 'Persons and Bodies: The Metaphysics of Human Persons' (Ph.D. Dissertation, Purdue University, 1997).

14. I omit temporal indexicals like 'now' and 'then' because in my view there are two primitive indexicals that cannot be reduced to or eliminated in favour of the other: 'I' and 'now'. 'Now' expresses an irreducible fact about temporal reality – presentness – and it implies an A-series view of time. The fact that 'I' and 'now' are both primitive may have something to do with the fact that finite, conscious beings are intrinsically temporal entities.

15. See Madell, *Mind and Materialism*, pp. 103–25.

16. See Madell, *Identity of the Self*; H. D. Lewis, *The Elusive Self* (Philadelphia: Westminster Press, 1982).

17. If human beings exercise libertarian agency, then (1) they have the power to initiate change as a first mover and (2) they have the power to refrain from exercising their power to initiate change and (3) they act for the sake of reasons as irreducible, teleological ends for the sake of which they act. It has been argued that these features of libertarian agency are not physical properties and powers and, thus, libertarian agents are not physical objects. See John Foster, *The Immaterial Self* (London: Routledge, 1991), pp. 266–80; Grant Gillett, 'Actions, Causes, and Mental Ascriptions', in Howard Robinson (ed.), *Objections to Physicalism* (Oxford: Clarendon Press, 1993), pp. 81–100; J. P. Moreland, 'Naturalism and Libertarian Agency', *Philosophy and Theology*, 10 (1997), pp. 351–81. But cf. Timothy O'Connor, 'Agent Causation', in Timothy O'Connor, *Agents, Causes, & Events* (NY: Oxford University Press, 1995), pp. 178–80.

18. Foster, *Immaterial Self*, pp. 266–80.

19. Cf. Keith Yandell, 'A Defence of Dualism', *Faith and Philosophy*, 12 (1995), pp. 548–66; Charles Taliaferro, 'Animals, Brains, and Spirits', *Faith and Philosophy*, 12 (1995), pp. 567–81.

20. See Swinburne, *Evolution of the Soul*, pp. 11–16; Alvin Plantinga, *Warrant and Proper Function* (New York: Oxford University Press, 1993), pp. 65–77.

21. Saul Kripke, *Naming and Necessity* (Cambridge, MA: Harvard University Press, 1972), pp. 148–55.

22. Cf. David Papineau, 'Arguments for Supervenience and Physical Realization', in Elias E. Savellos and Umit D. Yalcin (eds), *Supervenience: New Essays* (Cambridge: Cambridge University Press, 1995), pp. 226–43.

5.1

'A REFUTATION OF DUALISM'

Paul Churchland

ARGUMENTS FOR DUALISM

Here we shall examine some of the main considerations commonly offered in support of dualism. Criticism will be postponed for a moment so that we may appreciate the collective force of these supporting considerations.

A major source of dualistic convictions is the religious belief many of us bring to these issues. Each of the major religions is in its way a theory about the cause or purpose of the universe, and Man's place within it, and many of them are committed to the notion of an immortal soul—that is, to some form of substance dualism. Supposing that one is consistent, to consider disbelieving dualism is to consider disbelieving one's religious heritage, and some of us find that difficult to do. Call this the *argument from religion*.

A more universal consideration is the *argument from introspection*. The fact is, when you center your attention on the contents of your consciousness, you do not clearly apprehend a neural network pulsing with electrochemical activity: you apprehend a flux of thoughts, sensations, desires, and emotions. It seems that mental states and properties, as revealed in introspection, could hardly be more different from physical states and properties if they tried. The verdict of introspection, therefore, seems strongly on the side of some form of dualism—on the side of property dualism, at a minimum.

A cluster of important considerations can be collected under the *argument from irreducibility*. Here one points to a variety of mental phenomena where it

Paul Churchland, 'A Refutation of Dualism', in Paul Churchland, *Matter and Consciousness*, rev. edn (Cambridge, MA: The MIT Press, 1988), pp. 13–21.

seems clear that no purely physical explanation could possibly account for what is going on. Descartes has already cited our ability to use language in a way that is relevant to our changing circumstances, and he was impressed also with our faculty of Reason, particularly as it is displayed in our capacity for mathematical reasoning. These abilities, he thought, must surely be beyond the capacity of any physical system. More recently, the introspectible qualities of our sensations (sensory 'qualia'), and the meaningful content of our thoughts and beliefs, have also been cited as phenomena that will forever resist reduction to the physical. Consider, for example, seeing the color or smelling the fragrance of a rose. A physicist or chemist might know everything about the molecular structure of the rose, and of the human brain, argues the dualist, but that knowledge would not enable him to predict or anticipate the quality of these inexpressible experiences.

Finally, parapsychological phenomena are occasionally cited in favor of dualism. Telepathy (mind reading), precognition (seeing the future), telekinesis (thought control of material objects), and clairvoyance (knowledge of distant objects) are all awkward to explain within the normal confines of psychology and physics. If these phenomena are real, they might well be reflecting the superphysical nature that the dualist ascribes to the mind. Trivially they are *mental* phenomena, and if they are also forever beyond physical explanation, then at least some mental phenomena must be irreducibly nonphysical.

Collectively, these considerations may seem compelling. But there are serious criticisms of each, and we must examine them as well. Consider first the argument from religion. There is certainly nothing wrong in principle with appealing to a more general theory that bears on the case at issue, which is what the appeal to religion amounts to. But the appeal can only be as good as the scientific credentials of the religion(s) being appealed to, and here the appeals tend to fall down rather badly. In general, attempts to decide scientific questions by appeal to religious orthodoxy have a very sorry history. That the stars are other suns, that the earth is not the center of the universe, that diseases are caused by microorganisms, that the earth is billions of years old, that life is a physicochemical phenomenon; all of these crucial insights were strongly and sometimes viciously resisted, because the dominant religion of the time happened to think otherwise. Giordano Bruno was burned at the stake for urging the first view; Galileo was forced by threat of torture in the Vatican's basement to recant the second view; the firm belief that disease was a punishment visited by the Devil allowed public health practices that brought chronic plagues to most of the cities of Europe; and the age of the earth and the evolution of life were forced to fight an uphill battle against religious prejudice even in an age of supposed enlightenment.

History aside, the almost universal opinion that one's own religious convictions are the reasoned outcome of a dispassionate evaluation of all of the major alternatives is almost demonstrably false for humanity in general.

If that really were the genesis of most people's convictions, then one would expect the major faiths to be distributed more or less randomly or evenly over the globe. But in fact they show a very strong tendency to cluster: Christianity is centered in Europe and the Americas, Islam in Africa and the Middle East, Hinduism in India, and Buddhism in the Orient. Which illustrates what we all suspected anyway: that *social forces* are the primary determinants of religious belief for people in general. To decide scientific questions by appeal to religious orthodoxy would therefore be to put social forces in place of empirical evidence. For all of these reasons, professional scientists and philosophers concerned with the nature of mind generally do their best to keep religious appeals out of the discussion entirely.

The argument from introspection is a much more interesting argument, since it tries to appeal to the direct experience of everyman. But the argument is deeply suspect, in that it assumes that our faculty of inner observation or introspection reveals things as they really are in their innermost nature. This assumption is suspect because we already know that our other forms of observation—sight, hearing, touch, and so on—do no such thing. The red surface of an apple does not *look* like a matrix of molecules reflecting photons at certain critical wavelengths, but that is what it is. The sound of a flute does not *sound* like a sinusoidal compression wave train in the atmosphere, but that is what it is. The warmth of the summer air does not *feel* like the mean kinetic energy of millions of tiny molecules, but that is what it is. If one's pains and hopes and beliefs do not *introspectively* seem like electrochemical states in a neural network, that may be only because our faculty of introspection, like our other senses, is not sufficiently penetrating to reveal such hidden details. Which is just what one would expect anyway. The argument from introspection is therefore entirely without force, unless we can somehow argue that the faculty of introspection is quite different from all other forms of observation.

The argument from irreducibility presents a more serious challenge, but here also its force is less than first impression suggests. Consider first our capacity for mathematical reasoning which so impressed Descartes. The last ten years have made available, to anyone with fifty dollars to spend, electronic calculators whose capacity for mathematical reasoning—the calculational part, at least—far surpasses that of any normal human. The fact is, in the centuries since Descartes' writings, philosophers, logicians, mathematicians, and computer scientists have managed to isolate the general principles of mathematical reasoning, and electronics engineers have created machines that compute in accord with those principles. The result is a hand-held object that would have astonished Descartes. This outcome is impressive not just because machines have proved capable of some of the capacities boasted by human reason, but because some of those achievements invade areas of human reason that past dualistic philosophers have held up as forever closed to mere physical devices.

Although debate on the matter remains open, Descartes' argument from language use is equally dubious. The notion of a *computer language* is by now a commonplace: consider BASIC, PASCAL, FORTRAN, APL, LISP, and so on. Granted, these artificial 'languages' are much simpler in structure and content than human natural language, but the differences may be differences only of degree, and not of kind. As well, the theoretical work of Noam Chomsky and the generative grammar approach to linguistics have done a great deal to explain the human capacity for language use in terms that invite simulation by computers. I do not mean to suggest that truly conversational computers are just around the corner. We have a great deal yet to learn, and fundamental problems yet to solve (mostly having to do with our capacity for inductive or theoretical reasoning). But recent progress here does nothing to support the claim that language use must be forever impossible for a purely physical system. On the contrary, such a claim now appears rather arbitrary and dogmatic.

The next issue is also a live problem: How can we possibly hope to explain or to predict the intrinsic qualities of our sensations, or the meaningful content of our beliefs and desires, in purely physical terms? This is a major challenge to the materialist. But active research programs are already under way on both problems, and positive suggestions are being explored. It is in fact not impossible to imagine how such explanations might go, though the materialist cannot yet pretend to have solved either problem. Until he does, the dualist will retain a bargaining chip here, but that is about all. What the dualists need in order to establish their case is the conclusion that a physical reduction is outright impossible, and that is a conclusion they have failed to establish. Rhetorical questions, like the one that opens this paragraph, do not constitute arguments. And it is equally difficult, note, to imagine how the relevant phenomena could be explained or predicted solely in terms of the substance dualist's nonphysical mind-stuff. The explanatory problem here is a major challenge to everybody, not just to the materialist. On this issue, then, we have a rough standoff.

The final argument in support of dualism urged the existence of parapsychological phenomena such as telepathy and telekinesis, the point being that such mental phenomena are (a) real and (b) beyond purely physical explanation. This argument is really another instance of the argument from irreducibility discussed above, and as before, it is not entirely clear that such phenomena, even if real, must forever escape a purely physical explanation. The materialist can already suggest a possible mechanism for telepathy, for example. On his view, thinking is an electrical activity within the brain. But according to electromagnetic theory, such changing motions of electric charges must produce electromagnetic waves radiating at the speed of light in all directions, waves that will contain information about the electrical activity that produced them. Such waves can subsequently have effects on the electrical activity of other brains, that is, on their thinking. Call this the 'radio transmitter/receiver' theory of telepathy.

I do not for a moment suggest that this theory is true: the electromagnetic waves emitted by the brain are fantastically weak (billions of times weaker than the ever present background electromagnetic flux produced by commercial radio stations), and they are almost certain to be hopelessly jumbled together as well. This is one reason why, in the absence of systematic, compelling, and repeatable evidence for the existence of telepathy, one must doubt its possibility. But it is significant that the materialist has the theoretical resources to suggest a detailed possible explanation of telepathy, if it were real, which is more than any dualist has so far done. It is not at all clear, then, that the materialist *must* be at an explanatory disadvantage in these matters. Quite the reverse.

Put the preceding aside, if you wish, for the main difficulty with the argument from parapsychological phenomena is much, much simpler. Despite the endless pronouncements and anecdotes in the popular press, and despite a steady trickle of serious research on such things, there is no significant or trustworthy evidence that such phenomena even exist. The wide gap between popular conviction on this matter, and the actual evidence, is something that itself calls for research. For there is not a single parapsychological effect that can be repeatedly or reliably produced in any laboratory suitably equipped to perform and control the experiment. Not one. Honest researchers have been repeatedly hoodwinked by 'psychic' charlatans with skills derived from the magician's trade, and the history of the subject is largely a history of gullibility, selection of evidence, poor experimental controls, and outright fraud by the occasional researcher as well. If someone really does discover a repeatable parapsychological effect, then we shall have to reevaluate the situation, but, as things stand, there is nothing here to support a dualist theory of mind.

Upon critical examination, the arguments in support of dualism lose much of their force. But we are not yet done: there are arguments against dualism, and these also require examination.

Arguments against Dualism

The first argument against dualism urged by the materialists appeals to the greater *simplicity* of their view. It is a principle of rational methodology that, if all else is equal, the simpler of two competing hypotheses should be preferred. This principle is sometimes called "Ockham's Razor"—after William of Ockham, the medieval philosopher who first enunciated it— and it can also be expressed as follows: "Do not multiply entities beyond what is strictly necessary to explain the phenomena." The materialist postulates only one kind of substance (physical matter), and one class of properties (physical properties), whereas the dualist postulates two kinds of matter and/or two classes of properties. And to no explanatory advantage, charges the materialist.

This is not yet a decisive point against dualism, since neither dualism nor materialism can yet explain all of the phenomena to be explained. But the objection does have some force, especially since there is no doubt at all that physical matter exists, while spiritual matter remains a tenuous hypothesis.

If this latter hypothesis brought us some definite explanatory advantage obtainable in no other way, then we would happily violate the demand for simplicity, and we would be right to do so. But it does not, claims the materialist. In fact, the advantage is just the other way around, he argues, and this brings us to the second objection to dualism: the relative *explanatory impotence* of dualism as compared to materialism.

Consider, very briefly, the explanatory resources already available to the neurosciences. We know that the brain exists and what it is made of. We know much of its microstructure: how the neurons are organized into systems and how distinct systems are connected to one another, to the motor nerves going out to the muscles, and to the sensory nerves coming in from the sense organs. We know much of their microchemistry: how the nerve cells fire tiny electrochemical pulses along their various fibers, and how they make other cells fire also, or cease firing. We know some of how such activity processes sensory information, selecting salient or subtle bits to be sent on to higher systems. And we know some of how such activity initiates and coordinates bodily behavior. Thanks mainly to neurology (the branch of medicine concerned with brain pathology), we know a great deal about the correlations between damage to various parts of the human brain, and various behavioral and cognitive deficits from which the victims suffer. There are a great many isolated deficits—some gross, some subtle—that are familiar to neurologists (inability to speak, or to read, or to understand speech, or to recognize faces, or to add/subtract, or to move a certain limb, or to put information into long-term memory, and so on), and their appearance is closely tied to the occurrence of damage to very specific parts of the brain.

Nor are we limited to cataloguing traumas. The growth and development of the brain's microstructure is also something that neuroscience has explored, and such development appears to be the basis of various kinds of learning by the organism. Learning, that is, involves lasting chemical and physical changes in the brain. In sum, the neuroscientist can tell us a great deal about the brain, about its constitution and the physical laws that govern it; he can already explain much of our behavior in terms of the physical, chemical, and electrical properties of the brain; and he has the theoretical resources available to explain a good deal more as our explorations continue.

Compare now what the neuroscientist can tell us about the brain, and what he can do with that knowledge, with what the dualist can tell us about spiritual substance, and what he can do with those assumptions. Can the dualist tell us anything about the internal constitution of mind-stuff? Of the nonmaterial elements that make it up? Of the laws that govern their behavior? Of the mind's structural connections with the body? Of the manner of its operations? Can he explain human capacities and pathologies in terms of its structures and its defects? The fact is, the dualist can do none of these things, because no detailed theory of mind-stuff has ever been formulated. Compared to the rich resources and explanatory successes of current materialism, dualism is less a theory of mind than it is an empty space waiting for a genuine theory of mind to be put in it.

Thus argues the materialist. But again, this is not a completely decisive point against dualism. The dualist can admit that the brain plays a major role in the administration of both perception and behavior—on his view the brain is the *mediator* between the mind and the body—but he may attempt to argue that the materialist's current successes and future explanatory prospects concern only the mediative functions of the brain, not the *central* capacities of the nonphysical mind, capacities such as reason, emotion, and consciousness itself. On these latter topics, he may argue, both dualism *and* materialism currently draw a blank.

But this reply is not a very good one. So far as the capacity for reasoning is concerned, machines already exist that execute in minutes sophisticated deductive and mathematical calculations that would take a human a lifetime to execute. And so far as the other two mental capacities are concerned, studies of such things as depression, motivation, attention, and sleep have revealed many interesting and puzzling facts about the neurochemical and neurodynamical basis of both emotion and consciousness. The *central* capacities, no less than the peripheral, have been addressed with profit by various materialist research programs.

In any case, the (substance) dualist's attempt to draw a sharp distinction between the unique 'mental' capacities proper to the nonmaterial mind, and the merely mediative capacities of the brain, prompts an argument that comes close to being an outright refutation of (substance) dualism. If there really is a distinct entity in which reasoning, emotion, and consciousness take place, and if that entity is dependent on the brain for nothing more than sensory experiences as input and volitional executions as output, *then one would expect reason, emotion, and consciousness to be relatively invulnerable to direct control or pathology by manipulation or damage to the brain.* But in fact the exact opposite is true. Alcohol, narcotics, or senile degeneration of nerve tissue will impair, cripple, or even destroy one's capacity for rational thought. Psychiatry knows of hundreds of emotion-controlling chemicals (lithium, chlorpromazine, amphetamine, cocaine, and so on) that do their work when vectored into the brain. And the vulnerability of consciousness to the anesthetics, to caffeine, and to something as simple as a sharp blow to the head, shows its very close dependence on neural activity in the brain. All of this makes perfect sense if reason, emotion, and consciousness are activities of the brain itself. But it makes very little sense if they are activities of something else entirely.

We may call this the argument from the *neural dependence* of all known mental phenomena. Property dualism, note, is not threatened by this argument, since, like materialism, property dualism reckons the brain as the seat of all mental activity. We shall conclude this section, however, with an argument that cuts against both varieties of dualism: the argument from *evolutionary history*.

What is the origin of a complex and sophisticated species such as ours? What, for that matter, is the origin of the dolphin, the mouse, or the housefly? Thanks to the fossil record, comparative anatomy, and the biochemistry of proteins and nucleic acids, there is no longer any significant doubt on this matter. Each existing species is a surviving type from a number of variations on an earlier type of organism; each earlier type is in turn a surviving type from a number of variations on a still earlier type of organism; and so on down the branches of the evolutionary tree until, some three billion years ago, we find a trunk of just one or a handful of very simple organisms. These organisms, like their more complex offspring, are just self-repairing, self-replicating, energy-driven molecular structures. (That evolutionary trunk has its own roots in an earlier era of purely chemical evolution, in which the molecular elements of life were themselves pieced together.) The mechanism of development that has structured this tree has two main elements: (1) the occasional blind variation in types of reproducing creature, and (2) the selective survival of some of these types due to the relative reproductive advantage enjoyed by individuals of those types. Over periods of geological time, such a process can produce an enormous variety of organisms, some of them very complex indeed.

For purposes of our discussion, the important point about the standard evolutionary story is that the human species and all of its features are the wholly physical outcome of a purely physical process. Like all but the simplest of organisms, we have a nervous system. And for the same reason: a nervous system permits the discriminative guidance of behavior. But a nervous system is just an active matrix of cells, and a cell is just an active matrix of molecules. We are notable only in that our nervous system is more complex and powerful than those of our fellow creatures. Our inner nature differs from that of simpler creatures in degree, but not in kind.

If this is the correct account of our origins, then there seems neither need, nor room, to fit any nonphysical substances or properties into our theoretical account of ourselves. We are creatures of matter. And we should learn to live with that fact.

Arguments like these have moved most (but not all) of the professional community to embrace some form of materialism. This has not produced much unanimity, however, since the differences between the several materialist positions are even wider than the differences that divide dualism.

5.2

'A DEFENSE OF DUALISM'

John Foster

By "dualism" I mean the thesis that the mind and its contents are radically nonphysical, that is, that they are neither themselves physical, nor the logical product of anything physical, nor, except causally or nomologically, dependent on anything physical.[1] It is worth noting that dualism in this sense is compatible with monism. For while a dualist cannot hold that reality (or as I would prefer to say, ultimate reality)[2] is wholly physical, he can hold that it is wholly mental. He can even hold this view while accepting what for the purposes of this discussion I shall pretend to accept,[3] the reality (ultimate reality) of the physical world. This possibility, however, will not concern us till the very end.

It is nowadays generally assumed that dualism has been discredited. Even those who see problems for the alternatives usually are unwilling to countenance dualism as a possible solution. I believe that dualism is correct, and the purpose of this chapter is to defend it in two ways. Thus in section I, I shall consider the alternatives to dualism and try to show why they are unacceptable (some of the arguments here are familiar, but they are worth rehearsing). And in section II, I shall consider some of the main objections to dualism and try to show why they are ineffective. In addition to this twofold defense, there is a short postscript (section III), in which I consider the possibility of mentalistic monism.

John Foster, 'A Defense of Dualism', in John R. Smythies and John Beloff (eds), *The Case for Dualism* (Charlottesville: University Press of Virginia, 1989), pp. 1–23.

I. THE ALTERNATIVES TO DUALISM

I. Conceptual Materialism

The most radical alternative to dualism is "materialism," the thesis that mental facts (or states of affairs) are nothing over and above physical facts (or states of affairs). This thesis can be interpreted in two ways. I shall start by considering the most straightforward interpretation: all mental truths (true propositions about the mind) are logically deducible from physical truths (true propositions about the physical world). I shall call this version of the thesis "conceptual materialism." The label "conceptual" is not intended to signify that the materialist thesis is offered as a conceptual (a priori) truth but only to signify the deductive (a priori) character of the logical relation between mental truths and the physical truths from which they allegedly flow.

As defined, conceptual materialism is a very general thesis: it leaves open a wide range of possibilities. But, typically, what the conceptual materialist has in mind is something like this. Take a human organism O at a certain time t. Suppose, for the sake of argument, we have a complete description of the physical structure of O at t and know all the physical laws of nature. From this information we can, it is claimed, deduce a complete description (or as close to complete as we care to make it) of how O is designed to function in different physical environments.[4] Not all aspects of this total functional organization are relevant to the mental activities of O. So we next select those that are. For example, we select as one mind-relevant item the functional organization of O's visual system, noting how, through the reception and processing of different light inputs, this system equips O to behave in discriminatory ways with respect to the arrangement of colors in his environment. Likewise, we select as another mind-relevant item the functional organization of O's hunger system, noting how, by the monitoring of nutrient levels and stomach condition, this system disposes O to behave in food-seeking ways (partly under the guidance of the visual system) when appropriate. Once we have selected all the relevant items and, integrating them, have a complete description of the total mind-relevant organization of O, we then consider the physical state of O at t and work out its mind-relevant significance with respect to this organization. From this, it is claimed, we can deduce a complete description of O's state of mind at t.

It is, typically, something like this which the conceptual materialist has in mind—the mental description of an organism being deducible from its functional description and its functional description being deducible from its physical description and physical laws. But my objection to conceptual materialism applies quite generally. The objection, which is a very familiar one, is that such materialism fails to do justice to the nature of conscious experience. There are many ways of putting this objection. Here is one way which I find compelling. Consider the situation of someone who is congenitally blind. Could such a person derive from physical information about the sighted a full knowledge of the character of visual experience? Could he deduce from the physiology and functional organization of the sighted human organism (and any other physical truths that might be thought relevant) a full knowledge of what it is like, experientially, for such an organism to see? It seems clear that he could not. But why not if conceptual materialism is true?[5]

Does the conceptual materialist have any replies? Well, in the first place, he might say that what prevents the blind man from deducing the experiential conclusion is that, being congenitally blind, he is not conceptually equipped to understand it. But this is clearly hopeless. If conceptual materialism were correct, there would be nothing to prevent such a person from acquiring the requisite experiential concepts, assuming he was sufficiently intelligent and was conceptually equipped to understand the relevant physical truths. The presumption that his blindness prevents such acquisition is already a tacit acknowledgment that the physical truths do not implicitly specify, in full, the nature of the sighted organism's experience. In any case, it is not essential to the example that the blind person should lack the requisite concepts. We can suppose that his visual cortex is sufficiently operational to give him, from time to time, visual experiences of a rudimentary kind, though ones which are not, and which he does not take to be, perceptions of his physical environment. These experiences could equip him to understand the experiential conclusion. But it still seems clear that he could not deduce it from the physical premiss. For the physical information about the sighted, however comprehensive, would not logically establish that their experience was of the sort to which his experiential concepts, furnished by his own visual experiences, applied.

Alternatively, the conceptual materialist might claim that the blind man is not conceptually equipped to understand all the relevant physical premises. Thus he might argue that one of the physical truths which would be required as a premise is that the sighted organism is equipped by its visual system to behave in ways which are discriminatory with respect to physical color, for example, in the case of a motorist, to stop when the traffic lights are red and continue when they are green. This is a truth which the blind man cannot fully understand, not having an adequate conception of physical color. But this reply too is quite hopeless. The blind man can acquire an adequate conception of physical color insofar as it is described scientifically, that is, in terms of wavelengths of light and the reflective properties of pigment. What he lacks is merely a conception of how physical colors look to the sighted. But this deficiency is just one aspect of his not knowing what it is like, experientially, for the sighted organism to see. The only respect in which he fails to grasp what is meant by "the traffic lights are red" is that he does not know what sort of experience the sighted person has when he receives light of the relevant wavelength. But this knowledge is precisely what, if conceptual materialism were true, he should be able to deduce from the physical information available. So the blind man's inability to achieve an adequate conception of color merely reflects the falsity of the materialist's thesis.

The conceptual materialist still has one final line of defense. He might claim that the blind man can, from the physical truths, derive a full knowledge of the character of visual experience, and that what misleads us into supposing otherwise is that the physical truths do not afford that kind of knowledge which is available, through introspection, to the sighted. On this view, there is no more to the character of visual experience than the blind man can deduce; it is simply that, being blind and lacking even the capacity to visualize, he cannot conceptually focus on this character in the way the sighted can. He knows exactly what such experience is psychologically like but cannot achieve, in his imagination, the viewpoint of those who have it. This reply looks more promising than the others. At least the distinction between merely knowing the character of a certain type of experience and knowing it in introspective perspective is sound. To take a different example, there are some pitches which are too high for me to hear or frame a mental image of. Suppose P is the highest pitch I can hear or image. There is a perfectly good sense in which I know what it is like, experientially, to hear the pitch which is an octave higher than P: I can exactly fix the position of such an experience in the auditory spectrum. All I lack is the kind of knowledge available to someone who has the experience or can achieve, in his imagination, the viewpoint of one who has it. However, I do not think that this distinction can be of use to the conceptual materialist. For while it is possible for someone to know the character of a certain type of experience without knowing it in the introspective manner, it is surely only possible in those cases where the person can define that character by reference to other types of experience whose character he does know in that manner. I can grasp the experiental character of hearing the relevant pitch because I can introspectively grasp both the hearing of P and the octave relation. The problem for the blind man is that the physical truths provide no introspective reference points at all. And for this reason, I cannot see how he could derive from them, in any sense, a full knowledge of what it is like, experientially, for the sighted organism to see.

2. Metaphysical Materialism

The failure of conceptual materialism does not entail the failure of materialism as such. For the thesis that mental facts are nothing over and above physical facts can be interpreted in another way. It can be interpreted as meaning that all mental facts are the necessary consequences of physical facts by some mode of necessity which, while in a broad sense logical (i.e., stronger than mere natural necessity), is not that of deductive entailment. Since this mode of necessity is often called "metaphysical," I shall label this position "metaphysical materialism." It might be objected that this so-called interpretation of the materialist thesis does not do justice to the force of the phrase "nothing over and above." But this is a purely verbal issue. The fact remains that metaphysical materialism as defined is incompatible with dualism.

How could mental facts be the logically (stronger than naturally) necessary consequences of physical facts except by some relation of deductive entailment? Well, the metaphysical materialist invites us to accept a certain analogy. Consider the relationship between the two propositions (A) that this spoon is hot, and (B) that the molecules of this spoon are agitated. Let us assume that our ordinary (i.e., prescientific) concept of physical heat is as that property, whatever it is, which induces heat sensations in us. From this it immediately follows that (A) is not deducible from (B), since it is not an a priori truth that what induces such sensations is molecular agitation. At the same time, it is a truth, and one which science has established. And from this, together with the assumption, it follows that heat is (i.e., is identical with) molecular agitation. But, for reasons which Kripke has made familiar, this obliges us to say that there is no logically possible world in which (B) is true and (A) is false.[6] In this sense, if the spoon is hot, its being so is a logically necessary consequence of the fact that its molecules are agitated. In the same way, it is claimed, mental facts about a person are the logically necessary consequences of physical facts about his body. Thus our ordinary (i.e., prescientific) concept of pain, it is said, is as that state, whatever it is, which reveals itself to the subject under a certain introspective appearance and is expressed overtly through certain forms of behavior. We cannot deduce that a person is in pain from a physical description of his body (not even from one which includes a formulation of physical law), since such a description does not tell us how things appear introspectively: it does not address itself to the character of pain as a subjective experience. But we should, it is claimed, anticipate the scientific discovery that the state which meets our conceptual requirements—the state which, in the actual world, has the required introspective appearance and behavioral influence—is, in its intrinsic nature, physical. And if pain is (i.e., is identical with) a physical state, then it is a necessary truth (true in all logically possible worlds), though not a priori, that a person is in pain if and only if his body is in that state. Admittedly, it may well turn out that pain in one species of organism is a different physical state from pain in another, and it may even turn out that, within a single species, pain in one member is a different physical state from pain in another. But while this would prevent an exact analogy with heat, it does not affect the fundamentals of the account.

However, as Kripke has shown,[7] the suggestion of any analogy at all is totally misconceived. What allows us to identify physical heat with molecular agitation is that we can detach the sensible appearance of physical heat from its essential nature: we can regard the sensible appearance as just the contingent effect of physical heat on human experience. If we are to identify pain with a physical state (whether absolutely or in a way which is species/organism-relative) we must similarly detach the introspective appearance of pain from its essential nature. But how could this be done? Only by separating what pain is in itself from how pain feels to the person who has it.

And such a separation is surely impossible. Moreover, even if it were possible, it would be, from the standpoint of the materialist, self-defeating. For, if the experiential character of pain is not part of its essential nature, the identification of pain with a physical state does nothing to make the experiential facts necessary consequences of physical facts and hence contributes nothing to the materialist's program. Nor can I see any other way in which the materialist could attempt to justify his consequentialist thesis without reverting to some form of conceptual materialism (e.g., by analyzing experiential concepts in functional terms), and this we have already refuted. Of course, the materialist could simply assert that experiential facts are metaphysically necessitated by physical facts and challenge us to refute him. But without some explanation of how such necessitation might obtain, we can hardly take this assertion seriously.

3. The Token-Identity Thesis

The fact that experiential states, as mental types, cannot be identified with physical states does not, as such, entail that experiences (experiential events), as mental particulars, are not identical with physical events. Thus a position which is becoming increasingly fashionable is to hold that mental events are identical with certain neural events, but that the mental properties of these events are not identical with any of their physical properties or indeed with anything, such as their functional properties, whose instantiation could be deduced from purely physical truths. This position is not a form of materialism as defined; it does not claim that mental facts are, either deductively or by metaphysical necessity, nothing over and above physical facts, though in some versions it does claim that mental facts are supervenient on physical facts, that is, that there cannot be mental differences without physical differences. Rather, the position combines a kind of ontological monism with an attributive dualism. When someone is in pain, the pain event is part of the material world (e.g., the firing of his C fibers at a particular time); but its being a pain (its mental character) is something genuinely additional to, and not logically necessitated by, its physical properties or anything which physical science could describe. This position, or, strictly, the monist part of it, is known as the "token-identity thesis." It is thus contrasted with the stronger "type-identity thesis," which claims that the mental types of which mental events are the tokens are identical with certain physical types, that is, that mental properties are identical with physical properties.

Once again it is Kripke who has exposed the flaw in this weaker position.[8] Suppose Smith is in pain. Let us call the particular pain event (the particular experiential event in Smith's mind at that time) E. And let us call the particular neural event with which E is supposedly identical (e.g., some particular firing of Smith's C fibers) B. Now it is clear that the experiential property "being a pain" is an essential attribute of E (the experiential event); that is, there is no logically possible world in which E exists and is not a pain. The only remotely feasible way of denying this claim would be by adopting a functionalist account of experiential properties, as in certain versions of conceptual materialism. For this would allow one to say that E qualified as a pain only contingently, in virtue of the causal role which events of E's (presumably physical) intrinsic type played in the whole physical or psychophysical system. But, as we have already seen, the functionalist account is inadequate; the arguments that refute it as an adjunct to conceptual materialism refute it quite generally. But while "being a pain" is an essential attribute of E, it is surely not an essential attribute of B (the neural event). For surely there is a possible world (perhaps it has to be one with different psychophysical laws) in which B exists and has no experiential character at all. Of course, this would be rejected by someone who identified experiential properties with physical properties, but, as we have seen, this type-identity thesis is unacceptable. But if E is essentially a pain and B is not, then E and B cannot be numerically identical. For if they were, they would have all their properties, including their modal properties, in common.

Granted the rejection of functionalism and the type-identity thesis, the defender of token-identity has, as far as I can see, only one way of trying to resist this argument. He has to maintain that while the experiential character of B is not part of the essential nature of the type of physical event of which B is an instance, it is, nonetheless, essential to the identity of B itself. But even this reply fails, since the identity of B is wholly determined by physical factors. Thus, suppose we try to envisage a world W which results from the actual world by (a) removing B, (b) filling the gap with an event of exactly the same physical type, composed of exactly the same particle events, with exactly the same causal antecedents, but without B's experiential character, and (c) making whatever further adjustments this requires, for example, changes in psychophysical law and similar (putative) replacements of other B-type events. It is surely obvious that the W event which is the counterpart of B is none other than B itself. Being of exactly the same physical type, having exactly the same spatiotemporal location, being composed of exactly the same particle events in the same brain, and being caused in exactly the same way, the putative replacement just is numerically the same physical event. It follows that if W is genuinely possible, "being a pain" is not essential to B. And consequently, the only way in which we could hold it to be essential would be by claiming that the experiential character of B was logically determined, either deductively or metaphysically, by its physical properties and other physical factors on which its identity depends. This claim would exclude the possibility of W, but it would oblige us to accept a full-blooded materialism of the kind we have already rejected and which the token-identity thesis was designed to avoid.

4. The Logical Dependence Thesis

The token-identity thesis was one way of trying to get a compromise between full dualism and full materialism. Another way would be to claim that while mental facts are not logically determined by physical facts, they are at least logically dependent on them. There are several positions of this sort. Among the most familiar are the claim that any subject of mental states has to be (or at least to have been) embodied and the claim that the connection between mental states and their behavioral manifestations is not purely contingent. I do not have time to examine such claims in detail, though I find none of them at all convincing. My main objection to all of them is that, in the last analysis, they rest on an indefensible form of the verification principle. They all, in one way or another, appeal to the alleged fact that dualism generates skepticism— for example (and this is the case most often cited), skepticism about other minds—and that such skepticism can only be avoided by moving, to some extent, in the direction of conceptual materialism—for example, by making certain concessions to behaviorism. But the fact that a philosophical position generates an epistemological problem is not as such a reason for rejecting it. Moreover, in the particular case of other minds, the problem that dualism allegedly generates has been greatly exaggerated. Even from a dualist stand-point, most of our commonsense beliefs about the mental states of others can be justified by an inference to the best explanation. If it is said that such justification falls short of conclusive verification, this is quite true. But it is surely very implausible to maintain that in the case of statements about other minds, conclusive verification is available. The only area, in the topic of other minds, where dualism seems to generate a really acute epistemological problem is that concerned with sense qualia—for example, how can I tell that your color spectrum is not inverted with respect to mine? But here it seems to me that the problem is a genuine one and that a theory which did not allow it to arise would be defective.

5. The Restriction of Dualism to Experience

Assuming we reject the logical dependence thesis, we cannot, I think, avoid a dualistic account of experience: experiential states and experiential events are radically nonphysical, that is, are neither physical, nor the logical product of anything physical, nor, except causally or nomologically, dependent on anything physical. But we could still reject dualism with respect to the residual contents of the mind. Thus we could still claim that propositional attitudes, such as belief and desire, are physical states of the brain, or functional states whose instantiation is deducible from a physical description of the brain, or whole organism, together with certain physical laws. And we could still claim that propositional acts, such as thoughts and judgments, are physical events in the brain, or functional events whose occurrence is deducible from a brain/

organism-description and physical laws. My arguments against materialism and the token-identity thesis do not directly exclude such claims, since they have exclusively concerned the case of experience.

Nonetheless, it seems to me that once we have accepted experiential dualism, the extension of dualism to the rest of the mind becomes unavoidable. The first point to stress is that although, as formulated, my arguments against materialism and the token-identity thesis have only concerned the case of experience, they can be generalized to cover all those aspects of our mental life which are essentially conscious—all those aspects which, of their very nature, form part of how it is, subjectively, with the subject. For it was precisely the conscious character of experience that made it resistant to the materialist and identity accounts. This does not oblige us to adopt a dualist account of propositional attitudes, such as belief and desire, since these are not essentially conscious in the relevant sense: a person who is sound asleep can still be said to have beliefs and desires. But it does, I think, oblige us to adopt a dualist account of propositional and quasi-propositional acts, such as thoughts, judgments, and decisions. For these, it seems to me, are essentially conscious. It might be objected, by philosophers of a radically empiricist persuasion, that it is only the phenomenal, not the conceptual, aspects of these acts which are essentially conscious. For example, suppose that in the course of performing some larger arithmetical calculation, I make the judgment that $9 \times 7 = 63$. An empiricist might argue that the only essentially conscious element in this judgment is my mental voicing of the sequence of sounds "nine sevens are sixty-three" and that this phenomenal act only derives its conceptual significance, as a vehicle for my propositional act, from a surrounding mental framework (involving such items as my mastery of English and my knowledge of arithmetic) which is, or could be, subjectively silent. If this were so, then the conceptual aspects of the judgment—in effect, the propositional act itself—could be construed in a nondualistic way. However, I find this empiricist account very implausible. I think we can best see this by beginning with the case of perception. It is quite clear that in most cases of perception, at least after early infancy, there is a large element of conceptual interpretation within the conscious experience itself. Thus in visual perception, the experience consists of more than just the presentation of a color array; it includes seeing the color array as a physical scene of a certain sort. (Seeing Wittgenstein's ambiguous picture as a duck or as a rabbit is just a dramatic example of this.) Now consider the particular case of hearing the sequence of sounds "nine sevens are sixty-three." There is clearly an experiential difference between hearing it just as a sequence of sounds (this might be the experience of someone who did not understand English) and hearing it as a sentence of English expressing the proposition that $9 \times 7 = 63$ (this would be the normal experience of a numerate English-speaker). But given that a propositional interpretation of the sounds can be part of the total perceptual experience when the sounds are heard, it can also be part of the total conscious state when they are mentally voiced. And surely this will always be so when the mental voicing is the vehicle for a propositional act.

We are still left with the case of propositional attitudes, which, as I have conceded, are not essentially conscious. Here, the case of dualism rests on the fact that such states, while not in themselves states of consciousness, are essentially linked with states of consciousness. Let us focus on the example of belief. There is no denying that a person can hold a certain belief at times when he is not performing the corresponding act of judgment. But it is surely part of the essential nature of belief that it should dispose the subject to make such judgments when the need arises. Thus it is surely logically impossible for me to believe that $9 \times 7 = 63$ unless I am thereby disposed to judge that $9 \times 7 = 63$ when I address myself to the question. If so, then beliefs cannot be identified with physical states, such as neural networks, since such states would at best sustain such dispositions only contingently, that is, through the contingent obtaining of certain psychophysical laws. Nor, given that judgments themselves are nonphysical, can beliefs be construed as functional states of a kind whose instantiation could be deduced from purely physical truths. It might be objected that in rejecting the identity thesis, I am overlooking the distinction between types and tokens. Thus it may be that as a mental type, a belief state cannot be physical. But why shouldn't the tokens of this type—the particular instances of this belief state in particular minds at particular times—be physical? Why not say that my current token-belief that $9 \times 7 = 63$ is some current neural network in my brain, while allowing that this network only qualifies as a token-belief in virtue of its contingently disposing me to make the appropriate conscious judgment? But the trouble with this is that while we are free to recognize an ontology of token-beliefs, we cannot do so in a way which leaves their belief character (their character as token-beliefs) only contingent. For our only conception of a token-belief is as something which is, by its essential nature, the particular occurrence of some type of believing, for example, my believing now that $9 \times 7 = 63$. And if the token-beliefs are essentially token-beliefs, then their dispositional connection with conscious judgments must be essential too.

Given all this, the only way of avoiding a wholly dualistic account of belief would be to adopt a hybrid form of functionalism, in which belief is construed as a functional state defined partly in terms of its output in nonphysical conscious judgment and partly in terms of its output in physical behavior—in effect, the combination of certain mentalistic and certain behavioral dispositions. All I can say against this is that I find the behavioristic element implausible. It is inconceivable that someone should believe that $9 \times 7 = 63$ without being disposed to make the corresponding judgment. But it is surely quite conceivable that someone should hold this belief without being equipped with the right kind of neuromuscular system to express it overtly. Indeed, in the case of stroke victims, this frequently happens. It may be objected that such victims only retain their beliefs because they once possessed the neuromuscular capacity to express them. But we can surely also envisage cases in which someone acquires beliefs without ever having such a capacity.

As I see it, then, we are obliged to give a wholly dualistic account of belief. (Exactly what account we should give I shall not pursue; the fact that belief essentially involves a judgmental disposition may seem to support some kind of dualistic functionalism, but for reasons I shall not go into, I doubt if this is so.) Obviously, if we are dualistic about belief, we must be similarly dualistic about other propositional attitudes. Since we have already established dualism for experience and other essentially conscious states, this means, in effect, that we must accept dualism as such—accept the thesis that the mind and its contents are radically nonphysical.

II. Four Objections to Dualism

I have tried to show why the alternatives to dualism are unacceptable. If my arguments have been correct, there is a sense in which I could afford to rest my case there, since, if the alternatives are wrong, dualism must be right. The reason I continue is that dualism itself is thought to be vulnerable to certain objections, and these objections (or at least some of them) merit answers. Of course, I do not have space to consider all the objections. Some are nothing more than rhetoric (I would put into this category such objections as "nonphysical entities are queer" and "postulating nonphysical entities is ontologically extravagant"); others would require a separate chapter to deal with them effectively (in particular, those objections which concern the problem of other minds and the issue over private languages, though, in the case of other minds, I have given some indication in section I.4 of the line I would take). Apart from these, however, I have tried to cover those objections which I regard as the most important, either because of their intrinsic merits or because of the influence they have exerted.

As it turns out, the four objections I consider all concern, in one way or another, the dualist's account of psychophysical causation—his account of the causal relations between body and mind. Dualism itself, of course, does not entail that there are such relations. There is no contradiction in maintaining that the mind, as well as being nonphysical, is causally isolated from the physical world; and with the help of a suitable theism, it may even be possible to explain why things are empirically organized as if there were psychophysical causation, when there is not. But since I do not want my defense of dualism to force me into such an eccentric position, I shall work on the assumption that parallelism, in this extreme form, is untenable and that mind and body are indeed causally related. This still leaves the dualist with a choice between interactionism, which takes the causal relations to run in both directions, and epiphenomenalism, which takes them to run only from body to mind. Here my sympathies, again in line with common sense, are with the interactionist. And consequently, I would feel at least very uncomfortable if there were something which obliged me to choose between abandoning dualism altogether and adopting its epiphenomenalist version. That I do face such a choice is the substance of the fourth objection.

1. The Traditional Objection

Perhaps the oldest objection to dualism is that if the mind is nonphysical, the very idea of psychophysical causation—of the body causally affecting the mind or the mind causally affecting the body—is deeply puzzling, if not incoherent. How can such different kinds of thing—the physical and the nonphysical—come into causal contact? How can the material body gain purchase on the immaterial mind, or vice versa? However, put like this, I cannot see what the problem is supposed to be. Obviously, dualistic causation does not operate through physical contact, as when one billiard ball displaces another. But why should it not just be in the nature of things that in certain psychophysical conditions, certain types of neural event cause certain types of mental event, or vice versa? According to Thomas Nagel, we cannot understand how such causation would work.[9] Nagel assumes, I think correctly, though contrary to Hume's account, that causation involves some kind of objective necessitation. He then argues, in effect, that so long as we think of mental and physical events as radically different in their intrinsic nature, such necessitation is incomprehensible: "what we cannot understand is *how* . . . the brain process necessitates the sensation."[10] But what I cannot understand is how this "how"-question arises. Since the necessitation is causal, rather than logical, there cannot be any question of construing it as some kind of a priori entailment. Moreover, since the causation is direct (the brain event directly causing the mental event, or vice versa), there is no question of an intervening mechanism. Perhaps it is this very directness which Nagel finds puzzling. For in the physical world causal processes are, in general, spatio-temporally continuous, thus providing an intervening mechanism between a cause and any subsequent effect. But there is surely nothing incoherent or problematic about the notion of direct causation. And where causation is direct, I do not see in what sense there could be a question of how it operates, except as a request to specify the causally relevant properties and covering laws.

2. The Problem of Causal Pairings

While the traditional objection to dualistic psychophysical causation is totally misconceived, there is a related objection which is more troublesome and for which, ironically, I have to take the credit.[11] It is normally assumed that where two events are causally related, they are so wholly by virtue of the way in which, via their noncausal properties and relations, they fall under some natural law. Thus if, on a particular occasion, my heating of a lump of metal caused it to melt, it is assumed that what makes this true is that the metal was of a certain type and reached a certain temperature and that it is a law of nature (or a consequence of a law of nature) that whenever a lump of metal of that type reaches that temperature, it melts. However, when we apply this model to the case of psychophysical causation, dualistically conceived, we encounter a problem. Suppose that B is the event of Smith's brain being in state ϕ at time t and that E is a mental event of type ψ which occurs in Smith's mind a tenth of a second after t and as the direct causal result of B. What psychophysical law could we postulate to account for this causal episode? We might begin by postulating the law (L_1) that whenever a brain is in a state ϕ a mental event of type ψ occurs a tenth of a second later. But this would be inadequate. For suppose that Jones's brain is also in state ϕ at t, giving us the event B' which is a simultaneous duplicate of B, and that this causes in Jones's mind, a tenth of a second later, an event E' of type ψ, which is a simultaneous duplicate of E. *Ex hypothesi*, B is the cause of E and B' is the cause of E'. But the law L_1 does not account for these causal pairings. Because it only specifies the temporal relation between cause and effect, it is neutral between these pairings and the alternative, but false, hypothesis that B is the cause of E' and B' is the cause of E. The obvious remedy is to replace L_1 by the stronger law (L_2) that whenever a brain x is in state ϕ a mental event of type ψ occurs a tenth of a second later in that mind which x, or the x-containing organism, embodies—in other words, in the mind of that subject whose brain x is. L_2 would then yield the unique causal pairings of B with E and of B' with E'. But the problem with this is that, for a dualist, the relation of embodiment itself must be analyzed, wholly or partly, in causal terms: at least part of what makes a particular brain x the brain of a particular subject y is that things are psychophysically arranged in a way which gives x (and x alone) the capacity to have a direct causal influence on y (and y alone) and, for the interactionist, vice versa. It would be circular to account for this arrangement by laws like L_2 and, because of the original problem, impossible to account for it by laws like L_1. In view of this, it might seem that the right solution is to abandon dualism. For if we identified mental events with neural events, we could envisage laws that guaranteed unique causal pairings by specifying the precise spatiotemporal relation between cause and effect. Indeed, we could hope to account for psychophysical causation wholly in terms of the ordinary laws of physics and chemistry.

When I first wrote about this problem back in 1968, I argued that the right response, for the dualist, was to postulate psychophysical laws restricted to particular pairs of brains and minds (or brains and subjects). Thus in the case of Smith and Jones, we can secure the correct causal pairings by postulating a separate law for each person—the law (relevant to Smith) that whenever brain x_1 is in state ϕ, a ψ event occurs a tenth of a second later in mind M_1 (or to subject S) and the law (relevant to Jones) that whenever brain x_2 is in state ϕ, a

ψ event occurs a tenth of a second later in mind M_2 (or to subject J), where x_1 and M_1 are the brain and mind of Smith and x_2 and M_2 are the brain and mind of Jones. More recently, I have tried to meet the problem in a quite different way.[12] I have argued that even in the physical realm we can envisage cases in which the fundamental laws do not account for the causal pairings. Thus suppose that, for a certain kind K of metal, it is a law that when any spherical K lump reaches a specified temperature a flash occurs a tenth of a second later somewhere (unspecified) in the region of points no farther from the center of the sphere than twice its diameter. Suppose further that there is no stronger law which fixes the position of the flash more precisely. Now imagine the case in which two adjacent K spheres simultaneously reach the critical temperature and, a tenth of a second later, two flashes occur, both within the specified region for each sphere. It is coherent and indeed plausible to suppose that each flash is the effect of just one of the sphere-temperatures and that each sphere-temperature is the cause of just one of the flashes. But the causal pairings are not determined by the law and the noncausal conditions, since each flash falls within the specified region for each sphere. From this I concluded that we should abandon the assumption that causal relations can be wholly accounted for in terms of noncausal properties and laws. And once this assumption is abandoned, the problem of psychophysical causal pairings no longer arises; it no longer matters if the pairing of B with E and B' and E' is not determined by the noncausal conditions and the covering law.

Reviewing these alternative responses, I now think that in a sense, both were correct. On the one hand, the hypothetical case of the K spheres does indeed show that causal pairings can be law-transcendent; and, in that respect, the original objection to the dualist's position fails. On the other hand, it does seem quite plausible to envisage laws of the restricted kind as underlying the relation of embodiment. As we have said, at least part of what makes a particular brain x the brain of a particular mental subject y is that things are psychophysically arranged in a way which gives x (and x alone) the capacity to have a direct causal influence on y (and y alone)—and, for the interactionist, vice versa. It is hard to see in what this arrangement could consist except in certain psychophysical laws which specifically link x and y, and such laws would guarantee unique causal pairings. At all events, it is clear that the dualist has sufficient resources to meet the objection.

3. Davidson's Objection

Even if causal pairings can be law-transcendent, it is still plausible to insist that if an event x causes an event y, there is some covering law which ensures that in relevantly similar conditions any event of the (relevant) x-type stands in a relevantly similar relation to some event of the (relevant) y-type. According to Donald Davidson, even this relatively weak claim, combined with the acceptance of psychophysical causation, commits us to the token-identity thesis.[13]

The reason, argues Davidson, is that the "disparate commitments of the mental and physical schemes" preclude the existence of strict psychophysical laws.[14] "It is a feature of physical reality that physical change can be explained by laws that connect it with other changes and conditions physically described. It is a feature of the mental that the attribution of mental phenomena must be responsible to the background of reasons, beliefs, and intentions of the individual. There cannot be tight connections between the realms if each is to retain allegiance to its proper source of evidence."[15] As he explains the point in a subsequent essay,

> my general strategy for trying to show that there are no strict psycho-physical laws depends . . . on emphasizing the holistic character of the cognitive field. Any effort at increasing the accuracy and power of a theory of behaviour forces us to bring more and more of the whole system of the agent's beliefs and motives directly into account. But in inferring this system from the evidence, we necessarily impose conditions of coherence, rationality and consistency. These conditions have no echo in physical theory, which is why we can look for no more than rough correlations between psychological and physical phenomena.[16]

Davidson concludes that where there are causal relations between mental and physical events, the covering law must be physical. This in turn requires identifying mental events with physical events and claiming that it is in respect of their physical, not their mental, properties that mental events have physical causes and physical effects. He calls this position "anomalous monism": "monism, because it holds that psychological events are physical events; anomalous, because it insists that events do not fall under strict laws when described in psychological terms."[17]

When Davidson denies the possibility of strict psychophysical laws, he only intends this, I assume, to apply to those types of mental phenomena, such as beliefs and desires, which have propositional, or in some other way conceptual, content. He is not, I assume, excluding the possibility of a psychophysical law ensuring that a certain type of brain process always produces a certain type of nonconceptual sensation. However, even when we confine our attention to the relevant types of phenomena, Davidson's argument seems very strange. No doubt he is right to stress the holistic character of the mental: we cannot, I suspect, even make sense of the claim that someone has just one propositional attitude, not forming part of some coherent system of attitudes; and certainly, as Davidson sees, it is only by finding evidence of some larger system in a subject that we can be justified in ascribing a particular attitude to him. No doubt too Davidson is right in claiming that the considerations of coherence, rationality, and consistency which form an essential part of the evidence (or of the way the evidence is interpreted) "have no echo in physical theory." My difficulty is in not being able to see why these points should rule out strict psychophysical laws. Davidson seems to be arguing that because the epistemological methods of commonsense psychology and physical science are quite different, psychological and physical facts cannot stand in any tight lawlike connection. But this is just a non sequitur.[18] The only point which even seems to pose a threat to strict psychophysical laws—and it concerns the logical, not the epistemological, holism of the mental—is that the smallest viable unit of propositional mentality is a coherent system. But the most that follows from this is that some of the psychophysical laws would have to be very complicated, for example, ones which determine how complex neural networks causally sustain complex systems of belief and desire. Maybe such laws would be too complicated for us to discover; maybe even some of them could not be exhaustively specified; but that does not mean that they do not exist. Nor should we conclude that all psychophysical laws are, in respect of their psychological content, of this complexity. If there are laws determining how complex neural networks sustain complex systems of propositional attitudes, then a fortiori there are laws determining how complex networks sustain individual attitudes. Moreover, in the case of causal links from mind to body, there is nothing to prevent there being laws which determine how, given certain brain conditions, certain types of volition (such as the attempt to move one's arm in a certain way) cause certain types of neural reponse. The fact that such volitions are possible only in the framework of a complex cognitive field makes no difference.

All in all, it seems to me that while we can accept much of what Davidson says about the holistic character of the mind and the difference between the epistemological methods of psychology and physical science, there is nothing here which even looks like an argument against the existence of strict psychophysical laws.

4. An Objection to Dualistic Interactionism

Some dualists, while accepting that there are psychophysical causal relations, hold that they only run in one direction—from body to mind. They accept, for example, that if I am stung by a wasp the subsequent pain is caused by the neural response which the sting induces, but they deny that if I decide to smoke my pipe the subsequent bodily movements involving pipe and matches are caused by my decision. And, quite generally, they accept that a person's mental states are causally affected by the states of his body but deny that his mental states have any causal influence on the states of his body or on anything else in the physical world. This version of dualism is known as "epiphenomenalism," and the version it contrasts with, which accepts psychophysical causation in both directions, is known as "interactionism." I should add that most epiphenomenalists, as well as denying that the mind has any causal influence on the body, also deny that it has a causal influence on anything at all. In particular, they deny that mental states can cause, or contribute to the causation of, other mental states.

Like most other current philosophers, I regard epiphenomenalism as unnatural and implausible. In the first place, it is in radical conflict with our conception of ourselves as agents. If mental states have no causal influence on behavior, then behavior cannot be thought of as intentional in any decent sense, even if the subject happens to have certain intentions which it fulfills. And if behavior is not intentional, it does not qualify as action in a sense which distinguishes it from mere bodily movement. The epiphenomenalist might reply that the general conformity of our behavior to our intentions is not merely accidental; it is ensured by the very structure of our brains and their muscular extensions in the framework of physical and psychophysical law. But even so, the behavior would not be intentional in the requisite sense, since the intentions and the psychophysical laws that control their occurrence would be irrelevant to its production. Second, human behavior exhibits certain complex regularities that call for explanation and that, at present, we explain (at least partly) in psychological terms. These psychological explanations, though typically of a rational rather than a mechanistic kind, attribute a causal efficacy to the mental; they represent behavior as falling under the control of the subject's beliefs and desires, or under the control of the subject's decisions, which are responsive to (if not determined by) his beliefs and desires. And these explanations gain credence from the fact that, as well as being, in their own terms, successful, they cannot, at present, be replaced by nonpsychological explanations that cover the same ground. Third, it is difficult to see how, if epiphenomenalism were true, the mind could form a subject matter for overt discussion. Certainly, if mental states have no causal access to our speech centers, the notion of an introspective report collapses: even if the subject retains an introspective knowledge of his mental states, his utterances would not count as expressing that knowledge if it contributes nothing to their production. But it is not even clear how, on the epiphenomenalistic view, our language, as a medium for our utterances, makes semantic contact with the mind at all. In what sense, for example, could be word "pain," as overtly used, be said to signify a certain type of sensation, if neither the occurrence of the sensations nor our introspective conception of their type affects the overt use? Quite generally, it seems that if the mental contributes nothing to the way in which the linguistic practices involving "mental" terms are developed and sustained in the speech community and in no other way affects the production of utterances employing these terms, then, in respect of their overt use, the terms should be analyzed in a purely behaviorist or functionalist fashion—which would deprive the epiphenomenalist of the linguistic resources to enunciate his thesis. It is true, of course, that each language user may mentally interpret each term as signifying a certain kind of (dualistically conceived) mental state. But how could such interpretations have any bearing on the objective meaning of the terms, as employed in speech and writing, if they are causally idle?

None of these points shows that epiphenomenalism is logically untenable, in the sense of being incoherent or self-contradictory. Even the third point, if correct, only shows that when overtly expressed, epiphenomenalism is self-refuting—that the very attempt to provide an audible or visible formulation of the thesis presupposes its falsity. Nonetheless, we have, I think, very strong, and perhaps even conclusive, reasons for rejecting it. And, because of this, I should not want my defense of dualism to involve my acceptance of anything but an interactionist position.

It is at this point that the fourth objection arises. For there is an argument which purports to show that dualism of any but an epiphenomenalistic kind is scientifically unacceptable. The argument runs like this:

1. The body is a physical system.
2. As such, the body must be subject to ordinary physical laws.
3. Our theories as to what physical laws obtain are subject to revision. But our current scientific evidence strongly supports the view that at any level of description relevant to a theory of human behavior, these laws are, for all practical purposes, deterministic.
4. So we can reasonably conclude that any bodily event, of a sort which might be cited in a description or explanation of behavior, is causally determined by prior physical events and conditions.
5. But such a conclusion leaves no room for a nonphysical mind to have any causal influence on behavior.
6. Hence, on our present scientific evidence, we face a choice between epiphenomenalism and some kind of identity thesis (if only of the token-token variety).

If it is correct, this argument constitutes an objection to dualistic inter-actionism. It also, on the face of it, constitutes an objection to dualism as such, if epiphenomenalism is, as I would concede, unacceptable. And, nowadays, it is normally as an objection to dualism, and in support of the identity thesis, that the argument is offered.[19] But here we must be careful. It is true that epiphenomenalism is very implausible and, overtly expressed, may even be self-refuting. And this means that, other things being equal, we should reject it. But it does not mean that we should reject it at all costs. If the only alternative were the identity thesis, then, in my view, epiphenomenalism, despite its implausibility, would be the preferable option. For I think that my earlier arguments show that the identity thesis is incoherent. The choice between epiphenomenalism and the identity thesis only counts against dualism on the assumption, which I hold to be false, that epiphenomenalism is not only very implausible but less plausible than its rival. There is also a further point to bear in mind. If the identity thesis is only of a token-token kind, it is not clear how, even if it were coherent, it would avoid the implausibilities of epiphenomenalism. For if mental events have physical effects only by virtue of their physical properties, and if mental properties are not identical with physical properties, or with functional properties of a purely physicalistic kind, then mental properties are causally irrelevant. And if mental properties are causally irrelevant, the identity thesis does not accord the mind the kind of causal efficacy which common sense demands. It does not allow the mental an influence on behavior in any interesting sense. So to provide a genuine alternative to epiphenomenalism, the identity thesis would have to be of a full-blooded materialist form, involving, in addition to token-identity, some physicalistic construal of mental properties. This is something which defenders of token-identity do not always recognize. It is not, for example, recognized by Davidson.[20]

However, whether it is an objection to dualism as such or only to interactionism, I have to find some answer to the argument; for I am not willing to concede that epiphenomenalism and the identity thesis are the only empirically acceptable options. In fact, the error in the argument is not hard to identify. We must begin by distinguishing two ways in which science might provide evidence that the functioning of the body is wholly explicable in terms of deterministic physical law. The first way would be by direct research on the body itself—in particular, on the brain, since it is on brain activity, if on anything, that we might expect the mind to exert a direct causal influence. Thus, by monitoring neural activity in various parts of the brain (without disturbing normal functioning), scientists might build up a strong inductive case for the conclusion that the electrochemical state of any neuron at any time is determined by its immediately prior electrochemical state and the states of other neurons directly connected to it. The second way would be by discovering, without reference to the functioning of the human body, that the rest of the physical world seems to be subject to certain physical laws of a sort which, if they applied universally, would make the body a deterministic system. This is the evidence provided by the investigations of physics and chemistry into the properties of matter and energy in general. Now it is predominantly evidence of the second kind to which the argument appeals. The claim is not that a thorough sampling of brain activity reveals a wholly deterministic system, for no such sampling has been conducted. Rather, the claim is that the human body, including the brain, must be physically deterministic if it is to conform to those theories which apply to physical systems in general. But this evidence, just because it bears on the question of the human system only indirectly, is not decisive. It has to be weighed against what we know or have reason to believe, independently, about the relation between body and mind. In particular, it must be weighted against all that makes epiphenomenalism an implausible theory, and this, in turn, must be set against the background of the a priori objections to materialism and token-identity. When everything is taken into account, the most reasonable conclusion to draw is, surely, that through its attachment to a nonphysical mind, the brain is subject to certain influences which do not affect the other physical systems that science investigates and on whose behavior its nomological theories are based. It is conceivable that this conclusion will be called into question by future brain research (if it were, I should have to reconsider my rejection of epiphenomenalism). But as things stand, we are entitled to assume that it will not.

III. TURNING THE TABLES

Given the current fashion for materialism or positions that come close to it, there is a final irony. For while it is certain that our minds are radically nonphysical, it is far from certain that the physical world is not wholly mental. And here the possibility I have in mind is not the obvious one of subjective idealism—the thesis that the physical world is, in some way, a construct of the human mind or the logical product of the nomological constraints on human sense experience. As it happens, this is a thesis which I accept and have defended elsewhere,[21] but, for present purposes, I am willing to set it aside and adopt the commonsense position of physical realism. Rather, the possibility I have in mind is less extreme but more startling; that the physical world, while ultimately real and independent of human consciousness, is wholly mental in its intrinsic nature. I have called this position "mentalistic physical realism."[22]

At first sight the claim that the physical world might be intrinsically mental seems absurd. But if we find it so, it is because we are failing to appreciate the severe limitations on the extent to which the nature of the physical world can be specified in physical terms. As I have shown elsewhere,[23] any correct physical description of the physical world, or any aspect of it, is of a highly "topic-neutral" character: it reveals formal structure and nomological organization but conceals what the physical items thus structured and organized are like in themselves. Thus whatever occupants of physical space we take as fundamental, it is impossible to provide, in physical terms, a "transparent" (genuinely revealing) specification of their intrinsic properties beyond a specification of their shape and size and other aspects of their spatial or spatiotemporal arrangement; beyond this, we can, in physical terms, only specify their intrinsic properties "opaquely" (in a non-genuinely-revealing way), as those properties, whatever they are, which, in conjunction with the laws of nature, generate certain causal powers and sensitivities. Moreover, it is impossible to provide, in physical terms, a transparent specification of the intrinsic nature of physical space beyond a formal specification of its geometrical structure—a specification which does not reveal what physical points and physical distance are like in themselves. If we are normally unaware of these limitations on the scope of physical description, it is largely because, prior to philosophical reflection, we think of the physical world as intrinsically characterized by the qualities of its sensible appearance. Once we have recognized, as we must, that these sensible qualities are, in their physical realization, nothing but powers to affect human experience, the topic-neutrality of any correct physical description of space and its occupants becomes clear. And it is this topic-neutrality which leaves room for mentalistic physical realism—leaves room for the possibility that the physical world is, in its intrinsic nature, wholly mental.

This is not the right place to elaborate these points in detail—to present the full argument for the topic-neutrality thesis and develop concrete versions of the mentalistic hypothesis. All this, in any case, I have done in my book.[24] My reason for mentioning these points at all is to stress the extent to which current philosophy has got the real issues of mind and matter out of focus. And even here I have somewhat underplayed my hand. For what the topic-neutrality thesis shows is not just that the physical world might be intrinsically mental, but that, unless it is, its intrinsic nature is, to us at least, incomprehensible— composed of properties of which we can have no conception.[25] Whether this itself counts as an argument for mentalism is a moot point. But it certainly shows the extent to which the tables are now turned on the materialist.

NOTES

1. I am indebted to Howard Robinson for his helpful comments on an earlier draft of this paper.
2. Thus see my *The Case for Idealism* (London: Routledge and Kegan Paul, 1982), chap. I.
3. I, in fact, reject it. See ibid., part III.
4. On my interactionist view, which I defend in section II, this claim is, in fact, false.
5. Cf. H. Robinson, *Matter and Sense* (Cambridge: Cambridge University Press, 1982), pp. 4–5.
6. Thus see S. Kripke, *Naming and Necessity* (Oxford: Blackwell, 1980), pp. 131–34.
7. Ibid., pp. 148–54.
8. Ibid., pp. 146–47.
9. T. Nagel, *Mortal Questions* (Cambridge: Cambridge University Press, 1979), pp. 185–87.
10. Ibid., p. 187.
11. See my "Psychophysical Causal Relations," *American Philosophical Quarterly* 5, no. I (1968).
12. See my "In *Self*-Defense," in G.F. Macdonald, ed., *Perception and Identity* (London: Macmillan, 1979), pp. 168–70.
13. D. Davidson, "Mental Events," in L. Foster and J. Swanson, eds., *Experience and Theory* (London: Duckworth, 1970), pp. 79–101.
14. Ibid., p. 97.
15. Ibid., pp. 97–98.
16. "Psychology as Philosophy," in Davidson, *Action and Events* (Oxford: Oxford University Press, 1980), p. 231.
17. Ibid., p. 231.
18. This was pointed out by T. Honderich in "Psychophysical Lawlike Connections and Their Problem," *Inquiry* 24:191–93.
19. This, in effect, is how C. Peacocke argues for token-identity in his *Holistic Explanation* (Oxford: Oxford University Press, 1979), pp. 134–43.
20. For a fuller exposition of this point, see Robinson, *Matter and Sense*, pp. 8–13.
21. In my *The Case for Idealism*, part IV.
22. Ibid., p. 13.
23. Ibid., part II.
24. Ibid. For examples of mentalistic physical realism, see chaps. 7 and II.
25. Thus see ibid., pp. 122–23.

5.3

'A DEFENSE OF DUALISM'

Keith E. Yandell

I argue here (in Part II) for mind-body dualism — a dualism of substances, not merely of properties. I also investigate (in Part III) dualism's relevance to the question of whether one can survive the death of one's body. Naturally the argument occurs in a philosophical context, and (in Part I) I begin by making that context explicit.[1]

PART I: CONTEXT

Necessity

Standard definitions of logical necessity tell us something like this: a proposition *P* is logically necessary if and only if *not*-P is correctly expressed in a sentence *S* that has a proper logical inscription whose form is *Q and not-Q*. Logically necessary truth is exposed by specifying the formally contradictory structure of its denial — by what we might call *logical specification*. Yet, since every proposition has its modalities with necessity, the proposition expressed by *Some proposition has its modalities contingently* is necessarily false, but fails to exhibit the requisite form. Nor is it clear exactly how to remedy that defect, if defect it be. So logical specification will not reveal its necessity (or that of other examples), and we hear talk of "broad" logical necessity.

Related to these issues is the fact that while every necessarily true proposition is entailed by every other (and by every contingent proposition), it is false that every necessarily true proposition is strictly *contradicted by* the denial of

Keith E. Yandell, 'A Defense of Dualism', *Faith and Philosophy*, 12, 4 (4 October 1995), pp. 548–66.

every other necessary truth, let alone by the denial of any contingent proposition.[2] It is hard to see how to deal with that fact without some recourse to a notion of necessity broader than that provided by logically specifiable necessity.

The proposition *Water is* H_2O, assuming it to correctly report an essence that water mind-independently possesses, is necessarily true, but *Water is not* H_2O lacks contradictory structure. Similar remarks go for *Water is essentially* H_2O and *Water is not essentially* H_2O. So logical specification will not reveal their necessity, and we hear talk of "metaphysical" necessity.

I take it that talk of *broad logical necessity* supposes that logical impossibility sometimes is, but sometimes is not, identifiable via logical specification. Roughly, sometimes semantic considerations, and sometimes discovery of natural essences, are required if we are to expose logical contradiction. Talk of metaphysical necessity tends to mean something like this: *There are metaphysically necessary propositions* is understood in the context of these claims: (i) essentialism is true [every substance has an essence, and there are substances]; (ii) conventionalism in logic is false; (iii) propositions that correctly ascribe essences to substances are true with logical necessity; and (iv) not every logically necessary proposition is identifiable as necessary by logical specification. Roughly, then, insofar as our talk about substances is properly shaped (insofar as we get it right about what essences substances have) our essence-ascribing propositions will possess a logical necessity not (at least by current techniques) accessible to logical specification.[3] Further, talk of metaphysical necessities is in the tradition of Aristotle's remark that the principle of non-contradiction is a law both of thought and of things that are independent of thought. Without further wandering in logical minefields, I shall here take the line that there are logical necessities that are, and others that are not, logically specifiable, and that among these are correct ascriptions of essences to substances. I will use *necessarily false*, *logically impossible*, and *is self-contradictory* in such a way that propositions having these inelegancies need not have formally contradictory denials.

Mental Properties

As a rough characterization, let us say that a property Q is a mental property if and only if *X has Q* entails *X is [sometimes episodically and always dispositionally] self-conscious*. One could not implausibly suggest that *being conscious* is a mental property. It is not a mental property by my definition. While *X is self-conscious* entails *X is conscious*, it does not follow that from this that *being conscious* is a mental property; *X is self-conscious* entails *X has only consistent properties* but that does not make *having only consistent properties* a mental property.[4]

Physical Properties

Not every non-mental property is a physical property; *being prime* presumably is not a physical property, nor is *having only consistent properties* or *being entailed by the axioms of modal system S5*. Without pretense of precision, I shall refer to such properties as "abstract properties" and suggest that property Q is a physical property if and only if Q is neither mental nor abstract. On this account, *X has an abstract property* does not entail *X is abstract*; minds and bodies are not abstract and they all have the property *having only consistent properties* and the property *not being prime*. I will be as generous as one could reasonably ask as to what counts as a property, but the properties that concern me here will be properties on any plausible account thereof.

Properties and Property Instances

Some philosophers think that there are properties (e.g., *being red*) and there are *property instances* (e.g., *the chair's being red* and *the pencil's being red*). Other philosophers do not think that there are properties above and beyond property instances; remove all the red property instances and there is not some further *being red*. I will be concerned here only with property instances. It is metaphysically necessary that *(P1) Nothing exists that lacks all property instances* or *To exist is to posses some property instance*; that is, *X exists and for any property-instance Q, it is false that X has Q* is necessarily false. Further, it is necessarily the case that *(P2) No property instance fails to be a property instance of something*. Second-order property instances characterize first-order property instances, which in turn characterize things. *The pencil's being red* is a matter of a property instance characterizing one thing, *the chair's being red* a matter of another property instance characterizing something else. Cases of a property instance that characterizes nothing are cases of there not being a property instance. If there are any properties, as opposed to property instances, presumably they are abstract objects; in any case, such items will have property instances without being property instances themselves. Hereafter, I will use "property" as an abbreviation for "property instance."

Tiny Substances

Consider the notion of a *tiny substance: X is a tiny substance iff X has properties and is not itself merely a bundle of properties*. An item can be a tiny substance by existing merely momentarily. The truth of (P1) and (P2) tells us that *(P3) If there is anything at all then there are tiny substances*.[5]

Robust Substances

Consider the notion of a *robust substance: X is a robust substance iff X has properties, is not itself merely a bundle of properties, and (if it is temporal) remains the same over time and through change of nonessential properties.* A robust substance is always a tiny substance (and always more than tiny), and a tiny substance may be a robust substance. There are alleged accounts of minds or bodies or states or whatever that are non-substantival in the sense of their truth not requiring the existence of tiny substances. But since (P1–P3) are necessary truths, there *are* no non-necessarily-false accounts of minds or of bodies (or of anything) that are non-substantival in the sense of their truth not requiring the existence of tiny substances, because there *cannot* be any such accounts. Any alleged account of this sort would be self-contradictory. I take it to be plainly true that *(P4) If there are changes then there are robust substances.*

Essences

An item has a generic essence if (i) it has one or more properties by virtue of which it belongs to a kind such that its not belonging to that kind would entail its not being the thing that it is, and (ii) it is logically possible that there be other things of the same kind. An item has an individual essence if (i) it has one or more properties P that make it the thing it is such that its not having that or those properties would entail its not being the individual that it is, and (ii) it is logically impossible that any other thing have P. My concern here is with generic essences.

Dualism and Interactionism

It is standard fare to raise supposed difficulties for dualism by asking such questions as: How is something so different from the physical as is the non-physicalistically mental able to causally affect, or be causally affected by, the physical? How can what is not in space, as the non-physicalistically mental is not, affect, or be affected by, the physical, which is in space? Won't the connection between the mental and the physical, as well as the connection between the physical and the mental, be in every case simply a brute — and therefore unintelligible — connection? Such questions about the possibility of mind-body interaction express much of the core of what there is by way of an actual argument against mind-body dualism — an argument that goes something like this: 1. The only plausible version of dualism is interactionism; 2. If the only plausible version of dualism is interactionism, then if dualism is true, interactionism is true.[6] So: 3. If dualism is true, interactionism is true; 4. If interactionism is true, then there are causal effects of the mental on the physical and causal effects of the physical on the mental; So: 5. If dualism is

479

true, then there are causal effects of the mental on the physical and causal effects of the physical on the mental; 6. That there are causal effects of the mental on the physical and causal effects of the physical on the mental is unthinkable; 7. What is unthinkable is false; So: 8. That there are causal effects of the mental on the physical and causal effects of the physical on the mental is false; So: 9. Dualism is false.

"Unthinkable" here may just ultimately mean "is not compatible with physicalism" in which case it will be hard to see why a dualist should either disagree or regard this as a criticism, but penultimately at any rate presumably it means something like "violates some at least putative necessary truth." Major candidates seem to be *Like can only affect like*, *What is in space can only be affected by what is in space*, and *Ultimate connections cannot be brute*. We will look at these in turn.

Like Can Only Affect Like

There is no sense of "like" in which the principle "Like can only affect like" is true and in which excitation of retinal cones produces color sensations, imbalance of ear fluids gives rise to vertigo, viruses cause viral diseases and bacteria cause bacterial diseases, the Big Bang produces massive mass emigration, etc. The principle either disallows such cases as stubbing one's toe causing pain, recognizing an oncoming truck yielding terror, and noting an error in reasoning leading to an onscreen correction in the manuscript, or else simply legislates that in order to occur they must be physical-physical. The so-called "Causal likeness principle" (*If A causes Q in B, then A must itself have Q*) on which causality is viewed on the old pass-along-the-bucket fire brigade model survives in contemporary philosophy only as a way of criticizing interactionism. Since this principle is false, it should survive no longer, and anyone should be ashamed for basing criticisms of anything on it.

Logically Possible Knowledge of Abstracta

Friends of abstracta typically hold the metaphysical doctrine that the existence of abstracta provides the truth conditions for necessary truths and the epistemological doctrine that awareness of abstracta is somehow involved in our knowledge of such truths. The metaphysical view's truth is a necessary condition of the truth of the epistemological view, and since the view that persons are abstract objects has as little favor among friends of abstracta as elsewhere, this involves a doctrine of contact of some sort between non-abstract minds, however concretely construed, and abstracta. It seems plain that this view is not self-contradictory and is not a disguised twin of "Plutins plonk parastics." If the epistemological thesis in question is neither necessarily false nor gibberish, then the causal likeness principle, presumably necessarily true if true at all, is false (and hence necessarily false). Thus it is no real danger to anything or anyone except those who appeal to it to refute mind-body dualism.

What Is in Space Can Only Be Affected by What Is in Space

The contradiction in propositions properly expressed by sentences of the form (A) *A, which is non-spatial, causally affects spatial B* and (B) *Spatial B causally affects A, which is non-spatial* is not formal; these are not *Q and not-Q* affairs. Nor, I suggest, are they like *Ralph has drawn a rectangle but Ralph has not drawn a figure* or *Propositions have their modalities only contingently* which are necessarily false but not, so to say, syntactically so. So what, exactly, is wrong with (A) and (B) save that they associate with interactionist friends?

Ultimate Connections Cannot Be Brute

Presumably, on any account of what *Law L2 reduces to law L1* means, it will be false that every law *L* such that *L* relates instances of one physical sort to instances of another physical sort is reducible to still another physical law; presumably the proposition *L is an irreducible physical law* is neither self-contradictory nor false of all laws. Let *L** be an irreducible physical law and let *k1-phenomena* and *k2-phenomena* be the sorts of physical items *L** connects. Its connection of them will be irreducible, hence brute, hence "unthinkable." So what? The alternative is simply denying that there are any physical laws. Is that, particularly for a materialist, not "unthinkable"? It is not at all clear, physicalist prejudices aside, why brute mental-physical or physical-mental connections should be objectionable because they are brute, whereas brute physical-physical connections are not objectionable.[7]

There is an interesting version of the cosmological argument whose first premise is *If it is logically possible that there is an explanation of a true, logically contingent existential statement, then there is an explanation of its truth.* In its three-by-five card version it continues by claiming *That there is a world is a possibly explicable, true, logically contingent existential statement*; after all, it is logically possible that there not be a physical world (or a physical world plus finite minds). It then properly draws the conclusion that *That there is a world has an explanation* and rightly notes that *there being a world* is what is up for explanation and so cannot be any part of the explanation required. It then concludes that *there being a world* has an explanation that refers to something that is not the physical world (or the physical world plus finite minds). From there it is abstract objects or God, and abstract objects don't act.

Whatever the merits of the argument (they would have to be addressed after the argument was put carefully rather than caricatured as it has been here), its first premise rejects brute facts.[8] It will explanatorily rest only with what so exists that its existence is logically impossible to explain. The acceptance of this premise would explain physicalist enmity to brute facts, though I am not aware that it is used as a rationale in that way. The premise is, I suspect, incompatible with physicalism.

A Conclusion Concerning Interactionism

I suspect, then, that the argument against interactionism, and hence against dualism, more draws psychological support from the current philosophical culture than philosophical sustenance from sound and valid arguments. At any rate, the sorts of considerations that we have noted, while common enough in criticism of mind-body dualism, have little to commend them.

PART II: MIND-BODY DUALISM

Substance Dualism

If one holds property dualism, it does not follow that one embraces substance dualism. Substance dualism, I take it, is the view that mental properties are kind-defining and physical properties are kind-defining, that there are things of each kind so defined, and that for any item *A* that belongs to the kind *mental substance* and any item *B* that belongs to the kind *physical substance*, it is logically possible that *A* exist and *B* not exist. (Presumably it is also possible that *B* exist and *A* not exist, but I will not pursue that here.) A monotheistic dualist will restrict the range of "A" and "B" to mental substances other than God. Standardly, essentialists hold that no one non-composite thing can have more than one essence. This, plus the view that *having physical properties* and *having mental properties* define essences, leads to the view that human persons are substantively composite.

Materials for Modal Arguments

Let *X* range over only noncomposite substances. Let *W* be an *existence-entailed* property if and only if, for any substance *X*, *X exists* entails *X has W*; *having properties*, *having only consistent properties*, and *being self-identical* are existence-entailed properties. Let a property be a *kind-defining and deep difference making property* if and only if it is *not* an existence-entailed property, defines a kind, and something's having it is necessary to that thing's existing at all as well as to its having the sorts of causal powers and passivities it has. Then let *Q* range over only kind-defining and deep difference making properties and consider these forms of statements: 1. It is possible that some *X* have *Q1* and lack *Q2*; 2. It is possible that some *X* have *Q2* and lack *Q1*; 3. It is not possible, relative to any *X*, that both *X has Q1* and *X has Q2* are true; [and, to be explicit if redundant] 4. *Having Q1* and *having Q2* are kind-defining, deep difference making properties. Consider also these forms of statements: 5. It is possible that I exist and lack *Q1*;

6. *Having Q1* is not essential to me; 7. *Having Q2* is essential to me; 8. It is not possible that I exist and lack *Q2*. No essentialist can consistently embrace 5. and deny 6., or accept 7. and deny 8. From such materials as these, modal arguments for dualisms are built.

Modal Arguments and Dualisms

Standard arguments for property dualism and substance dualism appeal to modal arguments. Let # mean *It is logically possible that*. Also let *MP* range over some particular mental property, *PP* over any physical property, *MS* over some particular mental substance, and *PS* over any physical substance. The arguments typically and understandably focus on those physical properties with which the mental property in question might be thought to be identical and those physical substances with which the mental substance in question might be thought to be identical. The standard arguments have these forms:

Modal Argument for Property Dualism
    1. *#MP exists and PP does not exist.*
    2. *If #MP exists and PP does not exist*, then *MP is not identical to PP*;
So:
    3. *MP is not identical to PP.*

Modal Argument for Substance Dualism
    4. *#MS exists and PS does not exist*;
    5. *If #MS exists and PS does not exist*, then *MS is not identical to PS.*
So:
    6. *MS is not identical to PS.*

For our purposes, the relevant substitutions regarding properties are:

    7. *#I am self-conscious and I have no bodily states.*
    8. *If #I am self-conscious and I have no bodily states*, then *My being self-conscious is not identical to my having bodily states.*
So:
    9. *My being self-conscious is not identical to my having bodily states.*

The relevant substitutions regarding substances are:

    10. *#I exist as a self-conscious being and I have no body.*
    11. *If #I exist as a self-conscious being and I have no body*, then *My existing as a self-conscious being is not identical to my having a body.*
So:
    12. *My existing as a self-conscious being is not identical to my having a body.*

This gives us a rough map of the conceptual neighborhood for modal arguments for mind-body dualism. It remains to be seen whether sound and valid arguments for dualism can be found there. (The particular arguments just noted are problematic.)

The Scientific Realist Objection

One objection to the possible success of such arguments is the scientific realist objection. Having used # for *It is logically possible that*, let us use* for the very different notion *It is epistemically possible that* which amounts to something like *For all we know, it may be true that*. Goldbach's Conjecture presumably is either true or false, if true then necessarily true, and if false then necessarily false. Of the propositions #*Goldbach's Conjecture is true* and the proposition #*Goldbach's Conjecture is false*, one is necessarily true and one is necessarily false. But neither of the propositions* *Goldbach's Conjecture is true* and * *Goldbach's Conjecture is false* is false. The Scientific Realist Objection goes as follows. The property dualist argument requires that we know that 7. #*I am self-conscious and I have no bodily states*. But we do not know that 7. unless we can eliminate: 7A. **I cannot be self-conscious and have no central nervous system states*. But we cannot eliminate 7A. since someone may discover that the essence of *being self-conscious* is *being in bodily state CS* (where "CS" is defined physically) just as someone discovered that the essence of *being water* is *being H_2O*. Similarly, the substance dualist argument requires that we know 10. #*I exist as a self-conscious being and I have no body*. But we do not know that 10. unless we can eliminate: 10A. **I cannot exist as a self-conscious being and have no body*. But we cannot eliminate 10A. since someone might discover that the essence of *being a self-conscious being* is *being a body of CS type* (where "CS" is defined physically) just as someone discovered that the essence of *being water* is *being H_2O*.

The objection mistakenly ignores crucial differences between the relevant cases. The *Water is H_2O* case (assuming for the sake of the argument that the standard scientific realist account is correct) is that of a deep structure essential property, *being H_2O*, underlying and explaining such directly experienced features as *feeling wet, possessing buoyancy*, and the like. In the case of *being self-conscious*, it is the directly experienced property itself that is essential. The point can be made in what is by now canonical form. For any physical feature F, were we to discover that some Twin Earth being had F but lacked the phenomenological feature we refer to as *being self-aware*, F would not be identical on Twin Earth to self-awareness, no matter what physical feature F was. The argument for property dualism, then, cannot be undercut by appeals to alleged discoveries of physical deep structures regarding properties. Exactly similar considerations apply to the argument for substance dualism. It is the phenomenologically accessible property *having self-consciousness* that is an essential property of mine, whatever the related physical features may be. For any physical substance on Twin Earth, if it lacked that phenomenologically accessible property, then it would belong to a different kind than I do, no matter how similar our physical makeup; in the absence of the phenomenological feature *having self-consciousness* it will not be a person. So the scientific realist criticism of substance dualism also fails.

The modal arguments for property and substance dualism require that there be necessary truths that are not logically specifiable.[9] They also require that reflection on logical possibilities together with introspection sometimes be sufficient to establish that a property is of one kind rather than another and to reveal that a substance has a non-physical essence. This is, of course, a far cry from the stark empiricism for which all necessity was conventional, tautological, and empty of fact and for which only sensory observation (plus inference from what sensory observation justified) established anything. Given that this position is notoriously self-defeating, that a view is incompatible with it is hardly much of a criticism. The modal arguments require that there be essences — at least, those of persons — that are not discernible by physics (or physiology, chemistry, etc.); notoriously, physicalists deny this. But their denial is part of their physicalism, and presumably should be a *derivative* part thereof — a part for which there are good arguments that do not require the truth of physicalism as a premise. While of course the issues are complex, I think that it is far more clearly true that *Necessarily, if X is a person then X is self-conscious* than it is true either that *For any item X and essence E, if X has E then the only way in which it is discoverable that X has E is by some natural science procedure* or *For any item X, if X exists, then X is physical*. Even if *For any physical item X and essence E, if X has E, then the only way in which it is discoverable that physical X has E is by some natural science procedure* this will not, by itself, provide any problem for dualist modal arguments.

The Irrelevance of Imagination

No argument offered here requires that we infer from images, or from the ways in which we can or cannot combine images, that the relevant modal claims are true. Imagination, in the sense of imaging, reflecting on images, or putting labels on images, is entirely irrelevant. To suggest otherwise is either confused or disingenuous.

Mistaken Modal Arguments

There are plenty of modal arguments that are invalid. Perhaps the most famous is: *Necessarily, P entails Q; P; hence Necessarily, Q*. For any logically contingent proposition *P*, the argument *Possibly P, so P* is obviously invalid. In contrast, the argument forms *Possibly possibly P, so possibly P, Possibly necessarily P, so necessarily P, Possibly P is contingent, so P is contingent*, and *Possibly necessarily not P, so necessarily not P* are perfectly valid. Consider an argument parallel to one for property dualism:

P1. *#I am charitable and the state described in 1st Corinthians 13 does not exist.*

P2. *If #I am charitable and the state described in 1st Corinthians 13 does not exist then Being charitable is not identical to the state described in 1st Corinthians 13.*

So:

P3. *Being charitable is not identical to the state described in 1st Corinthians 13.*

Since P3. is false, one of P1. and P2. must be false. Since it is possible that charity is not the quality under discussion in *1 Corinthians 13* presumably P1. is true. But then P2. is false.

Consider two arguments parallel to some arguments for substance dualism:

P4. *#I exist and no plumbers exist.*

P5. *If #I exist and no plumbers exist* then *I am not identical to some plumber.*

So:

P6. *I am not identical to some plumber.*

But suppose that P6A. *I am a plumber* is true. Since P6A. is contingent, the conjunct *P4. and P6A.* is consistent. P6A. entails the denial of P6., and (thus) so does *P4. and P6A.*

But then the *P4–P6.* argument is invalid. If it is invalid, then P5. is false; so P5. is false. From P4. and P5. it follows neither that P6B. *It is not possible that I am identical to some plumber* nor P6. *I am not identical to some plumber.*

Consider the argument:

P8. *#I exist and no philosophy professors exist.*

P9. *If #I exist and no philosophy professors exist* then *I am not identical to some philosophy professor.*

So:

P10. *I am not identical to some philosophy professor.*

The problem here is that P10. is false, so that at least one of P8. and P9. must be false. Since I would still exist even if I lost my job, presumably P8. is true. So P9. is false. Thus these arguments, similar to some modal arguments for dualism, fail.

These arguments, nonetheless, are of interest for two reasons. Consider the following replacements:

(a) For P2. substitute: P2*. *If #I am charitable and the state described in 1st Corinthians 13 does not exist,* then *Being the state described in 1st Corinthians 13 is not an essential feature of charity.*

(b) For P5. substitute P5*. *If #I exist and no plumbers exist,* then *It is no part of my essence to be a plumber.*

(c) For P9. substitute P9*. If *#I exist and no philosophy professors exist*, then *It is no part of my essence to be a philosophy professor.*

Note, first, that these new premises, together with the original first premises, establish true negative conclusions regarding essences. It is not a necessary feature of the property *being charitable* to be referred to in the famous Pauline chapter nor is it any part of my essence to be either a plumber or a philosophy professor. That these conclusions are hardly earthshaking is nothing against the soundness or validity of the arguments that lead to them. Note, second, that they appeal to nothing but reflection.

Some Nonmistaken Modal Arguments (?)

Consider this argument relevant to property dualism:

Argument One
PD1. #I am self-conscious and I have no bodily states.
PD2. If #I am self-conscious and I have no bodily states, then My having bodily states is not essential to my being self-conscious.
So:
PDC. My having bodily states is not essential to my being self-conscious.

This argument seems as secure as the *revised* arguments about charity, plumbers, and philosophy professors.[10]

Consider this argument relevant to substance dualism in which the notion of a body is the notion of any physical substance, soft or hard:

Argument Two
SD1. *#I exist as a self-conscious being and I have no body.*
SD2. If *#I exist as a self-conscious being and I have no body*, then *My having a body is not essential to my existing as a self-conscious being.*
So:
SDC. *My having a body is not essential to my existing as a self-conscious being.*

This negative argument too seems correct. If PDC. and SDC. are true, then neither *being self-conscious* nor *self-conscious beings* are essentially physical. That, however, is not yet property or substance dualism.

Substance Dualism

Consider this argument for a positive property dualistic conclusion:

Argument Three
D1. *#There is a property instance of being self-conscious and there is no property instance of any physical property.*

> D2. If #*There is a property instance of being self-conscious and there is no property instance of any physical property*, then a property instance of *being self-conscious* does not have *being a physical property* as its essence.

So:

> D3. *A property instance of being self-conscious does not have being a physical property as its essence.*[11]

Consider this positive argument for substance dualism:

Argument Four

> D4. It is not #*I exist and I am not a self-conscious being.*
> D5. *Being a self-conscious being* is not an existence-entailed property.
> D6. If it is not #*I exist and I am not a self-conscious being* and *being a self-conscious being* is not an existence-entailed property, then it is (at least part of) my essence to be a self-conscious being.

So:

> D7. *It is (at least part of) my essence to be a self-conscious being.*

Next, consider

Argument Five

> D8. It is not #*I exist and my self-consciousness does not exist.*[12]
> D9. It is not #*My self-consciousness exists and I do not exist.*
> D10. If it is not #*I exist and my self-consciousness does not exist* and it is not #*My self-consciousness exists and I do not exist*, then the existence of my self-consciousness is necessary and sufficient for my existence.
> D11. The existence of my self-consciousness is necessary and sufficient for my existence.
> D12. If the existence of my self-consciousness is necessary and sufficient for my existence, then my essence includes nothing other than my being self-conscious.
> D13. *My essence includes nothing other than my being self-conscious.*

(Note that D11. does not say anything about whether the existence of my self-consciousness does, or does not, itself depend on something other than itself, as of course it does.) Next, consider:

Argument Six

> D14. If my essence includes nothing other than my being self-conscious, and my having a body is not essential to my existing as a self-conscious being, then it is no part of my essence to have a body.

So:

> D15. It is no part of my essence to have a body.
> D16. If it is no part of my essence to have a body, then it is no part of my essence to have any property the possession of which requires that I have a body.

So:

D17. It is no part of my essence to have any property the possession of which requires that I have a body.

D18. For any physical property Q, my possessing Q requires that I have a body.

So:

D19. It is no part of my essence to have any physical property.

D20. If it is no part of my essence to have any physical property and my essence includes nothing other than my being self-conscious, then my being self-conscious is not a physical property.

So:

D21. *My being self-conscious is not a physical property.*

These arguments, too, at least seem to escape the modal problems noted above. They bring us at least to the brink of mind-body dualism, for if we begin by granting that there are physical substances, show that there are substances whose essence is to have self-consciousness, and show that *being self-conscious* is not a physical property, then if *being self-conscious* is a mental property, there are mental substances.

Being Mental as Intrinsic, Neither Topic Neutral or Role-defined

The dualist must insist that *being self-conscious* is an introspectible, intrinsically phenomenological feature not reducible to anything like *a state that fulfills role R* where R is causally defined. It is not a topic-neutral feature and not reducible to any other feature. Its being so goes deeply against a variety of currently highly popular assumptions and research programs.[13] Roughly, to usefully prove that P is to deduce P from something more clearly true, or else to so elicit P's meaning that its truth shines through. And, as is typically the case for fundamental claims, perhaps the best the mind-body dualist can do here, having nothing more fundamental to which to appeal, is to critique accounts of *being self-conscious* on which it is not a mental property. This task is nothing like hopeless. Materialists themselves seem quite happy to provide powerful criticisms of every variety of materialism save the brand that they themselves favor. Alternatively, of course, the mind-body dualist may assert that *If item X is mental then item X is essentially mental*. If this is so, then functionalism is not even possibly true.[14]

PART III: DUALISM AND EXISTENTIAL SECURITY

Even if the property dualism and substance dualism arguments entirely succeed, it may still be true that:

M1. For any mental property *Q1*, there is some physical property *Q2* such that if *Q2* does not obtain, neither does *Q1*.

> M2. For any mental substance M, there is some physical substance P such that if P does not exist, neither does M.

Nothing in the modal arguments for property and substance dualism discussed here is sufficient to prove that mental substances do not (or do) depend for their existence on physical substances. Nothing in them, for example, proves that M3. *If property Q is not essential to X, then X's existence does not in fact depend on X's having Q, even though it is logically possible that it not so depend* or that M4. *If X is distinct from Y, then X's existence does not in fact depend upon Y's existence, even though it is logically possible that it not so depend* — not even where one restricts X and Y to referring to non-divine things. As Descartes reluctantly granted, the truth of dualism does not entail that the soul survives the death of the body, but only that its doing so is not logically impossible. Dualism without monotheism arguably leaves the claim that human persons survive death unsupported.

Survival and Mind-body Physicalism

What, then, is the significance of the truth of mind-body dualism, if it is true, for the issue of human survival? More than might appear from the previous section. On a physicalist account of persons, persons are either bodies or bundles of physical states (and/or properties). On neither sort of physicalism does survival seem promising.

Bundle Physicalism and Survival

Consider the sort of physicalism for which a person is a set of psychological states and/or dispositional states or processes, each of which is momentary. These states will include sensations, beliefs, preferences, desires, and the like, as well as tendencies to believe, desire, prefer, and so on. Let any particular set of such states that co-exist at some time be a *momentary psychological bundle* or MPB.[15] On this view, a particular person at a given time is one of the MPBs that exist at that time, and over time a particular person is a causally linked series of successive bundles.[16]

Consider the following scenario. Mary, a particular MPB, enters a transmission device that supposedly will beam her to Mars. The device misfires, sending one "Mary" to Venus and another "Mary" to Cleveland. Each new "Mary" is exactly as like the old Mary as the other, so each has equal claim to being her. Since "new Mary1" is not identical to "new Mary2," the old Mary cannot be identical to both new "Marys." The metaphysical identity conditions of an item are those features thereof that make it the item it is and not another; the epistemological identity conditions of an item are those features of an item that allow us to identify it as the item that it is. The relevant metaphysical features may or may not coincide with the relevant epistemological features. It is only metaphysical identity conditions that concern us here.[17] If Mary, on entry into the device, just is an MPB, and each new "Mary" is an MPB that is related in some tight causal connection to the in-the-device MPB — however it is that MPBs allegedly get strung together in a person-making series — then each new "Mary" is (epistemology aside) metaphysically as much of a new Mary as any Mary that would have come to be had Mary entirely avoided transmission devices.

It seems to me plainly a necessary truth that:

> (N) If person S exists at time T, then there are no possible conditions under which the coexistence with S of something just like S would have prevented S existing at T.

But while (on the bundle account) Mary would have existed on Mars had there not also been a "Mary" in Cleveland, or in Cleveland had there not been a "Mary" on Mars, the existence of two "Marys" (so to say) prevents Mary from enjoying a post-transmission existence. There is (on the bundle view) no fact of the matter regarding Mary's survival. But then *Mary survives* is not true (or false), and if *Mary survives* is not true (or false) then Mary does not survive. Her hopes of space traveling go unfulfilled. So, on the bundle account, N. is false. Hence the bundle account is false.

An anti-dualistic argument runs: such cases as the Mary case are logically possible; in them, there is no matter of fact about whether Mary has survived or not; were dualism true, there would be a fact of the matter in these possible cases; so dualism is false. Of course the dualist has a response: I do exist now. Necessarily, either I will exist a moment hence, or I will not. Were there nothing more to me than MPBs, it could be false that either I will exist a moment hence or not. So it is false that there is nothing more to me that MPBs. *Either I will exist a moment hence, or I will not* is a necessary truth; so any view on which it is not true is necessarily false. So the MPB-and-nothing-more view of persons is necessarily false. The anti-dualist argument and its response indicates at least part of the point of the view that persons are simple. *Simple* in this sense can, I think, be defined as follows. An item X has a *particular part* if any only if X belongs to kind K, X has parts, and at least one of X's parts also belongs to K. What we might call the *personalistic simplicity thesis* — that *Necessarily, if X is a person then X is simple* entails *Necessarily, if X is a person then X has no particular parts. Has no particular parts* is to be read strictly; it entails both *has no simultaneous particular parts* and *has no successive particular parts.* The MPB account of persons supposes that persons have successive particular parts, as the view that there is one cosmic mind of which each finite mind is a part supposes that the cosmic mind has simultaneous as well as successive particular parts. Both violate the personalistic simplicity thesis. Mind-body dualism typically, and perhaps necessarily, embraces it. The personalistic simplicity thesis typically, and perhaps necessarily, is part of monotheism, and in its application to God is to be distinguished from the view that ascribes a rather more dubious simplicity to God.

Substance Physicalism and Survival

Suppose that I am (identical to) a body B at time $T-1$, that I do not exist (i.e., on the view just assumed, am not identical to any body) at time T, and am "reconstituted" (i.e., B's twin is created) at time $T+1$.[18] On such a view, it is possible that two "B-twins" X and Y be created (twin with respect to whatever is supposed to make a single B-twin me again). Should this happen, there would then be no fact of the matter about my (re)existence or survival at $T+1$. After all, X is not numerically identical to Y, and so I cannot be identical to both X and Y. If there is no fact of the matter about my survival, then it is not true that I survive. So, on the reconstitution view, there are possible conditions under which the coexistence at some time with (what would otherwise have been) me of something just like me would prevent my existing. On the reconstitution view, then, N. is false. Hence the reconstitution view is false; a substance physicalist who thinks we survive must suppose that our bodies exist continuously. (Similar remarks apply if what is supposedly reconstituted is a mental rather than a physical substance.)

Very familiar evidence suggests that the fate of any human person's body is inelegant. It is logically possible that when, say, St. Paul died, God secretly removed his body to a heavenly freezer and replaced it by a copy which is what was buried. One could hold that St. Paul really is a hard, tiny physical pellet that is indestructible by any natural process. But these views are neither exegetically nor theologically, let alone philosophically, the sort of thing one would think of holding save under enormous conceptual duress. If they are what one is left with if one wants to hold both that persons are essentially physical and that persons survive death, one might understandably wonder if one or the other of those beliefs is false.

Conclusion

Mind-body dualism leaves open the question as to whether human persons survive death, and, if dualism is true, then it is both possible that God causes persons to survive and unproblematically compatible with what we know the fate of human bodies to be that God causes persons to survive. Reconstitution, body snatching, and pellet theories are unnecessary. That is not, of course, an argument for dualism, but a consequence of dualism of interest to many monotheists — a consequence perhaps not had by any other view of the essence of persons.

NOTES

1. I wish to indicate my indebtedness to the following philosophers on the indicated topics: **Property Dualism**: George Bealer, "Mental Properties," *The Journal of Philosophy* (1994), Vol. XCL, No. 4, 185–208; **Dualism**: Alan Donagan, "Realism and Freethinking in Metaphysics," *Theoria* (1976) Vol. 42, 1–19; **Mistaken Modal Arguments, Modal Arguments**: Richard Swinburne, *The Evolution of the Soul* (Oxford: Clarendon

Press, 1986); William P. Alston and Thomas W. Smythe, "Swinburne's Argument for Dualism," *Faith and Philosophy* (1994) Vol. 11, No. 1, 127–133; **Cartesian Dualism**: R. C. Richardson, "The Scandal of Cartesian Interactionism," *Mind* (1982), Vol. XCI, 20–37; Alan Donagan, "The Worst Excess of Cartesian Dualism," A. Donagan, N. Perovich, and M. V. Wedin (eds.), *Human Nature and Natural Knowledge* (Dordrecht: D. Reidel, 1986), 313–325; **Personal Identity**: Richard Swinburne and Sydney Shoemaker, *Personal Identity* (Oxford: Blackwell, 1984); Derek Parfit, *Reasons and Persons* (Oxford: Clarendon Press, 1984).

2. For some discussion of this, see the final chapter of the present author's *The Epistemology of Religious Experience* (Cambridge: Cambridge University Press, 1994).

3. We could redefine "water" so as to make "Water is not H_2O" equivalent to "Water is not water," but while the necessity that essentialistic scientific realism ascribes to water's being H_2O would be reflected in the structure of the denial of (redefined) "Water is H_2O," the proximate ground of the necessity would be in a real definition and the ultimate ground of the necessity would lie in the nature of water itself.

4. If one insists that mental properties come in two basic kinds, one entailing self-consciousness, and the other of that kind if and only if *X has Q* entails *X is conscious* but does not entail *X is self-conscious*, I will not argue. If both kinds of mental properties are kind-defining, it will follow that self-conscious beings are of a different kind than conscious-but-not-self-conscious beings. The issue likely to be of interest here concerns the ontological status of non-human animals. While that is an interesting and important issue, it is not the one I am concerned with here.

5. For a description and critique of Hume's argument that there are (and can be) only tiny substances, cf. the present author's "Continuity, Consciousness and Identity in Hume's Philosophy," *Hume Studies*, Vol. XVIII, No. 2, Nov., 1992, pp. 255–274.

6. It is false that it follows from *P1*'s being the most plausible version of theory *T* that if *T* is true, then *P1* is true, and were the argument in which premise 2. appears otherwise in order, it would require revision here. Since it is not otherwise in order, I will not worry about providing that revision.

7. Berkeley offered one's ability to create mental images — e.g., to daydream about being at the beach or, with our eyes closed, to picture our living rooms — as a nonphysical model for understanding God's creation of the world *ex nihilo*. In any case, it is true that (i) models themselves are understandable only by reference to data whose intelligibility is borrowed by, and not dependent on, the model, and (ii) there are cases of physical-mental and mental-physical causality that are intelligible without models and whose intelligibility can be borrowed by models. Hence (a) the intelligibility of causal claims cannot universally rest on our having models for them, and (b) it is arbitrary (as well as false) to think that all causal models must be physical-physical.

8. Strictly, it rejects brute existential facts — those properly recorded via assertions with such forms are *There is an X* or *There are X and Y*.

9. Or else real definitions; cf. note 4 above.

10. Appeal is often made here to the *necessary identity* doctrine that *If A is identical to B then A is necessarily identical to B*. If this doctrine is true, then it follows straight off that if it is possible that I exist and have no body, then I cannot be identical to any body. We shall then need a circumspect way of putting the necessary identity doctrine — perhaps in one version about properties and in another about substances. One will be a doctrine about possible relations among properties and the other a doctrine about possible relations among things — neither can be a doctrine about relations among terms and terms or among terms and things. The property doctrine perhaps will be something like the conjunct of these claims: PD1. If property *Q1* can be instantiated in *X* without property *Q2* being instantiated in *X*, then *Q1* is a different property than *Q2*; PD2. If property *Q1* is identical to property *Q2* then necessarily property *Q1* is identical to property *Q2*; PD3. If necessarily property *Q1* is identical to property *Q2*, then there is no possible world in which one of them is

instantiated and the other is not. The substance doctrine perhaps will be something like the conjunct of these claims: SD1. If substance M can exist without substance S existing, then M is a different substance than S; SD2. If substance M is identical to substance S then necessarily substance M is identical to substance S; SD3. If necessarily substance M is identical to substance S then there is no possible world graced with M and not with S or graced with S but not with M.

11. The temptation here is to argue: D3a. Any property that does not have *being a physical property* as its essence is not a physical property; So: D3b. *Being self-conscious* is not a physical property. But D3a. presupposes that *being self-conscious*, lacking *being a physical property* as its essence, cannot be physically instanced. Functionalism's varieties deny that presupposition. Functionalism requires that the essence of the mental is to be *role defined* and that anything, physical or not, that plays the right sort of (causal) role is mental in nature. It seems to me that *being self-conscious* is to be phenomenologically understood; its nature is intrinsic, not role-defined. Functionalism, in effect, makes *being self-conscious* a topic neutral property, which seems to me necessarily false of *being self-conscious*. But I will not insist on D3a. here, and will return below to the issue that it raises.

12. Reference to *my* self-consciousness is not problematic here; plainly "my self-consciousness" has a different referent than "self-consciousness in general" (which has no referent unless it is understood as "individual self-consciousnesses, collectively considered") or "someone else's self-consciousness," and its referent is the one required to make the premise true. The premise should be understood Cartesianly: what I am identical to at time T is a particular mental substance — a particular thing that has *being self-conscious* as its essence. While the premise stated is true, parallel claims in which "my self-consciousness" is replaced by, say, "my right hand," "my minivan," or "my body" are not true.

13. This is very different from having been refuted or even having been subjected to impressive critique. I have not tried here to discuss "the nature of the mental" — to deal with propositional attitudes and intentionality, let alone such (I believe) less central issues as privacy and alleged incorrigibility. There are myriad physicalistic and topic-neutral analyses of these notions. There is also the move of giving up on any such analysis and simply fiating that these notions have no purchase on reality. Useful perspective on these matters is given in Chapter 12 of *The Philosophical Papers of Alan Donagan* (ed. J. E. Malpas; Chicago: U. of Chicago Press, 1994) and Donagan's *Choice: The Essential Element in Human Action* (London: Routledge and Kegan Paul, 1987). There is also the suggestion that since the evolutionary process has not prepared us for dealing with hard metaphysical problems, we cannot expect to have any successful physicalistic or topic-neutral accounts but this fact should not make us suspicious of physicalism (a move analogous to Freudians inviting their critics to the psychoanalytic couch). Apparently, appeals to mystery are not limited to religion.

14. Cf. the remarks in note 10.

15. Notoriously, there are problems about what distinguishes one MPB at time T from another MPB at T.

16. There are various difficulties with an MPB view of personal identity. Note its apparent entailments regarding memory and morality. On an MPB view of things, a person is a collection of MPBs at one moment and another collection at another, membership in a series being constitutive of being a person over time. Series membership, in turn, is causally constituted; a series is formed when one collection gives causal rise to another, and that to another. Consider what memory presumably amounts to on this view. At one moment, in collection $C1$, a state obtains. At a later moment, in collection $C17$, another state obtains that represents the first state's having obtained and is caused by the state that it represents (indirectly, of course; the $C1$ state is long gone by the time $C17$ puts in an appearance). A state just like $C17$ but not caused by $C1$, or a state just like $C17$ and caused by $C1$ but occurring in a different series than the one that $C1$ occurred in — perhaps a state caused by hearing

the *C1*-series person describe *C1* by an especially apt representor — will not be a memory state relative to *C1*. (This entails that "same series" cannot be defined in terms of memory states, since nothing is a memory state that is not in the same series as the state that caused it and that it represents.) Consider also the account of moral responsibility that the MPB account offers. Actions are performed at times. Without worrying here about how temporally minimal a collection must be — about, so to speak, how long a single moment is — suppose that a bundle or collection *Cx* performs a wrong action that is punished. It will be a different collection — say, *Cy* — that is punished for doing what *Cx* did. If *Cx* performs an action, then *Cx* is a person, and (on the relevant doctrines) *Cy* as recipient of punishment is also a person. Collections are persons in one sense of "person" — *person(1)*, let us say. But if *Cy* is properly the recipient of punishment for *Cx*'s deed, then *Cy* must be a later collection in the same series as that to which *Cx* belongs. A series of collections is a person in a second sense — say, *person(2)*. A *person(1)* is a momentary being — a tiny substance that is not robust. A *person(2)* is not a momentary being and is not a robust substance; it is a series of momentary beings, a sequence of tiny substances, each tiny substance being numerically distinct from each other. Memory, then, on a MPB account is a matter of a state in a later *person(1)* being caused by an earlier *person(1)* who no longer exists. Responsibility, reward, and punishment are matters of a later *person(1)* being responsible, rewarded, or punished for what an earlier *person(1)* did. What justifies calling this memory or responsibility (if anything does) is simply that the later *person(1)* is in the same causal series as the earlier *person(1)*; numerical identity among earlier and later *persons(1)* is impossible. A *person(2)* "acts" only in the sense that its constitutive *persons(1)* act. A *person(2)* is nothing more nor less than one *person(1)* after another, each caused by its predecessor. At any given time, there are no *persons(2)* save insofar as there are *persons(1)* who had causal ancestors. To say that there are *persons(2)* is only to say that *persons(1)* causally succeed one another. Hence it is logically impossible that a *person(2)* at time *T* be identical, in whole or part, with a *person(2)* at time *T*−1 or with a *person(2)* at *T*+1; all that exists of a *person(2)* at time *T* is a *person(1)* at *T*, and the *person(1)* at *T* exists at no time other than *T* and hence cannot be numerically identical to anything earlier or later than *T*. Talk of the numerical identity of *persons(2)* over time is entirely chimerical. Memories occur only in worlds in which earlier beings are numerically identical to later ones. Responsibility obtains only in worlds in which earlier beings are numerically identical to later beings. If we are nothing but MPBs, we have no memories and we are responsible for nothing. Since it is far clearer that we have memories and we are responsible for our actions than that there is any reason whatever to think that we are nothing but MPBs, we are not merely MPBs. Had Hume's argument against robust substances succeeded, perhaps we would have to accept that there are no memories or responsibilities; but it did not succeed.

17. Even if we cannot find out the truth about Mary, it will not follow that there is no truth about her to be found. It is appropriate to wonder exactly what the transmission device did. Did it destroy Mary and make two Xerox copies? Did it clone Mary and send her to Venus and her clone to Cleveland? That we cannot tell which it did does not entail that it did not do one thing rather than another.

18. I will ignore here what seems to me another necessary truth: no person can cease to exist and then exist again — i.e. it is logically impossible that there be retention of personal identity over time gaps. This assumes (what also seems to me true) that (a) persons are substances and are not essentially composite substances, and (b) no substance that is not essentially composite can exist over time gaps. The idea that substance dualism is "anti-biblical" is the product more of eisegesis than exegesis; cf. John Cooper, *Body, Soul, and Life Everlasting* (Grand Rapids: Wm. B. Eerdmans Publishing Company, 1989).

5.4

'DUALISM AND PERSONAL IDENTITY'

Richard Swinburne

So far I have been analysing the structure of man's mental life. I have been arguing that there are mental events of various kinds—sensations, thoughts, purposings, desires, and beliefs—and that these interact with brain-events, which are physical events. I now come to the crucial question of the nature of that substance, the man (or human being) of which the mental events are states. Is a man just his body, an organized system of molecules, or does a man consist of two parts—body and soul?

I understand by substance dualism the view that those persons which are human beings (or men) living on Earth, have two parts linked together, body and soul. A man's body is that to which his physical properties belong. If a man weighs ten stone then his body weighs ten stone. A man's soul is that to which the (pure) mental properties of a man belong. If a man imagines a cat, then, the dualist will say, his soul imagines a cat. Talk of a man's body and its properties is of course perfectly natural ordinary-language talk; talk of a man's soul less so. The dualist would, however, claim that souls do feel and believe, even if we do not naturally talk in that way. (In ordinary talk perhaps minds, rather than souls, are, however, often given mental predicates—to be said to imagine things or feel weary, for instance.) On the dualist account the whole man has the properties he does because his constituent parts have the properties they do. I weigh ten stone because my body does; I imagine a cat because my soul does. Mixed mental properties, as I defined them in Chapter 1 are those mental properties which can be analysed in terms partly of a

Richard Swinburne, 'Dualism and Personal Identity', from *The Evolution of the Soul*, rev. edn (Oxford: Clarendon Press, 1997), pp. 145–60, 322–32.

physical component. Writing a letter is a mixed property because it involves purposing to write a letter (mental property) being followed by the hand so moving that a letter is written (physical property). The instantiation of the mental property is followed by the instantiation of the physical property. On the dualist view the mixed property belongs to the man, because its pure mental-property component belongs to his soul, and its physical-property component belongs to his body. I write a letter because my body makes certain movements and my soul purposed that it should.

A person has a body if there is a chunk of matter through which he makes a difference to the material world, and through which he acquires true beliefs about that world. Those persons who are men have bodies because stimuli landing on their eyes or ears give them true beliefs about the world, which they would not otherwise have; and they make differences to the world by moving arms and legs, lips and fingers. Our bodies are the vehicles of our knowledge and operation. The 'linking' of body and soul consists in there being a body which is related to the soul in this way.

Some dualists, such as Descartes, seem sometimes to be saying that the soul is the person; any living body temporarily linked to the soul is no part of the person. That, however, seems just false. Given that what we are trying to do is to analyse the nature of those entities, such as men, which we normally call 'persons', we must say that arms and legs and all other parts of the living body of a man are parts of the person. My arms and my legs are parts of me. The crucial point that Descartes[1] and others were presumably trying to make is not that (in the case of men) the living body is not part of the person, but that it is not essentially, only contingently, part of the person. The body is separable from the person and the person can continue even if the body is destroyed. Just as I continue to exist wholly and completely if you cut off my hair, so, the dualist holds, it is possible that I continue to exist if you destroy my body. The soul, by contrast, is the necessary core which must continue if I am to continue; it is the part of the person which is necessary for his continuing existence. The person is the soul together with whatever, if any, body is linked temporarily to it.

By saying that the person '*can*' continue if the body is destroyed I mean only that this is *logically* possible, that there is no contradiction in supposing the soul to continue to exist without its present body or indeed any body at all (although such a soul would not then, on the understanding which I have given to 'man' be a man or part of a man, although it would have been part of a man). Whether this normally happens, is another question; and one to which I shall come later. My concern is to show that a man has a part, his soul, as well as his body—whether or not in the natural course of things that part continues to exist without the body.

So much for what dualism is. Now for its general defence. My initial argument in its support has two stages. I argue first that knowledge of what happens to bodies and their parts, and knowledge of the mental events which occur in connection with them will not suffice to give you knowledge of what happens to those persons who are (currently) men. Talk about persons is not analysable in terms of talk about bodies and their connected mental life. And more generally, it is logically possible that persons continue to exist when their bodies are destroyed. Secondly, I argue that the most natural way of making sense of this fact is talking of persons as consisting of two parts, body and soul—the soul being the essential part, whose continuing alone makes for the continuing of the person.

So then for the first stage of the argument. It is, I suggest, a factual matter whether a person survives an operation or not. There is a truth here that some later person is or is not the same as some pre-operation person, but it is, I shall suggest, a truth of which we can be ignorant however much we know about human bodies and the fate of their organs.

How much of my body must remain if I am to survive an operation? Plausibly, with respect to all parts of my body other than the brain, if you remove them I survive. Cut off my arm or leg, replace my heart or liver, and I continue to exist; there is the same person before as after the operation. Remove my brain, on the other hand, and put it in the skull of another body, and replace it by a different brain, and intuitively the rest of the body that was mine is no longer. I go where my brain goes. We treat the brain as the core of the body which determines whose body it is. That is because with the brain goes the characteristic pattern of mental life which is expressed in behaviour. The brain gives rise to a man's mental states—his beliefs, including his apparent memories, and his desires, their expression in public behaviour, and his characterstic pattern of unintended response to circumstance. The brain gives rise to memory and character which we see as more intimately connected with personal identity than the digestive processes. But what if only some of my brain is removed? Do I survive or not?

The brain, as is well known, has two very similar hemispheres—a left and a right hemisphere. The left hemisphere plays a major role in the control of limbs and of processing sensory information from the right side of the body (and from the right sides of the two eyes); and the right hemisphere plays a major role in the control of limbs of and processing of sensory information from the left side of the body (and from the left sides of the two eyes). The left hemisphere normally plays the major role in the control of speech. Although the hemispheres have different roles in adults, they interact with each other; and if parts of a hemisphere are removed, at any rate early in life, the roles of those parts are often taken over by parts of the other hemisphere.[2] Brain operations are not infrequent, which remove substantial parts of the brain. It might be possible one day to remove a whole hemisphere, without killing the person, and to transplant it into the skull of a living body from which the brain has just been removed, so that the transplant takes. There would then appear to be two separate living persons. Since both are controlled by hemispheres originating from the original person p, and since apparent memory and character and their manifestation in behaviour are dependent on factors present in both hemispheres, we would expect each publicly to affirm such apparent memories and to behave as if he had p's character. It is possible that appearances might be misleading here—that one of the apparent persons was simply a robot, with no life of conscious experience at all, but caused to behave as if it had. But, if we suppose that appearances are not misleading here, the transplant will have created two persons, both with p's apparent memories and character. But they cannot both be p. For if they were, they would both be the same person as each other, and clearly they are not—they have now distinct mental lives. The operation would therefore create at least one new person—we may have our views about which (if either) resultant person p is, but we could be wrong. And that is my basic point—however much we knew in such a situation about what happens to the parts of a person's body, we would not know for certain what happens to the person.

I can bring the uncertainty out strongly by adapting Bernard Williams's famous mad surgeon story.[3] Suppose that a mad surgeon captures you and announces that he is going to transplant your left cerebral hemisphere into one body, and your right one into another. He is going to torture one of the resulting persons and free the other with a gift of a million pounds. You can choose which person is to be tortured and which to be rewarded, and the surgeon promises to do as you choose. You believe his promise. But how are you to choose? You wish to choose that you are rewarded, but you do not know which resultant person will be you. You may have studied neurophysiology deeply and think that you have detected some all-important difference between the hemispheres which indicates which is the vehicle of personal identity; but, all too obviously, you could be mistaken. Whichever way you choose, the choice would, in William's telling word about his similar story, be a 'risk'—which shows that there is something other to the continuity of the person than any continuity of parts of brain or body.

It is a fashionable criticism of an argument of this kind that it assumes that personal identity is indivisible. We do not make this kind of assumption with respect to inanimate things, such as cars and countries. These survive in part. If half the bits of my old car are used together with bits of another old car in the construction of a new car, my car has survived in part. And if the other bits of my old car are used in construction of another new car, then my old car has survived in part as one car and in part as another car. If we succeed in dividing humans, why should not human survival be like that? If half my brain is put into one body, and half into another body, do I not survive partly as one person and partly as another?

However, persons such as men are very different from inanimate beings such as cars. They have hopes, fears, and memories which make it very difficult to give sense to the idea of their partial survival. Consider again the victim in the mad surgeon story. If he survives to the extent to which his brain survives, his choice of who is to suffer will make no difference; however he chooses one person who is partly he will suffer and one person who is partly he will be rewarded. In that case he has reason both for joyous expectation and for terrified anticipation. But how can such an attitude of part joyous expectation and part terrified anticipation be justified, since no future person is going to suffer a mixed fate? It is hard to give any sense to the notion of there being a half-way between one having certain future experiences which some person has, and one not having them, and so to the notion of a person being divisible.

But even if this notion of partial survival does make sense, it will in no way remove the difficulty, which remains this. Although it *may* be the case that if my two brain hemispheres are transplanted into different bodies [and] I survive partly as the person whose body is controlled by one and partly as the person whose body is controlled by the other, it may not be like that at all. Maybe I go just where the left hemisphere goes. As we have seen, the fate of some parts of my body, such as my arms and legs, is quite irrelevant to the fate of me. And plausibly the fate of some parts of my brain is irrelevant—can I not survive completely a minor brain operation which removes a very small tumour? But then maybe it is the same with some larger parts of the brain too. We just don't know. If the mad surgeon's victim took the attitude that it didn't matter which way he chose, we would, I suggest, regard him as taking an unjustifiably dogmatic attitude. For the fact that a resultant person has qualitatively the same memory and character is certainly no guarantee that he is me—in whole or in part. For while I continue to exist quite untouched by any change of brain or character or memory, some other person p with my character could, through a long process of hypnosis, be given 'my' apparent memories in the sense of being led to believe that he had the same past experiences as I did. But that would not make me any less than fully me; and if I remain fully me, there is no room for p to be me, even in small part.

My argument has been that knowledge of what has happened to a person's body and its parts will not necessarily give you knowledge of what has happened to the person, and so, that persons are not the same as their bodies. I have illustrated my argument by considerations which, alas, are far from being mere thought-experiments. Brain transplants may well happen in a few decades time, and we need to be armed with the philosophical apparatus to cope with them. But it suffices to make my point to point out that the mere logical possibility of a person surviving with only half his brain (the mere fact that this is not a self-contradictory supposition) is enough to show that talk about persons is not analysable as talk about bodies and their parts.

My arguments so far, however, show only that some brain continuity (or other bodily continuity) is not sufficient for personal identity; which is something over and above that. They do not rule out the possibility that some bodily matter needs to continue *as well*, if personal identity is to continue. Thought-experiments of more extravagant kinds rule out this latter possibility. Consider life after death. It seems logically possible that any present person who is currently a man, having the mental properties which we know men to have and which I have described [elsewhere], could continue to be with loss of his present body. We understand what is being claimed in fairy stories or in serious religious affirmations which affirm life after death. It seems self-consistent to affirm with respect to any person who is the subject of mental properties that he continue to have them, while his body is annihilated. This shows that the very notions of sensation, purposing, etc. involve the concepts of a subject of sensation and purposing of whom it makes sense to suppose that he continues while his body does not.

This suggestion of a man acquiring a new body may be made more plausible, to someone who has difficulty in grasping it, by supposing the event to occur gradually. Suppose that one morning a man wakes up to find himself unable to control the right side of his body, including his right arm and leg. When he tries to move the right-side parts of his body, he finds that the corresponding left-side parts of his body move; and when he tries to move the left-side parts, the corresponding parts of his wife's body move. His knowledge of the world comes to depend on stimuli to his left side and to his wife's right side (e.g. light rays stimulating his left eye and his wife's right eye). The bodies fuse to some extent physiologically as with Siamese twins, while the man's wife loses control of her left side. The focus of the man's control of and knowledge of the world is shifting. One may suppose the process completed as the man's control is shifted to the wife's body, while his wife loses control of it. At that stage he becomes able to move parts of what was his wife's body as a basic action, not merely by doing some other action.

Equally coherent, I suggest, is the supposition that a person who is a man might become disembodied. A person has a body if there is one particular chunk of matter through which he has to operate on and learn about the world. But suppose that a person who has been a man now finds himself no longer able to operate on the world, nor to acquire true beliefs about it; yet still to have a full mental life, some of it subject to his voluntary control. He would be disembodied. Or suppose, alternatively, that he finds himself able to operate on and learn about the world within some small finite region, without having to use one particular chunk of matter for this purpose. He might find himself with knowledge of the position of objects in a room (perhaps by having visual sensations, perhaps not), and able to move such objects just like that, in the ways in which we know about the positions of our limbs and can move them. But the room would not be, as it were, the person's body; for we may suppose that simply by choosing to do so he can gradually shift the focus of his knowledge and control, for example, to the next room. The person would be in no way limited to operating and learning through one particular chunk of matter. Hence he would have no body. The supposition that a person who is currently a man might become disembodied in one or other of these ways seems coherent.

Not merely is it not logically necessary that a person have a body or brain made of certain matter, if he is to be the person which he is; it is not even necessitated by laws of nature.[4] For let us assume what I shall later call into question, the most that is claimed for natural laws, that they dictate the course of evolution, the emergence of consciousness, and the behaviour and mental life of men in a totally deterministic way. In 4000m BC the Earth was a cooling globe of inanimate atoms. Natural laws then, we assume, dictated how this globe would evolve, and so which arrangements of matter would be the bodies of conscious men, and so, also, just how those men would behave and what mental life they would have. My point now is that what natural laws still in no way determine is which animate body is yours and which is mine. Just the same arrangement of matter and just the same laws could have given to me the body (and so the behaviour and mental life) which are now yours, and to you the body (and so the behaviour and mental life) which are now mine. It needs either God or chance to allocate bodies to persons; the most that natural laws could determine is that bodies of a certain construction are the bodies of some person or other who in consequence of this construction behave in certain ways and have a certain mental life. Since the body which is presently yours could have been mine (logic and even natural laws allow), that shows that none of the matter of which my body is presently made is essential to my being the person that I am.

And so I come to the second stage of my argument. How are we to bring out within an integrated system of thought this fact which the first stage of my argument has, I hope, shown conclusively—that continuing matter is not (logically) essential for the continuing existence of persons. For persons are substances, and for substances of all other kinds continuing matter *is* necessary for the continuing existence of the substance. If a substance S_2 at a time t_2 is to be the same substance as a substance S_1 at an earlier time t_1 it must (of logical necessity) be made of the same matter as S_1, or at least of matter obtained from S_1 by gradual replacement. If my desk today is to be the same desk as my desk last year it must be made largely of the same wood; a drawer or two may have been replaced. But the desk would not be the same desk if all the wood had been replaced. In the case of living organisms such as plants, we do allow for total replacement of matter—so long as it is gradual. The full-grown oak tree possesses few if any of the molecules which formed the sapling, but so long as molecules were replaced only gradually over a period while most other molecules continued to form part of the organized tree, the tree continues to exist. That continuing matter was necessary for the continued existence of a substance was a central element in Aristotle's account of substances. But now we have seen that persons can survive (it is logically possible) without their bodily matter continuing to be part of them. In this situation we have a choice. Either we can say simply that persons are different—in their case continuing matter is not necessary for the continued existence of the substance. Or we can try to make sense of this fact by liberalizing Aristotle's account a little. We can say that the continuing existence of some of the stuff of which a substance is made is necessary for the continued existence of the substance. Normally the stuff of which substances are made is merely matter, but some substances (viz. persons) are made in part of immaterial stuff, soul-stuff. Given, as I suggested earlier, that persons are indivisible, it follows that soul-stuff comes in indivisible chunks, which we may call souls.

This liberalized Aristotelian assumption I will call the quasi-Aristotelian assumption: that a substance S_2 at t_2 is the same substance as an earlier substance S_1 at t_1 only if S_2 is made of some of the same stuff as S_1 (or stuff obtained therefrom by gradual replacement).

Given the quasi-Aristotelian assumption, and given, that for any present person who is currently conscious, there is no logical impossibility, whatever else may be true now of that person, that that person continue to exist without his body, it follows that that person must now actually have a part other than a bodily part which can continue, and which we may call his soul—and so that his possession of it is entailed by his being a conscious being. For there is not even a logical possibility that if I now consist of nothing but matter and the matter is destroyed that I should nevertheless continue to exist. From the mere logical possibility of my continued existence there follows the actual fact that there is now more to me than my body; and that more is the essential part of myself. A person's being conscious is thus to be analysed as an immaterial core of himself, his soul being conscious.[5]

If we are prepared to say that substances can be the same, even though none of the stuff (in a wide sense) of which they are made is the same, the conclusion does not follow. The quasi-Aristotelian assumption provides rather a partial definition of 'stuff' than a factual truth. To say that a person has an immaterial soul is not to say that if you examine him closely enough under an acute enough microscope you will find some very rarified constituent which has eluded the power of ordinary microscopes. It is just a way of expressing the point within a traditional framework of thought that persons can—it is logically possible—continue, when their bodies do not. It does, however, seem a very natural way of expressing the point—especially once we allow that persons can become disembodied. Unless we adopt the more liberal quasi-Aristotelian assumption, we shall have to say that there can be substances which are not made of anything, and which are the same substances as other substances which are made of matter.

There is therefore abundant reason for saying that a man consists of body plus soul. A man's physical properties (e.g. having such-and-such a shape and mass) clearly belong to his body and to the person in virtue of belonging to his body. If the man dies and ceases to exist (i.e. his soul ceases to exist), there need (logically) be no change in the way those properties characterize his body. A man's pure mental properties, however, belong to his soul and to the man in virtue of belonging to his soul; for it is logically possible that those properties continue to characterize the person who is that man, when his body is destroyed. Hence mixed properties belong to the person in virtue of their physical-component properties belonging to his body and their pure mental-component properties belonging to his soul.

Note that on the dualist view which I am expounding, although the identity of persons at different times is constituted by the identity of their souls (and these are not publicly observable things), it remains the case that all claims about personal identity are verifiable, in the sense that there can be evidence of observation for or against them. For although continuity of brain and of apparent memory (i.e. a man's apparent memory of who he was and what he did) do not constitute personal identity, they are evidence of it, and so evidence of sameness of soul.

And not merely are all claims about personal identity verifiable via observations of other things, but over a short period personal identity is itself experienceable by the subject, as directly as anything can be experienced, in the continuity of his perceptions and other mental events. Human perception is perception of change. The perceptual beliefs to which our senses give rise are not just beliefs that at one time things were arranged thus, and at another time in a different way, and at a third in yet a third way. For as a result of perception we come to know not merely what happened, but in what order things happened—that first things were arranged like this, and subsequently like that, and yet subsequently like that. Sometimes, of course, we infer from our perceptions and our general knowledge of how things happen in the world, the order in which those perceptions and so the events perceived[6] must have occurred. Knowing that, in general, cigarettes are first lit and then smoked and in the process get smaller, I may infer that my seeing the cigarette lit occurred before my seeing the cigarette half-smoked. But not all knowledge of the order of our perceptions can derive from inference. For first, we have much knowledge of the actual order of perceptions when as far as our general knowledge of the world goes the events perceived could as easily occur in one order as in the other—such as a ball moving on a particular occasion from left to right rather than from right to left. And, secondly, in order to infer the order of our perceptions we need that general knowledge of the order in which events of the kind perceived occur. Yet our beliefs about the latter (e.g. our knowledge that in general lit cigarettes get smaller) would be without justification (and so would not amount to the knowledge which we surely rightly believe them to be) unless they were grounded in many perceptions made by ourselves or others of actual such successions.

So the perceptual beliefs to which our senses give rise include (and must include if we are to have knowledge, grounded in experience) beliefs about the order in which things happen. That is, we perceive things happening in a certain order. The most primitive things which an observer sees include not just the train being here, but also the train moving from here to there, from there to the third place. When a train moves along a railway line, the observer S on the bank has the following successive perceptions: S sees (train

T at place p followed by T at place q); S sees (T at q followed by T at r); S sees (T at r followed by T at u), and so on. He acquires the belief that things were as perceived. But then that is not quite a full description of the beliefs which he acquires through perception, for, if those were all his data, he would have no grounds for believing that the second event which I have described succeeded the first event (rather than being one which occurred on an entirely different occasion). Why he does have such grounds is because he also acquires, through having the succession of perceptions, the further perceptual beliefs that the first perception is succeeded by the second perception, and that the second perception is succeeded by the third perception. He acquires, through experience, knowledge of temporal succession. And, more particularly, the further perceptual beliefs which he acquires are that *his* first perception is succeeded by his second perception, and so on. The content of his further perceptual beliefs is that there has been a succession of perceptions had by a common subject, viz. himself. Using the word 'experience' for a brief moment in a wide sense, we may say that the succession of perceptions is itself a datum of experience; S experiences his experiences as overlapping in a stream of awareness. As John Foster, to whom I owe this argument, puts it, 'It is this double overlap which provides the sensible continuity of sense experience and unifies presentations [i.e. perceptions] into a stream of awareness . . . It is in the unity of a stream that we primarily discern the identity of a subject'.[7] That is, one of a subject's basic data is of the continuity of experience, which means the continuity of the mental events of a common subject, the person.

In a famous passage Hume wrote: 'When I enter most intimately into what I call *myself*, I always stumble on some particular perception or other, of heat or cold, light or shade, love or hatred, pain or pleasure. I never catch *myself* at any time without a perception'.[8] It may well be that Hume never catches himself without a 'perception' (i.e. a conscious episode) but his bare datum is not just 'perceptions', but successions of overlapping 'perceptions' experienced by a common subject. If it were not so, we would have no grounded knowledge of succession. Hume says that he fails to find the common subject. One wonders what he supposed that the common subject would look like, and what he considered would count as its discovery. Was he looking for a common element in all his visual fields, or a background noise which never ceased? Is that the sort of thing he failed to find?[9] Yet the self which he ought to have found in all his mental events is supposed to be the subject, not the object of perception. And finding it consists in being aware of different mental events as had by the same subject.

Further, among the data of experience are not merely that certain mental events are the successive mental events of a common subject, but also that certain simultaneous mental events are states of a common subject. At a single moment of time you feel cramp in your leg, hear the noise of my voice, and see the movement of my arms. It is among the data of your experience (i.e. among basic data, not inferable from anything closer to experience) that these are all *your* mental events.

Yet that mental events are states of the same subject is something that knowledge of brains and their states and knowledge of which mental events were occurring would be insufficient to tell you. As I noted earlier, some sensory nervous impulses (including those from the right-side limbs and right sides of the two eyes) go in the first instance to the left brain hemisphere, and some (including those from the left-side limbs and the left sides of the two eyes) go to the right brain hemisphere; and the two hemispheres control different parts of the body (the left hemisphere controlling speech, as well as the right arm and leg). However, in the normal brain the signals to one hemisphere are immediately transmitted to the other, and the 'instructions' given by one are correlated with events in the other. But if the brain operation of cerebral commissurotomy (cutting the main tract between the two hemispheres) is performed the hemispheres act in a much more independent way, and it is a crucial issue whether by the operation we have created two persons. Experimenters seek to discover by the responses in speech, writing or other means whether one subject is co-experiencing the different visual, auditory, olfactory, etc. sensations caused through the sense organs or whether there are two subjects which have different sensations. The subject (or subjects) is aware of one or more kinds of sensation and the experimenter seeks to elicit information about his (or their) sensations from him (or them). That is not quite as easy as it sounds. If the mouth confesses to seeing a green object but not to hearing a loud noise, while the left hand denies seeing a green object, but claims instead to hear a loud noise, that is not enough in itself to show that no subject co-experienced a loud noise and saw a green object. For, first, mouth and hand may sometimes, as may any limb, give a reflex response to a question rather than a considered judgement (the reflex may be out of a subject's control without being in the control of some other subject), and the reflexes available to different limbs may relate to information of different kinds (the left hand may be able by pointing to give the answers to questions about objects presented to the left side of the visual field only without the subject being aware of the objects presented and/or the responses of the hand); and secondly, there may be kinds of belief (about his mental events) which the split-brain subject can convey only by one means rather than another. The effect of cerebral commissurotomy is not immediately evident, and various complex experiments are needed before any one hypothesis about what has happened can gain significant support.

That hypothesis about how many subjects of experience and action, that is, persons, there are will be best supported the better it can be filled out as a detailed claim about which beliefs, desires, and other mental events the one or more different subjects have, which explains in a simple way many observed data. For example, a hypothesis that there are two persons becomes more plausible if we can in certain circumstances attribute to each not merely distinct sensations and beliefs about them, but distinct beliefs and desires of a general character, that is, different views about what is good and bad in the world, and different inclinations to bring about long-term states of affairs, and these different beliefs and desires are continuing beliefs which explain whole patterns of limb movements—for example, the left hand and the mouth express different complex moral claims. For then the patterns of response of the different sets of limbs would be more analogous to the conscious responses of men by which they manifest beliefs of which they are conscious, than to patterns of mere unconscious reflex. And it would be simpler to suppose that similar patterns of response (of all limbs in normal persons, and of one set of limbs in split-brain persons) have similar explanations (viz, in distinct sets of beliefs and desires) than to suppose that the unity of response in the latter case does not arise from the unity of a person with a continuing mental life.[10]

What is clear in these cases is that what the investigator is trying to discover is something other than and beyond the pattern of the subject's responses, as it is also something other than and beyond the extent of the connections between the two hemispheres. That something is whether there are one or two subjects of experience and action, that is, persons. Whether one person is having both sensations is something of which he will be immediately aware, but which others have to infer (fallibly) from the complex public data. In considering simultaneous experience as in considering experience over time, we see that which persons are the same as other persons are facts additional to publicly observable facts. Dualism can make sense of why there is sometimes (i.e. in cases of cerebral commissurotomy) a difficult problem of discovering how many persons there are. Dualism, in claiming that a person is body plus soul, explains the problem as the problem of discovering the number of souls connected to a given brain. Since the outsider can only discover this by fallible inference from bodily behaviour and brain-states, discovering the answer can be difficult and we can always go wrong. However, co-experience is no artificial construct; it is as primitive a datum of experience for the subject as anything could be. The subject's awareness is an awareness of himself as the common subject of various sensations (and other mental events).

My conclusion—that truths about persons are other than truths about their bodies and parts thereof—is, I suggest, forced upon anyone who reflects seriously on the fact of the unity of consciousness over time and at a time. A framework of thought which makes sense of this fact is provided if we think of a person as body plus soul, such that the continuing of the soul alone guarantees the continuing of the person.

NOTES

1. There are passages in Descartes which can be interpreted as saying that the body is no part of the person and other passages which can be interpreted as saying that the

body is a part, but not an essential part, of the person. For examples and commentary, see pp. 63–6 of B. Smart, 'How Can Persons Be Ascribed M-Predicates', *Mind*, 1977, **86**, 49–66.

2. For a simple readable account of the current state of psychological research of the different roles of the two hemispheres, see S. P. Springer and G. Deutsch, *Left Brain, Right Brain*, W. H. Freeman, San Francisco, 1981.

3. For the original, see B. Williams, 'The Self and the Future', *Philosophical Review*, 1970, **79**, 161–80.

4. I owe this argument to an article by John Knox, Jr, 'Can the Self Survive the Death of Its Mind?', *Religious Studies*, 1969, **5**, 85–97.

5. See New Appendix C.

6. We learn through perceptions of the effects which we ourselves bring about that, in general, spatially near events are perceived at approximately the instant of their occurrence. See my *Space and Time*, Macmillan, London, second edition, 1981, p. 145.

7. J. Foster, 'In *Self*-Defence' in (ed.) G. F. MacDonald, *Perception and Identity*, Essays presented to A. J. Ayer, Macmillan, London, 1979, p. 176.

8. *A Treatise of Human Nature*, 1.4.6.

9. Because our awareness of ourselves is different in kind from our awareness of objects of experience, Berkeley chose to say that we have a 'notion' of the former but an 'idea' of the latter. 'To expect that by any multiplication or enlargement of our faculties we may be enabled to know a spirit as we do a triangle, seems as absurd as if we should hope to see a sound'—G. Berkeley, *Principles of Human Knowledge*, 1710, §142.

10. On the results and interpretation of such experiments, see Springer and Deutsch, op. cit., chs. 2 and 10, articles referred to therein (especially J. E. LeDoux, D. H. Wilson, and M. S. Gazzaniga, 'A Divided Mind: Observations on the Conscious Properties of the Separated Hemispheres', *Annals of Neurology*, 1977, **2**, 417–21), and, most recently, D. M. and Valerie Mackay, 'Explicit Dialogue between Left and Right Half-Systems of Split Brains', *Nature*, 1982, **295**, 690–1.

New Appendix C: The Modal Argument for Substance Dualism

In order to allay any suspicion that the argument in the main text commits some modal fallacy, I set it out in formal logical shape. The argument was originally designed to prove that I have a soul in 1984, and I leave it in that form. Updating is always possible for any year in which Premiss 1 is manifestly true. Likewise any name or other referring expression can be substituted for 'I', so long as Premiss 1 remains manifestly true. I use the usual logical symbols, '&' as 'and', '$\sim$' as 'not', '$\Diamond$' as 'it is logically possible that'. I define:

p='I am a conscious person and I exist in 1984'.

q='My body is destroyed in the last instant of 1984'.

r='I have a soul in 1984'.

s='I exist in 1985'.

x ranges over all consistent propositions compatible with (p & q) and describing 1984 states of affairs.

'(x)' is to be read in the normal way as 'for all x'.

The argument is then as follows:

p .... Premiss 1
$(x) \Diamond (p \ \& \ q \ \& \ x \ \& \ s)$ .... Premiss 2
$\sim \Diamond (p \ \& \ q \ \& \ \sim r \ \& \ s)$ .... Premiss 3

Premiss 2 says that it is possible that I survive into 1985, given that I am conscious in 1984, even if my body is totally destroyed and whatever else might be the case in 1984, compatible with these last two suppositions. Premiss 3 says that it is not possible that I who am conscious in 1984 survive into 1985 if my body is totally destroyed, unless there is a non-bodily part of me in 1984, namely, a soul. It follows from Premiss 2 and Premiss 3 that $\sim r$ is not within the range of x. But since $\sim r$ describes a 1984 state of affairs, it follows that it is not compatible with $(p \ \& \ q)$. Hence $(p \ \& \ q)$ entails r. But the addition to p of q, which describes what happens to my body at the end of 1984 can hardly affect whether or not p entails r. So I conclude that p by itself entails r. Hence, from Premiss 1, r.

Premiss 2 relies on the intuition that whatever else might be the case in 1984, compatible with $(p \ \& \ q)$, my stream of consciousness could continue thereafter. Premiss 3 is justified by the quasi-Aristotelian assumption that if I am to continue, some of the stuff out of which I am made has to continue. By my 'body' is understood all the matter which forms part of me. By my 'soul' is understood any immaterial stuff which forms part of me.

This modal argument has been subject to quite a bit of detailed criticism in philosophical journals, and a great more in private interactions, and I seek here to defend it against those criticisms.

First, I need to tidy it up slightly. 'In 1984' in p and r must be read as 'throughout 1984'. 'In 1985' in s may be read either as 'at some period during 1985' or as 'throughout 1985'. To say, as q does, that my body is destroyed in the last instant of 1984, is just to say that my body existed during a period terminating with the last instant of 1984, but not during any period beginning with that instant. To say that x ranges over propositions describing 1984 states of affairs, is to say that it ranges over propositions describing purported hard facts about 1984, and only such purported facts.

A purported hard fact about some time is, as I shall understand the term,[1] a purported fact about that time whose truth conditions lie solely at that time. By contrast, as I shall understand the term, a purported soft fact about some time is a purported fact about that time whose truth conditions lie in part at some other time, earlier or later. Thus, the sun rising over London at 8 a.m. on 31 December 1984 is a purported hard fact about 1984—whether the sun rose then or not is independent of what happened in 1983 or 1985. By contrast the sun rising for the last time ever over London at 8 a.m. on 31 December 1984 is a purported soft fact about 1984—it is one whose truth depends on what happens in 1985, 1986, and so on; the purported fact will only be a fact if the sun never rises again. Since its factual status (i.e. the truth of the proposition reporting it) depends (in part) only on what happens later than the year referred to, and not on what happens earlier, we may describe it as a soft future-related purported fact. The sun rising for the first time at 8 a.m. on 31 December 1984 over London is also a soft purported fact, but one whose truth depends (in part) on what happened before 1984. So we may call it a soft past-related purported fact about 1984. Or, to take another example, my being fifty years old in 1984 is a soft past-related purported fact, for its truth conditions lie in part in what happened fifty years earlier—my being born then. Whereas my feeling old or being healthy in 1984 are purported hard facts about 1984. Note that while p and r are both purported hard facts about 1984, and s is a purported hard fact about 1985, q is a purported future-related soft fact about 1984; it claims both that my body existed in a last period of 1984 and that it did not exist in a first period of 1985.

PREMISS 2

Most opponents of my argument admit its validity—the conclusion does follow from the premisses; but they challenge the premisses. The usual challenge is to Premiss 2. Most materialists these days are happy to allow that it is logically possible that a person be non-embodied or even become disembodied. But the most common criticism of Premiss 2 is that I have slid carelessly from this claim to the much stronger claim that it is logically possible that I become disembodied, and that there is no reason for believing the latter. I do not believe that there was any careless slip involved here. The arguments in the text concern 'any present person who is currently a man', for example, me.

The only arguments which can be given to show some supposition to be logically possible are arguments which spell it out, which tell in detail a story of what it would be like for it to be true and do not seem to involve any contradictions,[2] that is, arguments from apparent conceivability. Apparent conceivability is evidence (though not of course conclusive evidence) of logical possibility. The arguments have the form: take any actual human person, currently conscious in 1984, yet having his body destroyed at the end of 1984, conceive of anything you like (compatible therewith) being the case with his body during 1984, or happening to the bodies of other people, to the proportion of nitrogen in the surface of Jupiter or whatever else you choose in 1984; it is still conceivable that he goes on existing in 1985. If anyone does not see that at first, a story can be told in a lot more detail of what it would be like for it to be true, which would help the reader to see it. But of course whatever suppositions x we make must concern purported hard facts about 1984 and must be compatible with $(p \& q)$.

Like all worthwhile arguments, mine purported to start from premisses which many opponents might grant—namely premisses 1, 2, and 3 as they stand—to establish a conclusion which they did not previously recognize. I suggested that most people not already having a firm philosophical position on the mind/body issue will grant my premises. But someone already having a firm philosophical position contrary to mine can challenge my Premiss 2 by inserting an x which he claims to be compatible with p and q and which he claims will show the premiss to be false, where x states a philosophical thesis about the very issue in dispute, contrary to the one which I am seeking to prove. Examples proffered include 'I am purely material in 1984',[3] or 'I am identical with my body or some part of it'.[4] Now of course I claim that no such x is compatible with (p & q). Since I put forward Premisses 2 and 3 as purported necessary truths, my argument was designed to show that (given p) r is a necessary truth. The claim therefore that any x of the above type is compatible with (p & q) amounts to the denial of my conclusion. Now it is true that my argument will not convince anyone who claims to be more certain that the conclusion is false than that the premisses are true. But then that does not discredit my argument—for no argument about anything will convince someone in that position. My argument was designed for those prepared to set aside philosophical dogma concerned explicitly with the mind/body issue, and rely only on philosophical theses and intuitions about logical possibility relating to other or wider issues.

A philosophical worry lying behind this criticism of Premiss 2 is the view that what makes a substance that particular substance (its essence) cannot be discovered by mere thought experiment. The essence of Hesperus is not evident to someone picking it out by its observable characteristics (its 'stereotype'); we need scientific investigation to discover that. So, the worry is,[5] how can mere reflection on myself, show what my essence is. And if it cannot, maybe that essence is (in part or whole) my brain or something else bodily. And in that case, it would not be logically possible for me to survive the destruction of my body. Now it is true that the essence of Hesperus cannot be discovered by mere thought experiment. That is because what makes Hesperus Hesperus is not the stereotype, but what underlies it. But it does not follow that no one can ever have access to the essence of a substance, but must always rely for identification on a fallible stereotype. My claim is that for the person him or herself—for example, me—while what makes that person that person underlies what is observable to others, it does not underlie what is experiencable by the person. That this is so can be seen as follows. I pick out myself as the subject of certain conscious events, for example, these thoughts. Suppose that the thoughts had been had by someone else instead. In that case I could not have erroneously attributed them to myself. Nor could I erroneously suppose that certain thoughts now being had by me, were in fact being had not by me but by someone else instead. However, the appearances could be exactly the same if a planet quite other than Hesperus (made of quite different matter) appeared in the evening sky instead of Hesperus. So I have a grasp on what it is to be me which I do not have on what it is to be Hesperus, which allows me to pronounce on what, it is logically possible, can happen to me. But there is nothing special about me, to distinguish me from other conscious persons in this respect. And a similar claim is therefore warranted for them.

PREMISS 3

What, however, is more dubious in my Premiss 3, or rather the quasi-Aristotelian assumption which I use to support it—as I acknowledge in the text. Given Premiss 2, then, I wrote on p. 502, we have a choice: 'Either we can say simply that persons are different—in their case continuing matter is not necessary for the continued existence of the substance, or we can try to make sense of this fact by liberalizing Aristotle's account' (that continuing ordinary matter is necessary for the identity of substances) and allow immaterial stuff. The reason which I gave for adopting the latter alternative was to preserve an integrated system of thought. That led to the view that the continued existence of a person depends on the continued existence of a part of that person, made of immaterial stuff—what I shall call a Bonaventuran soul.[6] I now wish to bring out that the only viable alternative to this is to suppose that it depends on the continued existence of a soul in the sense of an individual property, which I shall call a Thomist soul. It will become apparent that such a view makes the difference between persons and inanimate substances even sharper and stronger than the Bonaventuran view.

Since substances are the substances they are in virtue of the stuff of which they are made and the properties (including relations to other substances) which they possess, if it is not being made of the same stuff which makes a person the same person as an earlier person, it must be having properties the same or continuous in certain respects with those of the earlier person, that is having certain relations to the earlier person. Many philosophers have sought to give an account of this kind. Both Locke[7] and Hume[8] considered that the identity of a later person with an earlier person depends on such features as the later person having the same apparent memories as, and apparent memories caused by, those of the earlier person. Apparent memories are properties possessed by a substance; they are abilities apparently to recall.

But a relational theory always runs into one of two difficulties. Either it has the consequence that indefinitely many later persons can satisfy the criteria for being the same person as a certain earlier person (the duplication difficulty), or it has the consequence that which later person is the same person as the earlier person depends on what happens to a third person (the arbitrariness difficulty). The duplication difficulty arises if more than one later person can have the relevant relational properties. Many distinct later persons could have the same apparent memories of doing the actions and having the experiences of the earlier persons. So an account which says that to be the same person as the earlier person you have to have apparent memories of their actions and experiences is subject to this difficulty. Any such account must be false—for the reason, that if two distinct later persons are the same as the earlier person they would be the same as each other—and, by hypothesis, they are not. The duplication difficulty is normally met by insisting that the relational properties include one which can be satisfied by at most one person. That person is the same as the earlier person who exemplifies some crucial relation—similarity of apparent memory, character, appearance, or whatever—in some way better than any other candidate. Thus a writer may claim that a later P_2 is the same as an earlier P_1 if and only if P_2 has the property of being the first person causally connected with P_1 to have similar apparent memories; or is in other ways the 'closest continuer'[9] of P_1. But then whether P_2 is the same person as P_1 will depend on what happens or does not happen to persons other than P_2, for example, whether P_1 causally generated some other similar person before generating P_2, or whether some person who would otherwise have been the 'closest continuer' dies prematurely. And is it not absurd to suppose that who P_2 is depends on what happens to someone else? Whether I am elected to some office may depend on how many votes are given to someone else, but that who I am can depend on such extrinsic factors seems absurd. This is the arbitrariness difficulty—my identity becomes an arbitrary matter.

There are philosophers who are prepared to accept that (in that stated sense) personal identity is an arbitrary matter. Derek Parfit[10] would acknowledge that personal identity is an arbitrary matter, but claim that that is not important, because identity is not important. What is important, claims Parfit, is not identity but 'survival'. What is important is not that I continue to exist, but that I 'survive'. And for Parfit a person can have many surviving selves in which he or she survives to different degrees. The normal meaning of 'survive' however is 'continue to exist'. Parfit is obviously giving this term a different meaning; an individual survives, for Parfit, in so far as another individual is related to him in certain ways (e.g., has similar apparent memories), and that relation, as we have seen, can be duplicated. But, despite Parfit, the satisfaction of such a relation is not the main thing that someone who wants to go on existing is hoping for. He who hopes to survive his death will not normally be satisfied by the knowledge that someone very like him will live again. Identity is regarded as important by most of us, and the philosopher must elucidate in what it consists.

Many writers have pointed out that for things without consciousness such as clouds, countries, and armies, identity clearly is (in my sense) an arbitrary matter. Whether a later country is the same as an earlier country will often depend on what happens to bits of territory not included in the later country, etc. But the point is just that these are non-conscious things, and their identity conditions are different from those of conscious beings. If I undergo some operation, or my brain state is copied in some way before my body is destroyed, there is clearly a truth here about whether or not I have survived this process, which is logically independent of what happens to other people. Before the process, I seek my continued existence. Afterward we may not know whether my endeavours have been fulfilled. But only someone already in the grip of a strong philosophical dogma could deny that there is a truth about whether or not I have survived an operation or brain-copying process, which is logically independent of what happens to anyone else.

There is, however, one kind of relational theory of personal identity which is immune to the duplication and arbitrariness objections. But it is one which I suspect the average modern reader would be less happy to adopt than he would be to adopt the Bonaventuran theory given above. Any relational theory of personal identity is bound to fail if the only properties considered are universals, that is, properties which could (maybe only in a 'different possible world' i.e. if things had been different) be instantiated in different individuals. For just because it is contingent in which person the property is instantiated, a property cannot suffice to make the person who he is. We normally think of properties as universals, and may indeed make it a matter of definition that to be a property something has to be a universal; but if we do thus make it a matter of definition, there can be no viable relational theory of personal identity. Clearly any relational theory open to the duplication objection has made personal identity depend on universals. And if a theory is open to the arbitrariness objection, this will be because a different person could have had the suggested identifying property. If relational properties are to provide the criterion of identity over time, they must be non-universals. The theory, that is, must state that to be P_1 a later person (P_2) must have a certain relation (R) to P_1 which can be possessed by no other person than P_1 in any other possible world. The relation must hold solely in virtue of factors intrinsic to P_2, if the criterion is to avoid the arbitrariness objection. Once we allow non-universal properties—which I shall call individual properties, the crucial relational property obviously just is the property of being identical with P_1, for in no possible world could any individual other than a certain individual (namely, P_1) have that property. Such a property constitutes an individual essence. A later person is the same person as an earlier person if and only if he has the same individual essence. Who an embodied person is depends on which individual essence is coinstantiated with his other properties.

Given the logical possibility for which I argued in the text, that any embodied person can become disembodied, there are—given individual essences—now available two possible theories of how this could come about. One is that there is again immaterial stuff, instantiation of his individual essence in which constitutes the continuing existence of a disembodied person. But on that theory we would have two kinds of new thing—immaterial stuff and individual properties which are essences. It is simpler to suppose that the individual essence can exist on its own without being instantiated in any stuff (exist, that is, in the full-blooded way in which substances exist, not in the pale way in which properties such as squareness 'exist' when there are no square objects). Then we can dispense with the notion of immaterial stuff. An individual essence can exist either on its own—and then we have a disembodied human, or united to a body—and then we have an embodied human. Individual essences are very strange properties indeed.

Duns Scotus seems explicitly committed to individual essences; and—though he had not thought through his views consistently—Aquinas was also, I believe, implicitly committed to them. Aquinas affirms that the human soul (which is a form, and so a property) is what makes an individual human person the person he is. When the soul of Socrates is instantiated in a body, we have Socrates. But Aquinas also held that the soul of Socrates could exist without the body and live some sort of a mental life, though it would not on its own be a human person. The soul of a human was thus a 'subsistent form' and in *Summa Contra Gentiles* though not in *Summa Theologiae* he calls it a substance.[11] (If we understand by a substance something which can exist on its own, that is what he must say that the soul is. But he does not always thus understand it.) So we can do without Bonaventuran souls (parts of persons made of immaterial stuff), if we allow Thomist souls—non-universal properties which can exist on their own and themselves possess properties—which are then themselves substances. I think that there is a lot to be said for Thomist souls,[12] but—suspecting that my readers would be marginally more tolerant of Bonaventuran souls—I commend the quasi-Aristotelian principle. But if you drop it and allow individual essences which can exist by themselves, then, when they are joined to matter to form embodied humans, they are substantial enough (not merely universals which cannot exist un-instantiated) to be parts of those humans (though not parts made of stuff), and so Premiss 3 is true for different reasons. So again, the argument goes through. It remains quite undefeated by any of the counter-arguments which any objector has raised. Humans have two substantial parts—body and soul.

NOTES

1. A distinction along these lines between hard and soft facts or properties has been current in the philosophical literature for some thirty years, but it has been more usual to understand by a purported 'hard fact' about a time one whose truth conditions lie only at that time or earlier, not later—i.e. to understand by a purported 'hard fact' what in my terminology is either a purported hard fact or a purported past-related soft fact. I need to understand these terms in my way in order to make my claim.
2. As I argue (with a qualification) at much greater length in *The Coherence of Theism*, revised edition, Clarendon Press: Oxford, 1993, ch. 3.
3. William P. Alston and Thomas W. Smythe, 'Swinburne's Argument for Dualism', *Faith and Philosophy* 1994, **11**, 127–33.
4. Dean W. Zimmermann, 'Two Cartesian Arguments for the Simplicity of the Soul', *American Philosophical Quarterly*, 1991, **28**, 217–26.
5. See, for example, T. Nagel, *The View from Nowhere*, Oxford University Press: Oxford, 1986, pp. 37–43.
6. St. Bonaventure held that the human soul consisted of 'spiritual' stuff (materia) informed by a form. See his II *Sentences*, 17.1.2, responsio.
7. John Locke, *An Essay Concerning Human Understanding*, 2.28.

8. David Hume, *A Treatise of Human Nature*, 1.46. Hume retracted this view in his appendix.
9. See R. Nozick, *Philosophical Explanations*, Clarendon Press: Oxford, 1981, ch. 1.
10. Derek Parfit, *Reasons and Persons*, Clarendon Press: Oxford, 1984, ch. 12.
11. For Aquinas' views see *Summa Theologiae*, Ia. 75 and 76 and *Summa Contra Gentiles*, 2, 46–end. One tension in Aquinas' account arises from his claim that a soul is individuated by the body which it is 'fitted' to occupy (see *Summa Contra Gentiles*, 2.81). Unlike normal forms, Aquinas held, it could fit only one body. Why that should be is, however, quite mysterious, if a soul is capable of existing without a body. Why should it not be joined again to a new but perhaps qualitatively similar body? And it is difficult to see how a soul could be fitted to occupy a particular body unless there was something intrinsic to it which made it different from other souls, and which would therefore be sufficient to individuate it. Scotus made this latter criticism in *Ordinatio*, II d 3 p 1 q7 nn. 230–1. For full analysis of the views on this issue of D. Scotus, and of the internal tensions within Aquinas' account of the soul, see my *The Christian God* (Clarendon Press: Oxford, 1994), pp. 47–50 and Additional Note 3. (In line 2 and line 4 of Additional Note 3, read 'subsistent forms' instead of 'substantial forms'.)
12. And indeed have defended it and put my account of personal identity in terms of it in *The Christian God*.

5.5

'THE RESURRECTION OF THE DEAD'

Stephen T. Davis

I

One traditional Christian view of survival of death runs, in outline form, something like this: On some future day all the dead will be bodily raised, both the righteous and the unrighteous alike, to be judged by God; and the guarantee and model of the general resurrection (that is, the raising of the dead in the last days) is the already accomplished resurrection of Jesus Christ from the dead.

My aim in this paper is to explain and defend this basic view of resurrection. There are many ways it might be understood, of course, and perhaps more than one is coherent and, even from a Christian point of view, plausible. I shall defend one particular interpretation of the theory – an interpretation advocated by very many of the Church Fathers, especially second-century fathers, as well as by Augustine and Aquinas.

It may help to clarify matters if I first provide a brief map of where we will be going in this paper. After introducing the topic I will discuss in turn what I take to be the three most important claims made by the version of the theory I wish to defend. Then I will consider one typical aspect of the traditional theory that has important philosophical as well as theological ramifications, namely, the notion that our resurrection bodies will consist of the same matter as do our present earthly bodies. Finally, since the version of the theory I wish to defend envisions a period of existence in a disembodied state, I will defend the

Stephen T. Davis, 'The Resurrection of the Dead', in Stephen T. Davis, *Death and Afterlife* (New York: St. Martin's Press; Basingstoke: Macmillan, 1989), pp. 119–44.

theory against some of the arguments of those contemporary philosophers who find the notion of disembodied existence incoherent.

II

Now there are several ways in which the basic concept of resurrection sketched in the opening paragraph can be fleshed out. One option is to understand the nature of the human person, and hence the nature of resurrection, in a basically materialist or physicalist way. Perhaps human beings are essentially material objects, perhaps some vision of identity theory or functionalism is true. Now I am attracted to this option, and hold it to be a usable notion for Christians. But having defended elsewhere a physicalist conception of survival of death through resurrection, I will discuss it no further here.[1]

Another option is to collapse talk of resurrection into talk of the immortality of the soul. A closely related move (and a popular one in recent theology) is to interpret resurrection in a spiritual rather than bodily sense (if this in the end differs significantly from immortality). Such a view will doubtless be based on some version of mind–body (or soul–body) dualism. Let us define dualism as the doctrine which says that (1) human beings consist of both material bodies and immaterial souls; and (2) the soul is the essence of the person (the real you is your soul, not your body). It then can be added that the body corrupts at death and eventually ceases to exist but the soul is essentially immortal.

It is surprising (to me at least) that so many twentieth-century Christian thinkers are tempted toward some such notion as this. For it is quite clear, both in scripture and tradition, that classical dualism is not the Christian position. For example, the biblical view is not that the soul is the essence of the person and is only temporarily housed or even imprisoned in a body; human beings seem rather to be understood in scripture as psycho-physical entities, that is, as unities of body and soul. And the notion that the body is essentially evil and must be escaped from (an idea often associated with versions of classical dualism) was condemned by virtually every orthodox Christian thinker who discussed death and resurrection in the first two hundred years after the apostolic age; the Christian idea is rather that the body was created by God and is good; the whole person, body and soul alike, is what is to be saved. Finally, the biblical notion is not that we survive death because immortality is simply a natural property of souls; if we survive death it is because God miraculously saves us; apart from God's intervention death would mean annihilation for us. Thus Irenaeus says: 'Our survival forever comes from his greatness, not from our nature'.[2]

It would be interesting to discuss this option further, and especially to ask why so many recent and contemporary Christian theologians are drawn toward it, how they might distinguish 'spiritual resurrection' from immortality of the soul, and how they might defend the theory against criticisms such as those just noted. However, I will not do so in this paper. As noted above, my aim here is rather to explore and defend a third way of understanding the traditional Christian notion of resurrection, a theory virtually all (but not quite all) of the Church Fathers who discussed resurrection held in one form or another.[3] I will call this theory 'temporary disembodiment'.

This theory of resurrection is based on a view of human nature which says that human beings are essentially material bodies *and* immaterial souls; the soul is separable from the body, but neither body or soul alone (that is without the other) constitutes a complete human being. Thus Pseudo-Justin Martyr says:

> Is the soul by itself man? No; but the soul of man. Would the body be called man? No, but it is called the body of man. If, then, neither of these is by itself man, but that which is made up of the two together is called man, and God has called *man* to life and resurrection, He has called not a part, but the whole, which is the soul and the body.[4]

What this theory says, then, is that human beings are typically and normally psycho-physical beings, that the soul can exist for a time apart from the body and retain personal identity, but that this disembodied existence is only temporary and constitutes a radically attenuated and incomplete form of human existence.

I call the theory temporary disembodiment because it envisions the following scenario: We human beings are born, live for a time as psycho-physical beings, and then die; after death we exist in an incomplete state as immaterial souls; and some time later in the eschaton God miraculously raises our bodies from the ground, transforms them into 'glorified bodies', and reunites them with our souls, thus making us complete and whole again.

Now temporary disembodiment has several theological and philosophical assets. For one thing, many Christian thinkers have seen a comfortable fit between it and the view of human nature expressed in the Bible and in the Pauline writings particularly. The apostle seems to hold that human beings consist both of material bodies and immaterial souls, that the body is not merely an adornment or drape for the soul, and is indeed good, since it can be the temple of the Holy Spirit (I Corinthians, 3:16–17; 6:19–20), and that the soul is in some sense separable from the body (II Corinthians 5:6–8; 12:2–3). What the body does is provide the soul with a vehicle for action in the world and expression of intentions and desires; and the soul provides the body with animation and direction.[5]

For another thing, the theory seems a neat way of reconciling the traditional view that the general resurrection does not occur until the eschaton with Jesus' statement to the good thief on the cross, '*Today* you will be with me in paradise' (Luke 23:43). The explanation (which naturally goes far beyond

Jesus' simple statement) is as follows: The thief would be with Jesus in paradise that very day in the form of a disembodied soul, only to be bodily raised much later. The theory may also help resolve a similar tension that is sometimes said to exist in Pauline thought, with texts like I Corinthians 15 and I Thessalonians 4 pointing toward the idea of a future, eschatological, resurrection (with those who die beforehand existing till then in a kind of bodiless sleep) and texts like II Corinthians 5:10 and Philippians 1:23 suggesting the idea that death for the Christian is an immediate gain since one is immediately at home with the Lord. (How one can simultaneously be both 'at home with the Lord' and 'in an incomplete state' is a tension that perhaps remains in the theory.)

Finally, the problem of personal identity after death seems in one regard more manageable on this theory than on at least some others, for there is in this theory no temporal gap in the existence of persons (although there is a gap in their existence as complete, unified persons). There is no moment subsequent to our births in which you and I simply do not exist – we exist as soul-bodies or as mere souls at every moment till eternity.

III

There are three main aspects of temporary disembodiment that require discussion both from a philosophical and a theological perspective. Let me now consider them in turn. The first is the notion that after death the soul exists for a time, that is, until the resurrection, in an intermediate state without the body. The second is the notion that at the time of the parousia the body will be raised from the ground and reunited with the soul. And the third is the notion that the body will then be transformed into what is called a 'glorified body'.

The first main claim of temporary disembodiment, then, is that after death the soul temporarily exists without the body. This differs from physicalist concepts of resurrection on which the person does not exist at all in the period between death and resurrection. Temporary disembodiment need not be based on classical dualism as defined earlier, but is based on one tenet of classical dualism, namely, the claim that human beings consist (or in this case at least normally consist) of both material bodies and immaterial souls. (The soul is not said to be the essence of the person, however, and is said to survive death not because immortality is one of its natural properties but because God causes it to survive death.)[6]

Now almost all Christians believe that there is some kind of interim state of the person between death and resurrection. But beyond this point there are very many theological differences. Some, for example, think of the interim state as purgatorial in nature, and others do not. Some hold that spiritual change, for example, repentance, is possible during the interim period, and others do not. Some think the soul rests or sleeps, that is, is not active or conscious, during the interim period, and others do not. It is not part of my purpose in this paper to express an opinion on either of the first two items of disagreement. However, I will argue on the third that the soul is conscious in the interim state. The biblical metaphor of sleep (cf. Luke 8:52; I Corinthians 15:20) is not to be taken as a literal description. This is because it is difficult to make sense of the notion of a disembodied thing being in the presence of God ('Today you will be with me in paradise') if that thing is unconscious and thus unaware of the presence of God.[7] Furthermore, since sleeping is essentially a bodily activity, it seems incoherent to suggest that a soul *could* sleep.

The state of being without a body is an abnormal state of the human person. This is one of the clear differences between temporary disembodiment and immortality of the soul, for the second doctrine (at least in versions of it influenced by Plato) entails that disembodiment is the true or proper or best state of the human person. On the theory we are considering, however, the claim is that a disembodied soul lacks many of the properties and abilities that are normal for and proper to human persons. Disembodied existence is a kind of minimal existence.

Which properties typical of embodied human persons will disembodied souls have and which will they lack? Clearly they will lack those properties that essentially involve corporeality. They will possess no spatial location, for example, at least not in the space–time manifold with which we are familiar. They will not be able to perceive their surroundings (using the spatial word 'surroundings' in a stretched sense) – not at least in the ways in which we perceive our surroundings (that is, through the eyes, ears, and so on). They will not be able to experience bodily pains and pleasures. They will not be able to engage in bodily activities. Taking a walk, getting dressed, playing catch – these sorts of activities will be impossible.

But if by the word 'soul' we mean in part the constellation of those human activities that would typically be classified as 'mental', then the claim that our souls survive death entails the claim that our mental abilities and properties survive death. This means that human persons in the interim state can be spoken of as having experiences, beliefs, wishes, knowledge, memory, inner (rather than bodily) feelings, thoughts, language (assuming memory or earthly existence) – in short, just about everything that makes up what we call personality. H. H. Price, in his classic article 'Survival and the Idea of "Another World" ', argues convincingly that disembodied souls can also be aware of each other's existence, can communicate with each other telepathically, and can have dreamlike (rather than bodily) perceptions of their world.[8]

But Aquinas argues that the disembodied existence of the person in the interim state is so deficient that attainment of ultimate happiness is impossible. No one in whom some perfection is lacking is ultimately happy, for in such a state there will always be unfilfilled desires. It is contrary to the nature of the soul to be without the body, Aquinas says, and he takes this to mean both that the disembodied state must only be temporary, and that the true bliss of the human person is only attained after re-embodiment, that is, in the general resurrection. He says: 'Man cannot achieve his ultimate happiness unless the soul be once again united to the body'.[9]

IV

The second main claim of the theory that I am calling temporary disembodiment is that at the general resurrection the body will be raised from the ground and reunited with the soul. As the second-century writer Athenagoras says:

> There must certainly be a resurrection of bodies whether dead or even quite corrupted, and the same men as before must come to be again. The law of nature appoints an end . . . for those very same men who lived in a previous existence, and it is impossible for the same men to come together again if the same bodies are not given back to the same souls. Now the same soul cannot recover the same body in any other way than by resurrection.[10]

As Athenagoras stresses, the idea is that each person's selfsame body will be raised; it will not be a different and brand new body but the old body. Aquinas (echoing the argument of very many of the fathers) notes the reason for this: 'If the body of the man who rises is not to be composed of the flesh and bones which now compose it, the man who rises will not be numerically the same man'.[11] Furthermore, in the resurrection there will be only one soul per body and only one body per soul. As Augustine says: 'Each single soul shall possess its own body'.[12] Otherwise (for example, if souls split and animate more than one body or if multiple identical copies of one body are animated by different souls) the problem of personal identity is unsolvable, and the Christian hope that we will live after death is incoherent.

The fathers and scholastics insisted, then, that both body and soul must be present or else the person does not exist. 'A man cannot be said to exist as such when the body is dissolved or completely scattered, even though the soul remain by itself' – so says Athenagoras.[13] And Aquinas agrees: 'My soul is not I, and if only souls are saved, *I* am not saved, nor is any man'.[14] Thus the Christian hope of survival is not the hope that our souls will survive death (though on temporary disembodiment that is one important aspect of it), but rather the hope that one day God will miraculously raise our bodies and reunite them with our souls.

What is it, then, that guarantees personal identity in the resurrection? What is it that ensures that it will really be *us* in the kingdom of God and not, say, clever replicas of us? Aquinas argues as follows: since human beings consist of bodies and souls, and since both souls and the matter of which our bodies consist survive death, personal identity is secured when God collects the scattered matter, miraculously reconstitutes it a human body, and reunites it with the soul.[15] And this surely seems a powerful argument. If God one day succeeds in doing these very things, personal identity will be secure. It will be us and not our replicas who will be the denizens of the kingdom of God.

V

The third main claim of temporary disembodiment is that in the resurrection the old body will be transformed into a 'glorified body' with certain quite new properties. This claim is based primarily on Paul's discussion of the resurrection in I Corinthians 15, and secondarily on the unusual properties the risen Jesus is depicted as having in some of the accounts of the resurrection appearances (for example, the apparent ability of the risen Jesus in John 20 to appear in a room despite the doors being locked). In the Pauline text just mentioned the apostle notes that some ask, 'How are the dead raised? With what kind of body do they come?' His answer is an argument to the effect that the new 'glorified' or 'spiritual' body (*soma pneumatikon*) is a transformation of the old body rather than a *de novo* creation (much as a stalk of grain is a transformation of a seed of grain, that is, it exists because of changes that have occurred in the seed and can be considered a new state of the grain). Further, Paul argues, while the old or natural body is physical, perishable, mortal, and sown in weakness and dishonour, the glorified body is spiritual, imperishable, immortal, and sown in strength and honour. The first body is in the image of the man of dust; the second body is in the image of the man of heaven.

The term 'spiritual body' might be misleading; it should not be taken as a denial of corporeality or as a last-minute capitulation to some version of the immortality of the soul as opposed to bodily resurrection. By this term Paul means not a body whose stuff or matter is spiritual (whatever that might mean) or an immaterial existence of some sort; rather he means a body that is fully obedient to and dominant by the Holy Spirit. Paul says: 'Flesh and blood cannot inherit the kingdom of God' (I Corinthians 15:50). What enters the kingdom of heaven, then, is not this present weak and mortal body of flesh and blood but the new glorified body. This new body is a physical body (Paul's use of the word *soma* implies as much),[16] and is materially related to the old body (taking seriously Paul's simile of the seed), but is a body transformed in such ways as make it fit to live in God's presence. If by the term 'physical object' we mean an entity that has spatio-temporal location and is capable of being empirically measured, tested, or observed in some sense, then my argument is that the new body of which Paul speaks is a physical object.

Temporary disembodiment, then, entails that human souls can animate both normal earthly bodies and glorified resurrection bodies. Continuity between the two bodies is provided by the presence of both the same soul and the same matter in both bodies. Thus Augustine says:

> Nor does the earthly material out of which men's mortal bodies are created ever perish; but though it may crumble into dust and ashes, or be dissolved into vapours and exhalations, though it may be transformed into the substance of other bodies, or dispersed into the elements, though it should become food for beasts or men, and be changed into their flesh, it returns in a moment of time to that human soul which animated it at the first and which caused it to become man, and to live and grow.[17]

The matter of our present bodies may be arranged differently in the resurrection, he says, but the matter will be restored.

Many of the theologians of the early church and of the medieval period stress also the perfection of the glorified body. It will be free of every bodily defect. It will be immune to evil because fully controlled by the spirit of God. It will not suffer. It will not grow old or die. It will have 'agility' – which is presumably an ability like that of the risen Jesus to come and go at will, unimpeded by things like walls and doors. It will exist in a state of fulfilled desire. It will need no material food and drink, but will be nourished by the elements of the eucharist.[18]

VI

Is the picture of resurrection just presented coherent? Is it plausible? The main objections that have been raised against it in recent philosophy revolve around the problem of personal idenity. Some philosophers argue that so far as disembodied existence is concerned this problem cannot be solved. That is, they argue that if some immaterial aspect of me survives death it will not be me that survives death. Since the view of survival of death I am defending essentially involves a period of disembodied existence, I had best try to defend the view against these sorts of objections. But a prior problem must be considered first – whether the fathers and scholastics were correct in their strong claim (I will call this claim 'the patristic theory') that if it is to be me in the kingdom of God the very matter of my original earthly body must be raised. Having discussed the point, I will then turn in section VII to the arguments of those philosophers who oppose the notion of disembodied existence because of the problem of personal identity.

Why did Aquinas and the fathers who influenced him insist that the same matter of my old body must be raised? Let us see if we can construct an argument on their behalf. Like many arguments in the area of personal identity, it involves a puzzle case. Suppose that I own a defective personal computer which I rashly decide to try to repair myself. Having taken it apart (there are now, say, 60 separate computer components scattered on my work bench), I find that I am unable to repair it. I call the outlet that sold me the computer, and the manager suggests I simply bring all 60 components to that office for repair. I do so, but through a horrible series of misunderstandings and errors, the 60 pieces of the computer are then sent to 60 different addresses around the country. That constitutes the heart of my story, but there are two separate endings to it. *Ending number one*: it takes three years for everything to be sorted out, for the pieces to be located and collected in one place, for the repairs to be made, and for the parts to be reassembled and restored, in full working order, to my desk. *Ending number two*: After three years of trying in vain to locate and collect the scattered pieces, the manager gives up, collects 60 similar parts, assembles them, and the resulting computer ends up on my desk.

Now I do not wish to raise the interesting question whether my computer *existed* during the three-year period. I am interested in the related question whether the computer now located on my desk is *the same* computer as the one that was there three years ago. And so far as ending number one is concerned, it seems most natural to affirm that the computer I now possess is indeed the same computer as the one that I possessed before. The computer may or may not have had a gap in its existence, that is, a period when it did not exist, but it seems clear that identity has here been preserved. And so far as ending number two is concerned, it seems most natural to deny that the computer I now possess is the same computer as the one that I possessed before. Furthermore, we would doubtless insist on this denial even if each of the 60 components the manager used to construct the computer I now possess was qualitatively identical to the 60 old components. What I now have is a qualitatively similar but numerically different computer.

Now I doubt that the Church Fathers often pondered personal identity test cases involving computers, and it is obvious that personal computers are different from human beings in many striking ways. But it was perhaps *the sort* of insight arrived at above that led them to take the strong stand they took on the resurrection. Only if God reassembles the very particles of which my body once consisted will it be me who is raised. Otherwise, that is, if other particles are used, the result will be what we would call a replica of me rather than me.

But despite the above argument, does it still not seem that Aquinas and the fathers in their strong stand have made the solution to the problem of personal identity more difficult than it need be? Even granting the point that some of the particles of the matter of which our bodies consist will endure for the requisite number of years, why insist that God must re-collect it, that is, that very matter, in the resurrection? For surely in the interim state it will be us (and not soul-like replicas of us) who will exist without any body at all; surely the fathers and scholastics insist on this much. Thus the soul alone must guarantee personal identity; what philosophers call the memory criterion (which is typically taken to include not just memory but all one's 'mental' characteristics and properties) must suffice by itself. Identity of memory, personality, and other 'mental' aspects of the person are sufficient conditions of personal identity. To admit this much is not necessarily to go back on the traditional notion that the soul is not the whole person and that the whole person must be raised. It is merely to insist that the existence of my soul entails *my* existence. Otherwise talk of my existence in the interim state is meaningless.

Now I do not claim that the patristic theory is logically inconsistent. It is possible to hold that when I die my soul will be me during the interim period but that it will no longer be me if my soul in the eschaton animates a body consisting of totally new matter, even if the new body is qualitatively identical to the old one. (Perhaps an essential property of my soul is that it can only animate *this* body – where 'this body' means in part a body consisting of *these* particles. So if *per impossible* my soul were to animate a different body the result would not be me. Or perhaps every configuration of particles that can possibly constitute a human body has it as one of its essential properties that it can be animated by one and only one soul.) But while logically consistent, this view seems to me exceedingly difficult to defend; it is hard to see how the suggested theses could be argued for.

Thus so far as the problem of personal identity is concerned, it is not easy to see why a defender of temporary disembodiment cannot dispense with all talk of God one day re-collecting the atoms, quarks, or whatever of our bodies. Perhaps human beings in this regard are unlike computers. Why not say God can award us brand new bodies materially quite unrelated to (although qualitatively similar to) the old ones? If the existence of the soul is sufficient for personal identity, and if the human soul never at any moment subsequent to its creation fails to exist, it will be us who exist after the resurrection in the kingdom of God whether or not our old bodies are reconstituted.

Furthermore, it needs to be noted here that identity of particles of bodily matter does not seem necessary to preserve the identity of an ordinary human person even during the course of a lifetime. As Frank Dilley says:

> We constantly replace our atoms over time and there is no reason to think that any eighty year old person has even a single atom in common with the newborn babe. If a person maintains personal identity over a process of total atom-by-atom replacement, it is difficult to see why such identity would not be preserved through a sudden replacement of all the atoms at once.[19]

Dilley's argument seems plausible, but we should notice that it does not necessarily follow. Perhaps gradual replacement of all the individual atoms of a human body is consistent with personal identity while all-at-once replacement of them is not. Perhaps some strong sort of material continuity is needed. One of the difficulties encountered by philosophers who discuss personal identity is that different persons' intuitions run in different directions. For example, in a slightly different connection, Peter Van Inwagen argues that sameness of person requires both (1) sameness of atoms and (2) regular and natural causal relationships between those atoms. So if God were now to try to raise Napoleon Bonaparte from the dead by omnisciently locating the atoms of which his body once consisted and miraculously reassembling them, the result would not be Napoleon.[20] Now I do not agree with Van Inwagen here; I see no reason for his second stipulation. I raise his argument merely to show that his intuitions run in a different direction than do Dilley's. Since Dilley's case of sudden-replacement-of-all-the-atoms-at-once seems to constitute something *un*natural and *ir*regular, Van Inwagen would doubtless deny that in such cases personal identity would be preserved.

What if there were, so to speak, some natural way of reassembling persons out of totally new matter? Derek Parfit considers in detail a series of test cases involving an imagined teletransporter.[21] This is a machine that is designed to send a person to distant places like Mars by (1) recording the exact state of all the body's cells (including those of the brain); (2) destroying the body and brain; (3) transmitting the information at the speed of light to Mars; where (4) a replicator creates out of new matter a body and brain exactly like the old one. Suppose Parfit enters the machine and is 'teletransported to Mars'. Would the resulting Parfit-like person on Mars *be* Parfit? Here again our intuitions might differ, even in this relatively simple case (that is, apart from complications like the original Parfit somehow surviving on earth or 15 Parfit-like persons appearing on Mars). Those (like the Church Fathers and Aquinas) who hold to some strong requirement about bodily continuity will deny it is Parfit. Those who stress the memory criterion are free to affirm that Parfit is now on Mars. So are those (for example, John Hick) who believe that identity is exact similarity plus uniqueness. Those who think that identity is exact similarity plus the right kind of causal origin or causal ancestry might go either way, depending on whether they think the operation of a teletransporter constitutes an appropriate sort of causal origin for the Parfit-like person on Mars.

The moral of the story thus far, I think, is that the fathers and Aquinas may be right in what they say about resurrection, but it is not clear that they are right. Their position may be consistent, but it does seem implausible to hold both (1) that it will be me in the interim period without any body at all (that is, the presence of my soul is sufficient for personal identity), and (2) that it will not be me in the eschaton, despite the presence of my soul, if the body which my soul then animates consists of new matter. There may be other (perhaps theological) reasons why we should hold that it is the very matter of our old bodies that is raised, but so far as the problem of personal identity is concerned, a strong case can be made that it will not matter.

Recent and contemporary Christian theologians who discuss resurrection seem for the most part to have departed from the Patristic theory. The more common thesis is that our glorified bodies will be wholly different bodies, not necessarily consisting of any of the old matter at all. As John Hick, an articulate spokesperson for this new point of view, says:

What has become a widely accepted view in modern times holds that the resurrection body is a new and different body given by God, but expressing the personality within its new environment as the physical body expressed it in the earthly environment. The physical frame decays or is burned, disintegrating and being dispersed into the ground or the air, but God re-embodies the personality elsewhere.[22]

Frequently connected with this view is an exegetical claim, namely, that by the term 'the body', St Paul meant not the physical organism but rather something akin to 'the whole personality'. What will be raised from the dead, then, is not the old body but rather the *person*, and in being raised the person will be given a brand new body by God.

It is not hard to see why such a view has come to be widely adopted. (1) As noted above, personal identity does not seem to require the resurrection of the old body. (2) The patristic theory seems to many contemporary Christians to be scientifically outmoded and difficult to believe; the idea that in order to raise me God must one day cast about, locate, and collect the atoms of which my earthly body once consisted seems to many people absurd. (3) Many such theologians want to hold in any case that the kingdom of God is not spatially related to our present world. It exists in a space all its own, and so can contain no material from this spatio-temporal manifold.

I am unable to locate any philosophical or logical difficulties in the 'modern' theory. It seems to me a possible Christian view of resurrection, and can fit smoothly with the other aspects of the traditional notion I am calling temporary disembodiment. Are there any theological reasons, then, for a Christian to retain the old theory, that is, to believe that our old bodies will be raised? Two points should be made here. The first is that the most natural reading of Paul in I Corinthians 15 is along the lines of the patristic theory. That is, Paul seems to be suggesting there that the old body *becomes* or *changes into* the new body, just as a seed becomes or changes into a plant. Thus, just as there is material continuity between the seed and the plant, so there will be material continuity between the old body and the new; the plant is *a new form* of the seed. Note also Paul's use in verses 42 and 43 of the expression: '*It* is sown . . . *it* is raised . . .', as if the one thing (a human body) is at one time in a certain state and at a later time in another state (see also vs 53 and 53).[23] Furthermore, as noted already, Paul's use of the term *soma* reveals that what he had in mind was a body; it is simply a lexical mistake to say that he merely meant 'the whole personality', or some such thing.[24]

The second point has to do with the difficulty of God one day collecting the atoms, quarks, or whatever fundamental particles human bodies consist of. This may well be the oldest philosophical objection ever raised against the Christian notion of resurrection. Virtually every one of the fathers who discussed resurrection tried to answer it, as did Aquinas. Such scenarios as this were suggested: What if a Christian dies at sea and his body is eaten by various fishes who then scatter to the seven seas? How can God later resurrect that body? Or what if another Christian is eaten by cannibals, so that the material of her body becomes the material of their bodies? And suppose God later wants to raise all of them from the dead, cannibals and Christians alike. Who gets what particles? How does God decide?

The move made by virtually all of the fathers in response to this objection is to appeal to omnipotence. You and I might not be able to locate and reconstitute the relevant atoms of someone's body, not surely after many years or even centuries have passed, but God can do this very thing. And as long as (1) the basic constituents of matter (for example, atoms) endure through time (as contemporary physical theory says they normally do); and (2) it is merely a matter of God locating and collecting the relevant constituents, I believe the fathers were right. An omnipotent being could do that.

But with the cannibalism case and other imaginable cases where God must decide which constituent parts shared at different times by two (or even two thousand) separate persons go where, the matter is more serious. The problem does not seem insoluble, but much more needs to be said. Perhaps some constituent parts of human bodies are essential to those bodies and some are not. That is, perhaps God will only need to collect the essential parts of our bodies and use them, so to speak, as building blocks around which to reconstruct our new bodies. And perhaps omnipotence must accordingly guarantee that no essential part of one person's earthly body is ever a constituent part, or an essential constituent part, of someone else's body. If these stipulations or ones like them are followed (for example, Augustine's idea that atoms will be raised in that human body in which they first appeared),[25] it still seems that the fathers were correct – an omnipotent being will be able to raise us from the ground.

Reacting against these and similar patristic appeals to omnipotence in order to rationalise resurrection, Paul Badham argues as follows:[26]

> Given belief in a once-for-all act of creation on the pattern of Genesis 1, then the act of resurrection cannot be difficult for an all-powerful God. Given that God made the first man by direct action, the restoration of a decomposed man becomes an easy task. Given that man consists of particles, it is easy to believe that omnipotence could reassemble these particles. But today each of these premises has lost its validity, and hence the conclusions drawn from them cannot stand. That man as a species is part of a slowly evolving process of life and in every respect continuous with the processes of nature from which he has emerged does not provide a congenial background for the idea of resurrection. Further, our increasing knowledge of the incredible complexity and constant changing of our physical components makes it difficult to see the resurrection as simply involving the re-collection of our physical particles. We are not composed of building bricks but of constantly changing living matter.

It is not easy to see exactly what the arguments here are meant to be. For one thing, Badham is right that nature is incredibly complex, as are human bodies; our bodies surely do consist of constantly changing living matter. But does any of this deny – or indeed does contemporary physics deny – the idea that our bodies consist of particles? I think not. Furthermore, it is hard to see how a commitment to evolutionary theory (a commitment I make) undercuts the ability of an omnipotent being to raise us from the dead. Perhaps it does undercut a simplistic argument which we occasionally find in the fathers, an argument which says, 'Since God already did the difficult job of creating me *de novo* by assembling the particles of my body, God can also do the far easier job of reassembling them in the eschaton.'[27] But surely claims about what is easy and what is hard for an omnipotent being to do are suspect anyway. The point the fathers were making is that whatever difficulties resurrection presents are difficulties that can be overcome by an omnipotent being. That point still stands, and is not rendered improbable or implausible by evolution.

VII

Several philosophers have argued in recent years that the concept of disembodied existence is incoherent or at least that no disembodied thing can be identified with some previously existing human person. Antony Flew,[28] Bernard Williams,[29] D. Z. Phillips,[30] Terence Penelhum,[31] and John Perry,[32] among others, have jointly presented what might be called the standard arguments against survival of death in disembodied form. P. T. Geach,[33] has similarly argued against the notion of *permanent* disembodied existence, though he supports something like the theory I am calling temporary disembodiment. Now I am inclined to hold that the standard arguments have been successfully answered by defenders of disembodied existence;[34] that is, I believe the notion of survival of death (and even permanent survival of death) in disembodied form is intelligible and logically possible. Furthermore, one result of recent discussion of the puzzle cases in the area of personal identity is that many philosophers are now prepared to defend the notion that we can imagine cases where the memory criterion will suffice by itself. But since the arguments of Flew, Williams, Phillips, and Penelhum have been discussed thoroughly in the journals, let me instead focus on the case John Perry makes in his excellent little book, *A Dialogue on Personal Identity and Immortality*.

Perry seems, in this dialogue, to speak primarily through the character of Gretchen Weirob, a mortally injured but still lucid philosopher who does not believe in life after death. And Weirob seems to present three main arguments against the conceivability or possibility of survival of death. All are versions of arguments we find elsewhere in the literature, but the virtue of Perry's work is that they are presented with great clarity and forcefulness. Perry's first argument has to do with the soul and personal identity; the second concerns memory and personality identity; and the third is an argument about the possibility of duplication of persons.

The first argument says that immaterial and thus unobservable souls can have nothing to do with establishing personal identity. Personal identity does not consist in sameness of soul, for if it did we would never know who we are or who others are. Since souls are not observable, no thesis having to do with souls is testable (not even the thesis, 'My soul is me'). So I cannot know whether other human beings have souls, or even whether I have a soul; I have no idea whether I have one soul or several, or whether I have one soul for a time and then later a different soul. Thus there are no criteria for, and hence no way to make informed judgements about, 'the same soul'. It is possible simply on faith to assume criteria like, 'Same body, same soul', or 'Same mental traits, same soul', but since we never independently observe souls there is no way to test these principles, and thus no reason to think they hold. But since we evidently are able to make correct personal identity judgements about persons, it follows that personal identity has nothing to do with souls. Personal identity must instead be based upon bodily criteria. Thus, concludes Perry, no thesis about my survival of death via the survival of my soul is coherent.

Perry's second argument is that the memory criterion of personal identity, which those who believe in immortality must rely on, is never sufficient to establish personal identity. This is because of the obvious fact that memory is fallible. Without some further criterion, we will never be able to distinguish between apparent memories and genuine memories. In fact, believers in immortality are committed to a kind of circularity – they claim that genuine memory explains personal identity (that is, a purported Jones in the afterlife really is Jones just in case the purported Jones genuinely remembers from Jones's point of view events in Jones's past), and they claim that identity marks the difference between apparent and genuine memories (the purported Jones can have genuine memories of events in Jones's past just in case the purported Jones *is* Jones – otherwise the memories are merely apparent memories). Thus again, the thesis that our souls survive death, which must rely on the memory criterion of personal identity, is incoherent.

Finally, Perry argues that the thesis of survival of death through immortality is rendered incoherent by the possibility of multiple qualitatively identical persons in the afterlife. Weirob says:[35]

> So either God, by creating a Heavenly person with a brain modeled after mine, does not really create someone identical with me but merely someone similar to me, or God is somehow limited to making only one such being. I can see no reason why, if there were a God, He should be so limited. So I take the first option. He would create someone similar to me, but not someone who would *be* me. Either your analysis of memory is wrong, and such a being does not, after all, remember what I am doing

or saying, or memory is not sufficient for personal identity. Your theory has gone wrong somewhere, for it leads to absurdity.

When told by one of the discussants that God may well refrain from creating multiple qualitatively identical persons in the afterlife and that if God does so refrain the immortality thesis is coherent, Weirob replies that a new criterion has now been added. What suffices for personal identity (that is, what makes it such that the purported Jones in the afterlife *is* Jones) is not just memory but rather memory plus lack of competition. An odd way for someone to be killed in the afterlife, she remarks – all God has to do is create, so to speak, an identical twin to Jones, and then *neither* is Jones; Jones has not survived death. Identity is now made oddly to depend on something entirely extrinsic to the person involved. Thus if memory does not secure personal identity where there are two or more Jones's in the afterlife, it does not secure personal identity at all. Weirob concludes it is best simply to abandon any thought of survival of death – when my body dies, I die.

Perry's first argument in favour of the notion that survival of death is incoherent is based on an element of truth, but is used by him in an erroneous way. Throughout his book he seems illicitly to jump back and forth between talk about criteria of personal identity and talk about evidence for personal identity. It is surely true that the soul is not observable, and that the presence or absence of a soul or of a certain soul is not something for which we can successfully test. What this shows, as I suppose, is that the soul is not *evidence for* personal identity. We cannot, for example, prove that a given person really is our long-lost friend by proving that this person really has our long-lost friend's soul. But it still might be true that the soul is *a criterion of* personal identity. That is, it still might be the case that the person really is our long-lost friend just in case this person and our long-lost friend have the same soul. It might even be true to say that a purported Jones in the afterlife is the same person as the Jones who once lived on earth just in case the purported Jones has Jones's soul. How we might test for or come to know this is another matter. Maybe only God knows for sure who has what soul. Maybe the rest of us will never know – not apart from divine revelation anyway – whether the purported Jones has Jones's soul. But it can still be true that if they have the same soul, they are two different temporal episodes of the same one person.

And the claim that personal identity consists in or amounts to the presence of the soul does not rule out the possibility of our making reliable personal identity judgements on other grounds, as Weirob seems to claim it does. Those who believe in the possibility of disembodied existence need not deny that there are other criteria of personal identity (for example, if the person before me has the same body as my long-lost friend, this person *is* my long-lost friend) and other ways of producing evidence in favour of or against personal identity claims.

Perry's second argument is also based on an element of truth – memory certainly is fallible; we do have to distinguish between apparent memories and genuine memories. So unless I have access to some infallible way of making this distinction, the mere fact that the purported Jones seems to remember events in Jones's life from Jones's point of view will not establish beyond conceivable doubt that the purported Jones is Jones (though it might count as evidence for it). As above, however, this does not rule out the possibility that memory is a criterion of personal identity – if the purported Jones does indeed remember events in Jones's life from Jones's point of view, then the purported Jones is Jones.

It is sometimes claimed that the memory criterion is parasitic on the bodily criterion and that use of the memory criterion never suffices by itself to establish identity. But such claims are surely false. We sometimes do make secure identity claims based on the memory criterion alone – for example, when we receive a typed letter from a friend. We hold that it is our friend who wrote the letter solely on the basis of memories and personality traits apparently had by the letter's author that seem to be memories and personality traits our friend has or ought to have. Of course if doubts were to arise we would try to verify or falsify the claim that our friend wrote the letter by the use of any evidence or criterion that might seem promising. We might check the letter for finger prints; we might try to see if it was written on our friend's typewriter; we might even telephone our friend. What this shows is not that we must always rely on the bodily criterion; there are equally cases where we might try to verify an identity claim originally based on the bodily criterion by means of memories. What it shows is that in cases of doubt we will look at both criteria.

But in the cases where the bodily criterion cannot be used – for example, during the interim period postulated in temporary disembodiment – can identity claims rationally be made? Can we ever be sure that a disembodied putative Stephen Davis *is* Stephen Davis? The problem is especially acute since memory is notoriously fallible; without recourse to the bodily criterion, how can we distinguish between actual memories and purported memories? I would argue that secure identity claims can be made without use of the bodily criterion, and that this can be achieved in cases where there are very many memories from very many different people that cohere together well. The context would make all the difference. If there are, say, 100 disembodied souls all wondering whether everyone in fact is who he or she claims to be, it would be irrational to deny that their memories are genuine if they all fit together, confirm each other, and form a coherent picture. Doubt would still be conceivable, but not rational. And something like this is precisely what defenders of temporary disembodiment claim will occur during the interim period.[36]

The third or duplication argument is one that critics of disembodied existence frequently appeal to, but is is one of the advantages of Perry's *Dialogue* that he grasps the defender's proper reply to it, and then moves to deepen the objection. After the comment from Weirob quoted above, Perry has Dave Cohen, a former student of hers, say: 'But wait. Why can't Sam simply say that if God makes one such creature, she is you, while if he makes more, none of them is you? It's possible that he makes only one. So it's possible that you survive'. This seems to me the correct response. Of course immortality or resurrection would be difficult to believe in if there were, say, 14 qualitatively identical Weirobs in the afterlife, each with equal apparent sincerity claiming to be Gretchen Weirob. But surely you can't refute a thesis, or the possible truth of a thesis, by imagining possible worlds where the thesis would be exceedingly hard to believe. Survival of death theses might well make good sense if in the afterlife there is never more than one person who claims to be some pre-mortem person. And since it is possible there will be but one Gretchen Weirob in the afterlife, survival of death is possible.

In response to this point Perry deepens the objection with Weirob's points about there now being two criteria of personal identity (memory and lack of competition) and about the oddness of God's ability to prevent someone's surviving death by creating a second qualitatively identical person. Both points seem to me correct, but do not render the survival thesis incoherent or even, as Weirob claims, absurd. What exactly is wrong with saying (in the light of God's evident ability to create multiple qualitatively identical persons) that memory plus lack of competition are criteria of personal identity? Lack of competition is a criterion that technically applies in this life as well as the next – we never bother to mention it because it rarely occurs to us that God has the ability to create multiple qualitatively identical persons here as well. And I suppose it *is* odd that God can prevent someone's survival in the way envisioned, and that personal identity is here made in part to depend on something entirely extrinsic to the person. These facts are odd, but they do not seem to me to impugn the possibility of the survival thesis.

Christians strongly deny that there will be multiple qualitatively identical persons in the eschaton. They would hold, however, that God has the ability to create such persons, so it is perfectly fair for critics to ask: How would it affect your advocacy of resurrection if God were to exercise this power? Now I prefer to hold that the existence of multiple qualitatively identical Joneses in the eschaton would place far too great a strain on our concept of a human person for us to affirm that Jones has survived death. Our concept of a person, I believe, includes a notion of uniqueness – there is and can be only one instance of each 'person'. Uniqueness or 'lack of competition' (as Weirob puts it) is a criterion of personal identity. So I would argue at the very least that we would not know what to say if there were more than one Jones in the afterlife (perhaps our concept of a human person would have to be radically revised to include amoeba-like divisions, or something of the sort). More strongly, I would argue that Jones (the unique person we knew on earth) has not survived death.

Accordingly, I see no serious difficulty for the survival thesis here. Although the view I am defending – temporary disembodiment – does not require the coherence of any notion of permanent disembodiment (like, for example, the doctrine known as immortality of the soul), I nevertheless would hold both to be coherent. As noted above, however, Geach argues strongly that only temporary disembodiment is coherent; what alone makes the problem of personal identity manageable as regards a disembodied person is its capacity or potential eventually to be reunited with a given body. Otherwise, he says, disembodied minds cannot be differentiated.[37] If Geach is right, only temporary disembodiment is coherent – immortality of the soul is not. Or at least, those who believe in the latter doctrine must add an item to their theory – perhaps something about a permanently disembodied soul permanently retaining the (forever unrealised) *capacity* to be reunited with a given body.

VIII

As can be seen from the preceding discussion, I do not consider that what I have been calling the patristic theory is normative for Christians today. The 'modern' theory seems to me an acceptable interpretation of resurrection. God's ability to raise us from the dead in the eschaton does not seem to depend on God's ability to locate and reunite the very particles of which our bodies once consisted. Nevertheless, the patristic theory also constitutes an acceptable understanding of resurrection for Christians. The standard objections to it are answerable, and the most natural exegesis of I Corinthians 15:35–50 supports it. Furthermore, respect for Christian tradition must (or so I would argue) grant great weight to views held by virtually all the fathers of the church unless there is serious reason to depart from what they say. It seems to me quite possible that God will one day raise us from the dead in the very way that the fathers and Aquinas suggest.

My overall conclusion is that the theory of resurrection I have been considering (which can be interpreted in either the patristic or the 'modern' way) is a viable notion for Christians. Temporary disembodiment seems eminently defensible, both philosophically and theologically. I do not claim it is the only viable option for Christian belief about life after death; I do claim it is an acceptable way for Christians to understand those words from the Apostles' Creed that say, 'I believe in . . . the resurrection of the body'.

Much contemporary philosophy tends, in its understanding of human nature, in a behaviourist or even materialist direction. No believer in temporary disembodiment can embrace philosophical materialism, but such believers can have great sympathy with any view which says that a disembodied person would hardly be a human person, not surely in the full sense of the word. They too embrace the notion that a disembodied person is only a minimal person, a mere shadow of a true human person – not completely unlike a person who is horribly disabled from birth or from some accident but who continues to live.

Such Christians will accordingly embrace the notion that full and true and complete human life is bodily life. That is why they look forward to 'the resurrection of the body'. As Pseudo-Justin says:[38] 'In the resurrection the flesh shall rise entire. For if on earth He healed the sickness of the flesh, and made the body whole, much more will He do this in the resurrection, so that the flesh shall rise perfect and entire'.[39]

NOTES

1. See Stephen T. Davis, 'Is Personal Identity Retained in The Resurrection?' *Modern Theology*, 2 (4) (1986).
2. Cyril Richardson (ed.), *Early Christian Fathers* (Philadelphia: The Westminster Press, 1953) p. 389.
3. See Harry A. Wolfson, 'Immortality and Resurrection in the Philosophy of the Church Fathers', in Krister Stendahl (ed.), *Immortality and Resurrection* (New York: Macmillan, 1965) pp. 64–72. See also Lynn Boliek, *The Resurrection of the Flesh* (Grand Rapids, Michigan: Wm B. Eerdmans, 1962).
4. Alexander Roberts and James Donaldson (eds), *The Ante-Nicene Fathers* (New York: Charles Scribner's Sons, 1899) pp. 297–8.
5. Robert H. Gundry, *Soma in Biblical Theology: With Emphasis on Pauline Anthropology* (Cambridge: Cambridge University Press, 1976) p. 159.
6. Wolfson, op. cit., pp. 56–60, 63–4.
7. It does not seem to make sense to speak of some disembodied thing x being 'in the presence of' some other thing y, where 'in the presence of' means 'in the spatial vicinity of'. The notion may be coherently understood, however, as something like 'being acutely aware of and sensitive to'. This is why I am unable to provide a sensible construal of the notion of a disembodied and unconscious person being in the presence of God.
8. H. H. Price, 'Survival and the Idea of "Another World",' in John Donnelly (ed.), *Language, Metaphysics, and Death* (New York: Fordham University Press, 1978) pp. 176–95. I do not wish to commit myself entirely to Price's theory; among others, John Hick has detected difficulties in it. See *Death and Eternal Life* (New York: Harper & Row 1976) pp. 265–77. But Price's main point – that disembodied survival of death is possible – seems to me correct.
9. Thomas Aquinas, *Summa Contra Gentiles*, trans. by Charles J. O'Neil; Book IV (Notre Dame, Indiana: The University of Notre Dame Press, 1975) IV, 79.
10. Athenagoras, *Embassy for Christians and the Resurrection of the Dead*, trans. Joseph H. Crehan, S. J. (London: Longmans, Green, 1956) pp. 115–16.
11. Aquinas, op. cit., IV, 84.
12. Augustine, *The Enchiridion on Faith, Hope, and Love* (Chicago: Henry Regnery, 1961) LXXXVII.
13. Athenagoras, op. cit., p. 115.
14. Cited in P. T. Geach, *God and the Soul* (London: Routledge & Kegan Paul, 1969) pp. 22, 40.
15. Aquinas, op. cit., IV, 81.
16. See Gundry, op. cit., pp. 164ff. For this and other points made in this paragraph, see C. F. D. Moule, 'St Paul and Dualism: The Pauline Concept of Resurrection', *New Testament Studies*, 12 (2) (1966), and Ronald J. Sider, 'The Pauline Conception of the Resurrection Body in I Corinthians XV. 35–54', *New Testament Studies*, 21 (3) (1975).
17. Augustine, op. cit., LXXXVIII.
18. See Irenaeus, in Richardson, op. cit., p. 388; Augustine, op. cit., XCI; Aquinas, op. cit., IV, 83–7.

19. Frank Dilley, 'Resurrection and the "Replica Objection" ', *Religious Studies*, 19 (4) (1983) p. 462.
20. Peter Van Inwagen, 'The Possibility of Resurrection', *International Journal for Philosophy of Religion*, IX (2) (1978) p. 119.
21. Derek Parfit, *Reasons and Persons* (Oxford: Oxford University Press, 1986) p.199f. I mention here only the most simple of the test cases involving teletransportation that Parfit discusses. Nor will I consider in this paper what I take to be the central theses of Part III of his book.
22. Hick, op. cit., p. 186.
23. Commenting on Paul's argument in I Corinthians 15:53, Tertullian says: 'When he says *this* corruptible and *this* mortal, he utters the words while touching the surface of his own body' (Tertullian, *On the Resurrection of the Flesh*, in Roberts and Donaldson (eds) *the Ante-Nicene Fathers*, III ([New York: Charles Scribner's Sons, 1899] L1).
24. Gundry makes this point convincingly (see op. cit., p. 186). See also Sider, op. cit., pp. 429–38, and Bruce Reichenbach, 'On Disembodied Resurrection Persons: A Reply', *Religious Studies* 18 (2) (1982) p. 227.
25. Augustine, op. cit., LXXXVIII. See also Augustine, *The City of God* (Grand Rapids Michigan: Wm. B. Eerdmans, 1956) V, XXII, p. 20.
26. Paul Badham, *Christian Beliefs about Life after Death* (London: MacMillian Press, 1976) p. 50. Despite my disagreement with him on this point, it must be admitted that in his book Badham does successfully rebut several unconvincing patristic arguments about bodily resurrection.
27. See, for example, Irenaeus, *Against Heresies*, in Roberts and Donaldson (eds), *The Ante-Nicene Fathers*, I (Grand Rapids, Michigan: Wm. B. Eerdmans, n.d.) V, III, 2. See also Tertullian, op. cit., XI.
28. See Flew's article on 'Immortality' in Paul Edwards (ed.) *The Encyclopedia of Philosophy* (New York: MacMillan, 1967), and the articles collected in Part III of Flew's *The Presumption of Atheism and Other Essays* (London: Elek/Pemberton, 1976).
29. See the articles collected in Bernard Williams, *Problems of the Self* (Cambridge: Cambridge University Press, 1973).
30. D. Z. Phillips, *Death and Immortality* (New York: St. Martin's Press, 1970).
31. Terence Penelhum, *Survival and Disembodied Existence* (New York: Humanities Press, 1970).
32. John Perry, *A Dialogue on Personal Identity and Immortality* (Indianapolis, Indiana: Hackett, 1978).
33. Geach, op. cit., pp. 17–29.
34. Among others, see Richard L. Purtill, 'The Intelligibility of Disembodied Survival', *Christian Scholar's Review*, V (1) (1975), and Paul Helm, 'A Theory of Disembodied Survival and Re-embodied Existence', *Religious Studies*, 14 (1) (1978). See Also Bruce Reichenbach, *Is Man the Phoenix?: A Study of Immortality* (Washington, DC: University Press of America, 1983).
35. Perry, op. cit., p. 3.
36. I will not try to answer Perry's circularity charge noted above because I believe Parfit has decisively done so via the notion that he calls quasi-memories, See op. cit., pp.220ff.
37. Geach, op. cit., pp. 23–8.
38. Roberts and Donaldson, op. cit., p. 295.
39. I would like to thank professors John Hick, Jim Hanink, Jerry Irish, Kai Nielsen, and Linda Zagzebski for their very helpful and incisive comments on earlier drafts of this paper.

SUGGESTED READING

DEFENCES OF PHYSICALISM

Heil, John (1992), *The Nature of True Minds*, Cambridge: Cambridge University Press.

Kim, Jaegwon (1996), *Philosophy of Mind*, Boulder, CO: Westview Press.

— (1998), *Mind in a Physical World*, Cambridge, MA: MIT Press.

Papineau, David (1993), *Philosophical Naturalism*, Oxford: Blackwell.

Searle, John (1992), *The Rediscovery of the Mind*, Cambridge, MA: MIT Press.

DEFENCES OF DUALISM

Cooper, John W. (1989), *Body, Soul, & Life Everlasting*, Grand Rapids, MI: Eerdmans.

Foster, John (1991), *The Immaterial Self*, London: Routledge.

Hart, W. D. (1988), *The Engines of the Soul*, Cambridge: Cambridge University Press.

Hasker, William (ed.) (1995), 'Christian Philosophy and the Mind-Body Problem', Theme Issue, *Faith and Philosophy*, 12 (October).

— (1999), *The Emergent Self*, Ithaca, NY: Cornell University Press.

Madell, Geoffrey (1988), *Mind & Materialism*, Edinburgh: Edinburgh University Press.

Moreland, J. P. and Scott B. Rae (2000), *Body & Soul*, Downer's Grove, IL: InterVarsity Press.

Robinson, Howard (1982), *Matter and Sense*, Cambridge: Cambridge University Press.

— (ed.) (1993), *Objections to Physicalism*, Oxford: Clarendon Press.

Smythies, John R. and John Beloff (eds) (1989), *The Case for Dualism*, Charlottesville: University Press of Virginia.

Swinburne, Richard (1997), *The Evolution of the Soul*, rev. edn, Oxford: Clarendon Press.

Taliafero, Charles (1994), *Consciousness and the Mind of God*, Cambridge: Cambridge University Press.

LIFE EVERLASTING

Davis, Stephen T. (ed.) (1989), *Death and Afterlife*, New York: St. Martin's Press.

Edwards, Paul (ed.) (1992), *Immortality*, New York: Macmillan.

Habermas, Gary and J. P. Moreland (1998), *Beyond Death*, Wheaton, IL: Crossway Books.

Hick, John H. (1976), *Death and Eternal Life*, San Francisco: Harper & Row.

PART VI
CHRISTIAN THEOLOGY

CHRISTIAN THEOLOGY: INTRODUCTION

Michael Murray

1. Philosophy and Christian Theology

In this section we turn our attention to recent work in contemporary philosophy that bears on distinctively theological claims. Can one make sense of God's taking on a human nature? Does the notion of eternal punishment for sin make sense? Is the practice of petitioning an all-good, all-knowing, perfectly benevolent God sensible? Some of these questions focus on claims made in a number of the Western theistic religious traditions, while others focus on claims distinctive to the Christian tradition. Although reflection on theological questions from a philosophical standpoint has gone on from within all three major Western theistic traditions (Judaism, Islam and Christianity) we shall, in this section, focus on the way in which recent philosophy of religion has been directed towards distinctively Christian claims.

In the history of Christian theology, philosophy has sometimes been seen as a natural complement to theological reflection, while at other times the advocates for the two disciplines have regarded them as mortal enemies. Some early Christian thinkers such as Tertullian were of the view that any intrusion of secular philosophical reason into theological reflection was out of order. Thus, even if certain theological claims seemed to fly in the face of the standards of reasoning defended by philosophers, the religious believer should not flinch. Other early Christian thinkers, such as St Augustine of Hippo, argued that philosophical reflection complemented theology, but only when these philosophical reflections were firmly grounded in a prior intellectual commitment to the underlying truth of the Christian faith. Thus, the legitimacy of philosophy was derived from the legitimacy of the underlying faith commitments.

Into the High Middle Ages, Augustine's views were widely defended. It was during this time, however, that St Thomas Aquinas described another model for the relationship between philosophy and theology. According to the Thomistic model, philosophy and theology are distinct enterprises. The primary difference between the two is their intellectual starting points. Philosophy takes as its data the deliverances of our natural mental faculties: what we see, hear, taste, touch and smell. These data can be accepted on the basis of the reliability of our natural faculties with respect to the natural world. In contrast, theology takes as its starting point the special revelations contained in the Bible. These data can be accepted on the basis of divine authority, in a way analogous to the way in which we accept, for example, the claims made by a physics professor about the basic facts of physics.

On this way of seeing the two disciplines, if one of the premises of an argument is known from revelation, the argument falls into the domain of theology; otherwise it falls into philosophy's domain. Since this way of thinking about philosophy and theology sharply demarcates the disciplines, it is possible in principle that the conclusions reached by one might be contradicted by the other. According to advocates of this model, however, any such conflict must be merely apparent. Since God both created the world which is accessible to philosophy and revealed the texts accessible to theologians, the claims yielded by one cannot conflict with the claims yielded by another unless the philosopher or theologian has made some prior error.

Since the deliverances of the two disciplines must then coincide, philosophy can be put to the service of theology (and perhaps vice versa). How might philosophy play this complementary role? First, philosophical reasoning might persuade some who do not accept the authority of purported divine revelation of the claims contained in religious texts. Thus, an atheist who is unwilling to accept the authority of religious texts might come to belief that God exists on the basis of purely philosophical arguments. Second, distinctively philosophical techniques might be brought to bear in helping the theologian clear up imprecise or ambiguous theological claims. Thus, theology might provide us with information sufficient to conclude that Jesus Christ was a single person with two natures, one human and one divine, but leave us in the dark about exactly how this relationship between divine and human natures is to be understood. The philosopher can provide some assistance here, since, among other things, he or she can help the theologian discern which models are, for example, logically inconsistent and thus not even candidates for understanding the relationship of divine and human natures in Christ.

For most of the twentieth century, English language philosophy went on without much interaction with theology at all. While there are a number of complex reasons for this divorce, two are especially important. The first is that atheism was the predominant opinion among English language philosophers throughout much of that century. The second is that a great deal of academic theology moved away from defending the claims of orthodox Christian theism in traditional ways, often seeking devices for re-interpreting these claims in ways congenial to contemporary modes of thought which often ran contrary to the methods employed in analytic philosophy.

In the last twenty years, however, the number of philosophers who are theists has increased dramatically. These theistically inclined philosophers soon began returning to many of the traditional claims of orthodox Christianity and applying the tools of philosophy in ways that are somewhat more eclectic than those described in the Augustinian or Thomistic models described above. In keeping with the recent academic trend, contemporary philosophers of religion have been unwilling to maintain hard and fast distinctions between the two disciplines. As a result, it is often difficult in reading recent work to distinguish what the philosophers are doing from what the theologians of past centuries regarded as strictly within the theological domain. However, like theologians of the medieval period, much recent work in philosophy of religion seems to fall into one of two categories. The first category includes attempts to demonstrate the truth of religious claims by appeal to evidence available apart from purported divine revelations. This is the sort of work represented in Parts 2 and 4 of this book. The second category includes attempts to demonstrate the consistency and plausibility of theological claims using philosophical techniques. This sort of work is represented in Part 3 and the current section of the book.

2. TRINITY

From the beginning Christians have affirmed the claim that there is one God and that three persons are God: God the Father, God the Son and God the Holy Spirit. In AD 675, the Council of Toledo framed this pair of claims as follows:

> Although we profess three persons we do not profess three substances but *one substance* and three persons . . . If we are asked about the individual Person, we must answer that he is God. Therefore, we may say God the Father, God the Son, and God the Holy Spirit; but they are not three Gods, he is one God . . . Each single Person is wholly God in himself and . . . all three persons together are one God.

Such formulations set forth the Christian doctrine of the Trinity. Cornelius Plantinga, Jr., reflecting on the Council of Toledo's profession, remarks that it 'possesses great puzzling power'.[1] No doubt this is an understatement. The Christian doctrine is puzzling, and this has led some of Christianity's critics to advance the claim that it is, in fact, incoherent.

Perhaps the initial puzzling power of the doctrine of the Trinity is not immediately obvious. After all, someone might think that one thing, Fred, can be 'many things' all at the same time, for example, a butcher, a baker and a candlestick maker. So why can't God be Father, Son and Holy Spirit all at the same time? Likewise, multiple distinct things can all be 'one thing' at the same time. Thus, each member of the Baltimore Orioles baseball team can be Orioles taken individually, as well as 'the Orioles' taken collectively. One might then think that defenders of the Trinity might be able to construct models out of such examples that would preserve the logical coherence of the doctrine. But things will not be quite that easy. To see why, we can take a brief detour and then come back to the two examples above.

Traditional Christian theologians have held that however the doctrine of the Trinity is understood, there are two extreme positions that are to be ruled out. These positions are modalism and tritheism. According to modalism, God is one single entity, object, or substance, and each person of the Trinity is simply a mode or a 'way in which the one divine substance manifests itself'. This view has been rejected because it seems to sacrifice the distinctness of the divine persons in order to maintain the notion of divine unity. According to tritheism, in contrast, the divine persons are each distinct individual persons which are so closely related that they together count as a single thing in some fashion. This view has been rejected for the opposite reason, namely, it preserves the distinctness of persons without maintaining any robust sense of the 'oneness' of God.

One can now see why the 'butcher, baker, candlestick maker' and the 'Orioles' examples will not help us in providing a model for the Trinity. The first, like modalism, leans too heavily towards oneness at the expense of the distinctness of the three persons. It holds, that is, that there is really only one Fred, but that Fred can manifest himself in different ways by carrying out three different tasks. The second, like tritheism, leans too far in the opposite direction. On this example, the individual Orioles only form the 'single team' because of certain agreements they have made to act cooperatively on the baseball team. There is no genuine, organic unity here.

Nonetheless, most models of the Trinity that have been proposed and defended have leaned in modalist or tritheistic directions. In order to help sort out which sorts of models can be regarded as plausible, we need first to get clear about just what the Christian means to affirm in confessing the existence of three persons and one God. What is 'a person' according to the doctrine, and what is 'a God'? One can easily see some initial difficulties in even these questions. Even if we can come up with a single coherent description of God in the way sketched out in Part 3 of this book, we are still left with the ambiguous notion of person. Sometimes we use the word person in a metaphysical sense, to refer to an individual, rational substance. Other times we use it in a psychological sense to refer to a 'centre of consciousness or rational awareness'. In other cases we might have in mind a functional notion of person, according to which a person is whatever sort of thing is capable of entering into certain sorts of relationships, such as love, friendship and so forth. Or we might use 'person' in a moral or forensic sense, according to which a person is a subject of moral accountability, praise, or blame. And there are others.

Since Christians claim that the doctrine of Trinity is discovered through divine revelation, perhaps the relevant conception of person should be drawn from revealed texts. Unfortunately, the Bible itself does not seem to narrow down the alternatives to a single candidate. As a result, there is a good deal of remaining latitude in constructing a model for the Trinity.

Recent defences of orthodox conceptions of the Trinity understand the notion in a way that highlights the centrality of persons as distinct centres of rational, conscious and morally significant volitional activity. Most have concluded that this conception of personhood is incompatible with regarding the three divine persons as somehow mere aspects or modes of presentation of an underlying singular entity. As a result, these recent defences have leaned in the direction of regarding the divine persons as distinct entities whose unity arises in virtue of certain necessary relations that exist among them. In this way, these models lean more in the tritheistic direction. Still, the necessary relations that these models attribute to the divine persons unify them in special and unique ways.

In the model set out by Swinburne in the following essay, Swinburne claims that each of the three divine persons has all of the essential characteristics of divinity: omniscience, omnipotence, omnipresence, moral perfection and so forth. He further claims that the persons have necessarily harmonious wills, so that their volitions never come into conflict, and that there is a perfectly loving relation that also necessarily obtains among them. Further, this view is compatible with traditional claims of dependence relations among members of the Trinity. Traditional formulations of the doctrine hold that the Father generates the Son and that Father and Son jointly give rise to (or *spirate*, literally 'breathe forth') the Holy Spirit. Such relations are possible as long as one causes the other in such a way that the causing relation has always obtained, and it is impossible for the relation not to obtain.

On this sort of view, there is one God because the community of divine persons is so closely inter-connected that though they are three distinct persons they nonetheless count as a single entity in another respect. For if we were to consider a set of three human persons, for example, who exhibited these characteristics of necessary unity, volitional harmony and love, it is hard to regard them as distinct in the way we do ordinary persons. And that is, of course, just what the doctrine aims to put forth.

Perhaps this view seems to lean too strongly in the tritheistic direction. How should the social Trinitarian respond to this worry? One way, which I can only hint at here, is to begin to focus our attention on exactly what is required in order for many 'things' to jointly constitute another single 'thing'. My (one) body is composed of (many) atoms. My (one) car is composed of (many) parts. In order to assess whether or not social Trinitarianism is viciously tritheistic, we need to ask what principles govern the relationship between parts and wholes generally. We know many atoms can make a single body and many ingredients can make a single cake. Can many persons constitute a single divine entity? One thing is sure: the answer is not an obvious 'no'. And this, perhaps, leaves the door open for the social Trinitarian to make the case that divine unity is not lost on his view after all. Saving such unity, however, will require more metaphysical work than we can do here.

3. INCARNATION

The doctrine of the Incarnation concerns Jesus Christ, the second person of the Trinty, and claims concerning him that at a time roughly two thousand years in the past he took on himself a fully human nature in addition to his divine nature. As a result, he was one person in full possession of two distinct natures, one human and one divine. The Council of Chalcedon in 451 put forth the canonical statement of the doctrine as follows:

> We confess one and the same our Lord Jesus Christ . . . the same perfect in Godhead, the same in perfect manhood, truly God and truly man . . . acknowledged in two natures without confusion, without change, without division, without separation – the difference of natures being by no means taken away because of the union, but rather the distinctive character of each nature being preserved, and combining into one person and hypostasis – not divided or separated into two persons, but one and the same Son and only begotten God, Word, Lord Jesus Christ.

Critics have held this doctrine to be 'impossible, self-contradictory, incoherent, absurd, and unintelligible'. The central difficulty for the doctrine is that it seems to attribute to one person characteristics that are not logically compatible. Thus, it seems on the one hand that human beings are necessarily created, finite, not-omnipresent, not-omniscient, not-omnipotent and so forth. On the other hand, divine beings are essentially the opposite of all those things. Thus, one person could bear both natures, human and divine, only if such a person could be both finite and not-finite, created and un-created, and so forth. And this is surely impossible.

Two main strategies have been pursued in an attempt to resolve this apparent paradox. The first is the kenotic strategy. The kenotic view finds its motivation in a New Testament passage which claims that Jesus

> being in very nature God, did not regard equality with God something to be grasped, but made himself nothing, taking the very nature of a servant, being made in human likeness. And being found in appearance as a man, he humbled himself and became obedient to death. (Phil. 2:6–8)

According to this view, in becoming incarnate, God the Son voluntarily and temporarily laid aside some of his divine attributes in order to take on a human nature and thus his earthly mission.

The main difficulty with this basic version of the kenotic view is that it entails that a thing can lay aside properties essential for its being a member of a certain kind and still remain a member of that kind. In other words, it allows that God the Son could (temporarily) be non-omnipotent, non-omniscient and so forth, and still be God. But if those attributes are essential to divinity, that is, essential for something's being counted as God, then this solution is simply mistaken. Some have offered more refined versions of the kenotic theory, arguing that the basic view mischaracterises the divine attributes. Rather, God's properties should be characterised as: omniscient-unless-incarnate, omnipotent-unless-incarnate and so forth. Thus, when the powers of omnipotence are laid aside at the incarnation, Jesus can be fully human while retaining these divine attributes without contradiction.

The other main strategy, developed recently by the philosopher Thomas V. Morris, is the 'two minds view'. This view, explained in the selection below, unfolds in two steps, one defensive, the other constructive. First, Morris claims that the incoherence charge against the incarnation rests on a mistake. The critic assumes that, for example, humans are essentially non-omniscient. But what are the grounds for this assertion? Unless we think that we have some special direct insight into the essential properties of human nature, our grounds are that all of the human beings we have encountered have that property. But this merely suffices to show that the property is common to humans, not that it is essential. As Morris points out, it may be universally true that all human beings, for example, were born within ten miles of the surface of the earth, but this does not mean that this is an essential property of human beings. An offspring of human parents born on the international space station would still be human. If this is right, the defender of the incarnation can reject the critic's characterisation of human nature, and thereby eliminate the conflict between divine attributes and human nature so characterised.

This merely provides a way to fend off the critic, however, without supplying any positive model for how the incarnation should be understood. In the second step, then, Morris proposes that we think about the incarnation as the realisation of one person with two minds: a human mind and a divine mind. If possession of a human mind and body is sufficient for something's being a human, then 'merging' the divine mind with a human mind and conjoining both to a human body will yield one person with two natures. During his earthly life, Morris proposes, Jesus Christ had two minds, with consciousness centred in the human mind. This human mind had partial access to the contents of the divine mind, while God the Son's divine mind had full access to the corresponding human mind.

The chief difficulty the view faces is the coherence of holding that a single person can possess two distinct minds. Does this view propose an Incarnate

Christ with multiple personality disorder? Morris claims that this objection lacks merit. In fact, contemporary psychology seems to provide resources which support the viability of such a model. As Morris points out elsewhere, the human mind is typically characterised as a system of somewhat autonomous subsystems. The normal human mind, for example, includes the workings of the conscious mind, the seat of awareness and the unconscious mind. Morris proposes that similar sorts of relations can be supposed to obtain between the divine and human mind of Christ.

4. HELL

According to traditional Christian doctrine, each human being sins and consequently separates himself or herself from God. As a result of this separation, human beings are naturally destined to spend their eternal existence separated from God in hell. Some regard hell as a place of physical suffering. Others have held it to be a place of psychological suffering induced because of the horrible recognition that one is eternally separated from God due to one's wrongdoing. However, it is possible, on the Christian view, for the natural consequences of sin to be reversed, allowing one to spend eternity in beatific union with God. On the Christian view, that way is provided by Christ who became incarnate, suffered, died and was resurrected. These activities of Christ are sufficient to purge the natural consequences of sin for all who repent of their sin and trust in Christ's redemptive work.

There are a number of different variants on this general picture. One of the key variables concerns how we understand the natural consequences of sin, and specifically how and why they result in eternal separation from God. This is important, since critics of the traditional doctrine often claim that there is no plausible way to understand the claim that earthly sins can result in or merit eternal separation from God. A second key variable concerns exactly what it is believed Christ's incarnation, death and resurrection accomplish. How can it be that these historical events have any impact on the consequences of the sins of others? Some have argued that there is no way in which the consequences of the sins of one person can be remedied by the activities of another and that as a result the Christian story of redemption cannot be sustained. The final variable concerns the ways in which sinful human beings are able to avail themselves of Christ's saving work. Some have held that redemption can only be secured by coming to hold very specific beliefs – beliefs, in fact, that could only be acquired through direct or indirect contact with the content of Christian revelation. This seems to rule out a number of people, and some have claimed that such exclusion is unfair or unloving. Others have held that redemption can be secured in other ways, such as appropriate responsiveness to the information about God available to one, or by opportunities to repent and believe immediately after the end of one's earthly life.

In the essay below, Michael Murray explores the plausibility of these variants. Murray argues that there are two main models that are available for explaining how sin separates human creatures from God and how the natural effects of sin are reversed by Christ's life, death and resurrection. On the first model, human sin incurs a debt towards God that can only be paid by the sacrifice of a perfect offering. That offering, on this model, is exhibited in Christ's passion. On the second model, the aim of the human earthly life is to cultivate the image of God impressed on human beings at creation. Sin, however, leads us to form character traits which are inconsistent with God-likeness, which traits further prevent one from orienting one's life toward God all on one's own. As a result, an infusion of divine grace is necessary to allow one to become re-oriented in this way.

Murray argues that the Christian can plausibly accept both models. The first model seems to have support in Christian revelation and gives a clear explanation of the role of Christ's death and resurrection in the scheme of salvation. However, the first model leaves a number of questions unanswered. For example, it does not tell us why sin and its effects cannot simply be remitted by God. It also leaves few resources for explaining the traditional claim that the earthly life represents humanity's only opportunity to turn to God for redemption. The second model, however, does explain these features. Since sinfulness brings one to have a fully formed self-oriented character, God cannot simply redeem the creature without taking away creaturely freedom and its meaningfulness. Further, since we may reach a time after which moral reform is no longer possible in a way consistent with human freedom, it may be that no one after the course of his or her earthly life would freely choose to turn to God. Still, the second model does not have an obvious explanation of the necessity of Christ's death and resurrection. Murray contends that the two views each have significant explanatory power and are complementary. As a result, he argues that the Christian should accept both models.

5. ATONEMENT

Closely related to the Christian doctrine of postmortem punishment is the doctrine of the atonement. As noted above, Christians hold that sin separates human creatures from God, and that reconciliation can occur in virtue of something that happens through the incarnation, life, death and resurrection of Jesus Christ. But how are these claims of separation and reconciliation to be understood? The answer to these questions makes up the doctrine of atonement. Throughout the history of Christian theology, a variety of models has been proposed. Most of these models fall into one of four types.[2]

Ransom theories contend that sin has rendered humans enslaved to the Devil. In order to free His beloved creatures from this enslavement God was required to pay a ransom, and the price was the death of His sinless incarnate Son.

Penal substitution models contend that through sin humans have incurred a moral debt which needs to be paid. These views hold that the price to be paid is spiritual death and separation from God. No one man can pay the debt of any other since all men have sinned equally. Thus, God chose to send His incarnate Son, free from original or committed sin, to die on behalf of others, and so satisfy their debt.

Sacrifice models are similar to substitution models, but differ in that they do not think that any moral debt of human creatures can be transferred and satisfied by another. Sacrifice theories acknowledge that wrongdoers incur an obligation to 'make things right' with the person wronged. Sometimes this means making restitution. Other times it means undertaking acts of penance which demonstrate the wrongdoer's genuine remorse. Thus, if I, in a fit of anger, throw a brick through the window of your house, I might come to seek forgiveness. In doing so I agree to fix the broken window (restitution) but might also do something more, such as bring you a gift as way of demonstrating my genuine remorse. This latter is the act of penance. However, sometimes restitution and suitable penance cannot be carried out by the wrongdoer himself because restitution or suitable penance is beyond his means. In the case of human sinfulness towards God, this is exactly the case. As a result, God sent Christ to earth, where Christ willingly offered his life as a restitution and penance for the sin of the world. Thus, although human sinful creatures cannot make restitution or penance for their wrongdoing on their own, they can, in their repentance, offer up to God the sacrifice of Christ which was made on their behalf.

Finally, moral exemplar theories hold that the atonement is secured by moral reform of the sinner. But such moral reform was not fully possible without someone to set the moral example for fallen creatures. Christ became incarnate, on these theories, in order to set this example and thus provide a necessary condition for moral reform and thus restoration of the relationship between creature and Creator.

Ransom theories have no defenders in the recent literature. While each of the remaining theories has defenders, each faces certain key difficulties as well. Substitution theories, for example, require a few central controversial claims. For one, these theories seem to entail that a person can incur an infinite moral debt for a finite amount of earthly wrongdoing. Second, they entail that the moral debt in question cannot simply be forgiven by God, but that it must be settled by full payment. Some have argued that this entails that God does not forgive sin at all. Forgiveness involves remitting some of the payment owed. On these theories, however, the debt is paid in full. Most controversial, however, is the claim that moral debts of the sort in question here are transferable. That is, on this view it seems that the punishment of one can be fairly borne by another. While this might be acceptable in certain cases where monetary fines are involved, many think that it cannot apply to specifically moral debts.

Sacrifice theories do not encounter these difficulties. Instead they, like moral exemplar theories, face difficulties of two main sorts. First, both views seem unable to account for the biblical emphasis on the necessity of Christ's passion to remedy the problems brought forth by sin. It is hard to see why Christ's passion plays any essential role in establishing him as moral exemplar. Further, it is hard to see why Christ's death would provide a suitable sacrifice. Why would it not suffice for Christ to dwell among us and live a perfect human life, resisting all earthly temptation? Second, both views seem unable to account for the necessity of the horrible nature of Christ's death on the cross. The reason for this is that both hold that God either could or does forgive the sin of creatures without such grave sacrifices being offered. As a result, one is left to wonder why a solution which does not involve such horrific suffering is preferred to simple forgiveness. This is especially problematic for the moral exemplar theories, which lay almost exclusive emphasis on the importance of Christ's moral example during his life and on the centrality of creaturely moral reform for reconciliation with God.

Defences of substitution models seem to be on the wane in recent literature, with sacrifice and exemplar theories becoming more widely defended. Can the substitution model overcome the difficulties posed for it above? In the selection below, Stephen Porter argues that it can. Porter defends what he calls a 'modified penal substitution theory' according to which punishment is a fitting response to human sin, and yet also such that it might nonetheless be fairly borne by a surrogate, in this case, the perfect Christ. Porter admits that our moral intuitions generally incline us to view punishment of a surrogate as a bad thing, and that some case needs to be made for its permissibility in this instance. In run of the mill cases of punishment, the good reasons for punishment (such as reform of the wrongdoer, making reparation, deterrence and so forth) usually weigh in favor of not transferring the punishment to a surrogate. But here, Porter argues, the good reasons for punishing human sinners are not undercut, and that, in fact, there are outweighing reasons for allowing Christ to bear the punishment due human sinners.

Specifically, Porter claims that the goods that come from God's punishment of sin (namely, reparation, manifesting an objective correction to distorted human values and moral education/reform) justify the punishment. What is more, Porter claims, these ends are more fittingly served through the suffering of Christ on our behalf. The reasons for this are twofold. First, were we to bear the punishment directly, it might further serve to alienate us from God. Second, the gravity of human sin against an infinite God cannot be suitably expressed by punishment of merely finite humans. Punishment of an infinite God–man better expresses the seriousness of sin.

In Porter's account we have an attempt to respond to the three objections raised earlier against substitution views. First, the (infinite) severity of the punishment is required in order to express adequately the gravity of human sin against an infinite and perfect God. Concerning the second objection (namely, that paying the full price of sin means that there is no forgiveness on

God's part), Porter can reply that the objection is simply misguided. God can forgive without any punishment being exacted. However, certain goods arise as a result of punishment being meted out, and God thus metes out punishment suitable for securing those goods. The third difficulty (i.e., the non-transferrability of moral debts) initially seemed to be the most formidable of the three. Porter argues, however, that as long as (1) offender, offended, and surrogate are willing participants, and (2) the goods of punishing can be secured through the punishment of the surrogate, then substitution is permissible, perhaps even preferable. The reason it is permissible, however, is not because the moral debt is 'transferred' from sinner to Christ (as the objection assumes) but simply because punishing wrong is a good and punishing a surrogate can equally or better serve the aims of punishing.

6. PRAYER

The practice of petitionary prayer is widespread among adherents of the Western theistic traditions, yet there is something deeply puzzling about this practice. Why, one might wonder, would an all-good, all-knowing and all-powerful God want ignorant, weak and sinful human beings to petition Him, and why would such a being be moved to act in the light of such petitions? After all, if God were perfectly good, He would want to provide us with any good that would improve our true well-being and further would deny us anything that would detract from our well-being. Thus, if one prays for something that it would be truly good to have, a perfectly good God would have already intended to give that good thing, whether it was prayed for or not. Likewise, if the thing prayed for were not good for us, God would not give it to us regardless.

These worries about petitionary prayer are made even more difficult when one considers that the Christian practice of petitionary prayer enjoins believers not simply to pray for their needs but to pray for them repeatedly, and to pray for these needs together with others. Even if there are reasons that move God to respond to creaturely petitions, why would creatures need to pray repeatedly or in conjunction with others?

Various authors have addressed these and other related concerns. In the essay included below, Eleonore Stump argues that petitionary prayer furthers the aim of securing friendship between God and creatures. If God were simply to lavish all possible goods on creatures, then He would run the risk either of spoiling the creature and making him or her indulgent, or of overwhelming the creature thus making friendship impossible.

Some philosophers have proposed other reasons for the practice of petitionary prayer. Among them is that petitionary prayer serves as a hedge against idolatry. Biblical texts consistently warn that as creatures begin to see themselves as independent and self-sufficient, they will begin to think of themselves as the source of their well-being. As a result, one might surmise that petitionary prayer is a way to prevent creatures from viewing themselves or other aspects of nature as primarily responsible for their welfare, thus preventing a pernicious form of idolatry. Second, petitionary prayer sometimes permits creatures to learn more about the nature and will of God. By petitioning God for certain goods and seeing whether or not such goods are supplied or not, we can begin to learn about God's will. In this way, human petition and divine response can aid in promoting spiritual maturity in a way analogous to parents promoting maturity in their earthly children by granting or refusing to grant their requests.

As noted, however, there are further challenges to the practice of petitionary prayer that spring from the fact that Christians are commanded to enjoin others at times to petition God on their behalf. What could explain such an odd practice? One of my more cynical students once said that such a practice seemed either to make the economy of divine blessing dependent on popular vote or to make God into a divine vending machine, dispensing goodies if enough 'coins' are inserted. Can the theist offer any more satisfying explanation for cooperative petitionary prayer than this? Some have argued that perhaps the aim of this sort of petitionary prayer is the development of close interpersonal relationships among members of the Christian community. If I know that God has made granting some of my petitions dependent on the intercession of others, two things will result, each of which can serve to promote such relationships. First, I shall be inclined to share with other members of the community my deepest concerns and fears. Second, I shall begin to see other members of the community as possessing the means to give me genuine assistance in the meeting of my needs, even if meeting them is beyond their individual resources. The reason for this is that I recognise that by petitioning God they help bring about the meeting of those needs. If something like this model is correct, we have an explanation of why God might require such cooperative petitions and why He might make certain provisions hang on such petitions being offered.

NOTES

1. 'Social Trinity and Tritheism', in Ronald J. Feenstra and Cornelius Plantinga, Jr. (eds), *Trinity, Incarnation, and Atonement* (Notre Dame: University of Notre Dame Press, 1989), p. 21.
2. The reader should note that the classification of atonement theory types I offer here is somewhat different than that offered by Stephen Porter in the selection on atonement that follows.

TRINITY
6.1

'A DEFENSE OF THE DOCTRINE OF THE TRINITY'

Richard Swinburne

[. . .]

Could There be More than One Divine Individual?

[. . .]

A divine individual who exists of ontological necessity would be such that there is no cause active or permissive of his existence at any time. But, if he is the creator and sustainer of any universe there may be, any other substance can only exist if he is, at least in part, the cause of its existence. Hence there cannot be, beside an ontologically necessary divine being, another such.

But what if the necessity of a divine individual is understood as metaphysical necessity?

. . . Now there certainly could be two or more individuals who were necessarily perfectly free, and omniscient.

The problem arises with omnipotence. Could there be two omnipotent individuals who existed of metaphysical necessity (i.e. everlastingly, and uncaused or inevitably caused by a backwardly everlasting uncaused substance)?

An omniscient and perfectly free individual will always be perfectly good.

Richard Swinburne, 'A Defense of the Doctrine of the Trinity', from 'The Trinity', *The Christian God* (New York: Clarendon Press, 1994), pp. 170–91.

I have spelled this out earlier as follows. I understand all the acts which an individual can do simultaneously as one possible act available to such an individual. Then a perfectly good individual will act as follows. He will do no bad act, and where there is a unique best act he will do it. Where there are equal best acts he will do one of them; and where there is a best kind of act, but no best of the kind but rather an infinite number of acts each less good than another act, he will do one act of that kind. Otherwise his perfect goodness does not restrict how he will act. I called the acts that such an individual does and has to do in virtue of his perfect goodness—for instance, the best act in the circumstances if there is one—acts of essence; and the acts which he does but does not have to do, despite his perfect goodness, acts of will. These latter are acts between which he chooses, and between which no balance of reason dictates how he will choose. A divine individual's compatibilist power is his omnipotence, the power to do anything logically possible, if he so chooses; his absolute power is the power to choose and do, and that is limited not merely by logical possibility but by perfect goodness.

So could there be two omnipotent individuals having also the previously cited divine properties? An initial gut reaction is 'No'. Would not the omnipotence of one such individual be subject to frustration by the other individual and so not be omnipotence? Not in general—for the omnipotence of such an individual, being also perfectly good, is only the power to do good actions within ranges of the kind available to a perfectly good being. Each individual would be bringing about many good states, within himself, in relation to the other individual, and creating and sustaining without. Since each would recognize the other as having the divine properties, including perfect goodness, it is plausible to suppose that each would recognize a duty not to prevent or frustrate the acts of the other, to use his omnipotence to forward them rather than frustrate them. If the second individual creates a universe which the first individual by himself would not have chosen to create, there would be wrong in the first individual attempting to prevent or frustrate this creative work; on the contrary, it would be good that he should give it his backing.

The only possibility of conflict between the acts of individuals with the above properties would arise where each tried to do an act compatible with his perfect goodness but incompatible with the act which the other was trying simultaneously to do. Thus, it might be an equally good event that Abraham be called by a divine individual to settle in Iraq as that he be called to settle in Iran, and thus there might be before both divine individuals two equally good possible acts. One might try to perform the one, and the other the other. Or (if we call the present direction of revolution of the Earth round the Sun clockwise) it might be equally good that the Earth revolve anticlockwise as that it revolve clockwise, and thus again there might be before both divine individuals two equally good possible acts of bringing about these states of affairs. One might choose the one and the other the other. There could not be two divine individuals unless there was some mechanism to prevent inter-ference and the mechanism could not limit their power in the compatibilist sense, only in the absolute sense (by making it no longer good to do acts of a certain sort). It could do that only by there being something which made it a bad thing for each to act in an area where the other was operative, for instance, an agreement between them not to do so. But how are the lines of distribution of the proper exercise of power to be drawn up? By one divine individual? But there is nothing to guarantee that at the moment at which he draws up a proposal for distributing power, the other divine individual might not draw up a different proposal; and, even with the best will in the world, only luck could prevent an actual collision of wills. (Compare the situation where two people are approaching each other along a pavement, and each tries to move to that side of the pavement where he guesses the other will not go; they may or may not collide.) Only if one lays down what the rules are, and his decision is accepted because he has the authority to lay down the rules, will the collision necessarily be avoided. But a difference in authority would have to arise from some other difference of status between the divine individuals; in some way one would have to be the source of being of the other. And for other reasons it surely must be that if there are two divine individuals, one is the ultimate source of being.

[. . .]

If there can be more than one divine individual, one divine individual can derive his existence from another divine individual, so long as the derivation is inevitable. For each of two divine individuals G_1 and G_2 it can be the case that there is no cause of it existing at any time while it exists, neither active cause nor permissive cause, except (directly or indirectly) an uncaused and back-wardly everlasting substance, namely a divine individual, who causes his existence inevitably in virtue of his properties. If G_1 inevitably in virtue of his properties throughout some first (beginningless) period of time actively causes G_2 to exist, and thereafter permissively causes (i.e. permits) the continued existence of G_2 while G_2 is such that G_1 only exists at each period of time which has a beginning because G_2 permits G_1 to exist, then both would be metaphysically necessary—once existent, they inevitably always exist, and there is no time at which they do not exist. The eternal (active and then permissive) bringing about of G_2 by G_1 would be an act of essence by G_1, just as the (permissive) bringing about of G_1 by G_2 would be an act of essence by G_2, and the former would provide a mechanism by which to ensure that there was no conflict of action between them. For G_1 would prescribe what the mechanism was. The same will hold in the simpler case with which I will work henceforward, that G_1 is everlastingly (inevitably in virtue of his properties) the active cause of G_2; while G_2 is for every period of time which has a beginning (inevitably in virtue of his properties) the permissive cause of G_1.

There are many different ways in which unity of action can be secured among individuals who might otherwise impede each other's efforts. One of them could take all the decisions and the others simply execute those decisions. Another way is to have a vote on every issue and for each then to carry out the result of the vote. A third way is to have a division of functions. One individual takes decisions on certain kinds of issues, and the others support him in these. Another individual takes decisions on other issues, and the others support him in those, and so on. Which would be the best way for divine individuals to secure unity of action, to determine a choice between alternatives equally available to a perfectly good individual? The first way would seem an imperfect way of sharing power between divine individuals, and so one which G_1 would not adopt. The second way, taken strictly, is not a possible way when there are only two individuals, for, unless chance produces a prior coincidence of their views, votes will always be tied. (Marriage cannot be a democracy.) And even where there are more than two individuals, but many alternative actions (such that there is no overriding reason for doing one rather than another), is there any reason to suppose that there will often be a majority in favour of one course of action? Only the third way would seem a viable way of securing unity of action in shared power among divine individuals.

Such unity of action could be secured if the first individual solemnly vows to the second individual in causing his existence that he will not initiate any act (of will) in a certain sphere of activity that he allocates to him, while at the same time the first individual requests the second individual not to initiate any such act outside that sphere. The vow of the first individual would create an obligation on him not to initiate any act (of will) within the second individual's allocated sphere of activity. So, although the first divine individual retains his omnipotence, it is, as before, limited by his inability to do other than what is perfectly good, and in virtue of his promise this limitation will ensure that he does not frustrate the actions of the second divine individual. Conversely, although all power is given to the second individual, it comes with a request that it should not be exercised in a certain way. The overall goodness of conformity to that request (not to conform would be not to conform to a reasonable request from the source of his being and power) will ensure that, although omnipotent, the second individual cannot frustrate any action of the first individual. The sharing of divinity could (logically) only occur subject to some restriction preventing mutual impediment of action. I have presented a highly fallible human judgement as to what the best such mechanism (and so the one which would be adopted) would be.

Each of the postulated divine individuals would be omnipotent in the sense that each could at any period of time do anything logically possible—for example, bring it about that the Earth moves round the Sun in a clockwise direction. But the omnipotence of each individual is limited by his perfect goodness, and if one individual has promised the other individual that he will not perform actions (when there is not a unique best action) in this area (e.g.

the area of movements of heavenly bodies), then his perfect goodness limits his omnipotence so that he does not do such an act. Thus each of two individuals with the earlier divine properties can be omnipotent.

[. . .]

So there can be more than one divine individual if it is necessary that the first divine individual brings about the existence of a second divine individual. It is possible that there be more than one divine individual only if it is necessary that there be more than one divine individual. But since nothing affects how a divine individual acts except reason, this can only be if the first divine individual has an overriding reason to bring about the existence of a second individual, that is, he brings this about as an act of essence.

I have talked only of a second divine individual. But similar arguments will obviously show that there can be a third divine individual only if it is necessary that there be a third divine individual, and that will be only if the first divine individual, or the second individual, or both together, have overriding reason for bringing about (everlastingly, or for an initial beginningless period) the third individual. If there is such overriding reason, then one way in which this could come about is if the first divine individual in bringing about the second individual requests him to confine his acts of will to a narrower field of activity, and one or the other or both together then bring about the existence of the third divine individual, with both divine individuals undertaking not to initiate acts of will in a certain sphere and requesting the third individual to confine his acts of will to that sphere. Such requests and undertakings would again limit the absolute power of each individual, but not the compatibilist power.

[. . .]

Is there overriding reason for a first divine individual to bring about a second or third or fourth such? I believe that there is overriding reason for a first divine individual to bring about a second divine individual and with him to bring about a third divine individual, but no reason to go further. If the Christian religion has helped us, Christians and non-Christians, to see any-thing about what is worthwhile, it has helped us to see that love is a supreme good. Love involves sharing, giving to the other what of one's own is good for him and receiving from the other what of his is good for one; and love involves co-operating with another to benefit third parties. This latter is crucial for worthwhile love. There would be something deeply unsatisfactory (even if for inadequate humans sometimes unavoidable) about a marriage in which the parties were concerned solely with each other and did not use their mutual love to bring forth good to others, for example by begetting, nourishing, and educating children, but possibly in other ways instead. Love must share and love must co-operate in sharing. The best love would share all that it had. A divine individual would see that for him too a best kind of action would be to share and to co-operate in sharing. Now a first divine individual is such that but for his choice there would be none other with whom to share. So the love of a first divine individual G_1 would be manifested first in bringing about another divine individual G_2 with whom to share his life, and the love of G_1 or G_2 would be manifested in bringing about another divine individual G_3 with whom G_1 and G_2 co-operatively could share their lives. G_2 and G_3 would then (i.e. for every period of time which had a beginning) co-operate in allowing G_1 to continue in being, for, but for their action, there would be no G_1. But their action would be an inevitable action, an act of essence; the power not to keep G_1 in being would be only compatibilist power, not absolute power. (The love of the first and second individuals might be manifested in an initial active causing and thereafter permissive causing, or in an everlasting active causing. The same consequences of everlasting mutually sustaining coexistence of divine individuals follow on either supposition.) All three would go on to co-operate further in backing (i.e. putting their causal power behind) the activities of each other in their respective spheres of activity.

If divine individuals can thus multiply, why should not the process continue further? The reason why it was an overall good that the first divine individual should bring about the second was that otherwise there would be none with whom to share totally; and the reason why it was an overall good that the first and second divine individuals should bring about a third was that otherwise there would be no one with whom to co-operate in sharing totally. But that argument does not provide a reason for any more bringing about.

[. . .]

I conclude (tentatively) that necessarily if there is at least one divine individual, and if it is logically possible that there be more than one divine individual, then there are three and only three divine individuals. The logical possibility seems to exist if there exists one divine individual with metaphysical but not ontological necessity, and if divine individuals lack thisness. Otherwise there is no possibility of there being more than one divine individual. I have presented a priori arguments why one might expect a divine individual to have only metaphysical necessity and to lack thisness, but those arguments can hardly be regarded as other than balance of probability arguments.

THE TRADITIONAL DOCTRINE

[. . .]

This doctrine involves the claim that there is only one God, but three divine individuals, each of whom is God; and whether that follows from my account depends on how 'there is only one God' and 'each divine individual is God' are to be understood. If 'there is only one God' meant 'there is only one divine individual', then the doctrine of the Trinity would be manifestly self-contradictory. So clearly Church councils in affirming both must have understood 'there is only one God' in a somewhat subtler sense—since no person and no Council affirming something which they intend to be taken with utter seriousness can be read as affirming an *evident* contradiction. What in denying tritheism, the view that there are three Gods, were Councils ruling out? I suggest that they were denying that there were three *independent* divine beings, any of which could exist without the other; or which could act independently of each other.

On the account which I have given, the three divine individuals taken together would form a collective source of the being of all other things; the members would be totally mutually dependent and necessarily jointly behind each other's acts. This collective would be indivisible in its being for logical reasons—that is, the kind of being that it would be is such that each of its members is necessarily everlasting, and would not have existed unless it had brought about or been brought about by the others. The collective would also be indivisible in its causal action in the sense that each would back totally the causal action of the others. The collective would be causeless and so (in my sense), unlike its members, ontologically necessary, not dependent for its existence on anything outside itself. It is they, however, rather than it, who, to speak strictly, would have the divine properties of omnipotence, omniscience, etc.; though clearly there is a ready and natural sense in which the collective can be said to have them as well. If all members of a group know something, the group itself, by a very natural extension of use, can be said to know that thing; and so on. Similarly this very strong unity of the collective would make it, as well as its individual members, an appropriate object of worship. The claim that 'there is only one God' is to be read as the claim that the source of being of all other things has to it this kind of indivisible unity.

But then how is the claim that each of the individuals is 'God' to be understood? Simply as the claim that each is divine—omnipotent, perfectly good, etc. Each such being would be an all-perfect source of all things—what more could councils intelligibly mean by that claim that an individual is God? On this reading, unavoidable if we are to make any sense of the creeds, 'there is one God' is to be read in such a way that '*a* is God' and '*b* is God' and 'there is only one God' do not entail '*a=b*'.

[. . .]

On this understanding of what the creeds mean by saying that there is one God (θεός, *deus*) but three individuals who are each 'God' (i.e. divine, θεός, *deus*), the rest of their claims about the Trinity follow straightforwardly from my account. The individuals are said to be *hypostases* (ὑποστάσεις), that is, individuals, or *personae* (πρόσωπα); a *persona* is simply a rational individual—'person'. As it follows from my argument that there will be, so there is, according to the creeds, a difference between the persons in respect of which depends on which and also in respect of function, and the traditional names bring out both of these aspects of the differences. Traditionally, the first divine individual is called 'Father', the second 'Son' (or 'Word'), the third 'Spirit'. 'Father' seems a name appropriate to the original source. Both 'Son' and 'Word' suggest a second or third divine individual. Biblical tradition apportions both these names to Christ, and if the second person of the Trinity became incarnate, they are then appropriate names for that second person. Apart from insisting that the second person of the Trinity alone became incarnate, the early church had no very clear view about which members of the Trinity did what, although the name of 'Spirit' derived from many biblical sources was often recognized as giving the third individual a primary role in sanctification.

[. . .]

The Western Church's version of the Nicene Creed asserts that the Spirit 'proceeds from the Father and the Son', whereas the original version preserved by the Eastern Church asserts that the Spirit proceeds 'from the Father', though individual Eastern theologians taught that the procession from the Father is 'through the Son'. It seems to me that the Western version brings out the fact, which alone on my argument could account for it, that the generation of the Spirit is a co-operative act.

The three individuals all have the same essence, that is, they are each of the same essential kind, namely, divine. The mutual dependence of the three persons is naturally called περιχώρησις, 'interpenetration' or 'coinherence'. In acting towards the outside world (i.e. in creating or sustaining other substances), although (unless there is a unique best action) one individual initiates any action, the initiating act (whether of active or permissive causation) is backed by the co-causation of the others—hence the slogan *omnia opera Trinitatis ad extra indivisa sunt* ('all the acts of the Trinity towards the outside world are indivisible'). (In consequence of such co-causation, I shall often continue to write of 'God' doing this or that, except where it is important to bring out which member of the Trinity initiates such action.) But within the Trinity there must be, I argued, some asymmetry of dependence—God the Father is not caused to exist actively by the Son or Spirit. He is in this sense uncaused, although throughout any period which has a beginning he is permitted to exist by the others. And there is inevitably a similar asymmetry of dependence for each of the others. But since the Father had no option but to cause the Son, and Father and Son had no option but to cause the Spirit, and all exist eternally, the dependence of Son on Father, and of Spirit on Father and Son, does not diminish greatness. Each could not exist but as eternally causing or permitting the other or others to exist. A king who at some stage in his reign voluntarily shares his kingdom with another may well be thought to be greater than the other. But a king who for all his reign has to share his kingdom with another may reasonably be considered no greater than the other.

All of this is what we find in what the Nicene Creed has to say about the Trinity:

> We believe in one God (θεός), the Father Almighty . . . and in one Lord Jesus Christ, the only-begotten Son of God, begotten of the Father before all ages . . . true God of true God, begotten not made, of one substance (ὁμοούσιός) with the Father . . . And in the Holy Spirit that proceeds from the Father [and the Son] who with the Father and the Son is worshipped and glorified together.

The Council of Nicaea declared the Son to be ὁμοούσιός with the Father. It may well have meant by that only that Father and Son were both (to use the technical patristic term) 'of the same second substance', that is, both divine. But a stronger understanding of ὁμοούσιός soon arose, to the effect that Father, Son, and Spirit were all 'of the same first substance', namely, in some sense formed the same individual thing. I have explained the sense in which that also is true. The words 'and the Son' (*filioque*) describing the source of the Spirit's procession were not originally in the Nicene Creed, but were added later to the Western version, but, as I have noted, even the Eastern version seems to allow a certain asymnietry of dependence.

Likewise the account of the Trinity which I have derived fits in with what the Athanasian Creed has to say about it:

> the Catholic Faith is this: that we worship one God in Trinity, and Trinity in Unity; neither confounding the Persons, nor dividing the substance. For there is one Person of the Father, another of the Son, and another of the Holy Spirit. But the Godhead of the Father, of the Son, and the Holy Spirit is all one: the Glory equal, the Majesty coeternal . . . The Father uncreated, the Son uncreated, and the Holy Spirit uncreated . . . the Father eternal, the Son eternal, and the Holy Spirit eternal. And yet there are not three eternals but one eternal . . . So likewise the Father is Almighty, the Son Almighty, and the Holy Spirit Almighty. And yet there are not three Almighties, but one Almighty . . . Like as we are compelled by the Christian verity to acknowledge each Person by himself to be God and Lord; so we are forbidden by the Catholic religion to say that there are three gods or three Lords. The Father is made of none, neither created nor begotten. The Son is of the Father alone, not made, nor created but begotten. The Holy Spirit is of the Father and the Son; neither made, nor created, nor begotten but proceeding . . . In this Trinity none is before or after another, none is greater or less than another . . . He therefore that will be saved must thus think of the Trinity.

I derived the traditional formulas by reading the *deus* (θεός), which the Father, Son, and Spirit are each said to be, differently from the *deus* (θεός) which is used when it is said that there are not three *dei* but one *deus*. Unless we do this, it seems to me that the traditional formulas are self-contradictory. If we read all occurrences of *deus* as occurrences of the same referring expression, the Athanasian Creed then asserts that Father, Son, and Spirit are each of them the same individual thing, and also that they have different properties, for example, the Father begets but is not begotten. But that is not possible; if things are the same, they must have all the same properties. Alternatively, if we read all occurrences as occurrences of the same predicate, attributing the same property, the Athanasian Creed then claims that each of the three persons, which are not the same persons as each other, is divine; but there is only one divine thing which is a substance, God the Holy Trinity. But how can there be three divine things, and yet only one? Contradiction looms. There have been attempts to make sense of there being three divine persons, and yet only one divine substance, by means of the philosophical doctrine of relative identity, especially recently by Peter van Inwagen.[1] The reader will recall from Chapter 1 that a philosophical doctrine of relative identity claims that one thing, a, which is (ϕ and ψ) may be the same ϕ as b but not the same ψ as b; sameness is relative to the sortal (ϕ or ψ). The sort of example the doctrine has in mind is that some statue may be the same statue as an earlier statue but not the same lump of brass as the earlier one (because the lump of brass has been gradually replaced in the interval by new brass formed into the same shape). Van Inwagen then claims analogously that 'substance' (which he equates with 'being'), 'God', and 'person' are sortal terms, such that the Father is the same substance, and so the same God, as the Son; but not the same person as the Son. Likewise the Spirit is the same substance and God as the Son, but not the same person. From this it follows that there are three persons, each of which is God, but only one God. Van Inwagen has developed a very rigorous formal logic of relative identity, which, he claims, prevents us from drawing any contradictions from statements such as these.

However, the philosophical objections to any doctrine of relative identity remain. If 'the Father', 'the Son', and 'the Spirit' are to have clear uses, then each must have associated with it a substance-sortal (or more than one sortal, so long as the sortals carve up the world in the same way); they cannot have sortals associated with them which diverge in their subsequent applications. If 'the Father' is the name of a person who is not the same person as the Son or the Spirit, then it cannot also be the name of a God (or a substance) who is the same God (or substance) as the Son and the Spirit. And if we deny that 'the Father' etc. do have clear uses, we deny any clear content to the doctrine of the Trinity at all.[2]

In AD 1215 the Fourth Lateran Council claimed firmly, in purported refutation of the views of Joachim of Fiore, that the unity of the Godhead was not just a collective unity 'in the way that many human beings are said to make one people, and many believers one church'. Rather it is the same 'thing', 'that is divine substance, essence or nature' which 'truly is the Father, and is the Son, and is the Spirit', 'That thing is not begetting, nor begotten, nor proceeding, but is the Father who begets, and the Son who is begotten, and the Holy Spirit who proceeds, so that there may be distinction of persons but unity of nature. These expressions can certainly be read in such a way as to be claiming that there are three divine individuals and each is the same substance (in my sense), leading to the clear contradiction from which the doctrine of relative identity cannot help us to escape. It is so read if we read the *res*, "thing", which is said to be "substance" (*substantia*) as *a* substance in my sense. But if "substance" just means "essence" or "nature", as the Council glosses it, then there is *a* way of reading what it said along the lines which I have developed. There is a sense in which a divine individual is his essence, namely, that he lacks thisness—there is nothing more to a divine individual than the instantiation of the divine essence and any further individuating relational properties (e.g. "being begotten"). Hence what the Council *may* be saying is this: the Godhead is not just three individuals, each with its thisness, who have common essential properties. Rather, it is exactly the instantiation of the same essence of divinity which makes the Father God, as makes the Son God, as makes the Spirit God. They would be the same individual but for the relational properties which are distinct from the divine essence and which distinguish them.

Articulations in the Christian tradition of the doctrine of the Trinity are often distinguished into forms of social Trinitarianism that stress the separateness of the persons, and forms of relative Trinitarianism that stress the unity of the Godhead. What I have expounded is, I suppose, a moderate form of social Trinitarianism but one which stresses both the logical inseparability of the divine persons in the Trinity, and the absence of anything by which the persons of the Trinity are individuated except their relational properties.

The reason which I have given for why a divine individual must give rise to another and hence a third, that goodness is essentially diffusive and generous, was, I believe, implicitly or explicitly, at the heart of the thinking of many of those of early centuries who advocated the doctrine of the Holy Trinity. Of course the biblical texts had enormous influence, yet on their own they could have given rise to a hundred different theologies. Certainly emanations and trinities formed part of the common stock of religious ideas current in the Mediterranean of the first centuries AD, but these ideas took many different forms, and there were other ideas around. So why did Christians choose to see in the biblical texts Trinitarianism of the kind which subsequently became the orthodoxy? The answer is, I think, this. They had two basic convictions. One was that our complex and orderly universe derived its being from a single personal source of being, possessed of all perfection. The other was that perfection includes perfect love. There is something profoundly imperfect and therefore inadequately divine in a solitary divine individual. If such an individual is love, he must share, and sharing with finite beings such as humans is not sharing all of one's nature and so is imperfect sharing. A divine individual's love has to be manifested in a sharing with another divine individual, and that (to keep the divine unity) means (in some sense) within the godhead, that is, in mutual dependence and support.

[. . .]

The Christian revelation teaches the doctrine of the Trinity as a central element of its creeds. Any evidence from the circumstances of its origin that that revelation is true confirms the doctrine of the Trinity; just as any a priori grounds for supposing the doctrine of the Trinity to be true is evidence that the Christian revelation (and so any elements it contains) is true. What I have presented as a priori a marginally more probable account of the divine nature than any other, becomes enormously more probable if backed up by revelation.

NOTES

1. Peter van Inwagen, 'And yet there are not three Gods, but one God', in T. V. Morris (ed.), *Philosophy and the Christian Faith* (University of Notre Dame Press, 1988).
2. As van Inwagen points out, the same might still be said of some sentences purporting to describe the content of such deep physical theories as Quantum Theory. But in physics a scientist simply has to operate with the sentences, he is not required in any sense to believe the propositions which they express. Since belief in the Trinity is commended to Christians by the Church, the Church must be purporting to teach the doctrine as one of which there is some graspable content; and if a certain form of that doctrine has the consequence that there cannot be, the Church cannot coherently commend that form for belief, for there is nothing in which belief in it would consist.

INCARNATION

6.2

'THE TWO MINDS VIEW OF INCARNATION'

Thomas V. Morris

[. . .]

One might say "If Christ is God, then he cannot have begun to exist at a certain point in human history because God (and his Son) are necessarily eternal. But then nothing can count as a man, a creature, which does not have a beginning in time and which is thus coeval with God." The remark about "counting as a man" makes clear the structure of the reasoning. Like all other contemporary critics who issue a form of incoherence challenge, our critic is relying on a certain sort of conception of human nature and of divine nature for the generation of his argument. And, crucially, he is assuming that, with respect to questions concerning metaphysical status, the ontological status of an object's existence, properties essential for being God are logical complements of those essential for being human.

SOME CRUCIAL DISTINCTIONS

If the properties of possibly being annihilated, having a beginning in time, and metaphysical contingency were all essential human properties, any truly human being would have to exemplify each of them. Thus Jesus, if he was fully human, would have had them, and this argument could succeed. For

Thomas V. Morris, 'The Two Minds View of Incarnation', from 'Divine and Human Existence' and 'Jesus and the Attributes of Deity', *The Logic of God Incarnate* (Ithaca, NY: Cornell University Press, 1986), pp. 62–7, 69–70, 88–9, 102–7.

surely these are properties no divine person could have. But the question we must press is: What reason do we have to believe that they are essential human properties, necessary elements of what it is to be human?

In order to appreciate the impact of this question, we first must take care to draw a clear distinction between *common* human properties and *essential* ones. A common human property will be one which many or most human beings have. A limiting case of commonality would be a property which was universally shared by all humans alike. We need to be clear that a property's being common or even universal for members of a kind does not entail that it is essential for the kind, such that membership in the kind would be impossible without its exemplification. For example, the property of living at some time on the surface of the earth is a common human property. I think it is safe to assume it is now a universal property for humans. But it is not an element of human nature. It is not essential for being human. It is clearly possible that at some time in the future human beings will be born, live, and die on a space station or on another planet colonized by earth, without ever setting foot on the earth itself. This is an obvious example of our distinction. The property of living at some time on the surface of the earth may now be a universal human property, but it is not an essential one.

This simple but important distinction is often overlooked by theologians. Richard Norris, for example, has written: "We can speak of human nature, meaning something like 'that which is normally characteristic of all human beings.'"[1] I do not want to deny that Norris's use of the phrase 'human nature' is an allowable one in colloquial or informal contexts. It just is not the one which properly operates in metaphysics. For philosophical or theological anthropology, we need something much more precise and demanding than that. It is normally characteristic of human beings to have hair. Yet one can certainly be fully human, exemplify human nature, while lacking this adornment. It is also normally characteristic of human beings to come into existence and to have the metaphysical status of contingency. But of course our critic wants to block the possibility of there being a man who lacks these properties. So his argument depends on the more precise understanding of human nature I have assumed here.

Once we acknowledge a clear distinction between commonality and essence, what forces the Christian to count as essential any common human properties which would preclude a literal divine incarnation? I can think of nothing which would do this. If we develop our philosophical anthropology and our doctrine of God in isolation from each other and from the central tenets of Christian faith, it is no surprise that conflicts may arise, that "impossibilities" be generated. But it is a perfectly proper procedure (some would even say— rightly, I think—mandatory) for the Christian philosopher or theologian to develop his idea of human nature, his conception of what the essential human properties are, with certain presuppositions or controls derived from his doctrine of God and his belief in the reality of the Incarnation.

In a moment of insight apparently rare among contemporary theologians involved in the debate over the Incarnation, John MacQuarrie wrote a few years ago: "Part of the trouble with the doctrine of incarnation is that we discuss the divinity and even the humanity of Christ in terms of ready-made ideas of God and man that we bring with us, without allowing these ideas to be corrected and even drastically changed by what we learn about God and man in and through the incarnation."[2] This is precisely the problem. It is all a matter of epistemic priorities. The orthodox Christian can quite rationally argue that we are less sure that human nature essentially comprises properties incompatible with a divine incarnation that Christians are that Jesus was God Incarnate. This is not to say that the doctrine of the Incarnation should or even could have complete epistemic priority for the Christian over any conception whatsoever of humanity or divinity. Some prior idea of what it is to be God and what it is to be a man is required for even understanding the doctrine at all. But the prior conceptions requisite for any understanding of the doctrine at all are far from complete and unalterable. And I think it can be shown that the Christian of orthodox leanings can, in all epistemic propriety, develop his philosophical anthropology in such a way as to allow for a divine incarnation, thereby disallowing the sort of argument mounted by our critic.

Only a very few contemporary theologians who have written on the topic seem to have recognized that we can understand human nature in such a way that it can be coexemplified with divinity in one and the same subject. Herbert McCabe, for one, has said: "A human person just is a person with a human nature, and it makes absolutely no difference to the logic of this whether the same person does or does not exist from eternity as divine."[3] Surely, a *merely* human being will not have existed from eternity as divine. A mere human will furthermore be a contingent creation. But no orthodox theologian has ever claimed that Jesus was merely human. The claim is that he was fully human, but also divine. If contingency, coming into existence, and possibly ceasing to exist were essential human properties, the doctrine of the Incarnation would express a metaphysical, or broadly logical, impossibility. But I can think of no compelling argument, or any other type of good reason, to think they are elements of human nature, understood along our precise metaphysical lines.

It may be that these, or at least two of these, properties just mentioned are essential to being merely human. Any being which exemplifies human nature without also exemplifying divine nature would then have to exemplify them, otherwise it would not "count as" a mere human. But the Christian claim is that in order to be fully human, it is not necessary to be merely human. An individual is merely human just in case it has all the properties requisite for being fully human (the component properties of human nature) and also some limitation properties as well, properties such as those adduced by our critic. These limitation properties will not be understood as elements of human nature at all, but as universal accompaniments of humanity in the case of any created human being.

Perhaps a few more words should be said about this merely *x*/fully *x* distinction. Consider a diamond. It has all the properties essential to being a physical object (mass, spatiotemporal location, etc.). So it is fully physical. Consider now an alligator. It has all the properties essential to being a physical object. It is *fully* physical. But, there is a sense in which we can say that it is not *merely* physical. It has properties of animation as well. It is an organic being. In contrast, the gem is merely physical as well as being fully physical. Now take the case of a man. An embodied human being, any one you choose, has mass, spatiotemporal location, and so forth. He is thus fully physical. But, again, there is a sense in which he is not merely a physical object: he has organic and animate properties as well. So let us say he is fully animate. But unlike the alligator he is not merely animate; he has rational, moral, aesthetic, and spiritual qualities which mere organic entities lack. Let us say that he belongs to a higher ontological level by virtue of being human. And if, like you and me, he belongs to no ontological level higher than that of humanity, he is merely human as well as being fully human.

To repeat: the kind-nature exemplified distinctively by all human beings is that of humanity. To be a human being is to exemplify human nature. An individual is fully human just in case he fully exemplifies human nature. To be merely human is not to exemplify a kind-nature, a natural kind, distinct from that of humanity; it is rather to exemplify humanity without also exemplifying any ontologically higher kind, such as divinity.

Now, as I have said, according to orthodox Christology, Jesus was fully human without being merely human. He had all the properties constitutive of human nature, but had higher properties which, from an Anselmian perspective, form the upper bound of our scale. A philosophical anthropology developed from a distinctively Christian point of view will categorize all human properties logically incompatible with a divine incarnation as, at most, essential to being *merely human*. And, again, the Chalcedonian claim is not that Jesus was merely human. It is rather that he was, and is, fully human in addition to being divine.

I am suggesting that, armed with a couple of fairly simple metaphysical distinctions, we can begin to see how the doctrine of the Incarnation can possibly be true. I have considered only a few alleged divergences and metaphysical disparities between human nature and divine nature, specifically that range of properties concerning divine and human existence to which our critic's argument draws our attention. My suggestion is that such properties as those of possibly coming into existence, coming to be at some time, being a contingent creation, and being such as to possibly cease to exist are, although common human properties, not essential to being human. They, or some of them, may be essential to being *merely* human, but they can be held, in all epistemic and metaphysical propriety, not to be essential to being *fully* human, to exemplifying the kind-essence of humanity.

[. . .]

It is only with a clear focus on the difference between a property's being essential for being fully human, and its being essential merely to being a particular human that we can begin to turn back the incoherence charge against the Incarnation and display its metaphysical possibility. But these few distinctions alone will not do the full job of rebutting all alleged violations of the indiscernability principle. For merely to claim of all human properties incompatible with some kind-essential divine attribute that they are not part of the kind-essence of humanity may turn back the a priori incoherence charge, or at least a part of it, but it can appear to yield by implication an utterly fantastic figure of Christ.

On the resultant picture, will it not follow that Jesus was omniscient, omnipotent, necessarily existent, and all the rest, as well as being an itinerant Jewish preacher? And is this not outlandish to the greatest possible degree? Did the bouncing baby boy of Mary and Joseph direct the workings of the cosmos from his crib? Was this admittedly remarkable man, as he sat by a well or under a fig tree, actually omnipresent in all of creation? Did this carpenter's son exist necessarily? Such implications of orthodoxy can sound just too bizarre for even a moment's serious consideration. How could such a view possibly be squared with the biblical portrait of Jesus as a limited man among men? How could such a being possibly be said to have shared the human *condition*?

[. . .]

The Properties of the God-Man

Let us follow the Anselmian tradition in holding that God is omnipotent, omniscient, and omnipresent. Let us grant that these are attributes of deity, properties any divine being has. It seems to follow then quite directly from "Jesus is God the Son," where 'God the Son' denotes a divine being, that Jesus was omnipotent, omniscient, and omnipresent. But this is hard to swallow for two reasons: (1) it is difficult to see how anyone could be fully human while having such properties, and (2) according to the biblical portrayal of Christ, Jesus seems not to have had such properties. Our problem is to provide a model for the Incarnation which both recognizes these properties as properties of deity and yet at the same time reconciles this view with what seems so clearly to have been true of Jesus.

[. . .]

[One might claim that] no person is identical with any particular range of conscious experience, or collection of belief states, he might have. I think that the truth of this claim will follow from any modally plausible and metaphysically careful account of what a person is. With this in mind, we can begin to appreciate the early view that, in the case of God Incarnate, we must recognize something like two distinct ranges of consciousness. There is first what we can call the eternal mind of God the Son with its distinctively divine consciousness, whatever that might be like, encompassing the full scope of omniscience. And in addition there is a distinctly earthly consciousness that came into existence and grew and developed as the boy Jesus grew and developed. It drew its visual imagery from what the eyes of Jesus saw, and its concepts from the languages he learned. The earthly range of consciousness, and self-consciousness, was thoroughly human, Jewish, and first-century Palestinian in nature.

We can view the two ranges of consciousness (and, analogously, the two noetic structures encompassing them) as follows: The divine mind of God the Son contained, but was not contained by, his earthly mind, or range of consciousness. That is to say, there was what can be called an asymmetric accessing relation between the two minds. Think, for example, of two computer programs or informational systems, one containing but not contained by the other. The divine mind had full and direct access to the earthly, human experience resulting from the Incarnation, but the earthly consciousness did not have such full and direct access to the content of the overarching omniscience proper to the Logos, but only such access, on occasion, as the divine mind allowed it to have. There thus was a metaphysical and personal depth to the man Jesus lacking in the case of every individual who is merely human.

This account allows for the apparent intellectual and spiritual growth of Jesus in his humanity to be a real development. It can also help to explain, or at least to allow for, the cry of dereliction.[4] When this view is used to augment the apparatus of the previous argument, we have in principle a full and adequate account of the basic features of the metaphysics of the Incarnation. In particular, it allows us to avoid the absurdities to which orthodoxy has always seemed vulnerable. On it, we have in the person of Jesus no case of a God merely dressed up as a man. We have an individual who is fully human, and who shares in the human condition, experiencing the world in a human perspective. No Docetic absurdities are implied by the view. Nor is it Nestorian. Nor Appolinarian. There is one person with two natures and two ranges of consciousness. He is not the theological equivalent of a centaur, half God and half man. He is fully human, but not merely human. He is also fully divine.

The two-minds view seems to me, further, to be a clear improvement over kenoticism. When he became a man, God the Son did not give up anything of deity; he merely took on the nature and condition of humanity. We can capture full well the New Testament claim that in the Incarnation God the Son humbled himself, without following kenotic Christology in holding that he gave up any metaphysical attributes distinctive of deity. His humbling consisted rather in his rendering himself vulnerable to the pains, sufferings, aggravations, and agonies which became his as a man but which, in his exclusively divine form of existence, could not have touched him this way. It is not by virtue of what he gave up, but in virtue of what he took on, that he humbled himself. This sort of divine kenosis was a feature of the Incarnation, but so understood it is a feature which accords logically with strong claims concerning the modality and immutability of the attributes distinctive of and traditionally held to be constitutive of deity. No kenotic move with any of those attributes is required for ridding orthodoxy of any appearances of absurdity.

But can we really understand what it is to attribute two minds, or two ranges of consciousness, to one person? That depends on what is required for understanding the claim. Can we know what it is like to be a God-man? Well, can we know what it is like to be a bat? It is hard, if possible at all, to imagine what a sonar-consciousness is like. Likewise, we do not, and cannot, know what it is like to be God, at least not in the way we know what it is like to be a human being. It is no objection to my suggestions that we cannot in this sense know what it would be like to be a God-man with two related but distinct ranges of consciousness. But as a matter of fact, we can fill out some significant level of understanding concerning the claim by way of some analogies.

I have suggested already a computer or artificial intelligence analogy. Consider two or three others. First, an interesting, and interestingly parallel, dream phenomenon is reported by many people. I think I have had such an experience myself on more than one occasion. The dreamer is having a dream with a large cast of characters. The dreamer himself is one of those characters, perceiving the internal environs of the dream and taking part in its action "from within." But at the same time, the dreamer "as sleeper" is somehow aware, in what could be called an overarching level of consciousness, that it is just a dream that is going on, in which he is playing a role as one of the characters. If in fact there is in such an experience a twofold consciousness, one "within" the dream, the other "outside" the dream simultaneously, then we have, if not a model, then at least an analogy of some value in helping us to get some imaginative grip on the two-minds picture of the Incarnation. It is possible, though, that in such experiences the dreamer is very rapidly alternating between two perspectives. And of course such a case would provide no model or particularly good analogy at all.

Consider the common claim in twentieth-century psychology that there are various strata to the ordinary human mind. The postulated unconscious, or subconscious, mind would stand in an asymmetric accessing relation to the conscious mind somewhat parallel to that postulated between the divine consciousness and the earthly consciousness of God Incarnate. If modern psychology is even possibly right in this postulation, one person can have different levels or ranges of mentality. In the case of Jesus, there would then be a very important extra depth had in virtue of his being divine.

Finally, there are cases of brain hemisphere commisurotomy, multiple personality, and even hypnosis, in which we are confronted by what seems to be in some significant sense a single individual human being, one person, but one person with apparently two or more distinct streams or ranges of consciousness, distinct domains of experience. Now, of course, there are philosophers who claim that in many if not all cases of multiple, simultaneous ranges of experience associated with the stimulation of one human body, the requisite conditions are lacking for judging there to be a single person who is the ultimate bearer of the disparate sets of experience. Some theorists identify each discrete range of consciousness in the commissurotomy patient and each personality in the case of a multiple personality as a person. Such a claim is less often made with respect to different levels of consciousness or divergent streams of awareness associated with cases of hypnotism. But in any case, this sort of identification can be argued to be implausible. If one troubling aberrant personality is eliminated therapeutically from the behavioral repertoire of someone afflicted with multiple personalities, the therapist surely need not see the effect of her work as the killing of a person. Moreover, it is plausible, and indeed illuminating, to view normal persons as either having or even being systems of systems of mentality or experience. And, again, if it is even conceivable that one person have, simultaneously, such distinct ranges of mentality, we may have here, in at least some of the more unusual cases, vivid partial analogies which can help us to gain some firmer understanding of the two-minds view.

As a matter of fact, in some cases of multiple personality, there exists one personality with apparently full and direct knowledge of the experiences had, information gathered, and actions initiated by one or more other personalities, a sort of knowledge which is not had by any other personality concerning it. In other words, there seem to exist asymmetric accessing relations in such cases, interestingly though of course not perfectly parallel to the sort of relation claimed by the two-minds view to hold between the divine and human minds of Christ.

Does the two-minds view then present the Incarnation as a case of split personality on the part of God the Son? And if so, should not the recognition of this alone suffice for a rejection of the view as an unworthy, demeaning characterization of Christ? Does what initially can appear to serve as a partial explication of orthodoxy end up amounting to no more than a gross impiety?

First of all, the reference to some phenomena of multiple personality here is intended only to provide a partial analogy for some of what the two-minds view claims to be true in the case of Christ. It is to have no more than the limited but, I hope, helpful function of providing some understanding of, and imaginative grip on, the central elements of the two-minds view. It thus is intended to serve the same function as the computer analogy, the dream analogy, and the reference to the classic distinction between the conscious and unconscious, or subconscious, mind. It is not intended to be a complete modeling of the noetic features of the Incarnation.

Furthermore, the analogy or partial parallel is in no way demeaning to God the Son. To see this we must ask exactly what it is about the phenomena of multiple personality generally that renders the state of exhibiting such phenomena a bad state for a human being to be in, a state it would be better to be without. The answer is, I think, quite simple. Typical cases of multiple personality exhibit two negative features: They are not mental states, or arrangements, voluntarily entered into by the person who exhibits the phenomena, and they are not mental states, or arrangements, conducive to that attainment of goals valuable to the person involved. Both these features are, on any orthodox deployment of the two-minds view, absent from the case of Christ's exemplification of two minds. His taking on of a human mind was entirely voluntary. And according to any traditional account of the purpose of the Incarnation, it was conducive to, if not in fact necessary for, the attainment of goals valuable to God. So it seems to me that we have no reason from this quarter for hesitating to use whatever parallel phenomena we find in psychologically unusual human cases to help us to understand the relevant aspects of the Incarnation.

The two-minds view of Christ allows us to take seriously the human limitations of Jesus' earthly career without incurring the metaphysical and modal costs of kenoticism. I believe it is a very powerful picture, and that it can be an important ingredient in a solution to the single most difficult logical challenge to the doctrine of the Incarnation.

NOTES

1. Richard A. Norris, Jr., "Interpreting the Doctrine of the Incarnation," in *The Myth/Truth of God Incarnate*, ed. Durstan R. McDonald (Wilton, Conn.: Moorehouse-Barlow, 1979), p. 81.
2. John MacQuarrie, "The Humility of God," in McDonald, ed., p. 13.
3. Herbert McCabe and Maurice Wiles, "The Incarnation: An Exchange," *New Blackfriars*, 58 (December, 1977), 552.
4. Mark 15:34.

HELL
6.3

'HEAVEN AND HELL'

Michael J. Murray

Anyone who has spent much time talking to a non-Christian about the Christian faith has inevitably encountered the topic of hell. For non-Christians, and for many Christians as well, the doctrine of hell seems downright incompatible with the Christian view of God.

One of my students once explained his way of seeing the problem as follows. For him the Christian world-view made human existence out to be like an episode of the old show *Let's Make a Deal*. On the show, contestants were selected from the audience and given an opportunity to select blindly one of three curtains, each of which hid a certain prize. The prizes might be desirable (a new car) or undesirable (a goat or a chicken). The host offers the contestants financial incentives to take this or that door, but in the end, the contestants make what is essentially a blind choice, and take the prize they are given. Likewise, on the Christian picture, he explained, fallen human beings stumble around in a world in which they have to make choices, choices which amount to giving allegiance to one religion or another (or no religion at all). For the most part, the choices are made blindly since the evidence one way or the other is either ambiguous, or thin, or just nonexistent. Furthermore, along the way there are incentives or "temptations" to give one's allegiance to one religion or another. Even the Christian thinks that the devil stands ready to lure people away from the "right door." But at the end of the day, everyone

Michael J. Murray, 'Heaven and Hell', *Reason for the Hope Within* (Grand Rapids, MI: Erdmans, 1999), pp. 287–315.

blindly stakes their claim one way or the other. On the Christian view, those who select the single "correct" curtain are both lucky and rewarded (with eternal bliss). But what about those who choose any other curtain? They are immediately snatched away to live for eternity in a hell where they are burned alive but never die.

This is powerful imagery — imagery which illustrates a number of criticisms that have been raised against the traditional Christian doctrine of hell. Those criticisms can roughly be divided into two groups, those who claim that there is something *unjust* about hell, and those who claim that there is something *unloving* about a God who allows people to go (or sends them!) there. How should the Christian respond to these critical challenges? In recent years, Christian theologians and philosophers have taken up the challenge posed by the doctrine of hell and have sketched a wide variety of solutions to it. Some have defended the traditional notion of hell as the destiny of those without Christ, commencing immediately upon death and judgment and continuing for eternity without ceasing. Others have proposed what appear to be less harsh conceptions of hell, arguing that the duration of hell might be finite, either because one ceases to exist after a certain length of time or because one finally repents and is allowed to join the company of those in heaven. Others have argued that while hell exists, it is empty, because while anyone who would pass through the judgment unrepentant would go there, no one ever remains unrepentant in God's presence.

The most natural reading of the text of Scripture and the words of the Lord is certainly the one reflected in the first interpretation above. As a result, it is the one we should look to defend first. If such a defence turns out to be unsustainable, then we might have grounds for falling back to a different position.

In what follows I would like to show just how a Christian might argue that the natural reading *does* make good sense when it comes to the biblical teaching on hell. In the first part of the chapter I will explain the two central models that have been proposed for understanding the traditional doctrine of hell.

In the second part of the chapter, we can then turn and address the charges that the traditional view of hell renders God unjust or unloving. It is these charges which have led some to jettison the traditional view, in favor of alternatives, most commonly annihilationism (the view that those who are not saved are punished for a time and then cease to exist) and universalism (the view that all are ultimately saved).

[. . .]

The Penalty Model

With that said, we turn to the two models. The first I will call the "penalty model" while the second I will call the "natural consequence model." We can set out the penalty model as follows:

According to Scripture "all have sinned and fall short of the glory of God." The result of this sinfulness is that the sinner incurs a penalty, a penalty which Scripture describes as "death." However, the penalty of "death" mentioned in, for example, Romans 6:23 does not refer simply to the physical death all will experience. Instead, "death" refers to spiritual death, a death which involves separation of the person from God for eternity. As a result, each person who sins incurs this penalty. And since each person has only one life to give, each is thereby bound to be separated from God, unless the penalty incurred can be satisfied in some other fashion. To this end, God has established a means of satisfaction or payment of the penalty. God the Father wrought the Incarnation, yielding a person who was fully God and also fully human, yet without fault. And since he was faultless, and so had no penalty of his own to pay, he could, by offering himself in our place, satisfy the penalty on our behalf. As a result, those who are willing to allow the penalty to be paid on their behalf by Christ, must simply accept that gift by repenting of their former ways and placing their faith in Christ's work on the cross and in his victory in resurrection. Failure to do this means eternal separation from God with the attending punishment that this separation brings.

This is a view that many Christians espouse concerning sin, salvation, and eternal human destinies. There are many modifications of it to be found in this or that denomination or sect. But the above represents a rough approximation of the intersection of the beliefs of a very wide range of Christians.

OBJECTIONS TO THE PENALTY MODEL

[. . .]

One might object to the penalty model by pointing out that there is a grave disproportion between the amount of wrong one can do in this life, and the eternal duration and intensity of the punishment this wrong is claimed to merit. It seems that a necessary principle of fairness or justice is that penalties or punishments must be meted out in a way that is commensurate with the gravity of the offense. But since there is no offense that we finite beings could commit in a finite time that would merit infinite punishment, the punishment proposed by the penalty model is unfair.

How should one respond to this powerful criticism? There are at least two ways one might respond and I will look at each in turn. According to the *first* way, the objector is *right*: no wrongs we do in this life *can* merit infinite punishment. But, the defender continues, this does not mean that those in hell might not be rightly punished for eternity nonetheless. To see why, consider a criminal who commits a crime, is caught, and is then sentenced to twenty years in prison. While in prison, however, he continues to commit further crimes, and for these further crimes he receives additional sentencing time. The result is that while none of the crimes he commits merits a life sentence, the cumulative sentence for crimes committed before and while in prison is never exhausted. Likewise, one might hold, those who are judged and sentenced to hell might not have a sentence which initially merits an eternal punishment. But their unchecked sinful desires continue to lead them to sin even in hell and so continue to mount penalties which are never satisfied.

The *second* way to respond to this step in the critic's argument is to argue that the critic is mistaken in her belief that the sins we commit in this life *merit only a finite penalty*. If all sin is sin against God, then all sin is of infinite weight since it amounts to a transgression against an infinitely great being. This response, however, rests on two controversial assumptions. First, it assumes that all sins are sins against God, and second, it assumes that the gravity of an offense is in part dependent on the *type of being* offended.

While both of the claims have been criticized, neither seems especially problematic. Since the Christian holds that all moral commands find their source in God, it is reasonable to think that all transgressions are *at least* sins against God. It may be true, of course, that if I bring harm to an innocent person, I have sinned against *that person*, but there is no reason to think that this precludes my having sinned against God *as well*. We think something similar in cases of transgressions of laws of the state. Crimes which I commit against citizens in my community, are certainly crimes against *them*, but it is also perfectly reasonable to see these crimes as crimes "against the Commonwealth of Pennsylvania," at least if you live in my state.

The second assumption might seem slightly more controversial. If the gravity of the crime is increased with the greatness of the person offended, it seems that slapping Gandhi or Mother Teresa should merit a greater penalty, than slapping my next door neighbor. But this hardly seems right and our criminal law certainly takes no account of such differences. It is true that, when put this way, the principle in question seems implausible. But maybe *this* is not the principle that lies behind the penalty model. One might say, for example, that the weight of an offense depends, not on the *greatness of the person* offended, but on the greatness of the *type of being* offended. Thus, bringing injury to a tree, a frog, and a human would merit increasing penalties. Plants, animals, and humans are three quite different kinds of beings. While bringing injury to one *human* may merit the same punishment as bringing the same injury to any other *human*, it may merit a greater penalty than bringing the corresponding injury to a *dog*. In light of this, why is it implausible to think that offenses against God, who is infinitely greater than any human, merit a correspondingly greater penalty?

[. . .]

THE NATURAL CONSEQUENCE MODEL

I offer the penalty model above as one of the two main models of hell that have been defended by Christian orthodoxy and criticized by many in recent days. And while I think the penalty model is completely defensible, there is another model which may have more explanatory power. This second model, as we will see, has some features that are initially troubling. But all of these, except one, disappear on further investigation. Here, then, is the view in summary form:

> It is clear from the Genesis account of creation that one of the central aims God had in creating human beings was to make creatures in the "divine image." While the passage does not tell us all that this entails, it demonstrates that God was about the business of creating beings that were as much like God as they, finite and created as they were, could be. Many features of the divine nature could be replicated in creatures in characteristically finite ways: the ability to reason, to govern behavior on the basis of moral considerations, and to act freely, for example. This last feature is especially important since, because of it, humans are able to enter into a genuinely loving relationship with God. Without it, those who professed love for God (as the first great command dictates — Matt. 22:37) and who strove to be imitators of him (Eph. 5:1), would simply be robots or parrots, spitting back words of praise and behaving in ways that are simply a matter of preprogramming. Of course, such praise and behavior are not genuine expressions of love. In addition, having the ability to behave freely in these ways allows creatures to come close to exhibiting another divine attribute: self-existence. It is traditionally held that God has the attribute of self-existence (sometimes referred to as "a-seity" by philosophers and theologians [from the Latin phrase "a se" meaning "from oneself"]). Of course, no created thing can be self-existent (by definition!). But God might be able to make creatures who are self-existent at least in *certain respects*, and maybe in the most interesting and valuable respects, the respects which define what sort of person one is, and in particular, with respect to whether or not one will be a God-lover or not. God, wanting us to be creatures made in his image, wants us to be God-lovers. But recognizing that robots or preprogrammed parrots cannot be genuine God-lovers (although they can be preprogrammed to exhibit God-loving behaviors), God also gives us freedom, freedom to be self-made in a certain (very important) respect.
>
> As a result, God situates us, for a time, in this earthly life. And this earthly life is to act as a time of sanctification or, as some have called it, *soul-making*: a time when we have powers to make free choices to be a person of one sort or another. God's aim, of course, is that all will see

that being a God-lover is something to value over all else. But free creatures can, in virtue of their free powers, choose to reject this sort of life. They can instead become lovers of self and haters of God.

Once the course of one's life is complete, and one has, through conscious decision and behavior, become one sort of person or another, what then? For those who have become lovers of God, the natural consequence would be for them to enter into the divine presence to love God and enjoy him forever. But what of the others? What of those who simply have no interest in doing *that*? Why not, one might wonder, just accept them into the divine presence anyway? There are at least two reasons. The first is that doing this would amount to robbing the creature of the very freedom of self-determination that made their lives significant. The point of our earthly lives, on this account, is that we might be able to autonomously become creatures of one or another sort. But if we do not, after all, have that ability (because God will force the same "end" upon all of us), then our dignity is stolen. The second reason is that if those who lived lives in which they rejected God were nonetheless forced into God's presence forever, such a life would be utterly odious to them. It would be like forcing one who hates opera to sit through *Der Ring des Nibelungen* for eternity. This wouldn't be eternal bliss for *them*. It would be an eternal *nightmare*. As a result, the natural consequence for cultivating such a life would be eternal separation from God. And this is what hell is.

The Earthly Life and the Process of Sanctification

One of the more puzzling features of the Christian doctrine of hell is that hell is taken to be inescapable. The Lord teaches that for those in hell there is a chasm fixed so that those who are there cannot pass over into heaven. Similarly, we know that those who are in heaven remain there forever, eternally without sin. How can it come to pass, one might wonder, that those who can sin or refrain from sin while on earth, suddenly become, as Thomas Aquinas put it, "confirmed in good or evil" thereafter? The natural consequence view has an answer to this question. One interesting and noteworthy feature of human nature is our ability to make free choices. But a further interesting feature is that we are *habit formers*. That is, our behaviors can influence future behaviors by *disposing us* to desire or think in certain ways. When I was a teenager, I didn't like fine coffee, but by drinking it I came to "acquire a taste" for it. The result is that it is something that I now like and even seek out. My desire for coffee and my thinking about it has changed in virtue of behaviors I engaged in. And we can bring about changes in our dispositions in matters more complex than tastes for food as well. Numerous books on marriage enrichment, for example, prescribe that one of the best ways to preserve or restore romantic feelings for your spouse, is to do special things for them (buying surprise gifts, sending flowers, giving cards without occasion, etc.) As odd as it might be, we are beings for whom thought and desire often *follow* action. And the dispositions that we develop from such behaviors seem to become quite firmly entrenched over time.

Why would we be designed by God in such a way that the actions I perform form habits in me, the Christian might ask? One reason might be this: that were I to have to think through my choices completely every time I made one, it would take me forever to get around in the world. We can get in and out of restaurants in less than a day because we take preferences, formed by past choices, with us to the menu, and these preferences make our decision procedure much quicker. We can easily make selections among alternatives without agonizing over every option. Simply, it makes it possible for us to effectively navigate in the world.

But more than that, this is part of the way in which we can use the freedom that God has given us to *become a certain sort of person*. What does it mean to become a certain sort of person except to become disposed to think and desire and act in certain ways? So, it is essential for becoming a "person of a certain sort" that we have such disposition-forming capacities.

As we cultivate these dispositions, the range of choices open to us in a given circumstance becomes narrower and narrower. As I become more disposed to eat foods of the sort one finds in America, I find foods from distant and exotic cultures to be less palatable, to the point where I might have no desire for them whatsoever. Eating the eyes of fish or squirrel brains, delicacies in some cultures, is simply no longer one of the things I can choose, because there is nothing about the thought of such a thing that is attractive to me. We have a phrase to describe this phenomenon: "becoming set in your ways." The more "set in our ways" we become, the less options we have in choosing. We might then think of those in heaven and hell as those who are *maximally set in their ways*. That is, they are disposed to act as lovers of God or lovers of self *without fail*. The result is that those who are in heaven are no longer able to break the hold of the dispositions which they have acquired and likewise for those in hell.

The Role of Grace

One of the things that looks troubling about the natural consequence view is that it appears to teach straightforward works salvation. And because of this one should be inclined to think, at this point, that this view just cannot be reconciled with passages which claim that "he saved us, not because of things we have done, but because of his mercy. He saved us through the washing of rebirth and renewal by the Holy Spirit, whom he poured out on us generously through Jesus Christ our Savior, so that having been justified by his grace, we might become heirs having hope of eternal life" (Titus 1:9); or "It is by grace you have been saved through faith, and this not from yourselves, it is the gift of God, not as a result of works, so that no one can boast" (Eph. 2:8, 9). There is not a *hint* here that heaven is for those who have, by means of their choices in life, become lovers of God, as the natural consequence view seems to hold.

There is, however, more to the natural consequence (NC) story than what was set out above, the NC theorist will maintain. All other things being equal, the aim of our earthly lives is to cultivate God-loving characters so that we can become meaningfully related to God. But such meaning can only be had by allowing people to freely choose to become God-lovers or not. All other things being equal, we do this, on this view, by making choices to engage in God-loving or self-loving types of activity and thereby to make ourselves into one sort of person or another, again, all other things being equal. But all other things *aren't* equal. When it comes to being a self-lover, there is no problem. We are able, all on our own, to become utterly self-absorbed and self-centered lovers of self, and thereby to merit hell as a natural consequence. In other words, we are fully able to bring about *damnation by works*. Orthodox Christian belief has no quarrel with this.

But when it comes to being *God-lovers*, the Bible surely teaches something different. Sin has brought devastation to the world, a devastation which makes it impossible for us to cultivate God-loving habits, and thus a meaningful God-loving character. Not only is the world, as a result, filled with enticements that serve to draw us away from God, but our very souls are contaminated with the love of sin and self. The fallen world we have been placed in puts us in a position where becoming a God-lover by our own efforts is difficult to the point of impossibility. Sin is a crippling and debilitating influence that drags us all farther and farther from God unless its influence is graciously reversed. And thus, grace is necessary in order for us to be transformed into lovers of God.

The NC theorist will insist on all of this as much as the defender of the penalty model. And it is precisely here, on the NC view, that the need for grace becomes obvious. It is only by grace that anyone has the ability, in the first place, to choose to repent and seek reconciliation with God. In turn, it is only by God then granting the grace of reconciliation that the person is given the ability to be free of the power of sin and so to begin the process of becoming a lover of God, a process we call sanctification. So, the NC view includes the claim that divine grace is a *necessary condition* for being able to seek freely reconciliation with God and for being set free from the bondage to sin that prevents us from cultivating God-loving characters (i.e., from becoming sanctified).

Fire and Brimstone

The natural consequence view maintains that those who choose to be self-lovers are thereby separated from God for eternity, forever unable to enjoy the presence of God. While this tells us what the damned *do not* experience, what, according to the natural consequence view, *does* happen to those who are damned? On this view, it seems initially that hell is not so much a place where the damned suffer but rather just a place certain goods are lacking. Yet in Scripture hell is portrayed as more than just a *lack*. We see things like "eternal fire" and "raging fire" leading to "weeping and gnashing of teeth" and "torment."

As a rule, natural consequence theorists hold that talk of "fire" with respect to hell is metaphorical. But, they might argue, we are all obligated to take the talk of fire more or less metaphorically. After all, fire cannot really burn nonphysical souls. In any case, one would do better to understand the fires of hell as a metaphor for an intense and severe sort of suffering. The penalty model thinks of this suffering as a penalty. The natural consequence model instead thinks of the suffering of hell as an agonizing and conscious awareness of loss—an awareness which is the natural consequence for having become a self-lover.

It seems from the Scriptures that those in hell are aware of the fact that they have been judged and sent away from the divine presence as a result of this judgment. And parables such as the rich man and Lazarus, seem to indicate that those in hell are continuously aware of the loss that they suffer from being in hell (Luke 16:19–31). The NC view holds that the loss one feels is the sort of loss felt by someone who recognizes that they are responsible for missing out on the highest in human fulfillment and happiness. Thus, a deep, eternal regret nags at the person who becomes a lover of self.

One is, of course, likely to ask how reasonable it is to think that those in hell can recognize how badly off they are in their state of separation and still never seek reconciliation with God. If they are suffering in such agony, why not repent? The answer can be seen in what was already said earlier: since they are maximally disposed to be self-lovers, that is, they have become *set in their ways*, they might intellectually recognize how badly off they are in their condition, but still not *desire* to change it. NC theorists often liken this state to the state of an unwilling drug addict. The addict recognizes his ruined condition, and wishes that he no longer wanted to take drugs. But nonetheless, he *does* want to take them and thus continues to do so. Similarly, the one in hell, though recognizing that he would be better off if he loved God, still refuses to do so. And we need not resort to the drastic examples of the unwilling drug addict to illustrate this phenomenon. People who are addicted to smoking, or who simply love foods that are devastating to their health are not situated much differently. They see full well that the behaviors they are engaging in are harmful and destructive for them. They may even wish that they didn't desire to engage in these behaviors. But they nonetheless *do* desire to continue to engage in these behaviors.

A Problem and a Compromise

Above I have set out the natural consequence model and explored some of the additional explanatory power that this model seems to have. But there is one serious difficulty with the natural consequence model. The philosopher Eleonore Stump, in a context similar to the one we are discussing here, puts the problem this way:

> [On a view such as this] there seems no need, in fact no room, in this process for the atonement. If God can do the work of making a believer righteous in virtue of the believer's assent to God's work, then what is the role of atonement in salvation? Why shouldn't God have done the entire work of justification without the suffering and death of the incarnate Christ? On the other hand, if we can describe the Atonement in such a way as to make it an integral part of salvation, what is its relation to the process of justification by faith? How does the atonement contribute to justification . . . ?[1]

You might think that we have addressed this above when discussing the role of grace on the NC model. But all that is really said there is that the NC model is not a "works salvation" model since it positively *requires the operation of divine grace* in salvation and sanctification. But the problem raised here can be seen by considering this question: how exactly does the story of *Christ's death and resurrection* figure into the grace that we receive according to the NC model? Why, on this model, did God incarnate have to come to earth to *suffer and die*?

It is abundantly clear in Scripture that our sin has caused us to be cut off from God and that Christ's death is the remedy for this. It is also clear in Scripture that the effects of sin which serve to cut us off from God are numerous. But one of those effects is surely that our sins merit punishment. And one of the things that Christ's death achieves for us is the satisfaction of that punishment. Undoubtedly, this is a controversial claim among Christian theologians, but it is one that the teachings of Scripture make it hard to escape. The fact that justification is set out in terms of violation of "law" and resultant "condemnation" which necessitates "justification" and "satisfaction" or "propitiation" surely makes the salvation story look very much like the story proposed in the penalty model. And passages such as 2 Thessalonians 1:7–9 make it clear that part of what keeps us separated from God is a penalty that sin has brought upon us — a penalty that requires payment: "God is just . . . He will punish those who do not know God and do not obey the gospel of our Lord Jesus. They will be punished with everlasting destruction and shut out from the presence of the Lord and from the majesty of His power . . ."

This feature seems to be at the heart of the penalty model while there seems to be no role for it at all in the natural consequence model. One way to solve this problem would be adopt a hybrid model, that is a model which accepts *both* the penalty model *and* the natural consequence model. There is no reason why we could not append to the NC model the claim that in addition to destroying our ability to become God-lovers (God's intended purpose for us) sin also carries a penalty, a penalty which we could not pay on our own. Without the payment being made we cannot receive the grace necessary to cure the disease. So, the atonement made on the cross then is a necessary condition for receiving divine grace, which in turn is necessary for being made fit for spending eternity in God's presence.

On the hybrid view, then, it is true that there is a penalty, a penalty which Christ's death pays on behalf of those who accept it. But it is also true that those who fail to accept it put themselves into a state which leads them naturally to being self-lovers and thus naturally to spend eternity apart from God. Incorporating the natural consequence model brings along answers to questions that do not seem to be available on that model alone, questions, as noted above, such as why those in hell can never be saved.

Unloving/Unjust?

Now that we have had the chance to propose a model for understanding and defending the traditional doctrine of hell, let's turn to look at the objections to the view raised by its critics. As I said at the beginning, the charge of the critics most often amounts to the claim that there is something unloving or unjust or both about the traditional view of hell. Let's look at each of these charges in turn.

The discussions of these charges have been long, complex, and frequently intertwined. One might argue, for example, that a God who admits people to hell is unloving *because* he is unjust. Thus, we cannot completely unhook one charge from the other. We can try to do so for our purposes here by dividing up the objections as follows. We will discuss the four most central charges of this type in turn (all of these are meant to be understood as objections raised against the belief that God allows a hell of the sort described in what I will, from here forward, call the "hybrid model"):

1. God is *unjust* because the punishment received in hell does not fit the crime.
2. God is *unjust* because some who go to hell never had a chance to hear or understand the gospel.
3. God is *unloving* because true love would not allow the beloved to suffer such a fate.
4. God is *unloving* because he would not make the eternal consequences of heaven and hell depend on what we think and choose in earthly lives of this sort.

Charge 1: God is *unjust* because the punishment received in hell does not fit the crime.

Reply to Charge 1: A reply to this charge was already given in detail in the section entitled "Objections to the Penalty Model."

Charge 2: God is unjust because some who go to hell never had a chance to hear or understand the gospel.

Reply to Charge 2:[2] Before presenting what I take to be an adequate response to this charge, it is worthwhile to pause briefly in order to say a few words about a very common response to this charge offered by Christian apologists and theologians. The response can be put like this:

> The trouble with this charge is that it is based on a faulty presupposition. Since it claims that God is unfair in setting things up in the way that he has, it presupposes that God was somehow *obligated* to set it up so as to give each person the opportunity to be saved. But it is just wrong to think that God *owes us* salvation or even that he owes us a *shot at it*. Since salvation is an utterly unmerited gift, we can think of the situation along the lines of the following analogy. A rich philanthropist visits a homeless shelter. This philanthropist walks around a bit and then picks out three individuals and tells them that he will gladly buy them the house of their choosing. And away they go. Now those who were not picked might be saddened by the fact that they were not among those selected. But it would be sheer folly for any of these to claim that the philanthropist acted *unfairly*. He wasn't obliged to house any of them. He certainly cannot be faulted for not housing *all* of them. Likewise, God owes none of his fallen creatures salvation. And thus he cannot be criticized as somehow unfair for failing to save all of them, or even for failing to offer all of them an equal shot at salvation.

I think that the response offered above is, strictly speaking, correct. The defender of the traditional view here is saying that there is nothing *unfair* or *unjust* about God saving some of his creatures and not others. But while this is right, it does not really undermine the force of the charge. The reason is that even if this scenario does not raise any trouble for God's justice, it does seem to be inconsistent with his *love*. For imagine our philanthropist again, but this time imagine that he has infinite financial resources. In addition, this philanthropist claims to love all the people in the homeless shelter intensely and equally, as a parent loves a child. If this philanthropist goes to the homeless shelter and agrees to buy houses for only three of them, it seems to put the lie to the claim that he loves all of them, much less intensely. And the same lesson seems to apply in Charge 2 above. So, there is an issue here that needs to be addressed: isn't it somehow contrary to God's claim to *love* all of his children that he makes it that some of them never hear?

Solution One

Of course an answer to this first charge might not be hard to find at all. To see why, let's first consider carefully what it is that we find troubling about the fact that some perish never having heard. The trouble, it seems, is that those who don't hear are disadvantaged. They don't believe because they are not given the opportunity. But this claim presupposes that some who never hear *would believe if they did hear*. But why should we think that is true? For all we know, those who never hear are such that were they to hear they would not believe anyway. If this is right, God has not done anything unjust or unloving in not letting them hear in the first place. He has just allowed to occur what would have happened no matter what.

Someone might object to this solution by claiming that it is obviously false. The fact that people come to believe in Christ when the gospel is proclaimed in areas which were formerly unreached, shows that there are people in un-reached areas who would believe if they did hear. Notice, however, that this objection is mistaken. What Solution One denies is this: "that those who *never* hear, wouldn't believe if they did." Stated this way, we can never have evidence that such people would respond if they heard. Why? Because to have such evidence, we would have to notice that some such people *do* respond. But if that were to happen, they would (obviously) be among those who *did hear* and thus not be part of the relevant group (i.e., those who never hear) in the first place!

Solution Two

Solution One is a brief answer to the charge and many will find it unsatis-factory. Still, there aren't any especially good reasons to find it unsatisfactory. In fact, if God is the loving creator Christians claim he is, it makes eminently good sense. But there are other answers that can be developed. Let me gesture at a recipe for constructing another answer, though I won't actually construct it here. Part of what Charge 2 assumes is that those who do not have the gospel preached to them verbally do not have the necessary information to be saved. But the natural question that arises here is: what information *is* necessary exactly? Maybe it turns out that the information necessary for salvation can be discovered in nature, though it might take some efforts to discover it. So, for example, would it be enough if someone who had never believed the gospel nonetheless believed:

1. that God exists
2. that one is sinful

3. that sin separates us from God
4. that there must be some means of reconciliation

and as a result of believing 1–4 is moved by an act of will to repent and avail himself or herself of the reconciliation? These are difficult questions I don't intend to try to resolve here. As I said, this is a recipe for responding to Charge 2. How one responds depends on what one thinks the necessary beliefs are. If the necessary beliefs can be gleaned without receiving the verbal witness of the gospel, Charge 2 may be based on an utterly faulty presupposition.

Solution Three

One last solution that some have offered holds that those who did not hear in this life must then be given an opportunity to hear immediately after death but before judgment. There is, of course, no clear scriptural support for such "second chances" though it does not seem to be directly contradicted by any passages either. As a result, this is another response that one might consider to Charge 2.

Charge 3: God is unloving because true love would not allow the beloved to suffer such a fate. If God loved us all he would do whatever is necessary to guarantee that we are all saved.

Reply to Charge 3: Let's call Charge 3, the "universalist charge" since it reflects the sentiments underlying the position of most universalists. The criticism embodied in the universalist charge cuts to the heart of what most people find objectionable in the traditional doctrine of hell. Even those who, like myself, think that the traditional doctrine is true cannot help but struggle at times in thinking that true love for someone is inconsistent with assigning someone to hell forever.

What is it exactly that underlies this sentiment? Why do we all feel the tug of the objection that claims that God's love is inconsistent with the doctrine of hell? A look at the recent literature on the topic indicates at least two motivations. The first I will discuss here, the second below. The first motivation springs from the belief that a loving God would do whatever is necessary to prevent those who are destined for hell from going there. On our hybrid position above we have seen that this would mean doing two things:

1. Canceling the penalty due as a result of sin, and
2. Blocking the natural consequences which result from the life lived by the hell-bound person.

So, the critic who raises Charge 3 should be viewed as saying:
Revised Charge 3: God is unloving because true love would (i) cancel the

penalty due as a result of sin and (ii) block the natural consequences which result from the life lived by the hell-bound person.

Is this true? I think there is a lot to be said about (i). But let's leave that aside here since both traditionalist and universalist agree that God, out of his love, has sent his Son to "cancel the penalty of sin."

Must God "Block" the Natural Consequences?

Does love require that God do (ii) as well? Remember that on the hybrid view described above, the purpose of the earthly life is soul-making. That is, while on this earth God gives us meaningful freedom which allows us to become a person of a certain sort. And becoming a person of a certain sort means becoming a person who is resolute either in their love of self or in their love of God. Love of self, as we noted, is something which we can become resolutely settled in if we continue to spurn God's grace in this life. Love of God is something that we can strive for in this life, through the power of grace, and achieve when transformed by God in eternity. What the universalist is asking for, then, is that God reverse the natural consequences of a life of self-love.

[. . .]

"Blocking" Natural Consequences Makes Freedom Meaningless

What can the traditionalist who defends the hybrid view say here? The first thing one should say is that if God were to operate in this way he would make our freedom *meaningless*. What do I mean by this? Let me introduce a distinction here that might make the notion clear. We might think of our freedom of action in this life as having two components. When I act freely I first *make a choice among alternatives*. After making the choice, my body is set in motion in certain ways, ways which then have an impact on the world around me. So, if I, as a shortstop, decide to throw the ball to second base, I first make the decision to throw it there, and that in turn leads to my moving my muscles, which in turn leads to the ball moving towards the second baseman. Simple enough. What makes my freedom *real* we might say, is that I really can choose among alternatives. But what makes my freedom *meaningful* is that the choices I make have an impact on what happens in the world, that is, that because of my choosing, my muscles move in a certain way and the ball then flies through the air.

One could have real freedom *without* having meaningful freedom. Some philosophers, in the context of discussing the problem of evil have suggested, in fact, that God should have made the world in just this way. That is, God should have allowed us to make choices, but then should not have allowed those choices to have *real* consequences in the world. So, if I choose to shoot my neighbor, God would give me an illusion that I actually do it (so that I at least believe that my freedom is meaningful) but in fact, my evil choice has no real bad effect on the world (though it would have a bad effect on my character). But while God might have been able to set up the world in this way, to do so would be to make our freedom *meaningless*. For freedom to be meaningful, it is not only true that we have to be able to choose among alternatives. It must also be the case that the course of events varies with our choices. If I choose to become a self-lover, but God blocks my choices from having their effect, he has prevented my freedom from being what it was supposed to be, that is, a means by which I can engage in meaningful soul-making. I can engage in soul-making, but God won't let me become the person I choose to become. I can only become the sort of person he wants me to become. But then, of course, it looks like I don't have freedom to engage in soul-making after all.

Some might find nothing objectionable about such a picture in which humans have real but not meaningful freedom. Someone might ask us to imagine earthly parents who are watching their child making a choice that will have devastating consequences. The parents might allow the child to make the choice if the choice and its bad consequence will end up helping the child in the long run. In such cases, it may be better to allow them to make the bad choice. But if the bad choice will *only* be harmful (not to mention eternally destructive), no good parent would allow such a choice to be carried out, that is, to have its consequences. So, some might say, we all agree that it is more loving, in such cases, to permit the child to have real but not "meaningful" freedom. But is this really true? It is true that we override the decisions of our young children if the choice will have devastating consequences. I don't allow my child to toddle out into traffic or to drink battery acid. But when our focus shifts to adult children, the picture changes. If my son decides to choose a career, a mate, etc., which I believe (or know) will be destructive for him I may counsel him in the strongest terms not to do so. But if I were to kidnap him and surgically or chemically alter his brain so that he will not choose those things, I would be meddling in a way that displayed disrespect for his autonomy as a person. To interfere in this way would be to remove the *meaningfulness* of his freedom, and this would be to undermine both his human dignity and the real purpose of the earthly life: autonomous soul-making. Thus, if love requires respect for the freedom and individual autonomy of the person who is loved, the universalist charge is false because love does not require (ii).

It is worth noting here that the universalist may disagree with this way of seeing things, however. Some universalists agree with part of the account just given, but not all of it. These universalists agree that there is intrinsic worth in autonomous soul-making. As a result, they would argue, God leaves us free to try to become God-lovers by turning to him, accepting his grace, and struggling forward in the process of sanctification. But if that process fails, that is, if the person fails to turn to God and develop a God-loving character by choice, it is more loving for God to save that person *against their will*, so to speak, than to allow their choices to have their natural consequences, namely, being a self-lover, a God-hater, and thus separated from God for eternity.

Thus, as the universalists see it, it is more loving to interfere with the choices of those who want to be apart from God than it is to respect their freedom and autonomy. But it does seem that on this point it is the traditional view that is more in keeping with our impressions about how genuine love is to be expressed.

The discussion of Charge 3 leads naturally to Charge 4 which, you will recall, was put as follows:

Charge 4: God is unloving because he would not make the eternal consequences of heaven and hell depend on what we think and choose in earthly lives of this sort.

Reply to Charge 4: The charge raised here is one, again, that has been advanced in recent writings by universalists. Their central claim is that God has put us in an environment in which it is too hard for us to see that the point of this life is to become lovers of God. And even if God has provided us with enough evidence to make it clear to us that this is the purpose of this life, he has given us such frail human faculties that he could not reasonably have expected us to be able to succeed in the task.

[. . .]

It should be clear that this charge can be easily related to the one discussed above. The universalist might say, "On the hybrid view, to be a lover of God one must first turn to him and accept the grace that pays the penalty for our sin and gives us the power to break the bondage of sin. But to do *that* one must accept that initial grace and turn to God. And as we make choices in our daily lives, choices which might slowly but surely lead us away from God and into self-love, we unwittingly cut ourselves off from being able to will to turn to God in the first place. And, given our impaired condition and circumstances, it is almost impossible to prevent ourselves from cutting ourselves off from God in this way. And if God truly loves us, he would never put us in such a condition."

Thus, we might rephrase Charge 4 as follows:

Revised Charge 4: If God is hanging such great significance on the course of our earthly lives, he is obliged to make it very clear to us just what that significance is, and he is obliged to give us the tools and environment that allow us to meet the challenge. If he doesn't do these things, and then consigns to hell those who fail at the task, he is unloving. And surely he does *not* do these things, since many people do not even believe in an afterlife, never mind believing that the choices made in their daily lives have some connection to this eternal fate.

The claim of the defender of Charge 4, then, is that the task of human existence is not clear, and the tools for the task insufficient. Is this correct? To answer that question we must first answer the question of just how clear the task is supposed to be. One might think initially that it should be so clear that no one can possibly miss it, that is, as clear as modern advertising slogans. If mere human powers can implant these thoughts deeply in our minds, can't God do the same concerning this very central fact?

Can God Make It Clearer?

Some, myself included, have argued that God cannot make things quite that evident. One reason is that if he were to demonstrate to us that there were two courses, one leading to life and one to eternal separation in a forceful and obvious way, God would remove the freedom necessary for autonomous soul-making by subjecting us to a form of divine coercion.[3] So, if he cannot make the truth as fully evident as *that*, how evident must it be to make it fairly accessible while not coercively overpowering? For all we know, the answer is: just as accessible as it is.

Are We Properly Equipped to Achieve the Aims of This Life?

What about the claim, then, that the tools that God has given us are insufficient for the task? Is it true that our abilities to think about our fate and to make choices about it in this life are so drastically impaired that doing what is required of us is unfairly difficult? The problem with this question is that it is not really clear what it is asking. Assuming that we have adequately addressed the "is the task evident enough?" objection, the only thing it could be asking is whether or not we can choose to be lovers of God once we recognize that that is what we *ought* to do. No doubt doing this is hard. But its difficulty is part of what makes it soul-making. It is having to make the choices in the face of temptations that makes our choices *real* choices among alternatives. So the question is, once we recognize what the task of life is (becoming lovers of God rather than self), are the temptations to be lovers of self so strong that we don't have a fair opportunity to do otherwise? The universalist claims that the temptations are too strong, the traditionalist claims that divine grace overcomes the power of sin and allows us to choose to turn to God. It is by no means clear that the universalist is right on this score, and thus, we might say, there is no compelling reason to give up the traditional position on the basis of Charge 4.

No doubt, the issues raised here are deep and complex. Complete resolution of them would require a great deal more discussion than I can give them here. But the question we have been addressing in this section is whether or not the universalist has any successful objections against the traditionalist. What I have tried to show here is that it is far from clear that he does. As a result, I think we can conclude that we have seen no good reason to think that the plain sense of Scripture does not make good sense, and so no good reason to abandon the traditional doctrine of hell.

[. . .]

NOTES

1. "Aquinas on Atonement," in *Trinity, Incernation, and Atonement*, ed. Cornelius Plantinga and Ronald Feenstra (Notre Dame: University of Notre Dame Press, 1989), 198.
2. It is worth mentioning that there are a number of related objections that one can raise here. For example, one might say that God is unfair because he leaves the spreading of the gospel in the hands of lazy, sinful, selfish, and limited human beings, or because he does not make the gospel known by means of celestial fireworks or voices from the heavens. Unfortunately, space does not allow me to address all of the objections. Instead I will focus on the basic charge as stated.
3. See for example my essay "Coercion and the Hiddenness of God," *American Philosophical Quarterly* 30:1 (1993): 27–38, as well as essays by Daniel Howard-Snyder, "The Argument from Divine Hiddenness," *Canadian Journal of Philosophy* 26 (1996): 433–53, and Richard Swinburne, *The Existence of God* (Oxford: Clarendon Press, 1979), 153ff.

ATONEMENT
6.4

RETHINKING THE LOGIC OF PENAL SUBSTITUTION

Steven Porter

INTRODUCTION

The Christian understanding of the atonement vexed human minds from the start. The apostle Paul records that the crucifixion of Christ, commonly taken to be central to the atonement, was a 'stumbling block' to the Jews and 'foolishness' to the gentiles. But he goes on to claim that it was 'the power of God and the wisdom of God' to those called.[1] I will assume that, while the doctrine can certainly be perceived as a stumbling block or as foolishness, its actual nature displays the power and wisdom of God. The problem is to explicate exactly how this is so. More precisely, the problem of the doctrine of the atonement is to provide a rationally defensible explication of how Christ's person and work are efficacious for the salvation of human persons.

I will begin this paper with a brief overview of four historically noteworthy attempts to provide such an explication, and then turn to Richard Swinburne's reformulation of one of these. I will point out a weakness of Swinburne's approach, which is avoided on a modified theory of penal substitution.

FOUR HISTORICALLY DOMINANT THEORIES

The New Testament possesses both a unity and diversity when it comes to its atonement teachings. There is agreement in the univocal proclamation that

Christ is the saviour of humanity, but difference in the ways this salvific work is described. For instance, Christ is said to be a 'ransom' for many (Matt. 20:28); he 'saved' sinners from the 'wrath of God' (Rom. 5:9); he 'reconciles' the world to God (2 Cor. 2:19); he 'redeemed' humanity (Gal. 3:13); he is the 'mediator' between God and humans (1 Tim. 2:6); he makes 'propitiation' for sins (Heb. 2:17); and he is the perfect 'sacrifice' for sin (Heb. 9:26). Since there is no early orthodox formulation of the atonement which authoritatively synthesises these and other relevant passages, the various biblical ideas have provided the theological raw materials for the construction of a variety of atonement schemes. Here I will briefly outline the four dominant theories in church history.[2]

The ransom theory, put forth by such early fathers as Origen and Gregory of Nyssa, was the first detailed account of the atonement.[3] Due to a rightful emphasis upon Jesus' own claim to be a 'ransom for many' as well as a vivid awareness of the reality of evil, the ransom theorists saw Christ as delivering humanity from the powerful foes of sin, death and Satan by giving up his life as a ransom paid to Satan. Origen asserts of Christ:

> To whom gave He His life a ransom for many? It cannot have been to God. Was it not then to the evil one? For he held us until the ransom for us, even the soul of Jesus, was paid to him, being deceived into thinking that he could be its lord, and not seeing that he could not bear the torment of holding it.[4]

Gregory of Nyssa initiates the use of bait and hook metaphors as a means to explain the theory.[5] Christ's perfect human life is the bait which lures the ravenous fish (i.e., Satan) to turn over to God his rightful possession of sinful humanity in exchange for the possession of Christ. But Christ's divinity is the hook veiled beneath his humanity which snares Satan and crushes him in the resurrection. Since Satan's dominion over fallen humanity kept humans in bondage to sin and death, the overcoming of Satan entails the vanquishing of these forces as well.

While the ransom theory clearly presents a mechanism for how the life, death and resurrection of Christ accomplishes salvation, it has been consistently rejected since Anselm. This is largely due to the questionable supposition that Satan had just rights over fallen humans, as well as doubts that God would deceive Satan.

In *Why God Became Man*, Anselm of Canterbury proposes several objections to the ransom theory which are summed up in his statement,

> Finally, just as there is no injustice whatsoever in a good angel, similarly there is absolutely no justice in a bad one. There was nothing in the devil, therefore, which made God obliged not to use his mighty power against him for the purpose of liberating mankind.[6]

Since God could have justly overthrown the devil, the notion of Christ's life being a ransom paid to Satan loses its rational force.

In its place Anselm develops the satisfaction theory of the atonement positing Christ's obedient suffering and death as the necessary satisfaction of the debt sinners owe to God.[7] Anselm argues that humans have not rendered to God the honour due to him, and thus are in a position of debt. Justice demands that God punish human debtors with eternal death unless adequate satisfaction is provided. Anselm writes, 'It is a necessary consequence, therefore, that either the honour which has been taken away should be repaid, or punishment should follow.'[8] The problem is that God's creatures already owe God perfect obedience, and so they cannot engender any positive merit to restore the honour they have taken. But if punishment occurs, then all humans will be eternally separated from God, which would be a state unbefitting God. So it is necessary that satisfaction be made. And yet, while only humans ought to make satisfaction, only God is able to make it. Thus, writes Anselm, if 'no one can pay except God, and no one ought to pay except man: it is necessary that a God–Man should pay it.'[9] The obedient suffering and death of Christ is of such great worth that it restores the dignity owed to God, and thus makes possible the forgiveness of sins.

Of the many objections that have been proffered against Anselm's theory, there are two that often reappear. The first is that there is absent from Anselm's account a delineation of the principle of justice which necessitates God's requiring either satisfaction or punishment in order to forgive. Second, granting this necessity, there is some question as to how Christ's suffering and death is an appropriate satisfaction of the debts sinners owe to God. Peter Abelard, Anselm's contemporary, puts the essence of these objections poignantly:

> Indeed, how cruel and wicked it seems that anyone should demand the blood of an innocent person as the price for anything, or that it should in any way please him that an innocent man should be slain – still less that God should consider the death of his Son so agreeable that by it he should be reconciled to the whole world![10]

In order to avoid this troubling outcome, Abelard emphasised the subjective effects of the work of Christ in his explication of the atonement. In so doing, he initiated the third dominant atonement theory, namely, moral exemplarism.[11] The essence of this theory is that the cross is solely an exemplification of God's love, which serves to inspire others to love God in return. There is no objective mechanism that secures salvation, rather it is purely the manifestation of God's love that subjectively influences sinners to turn to God.

But while the cross of Christ presumably bespeaks the love of God, the question for atonement theorising is how it does so. If there is no good purpose for Christ's voluntary suffering and death as regards salvation, then there is no basis for it demonstrating God's love. A theory which provides an objective purpose for the crucifixion is needed to ground the subjective influence Abelard emphasised. Calvin's theory of penal substitution endeavours to furnish such an account.

The theory of penal substitution, as presented by Calvin, dissolves Anselm's disjunction of 'satisfaction or punishment' in favour of the sole necessity of punishment.[12] Calvin writes, 'for God's wrath and curse always lie upon sinners until they are absolved of guilt. Since he is a righteous Judge, he does not allow his law to be broken without punishment, but is equipped to avenge it.'[13] Since the just punishment for sin is eternal damnation, the demands of God's justice must be met in God's forgiveness of guilty sinners. Hence, the guilt of sinners is transferred to the innocent Christ and he vicariously suffers the punishment due sinners, thereby appeasing God's wrath and satisfying his justice.

But seeing the cross as fulfilling necessary punishment rather than necessary satisfaction does little to answer the objections posed earlier for the satisfaction theory. There still appears to be no justification for the necessity of God exacting punishment before he is able to forgive. And, given this strict view of the necessity of punishment, it is difficult to conceive how the punishment of Christ instead of sinners suffices the demands of justice. One sinner's necessary punishment of eternal damnation (let alone millions of sinners' necessary punishment) does not appear to be the kind of penalty that can be transferred to another.

THEORETICAL QUANDARIES: MYTH, MYSTERY, OR RATIONAL INVESTIGATION

How should one respond to the seemingly intractable problems that face each of the four atonement theories presented? One might decide that the Christian doctrine of the atonement is hopelessly implausible and that the truth about the conditions of salvation lie elsewhere than in the atonement myths generated by traditional theology.[14] Or one might maintain the traditional understanding of salvation through Christ while relegating the actual nature of the atonement to the realm of metaphor and mystery.[15]

I believe there are difficulties and dangers with both of these responses, but I will reject them both here for the single reason that they are default positions to be taken after one has exhausted rational investigations into the nature of the atonement. If there are still moves to be made in thinking more clearly about the atonement, then it is far too early to reduce the doctrine to either myth or mystery. Hence, to continue in the long tradition of careful reflection on the possible rationale for Christ's atoning work is the best response to the array of atonement theories.[16]

Rethinking Satisfaction

Of the four theories considered above, the satisfaction and penal substitution theories have received the greatest amount of attention by contemporary philosophers and seem to offer the most hope for the development of a rationally defensible atonement scheme.[17]

But, as presented earlier, Anselm's version of the satisfaction theory is problematic. The principal worry pertains to the grounds for it being necessary that God receive either full satisfaction for human sins or else deliver full punishment in order to justly forgive. Assuming that sin is like defaulting on a debt humans owe to God, then it seems God would have a right to collect on those debts. But it also appears consistent with divine justice for God to forego his right and freely forgive. Anselm needs to explain why this merciful option is unavailable to God.

The explanation Anselm gives is that forgiveness without repayment or punishment would be intolerable in God's morally ordered universe.[18] But how so? Human persons often forgive without demanding satisfaction or punishment, especially when the wrongdoer is apologetic and repentant, and this does not appear to be morally egregious. There is seemingly no moral principle available which would ground Anselm's position that either satisfaction or punishment is a necessary precursor to divine forgiveness.

This worry can be overcome though with a slight modification of Anselm's view. For if it is not necessary that God receive full satisfaction, but only good that he receive some satisfaction, then some sense could be given to the idea that God mercifully accepts the crucifixion as a sufficient payment for the debt of sin. Swinburne provides just such an account of the atonement and in so doing goes some way towards buttressing the satisfaction theory.[19]

Swinburne argues at length for an understanding of forgiveness between human persons which involves the process of repentance, apology, reparation and penance. Swinburne writes that these four components are 'all contributions to removing as much of the consequences of the past act as logically can be removed by the wrongdoer'.[20] When a wrongdoer intentionally harms another, Swinburne contends that the wrongdoer ought to repent and apologise for his offence. To repent is to own privately the wrong act and resolve to one's self not to act in such a way again, while to apologise is to express publicly this inner resolution. It is good that the victim withhold forgiveness until the wrongdoer repents and apologises, for to forgive without this would be to treat the situation without due moral seriousness.

In certain cases Swinburne holds that it is good for forgiveness to be withheld until reparation and penance are provided as well. In reparation the wrongdoer seeks to repair the damage done to the victim as much as is logically possible. In penance the wrongdoer goes beyond what is required in reparation and gives a gift to the victim as an attempt to show that his previous steps towards reconciliation were deliberate and serious. Requiring the acts of reparation and penance for forgiveness is good in that it treats the wrongdoer as a responsible agent and takes the harm done and its consequences as seriously as they can be taken.

Swinburne applies this general view of human forgiveness to the divine/human relationship. The idea here is that human sinners have acquired guilt before God, which is like being in debt, in failing to live their lives well. Swinburne argues that it would be good of God to forgive repentant and apologetic sinners their debt of guilt without requiring any further satisfaction. But it is also good of God to require reparation and penance in order to take the wrongdoer and his act with due seriousness. The problem is that it is difficult for sinners to provide substantive reparation and penance, for they owe God good acts anyway. So while God is free to choose any supererogatory act as a fulfilment of substantive reparation and penance, it is good of God to provide this through Christ's supererogatory life and death. For it was fitting for a life lived perfectly to be offered as reparation and penance when the wrong done was a life lived imperfectly. So, Christ offered up his life as a sacrifice to the Father as a means of reparation and penance for human persons. When sinners combine their repentance and apology with pleading the atoning work of Christ as a means of reparation and penance, God forgives them their sins and their guilt is removed.

Swinburne's view is an improvement on Anselm in that it replaces the necessity of satisfaction with a cogent moral framework in which repentance, apology, reparation and penance are good as conditions for forgiveness. But this otherwise plausible move generates a weakness. On Swinburne's theory God could freely choose any valuable act to serve as reparation and penance. God could have required merely Christ's valuable life for this purpose without requiring the crucifixion. Since the goods obtained by Christ offering reparation and penance on behalf of sinners could be accomplished without his suffering and death, it is implausible to think that a good God would require such an event for forgiveness.

Of course, there might be some other good which the cross served which made it a valuable act, and thus rendered it capable of being a part of the reparation and penance offered to God on behalf of sinners. But Swinburne does not suggest what this other good may be, and this is worrisome.[21]

Yet even if such a good is developed, God's choice of conditioning his forgiveness on the crucifixion in particular would be for an arbitrary reason.[22] For, on Swinburne's view, there is nothing about Christ's suffering and death which adds to the effectiveness of Christ being the means of substantive reparation and penance. Of all the valuable acts of Christ that God could have chosen as a means of reparation and penance, there is no reason given why God chose the suffering and death of Christ in particular. This arbitrariness forges a rift between the cross and the forgiveness of sins. On Swinburne's view, the reason for the crucifixion is not the forgiveness of sins. The notion that 'Christ died for our sins' must be taken to mean that Christ died for some other good purpose besides the forgiveness of sins which then makes his death suitable as a means for such forgiveness. There is nothing about the cross taken apart from God's choice to condition salvation upon it which has any meaning or significance pertaining to the forgiveness of sins. This disconnection as well as the ultimate arbitrariness of the cross weakens the explanatory force of Swinburne's theory. What is needed is a theory that avoids the Anselmian problems as Swinburne does, and yet intimately connects the crucifixion with the forgiveness of sins.

RETHINKING PENAL SUBSTITUTION

On the theory of penal substitution the crucifixion of Christ is morally necessary as punishment for sins.[23] But, as with Anselm, there is no clear justification of why it is that God must punish sinners and cannot simply forgive them. God has the right to demand full punishment, but there is seemingly no moral necessity obligating him to exercise that right.

Yet, even if some divine mystery makes punishment necessary, the additional problem arises as to how it is that the punishment of Christ suffices for the debt sinners owe. It is difficult to get away from the idea that the strict justice of morally necessary punishment would also demand that the guilty party pays his or her own debts. It has been suggested that God was lenient in mercifully allowing Christ to be the just substitute for the penalty due to others. But then one wonders why God could not have been lenient in withholding such severe punishment altogether? Is God lenient enough to let sinners escape their own punishment, but not lenient enough to let Christ avoid the pain and anguish of the cross?

I think the best response to these troubles is to maintain that God did exercise leniency in letting Christ take the punishment due sinners, and indeed that he could have withheld punishment altogether, including the punishment of Christ. But God didn't do the latter because it was good of him to punish Christ as a substitute for sinners. On this modified theory of penal substitution, it is good that God punish sinners (not necessary), and good that Christ take the punishment due sinners as a condition of God granting forgiveness (not necessary that he do so). It remains the case that salvation is necessarily through Christ, but this necessity is conditioned upon God's good decision to offer salvation only through the person and work of Christ.

Such a view of the crucifixion connects the nature of Christ's atoning work with the forgiveness of sins. It is not just any valuable act that Christ performs upon which forgiveness is based, but it is Christ's taking the penalty of human sins upon which forgiveness of those sins is based. The punishment of Christ is a fitting condition for the forgiveness of sins. So this view avoids the problem I pressed against Swinburne as well as the main objections to the traditional penal substitution view.

There are three main features of modified penal substitution. The first is the claim that punishment is not necessary for the forgiveness of sinners. There are many reasons to think this. First, there is a strong leaning in church history towards the view that God could have effected atonement for sins in any way that he pleased, but that the way he did was fitting for this or that reason. Almost all of the early Church Fathers, including Augustine, and the majority of medieval theologians, including Aquinas, took this line.[24] Second, that God is free to forgive without punishment squares with widespread moral intuition and moral experience that forgiveness without punishment is not only possible but also virtuous. Third, a traditional Christian belief is that God is sovereign over all things, and, while there are some logically impossible things that even a sovereign God cannot do, it seems odd that one of these impossibilities is forgiveness without punishment when humans do this regularly. In fact, Jesus taught that persons should forgive without demanding recompense, and more significantly he practised this teaching in his own life.[25] Finally, I will simply have to assert that I do not find the theological arguments in support of the necessity of punishment compelling.[26] So I propose that it is a reasonable shift to maintain that divine punishment of sinners is not morally necessary for forgiveness.

The second claim of modified penal substitution is that God is just and has good reasons to withhold his forgiveness until sinners receive some punishment. I say 'some' punishment because it is not my contention here that God is just and has good reasons to punish sinners for eternity in hell. What I will assume is that God is just to withdraw his providential care from rebellious sinners and abandon them to their ways for a time. At the very least, sinners deserve punishment of this kind for their wrongs against God and their fellows.[27] But what reasons might there be for God to execute this kind of punishment upon repentant and apologetic sinners?

First, as Swinburne holds, it is good of persons to demand substantive reparation and penance from repentant and apologetic wrongdoers. This takes the harm done and the process of reconciliation seriously. One way to accomplish this good is to punish wrongdoers. Punishment, then, is the infliction of harm for the intended purpose of exacting reparation that is owed for wrongdoing. Punishment is particularly appropriate as the means of reparation and penance when the wrong done is such that the damage cannot be repaired by positive means (e.g., rape or adultery). Punishment can take seriously the nature of the loss and 'undo the past' in a way that positive forms of reparation cannot. For instance, for a wife to be offered an expensive gift from her unfaithful husband as a means to make reparation for his adulterous betrayal seems petty in a way that her demanding her husband to move out for a period of time does not.

Fundamental to sin is a prideful usurpation of God's rightful place in one's life and thereby a rejection of God's offer of intimate friendship. Hence, sin is a form of rebellion that cannot be repaired by positive efforts, and thus, reparation and penance can be better captured via punishment. If God demanded some punishment prior to his forgiving repentant and apologetic sinners, this would treat sinners as responsible agents and take the wrongs done seriously, and it is good that God do this.

Second, such punishment would be good as an objective correction of the expression of distorted values in human sin. On the expressive theory of punishment, the chief end of retributive punishment is the vindication of the victim's value. John Hare writes of this view:

> The basic idea here is that the offender s wrongdoing demeans the victim by giving expression to the view that the offender's value is high enough to make this treatment of the victim legitimate or permissible . . . The demand for retributive punishment is then the demand that this false elevation of the offender's value be corrected visibly . . . it is the insistence on the recognition of a moral value, the correct relative value of wrongdoer to victim.[28]

For example, when little Johnny intentionally pushes sister Susan to the floor, he is considering himself to be more valuable than his sister. There is a devaluing of Susan and a corresponding overvaluing of Johnny expressed in the act. In this act a denial of the moral truth of Johnny and Susan's equal human worth is expressed. It is good that such a distortion of values be corrected as much as is logically possible so that the moral truth of equality is reaffirmed. Thus, it is good that Johnny be reprimanded and sent to spend time alone. The punishment is meant to inflict suffering on Johnny as a way of expressing his defeat. One good of punishment, then, is to express a correction of the original distortion of values by expressing a lowering of the overinflated value of the offender.[29]

In the case of human sin, one of the victims is God in the sense that the sinner expresses a devaluing of God and an inflated valuing of his own self in his prideful attempt to live independently of God. The point is not that God's value is actually reduced, but rather that the wrongdoing objectively expresses a distortion of values which is a denial of the moral truth of God's infinite value relative to a human individual's finite value. And it is good that this distortion and denial be recognised and corrected through the punishment of the sinner. If the sinner suffers a penalty proportionate in some measure to his offence, his elevated value is shown to be false and the moral truth is reaffirmed. This objective good can be called the expressive good.

The expressive good serves the further good purpose of providing an opportunity for the sinner to recognise in his punishment the true value of God, his own pride and the gravity of his wrong, which in turn draws the sinner towards healthy shame and virtuous humility. So on the expressive view of punishment there is the possibility of the further subjective good of what might be called moral education and moral formation.

Hence, on the position I am proposing, there are at least three kinds of goods that would be accomplished by God punishing sinners: the goods of substantive reparation and penance, the expressive good, and the goods of moral education and moral formation. So, I conclude that it would be just and good of God to punish human sinners to some degree as a condition of granting forgiveness of sins.

The third element of modified penal substitution is the claim that the goods derived from the punishment of sinners are better served when Christ voluntarily takes the punishment instead. But how might both the justice and greater goodness of this substitution be defended?

It is often purported that it would be unjust of God to punish Christ in the place of sinners. The main idea is that punishment is only just if the one being punished deserves the punishment, and Christ did not. Yet, if punishment is seen as a free exercise of a retributive right to punish in order to accomplish certain good ends, then how one goes about executing this punishment appears somewhat flexible. Since one does not have to punish at all, leniency of various kinds is allowable. The justification of God's right to punish lies in humans being in a position of debt before God, but his decision whether and how to execute that punishment is effected by the moral worth of such punishment. And if the good ends of punishment are better served by inflicting the punishment deserved by sinners onto the voluntary substitute of Christ then, while Christ does not deserve the punishment himself, there is no injustice in him taking it.

So while just punishment must always be directed towards a wrong that deserves such punishment, there is no injustice in someone else voluntarily serving that punishment if there are good reasons for such a transfer and the victim agrees to accept such a substitution as fulfilment of the offender's debt. It is simply that in most cases of serious crime there are few good reasons, and often very bad ones, for transferring the punishment. Given that deterrence and incapacitation are the main potential goods of criminal punishment, it is probably never good that such a penalty be transferred, for there is little hope of achieving these goods through a transfer.[30] But the same derivative goods are not at issue in the divine/human situation, and so it may be better for Christ voluntarily to serve the punishment that is due sinners.

Indeed, there are at least three reasons to think that it would be better for Christ to receive the punishment due sinners. First, Christ's vicarious punishment is a more costly form of reparation and penance than the direct punishment of sinners. That God himself is willing to suffer the punishment due sinners demonstrates just how seriously he takes the divine/human relationship and the process of reconciliation. For those repentant and apologetic sinners who are willing to see Christ's life and death as the means of entry into God's kingdom, the goods of substantive reparation and penance are more fully realised via the punishment of Christ.

Second, if God punished sinners to some degree, there would likely be further alienation between God and humans. It seems safe to assume that most persons are not mature enough to take punishment well. But if Christ is able to bear the punishment well, then persons will have cause to be exceedingly grateful for this substitution rather than bitter towards God.

Third, the expressive good would be better served through the punishment of Christ. For in human sin the view is expressed that a finite human is more valuable than an infinitely valuable God. So, any amount of punishment inflicted on a finite being would not suffice to express the degree of value distortion in human sin. While punishment as expression does not have to be quantitatively exact, it does need to vindicate the value of the victim adequately.[31]

But the punishment of Christ allows for an adequate expression of the value of God. The defeat on the cross of God incarnate gets at the value distortion in sin. For what is being expressed on the cross (i.e., finite humans ruling over an infinitely valuable being) is the exact kind of value distortion that is expressed in human sin. Only this time it occurs for the purpose of fulfilling the punishment sinners deserve, thereby expressing the true value of God. So Christ taking the debt of punishment on behalf of sinners makes possible the expressive good, and thus the goods of moral education and moral formation. For when a sinner considers the cross and realises that his sins were so grievous that it was good of Christ to suffer and die in response to those sins, the cross serves as an abiding expression of human depravity and the holiness of God. Further, the cross exemplifies the mercy and love of God for sinners in that God chooses to treat sinners differently than they deserve, because of the cross. But whether the sinner subjectively appreciates the meaning of the cross or not, Christ's suffering the punishment due sinners objectively expresses the great moral truth of God's value relative to rebellious sinners. So, for all these reasons, it is just and a greater good for God to visit on Christ the punishment that it would be just and good to visit on sinners.

CONCLUSION

Much more needs to be said. I hope enough has been said to demonstrate that the doctrine of the atonement is a burgeoning area of theological and philosophical inquiry, and that it is far from clear that the doctrine should be reduced to either myth or mystery. Moreover, my intention has been to present a theory of modified penal substitution as a fruitful way to articulate the traditional theory of penal substitution, and thereby provide a rationally defensible explication of how Christ's person and work are efficacious for human salvation.

NOTES

I would like to thank Doug Geivett, John Hare, Jeff Jensen, Michael Murray, Alicia Porter and Richard Swinburne for helpful comments relevant to this essay.

1. Cor. 1:23–4. Some take the longer passage in which these verses are a part to be a biblical argument against philosophical inquiry into the nature of revealed truth. I find this interpretation erroneous for reasons I cannot go into here.

2. For an overview of these and other theories see L. W. Grensted, *A Short History of the Doctrine of the Atonement* (Manchester: University Press, 1920).

3. For more on this theory, see Grensted, 32–55; Gustaf Aulen, *Christus Victor* (London: SPCK, 1953) 32–76.

4. Origin, *Commentary on Matthew*, xvi, 8. As quoted in Grensted, 38.

5. See Grensted, 39–44.

6. Anselm, 'Why God Became Man', in Brian Davies and G. R. Evans, eds., *Anselm of Canterbury: The Major Works* (Oxford: Oxford University Press, 1998) 274/1.7.

7. For more on Anselm's view, see Robert S. Franks, *The Work of Christ* (London: Thomas Nelson and Sons Ltd., 1962) 126–141; Steven S. Aspenson, 'In Defence of Anselm', *History of Philosophy Quarterly*, 7 (1990) 33–45.

8. Anselm, 286/I.13.

9. Anselm, 320/II.6.

10. Peter Abelard, 'Exposition of the Epistle to the Romans', Gerald E. Moffatt, trans., in Eugene R. Fairweather, ed., *A Scholastic Miscellany: Anselm to Ockham* (Philadelphia: Westminster, 1956) 283.

11. For more on Abelard's view, see Grensted, 103–110; Philip L. Quinn, 'Abelard on Atonement: "Nothing Unintelligible, Arbitrary, Illogical, or Immoral about It" ', In Eleonore Stump, ed., *Reasoned Faith* (Ithaca, NY: Cornell University Press, 1993) 281–300.

12. For more on Calvin's view, see Franks, 333–347; Robert A. Peterson, *Calvin's Doctrine of the Atonement* (Phillipsburg, NJ: Presbyterian and Reformed Publishing, 1983).

13. John Calvin, *Institutes of the Christian Religion*, Henry Beveridge, trans. (London: James Clarke and Co., 1957) Book II. 16.1.

14. For example, see John Hick, *The Metaphor of God Incarnate* (London: SCM Press, 1993) 112–126.

15. For example, Thomas F. Torrance considers the atonement an 'ineffable mystery'. See Torrance's *The Mediation of Christ* (Edinburgh: T&T Clark, 1992).

16. Of course, the nature of the atonement might still be somewhat of a mystery at the end of the day. Rational investigation into the nature of reality, including theological reality, while capable of getting one to the truth about things, at times only gets one to the best approximation of that truth. So while the precise nature of the atonement may not be known with certainty, there are nevertheless better and worse models of this reality.

17. Both of these theories mainly emphasise the relevance of Christ's death to the forgiveness of sins. While this narrow focus is beneficial for the purpose of analysis, it is also perilous in that it seemingly reduces the gospel to a message of the remission of sins. Certainly there is much more to salvation than the forgiveness of sins and much more to Christ than his sacrificial death. On this point I am in complete agreement with Dallas Willard's critique of myopic atonement theories. See Willard's, *The Divine Conspiracy* (New York: HarperCollins, 1998) 42–50.

18. Anselm, 286–287/Book I.13.

19. Richard Swinburne, *Responsibility and Atonement* (Oxford: Clarendon Press, 1989). For an extended treatment see Philip L. Quinn, 'Swinburne on Guilt, Atonement, and Christian Redemption', in Alan G. Padgett, ed., *Reason and the Christian Religion* (Oxford: Clarendon Press, 1994) 277–300.

20. Swinburne, 81.

21. Swinburne does maintain that Christ's life and death are a peculiarly appropriate means for reparation and penance in that they make up a perfect human life offered up for persons who led ruinous lives. Swinburne, 157. But, first, why is suffering and death by crucifixion a part of a perfect human life? And second, even if it is, I

question whether such a result would by itself justify God's requiring the crucifixion. Wouldn't it have been better for God to provide substantive reparation and penance through Christ's meritorious life alone and leave the whole mess of the crucifixion out of it?

22. In this instance Swinburne is more Scotist than Thomist in his theory of the atonement in that the crucifixion is chosen arbitrarily rather than for a fitting reason. For a discussion of this difference between Aquinas and Scotus see Grensted, 158–163.

23. Calvin thought that the necessity of the crucifixion was conditional on God's decree, but later proponents of the penal theory clearly take the punishment of Christ to be necessary in an absolute sense. See Louis Berkhof, *Systematic Theology* (Grand Rapids: Eerdmans, 1996) 368–370.

24. For the point about the Church Fathers see Grensted, 54. For Augustine, see *De Agone Christi*, c. xi; *De Trinitate*, xiii. 10. And for Aquinas, see *Summa Theologiae*, 3a. 46.2 ad 3.

25. See Matthew 5:38–48, Mark 2:5, Luke 7:40–50, Luke 15:20–24, etc.

26. The biblical proof texts for the necessity of divine punishment seem lacking. The fact of divine punishment as a penalty for sin is clear in Scripture. But it does not follow from the fact that God has and will punish sins that it is morally necessary that he do so. What does follow is that it must be good of God to punish sins. For an example of the type of argument I do not find compelling see Berkhof, 370–372.

27. I largely assume here that punishment for wrongdoing is justified on retributive grounds. The main question at this point is whether it is good of God to exercise his right to punish, and, if so, whether transferring the punishment to Christ is justified. For a discussion of the justification of retributive punishment, see C. L. Ten, *Crime, Guilt, and Punishment* (Oxford: Clarendon Press, 1987) 38–81. For a discussion of the justice of hell, see Michael J. Murray, 'Heaven and Hell', in Murray, ed., *Reason for the Hope Within* (Grand Rapids: Eerdmans, 1999) 287–317.

28. John E. Hare, *The Moral Gap* (Oxford: Clarendon Press, 1996) 247. I am deeply indebted to Hare's work on the connection between expressive punishment and penal substitution. See Hare, 243–259.

29. For more on the expressive theory see Jean Hampton, 'The Retributive Idea', in Jeffrie G. Murphy and Jean Hampton, eds., *Forgiveness and Mercy* (Cambridge: Cambridge University Press, 1988) 111–161.

30. This is part of the answer to David Lewis's query in his 'Do We Believe in Penal Substitution?,' *Philosophical Papers*, 26 (1997) 203–209.

31. See Hampton, 134.

PRAYER
6.5

'PETITIONARY PRAYER'

Eleonore Stump

Ordinary Christian believers of every period have in general taken prayer to be fundamentally a request made of God for something specific believed to be good by the one praying. The technical name for such prayer is "impetration"; I am going to refer to it by the more familiar designation "petitionary prayer." There are, of course, many important kinds of prayer which are not requests; for example, most of what is sometimes called "the higher sort of prayer"— praise, adoration, thanksgiving—does not consist in requests and is not included under petitionary prayer. But basic, common petitionary prayer poses problems that do not arise in connection with the more contemplative varieties of prayer, and it is petitionary prayer with its special problems that I want to examine in this paper.

Of those problems, the one that has perhaps been most discussed in the recent literature is the connection between petitionary prayer and miracles. For instance, if one believes in divine response to petitionary prayer, is one thereby committed to a belief in miracles? But as much as possible I want to avoid this issue (and several others involving petitionary prayer) in order to concentrate on just one problem. It is, I think, the problem stemming from petitionary prayer which has most often occurred to ordinary Christian believers from the patristic period to the present.

Put roughly and succinctly, the problem comes to this: is a belief in the efficacy and usefulness of petitionary prayer consistent with a belief in an

Eleonore Stump, 'Petitionary Prayer', *American Philosophical Quarterly*, 16, 2 (April 1979), pp. 81–91.

omniscient, omnipotent, perfectly good God? It is, therefore, a problem only on certain assumptions drawn from an ordinary, orthodox, traditional view of God and of petitionary prayer. If one thinks, for example, as D. Z. Philipps does,[1] that all "real" petitionary prayer is reducible to the petition "Thy will be done," then the problem I want to discuss evaporates. And if one thinks of God as the unknowable, non-denumerable, ultimate reality, which is not an entity at all, as Keith Ward does,[2] the problem I am interested in does not even arise. The cases which concern me in this paper are those in which someone praying a petitionary prayer makes a specific request freely (at least in his own view) of an omniscient, omnipotent, perfectly good God, conceived of in the traditional orthodox way. I am specifying that the prayers are made freely because I want to discuss this problem on the assumption that man has free will and that not everything is predetermined. I am making this assumption, first because I want to examine the problem of petitionary prayer as it arises for ordinary Christian believers, and I think their understanding of the problem typically includes the assumption that man has free will, and secondly because adopting the opposite view enormously complicates the attempt to understand and justify petitionary prayer. If all things are pre-determined—and worse, if they are all predetermined by the omnipotent and omniscient God to whom one is praying—it is much harder to conceive of a satisfactory justification for petitionary prayer. One consequence of my making this assumption is that I will not be drawing on important traditional Protestant accounts of prayer such as those given by Calvin and Luther, for instance, since while they may be thoughtful, interesting accounts, they assume God's complete determination of everything.

I think that I can most effectively and plausibly show the problem which interests me by presenting a sketchy analysis of the Lord's Prayer. It is a prayer attributed to Christ himself, who is supposed to have produced it just for the purpose of teaching his disciples how they ought to pray. So it is an example of prayer which orthodox Christians accept as a paradigm, and it is, further-more, a clear instance of petitionary prayer. Consequently, it is a particularly good example for my purposes. In what follows, I want to make clear, I am not concerned either to take account of contemporary Biblical exegesis or to contribute to it. I want simply to have a look at the prayer—in fact, at only half the prayer—as it is heard and prayed by ordinary twentieth-century Christians.

As the prayer is given in Luke 11, it contains seven requests. The last four have to do with the personal needs of those praying, but the first three are requests of a broader sort.

The first, "Hallowed be thy name," is commonly taken as a request that God's name be regarded as holy. I am not sure what it means to regard God's name as holy, and I want to avoid worries about the notion of having attitudes towards God's *name*. All the same, I think something of the following sort is a sensible interpretation of the request. The common Biblical notion of holiness has at its root a sense of strong separateness. And it may be that to regard God's name as holy is only to react to it very differently from the way in which one reacts to any other name—and that could happen because it seems specially precious or also (for example) because it seems specially feared. On this understanding of the request, it would be fulfilled if everyone (or almost everyone) took a strongly emotional and respectful attitude towards God's name. But it may be that this is too complicated as an interpretation of the request, and that to regard God's name as holy is simply to love and revere it. In that case, the request is fulfilled if everyone or almost everyone regards God's name very reverentially. And there are New Testament passages which foretell states of affairs fulfilling both these interpretations of the request—prophesying a time at or near the end of the world when all men fear or love God's name, and a time when the inhabitants of earth are all dedicated followers of God.[3]

The second request in the Lord's Prayer is that God's kingdom come. Now according to orthodox Judaco-Christian beliefs, God is and always has been ruler of the world. What then does it mean to ask for the advent of his kingdom? Plainly, there is at least some sense in which the kingdom of heaven has not yet been established on earth and can be waited and hoped for. And this request seems to be for those millenial times when everything on earth goes as it ought to go, when men beat their swords into plowshares (ls. 2:4) and the wolf dwells at peace with the lamb (ls. 11:6, 65:25). This too, then, is a request for a certain state of affairs involving all or most men, the state of affairs at the end of the world prophesied under one or another description in Old and New Testament passages (cf., e.g., Rev. 21:1–4).

And it seems closely related to the object of the third request, "Thy will be done on earth as it is in heaven." There is, of course, a sense in which, according to Christian doctrine, God's will is always done on earth. But that is the sense in which God allows things to happen as they do (God's so-called "permissive will"). God permits certain people to have evil intentions, he permits certain people to commit crimes, and so on, so that he wills to let happen what does happen; and in this sense his will is always done. But in heaven, according to Christian doctrine, it is not that God permits what occurs to occur, and so wills in accordance with what happens, but rather that what happens happens in accordance with his will. So only the perfect good willed unconditionally by God is ever done in heaven. For God's will to be done on earth in such a way, everyone on earth would always have to do only good. This request, then, seems to be another way of asking for the establishment of God's kingdom on earth; and it also seems linked with certain New Testament prophecies—there will be a "new earth," and the righteous meek will inherit it (cf., e.g., Mt. 5:5 and Rev. 5:10 and 21:1–4).

What I think is most worth noticing in this context about all three of these first requests of the Lord's Prayer is that it seems absolutely pointless, futile, and absurd to make them. All three seem to be requests for the millenium or for God's full reign on earth. But it appears from New Testament prophecies that God has already determined to bring about such a state of affairs in the future. And if God has predetermined that there will be such a time, then what is asked for in those three requests is already sure to come. But, then, what is the point of making the prayer? Why ask for something that is certain to come whether you beg for it or flee from it? It is no answer to these questions to say, as some theologians have done, that one prays in this way just because Jesus prescribed such a prayer. That attempt at an answer simply transfers responsibility for the futile action from the one praying to the one being prayed to; it says nothing about what sense there is in the prayer itself. On the other hand, if, contrary to theological appearances, the things prayed for are not predetermined and their occurrence or nonoccurrence is still in doubt, *could* the issue possibly be resolved by someone's asking for one or another outcome? If President Jimmy Carter, say, (or some other Christian) does not ask for God's kingdom to come, will God therefore fail to establish it? Or will he establish it *just because* Jimmy Carter asked for it, though he would not have done so otherwise? Even Carter's staunchest supporters might well find it frightening to think so; and yet if we do not answer these questions in the affirmative, the prayer seems futile and pointless. So either an omniscient, omnipotent, perfectly good God has predetermined this state of affairs or he hasn't; and either way, asking for it seems to make no sense. This conclusion is applicable to other cases of petitionary prayer as well. To take just one example, suppose that Jimmy Carter prays the altruistic and Christian prayer that a particular atheistic friend of his be converted and so saved from everlasting damnation. If it is in God's power to save that man, won't he do so without Jimmy Carter's prayers? Won't a perfectly good God do all the good he can no matter what anyone prays for or does not pray for? Consequently, either God of his goodness will save the man in any case, so that the prayer is pointless, or there is some point in the prayer but God's goodness appears impugned.

We can, I think, generalize these arguments to all petitionary prayer by means of a variation on the argument from evil against God's existence. (The argument that follows does not seem to me to be an acceptable one, but it is the sort of argument that underlies the objections to petitionary prayer which I have been presenting. I will say something about what I think are the flaws in this argument later in the paper.)

(1) A perfectly good being never makes the world worse than it would otherwise be if he can avoid doing so.

The phrase "than it would otherwise be" here should be construed as "than the world would have been had he not brought about or omitted to bring about some state of affairs." In other words, a perfectly good being never makes the world, in virtue of what he himself does or omits to do, worse than it would have been had he not done or omitted to do something or other. *Mutatis mutandis*, the same remarks apply to "than it would otherwise be" in (4) and (7) below.

> (2) An omniscient and omnipotent being can avoid doing anything which it is not logically necessary for him to do.
>
> ∴(3) An omniscient, omnipotent, perfectly good being never makes the world worse than it would otherwise be unless it is logically necessary for him to do so. (1, 2)
>
> (4) A perfectly good being always makes the world better than it would otherwise be if he can do so.
>
> (5) An omniscient and omnipotent being can do anything which it is not logically impossible for him to do.
>
> ∴(6) An omniscient, omnipotent, perfectly good being always makes the world better than it would otherwise be unless it is logically impossible for him to do so. (4, 5)
>
> (7) It is never logically necessary for an omniscient, omnipotent, perfectly good being to make the world worse than it would otherwise be; it is never logically impossible for an omniscient, omnipotent, perfectly good being to make the world better than it would otherwise be.
>
> ∴(8) An omniscient, omnipotent, perfectly good being never makes the world worse than it would otherwise be and always makes the world better than it would otherwise be. (3, 6, 7)

This subconclusion implies that unless the world is infinitely improvable, either the world is or will be absolutely perfect or there is no omniscient, omnipotent, perfectly good being. In other words, (8) with the addition of a pair of premisses—

> (i) The world is not infinitely improvable, and
> (ii) It is not the case that the world is or will be absolutely perfect (i.e., there is and always will be evil in the world)—

implies the conclusion of the argument from evil. That is not a surprising result since this argument is dependent on the argument from evil.

> (9) What is requested in every petitionary prayer is or results in a state of affairs the realization of which would make the world either worse or better than it would otherwise be (that is, than it would have been had that state of affairs not been realized).

It is not always clear whether a petitionary prayer is requesting just an earthly state of affairs, or God's bringing about that earthly state of affairs. So, for example, when a mother prays for the health of her sick son, it is not always clear whether she is requesting simply the health of her son or God's restoration of the health of her son. If we can determine the nature of the request on the basis of what the one praying desires and hopes to get by means of prayer, then at least in most cases the request will be just for some earthly state of affairs. What is important to the mother is simply her son's getting well. For a case in which the request is for God's bringing about some earthly state of affairs, we might consider Gideon's prayer concerning the fleece, discussed below. In any event, I intend "state of affairs" in this argument to range broadly enough to cover both sorts of cases.

∴(10) If what is requested in a petitionary prayer is or results in a state of affairs the realization of which would make the world worse than it would otherwise be, an omniscient, omnipotent, perfectly good being will not fulfill that request. (8)

∴(11) If what is requested in a petitionary prayer is or results in a state of affairs the realization of which would make the world better than it would otherwise be, an omniscient, omnipotent, perfectly good being will bring about that state of affairs even if no prayer for its realization has been made. (8)

It might occur to someone here that what is requested in at least some petitionary prayers is that God bring about a certain state of affairs *in response to the particular petitionary prayer being made*. In such cases, of course, it is logically impossible that God bring about what is requested in the petitionary prayer in the absence of that petitionary prayer. It is not clear to me that there are such cases. The familiar entreaties such as "Hear the voice of my supplications" (Ps. 28:2) in the Psalms seem to me not to be cases of the relevant sort, because they seem to be an elaborate "Please" rather than anything influencing the nature of what is requested in the prayer. Perhaps one of the best candidates for such a case is Gideon's prayer about the fleece: "If you will save Israel by my hand, as you have said, I will put a fleece of wool on the floor and if the dew is on the fleece only and it is dry on all the earth, then I will know that you will save Israel by my hand, as you have said" (Judges 6:36, 37; cf. also 6:39). Gideon here is requesting that God give him a sign by means of the fleece of wool. Does his prayer amount to a request that God produce dew only on the fleece and not on the surrounding ground, or does it come to a request that God do so in response to Gideon's prayer? If there are cases in which the request implicitly or explicitly includes reference to the prayer itself, then in those cases the inference from (8) to (11) is not valid; and such cases ought simply to be excluded from consideration in this argument.

∴(12) Petitionary prayer effects no change. (9, 10, 11)

There is, of course, a sense in which the offering of a prayer is itself a new state of affairs and accompanies or results in natural, psychological changes in the one praying, but step (12) ought to be understood as saying that no prayer is itself efficacious in causing a change of the sort it was designed to cause. An argument which might be thought to apply here, invalidating the inference to the conclusion (13), is that prayer need not effect any change in order to be considered efficacious, provided the offering of the prayer itself is a sufficient reason in God's view for God's fulfilment of the prayer. In other words, if, for certain reasons apart from consideration of a prayer for a state of affairs S, God has determined to bring about S, a prayer for S may still be considered to be efficacious if and only if God would have brought about S just in response to the prayer for S. But I think that even if this view is correct, it does not in fact invalidate the inference to (13). There is a difference between being efficacious and having a point. This argument about the efficacy of prayer seems to assume that not all answers to prayer will be of the overdetermined type. And as long as a believer is not in a position to know which states of affairs are divinely determined to occur regardless of prayers, there is some point in petitionary prayer—any given case may be one in which God would not have brought about the desired state of affairs without prayer for it. But if it is the case for every fulfilled prayer that God would have brought about the desired state of affairs without the prayer, it does seem that there is no point in petitionary prayer, except for those cases (which I think must at best form a very small minority) in which the real object of the one praying a petitionary prayer is not so much to see the realization of the state of affairs he is requesting as to have some influence on or contact with the Deity by means of petitionary prayer; and such cases may then simply be excepted from the conclusion of the argument.

∴(13) Petitionary prayer is pointless. (12)

The basic strategy of this argument is an attempt to show that there is an inconsistency between God's goodness and the efficacy of petitionary prayer; but it is possible to begin with other divine attributes and make a case for a similar inconsistency, so that we can have other, very different arguments to the same conclusion, namely, that petitionary prayer is pointless. Perhaps the most formidable of such alternative arguments is the one based on God's immutability, an argument the strategy of which can be roughly summarized in this way. Before a certain petitionary prayer is made, it is the case either that God will bring about the state of affairs requested in the prayer or that he will not bring it about. He cannot have left the matter open since doing so would imply a subsequent change in him and he is immutable. Either way, since he is immutable, the prayer itself can effect no change in the state of affairs and hence is pointless. Even leaving aside problems of foreknowledge and free will to which this argument (or attempted objections to it) may give rise, I think that orthodox theology will find no real threat in the argument because of the doctrine of God's eternality. However problematic that doctrine may be in itself, it undercuts arguments such as this one because it maintains God's atemporality. My thirteen-step argument against petitionary prayer is, then, not the only argument rejecting petitionary prayer on theistic principles, but it (or some argument along the same lines) does, I think, make the strongest case against petitionary prayer, given Christian doctrine.

The premiss that is most likely to appear false in the argument, at first reading, is (9) because one is inclined to think that there are many petitionary prayers which, if they are granted, would not make the world either better or worse than it would otherwise be. Such a view might be accommodated without damaging the argument simply by weakening (9) and the conclusion: many petitionary prayers, and surely the most important ones, are such that if fulfilled they make the world either a better or a worse place. But I think it is possible to argue plausibly for (9) in the strong form I have given it. Take, for instance, the case of a little boy who prays for a jack-knife. Here, we might think, we have an example of a petitionary prayer the fulfilment of which makes the world neither better nor worse. But, on the one hand, if the little boy has prayed for a jack-knife, surely he will be happier if he gets it, either because he very much wants a jack-knife or because God has honored his request. Consequently, one could argue that fulfilling the request makes the world better in virtue of making the one praying happier. Or, on the other hand, if we think of the little boy's prayer for a jack-knife from God's point of view, then we see that fulfilment of the prayer involves not just the little boy's acquiring a jack-knife but also God's bringing it about in answer to prayer that the little boy acquire a jack-knife. Fulfilling the prayer, then, will have an influence on at least the little boy's religious beliefs and perhaps also on those of his parents and even on those of the people in his parents' community. One might argue that the influence in this case would be deleterious (since it is conducive to wrong views of the purpose of prayer and of relationship with God), and consequently that fulfilling this prayer would make the world a worse place than it would otherwise be. So I think it is possible to argue plausibly that the fulfilment of even such a prayer would make the world either a worse or a better place.

Christian literature contains a number of discussions of the problem with petitionary prayer and various attempts to solve it. For the sake of brevity. I want to look just at the proposed solution Aquinas gives. It is the most philosophically sophisticated of the solutions I know; and, in the wake of the twentieth-century revival of Thomism, it is the solution adopted by many theologians and theistic philosophers today. Thomas discusses problems of petitionary prayer in his Sentence commentary and in the *Summa contra gentiles*,[4] but the clearest exposition of his views is in the question on prayer in the *Summa theologiae*, where he devotes an entire article to showing that there is sense and usefulness in petitionary prayer.[5] The basic argument he relies on to rebut various objections against the usefulness of prayer is this. Divine Providence determines not only what effects there will be in the world, but also what causes will give rise to those effects and in what order they will do so. Now human actions, too, are causes. "For," Thomas says, "we pray not in order to change the divine disposition but for the sake of acquiring by petitionary prayer what God has disposed to be achieved by prayer."[6]

Perhaps the first worry which this argument occasions stems from the appearance of theological determinism in it: God determines not only what effects there will be but also what the causes of those effects will be and in what order the effects will be produced. It is hard to see how such a belief is compatible with freedom of the will. In the preamble to this argument, however, Thomas says he is concerned *not* to deny free will but, on the contrary, to give an account of prayer which preserves free will. So I want simply to assume that he has in mind some distinction or some theory which shows that, despite appearances, his argument is not committed to a thorough-going determinism, and I am going to ignore any troubles in the argument having to do with the compatibility of predestination or foreknowledge and free will.

For present purposes, what is more troublesome about this argument is that it does not provide any real help with the problem it means to solve. According to Thomas, there is nothing absurd or futile about praying to God, given God's nature, because God has by his providence arranged things so that free human actions and human prayers will form part of the chain of cause and effect leading to the state of the world ordained in God's plan. And so, on Thomas's view, prayer should not be thought of as an attempt to get God to do something which he would not otherwise do but rather as an effort to produce an appropriate and preordained cause which will result in certain effects since God in his providence has determined things to be so. Now surely there can be no doubt that, according to Christian doctrine, God wants men to pray and answers prayers; and consequently it is plain that God's plan for the world includes human prayers as causes of certain effects. The difficulty lies in explaining how such a doctrine makes sense. Why should prayers be included in God's plan as causes of certain effects? And what sense is there in the notion that a perfect and unchangeable God, who disposes and plans everything, fulfills men's prayers asking him to do one thing or another? Thomas's argument, I think, gives no help with these questions and so gives no help with this problem of petitionary prayer.

This argument of Thomas's is roughly similar in basic strategy to other traditional arguments for prayer and is furthermore among the most fully developed and sophisticated arguments for prayer, but it seems to me inadequate to make sense of petitionary prayer. I think, then, that it is worthwhile exploring a sort of argument different from those that stress the connection between God's omniscience or providence and men's prayers. In what follows I want to offer a tentative and preliminary sketch of the way in which such an argument might go.

Judaeo-Christian concepts of God commonly represent God as loving mankind and wanting to be loved by men in return. Such anthropomorphic talk is in sharp contrast to the more sophisticated-sounding language of the Hellenized and scholastic arguments considered so far. But a certain sort of anthropomorphism is as much a part of Christianity as is Thomas's "perfect being theology," and it, too, builds on intricate philosophical analysis, beginning perhaps with Boethius's attempt in *Contra Eutychen et Nestorium* to explain what it means to say of something that it is a person. So to say that God loves men and wants to be loved in return is to say something that has a place in philosophical theology and is indispensable to Christian doctrine. Throughout the Old and New Testaments, the type of loving relationship wanted between man and God is represented by various images, for example, sometimes as the relationship between husband and wife, sometimes as that between father and child. And sometimes (in the Gospel of John, for instance) it is also represented as the relationship between true friends. But if the relationship between God and human beings is to be one which at least sometimes can be accurately represented as the love of true friendship, then there is a problem for both parties to the relationship, because plainly it will not be easy for there to be friendship between an omniscient, omnipotent, perfectly good person and a fallible, finite, imperfect person. The troubles of generating and maintaining friendship in such a case are surely the perfect paradigms of which the troubles of friendship between a Rockefeller child and a slum child are just pale copies. Whatever other troubles there are for friendship in these cases, there are at least two dangers for the disadvantaged or inferior member of the pair. First, he can be so overcome by the advantages or superiority of his "friend" that he becomes simply a shadowy reflection of the other's personality, a slavish follower who slowly loses all sense of his own tastes and desires and will. Some people, of course, believe that just this sort of attitude towards God is what Christianity wants and gets from the best of its adherents; but I think that such a belief goes counter to the spirit of the Gospels, for example, and I don't think that it can be found even in such intense mystics as St. Teresa and St. John of the Cross. Secondly, in addition to the danger of becoming completely dominated, there is the danger of becoming spoiled in the way that members of a royal family in a ruling house are subject to. Because of the power at their disposal in virtue of their connections, they often become tyrannical, willful, indolent, self-indulgent, and the like. The greater the discrepancy in status and condition between the two friends, the greater the danger of even inadvertently overwhelming and oppressing or overwhelming and spoiling the lesser member of the pair; and if he is overwhelmed in either of these ways the result will be replacement of whatever kind of friendship there might have been with one or another sort of using. Either the superior member of the pair will use the lesser as his lackey, or the lesser will use the superior as his personal power source. To put it succinctly, then, if God wants some kind of true friendship with men, he will have to find a way of guarding against both kinds of overwhelming.

It might occur to someone to think that even if we assume the view that God wants friendship between himself and human beings, it does not follow that he will have any of the problems just sketched, because he is omnipotent. If he wants friendship of this sort with men, one might suppose, let him just will it and it will be his. I do not want to stop here to argue against this view in detail, but I do want just to suggest that there is reason for thinking it to be incoherent, at least on the assumption of free will adopted at the beginning of this paper, because it is hard to see how God could bring about such a friendship magically, by means of his omnipotence, and yet permit the people involved to have free will. If he could do so, he could make a person freely love him in the right sort of way, and it does not seem reasonable to think he could do so. On the face of it, then, omnipotence alone does not do away with the two dangers for friendship that I sketched above. But the institution of petitionary prayer, I think, can be understood as a safeguard against these dangers.

It is easiest to argue that petitionary prayer serves such a function in the case of a man who prays for himself. In praying for himself, he makes an explicit request for help, and he thereby acknowledges a need or a desire and his dependence on God for satisfying that need or desire. If he gets what he prayed for, he will be in a position to attribute his good fortune to God's doing and to be grateful to God for what God has given him. If we add the undeniable uncertainty of his getting what he prays for, then we will have safeguards against what I will call (for lack of a better phrase) overwhelming spoiling. These conditions make the act of asking a safeguard against tyrannical and self-indulgent pride, even if the one praying thinks of himself grandly as having God on his side.

We can see how the asking guards against the second danger, of oppressive overwhelming, if we look for a moment at the function of roughly similar asking for help when both the one asking and the one asked are human beings. Suppose a teacher sees that one of his students is avoiding writing a paper and is thereby storing up trouble for himself at the end of the term. And suppose that the student *asks* the teacher for extra help in organizing working time and scheduling the various parts of the work. In that case I think the teacher can without any problem give the student what he needs, provided, of course, that the teacher is willing to do as much for any other student, and so on. But suppose, on the other hand, that the student does not ask the teacher for help and that the teacher instead calls the student at home and simply presents him with the help he needs in scheduling and discipline. The teacher's proposals in that case are more than likely to strike the student as meddling interference, and he is likely to respond with more or less polite variations on "Who asked you?" and "Mind your own business." Those responses, I think, are healthy and just. If the student were having ordinary difficulties getting his work done and yet docilely and submissively accepted the teacher's unrequested scheduling of his time, he would have taken the first step in the direction of unhealthy passivity towards his teacher. And if he and his teacher developed that sort of relationship, he could end by becoming a lackey-like reflection of his teacher. Bestowing at least some benefits only in response to requests for them is a safeguard against such an outcome when the members of the relationship are not equally balanced.

It becomes much harder to argue for this defence of prayer as soon as the complexity of the case is increased even just a little. Take, for example, Monica's praying for her son Augustine. There is nothing in Monica's praying for Augustine which shows that *Augustine* recognizes that he has a need for God's help or that *he* will be grateful if God gives him what *Monica* prays for. Nor is it plain that *Monica*'s asking shields Augustine from oppressive overwhelming by God. So it seems as if the previous arguments fail in this case. But consider again the case in which a teacher sees that a student of his could use help but does not feel that he can legitimately volunteer his help unasked. Suppose that John, a friend of that student, comes to see the teacher and says, "I don't know if you've noticed, but Jim is having trouble getting to his term paper. And unless he gets help, I think he won't do it at all and will be in danger of flunking the course." If the teacher now goes to help Jim and is rudely or politely asked "What right have you got to interfere?," he'll say, "Well, in fact, your friend came to me and *asked* me to help." And if John is asked the same question, he will probably reply, "But I'm your friend; I had to do *something*." I think, then, that because John asks the teacher, the teacher is in a position to help with less risk of oppressive meddling than before. Obviously, he cannot go very far without incurring that risk as fully as before; and perhaps the most he can do if he wants to avoid oppressive meddling is to try to elicit from *Jim* in genuinely uncoercive ways a request for help. And, of course, I chose Monica and Augustine to introduce this case because, as Augustine tells it in the *Confessions*, God responded to Monica's fervent and continued prayers for Augustine's salvation by arranging the circumstances of Augustine's life in such a way that finally Augustine himself freely asked God for salvation.

One might perhaps think that there is something superfluous and absurd in God's working through the intermediary of prayer in this way. If Jim's friend can justify his interference on the grounds that he is Jim's friend and has to do *something*, God can dispense with this sort of petitionary prayer, too. He can give aid unasked on the grounds that he is the *creator* and has to do something. But suppose that Jim and John are only acquaintances who have discussed nothing more than their schoolwork; and suppose that John, by overhearing Jim's phone conversations, has come to believe that all Jim's academic troubles are just symptoms of problems he is having with his parents. If John asks the teacher to help Jim with his personal problems, and if the teacher begins even a delicate attempt to do so by saying that John asked him to do so, he and John could both properly be told to mind their own business. It is not the *status* of his relationship or even the depth of his care and compassion for Jim which puts John in a position to defend himself by saying "But I'm your friend." What protects John against the charge of oppressive meddling is rather the degree to which Jim has freely, willingly, shared his life and thoughts and feelings with John. So John's line of defence against the charge of oppressive meddling can be attributed to God only if the person God is to aid has willingly shared his thoughts and feelings and the like with God. But it is hard to imagine anyone putting himself in such a relation to a person he believes to be omnipotent and good without his also *asking* for whatever help he needs.

Even if the argument can be made out so far, one might be inclined to think that it will not be sufficient to show the compatibility of God's goodness with the practice of petitionary prayer. If one supposes that God brought Augustine to Christianity in response to Monica's prayers, what is one to say about Augustine's fate if Monica had not prayed for him? And what does this view commit one to maintain about people who neither pray for themselves nor are prayed for? It looks as if an orthodox Christian who accepts the argument about petitionary prayer so far will be committed to a picture of this sort. God is analogous to a human father with two very different children. Both Old and New Testaments depict God as doing many good things for men without being asked to do so, and this human father, too, does unrequested good things for both his children. But one child, who is healthy and normal, with healthy, normal relations to his father, makes frequent requests of the father which the father responds to and in virtue of which he bestows benefits on the child. The other child is selectively blind, deaf, dumb, and suffering from whatever other maladies are necessary to make it plausible that he does not even know he has a father. Now either there are some benefits that the father will never bestow unless and until he is asked; and in that case he will do less for his defective child, who surely has more need of his help than does the healthy child. Or, on the other hand, he will bestow all his benefits unasked on the defective child, and then he seems to make a mockery of his practice with the normal child of bestowing some benefits only in response to requests—he is, after all, willing to bestow the same benefits without being asked. So it seems that we are still left with the problem we started with: either God is not perfectly good or the practice of petitionary prayer is pointless. But suppose the father always meets the defective child's needs and desires even though the child never comes to know of the existence of his father. The child knows only that he is always taken care of, and, when he needs something, he gets what he needs. It seems to me intuitively clear that such a practice runs a great risk, at least, of making the defective child willful and tyrannical. But even if the defective child is not in danger of being made worse in some respects in this situation, still it seems plain that he would be better off if the father could manage to put the child in a position to know his father and to frame a request for what he wants. So I think a good father will fulfill the child's needs unasked; but I think that he can do so without making a mockery of his practice of bestowing benefits in response to requests only if putting the child in a position to make requests is among his first concerns.

And as for the question whether God would have saved Augustine without Monica's prayers, I think that there is intermediate ground between the assertion that Monica's prayers are necessary to Augustine's salvation, which seems to impugn God's goodness, and the claim that they are altogether without effect, which undercuts petitionary prayer. It is possible, for example, to argue that God would have saved Augustine without Monica's prayers but not in the same amount of time or not by the same process or not with the same effect. Augustine, for instance, might have been converted to Christianity but not in such a way as to become one of its most powerful authorities for centuries.

With all this, I have still looked only at cases that are easy for my position; when we turn to something like a prayer for Guatemala after the earthquake—which begins to come closer to the sort of petitions in the first half of the Lord's Prayer—it is much harder to know what to say. And perhaps it is simply too hard to come up with a reasonable solution here because we need more work on the problem of evil. Why would a good God permit the occurrence of earthquakes in the first place? Do the reasons for his permitting the earthquake affect his afterwards helping the country involved? Our inclination is surely to say that a good God must *in any case* help the earthquake victims, so that in this instance at any rate it is pointless to pray. But plainly we also have strong inclinations to say that a good God must in any case prevent earthquakes in populated areas. And since orthodox Christianity is committed to distrusting these latter inclinations, it is at least at sea about the former ones. Without more work on the problem of evil, it is hard to know what to say about the difference prayer might make in this sort of case.

I think it is worth noticing, though, that the first three requests of the Lord's prayer do not run into the same difficulties. Those requests seem generally equivalent to a request for the kingdom of God on earth, that state of affairs in which, of their own free will, all men on earth are dedicated, righteous lovers of God. Now suppose it is true that God would bring about his kingdom on earth even if an individual Christian such as Jimmy Carter did not pray for it. It does not follow in this case, however, that the prayer in question is pointless and makes no difference. Suppose no one prayed for the advent of God's kingdom on earth or felt a need or desire for those millenial times strongly enough to pray for them. It seems unreasonable to think that God could bring about his earthly kingdom under those conditions, or, if he could, that it would be the state of affairs just described, in which earth is populated by people who *freely* love God. And if so, then making the requests in the first half of the Lord's Prayer resembles other, more ordinary activities in which only the effort of a whole group is sufficient to achieve the desired result. One man can't put out a forest fire, but if everyone in the vicinity of a forest fire realized that fact and on that basis decided not to try the fire would rage out of control. So in the case of the opening petitions of the Lord's Prayer, too, it seems possible to justify petitionary prayer without impugning God's goodness.

Obviously, the account I have given is just a preliminary sketch for the full development of this solution, and a good deal more work needs to be done on the problem. Nonetheless, I think that this account is on the right track and that there is a workable solution to the problem of petitionary prayer which can be summarized in this way. God must work through the intermediary of prayer, rather than doing everything on his own initiative, for man's sake. Prayer acts as a kind of buffer between man and God. By safeguarding the weaker member of the relation from the dangers of overwhelming domination and overwhelming spoiling, it helps to promote and preserve a close relationship between an omniscient, omnipotent, perfectly good person and a fallible, finite, imperfect person. There is, of course, something counter-intuitive in this notion that prayer acts as a buffer; prayer of all sorts is commonly and I think correctly said to have as one of its main functions the production of closeness between man and God. But not just any sort of closeness will result in friendship, and promoting the appropriate sort of closeness will require inhibiting or preventing inappropriate sorts of closeness, so that a relationship of friendship depends on the maintenance of both closeness and distance between the two friends. And while I do not mean to denigrate the importance of prayer in producing and preserving the appropriate sort of closeness, I think the problem of petitionary prayer at issue here is best solved by focusing on the distance necessary for friendship and the function of petitionary prayer in maintaining that distance.

As for the argument against prayer which I laid out at the start of the paper, it seems to me that the flaw lies in step (7), that it is never logically necessary for God to make the world worse than it would otherwise be and never logically impossible for him to make the world better than it would otherwise be. To take a specific example from among those discussed so far, orthodox Christianity is committed to claiming that the advent of God's kingdom on earth, in which all people freely love God, would make the world better than it would otherwise be. But I think that it is not possible for God to *make* the world better in this way, because I think it is not possible for him to *make* men *freely* do anything. And in general, if it is arguable that God's doing good things just in virtue of men's requests protects men from the dangers described and preserves them in the right relationship to God, then it is not the case that it is always logically possible for God to make the world better and never logically necessary for him to make the world worse than it would otherwise be. If men do not always pray for all the good things they might and ought to pray for, then in some cases either God will not bring about some good thing or he will do so but at the expense of the good wrought and preserved by petitionary prayer.

It should be plain that there is nothing in this analysis of prayer which *requires* that God fulfil every prayer; asking God for something is not in itself a sufficient condition for God's doing what he is asked. Christian writings are full of examples of prayers which are not answered, and there are painful cases of unanswered prayer in which the one praying must be tempted more to the belief that God is his implacable enemy than to the sentimental-seeming belief that God is his friend. This paper proposes no answer for these difficulties. They require a long, hard, careful look at the problem of evil, and that falls just outside the scope of this paper.

And, finally, it may occur to someone to wonder whether the picture of God presented in this analysis is at all faithful to the God of the Old or New Testaments. Is this understanding of God and prayer anything that Christianity ought to accept or even find congenial? It seems to me that one could point to many stories in either the Old or New Testament in support of an affirmative answer—for example, Elijah's performance on Mt. Carmel (I Kings 18), or the apostles' prayer for a successor to Judas (Acts 1: 24–26). But for a small and particularly nice piece of evidence, we can turn to the story in the Gospel of Luke which describes Jesus making the Lord's Prayer and giving a lecture on how one is to pray. According to the Gospel, Jesus is praying and in such a way that his disciples see him and know that he is praying. One of them makes a request of him which has just a touch of rebuke in it: teach us to pray, as *John* taught *his* disciples to pray (I. k. 11:1). If there is a note of rebuke there, it seems just. A religious master should teach his disciples to pray, and a good teacher does not wait until he is asked to teach his students important lessons. But Jesus is portrayed as a good teacher of just this sort in the Gospel of Luke.[7] Does the Gospel, then, mean its readers to understand that Jesus would not have taught his disciples how to pray if they had not requested it? And if it does not, why is Jesus portrayed as waiting until he is asked? Perhaps the Gospel means us to understand that Jesus does so just in order to teach by experience as well as by sermon what is implicit throughout the Lord's Prayer: that asking makes a difference.

NOTES

1. *The Concept of Prayer* (New York, 1966), pp.112ff.
2. Cf. *The Concept of God* (New York), pp. 62, 101, 111 and 185.
3. Cf., e.g., Isa. 2: 2–21, 45:23, and 65:23; Matt. 24; Mk. 13; Lk. 21; and Rev. 6:15–17.
4. See *In. IV Sent.*, dist. XV q.4, a. 1, and *Summa contra gentiles*, I.III. 95, 96.
5. See 2a–2ae, q. 83. a. 2.
6. See reply, 2.2. "Non enim propter hoc oramus ut divinam dispositionem immutemus: sed ut id impetremus quod Deus disposuit per orationes sanctorum implendum."
7. See, for example, the lessons taught in the two incidents described in Lk. 21: 1–6.

SUGGESTED READING

Trinity

Brown, David (1989), 'Trinitarian Personhood and Individuality', in Feenstra and Plantinga (eds), *Trinity, Incarnation, and Atonement*, pp. 48–78.

Plantinga, Cornelius, Jr. (1989), 'Social Trinty and Tritheism', in Ronald Feenstra and Cornelius Plantinga, Jr. (eds), *Trinity, Incarnation and Atonement*, Notre Dame: University of Notre Dame Press, pp. 21–47.

van Inwagen, Peter (1995), 'And yet they are not three Gods but one God', in Peter van Inwagen, *God, Knowledge, and Mystery*, Ithaca: Cornell University Press, pp. 222–59.

Incarnation

Feenstra, Ronald J. (1989), 'Reconsidering Kenotic Christology', in Feenstra and Plantinga (eds), *Trinity, Incarnation, and Atonement*, pp. 128–52.

Morris, Thomas V. (1986), *The Logic of God Incarnate*, Ithaca: Cornell University Press.

Relton, H. Maurice (1929), *A Study in Christology*, London: Macmillan.

Senor, Thomas (1991), 'God, Supernatural Kinds, and the Incarnation', *Religious Studies*, pp. 353–70.

Swinburne, Richard (1989), 'Could God Become Man?' in Godfrey Vesey (ed.), *The Philosophy in Christianity*, Cambridge: Cambridge University Press.

HELL

Craig, William Lane (1989), 'No Other Name: A Middle Knowledge Perspective on the Exclusivity of Salvation through Christ', *Faith and Philosophy*, 6, pp. 297–308.

Kvanvig, Jonathan (1993), *The Problem of Hell*, Oxford: Oxford University Press.

Swinburne, Richard (1983), 'A Theodicy of Heaven and Hell', in Alfred J. Freddoso (ed.), *The Existence of God*, Notre Dame: University of Notre Dame Press, pp. 37–54.

ATONEMENT

Jensen, Paul (1993), 'Forgiveness and Atonement', *Scottish Journal of Theology*, 46, pp. 141–59.

Quinn, Philip (1989), 'Aquinas on Atonement', in Feenstra and Plantinga, (eds), *Trinity, Incarnation, and Atonement*, pp. 153–77.

Stump, Eleonore (1998), 'Atonement according to Aquinas', in Thomas V. Morris (ed.), *Philosophy and the Christian Faith*, Notre Dame: University of Notre Dame Press, pp. 61–91.

Swinburne, Richard (1994), *The Christian God*, Oxford: Oxford University Press, ch. 8.

PETITIONARY PRAYER

Hoffman, Joshua (1985), 'On Petitonary Prayer', *Faith and Philosophy*, 2, pp. 30–7.

Murray, Michael and Kurt Meyers (1994), 'Ask and it will be given to you', *Religious Studies*, 31, pp. 475–84.

Tiessen, Terrance (2000), *Providence and Prayer*, Downers Grove, IL: Inter-Varsity Press.

NOTES ON THE EDITORS

William Lane Craig is Research Professor of Philosophy at Talbot School of Theology in La Mirada, California. He is the author, co-author, or editor of over twenty books, including *The* Kalam *Cosmological Argument* (Macmillan, 1979), *Divine Foreknowledge and Human Freedom* (Brill, 1990), *Theism, Atheism, and Big Bang Cosmology* (Clarendon Press, 1993), *Naturalism: A Critical Analysis* (Routledge, 2000), and *God, Time, and Eternity* (Kluwer, 2001), as well as numerous articles in professional journals such as *The Journal of Philosophy, Philosophy, Philosophical Studies, American Philosophical Quarterly, Australasian Journal of Philosophy, British Journal for the Philosophy of Science, International Studies in the Philosophy of Science, Astrophysics and Space Science, International Journal for Philosophy of Religion, Faith and Philosophy* and *Philosophia Christi.*

Kevin Meeker is Assistant Professor of Philosophy at the University of South Alabama in Mobile, Alabama. He is the co-editor of *The Philosophical Challenge of Religious Diversity* (Oxford, 2000) and is the author of several articles in professional journals such as *Australasian Journal of Philosophy, International Journal for Philosophy of Religion, Philosophia, Journal of the History of Philosophy* and *Hume Studies.*

J. P. Moreland is Distinguished Professor of Philosophy at Biola University in La Mirada, California. He is the editor, author, or co-author of fourteen books, including *Does God Exist? The Debate between Theists and Atheists* (Prometheus, 1993), *Naturalism: A Critical Analysis* (Routledge, 2000), *Body and Soul* (InterVarsity, 2000) and *Universals* (McGill-Queen's, 2001), as well as numerous articles in professional journals such as *American Philosophical Quarterly*, *Philosophy and Phenomenological Research*, *Australasian Journal of Philosophy*, *Southern Journal of Philosophy*, *Religious Studies*, *Metaphilosophy* and *Faith and Philosophy*.

Michael Murray is Associate Professor and Chair of Philosophy at Franklin and Marshall College. He has published two books: *Reason for the Hope Within* (Eerdmans, 1999) and *Philosophy of Religion: The Big Questions* (Blackwell Publishers, 1999) with Eleonore Stump. He is also the author of over twenty articles in books and professional journals such as *American Philosophical Quarterly*, *Philosophy and Phenomenological Research*, *Religious Studies*, *Faith and Philosophy* and *The Leibniz Review*, and has a third book forthcoming, *Leibniz's Philosophical Theology: An Annotated Translation of Leibniz's Commentary on Article 17 of Gilbert Burnet's Commentary on the Thirty-Nine Articles of the Church of England*.

Timothy O'Connor is Associate Professor of Philosophy at Indiana University. He is the editor of *Agents, Causes, and Events* (1995) and the author of *Persons and Causes: The Metaphysics of Free Will* (2000), both with Oxford University Press. He also has written over twenty professional articles on topics in metaphysics, philosophy of mind and philosophy of religion in journals such as *American Philosophical Quarterly*, *Philosophy and Phenomenological Research*, *Noûs*, *Philosophical Perspectives*, *Philosophical Topics*, and *Journal of the History of Philosophy*. He is currently writing a book on the cosmological argument from contingency for theism.

ACKNOWLEDGEMENTS

Grateful acknowledgement is made to the following copyright holders for permission to reproduce material in this book. Every effort has been made to trace copyright holders but if any have inadvertently been overlooked, the publishers will be pleased to make the necessary arrangements at the first opportunity.

Ian Hacking, 'The Logic of Pascal's Wager', *American Philosophical Quarterly*, 9, 2 (1972), pp. 186–92. Reprinted by permission of *American Philosophical Quarterly* and the author.

George Schlesinger, 'A Central Theistic Argument', in Jeff Jordan (ed.), *Gambling on God: Essays on Pascal's Wager* (Lanham, MD: Rowman & Littlefield, 1994), pp. 83–99. Reprinted by permission of Rowman & Littlefield.

Alvin Plantinga, 'Is Belief in God Rationally Acceptable?', from: 'Is Belief in God Properly Basic?', *Nous*, 15 (1981), pp. 41–51. Reprinted by permission of Blackwell Publishers; and 'Intellectual Sophistication and Basic Belief in God', from 'The Foundations of Theism: A Reply', *Faith and Philosophy*, 3, 3 (July 1986), pp. 298–313.

Philip L. Quinn, 'Defeating Theistic Beliefs', from 'The Foundations of Theism Again: A Rejoinder to Plantinga', in Linda Zagzebski (ed.), *Rational Faith* (Notre Dame, IN: University of Notre Dame Press, 1993), pp. 35–47. Reprinted by permission of the University of Notre Dame Press and the author.

Stephen T. Davis, 'The Cosmological Argument and the Epistemic Status of Belief in God', *Philosophia Christi*, series 2, 1, 1 (1999), pp. 5–15. Copyright © 1999. Reprinted by permission of *Philosophia Christi*.

William Lane Craig, 'The *Kalam* Cosmological Argument'. Copyright © William Lane Craig. Reprinted by permission of the author.

John Leslie, 'The Prerequisites of Life in our Universe', in G. V. Coyne (ed.), *Newton and the New Direction in Science* (Vatican City: Speculo Vaticana, 1988), pp. 97–119. Reprinted by permission of *Newton and the New Direction in Science*.

Robin Collins, 'Design and the Many-Worlds Hypothesis' (© June 2000). Reprinted by permission of the author.

Stuart C. Hackett, 'The Value Dimension of the Cosmos: A Moral Argument', *Reconstruction of the Christian Revelation Claim* (Grand Rapids, MI: Baker Book House Company, 1984), pp. 111–17, 152–6. Reprinted by permission of Baker Book House Company.

J. P. Moreland, 'Searle's Biographical Naturalism and the Argument from Consciousness', *Faith and Philosophy*, 15, 1 (January 1998), pp. 68–91. All rights reserved. Reprinted by permission of *Faith and Philosophy*.

Alvin Plantinga, 'The Ontological Argument', from 'God and Necessity', *The Nature of Necessity* (Oxford: Clarendon Press, 1974), pp. 196–221. © Oxford University Press 1974. Reprinted by permission of Oxford University Press.

Quentin Smith, 'The Conceptualist Argument for God's Existence', *Faith and Philosophy*, 11, 1 (January 1994), pp. 38–49. All rights reserved. Reprinted by permission of *Faith and Philosophy*.

Robert Prevost, 'Divine Necessity', from 'Necessity and Explanation', *Possibility and Theistic Explanation* (Oxford: Clarendon Press, 1990), pp. 130–50.

Alan Padgett, 'God and Timelessness', from 'A Coherent Model of Absolute Timelessness', *God, Eternity and the Nature of Time* (New York: St. Martin's Press; Basingstoke: Macmillan 1990), pp. 56–76, 150. Copyright © Alan Padgett. Reprinted by permission of St. Martin's Press LLC and Macmillan Ltd.

Alvin Plantinga, 'On Ockham's Way Out', *Faith and Philosophy*, 3 (1986), pp. 235–69. Reprinted by permission of *Faith and Philosophy*.

Alfred J. Freddoso, 'On Divine Middle Knowledge', in 'Introduction', from Luis de Molina, *On Divine Foreknowledge*, translated with an introduction and notes by Alfred J. Freddoso (Ithaca, NY: Cornell University Press, 1988), pp. 47, 68–75. Copyright © 1988 Cornell University. Used by permission of the publisher, Cornell University Press.

Thomas P. Flint and Alfred J. Freddoso, 'Maximal Power', in Alfred J. Freddoso (ed.), *The Existence and Nature of God* (Notre Dame, IN: University of Notre Dame Press, 1983), pp. 81–113. © 1983 by University of Notre Dame Press. Reprinted by permission of the publisher.

William P. Alston, 'What Euthyphro Should Have Said' (not previously published). Copyright © William Alston. Reprinted by permission of the author.

William L. Rowe, 'The Problem of Evil and Some Varieties of Atheism', *American Philosophical Quarterly*, 16, 4 (October 1979), pp. 335–41. Reprinted by permission of *American Philosophical Quarterly*.

Paul Draper, 'Pain and Pleasure: An Evidential Problem for Theists', *Nous*, 23 (1989), pp. 331–50. Reprinted by permission of Blackwell Publishers.

William P. Alston, 'Some (Temporarily) Final Thoughts on Evidential Arguments from Evil', in D. Howard-Snyder (ed.), *The Evidential Argument from Evil* (Bloomington, IN: Indiana University Press, 1996), pp. 311–32. Reprinted by permission of Indiana University Press.

Peter van Inwagen, 'The Magnitude, Duration, and Distribution of Evil: A Theodicy', *Philosophical Topics*, 16, 2 (Fall 1988), pp. 161–87. Reprinted by permission of *Philosophical Topics* and the author.

Eleonore Stump, 'The Problem of Evil', *Faith and Philosophy*, 2, 4 (October 1985), pp. 392–423. Reprinted by permission of *Faith and Philosophy*.

Paul Churchland, 'A Refutation of Dualism', in Paul Churchland, *Matter and Consciousness*, rev. edn (Cambridge, MA: The MIT Press, 1988), pp. 13–21. Reprinted by permission of The MIT Press.

John Foster, 'A Defence of Dualism', in John R. Smythies and John Beloff (eds), *The Case for Dualism* (Charlottesville: University Press of Virginia, 1989), pp. 1–23. Reprinted by permission of the University Press of Virginia.

Keith E. Yandell, 'A Defence of Dualism', *Faith and Philosophy*, 12, 4 (4 October 1995), pp. 548–66. All rights reserved. Reprinted by permission of *Faith and Philosophy*.

Richard Swinburne, 'Dualism and Personal Identity', from *The Evolution of the Soul*, rev. edn (Oxford: Clarendon Press, 1997), pp. 145–60, 322–32. © Richard Swinburne 1986 (revised edition, 1997). Reprinted by permission of Oxford University Press.

Stephen T. Davis, 'The Resurrection of the Dead', in Stephen T. Davis, *Death and Afterlife* (New York: St. Martin's Press; Basingstoke: Macmillan, 1989), pp. 119–44. Copyright © Stephen T. Davis. Reprinted by permission of St. Martin's Press LLC and Macmillan Ltd.

Richard Swinburne, 'A Defence of the Doctrine of the Trinity', from 'The Trinity', *The Christian God* (New York: Clarendon Press, 1994), pp. 170–91. © Richard Swinburne 1994. Reprinted by permission of Oxford University Press.

Thomas V. Morris, 'The Two Minds View of Incarnation', from 'Divine and Human Existence' and 'Jesus and the Attributes of Deity', *The Logic of God Incarnate* (Ithaca, NY: Cornell University Press, 1986), pp. 62–7, 69–70, 88–9, 102–7. Copyright © 1986 Cornell University. Used by permission of the publisher, Cornell University Press.

Michael J. Murray, 'Heaven and Hell', *Reason for the Hope Within* (Grand Rapids, MI: Eerdmans, 1999), pp. 287–315. Reprinted by permission of the author and WM. B. Eerdmans Publishing Company.

Steven Porter, 'Rethinking the Logic of Penal Substitution'. Copyright © Steven Porter, 2000. Reprinted by permission of the author.

Eleonore Stump, 'Petitionary Prayer', *American Philosophical Quarterly*, 16, 2 (April 1979), pp. 81–91. Reprinted by permission of *American Philosophical Quarterly*.

INDEX